UNDERSTANDING
MEMORY

CAROLYN ENSLEY

OXFORD
UNIVERSITY PRESS

OXFORD
UNIVERSITY PRESS

Oxford University Press is a department of the University of Oxford.
It furthers the University's objective of excellence in research, scholarship,
and education by publishing worldwide. Oxford is a registered trade mark of
Oxford University Press in the UK and in certain other countries.

Published in Canada by
Oxford University Press
8 Sampson Mews, Suite 204,
Don Mills, Ontario M3C 0H5 Canada

www.oupcanada.com

Library and Archives Canada Cataloguing in Publication

Title: Understanding memory / Carolyn Ensley.
Names: Ensley, Carolyn, author.
Description: Includes bibliographical references and index.
Identifiers: Canadiana (print) 20190154527 | Canadiana (ebook) 20190154535 | ISBN 9780199014989
(softcover) | ISBN 9780199034598 (loose-leaf) | ISBN 9780199014996 (EPUB)
Subjects: LCSH: Memory—Textbooks. | LCGFT: Textbooks.
Classification: LCC BF371 .E57 2020 | DDC 153.1/2—dc23

Cover image: Tuan Tran/Getty Images
Cover and interior design: Farzana Razak

Oxford University Press is committed to our environment.
This book is printed on Forest Stewardship Council® certified paper
and comes from responsible sources.

Printed and bound in Canada

1 2 3 4 — 23 22 21 20

Brief Contents

Contents

7 Generic Memory 155

8 Forgetting 185

Publisher's Preface

In preparing this new book, we had one paramount goal: to produce the most comprehensive, current, and applied introduction to the study of memory, with a focus on current models of memory systems and how these models are relevant to our everyday lives. We hope that this section will help you see why *Understanding Memory* is the most exciting and innovative memory textbook available to students today.

What Makes This a One-of-a-Kind Textbook

DIY Experiment Boxes

Appearing in every chapter, the DIY Experiment Boxes provide practical demonstrations of concepts in ways that students can experience for themselves.

DIY EXPERIMENT	BOX 1.1

The Mysterious Origins of the Method of Loci

Read the following story about the origins of the method of loci, and retell the story when you encounter Box 1.3 at the end of this chapter.

One of the most well-known accounts of memory in ancient Greece is the legend of Simonides of Ceos (ca 556–468 BCE), a Greek lyric poet who claimed he was inspired to create the method of loci after he attended a disastrous banquet for a nobleman named Sopras. According to the legend, retold by both Cicero (ca 105–43 BCE) and Quintilian (ca 35–100 CE), Simonides recited a poem about boxing for the guests at the banquet, making frequent reference to the gods Castor and Pollux. Sopras chided Simonides about the references after, stating that he would only pay him half his fee and that Simonides should charge Castor and Pollux for the other half, presumably because Simonides's poem was long and made many references to the strengths of these gods. Simonides was then allegedly told that he must leave the banquet hall because two men were outside waiting for him. However, when Simonides looked for the men outside, no one was to be found. At this point, according to the story, the banquet hall collapsed, crushing all attendees beyond recognition, but sparing Simonides who was outside. Families desperately wanted their loved ones identified and Simonides obliged them by recalling the seating arrangement of all guests, making it possible for the families to claim the correct bodies. Simonides later credited this experience as the inspiration for the method of loci. Later philosophers, including Cicero, would cite the story as fiction; however, the method of loci was a popular memory aid for scholars from ancient times to the Renaissance, regardless of where the idea originated.

MEMORY ACTIVITY	

Visualizations Help Memory

People better remember material that they have visualized (e.g., Marks, 1973). In this activity, we will take advantage of the benefits of visualization while learning the memory functions of different areas of the brain that are listed in Table 1.2.

First, trace or copy this image of a brain onto the centre of a piece of paper:

Next, use Figure 1.10 as a guide and divide your image into the four lobes of the brain and label each lobe. Next, review the function of each lobe of the brain one by one, devising an easy-to-draw mental image for each concept that needs to be learned; for example, you may envision a "car" for the primary motor cortex and an "I" for attention. Record each image on the paper in the general region of the associated cortex. You should develop a drawing like the one below:

Memory Activities

This feature, which appears near the end of every chapter, encourages students to practise memory-building activities while helping them to study the concepts covered in the chapter.

Pedagogical Features

Each chapter of *Understanding Memory* includes pedagogical features that keep the book engaging and student-friendly:

- Learning objectives
- Chapter-opening vignettes that provide students with a concrete, relatable, and interesting example that starts them thinking about the concepts that will be described in the chapter
- Relevant Research boxes that outline key research on the topics under discussion, describing both how the research was conducted and contextualizing the importance of the findings
- Case Study boxes that tie chapter topics to real-world events and/or popular culture, helping students relate to the concepts under discussion
- End-of-chapter questions
- List of key figures in each chapter

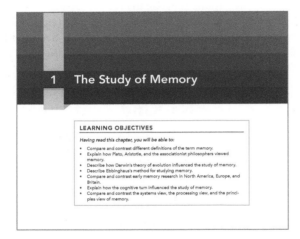

1   The Study of Memory

LEARNING OBJECTIVES

Having read this chapter, you will be able to:

- Compare and contrast different definitions of the term *memory*.
- Explain how Plato, Aristotle, and the associationist philosophers viewed memory.
- Describe how Darwin's theory of evolution influenced the study of memory.
- Describe Ebbinghaus's method for studying memory.
- Compare and contrast early memory research in North America, Europe, and Britain.
- Explain how the cognitive turn influenced the study of memory.
- Compare and contrast the systems view, the processing view, and the principles view of memory.

EXTREME EPISODIC MEMORY: HYPERTHYMESIA

Marilu Henner (b. 1952) is a well-known actress and dancer who has starred in television and movies since the 1970s. In 2010, Henner revealed in an interview on *60 Minutes* that she has **hyperthymesia** and is able to remember, in detail, each day of her life, going back decades. This is an example of superior **episodic memory** or memory for personal events. To show the interviewer at *60 Minutes* just how detailed her memory is, Henner took them through her shoe closet and picked up different pairs of shoes and told the reporter when she got them, when she first wore them, and what day of the week it was. For example, she explained, "I first wore these shoes on October the 7th, 2007. These I wore on April the 21st of this year; it was Tuesday; and these I got in 1982, April 9th. It was a Friday." The next day Henner was interviewed on *The Early Show* and, during the interview, described the process of recalling these events using the analogy of a DVD with the "select a scene" feature on. Henner explains that when she recalls a year; for example, she "sees" each of the days of the year mapped out in a sequence and she is able to access whichever day she chooses. The interviewer asked Henner to talk about 1975, a year she has chosen at random. The first thing that Henner recalls is that her birthday was on Sunday, April 6, that Christmas was on a Thursday, and that Thanksgiving was on November 27. As she thinks more about the year, more details are filled in. She recalls a first date with a new boyfriend on August 12 and rehearsals for her first Broadway show. Henner tells an interviewer that the experience is like time travel. While she is explaining this experience she recalls what outfit she wore on that first date (which was a Tuesday), Henner explains that while she remembers exciting first dates and Broadway rehearsals, she also remembers mundane details. Her autobiographical memory is highly accurate for all events in her life. Hyperthymesia is an extremely rare condition that was first identified in 2006. Experts on the subject have only identified 25 people who are truly able to recall their lives day by day. Six of the people with hyperthymesia have been studied in depth by researchers and they all report vivid visual memories. Because people with hyperthymesia show typical patterns of recall for generic memories (like facts), this suggests that episodic memory is somehow distinct from other types of long-term memory. In this chapter, we will explore what makes episodic memory different from generic memory and attempt to explain exactly what causes hyperthymesia.

Ancillary Resource Center

Online Resources

Understanding Memory is part of a comprehensive package of learning and teaching tools that includes resources for both students and instructors:

- A comprehensive instructor's manual provides an extensive set of pedagogical tools and suggestions for every chapter, including a sample syllabus, lesson plans, chapter summaries, suggested in-class and online activities/assignments, and suggested additional resources.
- PowerPoint slides summarize key points from each chapter and incorporate graphics and tables drawn from the text.
- An extensive Test Generator enables instructors to sort, edit, import, and distribute a bank of questions in multiple-choice, true–false, short-answer, and essay formats.
- A Student Study Guide includes chapter summaries, recommended online resources to help students review the textbook and classroom material and to take concepts further, and study questions and answers for self-quizzing.

Visit **www.oup.com/he/Ensley** for access to these materials. For instructors who require a password, please contact your sales representative.

Premium Digital Content

In addition to the online materials that come with the book, these additional supplements are available to enhance student understanding of key concepts:

- Discovery Lab interactive activities and experiments allow students to explore and interact with processes, phenomena, and structures in human memory. These activities show students how memory experiments are run while also exemplifying models of memory formation (particularly related to visual or auditory memory), providing a rich learning experience that students cannot get from reading a textbook.
- PowerPoint Presentation labs save time in course preparation by providing prepared walk-throughs of classic and explanatory experiments in order to help students better understand models of memory formation without running through the full lab (in cases where time or resources are limited, such as in large lectures or in online courses).

At Oxford University Press, we create high quality, engaging, and affordable digital supplements in a variety of formats, and deliver it to you in the way that best suits your needs. For information on how you and your students can access these materials, please contact your sales representative for your options.

Author's Preface

A few years ago, I was considering developing an undergraduate lecture course on memory. I wanted the course to appeal to most third- and fourth-year psychology students and I wanted the course to have practical value. I decided that the curriculum would include traditional memory theory as well as applied topics relating to social, developmental, health, forensic, and clinical psychology. I hoped that the applied topics would not only appeal to students but also teach students to look for the possible impacts that memory can have in any circumstance where a student might be trying to understand and explain human behaviour. So, armed with a solid idea for a great course, I began to search for a text. Much to my surprise, there were no memory texts that include both memory theory and applied memory topics. I knew I couldn't proceed with my course without a great text, so I turned my attention from developing a course to writing a text on memory that I felt was truly needed: a comprehensive book that covers memory theory, the neuroscience of memory, and applied memory topics.

Now, many years later, I present *Understanding Memory*. Each of the 14 chapters in this book includes current research, neuroscience, relatable examples, and DIY experiments to help students engage with the material while they read. The text is geared toward a North American audience, so I include both Canadian and American research examples throughout. My hope is that after reading this book, students will not only understand memory theory and the neuroscience of memory but also understand how to apply that theory to real-world situations.

The text first orients students to the material, then builds on their understanding and application through memory theories, and finally uses this foundational understanding to inform an exploration of applied topics in an in-depth manner. In Chapter 1, I include a review of the history of memory research as well as the principles of neuroscience that should be well understood before reading this book. Chapters 2 through 7 discuss different types of memory (sensory memory, short-term/working memory, long-term memory, episodic memory, and generic memory). In Chapter 8, we turn to an oft-overlooked but vital topic in memory: forgetting. In Chapter 9, memory is discussed from a life-course perspective. Finally, in each of Chapters 10 through 14, I explore a different applied topic in detail. Chapter 10 looks at memory's impact on social interactions. In Chapter 11, I relate the many ways that memory can impact crime investigations and legal proceedings. Chapter 12 talks about how memory affects our choices of both products and politicians. In Chapter 13, I explore memory and healthcare, and I also discuss memory disorders. Chapter 14, as the concluding chapter, covers memory experts and memory's impact on expertise. I would recommend reading and assigning the chapters in numerical order, although Chapter 9, Memory across the Lifespan, could also be covered early in a course. The applied chapters can be assigned and read interchangeably based on an instructor's discretion, interest, and time.

I welcome your comments and feedback at understandingmemory@rogers.com.

Acknowledgments

I would like to thank Dave Ward for signing me on to write this book and Amy Gordon and Rhiannon Wong for their editorial support. I would also like to thank my colleagues at Wilfrid Laurier University, Dr Anne Wilson and Dr Christian Jordan, for their helpful suggestions, as well as Mathew Darcel for his research assistance. My sincere thanks also to the reviewers for providing helpful insight throughout the writing process:

- Francesco Berladetti, University of Calgary
- Patrick Carolan, Simon Fraser University
- Victoria Chong, Simon Fraser University (student reviewer)
- Nicole Conrad, Saint Mary's University
- Silvia Corbera Lopez, Central Connecticut State University
- Myra Fernandes, University of Waterloo
- Vivian C. Hsu, Penn State Abington
- Stefan Köhler, Western University
- David Lane, St Thomas More College
- Jason Leboe-McGowan, University of Manitoba
- Christine R.P. Lofgren, University of California, Irvine
- Tammy Marche, St Thomas More College
- Jeremy W. Newton, Saint Martin's Univeristy
- Henry L. "Roddy" Roediger, III, Washington University
- Hannah Wade, Saint Mary's University (student reviewer)
- Jill A. Yamashita, California State University, Monterey Bay
- Jacqueline Zimmerman, University of Toronto
- Phillip R. Zoladz, Ohio Northern University

as well as those who chose to remain anonymous.

Finally, I would like to thank my husband Henry and my sons Jon, James, and Josh for encouraging me to take on this project and for supporting me throughout the writing process.

This book is dedicated to my parents who I remember every day.

—Carolyn Ensley

1   The Study of Memory

LEARNING OBJECTIVES

Having read this chapter, you will be able to:

- Compare and contrast different definitions of the term *memory*.
- Explain how Plato, Aristotle, and the associationist philosophers viewed memory.
- Describe how Darwin's theory of evolution influenced the study of memory.
- Describe Ebbinghaus's method for studying memory.
- Compare and contrast early memory research in North America, Europe, and Britain.
- Explain how the cognitive turn influenced the study of memory.
- Compare and contrast the systems view, the processing view, and the principles view of memory.

TOTAL RECALL?

In the 1990 movie *Total Recall*, the lead character attempts to purchase memories of a vacation to Mars only to find out his memory was previously erased and the life he is currently living is a lie. In the 1999 movie *The Matrix*, the lead character feels like he is leading a normal life and then discovers he, like most other Earthlings, is really in a coma and both his experiences and his memories are being generated by a computer. In the 2004 movie *Eternal Sunshine of the Spotless Mind*, the lead characters have their memories erased in order to forget they were ever in a relationship. All of these movies were labelled science fiction, but many viewers wondered, "Will that ever be possible?" Clearly writers and moviegoers alike have a fascination with the mysterious nature of memory and experience. However, speculation about how memory operates is not unique to the twenty-first century. In fact, there are theories about memory and its impact on life dating back to the beginning of recorded history in western society. In this chapter, we will explore the trajectory of memory research from the earliest recordings to the present day. We will see that memory research has rarely deviated from explaining real-life events, perhaps because of an unconscious desire of all people to harness memory and control it, as was done in these blockbuster films.

What Is Memory?

The term *memory* has different meanings in different contexts. It can refer to the use of a past experience on current behaviour. For example, you can say that you used your memory of how to read in order to interpret the words on this page. Memory can also refer to a body of knowledge. You can say that your memory is the sum of all the facts and experiences that you can recall. In addition, memory can refer to an ability; you can say that you use memory to encode, store, and/or recall information. Finally, memory can refer to neural connections in the brain that are formed during experiences. In this book, we will explore each of these aspects of memory: memory as a guide to behaviour, memory as a body of knowledge, memory as an ability, and memory as a biological construct. A full understanding of how memory operates and influences us must consider each of these distinct definitions.

memory
a record of learning

learning
a behaviour that facilitates the acquisition of new information

short-term memory
the contents of a person's awareness

long-term memory
all the memories a person has stored in memory

Although both concepts have a lot in common, it's important to note that **memory** is different from **learning**. Learning is behaviour that facilitates the acquisition of new information. Memory, on the other hand, is a record of learning. A person uses learning to acquire a language, but uses memory to recall the rules and vocabulary in order to speak that language. You learned how to read over a long period of time, and you now use your memory for words and rules of punctuation to read the words on this page. Learning is a process; memory is what remains.

There are two main ways that the concept of memory is further subdivided. The first is into **short-term memory** and **long-term memory**. Short-term memory refers to memories that a person is currently consciously aware of, while long-term memory refers to all of the memories that a person could potentially bring into consciousness should she or he wish to. Your short-term memory at the moment is comprised, in part, of the sentence you just read

We have different memory systems because of our evolutionary history. Frogs (left) use an implicit memory system to catch flies and avoid predators while chimpanzees (right) rely on a consciously accessible explicit memory system to cope with the demands of their more complex environment.

and the meaning of that sentence. The meaning of each word is stored in your long-term memory, along with all of your other knowledge, ready for when you need it. Think about your first day of university. Until this moment, the memory of that day resided in your long-term memory, but you were able to bring it into short-term memory very easily. Over time, thoughts of your first day of university that are currently in short-term memory will be replaced with new information because short-term memory has a limited capacity. However, the memory of your first day at university will remain in long-term memory indefinitely. Short-term memory is discussed in detail in Chapter 3, and long-term memories are discussed in Chapters 4 and 5.

Second, memory is divided into the implicit memory system and the explicit memory system. This division is based on two neural circuits that have formed over the course of human evolution. The first neural circuit is called the **implicit memory system**. As animals evolved the ability to move, being able to change behaviour based on experiences within the environment presented a significant survival advantage. For example, an animal that remembered feeling threatened in a particular location would have been more likely to survive and reproduce than an animal that could not remember being threatened (and subsequently fell prey to the threat at a later date). Similarly, an animal that could form memories of how to perform new actions would have had a survival advantage over an animal that could not form these types of memories. This type of memory is referred to as implicit memory because it functions outside of awareness. Implicit memory is necessarily independent of conscious experience because it evolved long before consciousness evolved, but was retained after consciousness evolved because implicit memory still had survival value. The implicit memory system stores and retrieves information based only on sensory input and primarily utilizes parts of the brain that appeared early in animal evolution. Because of when and how it evolved, the neural circuit involved in implicit memory does not interface with the parts of the brain that give rise to conscious awareness (Kolb & Whishaw, 2012). Implicit memory is discussed in detail in Chapter 5.

implicit memory system

a memory system that evolved to help animals adapt to their environments and learn new behaviours. This system operates outside of awareness.

explicit memory system

a memory system that evolved so that animals could be consciously aware of previous experiences and could use consciousness to deliberately recall information. This system operates within consciousness.

oratory

the art of public speaking

mnemonic

a device that aids in improving memory

metaphor

a figure of speech in which a term or phrase is applied to something to which it is not literally applicable in order to suggest a resemblance

The second neural circuit is the **explicit memory system**. Many researchers, including Bryan Kolb of the University of Lethbridge, argue that explicit memory evolved when, at some point in evolutionary history, some animals developed the ability to form a mental representation of their environment. This mental representation, which we refer to as consciousness, was used to guide the animal's actions and gave the animal a survival advantage in complex ecological niches. Supporters of this view suggest that a new type of memory evolved to be integrated into conscious experience. The existing implicit memory system could not serve this purpose because it takes information from the senses and stores it, and then retrieves information based on matching sensory experience. The new memory system needed to be under conscious control, as it needed to be possible to intentionally retrieve information. Thus, animals with consciousness evolved a neural circuit that started and ended with conscious experience; an animal could now deliberately recall information and have that information as part of its conscious experience. The explicit memory system is responsible for all memory within awareness, including short-term memory and deliberate memory recall. Because the neural circuits for explicit and implicit memory are independent from one another, they can be considered different types of memory (Kolb & Whishaw, 2012).

Memory is fundamental to human experience. When humans lose memory function because of injury or disease, they typically lose their ability to function as autonomous beings. Memory allows for mental time travel, and it supports culture, education, and language. For these reasons, memory has been of interest to humans for all of recorded history. Next, we will explore the ways that memory has been conceptualized and studied from the time of the ancient Greeks to present day. This account illustrates the fact that our understanding of memory is intrinsically tied to technology.

The History of the Study of Memory
Theories of Memory in Ancient Greece and Ancient Egypt

The topic of memory is as old as recorded history in the western world; both the Egyptians and the Greeks had deities devoted to memory. In ancient Egypt, Thoth was the god of memory, wisdom, and knowledge and was usually depicted with the head of an ibis and the body of a man holding the tools of a scribe. Thoth was a very high-ranking god and was given credit for authoring important works of science, religion and philosophy, astronomy, astrology, mathematics, medicine, theology, and **oratory**. The high status of Thoth and the vast array of intellectual accomplishments attributed to him implies that the Egyptians saw memory as fundamental to all aspects of intellectual life. In ancient Greece, Mnemosyne (pronounced "new-mow-seen") was the goddess of memory, from whose name the word **mnemonic** is derived. Mnemosyne was the mother of nine Greek muses, each of whom had a specialized skill related to memory: epic poetry, history, music, lyric poetry, tragedy, hymns, dance, comedy, and astronomy.

Plato and Aristotle

The earliest known *theories* of memory that attempted to explain how memory operated were put forth by Plato (428–348 BCE) and Aristotle (384–322 BCE), two great philosophers whose ideas would inspire all the

Dubois, L.J.J. (Leon Jean Joseph)/NYPL

Thoth, the Egyptian god of memory and wisdom

great thinkers yet to come. Plato used many **metaphors** to describe memory, but the best known is his wax tablet metaphor. In this metaphor, Plato argued that memories were encoded "like words carved onto a wax tablet" and that whether a memory was accessible later depended on how soft the tablet was and how deeply the words were carved in the wax. Plato was a **rationalist** and believed that knowledge came from reason and not from observation, which made memory unknowable (Bruce, 1998).

Unlike Plato, Aristotle was an **empiricist** and argued that it was possible to gain knowledge from observation. Aristotle developed a rudimentary scientific method and used it to put forth some basic ideas about memory, which he presented in his work *On Memory and Reminiscence*. In this treatise, Aristotle argues that memories are triggered by association, and that thinking about a given concept causes the recollection of all things associated with that concept. Aristotle's idea of **associations** would be proven true by the nineteenth-century memory researcher Hermann Ebbinghaus 2000 years later. Aristotle also accurately distinguished between semantic and episodic memory (a distinction that would not be made by psychologists until 1972) and implicit and explicit access to information (Ross, 1930). The concepts of semantic and episodic memory will be discussed in more detail in Chapters 5 and 6.

Ancient Greek Memorization: The Method of Loci

In Greco-Roman times, public figures were trained in oratory and **rhetoric** and expected to learn and deliver long complex speeches with perfect accuracy. The work of Cicero (106–43 BCE) shows that the Greeks and Romans understood memory well enough to develop an effective mnemonic known as the **method of loci** by at least 400 BCE, although who invented it and when is not clear (see Box 1.1; Yates, 1966). Regardless of its origins, all descriptions of the method of loci were comprised of three steps. First, the thinker was to envision a great house containing a variety of objects in connected rooms and memorize a fixed path

Mnemosyne, the goddess of memory in ancient Greece

through this house. The second step was to associate the first to-be-remembered item with the first location in the house, the second to-be-remembered item with the second location in the house, and so on (see Figure 1.1). Finally, the memorizer needed to rehearse the speech. When the memorizer wished to recall the items placed in the imagined house, the memorizer would simply imagine walking the set path. Cicero hypothesizes that the method of loci is effective because memory is closely linked to time and order and that vision is the most powerful of the senses (Yates, 1966). The modern explanation for the effectiveness of the method is discussed in Chapter 14.

The method of loci survived the fall of Rome by being included in a text written by Martianus Capella, which formed the basis for education in the Middle Ages. When rhetoric fell out of favour as a cornerstone of education, the mnemonic fell out of favour as well. However, as you will see in Chapter 14, people who compete in modern memory competitions rely heavily on the method of loci.

rationalist

a person who believes that using reason, rather than experience, authority, or spiritual revelation, provides the primary basis for knowledge.

empiricist

a person who believes that knowledge is gained through observation

Delaware Art Museum, Wilmington, USA/Samuel and Mary R. Bancroft Memorial/Bridgeman Images

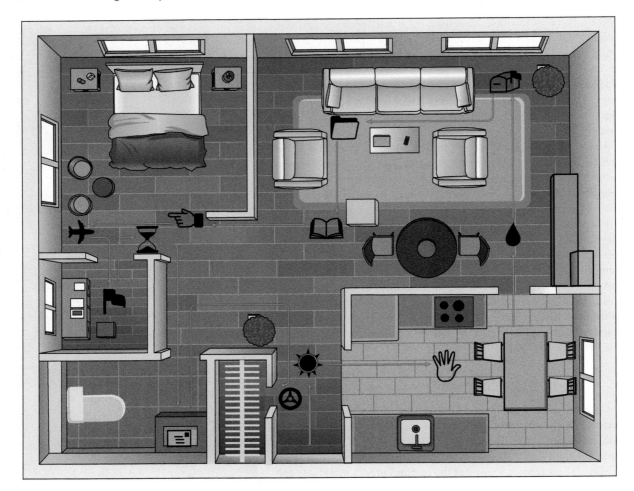

Figure 1.1   The three steps of the method of loci

The method of loci has been used to memorize lists of items for thousands of years. The method of loci involves these simple steps: Imagine a great house that you know well; memorize a path through that great house with familiar stops along the way; imagine placing objects at familiar stops along the path. When you wish to recall the list, imagine yourself walking the route through the house and the list will come to mind in order! This illustration shows how the method of loci might be used in a modern setting.

Source: Author generated using kpalimski/iStockphoto

associations

links between ideas
that give rise to
memories

From the Fall of Rome through the Eighteenth Century

Between the years 406 and 600, the Roman Empire lost its power and the Christian church became the sole source of knowledge in western society. Greek philosophy was no longer taught and Aristotle's ideas about empiricism were forgotten. Instead Saint Augustine (354–430), an influential philosopher at the time, expanded on Plato's rationalism to stipulate that true knowledge could only be obtained through religious contemplation. Once again, the prevailing view was that memory was unknowable. Saint Augustine also argued that humans were permanently

DIY EXPERIMENT

BOX 1.1

The Mysterious Origins of the Method of Loci

Read the following story about the origins of the method of loci, and retell the story when you encounter Box 1.3 at the end of this chapter.

One of the most well-known accounts of memory in ancient Greece is the legend of Simonides of Ceos (ca 556–468 BCE), a Greek lyric poet who claimed he was inspired to create the method of loci after he attended a disastrous banquet for a nobleman named Sopras. According to the legend, retold by both Cicero (ca 105–43 BCE) and Quintilian (ca 35–100 CE), Simonides recited a poem about boxing for the guests at the banquet, making frequent reference to the gods Castor and Pollux. Sopras chided Simonides about the references after, stating that he would only pay him half his fee and that Simonides should charge Castor and Pollux for the other half, presumably because Simonides's poem was long and made many references to the strengths of these gods. Simonides was then allegedly told that he must leave the banquet hall because two men were outside waiting for him. However, when Simonides looked for the men outside, no one was to be found. At this point, according to the story, the banquet hall collapsed, crushing all attendees beyond recognition, but sparing Simonides who was outside. Families desperately wanted their loved ones identified and Simonides obliged them by recalling the seating arrangement of all guests, making it possible for the families to claim the correct bodies. Simonides later credited this experience as the inspiration for the method of loci. Later philosophers, including Cicero, would cite the story as fiction; however, the method of loci was a popular memory aid for scholars from ancient times to the Renaissance, regardless of where the idea originated.

cursed to live in ignorance because Eve ate from the tree of knowledge in the Garden of Eden, making seeking knowledge about nature akin to making a deal with the devil (Walsh, Teo, & Baydala, 2014).

The Enlightenment

From the time of Saint Augustine until the nineteenth century, independently seeking knowledge was considered a sin. However during the seventeenth and eighteenth centuries, a period commonly known as the **Enlightenment**, a number of philosophers, including Thomas Hobbes (1588–1679), John Stuart Mill (1806–73), David Hume (1711–76), and John Locke (1632–1704), argued for using reason as a source for ideas rather than referring to religious tradition, and revived Aristotle's ideas about factors that influence the strength of an association in memory. These **associationists** suggested that the strength of an association may be influenced by its vividness, its distinctiveness, the amount of study time, repetition, and the topic's personal relevance to the individual (Bower, 2000; Walsh et al., 2014). For example, according to associationism, thinking of one's birthday will be more likely to bring into consciousness memories of the location of past birthday celebrations than memories of the name of the server at the restaurant where the celebration took place. This is because memories of past celebrations would be vivid, personally relevant, and likely thought about many times in the days following the celebration, whereas the name of the server would not create a vivid memory, would not be personally relevant, and would not have been thought about after the party.

rhetoric

the art of speaking in a way that informs, persuades, or motivates particular audiences in specific situations

method of loci

a mnemonic that involves visualizing to-be-remembered images at different locations along a well-known path

Enlightenment

an era from the 1650s to the 1780s in which cultural and intellectual forces in western Europe emphasized reason, analysis, and individualism rather than traditional lines of authority

This painting depicts Adam and Eve, with the snake above them tempting them to pick forbidden fruit from the tree of knowledge. At the time this painting was created, the western church argued that seeking knowledge about natural objects involved making a pact with the devil.

associationist

a philosopher who believed that ideas are brought to consciousness through associations with other ideas

nonsense syllables

pronounceable strings of letters that are not actual words, examples in English would include dak, ver, and maz

learning curve

a negatively accelerating function in which additional practice is very helpful in the early stages of learning but has less benefit over time

The Theory of Evolution and Its Impact on the Study of the Human Mind

While the associationists had ideas about memory, they didn't study memory. In fact, the human body and its functions were not formally studied in Europe until Charles Darwin (1809–82) published *On the Origin of Species* in 1859, which proposed the theory of evolution. Darwin's work, combined with the work of other nineteenth-century naturalists and geologists, changed the academic climate in Europe, eventually leading researchers to explore all aspects of human biology and psychology for the first time. Humans were not seen as being made in the image of God with minds that were unknowable as much as they were seen as having evolved from other animals with minds that were biological. The *Punch Almanac* cartoon shown on the opposite page illustrates this philosophical shift well by stating that "Man is but a worm" (Walsh et al., 2014).

Darwin believed that there was continuity between nonhuman animals and humans, and that human memory must therefore have its roots in nonhuman animal memory. This new view meant that methods that could not be used on humans to study memory, such as lesioning the brain to see what parts of the brain are required for memory, or controlling all stimulation an animal receives throughout life, could be used on animals and the results generalized to humans. Darwin may also have identified implicit memory (memory without awareness), writing in a notebook that he had observed that humans make selections and classifications seemingly without awareness (Ray, 2013).

The Beginning of Experimental Psychology and the Work of Gustav Fechner and Hermann Ebbinghaus

Darwin's work brought on a flurry of research in human biology and encouraged researchers to study the human mind for the first time. The first psychological experiments were conducted by Gustav Fechner, a German physician and physicist, in the 1860s. Fechner's work in psychophysics established that empirical methods could be used to derive theories that predicted human experience. Inspired by Fechner, Hermann Ebbinghaus (1850–1909), a German who had studied philosophy in university, embarked upon an investigation of human memory in the 1880s after establishing the first psychology laboratory at the University of Leipzig in 1879. Ebbinghaus chose to put Aristotle's ideas about memory resulting from associations to the empirical test. He created a simple hypothesis: If Aristotle (and by extension the associationists) is correct and memories are connected through association, then learning a list containing items for which a person has preconceived associations between the items should take less time than learning a list in which the person has no preconceived associations between the items. To test this hypothesis, Ebbinghaus created 2300 **nonsense syllables** (consonant-vowel-consonant) and memorized these lists until he could repeat them without error (such as is shown in list A in Figure 1.2). He then compared the amount of time it took to learn a new list in two conditions: one condition where he had learned nonsense syllables together before (e.g., list B in Figure 1.2) and one where the nonsense syllables were borrowed at random from a variety of other lists (such as list C in Figure 1.2). If memory was based on associations, learning should be faster in the associated condition than in the random condition, which is exactly what Ebbinghaus found in his experiments (Walsh et al., 2014).

Ebbinghaus used his data to develop a number of theories. First, he devised the **learning curve** based on his observation that additional practice is very helpful in the early stages of learning but has less benefit over time (see Figure 1.3a). Ebbinghaus also showed that spreading practice out over time leads to better learning than completing all practice in one setting; this distinction is currently known as the distinction between **distributed practice** and **massed practice**. In addition, Ebbinghaus found that most forgetting occurs soon after learning and thus developed the negatively sloped **forgetting curve** shown in Figure 1.3b. Ebbinghaus's work on forgetting revealed that it takes less time to learn material when the material has been learned before and then forgotten, compared to learning the material the first time, a concept he termed **savings**. The discovery of savings was very important because it suggested that some trace of learned material may still exist even after it is no longer possible for a person to consciously recall the material. Ebbinghaus's theories have stood the test of time and are still used to predict patterns in learning and forgetting.

"Man is but a worm." This cartoon was published in Punch's Almanac in 1881. It was inspired by a worm-related publication by Darwin earlier that year. Although satirical, this comic shows that in the 1880s it was accepted that humans evolved and that memory was the result of evolution and had a biological, instead of ethereal, basis.

distributed practice
practice that takes place over several learning sessions

massed practice
learning that occurs during one long practice session

A		B		C	
DUR	KLO	DUR	IMM	DUR	IRG
POY	GUV	POY	GUV	KLO	YUV
YAT	MUB	YAT	TUH	TOS	OON
FEN	RAV	FEN	VID	ERF	CEN
JIT	LIG	TEG	LIG	OLT	LIG
BIF	WUC	ELB	WUC	NUG	UNN

Figure 1.2 An example of Ebbinghaus's stimuli and hypothesis

Ebbinghaus would learn a list like the one shown in box A. He would then attempt to learn new lists. Some had similar associations in them like in box B, and some were random lists made up of syllables not studied together before. Ebbinghaus predicted that after learning box A, it would be faster to learn box B than box C because of the common associations in boxes A and B, and this is what he found when he conducted his experiments.

forgetting curve

a negatively accelerated function over time predicting that most forgetting occurs soon after learning, and that as time goes on less and less additional forgetting occurs

savings

refers to the fact that it takes less time to learn material on subsequent attempts, compared to the first time

behaviourist era

a time in the history of psychology when the majority of research focused on the observable effects of experience on behaviour

parsimony

the notion that when given the choice, the hypothesis that makes the fewest assumptions should be chosen

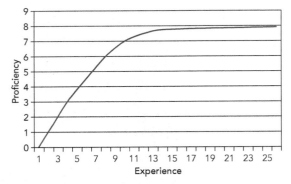

Figure 1.3a Ebbinghaus's learning curve

A typical illustration of Ebbinghaus's learning curve, which shows that experience has a bigger effect early in learning than later on.

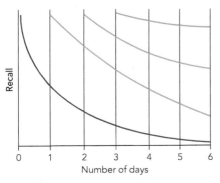

Figure 1.3b Ebbinghaus's forgetting curve

A typical illustration of Ebbinghaus's forgetting curve. The red line shows recall over time when there is only one learning session. The green lines show recall over time when there are additional practice sessions on three subsequent days. Note that when there is repeated practice there is very little forgetting.

Trends in Memory Research from 1890 to 1970

As the field of psychology began to gain popularity around the world, memory became an increasingly popular topic of study. In the early twentieth century, three main groups of memory researchers emerged in the western world: the verbal learning tradition in the United States, the Gestalt tradition in Europe, and the schema tradition in Britain.

North America: Verbal Learning, Skill Learning, and Transfer

In the United States, researchers focused on expanding on the work of Ebbinghaus and examined learning and memory for nonsense syllables or words. Because the research focused on memory for lexical items, it is typically referred to as the verbal learning tradition. The verbal learning tradition was heavily influenced by the emergence of behaviourism in the early part of the twentieth century. During the **behaviourist era**, the majority of psychological research focused on observable changes in behaviour brought about by experience. Prominent behaviourist researchers in the United States included Edward Tolman (1886–1959), Edward Thorndike (1874–1949), John B. Watson (1878–1958), and B.F. Skinner (1904–90). All of these researchers were interested in observable aspects of learning (such as how the consequences of behaviour influenced subsequent behaviour), but in the interest of **parsimony** were not comfortable making assumptions about the inner, unobservable, mechanisms that may be related to behaviour. Researchers supporting behaviourism were in positions of great power during this time, and it was

Hermann Ebbinghaus (1850–1909). Ebbinghaus was the first person to explore memory using empirical methods.

Serena Williams (left), considered one of the greatest athletes of all time, and Gary Kasparov (right), considered one of the greatest chess players of all time

nearly impossible to get funding for research, publish journal articles, or teach courses that contradicted behaviourist principles. Thus, memory research during the behaviourist era revolved around predicting how memory-related behaviours, such as recall and recognition, might vary across conditions. No attempts were made to model the cognitive structures that made memory possible because behaviourists were strict empiricists: If something could not be observed, no conclusions about how it operated could be made. The methodological rigour that was developed during the behaviourist era in order for a behaviourist to conclude, with confidence, that an observed change in behaviour was the result of the experimental manipulation helped legitimize psychology in the realm of science and remains a crucial element of quality memory research to this day.

physical skill
how to perform a task using the body, such as riding a bicycle or playing a violin

In the 1920s, research into how people learn to do activities or master different skills began to appear quite frequently in psychological research journals. Of interest were both **physical skills**, such as sports or playing musical instruments, and **cognitive skills**, such as learning how to play chess. Research usually involved monitoring the amount of time spent on the skill and the observable change in performance. The study of skill was probably the first study of applied memory.

In response to research on skills, researchers in the 1950s began to study learning **transfer**, that is, how much more easily one can learn how to do a task if one has already learned to do another task. For example, Miller (1956) found when participants were presented with lists of letters to be recalled, they were better able to recall portions of the list that contained familiar groupings of letters, such as CIA (for Central Intelligence Agency), than they were unfamiliar letter groupings such as ICA. This is an example of transfer because knowledge of the acronym CIA directly benefited recall of the letters CIA in the recall task. At this time other researchers, such as Lyman Porter and Carl Duncan of Northwestern University, also identified **negative transfer**, a reduction in memory performance as a result of prior knowledge. Porter

Miss Millicent Woodword (age 19) was Europe's fastest typist in the 1920s, typing 239 words per minute. The average typing speed in present-day Canada is 40 words per minute.

cognitive skill

how to perform a task that requires thinking, such as playing chess or completing a Sudoku

transfer

the extent to which learning of one ability accelerates learning of another ability

negative transfer

the extent to which learning of one ability interferes with the learning of another ability

Gestalt approach

to always see the whole as greater than the sum of the individual parts

schema

a cognitive framework that helps to organize and interpret information

and Duncan (1953) created three lists of words (lists A, B, and C). Participants had two learning sessions, and in each session they learned different pairings. Half of the participants learned pairs from lists A and B and then learned pairs from lists A and C, while the other half of participants learned pairs from lists A and B, then learned a second, different set of pairs from lists A and B. Porter and Duncan (1953) found no difference in the recall for the second list for participants in the A–C group but substantially worse performance for participants in the A–B group, indicating that having learned one set of A–B pairings interfered with learning a new set of A–B pairings (negative transfer). The results of negative transfer experiments led researchers to see for the first time that forgetting is not necessarily the result of a memory decaying, but can also result from learning new material. This would lead to *interference theories of forgetting*, which are discussed in detail in Chapter 8.

Europe: Gestalt Psychology

While behaviourism dominated in psychology departments in the United States and Canada during the first half of the twentieth century, the Gestalt approach led by Max Wertheimer (1880–1943), Kurt Koffka (1886–1941), and Wolfgang Köhler (1887–1967) dominated research in Germany. The **Gestalt approach** was to always assume that the whole was greater than the sum of its individual parts (see Figure 1.4). Unlike the verbal learning tradition, the Gestalt tradition emphasized the study of internal representations rather than observable responses. Several young researchers escaped Nazi Europe and brought the Gestalt approach to universities in North America. This group, which included George Mandler and Endel Tulving (who eventually conducted research at Canadian universities), rejected the verbal learning approach and instead studied how the internal organization of material influences memory.

Figure 1.4   Gestalt theory

The arrangement of these three acute angles gives rise to the appearance of a triangle floating in their centre. This is an example of a case where what is perceived when all elements are considered together, in context, is greater than what is perceived when they are perceived individually, and is therefore an example of the whole being greater than the sum of the parts.

Britain: Schema Theory

Frederic Bartlett was the first professor of experimental psychology at the University of Cambridge in England. In the 1930s, Bartlett (1932) discovered that learners often only actually recall small parts of the material that they have learned, and then fill in the missing pieces based on general knowledge about the subject. Bartlett hypothesized that people were guided by **schemas**. Schemas contain knowledge about what to expect in a given situation. For example, a person who was at a wedding may only really remember the bride, the groom, and the date, but may be able to reconstruct the event using their schema for a wedding, and may also "remember" a church, flowers, and vows based on the schema, not on actual recollection. Some of Bartlett's most compelling work showed the effect of culture on people's ability to remember stories. In a famous study, Bartlett had British participants read a Canadian Indigenous folklore story called "The War of the Ghosts," imploring them to remember as many details as possible. He then tested participants' recall for parts of the story at various intervals. Bartlett found that when elements in the story did not match a schema possessed by the reader, the reader would exchange the story element for something more familiar. For example, participants who were not familiar with canoes recalled people riding in boats because the British participants had an existing schema for riding in boats but not for riding in canoes. Research on schemas grew in popularity worldwide in the early 1970s.

Early Research into the Neuroscience of Memory

In 1825, future phrenologist Franz Gall (1758–1828) proposed that memory, like all human traits, was localized, meaning we have one memory area in the brain (Gall, 1835). This notion was supported by the work of Paul Broca (1824–80), who found that damage to a specific area in the left hemisphere resulted in profound **agnosia** (loss of vocabulary) and of Carl Wernicke (1848–1905), who found that damage to a different area of the left temporal lobe resulted in profound **agrammatism** (loss of grammar). The apparent localization of the memory for words and rules of grammar suggested that memories were in fact localized to specific parts of the brain.

In 1921, Richard Semon (1859–1918), a German zoologist and evolutionary biologist who studied memory, argued in his book *The Mneme* that specific stimuli left permanent memory traces or **engrams** in the brain. Semon's hypothesis revived Plato's memory analogy suggesting that memories were like impressions carved into a wax tablet. In his thesis, Semon suggested that the stimuli produce "[a] permanent record . . . written or engraved on the irritable substance" (Semon, 1921, p. 24). Semon believed that these engrams then instructed the body how to behave and he used his theory to explain the involuntary coordination between body parts. Semon's work was published after he died by suicide in 1918 allegedly because he was depressed over Germany's defeat in World War I. Karl Lashley (1890–1958), an eminent American zoologist, set out to confirm that Semon's (1921) engrams were localized in specific neurons by carefully measuring rat behaviour, such as food-seeking behaviour, before selectively lesioning their brains. Lashley argued that if engrams were localized, then a rat would have an engram for food-seeking behaviour and that it would be possible to destroy the engram through lesioning and eliminate the food-seeking behaviour. However, Lashley found that no amount of lesioning resulted in the cessation of food-seeking behaviour, suggesting that rats did not in fact possess localized engrams that controlled their behaviour. Lashley (1929) instead argued that all parts of the brain contributed equally to the formation of memories. Lashley is often lauded for disproving Semon's notion that engrams are localized; however, Semon (1921) never actually specified whether engrams were located on single neurons or distributed across neurons (Schacter, Eich, & Tulving, 1978).

Donald Hebb (1904–85), a Canadian psychologist who became a student of Lashley's at Harvard in the 1930s, challenged Lashley's notion that the brain was a passive recipient of memories through the mere presentation of stimuli and instead argued in his seminal work *The Organization of Behavior* (Hebb, 1949) that the brain actively creates memories in a two-stage process. In the first stage, a new pattern of activation reverberates throughout the brain for some time. In the second stage, connections between neurons that are firing simultaneously become stronger. Hebb (1949) argued that moving from stage one to stage two took time, which would explain why people who suffer from head trauma are often unable to recall events that immediately preceded the trauma. Hebb's ideas about memory consolidation were later proven to be an accurate description of the neuroscientific processes involved with memory formation. (This is discussed in more detail in Chapter 4.)

MRC Cognition and Brain Unit and the Department of Experimental Psychology at the University of Cambridge

Sir Frederic Bartlett proposed that memories were largely reconstructed on demand using schemas.

agnosia

the loss of memory for words

agrammatism

the loss of the ability to create grammatically correct sentences

engram

a specific location in the brain holding the trace of a specific memory

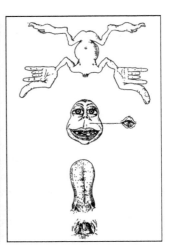

Dr Wilder Penfield (left) was the first to map the human brain. Penfield stimulated parts of the brain of conscious patients and observed what was elicited by the stimulation. Penfield and Boldrey's (centre) homunculus (right) is featured in every textbook that discusses the brain and behaviour.

Wilder Penfield (1891–1976) was a Canadian neurosurgeon working at McGill University at the same time as Hebb. Penfield treated people with epilepsy by lesioning their brains and set out to map the brain in order to allow him to avoid damaging areas of the brain that were critical to normal functioning. Penfield mapped the brain by interacting with conscious patients while simultaneously stimulating different parts of their brains. Penfield (1952) famously reported that stimulating the temporal lobes could lead to the vivid recall of specific memories, which led the academic community to believe once again in the concept of localized memories. What wasn't noted at the time was that only a small percentage of Penfield's patients reported any vivid memories when their temporal lobes were stimulated, and those who did often "recalled" things that could not really be memories (like seeing oneself standing on the side of the road). Modern critics speculate that those who reported "memories" during Penfield's neural-stimulation sessions were more likely reporting dream-like experiences than actual memories. Thus, Penfield never actually produced good evidence for localized memories, even though many people have been led to believe that he did. Hebb and Penfield are still Canadian heroes, however, for establishing the study of neuroscience and for ground-breaking research that has prevented thousands of people from suffering functional loss due to brain surgery. In addition, Penfield's homunculus is featured in every textbook that touches on brain and behaviour.

The Cognitive Revolution

In the late 1950s, a number of events occurred that ended the behaviourist era. First, a small but vocal group of researchers began to argue that behavioural mechanisms (such as reward and punishment) could not adequately explain many important psychological phenomena. For example, in 1959, Noam Chomsky published "A Review of B.F. Skinner's Verbal Behavior," which effectively discredited the behavioural explanation for language acquisition by noting that children's language is very creative and that children around the world make similar grammatical errors when learning language. This suggested that innate mechanisms, not adult guidance, underlie language development. Also in 1958, British psychologist Donald Broadbent (1926–93) published *Perception and Communication*, which included many experimental findings that, to be adequately explained, required an exploration of mental events. In 1960, Massachusetts Institute for Technology (MIT) professor George Miller (1926–2012) published *Plans and the Structure of Behavior*, which argued that planning, and not just a sequence of stimulus–response actions, governed behaviour, which was a radical break from behaviourism. Finally, in 1961, American psychologists Allan Newell and Herbert Simon proposed an information-processing approach to studying cognition, in part because the case of H.M. suggested that human cognition consists of distinct mental modules (see Box 1.2). The information-processing approach suggested by Newell and Simon was very well received and culminated in what is commonly known as the **cognitive revolution** in psychology. The cognitive revolution changed the nature of memory research from that which described overt behaviour resulting from learning to that which fostered the development of models of how information is coded by the human cognitive system.

Advances in computer technology at this time inspired researchers to begin to use computer analogies for many types of cognitive functions, including memory. Researchers asserted that, like a computer, human memory must require the same three capacities to use memory: the capacity to encode, the capacity to store, and the capacity to retrieve information. Researchers assumed that while these three stages may interact, encoding, storage, and retrieval are distinct types of processes, just like they are different processes within a computer. This computer analogy would heavily influence the modal model of memory that is discussed in the next section.

cognitive revolution
the period in the early 1960s during which psychologists began to use the experimental methods developed by the behaviourists to develop theories about cognitive functioning

anterograde amnesia
the loss of the ability to form new memories

CASE STUDY

BOX 1.2

A Dramatic Change in the Neuroscience of Memory: The Case of Henry Molaison

In 1952, Penfield and Hebb had the scientific community convinced that memories were localized but that memory as an ability was part of general intellectual ability. Then, in 1957, everything changed when William Scoville (1906–84) and Brenda Milner (b. 1918) reported the case of Henry Gustav Molaison (1926–2008) or H.M. H.M. had a bilateral medial temporal lobectomy (in other words, the midsection of his temporal lobes was removed from both hemispheres of his brain), which also removed most of his hippocampus and amygdala in an attempt to cure his epilepsy. As a result of the surgery, H.M. developed profound **anterograde amnesia**; H.M. could not form new memories. What was important about H.M. in terms of understanding the neuroscience of memory was not the fact that he developed a complex case of amnesia but rather that he retained his other cognitive abilities, including language, perception, and reasoning. Thus, the case of H.M. showed that memory was a distinct cerebral function that was separate from other cognitive abilities. The case of H.M. would inform the direction of subsequent research on the neuroscience of memory (Squire & Wixted, 2011). Over time, researchers noticed that H.M. was able to sustain information in the short term but not the long term and was able to learn new motor tasks but not new facts. These two findings led researchers to eventually establish that short-term memory retention, long-term memory, and procedural memory are all biologically distinct. It is fair to say that the case of H.M. helped bring about the cognitive revolution in the 1960s. H.M. is mentioned throughout this book.

baby boom

a large cohort of North Americans born between 1945 and 1963

modal model of memory

a heuristic, first introduced by Atkinson and Shiffrin (1968), for thinking about how memory processes work. The modal model includes three main components: sensory memory, short-term memory and long-term memory.

heuristic

a loosely defined approach to solving a problem

episodic memory

a type of long-term memory comprised of memories of specific situations, experiences, or events

semantic memory

a type of long-term memory comprised of meanings and concepts

procedural memory

a type of long-term memory comprised of knowledge of how to perform actions

triarchic model of memory

a model of memory proposed by Endel Tulving in which different types of memory are distinguished by different types of consciousness

autonoetic consciousness

the ability for one to imagine oneself in past, future, or counterfactual situations

The cognitive revolution occurred at the same time the **baby boom** generation was becoming old enough for university; the increased demand for university education at that time led to the creation of many new universities and a dramatic increase in published work in all areas of psychology. Within the body of psychological research, memory research tripled between 1940 and 1970. In 1960, approximately 588 journal articles were published that referred to the topic of memory; in 1970, this number was 2386.

Key Events in Memory Research Following the Cognitive Revolution

The Modal Model of Memory

In 1968, Richard Atkinson and Richard Shiffrin published "Human Memory: A Proposed System and Its Control Processes," which is commonly referred to as the **modal model of memory**. The modal model is a **heuristic** for thinking about memory, not an accurate model, but it has nonetheless been very influential in guiding discussions on memory. The model consists of a sensory store, a short-term store, and a long-term store, as well as a control process that serves multiple important functions. First, the control process selects a subset of the material from the sensory store to become active in the short-term store. Second, control processes are used to rehearse material in the short-term store; rehearsed material can then enter the long-term store. Finally, the control process can activate material from the long-term store and bring it to the short-term store. It is presumed that it is the contents of the short-term store that people use to interact with the outside world. The modal model is a heuristic and not a model because there are many exceptions to memory operating in this way. For example, sensory information does not need to pass through a short-term store to get to the long-term store. In fact, it may be better to understand the sensory information as activating information in the long-term store that then becomes active in the short-term store. Although the modal model is descriptive and not predictive (it is just a guideline), it heavily influenced subsequent memory research. As researchers strove to find evidence for the validity of this heuristic, they discovered a great deal about the nature and extent of short-term memory, long-term memory, and attention. Many models of short-term memory and working memory have been developed since 1968, each working as an improvement on the last. We will discuss these models in depth in Chapter 3.

Multiple Memory Systems

Following the cognitive revolution, research demonstrating that memory could be short term or long term, semantic or episodic, verbal or nonverbal. etc. led to the question as to the extent to which these systems were physiologically and psychologically distinct from one another. Many researchers took to answering this question by looking at memory performance in individuals with brain lesions and by looking at blood-flow patterns in the human brain when a person was completing various types of memory-related tasks. The results indicated that different types of memory tasks did indeed involve different parts of the brain; the medial temporal lobe and the hippocampus were needed for encoding new episodic memories, the left temporal lobe was essential for verbal memory, the right parietal lobe was important for visual memory, the amygdala was essential for memories of emotional nature, and the cerebellum, premotor cortex, and basal ganglia were involved in learning new motor skills (Bower, 2000; see Figure 1.5 and Table 1.1). The fact that researchers found, almost immediately, that there were physiological correlates to the different types of memory lent credence to the argument that the memory systems were distinct, and spurred on research in the cognitive neuroscience of memory, which continues to become more and more detailed with advances in the technology.

The Episodic/Semantic Memory Distinction

In 1972, Endel Tulving argued that there is an important distinction between **episodic memory**, which he defined as our memory for specific events that have happened (like a party you went to), and **semantic memory**, which he defined as our knowledge about words and concepts. Tulving argued that these types of memory, as well as **procedural memory** (knowledge of how to perform actions), were distinct because they were associated with different types of conscious awareness. Tulving developed the **triarchic model of memory** to reflect these differences. According to the model, episodic memories are linked to **autonoetic consciousness**, or an awareness of one's self within the memory. For example, if you not only remember the name of the restaurant you went to for your last birthday, but you can also recall being at that restaurant, you are experiencing autonoetic consciousness. In contrast, semantic memories are associated with **noetic consciousness**, which is a conscious experience based on knowledge. For example, if asked what day you were born, the correct day, month, and year will come into your conscious awareness, but it will not be accompanied by a memory of a personal experience, making the conscious experience associated with the recall of semantic information qualitatively different from the recall of episodic information. Lastly, Tulving argued that procedural memories are associated with **anoetic consciousness**, or sensation and perception without cognitive content. For example, when asked to recall a procedural memory

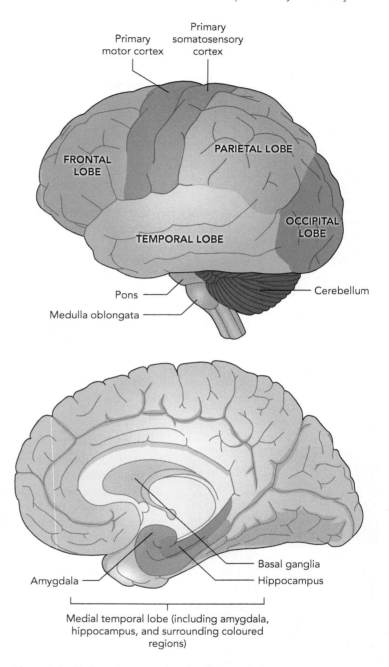

Figure 1.5 Brain regions associated with memory

See Table 1.1 for a broad overview of functions of each region. There will be greater detail on these structures later in this chapter.

Source: (top) Adapted from https://commons.wikimedia.org/wiki/File:Blausen_0101_Brain_LateralView.png; (bottom) Adapted based on Raslau, F.D., Mark, I.T., Klein, A.P., Ulmer, J.L., Mathews, V., & Mark, L.P. (2015). Memory part 2: The role of the medial temporal lobe. *American Journal of Neuroradiology* 36(5), 846–9, Figure 1.

Table 1.1   Types of memory and their associated brain regions

Type of Memory	Associated Brain Region
Episodic memories	Medial temporal lobe and hippocampus
Verbal memories	Left temporal lobe
Visual memory	Right parietal lobe
Motor-skill memories	Cerebellum, premotor cortex, basal ganglia
Emotional memories	Amygdala

such as riding a bicycle, a person will be unable to bring that memory into conscious awareness, even though they may be perfectly able to ride a bicycle if one is available. Tulving suggested that the majority of previous "verbal learning" research (where participants memorized word pairs such as "queen–apple") was actually testing episodic memory, not semantic memory; participants had to remember the specific learning instance (or episode) in order to remember the pair of items. Tulving also argued that there were so many differences in episodic memory and semantic memory that they must represent different memory systems. Tulving's theory was extremely important to memory research and has been the topic of theoretical debate for more than 40 years, with some researchers thinking semantic memories are derived from episodic memories and others arguing that the two types of memories are distinct. The debate was settled using neuroimaging techniques and will be discussed in more depth in subsequent chapters. Note that Aristotle implied episodic and semantic memory were distinct in his work published in 350 BCE!

noetic consciousness

a state of mind associated with knowledge and intellect

anoetic consciousness

a state of mind associated with pure perception and emotion without cognitive content

The Explicit/Implicit Memory Distinction

In 1986, Jim Cheesman and Philip Merikle demonstrated clear evidence for implicit memory, or memory without awareness, a type of memory that could influence behaviour but was not explicitly accessible and differed from **explicit memory**. This led to a flurry of research examining the distinction between memory that we could remember knowing (explicit memory, such as recalling a list of words) and memory that we could not (implicit memory, such as **priming effects** of very briefly presented stimuli). Neuroimaging research conducted suggests that the implicit/explicit distinction is valid; different areas of the brain are active during tasks designed to elicit each memory type (Schacter, 1987). Chapter 5 explores the explicit/implicit memory distinction in more detail.

The Emergence of Applied Memory Research

By 1975, there were dozens of well-replicated models of memory that could explain sensory, short-term, working, semantic, episodic, autobiographical, implicit, and visual memory. However, in 1978, renowned psychologist Ulric Neisser questioned the ecological validity of these models that were constructed by studying typical people completing *artificial* tasks in *laboratory*

Ulric Neisser inspired cognitive psychologists to study applied topics.

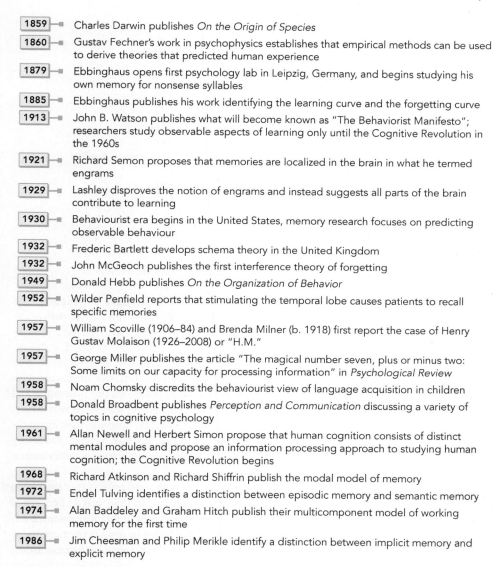

1859 — Charles Darwin publishes *On the Origin of Species*

1860 — Gustav Fechner's work in psychophysics establishes that empirical methods can be used to derive theories that predicted human experience

1879 — Ebbinghaus opens first psychology lab in Leipzig, Germany, and begins studying his own memory for nonsense syllables

1885 — Ebbinghaus publishes his work identifying the learning curve and the forgetting curve

1913 — John B. Watson publishes what will become known as "The Behaviorist Manifesto"; researchers study observable aspects of learning only until the Cognitive Revolution in the 1960s

1921 — Richard Semon proposes that memories are localized in the brain in what he termed engrams

1929 — Lashley disproves the notion of engrams and instead suggests all parts of the brain contribute to learning

1930 — Behaviourist era begins in the United States, memory research focuses on predicting observable behaviour

1932 — Frederic Bartlett develops schema theory in the United Kingdom

1932 — John McGeoch publishes the first interference theory of forgetting

1949 — Donald Hebb publishes *On the Organization of Behavior*

1952 — Wilder Penfield reports that stimulating the temporal lobe causes patients to recall specific memories

1957 — William Scoville (1906–84) and Brenda Milner (b. 1918) first report the case of Henry Gustav Molaison (1926–2008) or "H.M."

1957 — George Miller publishes the article "The magical number seven, plus or minus two: Some limits on our capacity for processing information" in *Psychological Review*

1958 — Noam Chomsky discredits the behaviourist view of language acquisition in children

1958 — Donald Broadbent publishes *Perception and Communication* discussing a variety of topics in cognitive psychology

1961 — Allan Newell and Herbert Simon propose that human cognition consists of distinct mental modules and propose an information processing approach to studying human cognition; the Cognitive Revolution begins

1968 — Richard Atkinson and Richard Shiffrin publish the modal model of memory

1972 — Endel Tulving identifies a distinction between episodic memory and semantic memory

1974 — Alan Baddeley and Graham Hitch publish their multicomponent model of working memory for the first time

1986 — Jim Cheesman and Philip Merikle identify a distinction between implicit memory and explicit memory

Figure 1.6   A timeline of significant events in the history of the study of memory

explicit memory

a memory that an individual can bring into conscious awareness

priming effect

when the recognition of an item is facilitated by previous exposure to a related item

ecologically valid

when the parameters of an experiment mirror the real-world situations to which the results of the experiments are to be applied

exceptional memory

memory that exceeds what is typical in the population; for example, being able to remember events from every day for the past 20 years or being able to recite *pi* to 200 decimal places

autobiographical memory

one's recall of experiencing events from one's own life

settings; none of the results could be applied to the real world. Neisser's opinion was very influential and thus began a frenzy of research in **ecologically valid**, or applied, memory. Researchers began to study how memory operated in different aspects of everyday life of both typical individuals and individuals with cognitive disorders. They also began to research **exceptional memory**, investigating how was it that actors could remember thousands of lines of prose, how musicians learned music, how taxi drivers could remember the routes around huge cites, and how some people could learn long sequences of numbers, such as the first 80 digits comprising the value of *pi*. For the first time, researchers also examined **autobiographical memory**, or

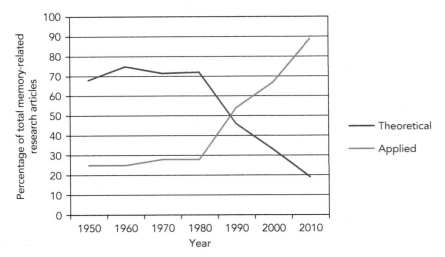

Figure 1.7   Publication frequency for articles addressing applied and theoretical memory research questions from 1950 to 2010

The proportion of theoretical and applied memory topics in the memory literature 1950 to 2010 is based on the PsycINFO database. Note the growing trend toward applied memory research starting in about 1980.

one's memory of one's own life, and learned how the sense of self is intimately connected with memory. For example, researchers found that one's self-concept is based on one's memory, and one's memory is biased by one's self-concept. What was astounding, and somewhat reassuring, was that despite the thousands of research studies on applied memory, time and time again researchers found the same patterns that they had established in the lab; thus, models of memory constructed in controlled settings could be used to explain and predict memory behaviour in the real world (Banaji & Crowder, 1989).

A review of peer-reviewed articles from the years 1950 through 2010 reflects this shift from purely theoretical research to research of real people in real settings. In 1950, just 25 per cent of memory research related to applied topics; as of 2010, a full 89 per cent of memory research addressed an applied question (see Figure 1.7). The most popular topics in applied memory today are related to psychological therapy and counselling, autobiographical memory, forensic topics such as eyewitness testimony, and education.

Theoretical Approaches to Studying Memory
The Systems Approach to Memory

systems approach

an approach to memory that presumes that memory is comprised of multiple independent systems, such as a short-term memory system, a long-term memory system, a procedural memory system, etc.

Different memory researchers approach memory phenomena in different ways. Some prefer to model memory as a series of systems (the **systems approach**); proponents of this view feel we have many different systems, each of which is specialized for a different type of information or task. The systems approach is based largely on the observation that people who sustain brain damage often lose the ability to form or recall memories of one type but not another, leading researchers to assume that different regions of the brain control separate memory systems.

Proponents of the systems approach have proposed many systems, including systems related to semantic memory, episodic memory, procedural memory, and short-term memory.

The systems approach is based on four principles:

1. **The systems must be functionally distinct.** Variables must have different effects on the two systems.
2. **The systems must have different neurological substrates.** They must operate in different areas of the brain.
3. **The systems must be uncorrelated with one another.** Performance of one memory system does not predict performance of another memory system.
4. **The systems must be functionally incompatible.** The job of one cannot be carried out by the other.

The four principles of the systems approach have led its advocates to identify many different components of the memory system; for example, sensory memory, short-term memory, and long-term memory all meet the criteria to be regarded as distinct memory systems.

Critics of the systems approach, such as Ian Neath and Aimée Surprenant, point out that the criteria used to identify different memory systems do not work perfectly. Surprenant and Neath (2013) argue that according to the four principles of the systems approach, **recall** (the process you would use to answer the question "What is your middle name?") and **recognition** (the process you would use to answer the question "Is the word 'moot' part of the English language?") should be characterized as different memory systems because they meet all four criteria of different systems. Because word frequency affects recall differently than recognition, the two can be considered functionally distinct, meeting the first criteria. Different brain areas are active during recall and recognition, which means the two have different neural substrates, meeting the second criteria. Performance on a recall task is uncorrelated with performance on a recognition task, meeting the third criteria. Finally, there are many situations in which we can recognize something but not recall it, as with tastes, showing that recall can be used to perform recognition, and recognition cannot be used to perform recall, meeting the fourth criteria (Surprenant & Neath, 2013). However, Surprenant and Neath (2013) argue that if recall and recognition should be characterized as different memory systems according to the systems approach, then a person must be using a different memory system to answer the recall question "Who was the first prime minister of Canada?" and the recognition question "Who was the first prime minister of Canada, John A. Macdonald, William Lyon Mackenzie King, or Wilfrid Laurier?" even though both ask for the same piece of information.

Alan Baddeley, who helped develop the systems approach, responds to these criticisms by remarking that, in his view, understanding memory requires the consideration of both memory stores and the processes that operate on them, much like understanding the brain requires understanding anatomical features and the physiological processes that interact with the anatomical features (Baddeley, Eysenck, & Anderson, 2015). The two best-known alternatives to the systems approach are the processing approach and the principles approach.

The Processing Approach to Memory

Some researchers prefer the **processing approach**, in which memory is based on the type of processing that the to-be-remembered item receives. Proponents of the processing approach, including Toronto-based researchers Fergus Craik and Robert Lockhart, argue that

processing approach

an approach to memory that presumes that memory traces vary based on how the to-be-remembered information has been processed

all memories use similar cognitive resources, but that there are differences in performance across different tasks because different tasks involve processing information in different ways. The processing approach developed from the observation that information that is processed more deeply tends to be remembered better than other information. For example, Craik and Lockhart (1972) presented participants with 60 words that participants had to process based on the word's visual characteristics ("Was the word presented on italics?"), the word's phonemic characteristics ("Did the words start with the sound 'dee'?") or the word's contextual characteristics ("Can you meet one in the street?"). Craik and Lockhart (1972) argued that the contextual questions invoked the deepest processing, Craik and Lockhart (1972) found that memory was best for words processed in the contextual condition and that better recall was shown for items that were processed more deeply. Craik and Lockhart (1972) also noted that this result cannot be well explained by a systems approach to memory, as the systems approach focuses on differences among memory stores, rather than how different types of processing may affect encoding. Processing approaches have been successful at denoting differences in memory when different cognitive processes are in play, such as when participants think of items in terms of themselves (or not) or when participants visualize to-be-remembered items (or not).

Critics of the processing approach note that it is very difficult to conduct experiments in which processing is well controlled. In order to do so, the experimenter must determine the nature and extent of processing that a given item receives, such as whether it was processed on a shallow or deep level. The amount and extent of processing for a given item is impossible to control and quantify outside of the lab and as a result the processing view is not an ideal platform for studying applied memory (Surprenant & Neath, 2013).

The Principles Approach to Memory

principles approach

an approach to memory that looks to commonalities in memory research across different experimental settings

A third approach to modelling memory is based on general principles of memory derived from patterns seen across a wide scope of memory research. This is known as the **principles approach**. The principles view grew from the observation that the systems view and the processing view had little real explanatory power outside of the very controlled experimental conditions within which they were conceived. Surprenant and Neath (2013) list seven principles but stipulate that the number is by no means fixed at seven; there could easily be more.

The seven (current) principles are as follows:

1. **The cue-driven principle:** In all situations, memory is driven by a cue.
2. **The encoding-retrieval principle:** Conditions during encoding affect retrieval.
3. **The cue-overload principle:** Cues can be associated with more than one thing, which can have a negative impact on retrieval.
4. **The reconstruction principle:** Memory is constructive in nature and a myriad of factors can influence how the construction takes place.
5. **The impurity principle:** Because memory is constructive, any number of processes may be involved at the time of retrieval. This principle makes a pure systems approach or a pure processing approach to explaining memory impossible.
6. **The relative-distinctness principle:** A memory that is distinct will be better recalled than a memory that is not. This is essentially the inverse of the cue-overload principle; distinct memories have more unique cues.

7. **The specificity principle:** Tasks that require information about the context in which a memory was learned will be more susceptible to interference or forgetting. This explains, for example, why the ability to recall facts (semantic memory) appears to be more extensive than memory for events (episodic memory).

The principles approach to evaluating memory research is not tied to any specific experimental paradigm and can be used to explain any memory data. Because the principles view is based on the culmination of memory research to date, proponents of this view argue that the principles approach provides the more comprehensive lens through which to develop meaningful interpretations of applied memory research. The main criticism of the principles approach comes from advocates for the systems approach, who note that the presence of similarities across memory domains does not mean that differences between those domains should be ignored (Baddeley et al., 2015).

Combining the Systems, Processing, and Principles Approaches to Best Understand Memory Research

The systems approach, the processing approach, and the principles approach to studying memory each have unique advantages, and because each perspective is valuable, each perspective is reflected in this book, although in different ways. The systems view is reflected in the fact that there are different chapters devoted to all the major memory stores identified by the systems view including sensory memory, short-term memory, and types of long-term memory including generic memory and episodic/autobiographical memory. The book also includes many examples from the processing approach, which shows how the way in which a person interacts with information can affect the memory for that information. Finally, the principles approach is used to help augment explanations of a wide variety of memory phenomena.

A Brief Introduction to the Neuroscience of Memory

This text includes many discussions related to neuroscience. Because not all students have a background in neuroscience, the last part of this chapter provides an introduction to neuroscience. This introduction serves two purposes. First, it provides you with the basics of neuroscience

---

DIY EXPERIMENT   BOX 1.3

Can You Remember the Story You Read Earlier?

Earlier in this chapter (on p. 7) a story was told in Box 1.1: The Mysterious Origins of The Method of Loci. How much can you remember? Once you have tried your best to remember the story, go back and read it again. What were you able to remember and what did you leave out? How much of what you remembered do you think you reconstructed using schemas?

needed to understand more complex topics discussed later in the text. Second, it introduces some of the fundamental facts related to the neuroscience of memory that you will learn about in future chapters.

The Neuron

The human brain is comprised of billions of neurons such as the one shown in Figure 1.8. Neurons have a cell body surrounded by branch-like dendrites that receive signals from other neurons. An axon also extends from the cell body and serves to carry signals from the dendrites to the axon terminal. Neurons are not physically connected to one another; they are separated by tiny spaces called **synapses** or synaptic clefts. Neurons communicate with one another by sending neurotransmitters across these synapses (see Figure 1.8). Making connection across these clefts is crucial for the formation of new memories.

synapse

the location where a nervous impulse passes from one neuron to another neuron

The Action Potential

In a resting state, neurons have a slightly negative charge and are surrounded by sodium ions, which have a positive charge. When a neuron receives a signal to communicate, the sodium ion channels on the neuron's axon open and positively charged sodium ions rush inside. This influx of positively charged sodium ions causes the neuron to change from a negative charge of about –70 mV (a neuron's charge at rest) to a positive charge of about 40 mV in what is known as an **action potential.**

action potential

the brief reversal of polarity in a neuron that occurs when a neuron is stimulated

Neurotransmitters and Neural Transmission

Neurotransmitters are stored in synaptic vesicles within the axon terminal (see Figure 1.9). When the action potential reaches the axon terminal, the change in voltage triggers voltage-gated calcium channels that then signal the release of neurotransmitters into the synaptic cleft. The neurotransmitters bind with receptors on neurons in the synaptic gap. If the receptor has an excitatory effect on the postsynaptic neuron, then the neuron is briefly depolarized and an action

long-term potentiation (LTP)

a persistent strength-ening of a synapse based on recent patterns of activity

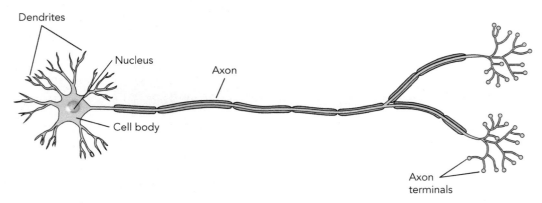

Figure 1.8   The neuron

A neuron is composed of a cell body, dendrites, an axon, and axon terminals.

Source: Based on Rudy, J. (2014). *Neurobiology of learning and memory*. Sinauer, p. 29, Figure 2.7

potential is triggered. If the receptor has an inhibitory effect on the postsynaptic neuron, on the other hand, then the neuron is hyperpolarized, making it less likely that an action potential will be triggered in the future.

When two neurons fire at the same time repeatedly, there are chemical changes at the synapse that make the pre-synaptic neuron more likely to trigger firing in the postsynaptic neuron in the future. This phenomenon is known as **long-term potentiation (LTP)** (Nicoll & Roche, 2013). Some neurons in areas of the brain involved in memory, such as the hippocampus, have specialized receptors that help ensure LTP occurs. For example, many hippocampal neurons have AMPA and NMDA receptors which, when activated, work to build more receptors like themselves nearby. AMPA and NMDA receptors are activated by amino acids of the same name and mediate the synaptic transmission of charged ions. Increasing the number of receptors on a neuron increases the probability that it will fire at the same time as a nearby neuron, which in turn increases the probability that LTP will occur at the synapse. LTP is essential for memory; when researchers prevent LTP from occurring, memories cannot be formed. (See Chapter 4.)

The Lobes of the Brain

The human brain is divided into four lobes: the frontal lobe, the temporal lobe, the parietal lobe, and the occipital lobe (as shown in Figure 1.5 on p. 17; see also Figure 1.10). The main function of each lobe is shown in Table 1.2. All four lobes are involved in memory in some way. The frontal lobe supports short-term memory maintenance (see Chapter 3) while the temporal lobe supports long-term memory formation

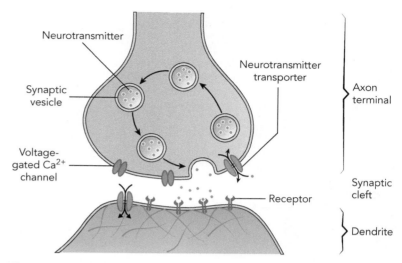

Figure 1.9   Neurotransmitters

Neurons communicate through neurotransmitters. Neurotransmitters are released from the axon terminal of one neuron and cross the synaptic gap to bind with receptors on a nearby neuron.

Source: Thomas Splettstoesser / CC BY-SA 4.0

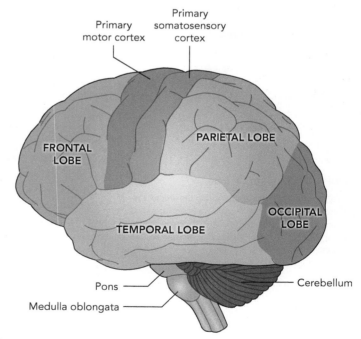

Figure 1.10   Lobes of the brain

Different lobes of the brain play different roles supporting memory. The frontal lobe supports short-term memory while the temporal lobe supports long-term memory formation. Individual memories may be stored in any lobe of the brain. (See Table 1.2).

Source: Adapted from BruceBlaus / CC BY 3.0

Table 1.2   Functions of the Lobes of the Brain

Frontal	Temporal	Parietal	Occipital
Primary motor cortex	Primary auditory cortex	Primary somatosensory cortex	Primary visual cortex
Attention	Language comprehension	Long-term memory storage of somatic information	Long-term memory storage of visual information
Language production	Encoding and retrieval processes		
Short-memory and working memory Long-term memory storage of motor information	Long-term memory storage of auditory information		

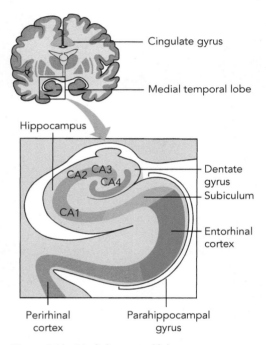

Figure 1.11   Medial temporal lobe

The medial temporal lobe is located within the area of the brain identified with a box (top image). The hippocampus, parahippocampal gyrus, and cingulate gyrus are all located in the medial temporal lobe (bottom image) and all play important roles in memory formation (see Chapter 4).

Source: Based on Eagleman, D. & Downar, J. (2016). *Brain and behavior*. New York: Oxford University Press. p. 283 (Figure 9.11, partial) and p. 278 (Figure 9.7, partial)

(see Chapter 4). All lobes store long-term memories related to the function of that lobe.

The Medial Temporal Lobe Structures

The medial temporal lobe is located deep within the cortex (see Figure 1.11). Many structures that are crucial for memory formation and maintenance are located within the medial temporal lobe area, including the hippocampus, the parahippocampal gyrus, and the cingulate gyrus. When H.M.'s medial temporal lobes were lesioned, he developed severe amnesia. (For more on H.M., see Box 1.2.)

The Cortex

The outermost layer of the human brain is referred to as the cortex (or the neocortex). Different areas of the cortex serve different functions (see Figure 1.12). For example, the prefrontal cortex is associated with attention and short-term memory (see Chapter 3), while Broca's area is associated with the production of speech. Long-term memories are stored throughout the cortex (see Chapters 4 and 5).

Most neuroscience topics discussed in the text relate back to these fundamental topics of neuronal functioning, receptors, long-term potentiation, and the roles of the prefrontal cortex, the medial temporal lobe, and the cortex in memory. Neuroscientific research enriches our understanding of memory as a biological construct.

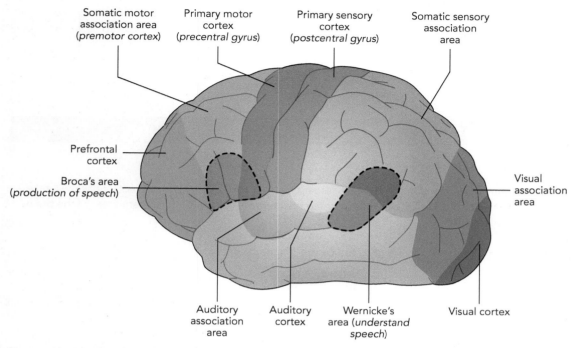

Figure 1.12   Motor and sensory regions of the cerebral cortex

CHAPTER REVIEW

- The ancient Greeks and Egyptians knew memory was important but did not study it scientifically.
- Hermann Ebbinghaus conducted the first formal memory research in the 1880s.
- Lashley, Hebb, and Penfield helped localize memory process in the brain in the first half of the century. However, they did not develop models of memory because the behaviourist philosophy of the time prohibited making inferences about internal processes.
- In the late 1950s, the case of H.M., who had severe anterograde amnesia, ignited an interest in memory processes and helped bring about the cognitive revolution. Following the cognitive revolution, researchers began to try to model memory.
- Researchers in the 1960s and 1970s defined many types of memory, such as semantic, episodic, implicit, and explicit memory, and studied how memory was organized.
- The first models of memory proposed that people possessed different memory systems, such as a short-term memory system and a long-term memory system, and that memory performance was dependent on these systems.

- More recently, researchers have questioned the systems view. Proponents of the processing view, for example, suggest that how information is processed, and not what system is involved, is key to modelling memory.
- Proponents of the principles view of memory conceptualize memory based on general themes, or principles, derived from decades of memory research.

MEMORY ACTIVITY

Visualizations Help Memory

People better remember material that they have visualized (e.g., Marks, 1973). In this activity, we will take advantage of the benefits of visualization while learning the memory functions of different areas of the brain that are listed in Table 1.2.

First, trace or copy this image of a brain onto the centre of a piece of paper:

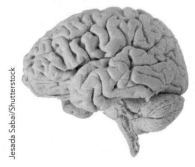

Jesada Sabai/Shutterstock

Next, use Figure 1.10 as a guide and divide your image into the four lobes of the brain and label each lobe. Next, review the function of each lobe of the brain one by one, devising an easy-to-draw mental image for each concept that needs to be learned; for example, you may envision a "car" for the primary motor cortex and an "!" for attention. Record each image on the paper in the general region of the associated cortex. You should develop a drawing like the one below:

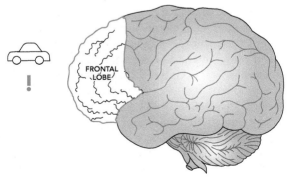

Figure 1.13   Brain

This diagram is deliberately incomplete because the best memory aids are developed using a person's own cues. After you complete the drawing, you can use the diagram to test your memory for the function of each area. Once you can recall the functions with the cues try recreating the drawing from scratch labelling each area not with the picture, but with the functions.

Questions

1. What aspects of ancient Greek philosophy regarding memory are still part of memory theory today?
2. How did the work of Darwin impact memory research?
3. What model of memory was Ebbinghaus's pioneering study of memory designed to address?
4. How did memory research differ in North America, Europe, and Britain in the early twentieth century?
5. How did searching for engrams lead to a better understanding of the neuroscience of memory?
6. What was the cognitive revolution? How was it related to memory research?
7. What lasting benefit did behaviourism have on the study of memory?
8. Describe how Endel Tulving linked different types of memory to different types of conscious experiences.
9. When was schema theory first proposed and by whom? Why was understanding schemas important for cognitive scientists in the 1970s?
10. What is the systems approach to modelling memory? What are some benefits to this approach?
11. What is the processing approach to memory? What are some benefits to this approach?
12. What is the principles view of memory? What are some possible benefits to this approach?

Key Figures

Aristotle p. 5
Richard Atkinson p. 16
Alan Baddeley p. 21
Frederic Bartlett p. 12
Fergus Craik p. 21
Charles Darwin p. 8
Hermann Ebbinghaus p. 8

Donald Hebb p. 13
Karl Lashley p. 13
Robert Lockhart p. 21
George Miller p. 15
Ian Neath p. 21
Ulric Neisser p. 18
Wilder Penfield p. 14

Plato p. 4
Aimée Surprenant p. 21
Richard Semon p. 13
Richard Shiffrin p. 16
William Scoville p. 15
Endel Tulving p. 12

2 Sensory Persistence and Information Persistence

LEARNING OBJECTIVES

Having read this chapter, you will be able to:

- Distinguish between the concepts of iconic memory, sensory persistence, and information persistence.
- Describe Sperling's (1960) paradigm for studying iconic memory.
- Describe the results of Sperling's (1960) partial- and whole-report experiments.
- Critique Sperling's (1960) model of iconic memory.
- Describe the modality effect and the suffix effect.

PATIENT X: A MAN WITH A DEFICIT IN AUDITORY SENSORY MEMORY

When Patient X was 42 years old, he suffered from a left putaminal hemorrhage (a type of stroke) that resulted in severe difficulties with verbal short-term memory. In many instances, Patient X cannot recall the syllable presented to him just one second earlier. When a series of digits are presented to Patient X verbally, he can't report more than four (99 per cent of people can recall more than four digits). However, when a series of digits are presented to Patient X visually, he can report six digits, which is well within normal range. Thus, Patient X's stroke seems to have affected his ability to retain auditory information, even for very short periods of time, but has not affected his ability to retain visual information. The case of Patient X lends support to the notion that people possess modality-specific short-term memory stores, and that these short-term memory stores rely on different parts of the brain. Because Patient X is able to recall visual information without impairment, Patient X's problem recalling digits cannot be attributed to a deficit in short-term memory (Kojima, Karino, Yumoto, & Funayama, 2014). As you will learn in the first section of this chapter, sensory persistence is modality specific, and thus a deficit in auditory-sensory persistence, rather than short-term memory, can explain the pattern of results observed in Patient X.

Sensory Memory

We are constantly bombarded with sensory information of no real importance, from the background noise in a busy park, to the feeling of the floor at one's feet, to the sights of things in our visual periphery while we are driving a car. Right now, as you read this, you are focused on visual information and thus can disregard inputs from your other senses, such as the feeling of your chair or sounds from the next room, because they are not relevant to your current task. Although much of the information that enters our sensory system is useless, we still need to be able to detect important and unpredictable stimuli when they arise: a child's call for help at the park, the floor suddenly becoming slippery, a deer darting from the woods toward the road, or the sound of someone knocking on the door. So how do we let in enough information to make sure we don't miss the things that are most important without overwhelming the system with things we don't need to know? When cognitive psychology was still in its infancy, researchers proposed that the first stage of the human information processing system is **sensory memory**, which allows for all information to be *available* for processing, but only a subset to be *selected* for processing. Sensory memory was assumed to be modality specific; a given representation was thought to contain information from only one sense (sight, sound, smell, taste, or touch). Together these sensory memory stores are called **sensory registers**. The most widely studied sensory registers are **iconic memory**, the register thought to maintain incoming visual information (Neisser, 1967), and **echoic memory** for incoming auditory information.

sensory memory
a general term referring to a very brief, very large-capacity memory store that retains information for a given sense (sight, hearing, taste, touch, or smell)

sensory register
a point where information from modality-specific sensory memories comes together into one store

iconic memory
a large-capacity, short-duration memory store for visual information

echoic memory
a large-capacity, short-duration memory store for auditory information

Iconic Memory

Iconic memory, first defined by Ulric Neisser in 1967, is a very brief memory store for visual information. Iconic memory is assumed to be the first stage of processing for all visual information, and all visual information enters iconic memory. Iconic memory is thought to hold information just long enough for that person to selectively attend to a subset of the material and process it further. Iconic memory is very brief because new, possibly important, visual information is constantly coming through the visual system.

The term *iconic memory* was inspired by the results of a series of experiments conducted by George Sperling in 1960. Sperling (1960) began his examination of iconic memory by asking participants to report as many letters as possible from a briefly presented display consisting of three rows of four letters (such as those shown in the second panel of Figure 2.1). The 50 ms presentation was so brief that it appeared only as a flicker to participants. This became known as Sperling's (1960) **whole-report paradigm**. Sperling found that participants were only able to report, on average, about 4.6 out of the 12 letters in the whole-report paradigm. Sperling (1960) had two possible explanations for this effect: either participants only *saw* 4.6 letters because the presentation was so brief, or participants could only *report* 4.6 letters before their visual sensory memory faded.

To test these two possible explanations, Sperling devised the **partial-report paradigm**. In the original partial-report paradigm, participants were presented with three rows of four letters (such as that shown in the second panel of Figure 2.1) for about 50 milliseconds (ms). After a delay ranging from 0 to 1000 ms, the participant was presented with a tone indicating which row of letters to report; a high tone indicating the top row, a mid-range tone indicating the middle row, and a low tone indicating the lowest row. The logic was that the capacity of iconic memory could be quantified as the number of letters a person can report from a randomly chosen row multiplied by the number of possible rows. If the whole-report performance was the result of only being able to see 4.6 letters, then performance on the partial-report task should be 4.6 ÷ 3, or about 1.3 letters per trial; however, if the whole-report score was because of rapidly fading memory, partial-report scores should be higher than whole-report scores for the duration of iconic memory. Indeed, at cue delays up to about 500 ms, Sperling found a **partial-report advantage**. Participants reported 3.4 out of 4 possible letters on average for a partial-report score of about 11 (3.4 items × 3 rows), compared to the whole-report score of 4.6. The partial-report advantage was observed up to cue delays of about 500 ms, at which point participants reported about the same number of items in the partial- and whole-report conditions. The duration of the partial-report advantage led Sperling to conclude that (a) for a brief period of time most visual information is available to participants and (b) after about 500 ms only a subset of information is available. Sperling inferred that iconic memory has an unlimited capacity, but a duration of less than 500 ms.

Sperling also found that presenting a bright flash of light immediately

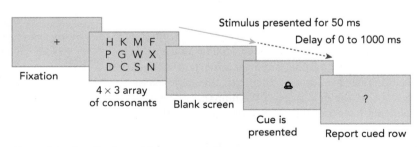

Figure 2.1   Sperling's partial-report paradigm

In Sperling's (1960) partial-report paradigm, participants are presented with a fixation cross followed by a 4 × 3 array of consonants that are presented for 50 ms. The letters are then replaced with a blank screen. Following a delay of 0 to 1000 ms, participants hear an audio cue indicating which row participants should report. Participants then report the letters they recall from the cued row.

after the presentation of the array eliminated participants' ability to report items. Sperling concluded that because the material in iconic memory could be effectively erased with a flash of light, the material must be perceptual in nature or **pre-categorical**, that is, not yet identified as specific numbers or letters. Sperling reasoned that if material in iconic memory had been processed to a point of being identified as specific numbers or letters (i.e., was **post-categorical**), then the material could be rehearsed and some items could be reported even following the flash of light. Sperling proposed that the best way to conceptualize iconic memory is as a store comprised of rapidly fading pre-categorical icons that have not yet been identified as a certain letter, number, or object (once a shape is identified as an "A," or a "2," or a "dog," it is considered categorical). Sperling

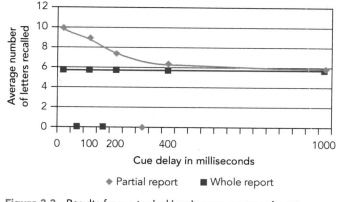

Figure 2.2   Results from a typical iconic memory experiment
This figure shows the number of items estimated to be available in sensory memory at different cue delays. Note that at a cue delay of about 500 ms, performance is similar to the whole-report condition and stays the same.

(1960, 1967) also made claims about the nature of the information in iconic memory, arguing that iconic memory only contained perceptual information and that icons needed to be "scanned" to extract categorical information (such as letter identity).

Critiques of Sperling's Concept of Iconic Memory

Although many experiments have replicated Sperling's findings, a plethora of experimental evidence contradicts the concept of iconic memory as a rapidly fading, pre-categorical memory store that is independent from other short-term memory stores. First, multiple experiments have demonstrated that some categorical information (e.g., whether the item is a letter or a number; whether the item is a vowel or a consonant) is available even when an array is presented only briefly (e.g., Merikle, 1980), which calls into question the notion that iconic memory is pre-categorical. Second, some of the partial-report advantage that is used as evidence for the existence of iconic memory may actually be the result of **output interference**. Output interference occurs when the very act of reporting recall (the "output") either distorts memories or allows material in short-term memory to be lost. Whole-report trials are more affected by output interference because these trials require more output (the maximum number of letters that can be reported on a whole-report trial is 12, while the maximum on a partial-report trial is 4). If output interference is reducing the amount of letters reported on whole-report trials, then this would in turn make the partial-report advantage seem larger and more rapidly changing than it actually is; the notion of iconic memory clearly predicts a large partial-report advantage (Haber, 1983). Third, several studies have shown that identity information in the partial-report task lasts much longer that location information (e.g., Mewhort, Campbell, Marchetti, & Campbell, 1981), which indicates that information in iconic memory is not well described as a fading icon; different aspects seem to fade at different rates. Thus, there is experimental evidence calling into question (a) that iconic memory is pre-categorical, (b) that iconic memory is vast and rapidly fading, and (c) that the information in iconic memory is essentially a duplicate of a visual stimulus in rapidly fading form (Haber, 1983).

pre-categorical
a stimulus that has not been processed to the point of having meaning. Because the stimulus has no meaning, whether it is a letter, number, word, or nonword is not known.

post-categorical
information that has been processed to the point of having meaning

output interference
when the act of retrieval itself interferes with retrieval

RELEVANT RESEARCH

BOX 2.1

Sensory Memory Improves Decision Making

Sensory memory may help people make quick decisions in a variety of rapidly changing situations. In the past this may have helped us survive in the wild, but we rely on the same abilities to process rapidly changing digital information.

There are many real-world situations where decisions must be made based on visual information that appears only briefly. For example, in the past, our ancestors would have had to decide how to act based on brief flashes of animals in the wild, while in present day we often have to make choices based on information flashed very briefly on a video screen. In these situations, when stimuli are seen and disappear, people must rely on visual sensory memory to make decisions. Alexandra Vlassova and Joel Pearson of the University of New South Wales were interested in better understanding how people use visual sensory memory to help them make decisions. In particular, the researchers were curious whether the visual information would continue to influence decision making after the stimulus was no longer available.

In their 2013 experiment, Vlassova and Pearson presented participants with a 250 ms array of random moving dots that were drifting to the right or to the left. The array was followed by either a mask (that would disrupt sensory memory) or a blank screen (that would not disrupt sensory memory). A tone sounded after a delay, which signalled participants to indicate as quickly and accurately as possible which way the stimuli were moving (see Figure 2.3). Vlassova and Pearson (2013) found that participants made more accurate decisions when the stimulus was followed by a blank screen than when followed by a mask, and that this accuracy advantage increased as response delay increased. Vlassova and Pearson (2013) conclude that participants use sensory memory when it is available to improve decision-making accuracy, and that the quality of information extracted from sensory memory improves with delay (up to about 500 ms). Thus, the results of Vlassova and Pearson (2013) suggest that when real-world decisions must be based on sensory memory, people will be more accurate if they pause before making a choice. So next time you are tracking animals in the woods, or making split decisions on a computer screen, and you need to repeatedly make choices based on what you see, you may decide to adopt a more hesitant strategy to take advantage of your sensory memory's natural tendency to improve with time.

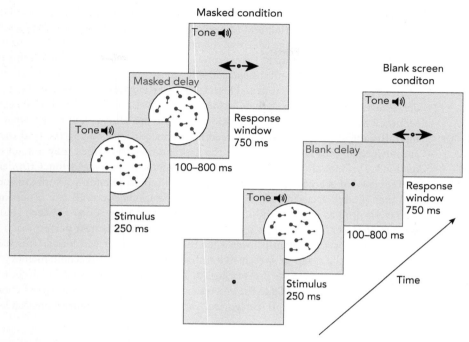

Figure 2.3 In Vlassova and Pearson (2013), each trial began with a fixation cross. After fixation, a random dot motion matrix was presented for 250 ms. In the masked condition, a mask was presented for varying durations before the response window; in the blank screen condition, a blank screen was presented for varying durations before the response window. When a tone sounded, participants indicated whether the stimulus was moving left or right.

Source: Slightly edited based on Vlassova & Pearson, 2013, p. 4, Figure 1

Echoic Memory

Echoic memory is a term frequently used to describe a brief pre-categorical auditory memory store that holds *all* incoming auditory long enough for the listener to select and further process the information of value. Conceptually, echoic memory is identical to iconic memory; the only difference between them is that echoic memory holds auditory, instead of visual, information. Some studies of echoic memory have been very similar conceptually to studies of iconic memory; researchers have presented large amounts of auditory information and then compared participants' ability to identify the items in partial- and whole-report conditions. For example, Darwin, Turvey, and Crowder (1972) presented auditory lists of numbers so they were heard as coming from the left, centre, or right of the listener. After the list presentation, a visual cue presented to the left, centre, or right indicated which list to report (partial report), or instead participants had to report as many items from any list as they would like. In these experiments, Darwin et al. (1972) found a partial-report advantage at short cue delays and attributed this finding to echoic memory, which they purported was similar to iconic memory: a large modality-specific pre-categorical store. The partial-report advantage was smaller than for iconic memory; at most just one more item could be recalled in the short-cue partial-report condition than on a whole-report trial, and this small partial-report advantage also lasted longer than the partial-report advantage in iconic memory experiments, with small but significant effects observed at cue delays of up to four seconds. Many researchers wondered if this paradigm was intrinsically problematic and instead chose to study echoic memory with different methods.

In an experiment by Conrad and Hull (1968), participants were presented with a list of numbers and had to read the list either out loud or silently. Conrad and Hull (1968) examined recall accuracy as a function of serial position. Conrad and Hull (1968) found what they called a **modality effect**: when participants read the items out loud during the trial they were better at remembering the last two items on the list than they were when they did not read the items out loud. This modality effect was attributed to echoic memory. Morton, Crowder, and Prussin (1971) explored echoic memory by looking at the impact of adding a suffix to auditory stimuli and then plotted accuracy of recall on a serial positions curve. In one condition, they added a buzzer sound as a suffix, and in the other condition they added a speech sound as a suffix. Morton et al. (1971) found that memory for the last item was near perfect when the suffix was a buzzer, but was significantly lower when the suffix was a speech sound. This **suffix effect** was thought to be the result of speech-like suffixes interfering with echoic memory. Crowder and Morton (1969) proposed the pre-categorical acoustic store (PAS) model to account for the suffix effect and the modality effect. The PAS was essentially the same as Neisser's concept of echoic memory: a large-capacity, pre-categorical, modality-specific memory store that lasted for about two seconds.

modality effect

the improved recall of the final items of a list when that list is presented verbally in comparison with a visual presentation

suffix effect

recall is better when to-be-remembered items are followed by a suffix that is a non-speech sound than when followed by a suffix that is a speech-like sound

Critiques of Echoic Memory and the Pre-Categorical Acoustic Store

As with iconic memory, a variety of experimental evidence contradicts the concept of echoic memory/PAS as a rapidly fading, modality-specific, pre-categorical memory store that is independent from other short-term memory stores. The biggest problem with echoic memory is the notion that it is pre-categorical. Neath, Surprenant, and Crowder (1993) demonstrated that the suffix effect could be created or eliminated with identical suffix stimuli depending on whether the listener was told the suffix was a speech sound or an animal sound in advance. If a pre-categorical modality-specific acoustic store was the only cognitive process being used to recall the items, then the results should have been the same in both conditions. Similarly, Spoehr and Corin (1978) showed a suffix effect when the listener saw the reader mouth the suffix but did not actually hear the suffix; again, if the serial recall of the items was being accomplished through a modality-specific pre-categorical store, there should have been no suffix effect when the suffix was mouthed but not heard.

stimulus persistence

residual neurological activity resulting from a stimulus presentation that fades rapidly over time

information persistence

the availability of stimulus information after the stimulus has been removed

Stimulus and Information Persistence as an Alternative Explanation for Iconic and Echoic Memory

The previous discussions call into question the notion that we possess high-capacity, pre-categorical memory stores for either visual or auditory stimuli. So how can we explain the ability to report stimuli that are no longer present? One possibility is that iconic memory and echoic memory are each artifacts of two other phenomena: **stimulus persistence** and **information persistence** (Nairne, 2003; Surprenant & Neath, 2013).

DIY EXPERIMENT

BOX
2.2

The Cocktail Party Effect

One of the best real-world demonstrations of echoic memory in action is the **cocktail party effect** (Cherry, 1953). The cocktail party effect occurs when individuals hear important information (such as their name or a taboo word) that they were otherwise ignoring (such as the voice of a speaker across a room). The effect occurs because information in the unattended stream is held in echoic memory long enough for important words to be detected. The cocktail party effect shows that listeners can both segregate auditory stimuli into different streams and then make a decision about which stream contains the most important information (Wood & Cowan, 1995). The cocktail party effect suggests that individuals automatically parse information in echoic memory based on its importance, letting through a person's name, but blocking out information not directly linked to the individual.

There is evidence from research by Anne Treisman and others that suggests that people are primed to detect personally important words such as their names (Driver, 2001), and words that are taboo in their society (Straube & Germer, 1979). This finding predicts that people's echoic memory will allow them to detect their names and taboo words in an unattended auditory channel. In the present experiment you will have participants attend to one auditory channel and ignore another and will test to see if participants can indeed hear their name and a few taboo terms while otherwise successfully ignoring a speaker.

Instructions: To complete this experiment, you will need at least three assistants, two smartphones, this textbook, a novel, two sets of in-ear earphones, a pad of paper, and a pencil.

First, assign your assistants to be Reader A, Reader B, and the Listener. The Listener should not hear the Readers making the recordings. Have Reader A select and read a one-minute passage from this textbook into one phone. Make sure it is a passage in which the word *memory* is mentioned frequently. Next, have Reader B randomly select and read a one-minute passage from a novel on a different phone and then replace ten nouns with four instances of the listener's name and six taboo words in random order read in a way that sounds natural.

When you are ready to begin the experiment, present the Listener with the regular stream from Reader A in their right ear and the taboo stream from Reader B in the left ear (or vice versa). The volume should be similar in both ears. Instruct the Listener to listen carefully to the passage about memory (in their right ear) and to record every time they hear the word *memory* spoken. Instruct them to ignore the stream in their other ear. At the end of both recordings, ask the Listener if they heard anything in the unattended ear. If the cocktail party effect has occurred, the Listener will have heard her or his name and the taboo words.

Questions
1. Why do you think that taboo words and names, but not other words, produce the cocktail party effect?
2. What role does sensory memory play in producing the cocktail party effect?

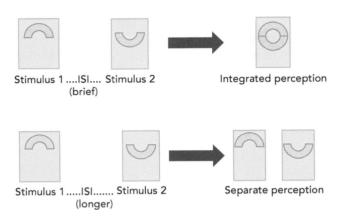

Stimulus 1 ....ISI.... Stimulus 2
(brief)

Integrated perception

Stimulus 1 .....ISI....... Stimulus 2
(longer)

Separate perception

Figure 2.4   An example of a temporal-integration paradigm

In a temporal-integration paradigm, two halves of a shape may be presented at varying interstimulus intervals. At short intervals, the stimuli appear as one; at long ISIs the stimuli appear to be distinct. Temporal integration is evidence for a brief period of stimulus persistence but its fleeting nature discounts the typical descriptions of iconic memory.

cocktail party effect

the phenomenon whereby a person attending to one auditory channel is able to detect important information conveyed in an unattended auditory channel

Stimulus Persistence

Stimulus persistence is residual neural activity that is produced by the presentation of a stimulus and fades quickly over time (or is replaced if a new stimulus is presented). Because we process different modalities with different parts of the brain, stimulus persistence is modality specific. Visual stimulus persistence has been studied in the visual modality using temporal-integration paradigm experiments (e.g., Loftus & Irwin, 1998). In these experiments, two stimuli are presented with varying interstimulus intervals (ISIs) and the participant indicates those trials where the stimuli appear distinct (see Figure 2.4). Stimulus persistence is estimated by noting the longest ISI where two stimuli appear as one. The results from these studies suggest that stimulus persistence is very brief and is estimated to last about 200 ms in ideal conditions, and thus cannot be used to explain the partial-report advantage in iconic memory experiments.

Stimulus persistence has also been studied for auditory stimuli. For example, Efron (1970) presented participants with tones of varying durations between 30 ms and 100 ms and asked the participant to adjust a light so that it came on as soon as the tone ended. Interestingly, Efron (1970) found that no matter how long the *actual* tone lasted, participants perceived the tone as at least 130 ms in duration. This strongly suggests that when a tone is presented, stimulus persistence continues for about 100 ms. However, this sensory store is far briefer than would be needed to explain the suffix effect or the modality effect in auditory-stimuli experiments. To explain phenomena from experiments where stimulus information seems to be used after this brief window of stimulus persistence, we turn to the notion of information persistence.

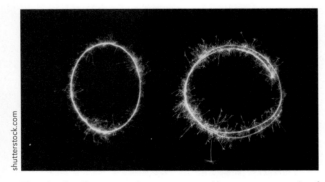

The visual trails we see when we use sparklers are an example of visual persistence.

Information Persistence

In a classic experiment, Vincent Di Lollo, then at the University of Alberta, presented participants with 12 dots placed at random on a 5 × 5 matrix, which had 25 potential locations for the dots. The dots were presented for 10, 40, 80, 120, 160, or 200 ms. Following an interstimulus interval (ISI) of 10 ms, dots were placed at random in 12 of the 13 remaining locations in the matrix. The participant's task was to indicate the location where dots had *not* appeared.

Di Lollo (1980) found that the number of errors increased as the duration of the first set of dots increased. Participants reported that at durations of 100 ms or less, the two arrays appeared to be presented simultaneously; however, when the first array appeared for more than 100 ms, the first and second arrays appeared to be presented sequentially, making the task more difficult (even though in both cases the arrays were in fact presented sequentially). Di Lollo (1980) thus reported an *inverse duration effect*: stimulus persistence appeared to decrease as the duration of the stimulus increased, which explains why, at longer durations, participants experienced sequential, instead of simultaneous, arrays. In a related experiment, David Irwin and James Yeomans (1986) varied the duration of the stimulus display in a partial-report paradigm experiment. Participants were presented with a 3 × 4 array of letters for either 50, 200, or 500 ms and were cued following a delay ranging from 50 to 500 ms (see Figure 2.6).

Irwin and Yeomans (1986) replicated Sperling (1960) and found a large effect of cue delay but found no effect of stimulus duration; partial report was equally accurate at 50 ms as at 500 ms. If partial report was being completed because of stimulus persistence, then an inverse duration effect should have been observed; reports should have been less accurate at longer durations (Di Lollo & Dixon, 1988). The fact that no such effect was found led the researchers to conclude that participants were using another resource, which they termed *information persistence*, to perform the task. Taken together, the results of Di Lollo (1980) and Irwin and Yeomans (1986) suggest that stimulus persistence and information persistence are two separate and dissociable phenomena. Stimulus persistence is pre-categorical and has a duration of about 500 ms (Vlassova & Pearson, 2013), while information persistence is categorical and has a duration up to 30 seconds (Neath, Bireta, & Surprenant, 2003). James Nairne and colleagues (2003) argue that the information-persistence component is not sensory in nature, but is the same type of memory as short-term memory (discussed in Chapter 3) and that participants completing partial-report paradigm experiments are probably utilizing information persistence to complete the task (Nairne, 2003). Information persistence cannot be considered sensory memory because it is not pre-categorical in nature; sensory memory, by definition, is modality specific.

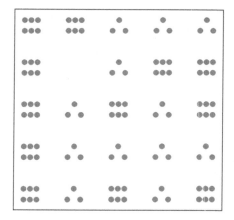

Figure 2.5 An example of an integrated display from Di Lollo (1980)

Di Lollo (1980) presented two sets of 12 dots sequentially and asked participants to identify the location that did *not* contain dots.

Source: Based on Di Lollo, 1980

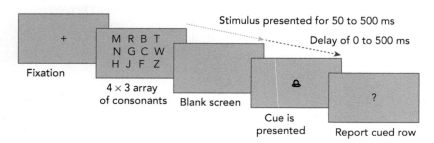

Figure 2.6 Irwin and Yeomans's (1986) partial-report paradigm

Irwin and Yeomans (1986) varied the duration of the stimulus array in a typical partial-report paradigm experiment. They found no effect of stimulus duration on the number of letters reported, leading them to conclude that participants were not using stimulus persistence to complete the task.

Source: Based on Irwin and Yeomans, 1986

The Neuroscience of Sensory Persistence and Information Persistence of Visual Information

Stimulus persistence results from sustained activation in the visual pathway between the retina and the primary visual cortex (V1) in the occipital lobe. In the retina, rods and M and P ganglion cells may remain active after the offset of a stimulus, as may cells in V1 (Irwin & Thomas, 2008). V1 is indicated in Figure 2.7.

While stimulus persistence results from sustained activation in the visual pathway, information persistence relies on sustained activation in cortical areas that lie beyond V1. Researchers studying the brains of macaque monkeys have found the anterior superior temporal sulcus (STS), which lies along the ventral stream (see Figure 2.7), to be active during iconic memory tasks (Keysers, Xiao, Földiák, & Perrett, 2005). This is not surprising because the STS is associated with objection recognition. The middle occipital gyrus (MOG), which is linked to change detection, is also active during iconic memory tasks and remains active for up to 2000 ms after the onset of a stimulus (Urakawa, Inui, Yamashiro, Tanaka, & Kakigi, 2010). Genetic factors that influence the production of a nerve-growth factor known as brain-derived neurotrophic factor (BDNF) also influence iconic memory; mutations in genes linked to BDNF are associated with shortened and less stable informational persistence (Beste, Schneider, Epplen, & Arning, 2011).

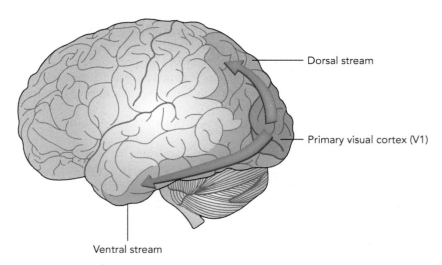

Figure 2.7   Ventral and dorsal streams

This image shows the primary visual cortex (V1), the ventral stream, and the dorsal stream. Sensory persistence is associated with sustained activity in the primary visual cortex while information persistence is associated with sustained activity in the ventral stream.

Summary

The original notion of sensory memory was that multiple modality-specific sensory registers held pre-categorical information until it was selected for processing. The consensus was that iconic memory lasted about one second (at the most) and echoic memory lasted about three seconds (at the most). Initial research using partial-report paradigms for the visual modality and modality effect and suffix effect for the auditory modality seemed to support this notion. However, more recent experimental results suggest that initial hypotheses about sensory memory were incorrect; there simply is no evidence for long-lasting pre-categorical memory in any modality. Instead, it appears as though we experience stimulus persistence only briefly after the presentation of stimuli. This persistence should not be considered memory any more than an afterimage on the retina of the eye should be considered memory. Material that is available more than about 100 ms after the removal of a stimulus should be attributed to information persistence, which is a part of active short-term memory, which we discuss in the next chapter.

CHAPTER REVIEW

- In 1960, George Sperling first proposed that humans possess a brief, large-capacity, pre-categorical visual store he called iconic memory. Researchers subsequently identified a brief, large-capacity, pre-categorical acoustic store they called echoic memory.
- Research since that time contradicts the notion of a long-lasting pre-categorical memory in any modality. Today, researchers instead argue that the results from Sperling's experiments can be attributed to stimulus persistence and information persistence.
- Sensory persistence is residual neurological activity resulting from a stimulus presentation that fades rapidly over time. Information persistence is the availability of stimulus information after it has been removed, and can be thought of as being part of short-term memory.
- Sensory persistence is associated with sustained activation in the visual pathway, while information persistence is associated with sustained activation in the ventral stream.

MEMORY ACTIVITY

Dispelling the Concept of Iconic Memory

The activity for this chapter involves summarizing experimental results on a simple graph in order to better remember the critique of Sperling's iconic memory model discussed in this chapter. This activity should generate a strong memory for the critique both because you will be processing the information on a deep level (see the discussion on The Processing Approach to Memory in Chapter 1) and because you will be creating a visual image (Marks, 1973).

continued

First, review the typical results from an iconic memory experiment and, on a graph similar to the one shown below, draw the recall curves typically seen in iconic memory experiments (for both whole-report trials and partial-report trials).

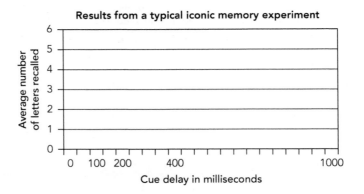

Results from a typical iconic memory experiment

Next, recall that one of the critiques of the iconic memory model is that the typical results in an iconic memory study show the effects of output interference. Look at your graph, and circle where output interference can be seen in the typical results of these studies.

Finally, briefly explain the contradiction between the iconic memory theory and the presence of the effects of output interference in typical studies of this theory.

Questions

1. Briefly describe Sperling's partial-report paradigm. Explain how the results led to a theory of iconic memory.
2. Describe persistence. Explain why research on persistence conflicts with Sperling's model of iconic memory.
3. Explain the difference between stimulus information that is pre-categorical and stimulus information that is post-categorical.
4. Differentiate between sensory and information persistence, including a description of the neuroscientific underpinnings of each phenomenon.

Key Figures

Vincent Di Lollo p. 38
Ulric Neisser p. 32
George Sperling p. 32

3 Short-Term Memory and Working Memory

LEARNING OBJECTIVES

Having read this chapter, you will be able to:

- Differentiate between the concepts of short-term memory and working memory.
- Explain how the case of H.M. influenced early models of memory.
- Sketch Broadbent's model.
- Critique Broadbent's model.
- Differentiate between Broadbent's model and the modal model.
- Sketch the modal model.
- Critique the modal model.
- Sketch Baddeley and Hitch's (1974) multicomponent model of working memory.
- Describe the central executive, the phonological loop, and the visuospatial sketchpad.
- Describe experimental research that led to the development of the multicomponent model put forth by Baddeley (2000).
- Describe the episodic buffer.
- Sketch Baddeley's (2000) multicomponent model of working memory.
- Discuss experimental research that led to the development of the multicomponent model put forth by Baddeley (2012).
- Sketch Baddeley's (2012) multicomponent model of working memory.
- Review early research that looked for a link between STM and the prefrontal cortex.
- Explain the sensory-recruitment model and provide evidence in support of this model from research using both verbal and visual stimuli.
- Describe the neurological regions that are central to working memory.
- Compare and contrast the brain regions involved in STM with those involved in working memory.

MENTAL CALCULATORS

On September 30, 2018, 14-year-old Tomohiro Iseda from Japan won the eighth Mental Calculation World Cup by scoring highest in a competition that included adding ten 10-digit numbers in seven minutes, multiplying two eight-digit numbers in 10 minutes, identifying the day of the week from a random date in one minute, computing the square root of a six-digit number in 10 minutes, as well as five "surprise tasks" that involved mental calculations. Mental calculators such as

Tomohiro Iseda scored first in the 2018 Mental Calculation World Cup.

Tomohiro Iseda rely on working memory to manipulate numbers and complete complex computations. In this chapter, you will discover that while working memory can be used for amazing mathematical feats, working memory is also used to complete everyday tasks that involve manipulating information, such as reasoning, learning, and comprehension.

Short-Term Memory

People are always thinking. Thoughts typically include events that have just happened and things that are planned or expected for the future. Initially, researchers believed that the cognitive mechanism that maintained thoughts briefly was simply a storage system and called this storage system **short-term memory (STM)**. However, in 1986 Alan Baddeley published an influential paper suggesting that the cognitive mechanism that was responsible for the temporary storage of information could also *manipulate* information, which led researchers to begin using the term **working memory** instead of short-term memory. At present, the term *short-term memory* only refers to the retention of material for a short period of time; for example, if you had to retain the numbers 4562 and 804 for 20 seconds you would use short-term memory. The term *working memory* is used when a person is manipulating information in some way while retaining it; for example, if you add 4562 and 804 using only your mental resources, you are using working memory instead of STM. In this section we will review early memory models, which conceived short-term memory as a storage mechanism. Models of working memory are discussed in detail later in this chapter.

short-term memory

a memory store that holds about four pieces of information for about 15 to 30 seconds without rehearsal

working memory

the part of short-term memory that is responsible for immediate conscious perceptual, cognitive, and linguistic processing

Models of Short-Term Memory

Donald Broadbent's Model

In 1957, William Scoville and Brenda Milner published the first paper discussing H.M., who had undergone surgery to control his epilepsy and had subsequently lost his ability to form new memories. (For an introduction to H.M., see Box 1.2 in Chapter 1.) Although H.M. could not create new long-term memories, H.M.'s short-term memory appeared intact; H.M. could carry on conversations and remember what happened a few seconds earlier provided he was not distracted. Scoville and Milner (1957) thus argued that H.M.'s pattern of memory loss suggested that long-term memory and short-term memory were controlled by different brain areas. Scoville and Milner (1957) argued that the medial temporal lobe and the hippocampi, which were destroyed by H.M.'s surgery, were responsible for long-term memory, while other regions that were not destroyed during H.M.'s surgery controlled short-term memory. This neurological dissociation between long-term memory and short-term memory served as an impetus for the first model that included the concept of short-term memory, which was published by Donald Broadbent in 1958 (see Figure 3.1). Broadbent's model is comprised of **primary memory**, which is short in duration, and **secondary memory**, which is a long-term memory store. According to this model, information must pass through primary memory to get to secondary memory. Importantly, primary memory and secondary memory are argued to COMPRISE entirely different memory systems. In Broadbent's model, primary memory encompasses two subsystems: the **S-system**, which holds sensory information in a pre-categorical form before it is selected for further processing, and the **P-system**, which consists of conscious thought. Material in the S-system fades rapidly. Material in the P-system must be rehearsed to be maintained; enough rehearsal may eventually lead this information to travel to secondary memory and be available in the long term.

Material in Broadbent's (1958) P-store is maintained in a speech-like code. Several experiments supported the notion that information maintained in the short term has phonological properties. Conrad (1964) compared the error rates for the recall of lists of letters that looked alike (e.g., X, K, Y) to lists of letters that looked different but sounded alike (e.g., C, V, B). Conrad (1964) found that participants were much more likely to make errors in the sound-alike condition than the look-alike condition, implying that a verbal coding was linked to the maintenance of these letters in short-term memory. In 1966, Alan Baddeley conducted a similar study but varied the phonological similarity of words instead of letters. In one condition, recall for phonologically similar words, such as *bet, get, men, pen,* was compared to recall for words that were not phonologically similar but were similar in how frequently they occurred in everyday use of English such as *pal, fin, hug, rag.* In another condition, participants' ability to recall items from a list of words with similar meaning, such as *small, tiny, thin,* was compared to recall for a list

primary memory
a synonym for short-term memory

secondary memory
a synonym for long-term memory

S-system
the part of primary memory that holds information in pre-categorical form

P-system
the part of primary memory that consists of conscious thought

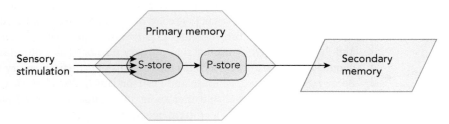

Figure 3.1   Broadbent's-dual-process model of memory

Broadbent's (1958) model indicated that incoming sensory information was held in a large-capacity S-store before being selected for higher-order processing and entering the limited capacity P-store. The S-store and the P-store comprised consciousness, or primary memory. Long-term memory was conceptualized as separate from the S-store and the P-store.

of words that were not related in meaning, such as *rack, horse, desk*. Baddeley (1966) found that memory for phonologically similar words was significantly worse than memory for phonologically different words, but that recall for semantically similar words was not different than recall for semantically different words. In addition, Murray (1968) showed that when participants were required to repeat the word *the* while being presented with a visual list of words, participants were far less likely to falsely identify phonologically similar words in a subsequent recognition task. Thus, the results from Conrad (1964), Baddeley (1966), and Murray (1968) all confirmed Broadbent's notion that the P-store contains speech-like codes. The results from Murray (1968) also suggest that *more* than just an acoustic code must be maintained, because participants in this experiment were able to report items even when inner speech was occupied during the retention interval.

The capacity of primary memory was of key interest to Broadbent and his contemporaries. In 1956, George Miller famously published the results of several experimental paradigms that converged on the conclusion that humans are limited to processing about seven items at any given time, plus or minus two. Miller (1956) proposed that items are not limited to single letters or numbers; instead, he suggested a span of more than seven items such as FBICIAABCCBC could be recalled if the items were chunked into units such that there were fewer than seven meaningful chunks, such as FBI, CIA, ABC, and CBC. However, the notion that we have a set capacity of chunks was soon dismissed when Simon (1974) found that the number of chunks that could be recalled was variable; the more information contained in each chunk, the fewer chunks that can be recalled.

Brown-Peterson paradigm

a paradigm designed to test the rate of primary memory decay by preventing the rehearsal of to-be-remembered items through the use of a concurrent counting task

In addition to its capacity, researchers in the 1960s and 1970s were also very interested in establishing the duration of primary memory. The **Brown-Peterson paradigm** (Peterson & Peterson, 1959) was designed to determine the rate at which information decays from a short-term memory store. In this paradigm, participants are presented with three consonants that they read aloud (e.g., D, H, R) and then are presented with a three-digit number that they also read aloud (e.g., 137). Participants are then required to count backwards from the number they have just read aloud by threes or fours for a predetermined length of time. This intervening arithmetic task is intended to prevent rehearsal, allowing short-term memory to decay naturally. After the interval is over, participants are asked to stop the arithmetic task and report the three letters presented at the beginning of the trial. Peterson and Peterson (1959) found that the probability of correctly reporting the letters was over 60 per cent after a three-second delay but decreased to less than 20 per cent after an 18-second delay (see Figure 3.2). Based on the results from the Brown-Peterson paradigm experiments, Peterson and Peterson (1959) concluded that primary memory has a duration of about 20 seconds; after 20 seconds the contents of primary memory will decay if not rehearsed. Peterson and Peterson (1959) also argue that any material that is still available after about 18 seconds with no rehearsal must reflect secondary, or long-term, memory.

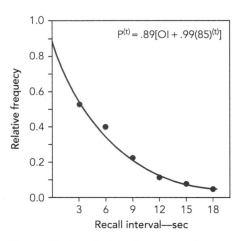

Figure 3.2 Results from Peterson and Peterson (1959)

This figure shows correct recalls with latencies below 2.83 seconds as a function of recall interval.
Source: Peterson & Peterson, 1959, p. 195

The Modal Model

Atkinson and Shiffrin (1968) expanded upon Broadbent's (1958) model by suggesting that memory is comprised of static memory stores as well as flexible, controllable memory processes. Atkinson and Shiffrin's dual-process model, which is shown in Figure 3.3, includes three different types of memory stores: a sensory register (SR) for each of the five senses, a short-term store (STS), and a long-term store (LTS). The sensory registers are modelled after Sperling's (1960) conception of sensory memory and are presumed to be large-capacity, modality-specific short-term stores where material decays very rapidly. Information enters the STS by being selected from an SR and the capacity and duration of the STS is very limited. In this way the STS is very similar to Broadbent's P-system. Material can be encoded in the LTS from the SR or the STS, and material from the LTS can only become active in the STS by being "copied" from the LTS. Material can enter the STS either through deliberate rehearsal processes or by passive exposure. Waugh and Norman (1965) and Murdoch (1972) both presented models that were very similar to Atkinson and Shiffrin (1968). In statistics, the term *mode* refers to the most frequent observation, and the term *modal* is used to describe something that shares characteristics with the most frequent observation. Because Atkinson and Shiffrin's (1968) model was so similar to other models presented around the same time, the model became known as the **modal model of memory**.

The most frequently cited support for the modal model comes from the observation of **serial-position curves** generated from **free-recall** experiments. In the free-recall paradigm, participants are presented with lists of items to learn and are then asked to report items from the list in any order that they like.

Researchers then compute how frequently items from each serial position are correctly recalled during free recall, which generates a serial-position curve. A consistent finding of free-recall experiments is that serial-position curves have a distinct U-shape; participants remember items at the beginning of the list well (known as the **primacy effect**) and items from the end of the list well (known as the **recency effect**). Figure 3.4 shows a typical serial-position curve from free-recall experiments conducted by Rundus (1971).

According to the modal model, the primacy and recency effects support the notion of two distinct memory systems. The recency effect results from material still being available in

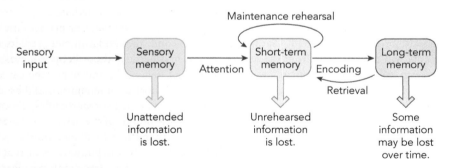

Figure 3.3 The modal model of memory

The modal model of memory was proposed by Atkinson and Shiffrin (1968). The first component in this model is a large-capacity, rapidly fading sensory memory store. Material can be selected from sensory memory and brought into short-term memory. Material in short-term memory must be rehearsed to be maintained. Material may enter long-term memory either directly from sensory memory or via short-term memory. Material can be copied from long-term memory into short-term memory.

Source: Based on Atkinson & Shiffrin 1968

modal model of memory

a heuristic, first introduced by Atkinson and Shiffrin (1968), for thinking about how memory processes work. The modal model includes three main components: sensory memory, short-term memory and long-term memory.

serial-position curve

a way of presenting data from free-recall experiments where proportion correct is presented on the vertical axis and the relative position of an item on the to-be-remembered list is shown on the horizontal axis

free recall

an experimental paradigm where participants are asked to report items from a list without regard to serial order

primacy effect

higher probability of free recall for items presented at the beginning of a to-be-remembered list as compared to items from the middle of the list

recency effect

recently acquired memories are more likely to be recalled than memories from further in the past

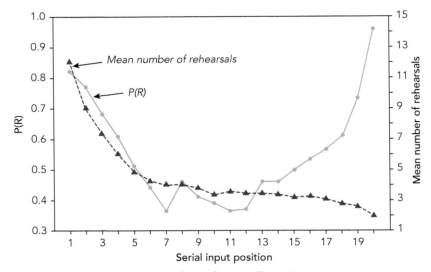

Figure 3.4 A typical serial-position curve from a free-recall experiment

This figure shows a typical serial-position curve from Rundus (1971). Participants were more likely to accurately report items from the beginning and end of the item list.

Source: Rundus, 1971, p. 67

short-term memory and the primacy effect results from items early in the list receiving more rehearsal and being established in long-term memory at the time of report. Items in the middle of the list do not receive sufficient rehearsal to enter long-term memory and are no longer available in short-term memory at the time of report; thus, they are rarely reported accurately.

The modal model makes several strong predictions about the serial-position curve. First, the modal model predicts that there will be a primacy effect and a recency effect at all list lengths; there will always have been more rehearsal of early items and more immediate availability of later items. This prediction is supported by Murdoch (1972), who found clear primacy and recency effects for list lengths of 10, 15, and 20 items. Second, the modal model predicts that participants will report items from the end of the list first because those items are available in short-term memory; if participants were not reporting items from the end of the list first, then no recency effect would be seen (because the items in short-term memory would be lost). Welch and Burnett (1924) did indeed find items from the end of the list reported first, followed by items from the front of the list, followed by items from the middle of the list, supporting this prediction. Third, the modal model predicts that items early in the list will be rehearsed more than items later in the list. Rundus and Atkinson (1970) tested this hypothesis by instructing participants to rehearse out loud while being presented with items for a free-recall task. Rundus and Atkinson (1970) found that items early in the 20-item list were rehearsed about 12 times, whereas items from the middle and the end of the list were rehearsed four or fewer times, confirming the prediction of the modal model. Rundus and Atkinson (1970) attribute the primacy effect to this increased rehearsal. Finally, the modal model predicts that delaying report and preventing rehearsal during that delay will impede the recency effect but not the primacy effect; this is because material in short-term memory will be lost during the delay but material encoded into long-term memory will not be affected. Glanzer and Cunitz (1966) show support for this prediction in an experiment in which the recency effect, but not the primacy effect, was eliminated when participants were asked to count backwards after each list item was presented.

Critique of the Modal Model

Although the modal model makes several correct predictions about performance on free-recall tasks, further experimentation called into question the simplistic tenets of the model. The modal model clearly predicts that impeding rehearsal on every trial with a task that occupies short-term memory should affect recall for all items. According to the modal model, no items will enter long-term memory without rehearsal, and no items will be available for report from short-term memory because the distraction task, and not items from the list, will occupy short-term memory. However researchers who have used a continual distraction paradigm, in which each list learned for serial recall was preceded and followed by a distracting task (such as verifying arithmetic problems or counting backwards by 7s), have still found substantial primacy and recency effects, even when there was a distracting task on every trial (e.g., Baddeley & Hitch, 1974; Bjork & Whitten, 1974; Watkins, Neath, & Sechler, 1989).

So why did the recency effect disappear in Glanzer and Cunitz (1966)? Bjork and Whitten (1974) suggest that the recency effect is related to two task demands of the free-recall procedure instead of the characteristics of short-term memory. These task demands are (a) the amount of time for which the item needs to be remembered (known as the **retention interval** or RI) and (b) the amount of time that separates items on the list (known as the **inter-item presentation interval** or IPI). The ratio of interest is the IPI divided by the RI. Nairne, Neath, Serra, and Byun (1997) varied the IPI/RI ratio and found that the ratio perfectly predicted the slope of the recency portion of the serial-position curves. Thus, the recency effect is not necessarily evidence for a separate short-term memory system; it could just as easily be an artifact of the IPI and RI chosen by the experimenter.

An alternative explanation for the recency effect is that it is the result of strategic task switching. When participants have a predictable distractor task, such as a task that is identical for every trial, they can quickly switch the focus of their cognitive resources between rehearsing items and the distractor task and, when they are successful, complete the distractor task *and* rehearse the material. When presented with a novel distractor task, however, such as counting backwards from a new number on each trial, rehearsal is no longer possible. Koppenaal and Glanzer (1990) found a recency effect when the distractor task was unchanging but not when it changed from trial to trial. In addition, Neath (1993) argued that if the recency effect was the result of multitasking demands, then participants would not show a difference between the changing and unchanging distractor conditions if they were not aware that they were going to complete a recall test at the end of the trial. This is because participants wouldn't attempt to rehearse if they did not expect to have to recall the items and thus the extra demands of the changing task would have no effect. As predicted, Neath (1993) found no difference in the performance of these "naïve" participants; they had similar recall whether they were doing an easy or difficult second task. If the recency effect was the result of material being available in short-term memory, then participants in the more difficult secondary task condition should have shown worse performance in the recall task. Neath (1993) also noted that it is only on the *third* trial of a changing distractor-task paradigm that a participant becomes aware of the fact that the distractor task is unpredictable and will begin to task switch accordingly. As a result, performance on the *first*

retention interval (RI)

the period of time between a learning event and a test of memory for that event

inter-item presentation interval (IPI)

the amount of time that separates the presentation of two items

trial of changing and unchanging distractor-task paradigm experiments should be no different, and this is what Neath (1993) found. Finally, Neath predicted that the recency effect would be eliminated if the distractor task changed on every trial because the demands of multitasking would make rehearsal impossible, and this is what Neath (1993) found. In both Koppenaal and Glanzer (1990) and Neath (1993), the researchers found that the recency effect could be created or eliminated depending on the demands of the task. The fact that the recency effect can be manipulated so easily presents a significant problem for proponents of the modal model, because according to the modal model the recency effect results from constant changes to short-term memory, and should therefore always be observed, regardless of the task demands.

Proponents of the modal model suggest that the distinctiveness of the primacy and recency effects is evidence for two separate memory systems. However, Tan and Ward (2000) hypothesized that the primacy effect may be the result of the ratio rule; participants may be able to rehearse items from the beginning of the list continually when items are presented at sufficiently slow rates, allowing the item to be reported at the end of the trial. To test this hypothesis, Tan and Ward (2000) varied the presentation rate of items in free-recall tasks and asked participants to rehearse out loud rather than covertly. Tan and Ward (2000) did indeed find typical primacy and recency effects in their experiment, both of which were greater in the slow presentation rate condition than the fast presentation rate condition, supporting the notion that when more rehearsal is possible, more recall will occur. But more interestingly, when Tan and Ward (2000) analyzed the proportion correct as a function of when the item was last rehearsed, instead of when it was presented in the item list, they found recency of rehearsal to perfectly predict recall; items that had been rehearsed recently were recalled; those that were not recently rehearsed were not recalled. This result suggests that rehearsal of early items does not necessarily serve to transfer those items to long-term memory, as the modal model suggests, but instead, serves to keep the items available for report at the time of test. The results from Koppenaal and Glanzer (1990), Neath (1993), and Tan and Ward (2000) all suggest that the serial-position curve does not provide evidence for the modal model, and further that the modal model cannot explain the serial-position curve.

In addition, the modal model is problematic in that none of the proposed memory stores in the modal model can operate independently from one another; information must pass through the short-term store on the way in and out of long-term memory, and long-term memory must be used to categorize information in the short-term store (Nairne, 1996, 2003). Thus, according to the modal model, performance of any and all tasks must involve accessing codes from both the short-term store and the long-term store. Nairne (1996, 2003) argues that due to the constant interaction between short-term memory and long-term memory that would be required according to the modal model, it is not possible to make a measurement of just short-term memory or just long-term memory; the codes are effectively inseparable. At this point it is reasonable to say that the modal model, while commonly presented as a de facto explanation of how memory works in many psychology textbooks, does not represent how memory *actually* works at all.

working memory

the part of short-term memory that is responsible for immediate conscious perceptual, cognitive, and linguistic processing

Working Memory

Earlier in this chapter, we discussed short-term memory (STM), which we defined as a memory store that holds about four pieces of information for about 15 to 30 seconds without rehearsal. We will now discuss **working memory**, which is a cognitive resource that allows for both the storage and manipulation of material held for a short period of time. Working memory is used when we solve problems, learn, and connect pieces of information together. Working memory is used for tasks such as performing arithmetic, re-ordering items into alphabetical order, or considering which of several sentence options conveys an idea most effectively. People who perform mental calculations competitively, like Tomohiro Iseda, apply pre-learned tricks for making mathematical calculations involving large numbers using working memory. While early accounts of short-term memory, such as Broadbent's (1958) model and the modal model, propose a short-term store that simply holds information for the individual but cannot change the information, subsequent research has suggested that information being held for short periods of time can also be manipulated, and new models have been proposed to include this new concept of working memory. We begin our discussion with the most widely cited model of working memory in the literature: the multicomponent model.

The Multicomponent Model

The best-known model of working memory is Alan Baddeley's multicomponent model. This model originally emerged in 1974 as an alternative to the modal model and has been modified several times since then to accommodate a growing body of data from studies on working memory. The model began with just three components, but when research emerged that could not be accommodated by the model, Baddeley revised the model. The most recent version of the model was developed in 2012. Baddeley himself admits that the model is a work in progress and that elements of the model may change with time, but asserts that, as it currently exists, the multicomponent model can account for most of the existing research on working memory.

In 1974, Alan Baddeley and Graham Hitch embarked on a research project to try to determine the relationship between STM and LTM. Their approach was quite simple. First, they asserted that there was good evidence that maintaining a set of digits (such as 5, 2, 3, 9, 5) occupied STM, and that the more digits that needed to be retained, the greater the demands on STM. Thus, they predicted that asking participants to repeat "3, 2, 1, 6, 7, 5" out loud over and over would require more of the limited capacity system than repeating "3, 2, 1" over and over. Next, they argued that if performance on a task was worse when a person was maintaining more digits, then that task must also rely on STM. Baddeley and Hitch (1974) note that previous experiments had shown that the impact of rehearsing digits affected some tasks differently than others. For example, Baddeley (1968) had participants complete a grammatical-reasoning task while rehearsing digit spans of different lengths. For the grammatical-reasoning task, the participant was presented with a statement such as "A follows B" and an illustration of the order of letters "A → B" and had to indicate as quickly and accurately as possible whether the statement matched the illustration. (In this example, the answer would be "no.") Participants rehearsed zero to eight digits out loud while performing the grammatical-reasoning task. Baddeley (1968) found that error rates on this task were unaffected by the number of digits being retained, but that response times increased as digit span increased. Baddeley and Hitch (1974) argued that the results from Baddeley (1968) suggested that the digit-span task and the grammatical-reasoning task require some of the same resources, but that the grammatical-reasoning task does not solely depend on the same resource that is involved in maintaining a digit span. If no resources were shared, then response time would not be affected by digit span. If all resources were shared, then error rates should increase with digit span. Baddeley and Hitch (1974) argued that the modal model's assumption that STM simply stored material was thus incomplete, and that it was necessary to conceptualize

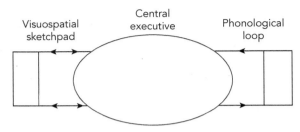

Figure 3.5   The multicomponent model of working memory

The multicomponent model of working memory was proposed by Baddeley and Hitch (1974). This model included three components: the phonological loop, the visuospatial sketchpad, and the central executive.

Source: Baddeley, 2012, p. 6

multicomponent model

a model of memory first proposed by Alan Baddeley in which working memory is comprised of a phonological loop, a visuospatial sketch-pad, and an episodic buffer, which are all controlled by a central executive

phonological loop

a portion of working memory in Baddeley and Hitch's multi-component model that consists of the short-term phono-logical store and an articulatory rehearsal mechanism

phonological-similarity effect

a decrement in recall performance that occurs when to-be-remembered words all sound similar (e.g., *pen, when, hen*)

STM as also involving an active *working* processor that supported mental activity and complex thought. Baddeley and Hitch (1974) presented the first **multicomponent model** of working memory, shown in Figure 3.5, as a response to this problem with the modal model.

The first version of the multicomponent model consists of three components: the *phonological loop*, which assists with acoustic or speech-based items; the *visuospatial sketchpad*, which is assumed to operate on visual items; and a *central executive*, which is attentionally limited and responsible for maintaining control over the other components.

The Phonological Loop

The **phonological loop** consists of a phonological store and an auditory processor. The phonological loop is used to retain and work with linguistic material in a speech-like form. Spoken words enter the phonological store automatically; however, visual material, like written words, must first be converted to a speech code by the auditory processor before entering the phonological store. The auditory processor periodically refreshes the contents of the phonological store, making it possible to retain information indefinitely. If not rehearsed, material decays in about two seconds. The characteristics of the phonological loop were designed to account for four prominent experimental findings: the effects of phonological similarity, articulatory-suppression tasks, word length, and irrelevant speech.

When to-be-remembered items have similar phonological characteristics, they are more difficult to remember then when the items are more phonologically distinct. This is known as the **phonological-similarity effect** (e.g., Baddeley, 1986; Conrad & Hull, 1964). Thus, a letter list consisting of rhyming letters like B-G-T-D-C would not be remembered as well as a list consisting of non-rhyming letters such as H-C-F-L-K (see Figure 3.6). This is a robust effect found for letters and words, regardless of whether items are presented visually or auditorially. The multicomponent model can account for this finding because the model makes the strong prediction that all linguistic material is maintained using speech-like coding and thus items are most likely to be confused if they share phonological characteristics.

When a person is asked to learn items while performing a concurrent task involving speech, recall for the items is significantly reduced. This is referred to as the **effect of articulatory suppression**. For example, when a participant must say the word *the* repeatedly while learning a word list, memory for the word list will be worse than if the concurrent articulation task was not required (Murray, 1968; Peterson & Johnson, 1971). The multicomponent model can account for this finding because the model predicts that occupying the articulatory processor will prevent coding of new visual items and maintenance rehearsal of all to-be-remembered items, which should result in worse performance on the recall task.

The number of words a person can recall is directly related to how long it takes to pronounce those words; a person is able to recall fewer long-sounding words than short-sounding words, even if the words contain the same number of syllables. This phenomenon is known as the **word-length effect** or the time-based word-length effect. For example, when a long-to-pronounce list like "baboon, weekday, foresee" is compared to a short-to-pronounce list like

(a)

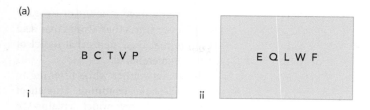

i   ii

(b)

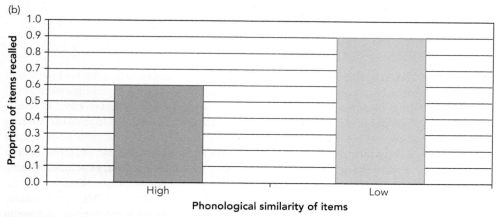

Figure 3.6   The effect of phonological similarity on letter recall

Figure 3.6.a.i is an example of letters with high phonological similarity. Figure 3.6.a.ii is an example of letters with low phonological similarity. Figure 3.6.b shows typical results from an experiment where the phonological similarity of visually presented items is varied across trials. Note that fewer items are recalled when the visually presented items are phonologically similar (as in list i) than when the items are phonologically different (as in list ii).

"picket, rugged, pistol," participants recall more from the short-to-pronounce group than the long-to-pronounce group (see, e.g., Baddeley, Thomson, & Buchanan, 1975; Baddeley & Wilson, 1985). Note that these words do not differ in number of letters or syllables, but rather in how long it takes to say them (and hence to rehearse them). The multicomponent model can account

effect of articulatory suppression

a decrement in recall for verbally presented words when the participant is given a concurrent task involving speech

word-length effect

a decrement in recall performance when words take longer to verbalize

DIY EXPERIMENT

BOX
3.1

Articulatory Suppression

It's easy to see the effects of articulatory suppression. Create two lists of 10 unrelated words on separate pieces of paper. Show the first list of words to a friend or family member for one minute without any special instructions. Take the list away and have your participant write down as many words as she or he can recall. Next show the same participant the second word list, but this time instruct the participant to repeat *cat* over and over out loud while reading the list. After one minute, take the list away and ask your participant to write down as many words as possible. Compare the number of correctly recalled words in each condition. If more words were recalled in the first condition, this shows an effect of articulatory suppression.

for the word-length effect because the model predicts that, given a fixed amount of time for rehearsal, words that take longer to rehearse will be rehearsed fewer times than words that take less time to pronounce. Because recall is said to be the result of rehearsal, items that took less time to pronounce and were thus rehearsed more will be better remembered.

When Colle and Welsh (1976) had participants view consonants either while listening to irrelevant speech or in quiet conditions, recall was better in the quiet condition. This effect came to be known as the **irrelevant-speech effect**. The multicomponent model explains the irrelevant-speech effect easily: The phonemes from the irrelevant-speech signal enter the phonological store and interfere with the coding of the visual items.

The Visuospatial Sketchpad

The **visuospatial sketchpad** is assumed to be a short-term memory store that retains both visual and spatial information in an **isomorphic** representation; that is, in a representation that retains the perceptual qualities of the real object. For example, people who are asked to report how many windows are in their home may use the visuospatial sketchpad to imagine walking through their house, counting the windows as they go. Material in the visuospatial sketchpad is assumed to be constantly decaying and, if resources are available, constantly refreshed. The characteristics of the visuospatial sketchpad are based on the results from experiments using mental-scanning and mental-rotation paradigms.

In a typical mental-scanning paradigm experiment (e.g., Kosslyn, 1976), participants memorize a map; the map is then removed from view and participants are asked to imagine moving from one location to another on the map, indicating to the experimenter when they have arrived. In mental-scanning paradigm experiments, researchers consistently find response times increase with the distance between points on the map (e.g., Kosslyn, 1976, 1980; Kosslyn & Pomerantz, 1977; Jolicoeur & Kosslyn, 1985). In a typical mental-rotation paradigm experiment (e.g., Shepard & Metzler, 1971), participants are shown two images of three-dimensional objects and are asked to indicate as quickly and accurately as possible whether both images are of the same object. On some trials the objects are mirror images of one another and rotated 0 to 180 degrees, and on other trials the objects are the same and rotated 0 to 180 degrees. Researchers have consistently found that response time for objects that are the same increases as the angle of rotation increases (e.g., Shepard & Metzler, 1971).

Research suggests that the visuospatial sketchpad interacts with other components of working memory. For example, Pearson, Logie, and Gilhooly (1999) presented participants with four, six, or eight shapes (e.g., circle, square, triangle) and asked them to use the shapes to create and draw a novel object that they were then to describe to the experimenter. Participants were also asked to generate a name for their novel object. Thus, the task required both the visuospatial sketchpad (to imagine the novel object) and the phonological loop (to maintain the names of the objects used and the name of the novel object). In some blocks of trials, participants performed a concurrent second task, which was either tapping their finger in a figure-eight pattern (spatial task) or repeating the word *go* every 500 ms (articulatory-suppression task). The researchers found that the spatial task disrupted the production of novel objects but did not affect memory for the objects that were used, while the articulatory-suppression task had no effect on the creation of the objects, but negatively impacted recall of the names of the shapes used to create the objects. The results from Pearson et al. (1999) thus show that the visuospatial sketchpad and the phonological loop can both be active in the same task without interfering with each other.

The visuospatial sketchpad can be used to imagine the manipulation of objects, while the phonological loop maintains the names for the objects being imagined. The results from Pearson et al. (1999) also show that while they may be active concurrently, the visuospatial sketchpad does not use the same cognitive resources as the phonological loop (Denis, Logie, & Comoldo, 2012). In addition, research suggests that the visuospatial sketchpad has limited capacity; people find it more difficult to maintain complex images than simple images and more difficult to maintain large images than small images (Kosslyn, 1975).

The Central Executive

Baddeley and Hitch (1974) suggested that working memory was controlled by an attentional mechanism called the **central executive**. The central executive is conceptualized as a supervisory system that controls the flow of information into the various supervisory components of the working-memory model. Material that receives attention from the central executive can become part of working memory. The central executive is also required for tasks that require complex cognitive processes, decision making, or searching for novel solutions to problems. For example, if you are at a paint store and you are trying to decide which colour of paint would look best in your living room, the central executive could bring a memory of what your living room looks like into the visuospatial sketchpad and then the central executive could be used again to develop a way to solve the problem, such as determining that the paint must match the floor and sofa. The central executive may be used a third time to decide whether the paint does indeed match the floor and the sofa.

One method for studying the effect of the central executive on working memory is to use what is known as the **n-back task**. In the *n*-back task, participants are presented with a series of items (usually letters or numbers) and are cued to report the item that was presented *n* items earlier, where *n* varies depending on the experiment. For example, in a typical two-back paradigm, participants would be told that they would be presented with a string of digits and after the presentation of each digit they would be cued to report the number that was presented two items earlier in the sequence. Thus, if the participant was shown "4, 2, 9," the participant would need to enter "4" after the digit "9" was presented. In other variations of the task, the cue is presented after digits at random. To complete the *n*-back task correctly, the central executive must continually update the contents of working memory such that, if needed, the *n*th item back is available for report. Research using the *n*-back task supports the notion that a central executive controls the content of working memory. For example, Scharinger, Soutschek, Schubert, and Gerjets (2015) presented participants with one central letter that was either flanked with three of the same letter on either side (e.g., FFF F FFF) or flanked by three different letters on either side (e.g., SSS F SSS). After each trial, participants had to indicate if the central letter they had just seen was the same as the central letter two trials earlier (this was a two-back test). Participants were also presented with blocks of trials where no flanker letters appeared (e.g., F or S appeared alone) but the same two-back test was given after each trial. Scharinger et al. (2015) found that participants were more accurate in the flanker condition than in the no-flanker condition and reasoned that this was because the central executive was recruited to inhibit the flankers, which in turn promoted attentional control and allowed for better *n*-back performance. Thus, the results of Scharinger et al. (2015) support the notion that attentional control provided by the central executive facilitates operations carried out in working memory.

central executive

a supervisory system that controls the flow of information in and out of working memory

n-back task (*n*-back procedure)

an experimental paradigm in which the participant must indicate whether the stimulus on the current trial matches the stimulus presented *n* trials before

The Addition of the Episodic Buffer to the Multicomponent Model

One problem with Baddeley and Hitch's (1974) three-component model (shown in Figure 3.5) is that it cannot explain how working memory is linked to LTM, even though there is significant evidence that the two processes must interact. For example, people can retain as many as 15 related words in working memory, but just five or six unrelated words (Brener, 1940). In addition, people can hold sentences consisting of even more than 15 words in working memory without issue, and can retain material that can't easily be visualized (e.g., the emotional tone of a sentence). The three-component model cannot explain this; the phonological loop has a capacity of about two or three items, and the visuospatial sketchpad is only useful for items that lend themselves to visual imagery. A second problem is that Baddeley and Hitch's (1974) model has difficulty accounting for digit spans of seven items, again because this exceeds the capacity limit of the phonological loop. A third problem with the three-component model is that it cannot explain how information from different modalities (such as vision and hearing) can come together to form a single percept (such as a person speaking). A final problem is that some amnesic patients who cannot access long-term memories are nonetheless able to recall stories in the short term that include details from a variety of modalities. This observation cannot be explained by the phonological loop alone. To accommodate these findings, Baddeley (2000) proposed a revision of the multicomponent model that included a fourth component, called the *episodic buffer*. The multicomponent model from Baddeley (2000) can be seen in Figure 3.7.

episodic buffer

a component of working memory that can hold about four chunks of multidimensional code

The Episodic Buffer

The **episodic buffer** is a storage system that can hold about four chunks of multidimensional code. This material can be visual, verbal, or semantic and can come from a variety of sources, including other parts of working memory, long-term memory, and perception. The link between the episodic buffer and LTM can account for the finding that people can retain related words better than unrelated words. Because the episodic buffer can hold chunks of multidimensional information, the new multicomponent model can also explain how people are able to hold long sentences in memory, why digit span exceeds the capacity of the phonological loop, and how people with amnesia can retain percepts combining information from different modalities in STM. Material is retrieved from episodic memory using conscious awareness, and the episodic buffer is assumed to be entirely under the control of the central executive. As an active processor, the episodic buffer can bind together different unrelated concepts. For example, the episodic buffer can be used for a person to take the concept of a car and the concept of glass and combine them to imagine a car made of glass. With this glass car conception in mind, a person is then able to think about specific problems presented by a glass car, such as privacy, visibility, whether it might break, and how terrible the car would look if it got dirty.

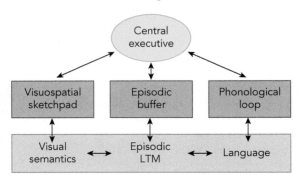

Figure 3.7   The multicomponent model from Baddeley (2000)

This model introduces the concept of the episodic buffer, which can hold four chunks of multidimensional material. The model also connects the various short-term stores with LTM.
Source: Baddeley, 2012, p. 16

Experimental evidence supports the notion that the episodic buffer requires attentional resources and operates independently of the phonological loop and the visuospatial sketchpad.
Langerock, Vergauwe, and Barrouillet (2014) had participants maintain words (a task that would
employ the phonological loop) while maintaining either an association between the word and
another item that also employed the phonological loop, or an association between the word
and another item that employed the visuospatial sketchpad. The cognitive load was varied across
trials by varying the number of to-be-remembered words. Langerock et al. (2014) found an effect
of cognitive load when participants had to maintain an association between an item in the phonological buffer and an item in the visuospatial sketchpad, but no effect of cognitive load in the
other condition. This result supports the notion that the episodic buffer in an attentional mechanism binds material of different modalities.

The Current Multicomponent Model of Working Memory

Alan Baddeley published the most current version of the multicomponent model in 2012. This
model can be seen in Figure 3.8. This model differs from Baddeley (2000) in two important
ways. First, the current model allows both the visuospatial sketchpad and the phonological loop
to have direct access to LTM. The link between the phonological loop and LTM is based on a
series of experiments that showed that the development of the phonological loop appears to be
correlated with language acquisition. Gathercole and Baddeley (1989) studied four- and five-
year-old children using a nonword repetition test (which assessed the capacity of the phonological loop), nonverbal intelligence, and vocabulary size. Gathercole and Baddeley (1989) found
a strong correlation ($r = .52$) between repetition performance and vocabulary. Gathercole and
Baddeley (1990) also found that a group of eight-year-old children with language delays but
normal nonverbal intelligence had more difficulty repeating nonwords than children without
language delays, suggesting that the ability to repeat words is linked to vocabulary development
in young children. Baddeley (2012) opted to link the phonological loop directly to LTM in the

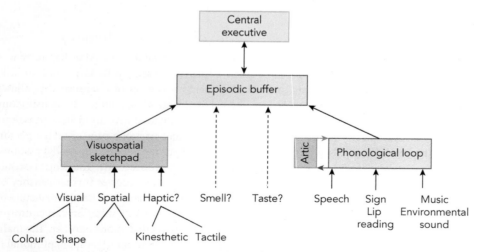

Figure 3.8 The multicomponent model of working memory from Baddeley (2012)

Source: Baddeley, 2012, p. 23

most current model because of the extensive experimental evidence connecting language learning to the phonological loop. Baddeley (2012) connects the visuospatial sketchpad directly to LTM because of an assumption that this would facilitate spatial learning in much the same way that a link between the phonological loop and LTM facilitates language learning.

In addition, Baddeley (2012) adjusted the connections to and from the episodic buffer. Baddeley (2000) stipulates that the material in the episodic buffer is multidimensional, implying that at some point in time prior to arriving in the episodic buffer, different dimensions of visual and auditory information must have been bound together. For example, for the episodic buffer to contain a percept of a red square, previous processing must have combined the red colour of the item and the square shape of the item into a single percept. In the multicomponent model presented in Baddeley (2000), only the central executive passed information to the episodic buffer (see Figure 3.7), implying the central executive was responsible for binding together these dimensions. Thus a clear prediction of Baddeley (2000) is that any task that occupies the capacity-limited central executive should impair the binding of perceptual features. For example, a paradigm that involves switching between tasks (which would tax the central executive) should impair the ability to bind together properties of objects. However, a series of experiments conducted by Baddeley and others found just the opposite; tasks demanding attention do not impair perceptual binding at all (Allen, Baddeley, & Hitch 2006; Baddeley, Hitch, & Allen, 2009). Baddeley (2012) suggests that the episodic buffer receives its multidimensional inputs from the phonological buffer and the visuospatial sketchpad, and adjusted the model accordingly. The current multicomponent model shows the episodic buffer at the epicentre of working memory, receiving material from the phonological loop and visuospatial sketchpad as well as interacting with the central executive. Baddeley speculates that the episodic buffer may receive information about smell and taste in much the same way it receives information about sights and sounds; however, the details of how this operates are not yet formal aspects of the multicomponent model of working memory. Baddeley also speculates that the episodic buffer receives information about emotions, explaining why emotion seems to influence working memory (Baddeley, 2007, 2012, 2015; Baddeley, Banse, Huang, & Page, 2012).

Cowan's Embedded-Processes Model of Working Memory

embedded-processes model

a model of short-term memory in which short-term memory is envisaged as the component of long-term memory that is currently active

In 1999, Nelson Cowan proposed the **embedded-processes model** while Alan Baddeley was working on the version of the multicomponent model proposed by Baddeley (2000). The embedded-processes model suggests that working memory is a set of processes that allows a subset of information to be maintained in a heightened state of activation. By focusing our attention, we can bring a subset of that material with heightened activation into conscious awareness. For example, by focusing attention on a particular part of a page of text, a person can bring the words from that part of the page into conscious awareness. The model assumes that we have a very brief sensory store lasting a few hundred milliseconds. The central executive controls attention and determines what sensory information receives further sensory or semantic processing. The processed sensory information will remain in a heightened state of activation for about 20 or 30 seconds without rehearsal. The focus of attention can comprise about three or four unrelated items, or more items if they are related to one another. The main difference between the embedded-processes model and the current multicomponent model is that the embedded-processes model assumes that links to locations in LTM are held in STM, whereas the multicomponent model suggests that material from LTM is downloaded into the episodic buffer.

In the embedded-processes model, short-term memory is simply the currently active portion of long-term memory. This intimate link between short-term and long-term memory makes it easy to explain many effects of serial recall that seem related to long-term memory. One such effect is the **concreteness effect**; concrete words such as *wall* are better recalled than abstract words such as *conscience* (Paivio, Yuille, & Madigan, 1968). The concreteness effect is usually attributed to there being more representations in long-term memory for concrete words. In addition, high-frequency words such as *cat* are usually better re-called than low-frequency words such as *vat*. The word-frequency effect is also attributed to long-term memory; high-frequency words have been encountered more often and thus have stronger representations in long-term memory. Both con-creteness and word frequency affect serial recall (Roodenrys & Quinlan, 2000; Walker & Hulme, 1999) and are easily explained by the embedded-processes model.

Cowan's (1999) model was developed to ac-count for experimental findings that could not be explained by Baddeley and Hitch (1974), includ-ing the simultaneous experience of material from multiple modalities as one percept. Baddeley's (2000) episodic buffer has most of the same char-acteristics of Cowan's (1999) model. All material decays and is subject to interference, but rehearsal or accessing the material in other ways, such as revisiting the item as part of the completion of a task, can reactivate the item and make it persist longer. Retrieval occurs when an item is within the focus of attention. A depiction of the embedded-processes model from Cowan (1988) can be seen in Figure 3.9.

Cowan's (1999) embedded-processes model does a good job at explaining most of the phe-nomena in the working-memory literature. Although the model has been well received, some researchers argue that the definition of activation in this model needs to be refined and that the model needs to more clearly explain how deactivation (e.g., decay) occurs.

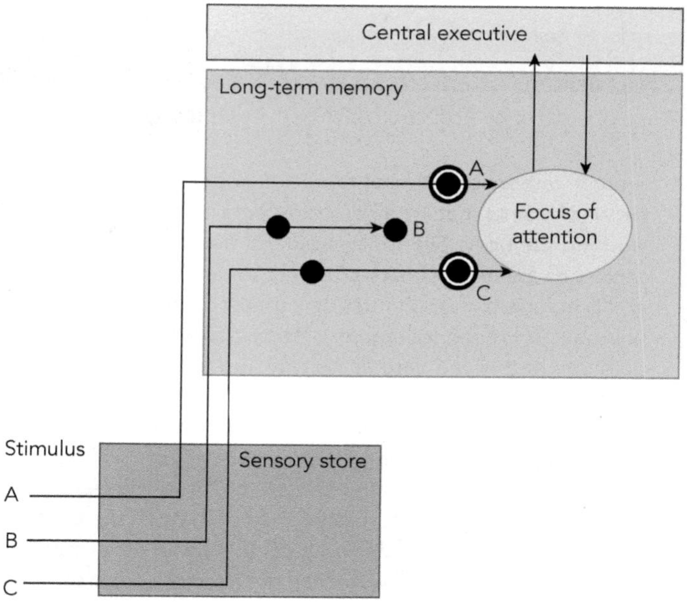

Figure 3.9   An example of Cowan's embedded-processes model of short-term memory

In this example, stimulus A is a familiar item that is selected by the central executive for further processing and becomes part of the focus of attention; stimulus A can be considered to be retrieved. Stimulus B is a familiar item but is not selected for further processing and less information about this item will be readily available. Stimulus C is a novel item. Its novelty attracts attention and becomes part of the focus of attention without the central executive directing such focus.

Source: Adapted from Cowan, 1988, Figure 1, page 180

concreteness effect

words that easily evoke visual images, such as *cat*, are better remembered than words that are less easy to imagine, such as *justice*

The Neuroscience of Short-Term Memory and Working Memory

Recall that STM and working memory are postulated to be different entities; STM stores about four pieces of information for about 30 seconds unrehearsed, while working memory refers to the mental manipulation of information in STM. The distinction between STM and working

BOX
3.2

RELEVANT RESEARCH

Does French Immersion Have Long-Term Effects on Executive Functioning?

French immersion (FI) programs are popular in Canada, and many parents choose FI for their children because of claims that FI has broad effects on a child's cognitive functioning, improving executive control and working memory. Ellen Bialystok and her colleagues at York University conducted a study that compared three groups of university students, monolingual students, students who had been in FI but had lost their ability to speak French fluently (lapsed bilinguals), and students who had been in FI who continued to be bilingual in French (bilinguals). Participants completed two tasks. The first was a flanker task in which participants had to indicate as quickly and accurately as possible which direction a red chevron (< or >) was pointing. In baseline blocks, the red chevrons were presented alone (i.e., <). In neutral blocks, the chevron was flanked by black squares (i.e., ■■ < ■■), and in mixed blocks, the red chevron was surrounded by black chevrons that were either congruent (i.e., < < < <) or incongruent (i.e., > > > < >). The second was a working-memory task. In this task, participants were shown an array of four stick figures and then shown individual stick figures across a series of trials. In the blocks that taxed working memory, participants had to indicate whether the stick figure on the current trial matched one from the initial display *and* was the same as a stick figure that appeared on the previous trials on some blocks or was *not* present in the last display in other blocks. The researchers found that the groups did not differ in their ability to perform the flanker task but did differ in their performance of the working-memory task; bilinguals were significantly more accurate in the working-memory task than lapsed bilinguals or monolinguals. The results suggest that FI may benefit working memory; however, that benefit is limited to individuals who continue to speak two languages. If French learning lapses, the benefit disappears.

memory is mirrored in neuroscientific findings that suggest that each entity is supported by different types of neural activity in different parts of the brain.

The Neuroscience of STM

The Search for a Neuroscientific Explanation of STM

In the 1930s, Yale professor Carlyle Jacobsen conducted a series of experiments in order to determine the primary function of the prefrontal cortex (PFC). Jacobsen trained two monkeys to perform a delayed-response task using a Wisconsin General Testing Apparatus (WGTA) like the one shown in Figure 3.10. The WGTA is comprised of a cage for an animal; a testing tray that can be moved within reach of the animal in the cage, or moved beyond its reach; and a screen that can be used to prevent the animal from reaching through the bars or seeing the tray during trial preparation. During training, the monkeys watched while the trainer placed food in one of two covered wells on the tray. There was a delay of several seconds and then the screen was lowered, which prevented the monkey from seeing or reaching the wells. The experimenter covered both wells. The screen was then lifted and the monkey was given one chance to reach out, displace the cover off one well, and take the reward if it had chosen correctly. The monkeys learned to perform the task almost perfectly. Next Jacobsen performed surgery on both monkeys, during which they received bilateral lesions to their PFC. After the lesions, the monkeys were presented

CASE STUDY

BOX
3.3

Dory's Story

In the 2003 Pixar film *Finding Nemo*, Dory is instrumental in helping Marlin find his lost son Nemo even though she suffers from what she calls *short-term memory loss*. Sometimes Dory will be having a conversation with Marlin when she suddenly forgets what they are talking about. Other times Dory begins a task that she doesn't complete because she forgets what she is supposed to do. Although Dory loses information in the very short term, her problem is more correctly called *working-memory loss* than *short-term memory loss*. As you

© 2003 Disney/Pixar

have learned in this chapter, working memory is the aspect of short-term memory that allows for the immediate completion of cognitive tasks. For example, working memory is involved in understanding speech and reading, doing calculations, and planning and completing unfamiliar tasks. All tasks that involve working memory require attention; one cannot comprehend a conversation, complete a calculation, or plan an action without focusing one's attention on that task. In every case, Dory forgets what it was she was just thinking about because she gets distracted ("Look! Krill!"); in other words, she forgets because her attention wanders elsewhere, not because the memory slips away. Dory's problem thus accurately reflects a real aspect of working memory: it can't operate without attention. In this chapter, we explore, among other things, the many ways that attention and memory in the short term are intertwined. By the end of this chapter, you will see that Dory's problem is indeed entirely plausible and isn't just a "fish tale."

> DORY
> Stop following me, okay?!
> MARLIN
> What are you talking about? You're showing me which way the boat went!
> DORY
> A boat? Hey, I've seen a boat. It passed by not too long ago. It went, um...
> This way! It went this way! Follow me!
> MARLIN
> Wait a minute. Wait a minute! What is going on? You already told me which way the boat was going!
> DORY
> I did? Oh no.

Source: Stanton, Andrew, Lee Unkrich, Graham Walters, John Lasseter, Bob Peterson, David Reynolds, Albert Brooks, et al. 2003. *Finding Nemo*. © Disney

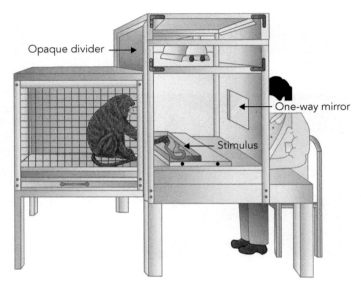

Opaque divider

One-way mirror

Stimulus

Figure 3.10   The Wisconsin General Testing Apparatus

The Wisconsin General Testing Apparatus (WGTA) is a structure used in experiments involving animals. The WGTA is comprised of a cage, a tray on wheels, and a screen that can be used to prevent the animal from reaching through the bars or seeing the tray during trial preparation.

Source: Nelson, E.E., Shelton, S.E., & Kalin, N.H. (2003). Individual differences in the responses of naïve rhesus monkeys to snakes. *Emotion, 3*(1), 3–11, p. 4

with the same delayed-response task in the WGTA; however, neither monkey could perform the task above results consistent with chance. However, the monkeys were able to retrieve the food if there was no delay between when the food was put in the well and when they were allowed to reach for it. Jacobsen (1936) concluded that poor performance in the delayed-response task was therefore not due to a problem with perception or movement and concluded that the PFC was responsible for what he termed *immediate memory*.

A few years later, however, Robert Malmo (1942) replicated Jacobsen's (1936) procedure with one added component: Malmo turned the lights off in the lab during half of the delayed-matching trials. On the trials when the room went dark during the delay, the monkeys were able to identify the correct well on about 85 per cent of trials, which should not have happened if the PFC was responsible for immediate memory. Malmo (1942) instead suggested that removing the PFC left the monkeys more susceptible to interference and thus more prone to errors on the delayed-matching task. From this point forward, researchers were in agreement that the PFC may mediate control of STM, but that STM is not localized in the PFC. Support for this argument came from Ghent, Mishkin, and Teuber (1962), who studied 24 individuals with PFC lesions and found no impairment in a digit-span task. In 1964, Brenda Milner conducted a series of experiments in patients with PFC damage. Milner (1964) used a delayed-recognition paradigm in which participants were shown a stimulus and then, following a 60-second delay, were shown another stimulus and were asked to indicate whether this second stimulus matched the first. Milner (1964) found that participants performed well on this task when she did not repeat the same stimulus across trials (e.g., if a circle was used on one trial it was not used on any other trial), but that the same participants had difficulty if the task used the same stimuli over and over (e.g., when digits were used and a participant saw the same digits at different points in the experiment). The results from Milner (1964) support the notion that STM is not localized in the PFC.

The Sensory-Recruitment Model

Short-term memory is conceptualized as a store; information is said to be *brought to* STM and held *in* STM. However, recent research suggests that the neuroscience underlying STM bears no resemblance to this analogy. STM does not appear to be a unitary mechanism localized in one place in the brain; in fact, the opposite appears to be true. John Serences and his colleagues used multi-voxel pattern analysis (MVPA) to see what parts of the brain were active when participants were holding different types of material in STM. The MVPA procedure involves monitoring overall brain activity across many presentations of the same stimulus and then running a pattern organizer than can detect regularities across presentations. When this method is used, the pattern categorizer is often able to accurately identify what stimulus a participant is viewing or thinking about based on the pattern of activity in the participant's brain. In their experiment, Serences, Ester, Vogel, and Awh (2009) first ran a learning phase during which participants were presented with red or green circles filled with lines of one of two different orientations. Participants were asked to attend to the colour of the stimulus on some trials and the line orientation on other trials while their brain activity was being recorded. The data from the learning trials was then run through a pattern-categorizer program that identified patterns of brain activity specifically associated with the participant attending to colour or line orientation. In the STM phase of the experiment, participants were presented with a stimulus from the learning phase that they had to hold in STM for 15 seconds, at which point they would be asked to report either the colour or line orientation of the stimulus. Sometime during the 15-second delay, participants were told whether they would have to report the colour or the line orientation of the stimulus. Serences et al. (2009) looked at brain activity right after the instruction was given and ran that activity through the pattern classifier. Serences et al. (2009) found that the pattern classifier correctly predicted that the person had been instructed to remember orientation or colour at rates significantly above chance. Thus, once given instructions about what feature to remember during the STM phase, participants' brain activity was similar to brain activity from the learning phase when they were attending to that dimension of the stimulus. These findings support the **sensory-recruitment model**, which asserts that STM is not localized to one brain region, but instead involves the activation of brain areas related to perceptual processing.

sensory-recruitment model

assumes that the brain areas that support STM for a stimulus are the same areas responsible for perceptual processing of that stimulus

STM for Phonological Information: The Phonological Loop

Paulesu, Frith, and Frackowiak (1993) used positron emission tomography (PET) scans to compare brain activity when participants were performing a variety of tasks. In experiment 1, the researchers presented participants with six English letters or six Korean letters one at a time on a computer monitor. At the end of the trial, participants were shown a probe item and were asked if it had been part of the preceding series. Paulesu et al. (1993) argued that because the participants only spoke English, they would only be able to use rehearsal and the phonological store on trials where English letters were presented. In a second experiment, participants were presented with a stream of letters and had to indicate whether each item rhymed with the letter B. In a second task, participants were shown a stream of Korean letters and had to indicate whether each letter shown matched a sample letter shown at the beginning of the experiment. Paulesu et al. (1993) argued that the rhyming task would engage the articulatory loop (as participants repeated the letter B) but not the phonological store, and that the Korean letter task would only engage the visual store. Paulesu et al. (1993) argued that regions that were active during the English letter task in experiment 1 but not during the rhyming task in experiment 2 allowed Paulesu et al. (1993) to isolate activity associated with the phonological store. Further, the researchers argued that regions that were active during the rhyming task in experiment 2 but not during the Korean letter shape–matching task in experiment 2 could isolate activity associated with the articulatory loop. Paulesu et al. (1993) found that Brodmann area 40 (BA 40) in the parietal lobe (see Figure 3.11) is linked to the phonological store, and that Broca's area in the frontal lobe (BA 44 and BA 45 in Figure 3.11) is linked to the articulatory loop. (Broca's area is also crucial for language production.) The results of Paulesu et al. (1993) were replicated by Smith, Jonides, and Koeppe (1996). Smith et al. (1996) used PET scans to examine brain activity during a delayed-recognition

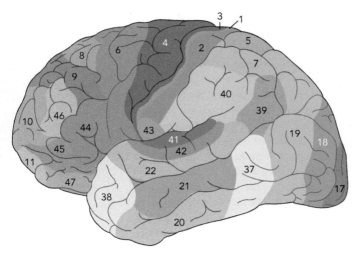

Figure 3.11   The Brodmann atlas of the brain

Brodmann area 40 in the parietal lobe is linked to the phonological store in STM while Brodmann areas 44 and 45 (Broca's area) in the frontal lobe are associated with the articulatory loop. Brodmann area 19 in the occipital lobe is associated with the visuospatial sketchpad.

Source: Eagleman, D. & Downer, J. (2016). *Brain and behavior*. New York: Oxford University Press. p. 65

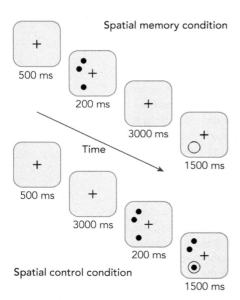

Figure 3.12   The spatial memory paradigm used in Smith, Vonides, and Koeppe (1996)

Source: Based on Smith, Jonides, & Koeppe, 1996, p. 12

task. Participants were shown four letters and then asked whether a probe was one of the four letters that was presented. On some trials, there was a delay between the presentation of the letters (during which participants needed to store the letter information), while on other trials there was no delay (and no need to store the letters). Smith et al. (1996) found that during the trials that required the phonological store and the articulatory loop, BA 40 and Broca's area were active. These areas were not active on trials where there was no delay. Taken together, the results of Paulesu et al. (1993) and Smith et al. (1996) strongly suggest that BA 40 is responsible for the phonological store, whereas Broca's area is responsible for the articulatory loop. This is reflected in the current multicomponent model, which distinguishes between the short-term store of verbal information and the process of rehearsing that information.

STM for Visuospatial Information: The Visuospatial Sketchpad

Smith et al. (1996) also studied the short-term visual store using PET scans. In the spatial memory condition, participants were presented with three dots on a computer screen for 200 ms and, following a delay of 3000 ms, an area of the screen would be highlighted for 1500 ms. Participants had to indicate whether the highlighted area had contained a dot during the stimulus presentation. On spatial control trials, participants were shown three dots for 200 ms and then a highlighted area appeared. Participants had to indicate whether a dot appeared within the highlighted area (see Figure 3.12). In order to complete the task, participants needed to keep spatial information in short-term memory in the spatial memory condition but not in the control condition. Smith et al. (1996) found that several areas in the right hemisphere were involved in the spatial memory task, including area 19 of the occipital cortex (see Figure 3.11), which has been found in previous experiments to be active in tasks where participants are asked to maintain visual images (e.g., Kosslyn et al., 1993), and area 40 of the parietal cortex, which is closely associated with spatial processing (Warrington & Rabin, 1970). It is well established that in normal visual processing, information about an object's location is processed separately from information about the characteristics of the object itself. Spatial information about an object, or the "where" stream, takes a dorsal path through the brain, whereas object characteristics, or the "what" stream, take a more ventral path. The findings from Smith et al. (1996) are consistent with this processing view; Smith et al. (1996) found activity in area 19 of the parietal lobe, which is part of the *where* pathway, and area 40 of the occipital lobe, which is part of the *what* pathway, to be active during their visuospatial STM task.

The Neuroscience of Working Memory

Short-term memory (STM) differs from working memory in that material in STM is held without changing, while material in working memory is held while it is being manipulated. This distinction between STM and working memory is reflected in the brain areas involved in tasks associated with each; while STM tends to involve brain areas specific to the type of information being maintained, the brain areas involved in working memory are more diverse and are often similar across different types of tasks. This is because working memory involves both attention and the integration of material across modalities.

Attentional Control: The Central Executive

Working memory involves manipulating material in STM. For example, look around the room you are currently in and choose any object. Focus your attention on the object and now imagine that the object is covered in blue fur. Now imagine the object is covered in green and yellow stripes. Now imagine it is bouncing up and down. You were able to imagine all these configurations of the object by manipulating an STM using working memory. First, you selected an object from the environment and then you performed controlled cognitive processes on that image, and both of these actions required your attention. **Attention** is a capacity-limited cognitive mechanism that is needed both to take in relevant information from the outside world (like the selection of an object in the room you are in) and to control cognitive operations (like imagining that object is now covered in blue fur). Simply holding information in memory does not require attention; for example, you can probably recall what colour of fur was mentioned in the previous sentence even though you were not actively thinking about that fur colour. Working memory is different in that it does require attention, and because it requires attention it involves different regions of the brain than STM. Attentional control is associated with the dorsolateral prefrontal cortex (PFC), the inferior parietal cortex, and the anterior cingulate (Banich et al., 2009; Bush, Luu, & Posner, 2000; Rothbart & Rueda, 2005; see Figure 3.13). These areas are collectively known as the **frontoparietal cognitive control network** (Duncan, 2010). Damage to any part of the frontoparietal cognitive control network leads to problems with attention. The anterior cingulate appears to be at the epicentre of the frontoparietal cognitive control network. The dorsal portion of the anterior cingulate is connected to the prefrontal cortex (PFC), parietal cortex, and motor cortex, and this area is most closely associated with controlling cognitive processes within working memory. For example, individuals with damage to the anterior cingulate have difficulty with the Stroop task, which involves naming the colour of ink a colour word is written in. The Stroop task is difficult when the ink colour and the word are incongruent (such as the word *red* written in blue ink). Performing the Stroop task involves cognitive control; the individual must suppress cognitive processes related to reading the word and instead focus attention only on the colour. The anterior cingulate cortex contains **spindle cells**, which are a recent evolutionary adaptation only found in great apes, cetaceans (like dolphins), and elephants. Spindle cells look different from typical neurons. Spindle cells are large and their soma (cell body) is cylindrical, like a spindle. Spindle cells typically have only one dendrite, whereas typical neurons have many. Spindle cells are only found in animals with large brains and it is

attention

a capacity-limited cognitive mechanism that is used for both stimuli selection and the control of cognitive tasks

frontoparietal cognitive control network

a collection of brain areas linked to attention and cognitive control that includes the dorsolateral prefrontal cortex (PFC), the inferior parietal cortex, and the anterior cingulate

spindle cells

large neurons found only in the anterior cingulate cortex and frontal lobes of a few large-brained mammals. These neurons likely evolved to transmit information quickly across long distances.

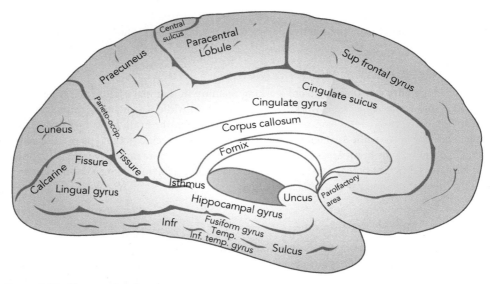

Figure 3.13 The anterior cingulate

This cortical area coloured orange is associated with attentional control. The anterior cingulate is part of the frontoparietal anterior control network that is linked to working memory.

thought that they facilitate fast communication across long distances within an animal's body. A meta-analysis of fMRI and PET scan studies that recorded brain activity while people performed a wide range of complex cognitive tasks, including those involving working memory, found that the anterior cingulate was the one area involved in all of the tasks (Duncan & Owen, 2000). The frontoparietal cognitive control network is reflected in the central executive of the current multicomponent model of working memory.

The Episodic Buffer

The episodic buffer, as it is currently conceptualized, is an integrated percept of all active short-term stores that can be accessed by the central executive but does not need the central executive to operate. Thus, the episodic buffer is supported by the same neurological mechanisms that support material in each short-term store, be it visual, auditory, or other sensory information. The role of the central executive seems to be voluntary; the central executive can interact with the episodic buffer, but its resources are not needed for representations to be within the buffer. Thus, the neurological substrates of attention (i.e., the anterior cingulate cortex) can interact with the episodic buffer but are not necessary for its existence. The concept of the episodic buffer is still in its infancy. Over time, more specific tests of the neuroscience of this area will likely provide a more definitive explanation as to what areas support it.

Summary

In the preceding discussion it was shown that STM is not localized to one brain region, but rather involves areas specific to be the material being retained. This supports the sensory-recruitment

Marijuana Smoking Really Does Mess with Short-Term Memory

No matter how you model short-term memory, short-term memory is impaired by frequent use of marijuana. Pope and Yurgelen-Todd (1996) had chronic pot smokers and non-users complete a series of short-term memory tasks while sober (they were isolated for 19 hours before the tasks were completed) and found that chronic users performed significantly worse on each and every task. The results from these experiments showed that the deleterious effect of marijuana on memory continues even after the subjective effects of the drug seem to have worn off. The question remained as to *why* marijuana has such a dramatic impact on memory. Ranganathan and D'Souza (2006) looked at the impact of marijuana on brain activity. One surprising finding from their research was that marijuana causes increased blood flow to memory-related areas, and the authors hypothesize that this increased blood flow may cause the development of irrelevant associations and confused mental activity. Unfortunately, these findings do not help clarify which model of short-term memory is best, as the multicomponent model and embedded-processes model of short-term memory both predict that random activation of ideas and a lack of control over attention (known effects of marijuana) will lead to impaired short-term memory performance.

Source: Ranganathan & D'Souza, 2006

model put forth by John Serences and his colleagues. Short-term memory for verbal material (the phonological store) is associated with activity in Brodmann area 40 (BA 40), while rehearsal of that material (the articulatory loop) involves Broca's area. Short-term memory for visual information activates area 19 of the occipital lobe, which maintains information about what the object looks like, and area 40 of the parietal lobe, which maintains the object's location. Working memory allows a person to manipulate material in STM. As with STM, the brain's areas associated with working memory depend in part on the type of stimuli being manipulated; visual areas are active for visual stimuli, speech areas are activated for verbal material, and so on. However, unlike STM, working memory involves the frontoparietal cognitive control network, which includes the dorsolateral prefrontal cortex (PFC), the inferior parietal cortex, and the anterior cingulate, which controls attention and performs complex cognitive processes on the material being manipulated. The anterior cingulate appears to be the epicentre of the components of the frontoparietal cognitive control network and is involved in both attentional control and cognitive processing. The episodic buffer may be connected to any of the neurological substrates associated with STM and will involve the frontoparietal cognitive control network any time that the episodic buffer is interacting with the central executive.

Working Memory and Emotional Regulation

There is a growing body of research demonstrating that emotion interacts with working memory; positive emotions are linked to better performance on a wide variety of tasks involving working memory including problem solving, categorization, word association, and decision making.

For example, a person experiencing positive emotions solves problems more quickly, categorizes words more quickly, makes faster word associations, and makes decisions more easily (Isen, 2008). In addition, many individuals with damage to the prefrontal cortex and surrounding area experience problems with both working memory and emotional control (Duncan, 2010). Researchers believe that working memory and emotional regulation both involve the frontoparietal cognitive control network. Positive emotions increase working-memory capacity because they release dopamine into the frontoparietal cognitive control network, which makes these brain areas operate more quickly and efficiently. Similarly, because both working memory and emotional regulation involve the frontoparietal cognitive control network, brain damage that affects one of these processes necessarily affects the other process as well, and people who excel at working-memory tasks tend to be better able to regulate emotional reactions. A number of research studies support this hypothesis.

Hawjin Yang and her colleagues (2013) compared participants' performance on STM and working-memory tasks in both positive and neutral emotional conditions. In order to induce positive emotions, half of the participants were given an unexpected bag of candy and told that their participation was very much appreciated prior to the experiment. The other half of the participants did not receive a gift. Next, all participants completed a word-span task where they were given a list of to-be-remembered words and asked to recall the list in serial order. This task assessed STM but not working memory, because while participants had to retain information, they did not have to manipulate it. Next, participants completed an operation-span test that involved solving a simple math problem while maintaining a list of unrelated words that would need to be recalled later. For example, participants would be shown "Is 8 ÷ 4 + 2 = 6? Yes/No PLANT" and would be required to answer the Yes/No question and retain the word PLANT until the end of the set of trials, when there would be a recall test for all the word items for that set of trials. There were between three and seven trials between each recall test. The operation-span task was a measure of working-memory because participants had to manipulate information in short-term memory. Yang, Yang, and Isen (2013) found a significant effect of emotion on performance on the working-memory task but not the STM task, which suggests that emotions impact the same brain regions as working memory, but not the same brain regions involved in STM.

Additional evidence for the connection between working memory and emotional regulation comes from neuroimaging studies. Susanne Schweizer and her colleagues (2013) collaborated with researchers at the University of Western Ontario to study the impact of working-memory training on both activity within the brain and emotion-related behaviour. The researchers examined fMRI data and behavioural data from participants before and after 20 days of **emotional working memory (eWM) training**. In the first phase of the experiment, all participants completed an eWM task and an emotional regulation (ER) task while their brain activity was recorded in an fMRI. The eWM task used the ***n*-back procedure** and included stimuli that varied in their emotional content; some of the visual stimuli evoked emotions (such as an angry face) and some of the words evoked emotional response (such as *evil*). The ER task involved viewing a series of 30-second films with different instructions for each film type. In the neutral condition, participants were shown neutral film footage (such as a weather report) and were instructed to simply pay attention. In the attend condition, participants were shown emotionally aversive films (such as scenes from wars) and were instructed to attend to the film but not try to change their emotional response to the film. In the regulate condition, participants were again shown aversive films but were instructed to try to regulate their emotional distress as much as possible. Participants rated their level of emotional distress after watching each film using a scale from 1 (extremely positive) to 10 (extremely negative).

emotional working memory (eWM) training

an *n*-back working-memory task that includes stimuli designed to evoke emotions, such as angry faces or emotional words

***n*-back procedure (*n*-back task)**

an experimental paradigm in which the participant must indicate whether the stimulus on the current trial matches the stimulus presented *n* trials before

Half of the participants (eWM group) practised the eWM task each day for 20 days, while the other half (placebo group) completed a shape-matching task. At the end of the 20 days, the participants returned to the lab and again completed the eWM task and ER task while in the fMRI. Schweizer et al. (2013) found that increasing the difficulty in the eWM task reliably increased activation in the frontoparietal cognitive control network and decreased activation in areas involved with emotional processing, such as the amygdala. Further, the researchers found that participants attempting to regulate their emotions in the ER task activated the same brain regions that were most active during the eWM task, the frontoparietal cognitive control network. These findings suggest that the same brain areas that control working memory also assist in emotional regulation. When the researchers examined fMRI data following 20 days of training, they found significant differences between the eWM and placebo groups. First, and not surprisingly, participants in the eWM training group were better able to manage eWM tasks with a greater number of intervening trials, and while doing the eWM task, there was more activation in the frontoparietal cognitive control network. In addition, the participants in the eWM group showed a significant improvement in their ability to perform the ER task and reported less distress during trials where they were asked to regulate their emotions. This reduction in reported distress coincided with increased activation in the same brain regions associated with the eWM task during the regulate trials. In sum, Schweizer et al. (2013) demonstrated both that the same brain regions are involved in working memory and emotional regulation tasks, and that eWM training improves performance in these regions and makes individuals better able to control their emotional responses to distressing stimuli.

RELEVANT RESEARCH

BOX 3.5

Taking Working-Memory Training from the Laboratory into Schools

Working memory plays a vital role in academic learning and working-memory skills are associated with improved academic performance (Gathercole, Pickering, Knight, & Stegmann, 2004). Many classroom activities require working memory and attentional control, including following instructions, mental computations, and seeing tasks through to their completion. Gathercole and Alloway (2008) showed that a substantial majority of children with poor working memory fail to meet expected standards for reading and math. Further, working-memory deficits are six times more common among children identified as having special education needs, suggesting that poor working memory places a child at high risk for poor academic achievement (Holmes & Gathercole, 2014). Joni Holmes and Susan Gathercole conducted an experiment to see if "brain-training" activities could be used to improve working-memory skills in children who were struggling in school. The researchers recruited 100 nine- and ten-year-old children with low academic performance for their study and assessed their reading and math skills. Half the children completed 20 sessions of Cogmed Working Memory Training (CWMT) over the course of the school year; the other half did not. During each CWMT session, children practised eight different memory tasks. The difficulty of the task was adjusted on each trial to ensure the task was neither too easy nor too difficult. At the end of the school year, math and reading were assessed again. Holmes and Gathercole (2014) found that the low-achieving children who completed the CWMT sessions made significantly greater gains in reading and math than the control group. The authors argue that the results of their study suggest that brain-training activities may be an effective educational intervention for low-achieving students.

CASE STUDY

Follow-Up to Dory's Story: Fact or "Fish Tale"?

Earlier in this chapter, Dory from Disney Pixar's *Finding Nemo* was used to emphasize the importance of attention in short-term memory, but could someone like Dory really exist? Although the creators of *Finding Nemo* may have added short-term-memory loss to Dory's character simply to make her character more interesting, Dory's character actually mirrors the characteristics of many people who develop short-term memory loss following brain injury, including H.M. H.M., who lost the ability to form new memories following

© 2003 Disney/Pixar

surgery to treat his epilepsy, had short-term memory that operated much like Dory's. Postle (2016) reports that, while being driven from his home in Hartford, Connecticut, to MIT by two post-graduate students, H.M. engaged in a game where each person selected a colour and accrued points each time a car of that colour passed in the opposite direction. Each player counted out loud and during gaps between passing cars the group engaged in conversation about the game. H.M. won the game by scoring 20 points first. There was then a lull in the conversation as the trio drove through the countryside. A few minutes later one of the students asked H.M. "What are you thinking about?" and H.M. replied that his count of cars was now up to 36. The topic of the conversation then changed. The students asked H.M., "Do you know today's date?" and "Do you know where we are going today?" H.M. could not answer the questions and changed the topic to something he could speak about, his childhood memories. After H.M. told a story about a train ride he took as a child (a story that he had already told several times during that trip), one of the students asked, "Do you remember what game we were playing a few minutes ago?" (Postle, 2016). H.M. did not remember the game, nor could he identify which colour of car he had been assigned or who had won the game. H.M. behaved in much the same way Dory does; as soon as his continuous thought about the car-counting game was interrupted and his attention diverted, he forgot about the game. Dory's story is no fish tale after all!

CHAPTER REVIEW

- In 1957, researchers William Scoville and Brenda Milner suggested that the case of H.M. implied that long-term memory involved the medial temporal lobes and the hippocampus while short-term memory relied on other parts of the brain.

- In 1958, Donald Broadbent published a model identifying primary memory, which was short in duration, and secondary memory, which was a long-term memory store.
- The term *short-term memory* refers to a storage mechanism that can maintain, but not change, information for short periods of time. Short-term memory is also sometimes referred to as primary memory.
- The term *working memory* refers to a short-term memory store that can also be used to manipulate information.
- Broadbent (1958) argued that primary memory was comprised of material in the S-system, which is pre-categorical and fades quickly, and material in the P-system, which is conscious thought. Broadbent further argued that material in the P-system must be rehearsed to be maintained.
- In 1968, Atkinson and Shiffrin used Sperling's notion of iconic memory and Broadbent's notion of a separate short-term and long-term memory system to develop what would become known as the modal model of memory, which included a sensory store, a short-term store, and a long-term store.
- The main support for the modal model were the primacy and recency effects frequently found in free-recall experiments. The short-term store accounted for the recency effect and the long-term store accounted for the primacy effect.
- The results from Koppenaal and Glanzer (1990), Neath (1993), and Tan and Ward (2000) all suggest that the serial-position curve does not provide evidence for the modal model, and further that the modal model cannot explain the serial-position curve.
- In 1974, Baddeley and Hitch published the multicomponent model of working memory. This model was the first to account for working memory, or the aspect of short-term memory that is responsible for the completion of cognitive tasks.
- The first version of the multicomponent model was comprised of the phonological loop, which handled acoustic information; the visuospatial sketchpad, which handled visual information; and the central executive, which supervised the flow of information in and out of the phonological loop and visuospatial sketchpad.
- The multicomponent model is consistent with the phonological-similarity effect, the articulatory-suppression effect, the word-length effect, and the irrelevant-speech effect.
- The episodic buffer was added to the multicomponent model in Baddeley (2000). The episodic buffer was argued to be a multidimensional storage system that could hold four chunks of information. The episodic buffer could also interact directly with long-term memory.
- In 2012, the multicomponent model was adjusted again to allow both the phonological loop and the visuospatial sketchpad to have direct access to long-term memory. In addition, the new model allowed for information to enter the episodic buffer without involving the central executive.
- Cowan's embedded-processes model of short-term memory suggests that short-term memory is simply the currently active portion of long-term memory. Cowan's model is ostensibly similar to Baddeley (2012).
- In the early twentieth century, Jacobsen (1932) proposed that short-term memory was located in the prefrontal cortex (PFC). However, a series of experiments showed that animals with PFC damage could still hold material in STM and that the PFC was likely related to attentional control, not memory.
- Recent neuroimaging research has shown that holding a stimulus in STM involves the same brain areas originally involved in processing that stimulus. This is known as the sensory-recruitment model. Brain areas associated with vocabulary and speech are associated with verbal STM. Brain areas associated with processing visual information are associated with visual STM.

- The frontoparietal cognitive control network controls functions associated with the central executive and consists of the dorsolateral prefrontal cortex (PFC), the inferior parietal cortex, and the anterior cingulate. The anterior cingulate cortex is intrinsically involved in all working-memory tasks.
- Positive emotions are associated with better performance on working-memory tasks. This is because the brain areas that control working memory are directly linked to brain areas associated with emotional experience. The frontoparietal cognitive control network is involved in both working-memory tasks and tasks that require emotional regulation.
- Tasks that improve working memory can be used to help improve emotional regulation.

MEMORY ACTIVITY

Generate an Acronym

Acronyms (such as Roy G. Biv for the colours of the rainbow) can help students better remember lists of items (Lakin, Giesler, Morris, & Vosmik, 2007). In this activity, you will practise developing your own acronym to help you remember the brain regions that comprise the frontoparietal cognitive control network (Duncan, 2010) discussed earlier in this chapter.

Here are the brain areas that comprise the frontoparietal cognitive control network:
>   dorsolateral prefrontal cortex
>   inferior parietal cortex
>   anterior cingulate

Create a word using the letters D, I and A (in any order) to help you recall the components of the frontoparietal control network later.

Questions

1. Differentiate between short-term memory and working memory.
2. Explain how the case of H.M. influenced early memory models.
3. Describe one task that would utilize short-term memory and one task that would utilize working memory.
4. Identify the components of the modal model of memory and describe the function of each component.
5. Explain how primacy and recency effects support the modal model.
6. Describe two findings from the literature that cannot be explained by the modal model.
7. Describe Baddeley and Hitch's (1974) multicomponent model of working memory, including each of the three components and how they interact.
8. Identify four well-established effects in the literature that support Baddeley and Hitch's (1974) notion of the phonological loop.
9. Identify at least two findings from the experimental literature that cannot be explained by Baddeley and Hitch's (1974) model of working memory.

10. Compare and contrast Baddeley and Hitch's (1974) multicomponent model of working memory and the multicomponent model of working memory described in Baddeley (2000).
11. Explain why research related to attention and perceptual binding led Baddeley (2012) to revise the multicomponent model of working memory.
12. Summarize research relating the phonological loop to language learning. Explain how this research has influenced the multicomponent model of working memory.
13. Explain why researchers initially thought that STM was controlled by the prefrontal cortex (PFC).
14. Explain the role of the PFC in STM tasks according to Malmo (1942) and Milner (1964).
15. Describe the sensory-recruitment hypothesis. Describe one experiment that supports this hypothesis.
16. Describe the method and results of a neuroimaging study that attempted to localize the phonological store and articulatory loop.
17. Describe the method and results of a neuroimaging study that attempted to localize visuospatial STM.
18. Identify the brain region most closely associated with attention.
19. Explain how the sensory-recruitment model can be used to explain the neuroscience of the episodic buffer.
20. Describe the *n*-back working-memory procedure and the emotional working-memory paradigm.
21. What is the link between working memory and emotional regulation? What are some ways that working memory can be used to improve emotional regulation?

Key Figures

4   Long-Term Memory

LEARNING OBJECTIVES

Having read this chapter, you will be able to:

- Explain the impact of the case of H.M. on the understanding of the neuro-science of memory.
- Recite Hebb's postulate and explain how Hebb's postulate was proven to be true.
- Describe the experiment that first demonstrated long-term potentiation.
- Explain how the types of receptors found on neurons in the hippocampus facilitate the learning of associations.
- Provide evidence that NMDA receptors are necessary for LTP.
- Explain how our understanding of the role of the hippocampus in memory has changed as a result of research with ibotenic acid.
- Discuss evidence that the hippocampus is involved in the development of cognitive maps.
- Describe the stability–plasticity dilemma.
- Describe the two-stage model of memory and explain how brain activity during SWS may serve to transfer hippocampal memories to the neocortex.
- Identify factors that may lead memories to be selected for consolidation.
- Describe an experiment that showed that SWS is important for the consolida-tion of memory for actions.
- Explain how the multiple-trace model differs from the two-stage model of memory.
- Compare and contrast consolidation and reconsolidation.
- Describe what multi-voxel pattern analysis (MVPA) indicates about brain activity during encoding and retrieval.

THE CASE OF H.M. IN MORE DETAIL

Henry Molaison (1926–2008; first introduced in Chapter 1), known as H.M. until his death in 2008, experienced his first grand mal seizure in the back of his parents' car on his fifteenth birthday in 1941. Over the next few years his seizures became more frequent and severe. Henry had to drop out of high school and was unable to work; he rarely left his parents' house in Hartford, Connecticut. When H.M. was in his twenties, he and his parents began to consult with a local surgeon named William Scoville. Scoville attempted to treat H.M. with medications but, when the medications didn't work, he proposed a new experimental surgery. Scoville was unable to identify exactly where H.M.'s seizures originated so he proposed that H.M.'s entire hippocampus be removed, as the hippocampus was known to be the epileptogenic (or seizure-causing) region in the brain. Scoville also removed most of the medial temporal lobe (MTL) surrounding the hippocampus. H.M. had the surgery in 1953 when he was 27 years old. While the surgery cured H.M.'s epilepsy, it left him with **anterograde amnesia**, the inability to form any new conscious memories, for the remainder of his life.

Shortly after H.M.'s surgery, Scoville came across a report from Brenda Milner and Wilder Penfield detailing a case of memory impairment following the unilateral removal of the temporal lobe in a patient. Milner was working at McGill University with Penfield and, soon after being contacted by Scoville, began to travel from Montreal to Hartford on a regular basis to study H.M. Milner's research on H.M. established several facts concerning the relationship between the MTL and long-term memory. These can be summarized as follows:

- The MTL and hippocampus are primarily connected to memory. Neither H.M.'s IQ nor his ability to use language was affected by his surgery.
- Memories formed more than a few years before MTL damage are not affected.

Henry Molaison (1926–2008) had his hippocampus and parts of his temporal lobe removed to treat his epilepsy. As a result, H.M. lost the ability to form most new memories and became among the most famous case studies in the history of psychology.

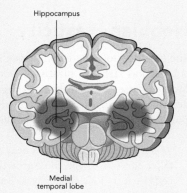

Figure 4.1 Hippocampus and MTL

The medial temporal lobe (MTL) surrounds the hippocampal region. Most of Henry Molaison's MTL was surgically removed.

Source: Based on Eagleman, D. & Downer, J. (2016). *Brain and behavior.* New York: Oxford University Press. p. 283; and Rudy, J. (2014). *Neurobiology of learning and memory.* Sinhauer. p. 293

anterograde amnesia
the loss of the ability to form new memories

- The MTL is involved in memories that can be consciously recalled (such as facts or events) but not memories for actions or other memories that cannot be consciously recalled.
- The MTL is not necessary for short-term memory.

The case of H.M. provided evidence that different parts of the brain were involved in different types of memory processes. But knowing that the MTL and the hippocampus are somehow intrinsic to long-term memory is only scratching the surface at explaining the neuroscience of long-term memory. Much more important than *where* memories are stored is *how* they are stored. The remainder of this chapter will explore neuroscientific theories explaining the mechanisms that underlie the formation and maintenance of long-term memory (LTM).

Long-Term Memory

A **long-term memory** is enduring, and in theory can last a lifetime. Psychologists recognize many different types of long-term memory including explicit and implicit long-term memory (Chapter 5), episodic and autobiographical long-term memory (Chapter 6), and fact-based generic long-term memory (also sometimes called semantic memory) (Chapter 7). This chapter discusses neuroscience topics that relate to all forms of long-term memory.

Hebbian Plasticity

The first step to understanding the neuroscience of long-term memory is to understand what is known as **Hebbian plasticity**. Donald Hebb (1904–85) was working at McGill University in Montreal when he published *The Organization of Behavior* in 1949. It was in this book that Hebb described the single most influential idea in the history of memory research known as **Hebb's postulate**, which states the following:

> When an Axon of cell A is near enough to excite a cell B and repeatedly or persistently takes part in firing it, some growth process or metabolic change takes place in one or both cells such that A's efficiency, as one of the cells firing B, is increased. (Hebb, 1949, p. 62)

Figure 4.2 provides a visual aid for understanding what Hebb meant. Note that, at the far right in Figure 4.2, the axon from the presynaptic neuron A touches the dendrites of the postsynaptic neuron B. Hebb's postulate suggests that when neurons arranged in this way both fire at the same time repeatedly, eventually activation of neuron A will cause the activation of neuron B. It is important to note that while neuron A can come to cause neuron B to fire, the reverse is not true; it is always the **presynaptic neuron** that comes to cause the **postsynaptic neuron** to fire. Hebb's postulate explained how memories could be formed by suggesting that the synapses, or connections, between neurons could change with experience; this flexibility came to be known as Hebbian plasticity.

long-term memory

all the memories a person has stored in memory

Hebbian plasticity

the notion that synapses are created by metabolic changes resulting from the simultaneous firing of neurons

Hebb's postulate

the notion that when cell A persistently causes the firing of cell B, there is a metabolic change such that cell A will more easily cause cell B to fire in the future

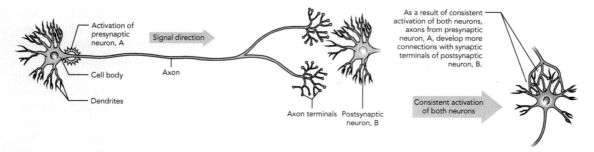

Figure 4.2   Hebb's postulate

Hebb's postulate suggests that if two neurons are close together such that the axon of the presynaptic neuron is close to the dendrites of the postsynaptic neuron, repeated simultaneous firing of both neurons will result in activation of the presynaptic neuron more frequently activating the postsynaptic neuron.

Sources: Adapted from Breedlove, M. (2105). *Principles of psychology.* New York: Oxford University Press. p. 65; and Eagleman & Downar. (2016). *Brain and behavior.* New York: Oxford University Press. p. 293

Hebb's postulate explains classical conditioning well. In classical conditioning, a neutral stimulus (such as a bell) is paired repeatedly with a stimulus (such as food) that elicits an involuntary response (such as involuntary salivation). Eventually the bell comes to elicit salivation when presented alone. As shown in Figure 4.3, Hebbian plasticity suggests that the learned association between the sound of the bell and salivation is the result of neurons in the auditory system firing at the same time as neurons in the digestive system, and axons from the auditory system being located near receptors for the digestive system.

When Hebb's postulate was first introduced in 1949, Hebb had no empirical evidence to support the idea. It was not until the 1970s that researchers in Sweden provided a biological explanation as to why the simultaneous firing of neurons increases the probability that these neurons will fire simultaneously in the future, a phenomenon known as *long-term potentiation.*

The Neuroscience of Long-Term Potentiation

The hippocampus is a complex structure that receives inputs from many parts of the brain, including the ventral and dorsal visual streams and the entorhinal complex (EC) (see Figure 4.4). The hippocampus receives highly processed information, processes it through its circuitry, and then projects that information back to the EC and many regions in the neocortex. Information passing through the hippocampus follows a very predictable path: The inputs from the EC go directly to an area known as the dentate gyrus (DG), then through the CA fields, then back out to the neocortex. The components of the hippocampus can be seen in Figure 4.4. In the 1960s, Norwegian electrophysiologist Per Andersen argued that because the circuitry of the hippocampus is so simple, it is possible to measure the strength of a connection between neurons in the EC and the DG (known as the **perforant path**) by measuring electrical activity in the granule cell-body layer of the DG. Andersen's graduate student Terje Lømo collaborated with

presynaptic neuron

a neuron that sends a signal across a synapse

postsynaptic neuron

a neuron that receives a signal across a synapse

perforant path

the connection between the entorhinal complex and the dentate gyrus in the hippocampus

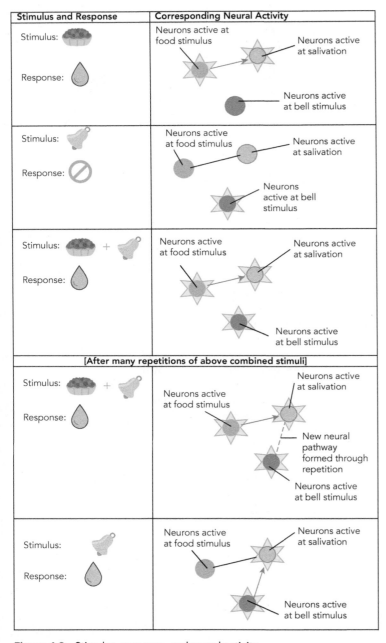

Stimulus and Response	Corresponding Neural Activity
Stimulus: Response:	Neurons active at food stimulus / Neurons active at salivation / Neurons active at bell stimulus
Stimulus: Response:	Neurons active at food stimulus / Neurons active at salivation / Neurons active at bell stimulus
Stimulus: + Response:	Neurons active at food stimulus / Neurons active at salivation / Neurons active at bell stimulus
[After many repetitions of above combined stimuli]	
Stimulus: + Response:	Neurons active at food stimulus / Neurons active at salivation / New neural pathway formed through repetition / Neurons active at bell stimulus
Stimulus: Response:	Neurons active at food stimulus / Neurons active at salivation / Neurons active at bell stimulus

Figure 4.3 Stimulus, response, and neural activity

This figure illustrates how Hebb's postulate predicts classically conditioned responses. Initially, there is no association between the neuron associated with the bell and the neuron associated with salivation; however, after these neurons fire at the same time repeatedly during conditioning, the neuron associated with the bell eventually comes to activate the neuron associated with salivation and a conditioned response occurs.

a British neuropsychologist Timothy Bliss and discovered long-term potentiation, confirming that Hebb's postulate was true.

In their 1973 experiment, Bliss and Lømo first measured the baseline strength of the perforant path in an anaesthetized rabbit by delivering single pulses of electricity and measuring the electrical activity in the cell-body layer of the DG. Next Bliss and Lømo (1973) delivered high-frequency electrical pulses in 15-second bursts (called **tetani**) to the perforant path every 30 minutes for three hours and measured the positive shift in electrical potential (known as **population spikes**) in the granule cell body of the DG in five-minute intervals. Because population spikes only occur after a neuron fires, population spikes are a good measure of recent neural activity. Bliss and Lømo found that at baseline, before the presentation of the tetani, the population spikes were very small, indicating that very few DG neurons were firing. However, after the presentation of the second tetanus, the population spikes increased significantly and continued to increase over time. The researchers presented the last high-frequency burst three hours after the first, but continued to see increases in population spikes for another three hours. Because the population spikes continued to appear long after the last electrical impulse was presented, the phenomenon was dubbed **long-term potentiation** (see Figure 4.5). Bliss and Lømo (1973) argued that the population spikes that appeared after the presentation of the last tetanus confirmed Hebb's postulate and reflected the concept of Hebbian plasticity.

Long-term potentiation is at the core of the Hebbian plasticity that allows for the formation of memories. After LTP was confirmed by Bliss and Lømo (1973), researchers went on to explore the molecular basis of LTP as it relates to memory.

Hippocampal Receptors and Their Role in LTP

Recall that Hebb's postulate states that "[w]hen an Axon of cell A is near enough to excite a cell B and repeatedly or persistently takes part in firing it, some growth process or metabolic change takes place in one or both cells such that A's efficiency, as one of the cells firing B, is increased" (Hebb, 1949, p. 62). When Bliss and Lømo (1973) found evidence for LTP, this confirmed Hebb's postulate was true, but the observation of LTP alone didn't explain the metabolic functions that lead to the strengthened associations between neurons. Those discoveries were made when a series of researchers studied in detail the characteristics of neurons located in the hippocampus (Rao & Finkbeiner, 2007).

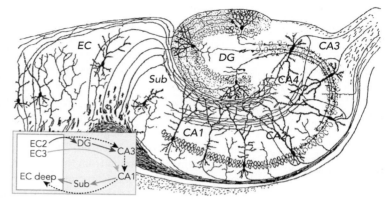

Figure 4.4 The hippocampus

There are four structures in the hippocampal area: the entorhinal cortex (EC), the dentate gyrus (DG), the subiculum, and the hippocampus. The hippocampus proper consists of the four *cornu ammonis* (CA) regions of CA1, CA2, CA3, and CA4. The hippocampus formation consists of the hippocampus, the dentate gyrus, and the subiculum.
Source: Based on Eagleman & Downer, 2016, p. 283

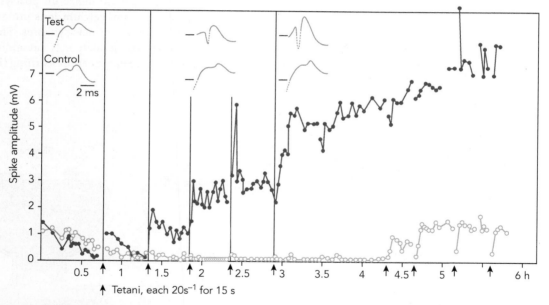

Figure 4.5 The results of Bliss and Lømo (1973)

These results show long-term potentiation (LTP) in the dentate gyrus (DG) of the hippocampus. In this study, the researchers presented a 15-second burst of electricity to the perforant path of an anaesthetized rabbit every 30 minutes for three hours and measured the population spikes in the granule cell body of the DG every five minutes. Solid circles show population spikes in the DG of the hemisphere receiving the tetani; open circles show population spikes in the hemisphere that did not receive the tetani. An increase in population spikes over time and an increase in population spikes even after the last tetani was presented show a long-term increase in DG cells as the result of stimulation of EC cells. This long-term activation is called long-term potentiation (LTP).
Source: Lømo, 2003, p. 610

One important feature of hippocampal neurons is that they contain two types of glutamate receptors; AMPA receptors and NMDA receptors. Glutamate is the most prevalent neurotransmitter in the brain and thus hippocampal neurons are poised to respond to a wide variety of neuronal activity. When glutamate comes in contact with a dendrite of a hippocampal neuron, the glutamate binds with both the NMDA and AMPA receptors (see Figure 4.6.a). The binding of the glutamate to the NMDA receptor initially does nothing because the receptor's calcium channel is blocked by a magnesium ion. However the binding of glutamate to the AMPA receptor opens a sodium channel allowing sodium ions to enter the neuron. The positively charged sodium ions that enter through the AMPA receptor sodium channel cause a moderate depolarization of the hippocampal neuron. This moderate depolarization of the hippocampal neuron dislodges the magnesium ion from the NMDA receptor and opens the NMDA calcium channel, allowing large numbers of calcium ions to enter (see Figure 4.6.b). This influx of calcium causes the hippocampal neuron to create additional silent receptors along the postsynaptic membrane. This strengthens, or potentiates, the synapse because now the neuron can respond more rapidly to glutamate (see Figure 4.6.c).

Activated NMDA receptors influence LTP through short- and long-term mechanisms. In the short term, the influx of calcium ions into an NMDA receptor results in more AMPA glutamate receptors becoming active in the postsynaptic area. The increase in the number of AMPA receptors in the postsynaptic area increases the probability that glutamate will bind with a postsynaptic neuron, meaning that each action potential initiated from a neuron with a high density of NMDA receptors will have a stronger influence on postsynaptic neurons; the synapse has been potentiated. In the longer term, calcium ions initiate the synthesis of new proteins that are needed for the development of new synapses. This research showed that hippocampal NMDA and AMPA receptors facilitate LTP, but additional research was needed to demonstrate that these receptors were *necessary* for learning (Rao & Finkbeiner, 2007).

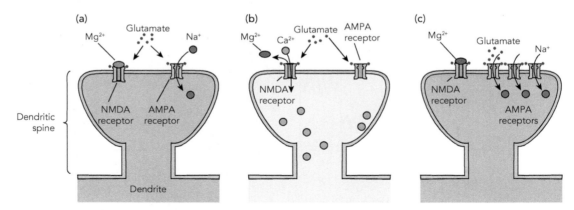

Figure 4.6   NMDA and AMPA receptors

Figure 4.6 shows how NMDA and AMPA receptors contribute to long-term potentiation. First, as shown in (a), glutamate molecules bind to AMPA and NMDA receptor sites. AMPA receptors then let in some positively charged sodium ions, depolarizing the area. Next, as shown in (b), the depolarization of the neuron dislodges the magnesium ions blocking the NMDA receptors, allowing an influx of positively charged calcium ions. Finally, the influx of calcium ions triggers the neuron to develop more AMPA receptor sites, making the neuron respond more rapidly to glutamate.

Evidence That NMDA Receptors Are Necessary for Learning

Richard Morris investigated the role of NMDA receptors in spatial learning in rats (whose hippo-campal receptors are similar to those of humans). For his study Morris used the Morris Water Maze, which is a 2-metre-wide pool filled with cold water made opaque with milk. When placed in the pool, rats (who dislike water) will instinctively swim around the pool looking for a way out. Hidden under the surface of the pool is a platform that allows the rats to get out of the water. Because the water is opaque, the first time a rat enters the pool the rat will swim continuously until it bumps into the platform by accident. However, on subsequent trials, a rat can attempt to use spatial memory for the platform to get out of the water more quickly. To test whether NMDA receptors were necessary for the formation of long-term spatial memory in rats, Morris and his colleagues administered a substance called AP5 to some of the rats in the study. AP5 stops NMDA receptors from working without affecting other synaptic functioning and thus, if NMDA is nec-essary for spatial learning, rats administered this substance will not learn the location of the platform. Morris, Anderson, Lynch, and Baudry (1986) administered AP5 to a group of rats who completed 15 trials in the Morris Water Maze across four days; another group did not receive AP5. On the critical trial, the platform is removed and the rat must swim for 60 seconds before being removed from the pool by the experimenter. Morris et al. (1986) measured the amount of time each rat spent in each of the four quadrants of the pool during the critical trial. Morris et al. (1986) found that rats who had not received AP5 spent most of their time in the quadrant where the platform had been located. However, rats who had received the AP5 swam in circles, showing no preference for the area of the pool where the platform had been and spending an equal amount of time in each quadrant, suggesting they had no memory for where the platform

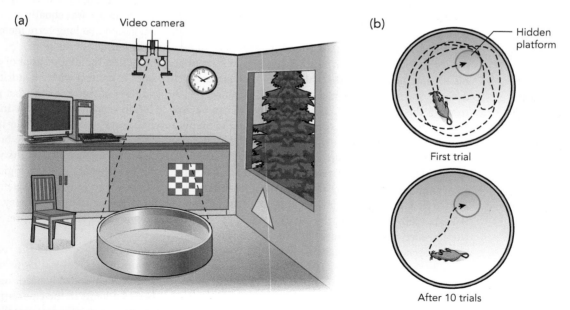

Figure 4.7 Example set-up and results of a Morris Water Maze

Source: Based on Rudy, J. (2014). Neurobiology of learning and memory. Sinauer. p. 165

was located. The results of Morris et al. (1986) demonstrate that NMDA receptor functioning is critical for spatial memory. Countless other studies have confirmed that NMDA receptors are essential for learning and memory of all kinds.

Revisiting the Role of the Hippocampus in Long-Term Memory

When H.M. showed profound anterograde amnesia following surgery that removed his hippocampus, researchers quickly concluded that the main role of the hippocampus was to form long-term memories. However, the hippocampus was not the only part of the brain damaged by H.M.'s surgery; the hippocampus is buried deep in the brain and tissue surrounding the hippocampus was also damaged. Therefore, it was not possible to say with certainty that the damage to the hippocampus caused the profound long-term memory deficit observed in H.M.

To better understand the role of the hippocampus in LTM, Larry Squire conducted a series of experiments in which the hippocampus was lesioned in animals. Again, because the hippocampus lies deep in the brain, other areas were damaged when Squire created the lesions; however, the areas that were damaged varied among animals. In some animals the hippocampus, parahippocampal gyrus (PHG), and caudal perirhinal cortex (PRC) were lesioned (the H+ group); in other cases, the hippocampus, PHG, PRC, and EC were lesioned (the H++ group). Squire used the delayed-nonmatch-to-sample (DNMS) task, in which an animal was rewarded if it chose a stimulus that was different from the stimulus in the previous trial, to compare the memory of animals with lesions in different areas of the brain. The delay in the task ranged from 15 seconds to 10 minutes. Squire (1992) reports that memory deficits tended to be greater in the H++ group, particularly when the delay was short; as the delay increased, performance was equally poor for both groups of animals. Squire (1992) proposed a model that suggested that long-term memory depended on the PHG, PRC, EC, and hippocampus, rather than the hippocampus alone.

ibotenic acid

a substance that destroys the neuron attached to dendrites it comes in contact with without affecting axons that pass through the injection site

In the 2000s, Elisabeth Murray and her colleagues began to lesion the hippocampi of animals using injections of **ibotenic acid**. When ibotenic acid comes in contact with a dendrite, it destroys the neuron attached to the dendrite; however, the acid does not affect axons that pass through the injection site. Thus, ibotenic acid can be used to lesion very specific regions in the brain. Recall that previous attempts to lesion the hippocampus always resulted in the destruction of additional regions simply because the hippocampus is located deep within the brain. When Murray used ibotenic acid to selectively lesion just the hippocampus, her results were surprising: She found that animals with these lesions performed the same as neurologically intact animals on DNMS tests as well as other tests of long-term memory. Murray thus demonstrated that the hippocampus per se is not necessary for long-term memory. Murray, Bussey, and Saksida (2007) argue that the PRC, not the hippocampus, stores complex stimulus representations needed to perform tasks like the DNMS task.

cognitive maps

an animal's internal representation of the spatial relationship among objects in the environment

Researchers have changed their view of the role of the hippocampus because of the results from ibotenic acid studies; many no longer believe that the hippocampus is critical for forming long-term memories. Researchers such as Howard Eichenbaum and Neal Cohen instead suggest that the role of the hippocampus is to learn the relationship between items in the environment and create **cognitive maps** (Eichenbaum & Cohen, 2004). A cognitive map is an animal's internal representation of the spatial relationship among objects in the environment. Animals performing the DNMS don't need to understand complex representations to perform the task and thus a hippocampal lesion does not affect performance. Eleanor Maguire found that patients with bilateral hippocampal damage had more trouble imagining novel spatial scenes from instructions such as "Imagine you are sitting on a park bench listening to birds sing." Patients with hippocampal damage created far less detailed scenes than controls, and the imagined scenes lacked what Maguire called "spatial coherence," or continuity among different elements being imagined. Maguire's hypothesis is consistent with Eichenbaum and Cohen's (2004) conception that the hippocampus plays a role in developing cognitive maps. Maguire's hypothesis is also consistent with the neuroscientific data that suggests that some memories can be formed even when the hippocampus is damaged. But perhaps the best evidence that the hippocampus is involved in spatial processing comes from a study by Maguire, Woollett, and Spiers (2006) that compared the hippocampi of taxi drivers in London, England, to bus drivers in the same city.

Eleanor Maguire noted several research studies that showed that the brain of some species of food-caching birds (such as chickadees) change with the seasons; at times when they need spatial memory the most, their hippocampus is largest. Maguire wondered if the hippocampi volume of humans might also vary based on spatial memory demands. To test this, Maguire decided to study taxi drivers in London, England, who have a job that demands dealing with spatial information full time. Before becoming a taxi driver in London, applicants must complete a course called The Knowledge. To pass the course, applicants must memorize 320 standard routes through central London as well as points of interest along each route, including streets, clubs, hospitals, hotels, theatres, government buildings, cemeteries, places of learning, restaurants, and historic buildings! It typically takes 34 months of training to complete The Knowledge. Working taxi drivers then use their spatial memory throughout their careers, making them a unique population who likely rely on cognitive maps more than any other group of workers in the world.

Maguire decided to compare the hippocampi of London taxi drivers to London bus drivers because the two groups are well matched in terms of their socioeconomic status and how they spend their days (e.g., both groups work while seated with their foot on a gas pedal holding a steering wheel). They also interact with strangers about the same amount. The main differences between the groups, argued Maguire, was that the taxi drivers had to complete The Knowledge course, and that taxi drivers had to constantly plan new routes, while bus drivers would drive the same route all day.

Maguire et al. (2006) compared taxi and bus drivers using a method called voxel-based morphometry (VBM), which measures the volume and density of grey matter for a given area in the brain using MRI images. When Maguire looked at the VBMs of taxi drivers, she found greater grey matter volume in the posterior hippocampal region. Maguire et al. (2006) also

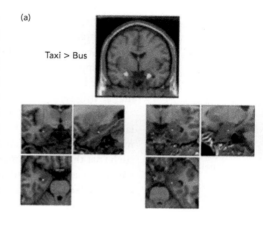

(a)

Taxi > Bus

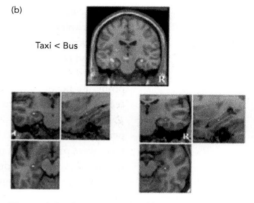

(b)

Taxi < Bus

Figure 4.8 A comparison of hippocampal volume and density in London taxi drivers and London bus drivers

Maguire, Woollett, and Squire (2006) found that the posterior hippocampal region was larger and contained more grey matter in taxi drivers than in bus drivers. The anterior hippocampal region was smaller and less dense in taxi drivers than in bus drivers.

Source: Adapted from Maguire et al., 2006, p. 1094

found that hippocampal volume and grey matter density increased with years of experience, while anterior hippocampal grey matter decreased with years of experience. Maguire et al. (2006) argue that the anterior region decreased in response to exceptional growth in the posterior hippocampal region. Maguire et al. (2006) found that the taxi drivers performed worse than the bus drivers on delayed recall of abstract complex figures, and attributed this performance difference to the reduced volume of the anterior hippocampal region.

relational binding

the process by which different memories of the same object are linked together

The hippocampus has also been found to play a critical role in **relational binding**, which is the process by which different memories of the same object are linked together. When the memory is visual, relational binding creates a viewpoint-independent representation of an object such that the object can be recognized from any viewing angle. Consider a situation where you encounter a fellow student several times, once sitting down the row from you in class, once sitting in front of you in class, and once when they give a presentation in the front of the class. Relational binding will connect those different memories of the same student and will allow you to identify that classmate from any viewpoint. Rosanna Olsen and colleagues of the Rotman Research Institute in Toronto conducted a study that compared facial recognition from different angles in a 23-year-old woman, known as H.C., whose hippocampi did not develop normally but who has an otherwise typical brain, and demographically matched controls. In the study phase of her experiment, Olsen presented H.C. and the controls with images of realistic computer-generated faces taken from five different viewpoints. In the test phase of her experiment, Olsen presented H.C. and the controls with faces from the study phase from either a repeated viewpoint or a novel viewpoint, as well as new faces, and asked participants to indicate whether they recognized the face from the study phase. Olsen found that H.C., who has a developmental abnormality in her hippocampus but no abnormalities in other areas of her brain, had impaired performance compared to demographically matched controls on the recognition test when the faces were presented at novel angles. The result from Olsen et al. (2015) supports the notion that the hippocampus is indeed necessary for relational binding.

In sum, research suggests that the hippocampus as well as many structures surrounding the hippocampus are involved in the production of long-term memories. Although it was once believed that the hippocampus was the seat of all LTM, recent research suggests that the role of the hippocampus may instead be to create cognitive maps and to perform relational binding rather than to be the long-term memory store. Some researchers have argued that these results are consistent with a more complex, two-stage model of long-term memory, where the hippocampus stores memories in the short term but the neocortex is responsible for long-term memory storage. While the two-stage model is controversial, it does provide an explanation for H.M.'s pattern of memory deficits and the pattern of memory deficits in animals with lesions restricted to the hippocampus while simultaneously explaining one of the great puzzles of human physiology: why we sleep.

stability–plasticity dilemma

a problem in neuroscience concerning how it is possible for the brain to keep existing memories stable while integrating new memories

The Two-Stage Model of Memory

In the 1990s, researchers were trying to answer two fundamental questions related to memory. The first question concerned why it was that the MTL and/or hippocampus is necessary for forming new memories, and for accessing recently learned memories, but is not necessary for the retention or recall of memories in the long term. The second question is referred to as the **stability–plasticity dilemma** and is related to the two primary functions of LTM. One role of LTM is to retain specific episodes (this result is called episodic memory and requires that memory be stable over time), and another role is to extract general patterns from these episodes to explain how the world works (this result is called generic memory and requires that memory be flexible, or plastic, over time). Thus, LTM must be able to retain old patterns of activation while forming new patterns of activation. The two-stage model of memory was developed to explain both the time-limited role of the hippocampus on LTM and the stability–plasticity dilemma. The two-stage model concentrates on explaining the formation of explicit memories, but there is also evidence for sleep-dependent consolidation for implicit memory (Diekelmann & Born, 2010).

Overview of the Two-Stage Model of Memory

According to many researchers, inferring that sleep is required for memory consolidation doesn't just explain why we sleep, it also solves the stability–plasticity dilemma (Carpenter & Grossberg, 1988). The **two-stage model** suggested by Marr, Willshaw, and McNaughton (1991) and McClelland, McNaughton, and O'Reilly (1995) posits that two systems affect memory: a **temporary store** (which relies on the hippocampus and adjacent temporal lobe structures) that learns quickly and holds on to information only briefly, and a **long-term store** (which relies on the neocortex) that learns slowly but holds on to information for long periods of time. Proponents of these two-stage models suggest that new information, which is gathered during wakefulness, is initially coded in both the temporary and the long-term stores. In subsequent periods of consolidation during sleep, the new information is reactivated repeatedly and is slowly organized and integrated into the long-term store. The two-stage model holds that because the same processes needed for reactivation are also used to process incoming stimuli, it is necessary to perform reactivation and redistribution processes during sleep, when there are no encoding demands from external stimuli. Plasticity is maintained because new information is constantly being incorporated into the long-term store, and stability is maintained because this consolidation doesn't disrupt existing memories. According to the two-stage model, the process of repeated reactivation and consolidation also serves to encourage the long-term consolidation of relevant information that integrates well with existing knowledge, and erases irrelevant details (Diekelmann and Born, 2007).

A Proposed Link between Sleep and Memory

Humans need sleep; without sleep, humans cannot survive. Yet the unconsciousness that characterizes sleep makes humans vulnerable to predators, and unable to collect survival-related resources like food and water (McClelland et al., 1995). Because sleep puts humans in peril and reduces their access to resources, some psychologists argue that sleep must serve some important purpose. Many explanations have been proffered; theorists have argued that sleep serves an energy-saving function (Berger & Phillips, 1995), that sleep restores energy resources and repairs cell tissues (Oswald, 1980), that sleep helps with the regulation of body temperature (Rechtschaffen & Bergmann, 1995), that sleep helps regulates metabolism, and that sleep helps immune functioning (Knutson & Van Cauter, 2008). A common problem with these theories is conserving energy, regulating temperature, regulating metabolism, and boosting immune functioning could all be achieved if an individual simply rested; these theories don't explain why humans require the loss of consciousness to survive. A possible answer to the question of why we sleep is emerging from memory research. When researchers look at what happens to people

two-stage model

a model of memory proposing that memories are consolidated through two processes: reactivation and redistribution

temporary store

in the two-stage model of memory, the temporary store holds new memories for short periods of time

long-term store

in the two-stage model of memory, the long-term store learns slowly and holds memories for long periods of time

who are deprived of sleep, they consistently find sleep deprivation to be linked to problems with memory and linked to irritability that is exacerbated by external stimulation. Many researchers argue that these two consequences of sleep deprivation (poor memory and the desire to reduce external stimulation) suggest a primary purpose of sleep is to consolidate memories, and that this process is only possible if external stimulation is cut off (Carr, Jadhav, & Frank, 2011; Marr et al., 1991; McClelland et al., 1995).

Stages of Sleep and the Two-Stage Model of Memory

Researchers have studied electrical activity in the brain during wakefulness and sleep using **electroencephalograms (EEGs)**. During wakefulness, people exhibit high-frequency beta waves while alert and lower-frequency alpha waves when relaxed. As a person begins to fall asleep (a period known as stage 1 sleep), lower-frequency theta waves begin to appear (see Figure 4.9.b). In stage 2 sleep, theta waves are interrupted by short bursts of electrical activity known as **sleep spindles** and K-complexes (see Figure 4.9.c). Stage 3 sleep or slow-wave sleep (SWS) is characterized by slow, high-amplitude EEG oscillations known as **slow oscillations**, sleep spindles, and **sharp-wave ripples** in the hippocampus. People cycle through stage 2 and stage 3 sleep several times before finally entering REM sleep (see Figure 4.9). REM sleep is characterized by ponto-geniculo-occipital **(PGO) waves** that move from the brainstem to the hippocampus (Figure 4.9.e) and **theta waves** (Figure 4.9.e) that are similar to those observed in a person who is awake.

Figure 4.10 shows how a typical person progresses through the stages of sleep and EEG activity associated with SWS and REM sleep. In a typical night, a person cycles up and down through these different stages, spending less time in stage 3 and more in REM sleep as the night progresses.

Advocates of the two-stage model of memory argue that each type of EEG activity observed during SWS reflects a different part of the process of reactivation and consolidation (see Figure 4.11). The slow oscillations are thought to synchronize activity in the neocortex, thalamo-cortical areas, and hippocampus. This synchronization is thought to lead to the spindles generated in the thalamo-cortical areas and the sharp-wave ripples observed in the hippocampus. The spindles and ripples reactivate memories in the hippocampus and those memories are then transferred, via continued slow-wave

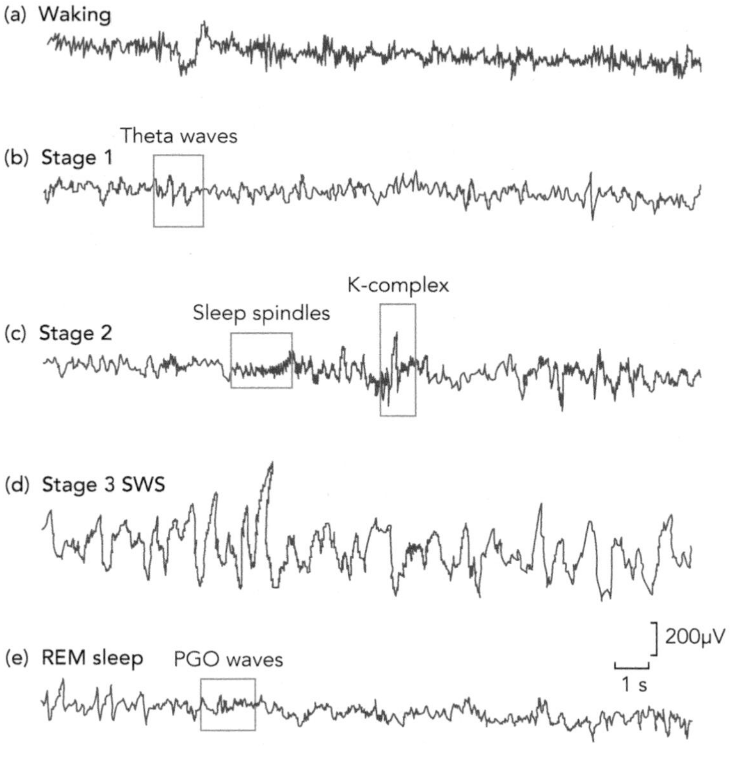

---

electroencephalogram (EEG)

a method for measuring the electrical activity occurring in the brain in real time using conductors applied to the scalp

sleep spindles

bursts of high-frequency high-amplitude EEG activity in the thalamo-cortical region of the brain

slow oscillations

slow-wave EEG activity in the neocortex

Figure 4.9   EEG patterns and sleep stages across a typical night's sleep

Source: Adapted from Breedlove, 2015, p. 265

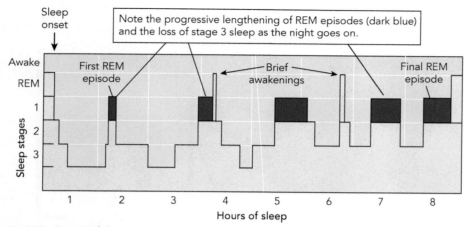

Figure 4.10   Stages of sleep

A person cycles through the sleep stages, each of which is associated with a different pattern of EEG activity, in a back-and-forth pattern throughout the night, tending to spend more time in slow-wave sleep (stage 3) in the beginning of the night and more time in REM sleep at the end of the night.

Source: Based on Breedlove, 2015, p. 265

oscillations, to the neocortex. Researchers believe that when spindles reach the neocortex, they stimulate calcium influxes into associated neurons, which strengthens synapses and consolidates the memory (Born & Wilhelm, 2012).

In one fascinating study, research looked for evidence that SWS served to reactivate and stabilize memories in a way that was not possible while the individual was awake. Rasch, Büchel, Gais, and Born (2007) had participants learn the location of pairs of cards in the presence of a distinct odour. The researchers then presented this odour to participants when the participants were in SWS or when they were awake. Immediately after the odour cue was presented, the experimenters introduced an interference task (waking them first if necessary) that involved having the participant learn new card-pair locations. Participants were then later tested on their memory for the original card-pair locations. Participants who had their memories reactivated when they were awake were more likely to make errors on the card-pair task, choosing locations from the interference task, while participants who had their memory reactivated during SWS made fewer errors on the card-pair task and were less affected by the interference task (Rasch et al., 2007). When the researchers looked at fMRI data for the two reactivation conditions, they found that reactivation during wakefulness mainly activated the prefrontal cortex while reactivation during sleep mainly activated the hippocampus. This suggests that reactivation of a memory serves different functions depending on whether it occurs during wakefulness or during sleep. While reactivation during wakefulness may serve to update existing information, reactivation during sleep serves to increase the likelihood that the memory will be coded in a more stable form in the cortex. As memories are reactivated and redistributed, they become less dependent on the hippocampus and less vulnerable to interference during wakefulness, promoting memory stability over time. While SWS serves to reactivate and redistribute memories to long-term storage, REM sleep is thought to support the consolidation of memories once they have been redistributed to the cortex (Diekelmann & Born, 2010).

sharp-wave ripples

high-amplitude bursts of EEG activity in the hippocampal region of the brain

PGO waves

high-amplitude bursts of activity that originate in the brainstem and move toward the hippocampus

theta waves

a pattern of EEG activity that is similar to activity observed when a person is awake

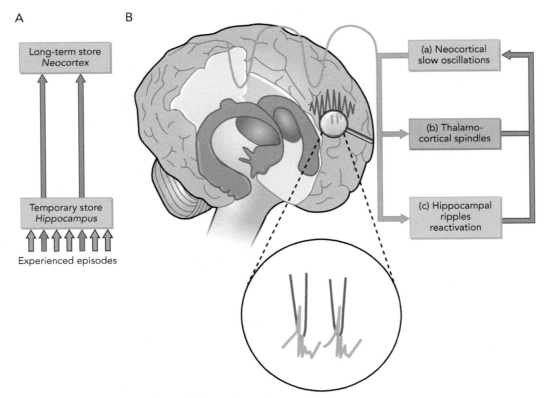

Figure 4.11   Memory reactivation and consolidation during sleep

Panel A shows how during slow-wave sleep (SWS) memories newly encoded into a temporary store in the hippocampus are reactivated to be redistributed to the long-term store in the neocortex. Panel B shows that system consolidation during SWS relies on a dialogue between the hippocampus and neocortex that is controlled by the neocortical slow oscillations (a). The depolarizing up phases of the slow oscillations drive the repeated reactivation of hippocampal memory representations together with sharp-wave ripples in the hippocampus and thalamo-cortical spindles (b). This synchronous drive allows for the formation of spindle-ripple events where sharp-wave ripples and associated reactivated memory information becomes nested into single troughs of a spindle [shown at larger scale in (c)].

Source: Adapted from Born & Wilhelm, 2012, p. 194

How Are Memories Selected for Reactivation and Distribution?

During the course of a typical day, an individual encodes a vast amount of information; however, research suggests that only a small amount of this information becomes part of long-term memory. A recent series of experiments by Ines Wilhelm and her colleagues suggests that people tend to consolidate memories that are relevant to that individual's future plans (Wilhelm, Diekelmann, Molzow, Ayoub, Mölle, & Born, 2011). In one study, Wilhelm had participants learn pairs of words and pairs of card locations before a period of sleep or wakefulness. Some participants were told that they would be tested later; others were not told. The researchers found that if participants knew they would be tested, participants who slept before they were tested had better memory performance than those who didn't sleep, but there was no effect of sleep on memory if the participants did not know they would be tested later. Wilhelm et al. (2011) also found that participants who knew they would be tested showed more slow-wave oscillations during sleep than those who did not know they would be tested. Together, these results suggest that knowing that information may be useful later may trigger EEG activity that promotes reactivation, redistribution, and consolidation of verbal and visuospatial memories. The research also suggests that students may benefit from completing their studying the night before a big exam and ensuring they get a good night's sleep before the test.

Sleep and Memory for Actions and Plans

Stefan Fischer and Jan Born conducted a study to see if memory for actions are also affected by SWS. They had participants learn two finger-sequence tapping tasks (task A and task B) in random order. Participants were then told that they would receive a monetary reward for performing particularly well on one of the sequences; half of the participants were told this would be task A, the other half were told it would be task B. Half of the participants slept during the delay between learning the tapping sequences and the test, half did not. Fischer found that while sleep benefited performance on both sequences, this effect was greater for performance on the sequence that the participant expected a greater reward for. For participants who did not sleep, performance was similar on both tapping tasks. This result suggests that, like verbal and visuospatial memory, memory for actions benefits from sleep, and that expecting a reward from that action enhances this benefit of sleep (Fischer & Born, 2009).

Sleep also has a direct benefit on the ability to implement future plans. Susanne Diekelmann and colleagues had participants learn to respond to a coloured dot on a computer screen at random intervals. Participants were then told that in two days they would have to complete the same task but that the dot would be a different colour, and that it was very important that they do this task well. If the wrong-coloured dot appeared they would have to inform the experimenter immediately or else, they were told, the whole experiment would be ruined. Thus, the instructions of the experiment suggested that the participants plan to tell the experimenter if the wrong-coloured dot appeared on the screen. (This was called the retrieval plan.) Half the participants were allowed to sleep right after the experiment; the other half were kept awake for the night. All participants then went home and spent the day awake and slept the next

RELEVANT RESEARCH

BOX
4.1

Why Is It So Hard to Remember Your Dreams?

When the Barenaked Ladies's song *Pinch Me* (released in 2000) included the lyric "It's like a dream—you try to remember but it's gone," the songwriters were on to something. Dreams are fleeting. Unless they are written down immediately when a person awakes, the dreams will be impossible to remember. How is it that sleep, which serves to consolidate memories, is also impossible to remember? Casimir Wierzynski at the California Institute for Technology argues that this is because sleep serves to first transfer memories from the hippocampus to the neocortex and then to reorganize those memories in the neocortex. Wierzynski argues that the reorganization of memories benefits from having as little input from the hippocampus as possible because activity in the hippocampus during reorganization would make the process more difficult (somewhat like it is more difficult to compose a sentence when someone is speaking). Indeed, Wierzynski has found that hippocampal activity is attenuated during REM sleep. Wierzynski suggests that because the hippocampus is not active during REM sleep, dreams that occur during REM are easily forgotten (Wierzynski, Lubenov, Gu, & Siapas, 2009).

DIY EXPERIMENT

Dream Journal

The two-stage model of memory consolidation suggests that sleep serves to reactivate and reorganize memories, and that dreams consist of images and concepts meant to tie these reactivated memories together. Try writing down your dreams as soon as you wake up (you have to write them down immediately or you will likely forget them) and use these recordings to guess what memories your brain was working to reorganize the night before. For example, you may dream that you are attending your public school, which may indicate that your brain was working on reactivating memories of your time at school while you were asleep.

night, returning to do the dot task the following day, during which the incorrect dot colour was always presented. While all participants who slept after being given the instruction about what to do if the dot was the wrong colour informed the experimenter of this apparent error, only 61 per cent of the participants who did not sleep did so. In a second experiment, Diekelmann manipulated whether participants spent most of their time in SWS or in REM sleep after learning about the retrieval plan. (Each group slept the same total amount of time.) Diekelmann found that 100 per cent of participants who experienced more SWS remembered the retrieval plan whereas only 55 per cent of participants who experienced mostly REM sleep remembered the plan. Combined, these results suggest that sleep enhances an individual's ability to make and carry out future plans, and that SWS plays a more important role in this process than REM sleep (Diekelmann, Wilhelm, Wagner, & Born, 2013). This research supports the notion that the two-stage model of memory can be used to explain the consolidation of implicit memories.

Multiple-Trace Theory

multiple-trace theory
a theory that suggests that generic memories are formed from multiple episodic traces

An alternative to the two-stage model of memory is the **multiple-trace theory** proposed by Lynn Nadel and Morris Moscovitch. According to this theory, each time a memory is retrieved, the hippocampus creates a new memory trace, and over time one memory can come to be stored as multiple traces (Nadel & Moscovitch, 1998). Nadel and Moscovitch (1998) suggest that generic memories are formed from multiple episodic traces that share features. For example, if a student learns during a lecture in an introductory psychology course that Ivan Pavlov was the first researcher to systematically explore classical conditioning and then later learns the same fact about Pavlov while reading a text, the student has multiple traces related to Ivan Pavlov being the first researcher to systematically explore classical conditioning. Multiple-trace theory suggests that individual episodic memories remain stored in the hippocampus and thus that damage to the hippocampus will impair an individual's access to episodic information. However, when there are multiple learning instances for the same fact (e.g., that Ivan Pavlov discovered classical conditioning), this fact will be accessible as a context-free generic memory and will be stored *outside* of the hippocampus. Thus, hippocampal damage will not affect the memory. In summary, the multiple-trace model suggests that only context-free information, such as information gleaned from multiple encounters with the same fact, will come to be stored outside of the hippocampus, while the two-stage model suggests that *all* episodic memories eventually become represented in the cortex through processes that take place during SWS.

Reconsolidation

Consolidation occurs when a hippocampus-dependent memory becomes hippocampus-independent over the course of weeks or years. Evidence for consolidation comes from experiments that demonstrated that interventions can impair or enhance memory, but only when the interventions are administered shortly after new learning (Nader and Hardt, 2009). For example, performance on memory-recall tasks can be impaired by electroconvulsive shock, protein-synthesis inhibition, or new learning. Memory can be improved by the administration of strychnine (a strong poison). However, because these interventions only work with newly learned material, they are evidence that memories can exist in two states: a labile state during which the memory is susceptible to enhancements and impairments, and a static state during which a memory cannot be enhanced or impaired by interventions. A memory in a static state is said to be consolidated (Alpern & Crabbe, 1972; Gordon, 1977).

In 2000, Glenn Schafe and Joseph LeDoux of New York University conducted an experiment examining consolidation of fear responses. In the first part of their experiment, rats were placed in a chamber and presented with a 30-second-long tone followed by a one-second foot shock. The normal fear response to shock, for a rat, is to freeze. The rats were immediately given an injection of either an inert substance or a chemical that would disrupt protein synthesis in the lateral and basal nuclei of the amygdala (LBA). The next day, the rats were placed in a chamber and presented with the tone again and the researchers measured immobility (freezing) in the rats following the tone. The rats given the inert chemical showed a typical fear response and froze when the tone was presented. The rats given the protein-synthesis inhibitor, on the other hand, did not freeze when the tone was presented, suggesting they had no memory of the foot shock. Schafe and LeDoux (2000) concluded that protein synthesis in the amygdala is necessary for the consolidation of fear memories.

Karim Nader, Glenn Schafe, and Joseph LeDoux (2000) also studied the effect of protein-synthesis inhibitors on the learning of fear responses in rats, but in their paradigm they tested whether a learned response could be forgotten. First, Nader et al. (2000) placed each rat in a chamber and presented it with a 30-second-long tone followed by a foot shock. One day later, when the fear memory should have been consolidated, half of the rats were placed in the chamber again and presented with the tone. The researchers measured immobility in the rat and then immediately injected the rat with either an inert substance or a substance that would inhibit protein synthesis in the amygdala. The rats that were not reminded of the tone were also either injected with an inert substance or a substance that would inhibit protein synthesis in the amygdala. One day later, all rats were presented with the tone and their immobility was measured. Nader et al. (2000) found that rats who had been reminded of the tone and then given the protein-synthesis inhibitor showed no memory for the fear conditioning, while the rats who were not reminded of the tone, or were given an inert substance, froze in response to the tone. Because only the rats who were reminded of the tone later forgot their fear response, Nader et al. (2000) concluded that reactivating a memory made that memory labile again, and that consolidation must occur after reactivation for the memory to be retained (see Table 4.1). This process became known as **reconsolidation**.

Since Nader et al. (2000) presented their findings showing memory loss when reactivation is not followed by consolidation, reconsolidation has been demonstrated in a variety of animals including

consolidation
a general term for neurological processes that make it possible for a memory trace to be sustained over time

reconsolidation
when a static memory is activated, becomes labile, and is returned to a static state again

Table 4.1   Method and results from Nader, Schafe, and LeDoux (2000)

Group	Learning Phase	Reminder	Test
No reminder, inert	tone and footshock	none, inert	fear response
No reminder, inhibitor	tone and footshock	none, inhibitor	fear response
Reminder, inert	tone and footshock	tone, inert	fear response
Reminder, inhibitor	tone and footshock	tone, inhibitor	no fear response

Nader et al. (2000) created a conditioned fear response in rats. Nader et al. (2000) found that if rats were reminded of their fear and then given a substance that inhibited consolidation, the fear response disappeared. This result suggests that memories must be reconsolidated after they are activated or the memory will be forgotten.
Source: Nader et al., 2000

crabs, snails, and honeybees, and for a various types of learning, including motor-sequence learning, object recognition, spatial memory, and episodic memory. Further, reconsolidation can occur through methods other than protein-synthesis inhibition, including heat shock, inhibiting NMDA receptors, anaesthesia, and interference through new learning. One interesting aspect of reconsolidation is that it appears to be context dependent; it only occurs when the memory is reactivated in a similar context to where it was learned. Thus reconsolidation only works when a rat is presented with the feared tone in the learning environment; being presented with the tone in another context does not reactivate the memory into a labile state (Terry & Holliday, 1972). Similarly, studies of reconsolidation in humans have shown that episodic memories are susceptible to reconsolidation through new learning but only if the interfering material is presented where the original learning took place (Hupbach, Hardt, Gomez, & Nadel, 2008). Research into reconsolidation is ongoing and its various applications will be discussed throughout this book.

What Happens in the Brain during Retrieval?

Humans are very good at retrieving event information. If asked, you could probably recall what you ate for dinner last night and the night before, how you spent your last birthday, and the topic from your last psychology lecture. One question that has concerned psychologists is how people are able to activate representations from specific events when asked (such as what you ate for dinner last night) instead of activating representations from other events (such as what you ate for dinner two nights ago) (Norman, Schacter, & Reder, 1996; Howard & Kahana, 2002).

Polyn, Natu, Cohen, and Norman (2005) decided to attempt to answer this question using fMRI data that was analyzed using a method known as **multi-voxel pattern analysis (MVPA)**. To conduct MVPA, researchers first collect fMRI data from several instances of the same cognitive event, such as viewing an image of a cat, or recalling the name of a childhood friend. Next, each image is partitioned into tiny segments called voxels; each voxel contains fMRI data from a small region of the brain. Finally, a computer program compares the voxel activity across the different instances of the same event (e.g., viewing a picture of a cat), looking for a pattern. If an MVPA is successful, it will isolate the voxels that are always active during the given event. The results of an MVPA are validated when participants again return to the fMRI and the MVPA correctly identifies those instances when the participant is viewing material from the training session (such as pictures of a cat).

multi-voxel pattern analysis (MVPA)

a popular analytical technique in neuroscience that involves identifying patterns in fMRI BOLD signal data that are predictive of task conditions

Polyn et al. (2005) devised a three-phase experiment so they could use MVPA to study retrieval. In the first phase (called the study phase), participants were scanned in an fMRI while viewing 90 different pictures from three categories: famous people, famous locations, and common household objects. During this phase, participants were not aware that they were participating in a memory experiment. When shown each picture, participants were asked to indicate either how much they liked the famous person, how much they wanted to travel to the famous location, or how frequently they used the common object. The second phase was the MVPA phase. Polyn et al. (2005) first divided the fMRI data for each participant into the three groups: famous people, famous locations, and common household objects. Next they ran an MVPA analysis on each category, which identified the voxels that were consistently active in each fMRI image. In the final phase, participants returned to the fMRI machine and were asked to recall as many items as possible from the study phase while their brain activity was recorded. Polyn et al. (2005) then compared the brain activity at each point in time to the voxel analysis for each category.

The results from one participant from Polyn et al. (2005) are shown in Figure 4.12. The lines of the graph reflect the similarity between brain activity at recall and the voxel pattern for a given category. The dots along the top of the figure indicate the category that the item recalled at that point in time belong to. Polyn et al. (2005) found that brain activity associated with a certain category during the learning phase matched brain activity while participants were recalling items for that category. For example, the participant whose data is shown in Figure 4.12 reported

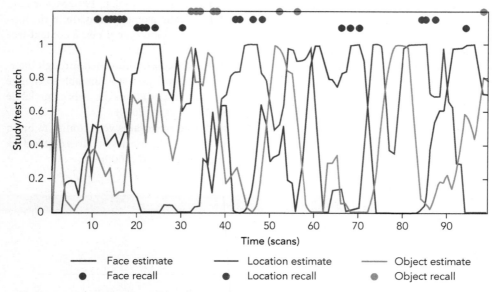

Figure 4.12   Example of results from Polyn et al. (2005)

This figure shows correspondence between the classifier's estimate of contextual reinstatement and verbal recalls for one participant in Polyn et al. (2005). Time is shown on the x-axis. For each brain scan, the classifier produced an estimate of the match between the current testing pattern and each of the three study contexts. Strength of estimate appears on the y-axis. The blue, red, and green lines correspond to the face, location, and object classifier estimates, respectively. The blue, red, and green dots correspond to the face, location, and object recalls made by the subject.

Source: Adapted from Polyn, Natu, Cohen, & Norman, 2005, p. 1964

several famous locations first. Just prior to listing the famous locations, the participant's brain activity was most similar to the brain activity observed when the participant was viewing pictures of locations during the study phase. The same was true when the participant was recalling famous faces and familiar objects; the pattern of activity found for a given category during the study phase was the same as the pattern of activity observed during free recall. The results from Polyn et al. (2005) suggest that successful, intentional retrieval of information involves configuring brain activity into the same state that it was in during encoding.

Summary

Long-term memory relies on a wide variety of neurological processes. Connections among neurons are strengthened through long-term potentiation (Bliss and Lømo, 1973). The hippocampus contains NMDA and AMPA receptors that facilitate LTP (Rao & Finkbeiner, 2007). NMDA receptors must be active in order for long-term memories to be formed (Morris et al., 1986). Although the hippocampus was once thought to store long-term memories, recent research suggests that the hippocampus may instead be responsible for developing cognitive maps and associations among elements in the environment, including those that comprise episodic memories (Eichenbaum & Cohen, 2001). The two-stage model of memory suggests that during slow-wave sleep (SWS), memories in the hippocampus are reactivated and slowly transferred to the neocortex where they remain for the long term (Carr et al., 2011; Marr et al., 1991; McClelland et al., 1995). Multiple-trace theory instead suggests that episodic memories remain in the hippocampus, but that when the same information is encountered multiple times, a context-free representation is created in the neocortex (Nadel & Moscovitch, 1998).

Research has also shown that new memories can be enhanced or diminished through intervention; however, memories eventually become consolidated and are not vulnerable to change through intervention at this time. When a memory is reactivated, however, it become labile again and must be reconsolidated if it is to be retained (Nader et al., 2000).

Finally, research has confirmed that brain activity during retrieval is very similar to brain activity during encoding and thus that the retrieval of long-term memories involves duplicating the pattern of activation produced during initial learning (Polyn et al., 2005).

CHAPTER REVIEW

- In 1953, Henry Molaison (H.M.) underwent surgery for epilepsy that involved the removal of his medial temporal lobe (MTL) and his hippocampi. After the surgery, H.M. displayed profound anterograde amnesia and was unable to learn and deliberately recall new information.
- Brenda Milner and her colleagues studied H.M. for the remainder of his life. Research involving H.M. revealed that the MTL and the hippocampus are heavily involved in the formation of explicit memory but are not crucial for other cognitive functioning. Research also revealed that the MTL is not necessary for short-term memory or for the maintenance and retrieval of memories more than two years old.

- In 1949, Donald Hebb first published Hebb's postulate: "When an Axon of cell A is near enough to excite a cell B and repeatedly or persistently takes part in firing it, some growth process or metabolic change takes place in one or both cells such that A's efficiency, as one of the cells firing B, is increased" (Hebb, 1949, p. 62).

- In the 1960s, researchers Timothy Bliss and Terje Lømo (1973) demonstrated a persistent increase in electrical activity after a learning episode had ended. This increase in electrical activity was termed *long-term potentiation* (LTP) and proved Hebb's postulate to be true.

- LTP proved Hebb's postulate to be true but did not explain the metabolic mechanisms that increase synaptic strength. Researchers later discovered that NMDA receptors in the hippocampus influence LTP through short- and long-term mechanisms. Richard Morris demonstrated that NMDA is necessary for LTP by showing that rats who receive AP5, which prevents NMDA receptors from functioning, could not form a memory for where a platform was located in a Morris Water Maze.

- Selective lesioning studies suggest that only the perirhinal cortex (PRC) is necessary for the completion of the delayed-nonmatching-to-sample (DNMS) task. These results led researchers to explore other possible functions of the hippocampus. Eichenbaum and Cohen (2004) and Maguire, Woollett, and Spiers (2006) both suggest that the hippocampus plays a crucial role in the formation of cognitive maps.

- In the 1990s, researchers were trying to explain the time-limited role of the MTL and hippocampus in memory as evidenced by the case of H.M. Researchers were also attempting to explain the stability–plasticity dilemma. The two-stage model of memory was developed to answer these two questions.

- According to the two-stage model of memory, there are two memory systems: one temporary store that learns quickly, and one long-term store that holds information for long periods. Information is initially encoded in both stores. In subsequent periods of consolidation during sleep, new information is reactivated repeatedly and is slowly organized and integrated into the long-term store. The theory holds that because the same processes needed for reactivation are used to process incoming stimuli, it is necessary to perform reactivation and redistribution processes during sleep, when there are no encoding demands from external stimuli. Plasticity is maintained because new information is constantly being incorporated into the long-term store, and stability is maintained because this consolidation doesn't disrupt existing memory.

- Researchers argue that each type of EEG activity observed during SWS reflects a different part of the process of reactivation and consolidation.

- Not all memories are selected for consolidation through this process. Research suggests that memories related to future plans may be more likely to be selected for consolidation than other memories.

- Although the two-stage model of memory was developed to explain the consolidation of explicit memories, there is evidence in the literature that implicit memory for actions may also be consolidated via slow-wave sleep.

- The multiple-trace theory is an alternative to the two-stage theory of memory. The models are very similar, except the multiple-trace theory assumes that episodic memories (memories for events) remain in the hippocampus whereas the two-stage model assumes that episodic memories are transferred to the neocortex.

- Recent research suggests that reactivated memories are malleable and must be reconsolidated if they are to be retained. Reactivating a memory brings that memory into a labile state and the memory must be consolidated again through a process called *reconsolidation*.

- Multi-voxel pattern analysis (MVPA) has been used to compare brain activity during encoding to brain activity during retrieval. The results from MVPA studies suggest that successful retrieval involves configuring brain activity into the same state that it was in during encoding.

MEMORY ACTIVITY

Using Cues to Self-Test

This chapter reviewed a great deal of complex information. One of the best ways to commit information like this to memory is through frequent self-testing (e.g., McDaniel, Anderson, Derbish, & Morrisette, 2007). There are many different ways to self-test but one of the most effective and easiest is just to use cues from the chapter and see what material you can generate from the cue. Below is an example of a list of concepts from the first section of this chapter. (It is by no means complete. You should always generate your own list to make sure you are covering everything!) Once you have a list like the one below, begin by developing a good definition for each concept. Next, use the concepts as cues and see how much of the material you can recall. After reviewing your attempt, wait a day and try testing yourself again. Repeat this process until you have mastered the material.

anterograde amnesia	Hebb's postulate	tetani
presynaptic neuron	long-term potentiation	the role of NMDA receptors in LTP
postsynaptic neuron	perforant path	
Hebbian plasticity	population spike	

Questions

1. If you knew of a patient who had her or his medial temporal lobe and hippocampi removed, what aspects of memory would you expect to be impaired? What aspects of memory would you expect to be unaffected?
2. Describe Hebb's postulate. Explain how Hebb's postulate can explain classical conditioning.
3. Describe the experiment by Bliss and Lømo (1973) and its impact on the understanding of the neuroscience of memory.
4. Identify two types of glutamate receptors found on neurons in the hippocampus. Describe the conditions under which each will cause a neuron to fire.
5. Explain how NMDA receptors influence LTP in the short and long terms.
6. Explain how Richard Morris demonstrated that NMDA receptors are necessary for LTP.
7. Compare and contrast the conclusions of studies that used lesioning and studies that used ibotenic acid to identify the brain regions necessary for performing a delayed-nonmatching-to-sample (DNMS) task.
8. Describe the function of the hippocampus according to Eleanor Maguire and her colleagues. Discuss the results of one experiment that supports her claim.
9. What is the role of slow-wave sleep (SWS) in memory consolidation according to the two-stage model of memory?
10. What are two key issues in the memory literature? What explanation does the two-stage model of memory provide for them?
11. Describe one experiment that supports the two-stage model of memory.
12. Provide a theory explaining how memories are selected for consolidation. Support the theory with the results from at least one experiment.
13. Describe an experiment that supports the claim that SWS is involved in the consolidation of implicit memories.
14. Compare and contrast the multiple-trace model and the two-stage model of memory.

15. Compare and contrast consolidation and reconsolidation.
16. Describe an experiment that demonstrated reconsolidation.
17. Explain how brain activity during retrieval relates to brain activity during encoding. Identify experimental evidence that supports your claim.

Key Figures

Howard Eichenbaum p. 82
Timothy Bliss p. 78
Neal Cohen p. 82
Per Andersen p. 77
Donald Hebb p. 76

Terje Lømo p. 78
Brenda Milner p. 75
Richard Morris p. 81
Morris Moscovitch p. 90
Elizabeth Murray p. 82

Lynn Nadel p. 90
Wilder Penfield p. 75
Larry Squire p. 82

5 Explicit and Implicit Memory

LEARNING OBJECTIVES

Having read this chapter, you will be able to:

- Differentiate between implicit and explicit memory.
- Describe explicit and implicit memory capabilities in people with anterograde amnesia.
- Describe the processing account of the dissociation between explicit and implicit tests of memory.
- Describe the main components of Mortimer Mishkin's neural circuit for implicit memory.
- Differentiate between the processes involved in encoding implicit and explicit memories.
- Describe artificial grammars and pattern-learning paradigms.
- Explain why classical conditioning is associated with implicit memory.
- Generate examples of the influence of implicit memory on personal preferences.
- Explain what studies of repetition priming have revealed about the nature of implicit memory.
- Describe the implicit-association test (IAT) and explain how the IAT can be used to measure stereotypes.
- Explain the illusory-truth effect and why this effect is attributed to implicit memory.
- Describe situations under which a person may form a memory under anaesthesia and explain why that memory is more likely to be implicit than explicit.
- Define procedural memory.

H.M. VS J.K.

When J.K. was in his late seventies, he began to develop symptoms of Parkinson's disease, a movement disorder linked to a dysfunction in the basal ganglia. A few years later, J.K. began to experience problems with his memory for familiar tasks, such as using doorknobs and turning off his radio, but J.K. had no difficulty remembering daily events or recalling facts. J.K.'s case is an example of a problem with **implicit memory**, or memory related to skills and other cognitive tasks outside of awareness. J.K.'s **explicit memory**, which is linked to conscious recall, was unaffected

Recall from Chapter 1 that H.M. developed severe **anterograde amnesia** after brain surgery to treat epilepsy. H.M. could not remember meeting doctors he had seen hundreds of times, and had no recollection of having eaten lunch just minutes after finishing his meal. Despite H.M.'s amnesia, H.M. had an above-average IQ and was able to do well on tests related to perception and was able to learn new skills, such as tracing a star shape in a mirror. H.M. had a deficit in explicit memory, while H.M.'s implicit memory seemed unaffected.

The cases of J.K. and H.M. demonstrate that implicit memory is functionally distinct from explicit memory. It is possible to have implicit memory without explicit memory (as in the case of H.M.) and it is possible to lose implicit memory and retain explicit memory (as in the case of J.K.). In the first part of this chapter, you will explore implicit memory and explicit memory as distinct entities. In the second half of the chapter, we will delve deeper into phenomena related to implicit memory.

implicit memory

a general term for memories that an individual cannot be consciously aware of, such as how to perform an action

explicit memory

a memory that an individual can bring into conscious awareness

anterograde amnesia

the loss of the ability to form new memories

The Implicit–Explicit Memory Distinction

According to Squire (1992), long-term memory is comprised of explicit, or declarative, memory and implicit, or nondeclarative, memory. Explicit memory is conscious while implicit memory is unconscious. Explicit memory refers to memory for facts, events, places, and anything else that can be described. Recalling your first day at university, your birth date, or something you learned in a lecture are all examples of explicit memory. Implicit memory refers to learning that is reflected in the ability to perform a task but that cannot be articulated. Knowing how to turn a door handle or drive a car reflects implicit memory, whereas being able to imagine what your front doorknob looks like or being able to articulate the rules for navigating a four-way stop reflects explicit memory.

A key distinction between explicit and implicit memory is related to consciousness. **Consciousness** is the mind's level of responsiveness to incoming sensory information. Consciousness enhances an animal's ability to construct a mental representation of the sensory world and select behaviours. It is impossible for a human to imagine what it is like to exist without consciousness; however, many animals, such as frogs, have no conscious experiences. When frogs are presented with visual information, they act a bit like zombies; they seem to act without thinking. If a frog is presented with a small, prey-like stimulus, it always snaps its tongue; however, if a frog is presented with a large, predator-like stimulus, it always jumps away. These tongue-snapping and jumping behaviours are reflexive responses triggered by specific types of

consciousness

the mind's level of responsiveness to incoming sensory information visual stimuli; no conscious awareness is involved. Despite not having consciousness, frogs have thrived on earth for tens of millions of years. Researchers Francis Crick and Christof Koch suggest that reflexive systems work well in a frog because only a limited number of responses are needed for a frog to survive; a frog's life involves waiting for food and catching it, and avoiding being eaten (Crick & Koch, 1998). However, as the number of reflexes needed to survive in an environment increases, reflexes become less efficient, and can potentially conflict with one another. For example, if an animal that lives in an environment where some small objects are a good source of food and other small objects are poisonous, neither a reflexive action to snap its tongue at all small objects nor a reflexive action to jump away from all small objects would be adaptive. At this point, it makes sense for the animal to produce a single sensory representation and allow the animal to use it to choose the best response. This sustained, complex representation is what we know as consciousness. During evolution, some animals lived in complex environments where survival benefited from introducing conscious experience and reducing reliance on reflexes. These animals developed more complex brains to sustain consciousness as well as a new explicit memory system for retaining conscious experiences; however, unconscious processing continued to exist side by side with conscious processing. Implicit memory is part of this unconscious system.

Elizabeth Warrington and Lawrence Weiskrantz conducted one of the first studies to compare explicit and implicit memory. Warrington and Weiskrantz (1970) presented people with amnesia (like H.M.) and matched controls with a list of five-letter words three times and then tested each individual using one of several measures including free recall (e.g., "Report as many of the words from the study list as you can."), yes/no recognition (e.g., "Did this item appear on the study list?") and word-fragment completion (e.g., "Identify the word that is consistent with this degraded image."). Warrington and Weiskrantz (1970) found that although participants with amnesia had worse recall and recognition performance than controls, participants with amnesia completed word fragments with words from the study list at the same rate as controls. This finding has since been replicated many times (see Shimamura, 1986 for a review). The observation that people with explicit memory deficits typically perform normally on tasks involving implicit memory is evidence that explicit memory and implicit memory are two separate memory systems.

The dissociation between explicit and implicit memory system isn't limited to tasks involving words. In a Gollin figure test (shown in Figure 5.1), individuals are shown a series

We are consciously aware of our explicit memories, such as facts learned in school. We are not consciously aware of implicit memories, such as how to ride a bicycle.

DIY EXPERIMENT

BOX 5.1

Priming

1. Read the following words out loud:
   grant   dodge   merit   craft   treat

2. Use the word *duck* in a sentence.

You probably generated a sentence like "I have to duck out of the way to avoid being hit" rather than "I saw a duck by the pond." This is because your implicit memory for words on the word list influenced how you interpreted the word with two meanings. Without being primed with the word *dodge* most people think of a type of bird when they see the word *duck*.

---

of figures depicting an object at various stages of completion; the object is more complete each time it is presented. The participant is asked to identify the object as soon as possible. Typically, a person needs to see several presentations (e.g., one from Set IV of Figure 5.1) before identifying the object for the first time but can recognize the object based on more incomplete representations if the experiment is repeated (e.g., a figure from Set II may be adequate for identification). This finding is replicated in people with amnesia; although people with amnesia have no explicit recollection of having seen the figures before, they are able to identify objects with less information if they have already seen the object before, suggesting implicit memory is intact. The topic of implicit memory for images is discussed in more detail later in this chapter.

People with anterograde amnesia also show motor learning with no explicit memory of having practised a skill. In the **pursuit-rotor task** (shown in Figure 5.2) a small disk moves in a circular pattern on a turntable that is turning in the opposite direction. The participant must hold a stylus on the small disk as it spins. Most people learn the pursuit-rotor task in about an hour. If people with anterograde amnesia are asked to perform the task again a week later, they master it much more quickly, even though they have no explicit memory of the first learning session. People without amnesia also master the pursuit-rotor task much more quickly when they have done so before.

pursuit-rotor task
a task used to assess procedural learning where the goal is to keep a stylus on a specific spot within a rotating circle that is embedded on a disk also rotating, but in the opposite direction

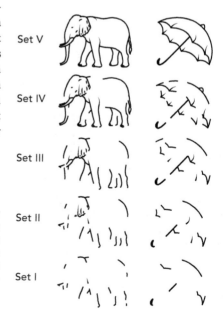

Set V

Set IV

Set III

Set II

Set I

Figure 5.1   An example of figures used in Gollin (1960)

Examples are of incomplete figures that have been used to test for the implicit memory for visual information in people with amnesia. Typically, a person with amnesia must see a fairly complete representation (e.g., one from Set IV) before identifying the object the first time that the figures are presented. Although the person with amnesia will have no recollection of having seen the figures before, she or he will identify the object much more quickly on subsequent presentations, showing the existence of implicit memory in the absence of explicit memory.
Source: Gollin, 1960, p. 290

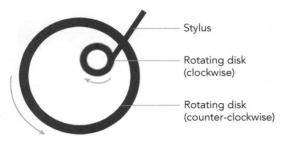

Stylus

Rotating disk
(clockwise)

Rotating disk
(counter-clockwise)

Figure 5.2   **Pursuit-rotor task**

In the pursuit-rotor task, the individual must hold the stylus on a metal disk that is rotating in one direction within another disk rotating in the opposite direction. People's ability to learn this skill relies on their implicit memory.

Although explicit memory is often linked to tasks involving language (such as recalling a word list or describing the events from the previous day), it is not limited to language. Nonspeaking animals often show evidence of explicit memory. In one type of experiment, rats are placed in an arena where there is a food reward. The experimenter waits for the rat to find the food reward and then removes the rat from the arena. Following a delay ranging from a few minutes to over a day, the rat is returned to the arena. The rat will immediately return to the location where it last found food. The location of the last piece of food is an explicit memory. If the delay is increased to more than three days, the rat will forget this explicit memory and, when placed in the arena, will search the arena for food. This searching behaviour reflects an implicit memory of how to perform the task. This simple type of experiment shows that rats have explicit and implicit memory and that they are separate from one another (explicit memory can be forgotten while implicit memory is retained; Kolb, 2016).

The Processing Account of Implicit and Explicit Memory

Some researchers argue that the dissociation in explicit and implicit task performance by people with amnesia results from differences in the level of processing required for the study items and the test items, rather than from separate explicit and implicit memory systems. Support for this processing view of explicit and implicit memory comes from experiments that revealed that whether a participant thought about a word in terms of its perceptual features (e.g., the letters it was comprised of) or its conceptual features (e.g., the word's meaning) affected performance on recognition, recall, and word-fragment tasks (e.g., Blaxton, 1989; Jacoby, 1983).

In her 1989 experiment, Teresa Blaxton first had participants study words in one of three conditions. In the perceptual processing condition, participants saw the word alone (e.g., XXX–*bashful*). In the first conceptual condition, participants saw the word with a synonym (e.g., timid–*bashful*). In the second conceptual condition, participants had to generate a word based on a synonym and a related letter (e.g., timid–*b?????*). Next, Blaxton (1989) tested participants using tasks that encouraged either perceptual processing or conceptual processing. Examples of the tasks are shown in Table 5.1. The conceptually driven tests were free recall, semantic-cue recall, and tests of general knowledge where a target word was the correct answer. The perceptually driven tasks were graphemic-cue recall and word-fragment completion. Importantly, the graphemic-cue recall task was an explicit memory test based on perceptual features of a word while the general knowledge test was an implicit memory test based on the conceptual features of the word. Blaxton (1989) argues that the memory systems' account of explicit and implicit memory predicts similar performance across study conditions for all explicit and implicit memory tasks and no effect for the level of processing manipulations at the time of study. However, Blaxton (1989) found a significant effect for level of processing at the time of study within each test type; conceptual processing led to the best performance on free-recall, semantic-recall, and general knowledge tests while perceptual processing led to the best performance on the word-completion and graphemic-cue tests (see Figure 5.3).

Table 5.1   Sample study and test items used in Blaxton (1989)

Target	Word Fragment	Graphemic Cue	Semantic Cue	General Knowledge Question
bashful	B_SH_U_	bushel	timid	Which of the seven dwarfs comes first alphabetically?
cheetah	_H_ _T_H	cheetos	jaguar	What is the fastest animal on earth?
cologne	C_ _ _GN_	colony	fragrance	What German city is famous for the scent it produces?
computer	C_ _PU_ _ _	commuter	processor	What is a Univac I?
copper	C_PP_ _	chopper	bronze	What metal makes up 10% of yellow gold?
freckle	F_EC_ _E	fickle	birthmark	What appears when the sun activates your melanocytes?
metropolis	M_T_ _ _OL_S	acropolis	township	In what fictional city did Clarke Kent and Lois Lane live?
plague	P_ _GU_	vague	epidemic	What disease was called the "Black Death"?
treason	_RE_ _ON	treasure	disloyalty	For what crime were the Rosenbergs executed?
universe	_ _IV_ _SE	unversed	cosmos	What was the Big Bang said to have created?

Source: Blaxton, 1989, p. 660

The processing account of explicit and implicit memory suggests that dissociations in performance across explicit and implicit tasks, such as those observed in Warrington and Weiskrantz (1970) and Blaxton (1989), result from a mismatch between the type of processing of target stimuli and the type of stimuli that produce optimal performance on a given task. On tasks based on perceptual information (like word-fragment completion or graphic-cue recall), targets processed at a perceptual level will produce the best performance, while on tasks based on conceptual information (such as semantic-cue recall or general knowledge) targets processed at a conceptual level will give the best performance. Thus, if participants process all targets at a perceptual level, they will show good performance on perceptual tasks and poor performance on conceptual tasks, creating an apparent dissociation. The processing account differs from the systems account, which suggests that the dissociations result from differing performance in separate implicit and explicit memory systems. Which account is correct? Interestingly, neuroscientific evidence suggests that the systems account and the processing account may both be correct. As we will see in the next section, Mortimer Mishkin (1982) proposes two distinct brain circuits: an explicit circuit that involves parts of the brain linked to conceptual information, and an implicit circuit that involves parts of the brain linked to perceptual processing. Thus, consistent with the systems account, explicit and implicit memory seem to involve different systems in the brain, and consistent with the processing account, explicit memory is linked to conceptual information while implicit memory is linked to perceptual information.

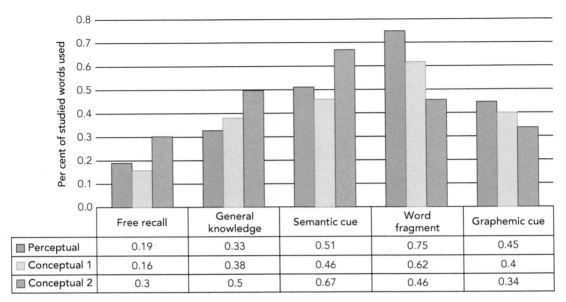

	Free recall	General knowledge	Semantic cue	Word fragment	Graphemic cue
Perceptual	0.19	0.33	0.51	0.75	0.45
Conceptual 1	0.16	0.38	0.46	0.62	0.4
Conceptual 2	0.3	0.5	0.67	0.46	0.34

Figure 5.3   The effect of level of processing on word use across different types of memory tests

The results from Blaxton (1989) show that performance on conceptual tests is highest when a word is studied in a conceptual context whereas performance on perceptual tests is highest when words are studied in a perceptual context. Blaxton (1989) argues that this result is consistent with a level-of-processing account of dissociations between explicit and implicit memory tasks and is inconsistent with a memory-systems view, which would predict more similar effects of study context across the three explicit tests (free recall, semantic-cued recall, and graphemic-cued recall) and implicit tests (general knowledge and word-fragment completion).

Source: Based on the results from Blaxton, 1989, p. 660

BOX
5.2

CASE STUDY

Implicit Memory without Explicit Memory

In a paper published in 2000, Antonio Damasio describes a patient named David whose left and right hemispheres were severely damaged by a virus. Damasio kept a record of people who visited David and whether those people had been kind to him. When Damasio asked David to recall people he had met recently, David was unable to do so. In addition, David was unable to recognize photographs of people he had met recently. However, when asked to identify photographs of people that David would ask for help if he needed it, David consistently chose people who had been kind to him, even though he had no idea who the people in the photographs he chose were. While David had no explicit memory of who had helped him, he clearly retained some implicit memory that he was able to use to complete the task.

The Neuroscience of Explicit and Implicit Memory

Explicit Memory

Mishkin (1982) proposed a neural circuit for explicit memory that involves the prefrontal cortex, the thalamus, temporal lobe structures including the hippocampus, and the entorhinal regions at the base of the forebrain (see Figure 5.4). When any of these areas is damaged, explicit memory disturbances can occur. Individuals with frontal lobe damage frequently have problems with short-term explicit memory. H.M. had surgery that lesioned his hippocampus and his temporal lobe, resulting in explicit memory loss. Chronic alcoholics often have a thiamine (vitamin B) deficiency that causes cell death in the thalamus and severe explicit memory loss known as Korsakoff syndrome. Alzheimer's disease, which is characterized by a loss of explicit memory, begins with the death of cells in the entorhinal region.

In Mishkin's model of explicit memory, there is an interactive flow of information throughout the brain. Individuals are consciously aware of explicit memories because all parts of the neural circuit for explicit memory eventually connect to the neocortex, which is the seat of conscious awareness. The temporal lobe is thought to be critical for forming long-term explicit memories and the prefrontal cortex is connected to working memory. Recall that H.M. had lesions in his hippocampus and surrounding medial temporal regions. Because H.M. was able to recall events from his childhood, but was unable to form new memories, researchers concluded that the medial temporal lobe and hippocampus were key to forming long-term memories but were not where long-term memories were actually stored. Explicit memory encoding is "top down"; concepts drive the reorganization of perceptual information. Processing begins in the cortex and this processing in turn affects how subsequent information is encoded. Take, for example, a person looking for the television remote. While searching, the person would only encode information about small objects and ignore larger ones, because the remote is a small

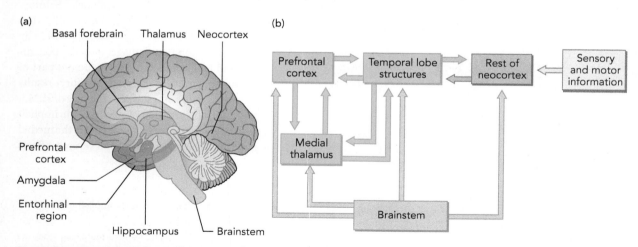

Figure 5.4 Neural circuit for explicit memory from Mishkin (1982)

The main components of this circuit are the prefrontal cortex, the thalamus, temporal lobe structures including the hippocampus, and the entorhinal regions at the base of the forebrain. If any of these areas is damaged, the individual will experience problems with explicit memory. Because the neocortex receives inputs from all parts of the circuit, explicit memories can become part of awareness.

Source: Adapted from Kolb, B., Whishaw, I., & Teskey, G.C. (2016). *An introduction to brain and behaviour*, 5e. MacMillan Publishing. p. 19

object. People play an active role in forming explicit memories and for this reason they create many cues that can be used for deliberate recall. The two-stage model of memory discussed in Chapter 4 can account for the consolidation of explicit memories.

The two main subtypes of explicit memory are *episodic memory* and *generic memory* (or knowledge). Episodic memory is discussed in detail in Chapter 6 and generic memory is discussed in detail in Chapter 7. The remainder of this chapter will focus on research relating to implicit memory.

Implicit Memory

Mortimer Mishkin and his colleagues proposed a neural circuit for implicit memory shown in Figure 5.5 (Mishkin, 1982). In this model, the basal ganglia in the midbrain is central to implicit memory. As can be seen in Figure 5.5, the basal ganglia receives inputs from the neocortex and dopamine-producing cells in the ventral tegmental area and substantia nigra nuclei in the brain stem. The basal ganglia then sends that information to the thalamus, which in turn sends information to the premotor cortex. Because dopamine is thought to be necessary for the normal functioning of the basal ganglia, dopamine is associated with implicit memory formation (Mishkin et al., 1997). Note that while the basal ganglia receive sensory and motor information from the neocortex, the neocortex does not receive information from the basal ganglia. Mishkin argues that this unidirectional arrangement explains why implicit memories do not enter consciousness: information must flow *to* the neocortex for an individual to become conscious of it, and implicit memories are not activated in the neocortex (see Figure 5.5).

Mishkin's model is supported by the observation that many people (such as J.K.) with Parkinson's disease, which impairs functioning in the basal ganglia, experience problems with implicit memory (Heindel, Salmon, Shults, Walicke, & Butters, 1989). Mishkin's model of implicit memory is also supported by the observation that damage to the hippocampus and temporal lobes (which are *not* part of the neural circuit for implicit memory) results in anterograde amnesia (as in the case of H.M.), but does not produce problems with implicit memory. Alzheimer's disease affects the medial temporal lobe of the cortex and severely affects

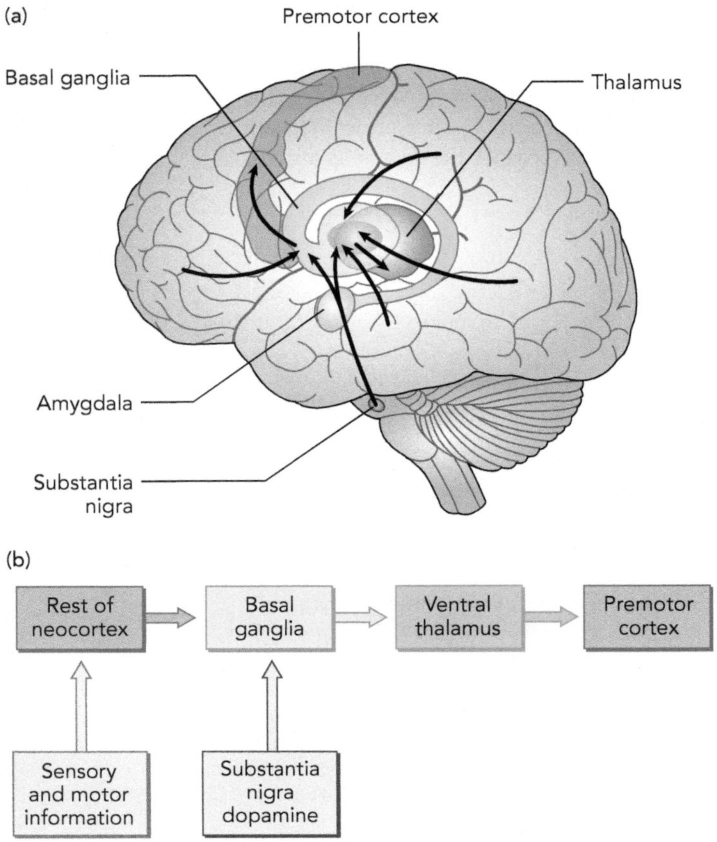

(a)

(b)

Figure 5.5 Neural circuit for implicit memory from Mishkin (1982)

In this circuit, information enters the circuit from the sensory and motor areas and dopamine-producing cells and is processed from the basal ganglia to the thalamus, which in turn sends information to the premotor cortex. Because this circuit is unidirectional and the neocortex is required for conscious experience, implicit memories remain outside of awareness.

Source: Adapted from Kolb et al., 2016, p. 20

explicit memory; however, many people with Alzheimer's disease retain implicit memory functioning, such as memory of how to swing a golf club, use household objects, and dress themselves.

Implicit information is encoded in much the same way it is perceived; information enters the system at the sensory receptors and then eventually makes its ways to cortical regions where it is identified. This type of process is referred to as "bottom up" because it begins with basic sensory signals and arrives at a percept. In order for a memory to be recalled, a probe must match an item stored in memory. Because implicit memories are encoded passively in a process that mimics perception, implicit memories are activated by perceptual information, as opposed to a person's desire to recall the information. Diekelmann and Born (2010) provide compelling evidence that the two-stage model of memory discussed in Chapter 4 applies to implicit memory and that slow-wave sleep (SWS) mechanisms are responsible for the consolidation of implicit memories.

Studying Implicit Memory

Researchers have devised many paradigms to study implicit memory, including the rotor-pursuit task, artificial grammars, pattern learning, and stem-completion tasks. Researchers also study implicit memory by studying language use, classical conditioning, and procedural memory.

DIY EXPERIMENT   **BOX 5.3**

Comparing Explicit and Implicit Memory for the Same Skill

Step 1: Use a computer and type the word *the* without looking at the keys.

Step 2: Without looking at an actual keyboard or moving your hands, attempt to locate where the letters T, H, and E are positioned on this image of a keyboard.

Step 3: Allow yourself to move your hands and attempt to locate T, H, and E on the keyboard diagram.

Alfonso de Tomas/Shutterstock

Chances are you found typing the word *the* very easy but had a hard time locating the T, H, and E without moving your hands, and easier when you were allowed to use your hands. This is because implicit memory is used for typing and thus the location of letters cannot easily be recalled with explicit instructions. It's easier to recall using implicit means, such as imaginary typing.

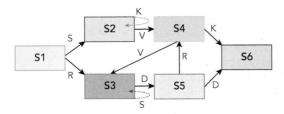

Figure 5.6   An example of an artificial grammar

A letter string is devised by randomly selecting an option at each juncture between S1 and S6. Circular arrows indicate steps that can be randomly selected to repeat. Possible strings include SKVK, RSDD, SKKVDD, RSSDRK.

artificial grammar

a set of rules governing how a string of letters can be combined

Artificial Grammars

In order to study how people use implicit memory, a researcher must devise a situation where participants gain knowledge without being explicitly aware of what that knowledge is. One such paradigm involves having participants learn **artificial grammars** without knowing they are doing so. An artificial grammar is simply a set of rules governing how a string of letters can be combined. An example of a possible artificial grammar is shown in Figure 5.6.

In 1967, as part of a study on artificial grammar, Arthur Reber created sentences using a grammar similar to the one shown in Figure 5.6 and also created letter strings of the same length using random selection. Participants were assigned to either learn and recall strings based on the artificial grammar (grammar group) or learn and recall random letter strings (control group). On each trial the participant was presented with a letter string for five seconds and then given a piece of paper on which to record the string (this study was conducted before computers were used to record data). Participants were not given any information about how the letters in the strings were selected. Participants were then given feedback on which letters they reported correctly. Reber (1967) found that while participants in the grammar group and the control group made a similar number of errors on the first few trials in the experiment, as the experiment progressed, participants in the grammar group recalled significantly more letters correctly than participants in the control group. This finding suggests that implicit knowledge of the artificial grammar was helping participants in the grammar group recall letter strings.

In a second experiment, Reber (1967) presented participants who had been exposed to an artificial grammar strings of letters that were either consistent or inconsistent with the grammar. Participants were able to identity the items that were consistent with the grammar even though they were unable to explicitly state what the grammatical rules were. The results of Reber (1967) suggest that complex information can be gleaned from patterns within stimuli without conscious effort and that patterns learned remain outside of an individual's awareness, lending support to the existence of a powerful implicit memory system that cannot be accessed explicitly.

Pattern-Learning Paradigms

pattern-learning paradigm

a paradigm in which participants must indicate the location of asterisks presented on a computer screen. Asterisks are presented very quickly to limit conscious processing of the stimuli.

The implicit **pattern-learning paradigm** is closely related to artificial grammars. In implicit pattern-learning paradigms, an asterisk (*) appears in one of four locations on a computer screen and the participant is instructed to press a key corresponding to the location as quickly and accurately as possible. Stimuli are presented very quickly so that the participant does not have time to consciously process a stimulus before the next stimulus is presented. For some participants, the location of the asterisk follows a consistent pattern that is repeated throughout a block of trials in the experiment (such as CBDABCDA), while participants in the control group are presented with asterisks at random. The results of implicit pattern-learning experiments consistently show a decrease in response times for participants in the pattern condition across trials, indicating that the participant has learned the pattern and can anticipate which stimulus is about to be presented (which speeds response time). Participants are not, however, able to explicitly describe the pattern that they have learned (see Stadler, 1995 for a review).

The implicit pattern-learning paradigm has been used to explore the role of attention in implicit learning. In 1987, Nissen and Bullemer included a divided-attention condition in an implicit pattern-learning task. In the divided-attention condition, participants responded to the location of the asterisk and then were presented with a high- or low-frequency tone. Participants were instructed to keep track of how many low-frequency tones had been presented; maintaining the tone count was intended to use some attentional resources. Nissen and Bullemer (1987) found that response times in divided-attention blocks were slower than in blocks that did not include the tone-counting task and concluded that this indicated that attention was involved in pattern learning. This result suggested that pattern learning involved some explicit processing, as only explicit processing involves attention.

Michael Stadler disagreed with Nissen and Bullemer's (1987) conclusion that the results from their experiment showed that attentional resources affect pattern learning in the implicit pattern-learning paradigm. Stadler speculated that the tone-counting task could have produced poor pattern learning because the task disrupted the participant's ability to recognize the pattern, not because the pattern-learning task required attention. Stadler noted that rather than being presented with the implicit pattern DCBACBDA (for example), participants in the divided-attention condition in Nissen and Bullemer's experiment were actually presented with something akin to "D," "tone task, add one to the count," "C," "tone task," "B," "tone task, add one to the count," "A," "tone task," "C," "tone task, add one to the count," and so on (again, this is just an example). Stadler argued that the tone task made the pattern unrecognizable and that performance suffered as a result. To test the hypothesis that Nissen and Bullemer's (1987) results occurred because of disrupted pattern organization and not because pattern learning requires attentional resources, Stadler (1995) devised an experiment with several conditions. In one condition, participants completed a typical implicit pattern-learning task with no other concurrent task, but the interval between the response to one asterisk and the presentation of the next asterisk was varied at random. Stadler speculated that this pause condition would disrupt the organization of the sequence without adding any additional attentional demands to the task. In a second condition, participants were presented with a list of seven letters before a block of several trials. Participants had to maintain the list and report it at the end of the trial block. Stadler argued that this task would introduce attentional demands but would not disrupt the organization of the pattern. In a third condition, Stadler replicated Nissen and Bullemer's tone-counting task; after each trial a tone was presented and participants had to keep track of how many times they heard a specific tone. Stadler (1995) argued that the tone-counting task would add attentional demands and would also disrupt pattern organization. In a final condition, a standard single-task implicit pattern-learning paradigm was used. Stadler also had four control conditions in which random asterisks were presented with a random pause between presentations, a memory load, a tone-counting task, or alone. Stadler argued that if organization problems produced the results in Nissen and Bullemer (1987), then response times would be most affected in the pause condition and the tone-counting condition of his experiment because these conditions impacted pattern organization. If Nissen and Bullemer (1987) were correct, on the other hand, then response times should be most affected in the memory load and the tone-counting conditions that involved attentional resources.

Stadler (1995) subtracted response times (RTs) for patterned blocks to those in the random condition for each of the four conditions in the experiment (see Figure 5.7). In Figure 5.7, a larger RT difference indicates more pattern learning. As is shown in Figure 5.7, Stadler found that the experimental manipulation affected pattern learning most in the random-pause condition and

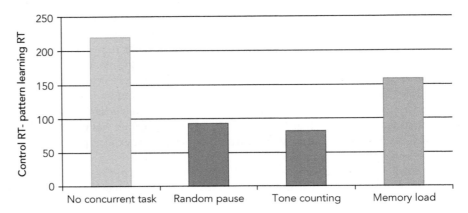

Figure 5.7   Results from Stadler (1995)

The difference in response times between the control and pattern-learning conditions across four concurrent task paradigms in Stadler (1995). A larger difference indicates more pattern learning. Pattern learning helped RTs the most with no concurrent task. Pattern learning was most affected by a random-pause condition and a tone condition and least affected by a condition that increased memory load. Stadler (1995) argues that because tasks that disrupt pattern organization affect pattern learning more than a task that demands attention, pattern learning is achieved with implicit memory.

Source: Adapted from Stadler, 1995, p. 674

the tone condition and affected pattern learning least in the memory-load condition. Stadler (1995) concluded that pattern organization is critical to the implicit pattern-learning task and that the results of Nissen and Bullemer (1987) likely reflected a disruption in pattern organization, rather than attentional resource involvement in this task. Stadler's (1995) results lend support to accounts of pattern learning that involve a memory system that is unconscious and automatic, lending empirical support to the extant definition of implicit memory.

The results from studies using artificial grammars and pattern-learning paradigms have demonstrated that complex pattern learning is achieved using implicit memory. The results converge with real-world evidence related to language learning and use. Not only do children acquire language without explicit instruction, but people who have acquired a language are able to detect grammatical errors without having explicit knowledge of the rule being violated. For example, a native English speaker can tell "Skaters in the park quickly pass us go" is not grammatically correct without being able to specify the rule that has been broken.

BOX 5.4

DIY EXPERIMENT

Read This!

Read the following words. The reason for doing so will become apparent later in the chapter.

RUFFIAN   KEROSENE   BOROUGH   APPROVAL   BACHELOR   HORIZON

Classical Conditioning

Early in the twentieth century, Ivan Pavlov noted that when a food reward was accompanied by a bell, dogs would learn to associate the bell with food and would eventually salivate when the bell was presented on its own. This type of learning is known as **classical condition**ing. Classical conditioning occurs when a **conditioned stimulus (CS)** (such as a bell) is paired repeatedly with an **unconditioned stimulus (US)** (such as food) that elicits an **unconditioned response (UR)** (such as salivation). Over time, the organism learns that the CS is a predictor of the US and the CS elicits the same response as the US, which is known as a **conditioned response (CR)**. For example, in a classical conditioning paradigm known as the eye-blink paradigm, the participant is presented with a neutral CS (usually a tone) followed by a gentle puff of air to the eye (the US), which causes the eye to blink (the UR). After a few trials the presentation of the tone (CS) alone causes the eye to blink (the CR). Conditioned responses are not under conscious control; the response is automatic and involuntary and classical conditioning is thus a form of implicit memory.

Research has found that classical conditioning is governed by the same neural mechanisms involved in other types of implicit learning. Classical conditioning is typically preserved in patients who have severe problems with explicit memory. Although H.M. could not explicitly recall events that occurred just a few minutes earlier, he displayed conditioned responses over the course of weeks. In one experiment a researcher administered a mild electric shock to H.M. when he shook his hand. H.M. responded to the shock by pulling his hand away. After a delay, the same researcher returned and extended his hand for H.M. to shake. Although H.M. did not recognize the researcher, and could not explicitly recall having his hand shocked, he refused to shake the researcher's hand. H.M. had been classically conditioned to avoid shaking hands with that researcher. This result is further evidence for the existence of an implicit memory system that is independent of the explicit memory system.

Because the main function of classical conditioning is to help an organism identify patterns in its environment, several pairings of a CS and a US are typically required for conditioning to occur. However, if a CS predicts a threat to survival, conditioning can occur after just one pairing. Most organisms will develop a conditioned taste aversion to a food item that is linked to illness after only one CS–US pairing. In addition, one terrifying incident (such as an accident, attack, or natural disaster) is often sufficient for a person to develop a phobia related to aspects of the event.

Classically conditioned associations are forgotten over time if the CS occurs frequently without the US. The process of forgetting conditioned responses is referred to as **extinction**. Extinction is adaptive; if a CS is not a good predictor of an US, then the CR may no longer be the appropriate response. For example, if an animal is threatened by another animal in a particular location, the animal may develop a conditioned fear response associated with that location and may either freeze or run away every time it is at that location. However, if the animal is at the location several times without being attacked by another animal, extinction will occur and it will no longer experience the fear response. This is adaptive because an animal acting in fear without the presence of a true threat is a waste of resources.

Two phenomena show that the extinction of a classically conditioned response does not mean that the association has been completely forgotten. The first is **spontaneous recovery**, which involves a weak CR to the CS long after the CS–CR association has been extinguished. Spontaneous recovery happens when an organism remembers the CS–CR association but forgets

classical conditioning
a learning process in which an innate response to a potent stimulus comes to be elicited in response to a previously neutral stimulus

conditioned stimulus (CS)
a previously neutral stimulus that, after becoming associated with the unconditioned stimulus, eventually comes to trigger a conditioned response

unconditioned stimulus (US)
a stimulus that produces an automatic response

unconditioned response (UR)
an automatic response to a stimulus

conditioned response (CR)
a response that is made as a result of classical conditioning

extinction
when the CS no longer elicits the CR

spontaneous recovery
a weak conditioned response that occurs when an organism remembers a CS–CR association but forgets that the association is no longer useful

RELEVANT RESEARCH

Using Implicit Memory to Prevent Conditioned Taste Aversion During Chemotherapy

Cancer treatments sometimes result in nausea and vomiting; cancer patients who undergo several courses of treatment often develop anticipatory nausea through classical conditioning. The hospital room becomes a conditioned stimulus that triggers the same feelings of nausea, even when no chemotherapy drugs have been given. There is no medical treatment for anticipatory nausea; however, it can cause significant distress in patients. Researchers have found that one way to combat anticipatory nausea is to use what is called an overshadowing technique. This approach involves

Cozine/Shutterstock

giving the patients a strongly flavoured (but harmless) drink before each session. The taste of the strong drink effectively overshadows perceptual processing of other aspects of the hospital environment and the conditioned stimulus for nausea becomes the strongly flavoured beverage instead of the hospital room. Anticipatory nausea can be avoided simply by presenting a different strongly flavoured drink during each chemotherapy session (Geiger & Wolfgram, 2013).

---

savings

when a CS–CR association is learned more quickly following the extinction of the same association

that the CS–CR association is no longer useful. If the CS–CR association were completely forgotten during extinction, spontaneous recovery would not occur. The second is **savings**, which involves faster learning of a CS–CR association following extinction of the same association. Savings implies that some aspect of the original memory remains intact after extinction. Both spontaneous recovery and savings are adaptive. Spontaneous recovery allows an organism to test to see if a previous response may be helpful in a new setting and savings helps expedite adaptation to new environments.

Individual preferences are largely a result of classical conditioning. When one is repeatedly exposed to a stimulus that is not harmful, one comes to prefer that stimulus over novel stimuli, a phenomenon known as the *mere exposure effect* (e.g., Zajonc, 2001). The **mere exposure effect** occurs when a previously neutral stimulus is paired with pleasant emotions over and over again; the neutral stimulus becomes a CS that evokes a CR of pleasant feelings. For example, seeing the same people in a favourite coffee shop several times a week can lead a person to feel positively about those people, even if they have never met. This is because the people (who are initially neutral stimuli) have been repeatedly paired with positive emotions associated with the coffee shop. The mere exposure effect can explain a wide variety of preference patterns, from why children become attached to familiar toys and blankets, to why university students rank the likeability of people they see often on campus (but do not know) higher than people they have not seen before. The mere exposure effect can also explain why people who review cars for a living always rank the make and model of their own car as preferable to all other cars they have test driven, even when newer car models have more comforts and features, and why fashion trends that seem

mere exposure effect

when a person comes to prefer stimuli merely because she or he has been exposed to the stimulus repeatedly

DIY EXPERIMENT

BOX
5.6

Eye-Blink Conditioning

For this experiment you will need a friend and something handheld that makes a clicking noise, like a stapler. Any electronic device that can make repeated sounds with the press of a single button will also work. The noise should not startle the other person.

moodboard/Getty Images Plus

Step 1: While holding the clicking device, sit directly opposite or beside your friend.
Step 2: Press the clicking device several times while observing your friend's eyes. Make sure your friend does not blink as a result of the clicking sound. If your friend blinks, the experiment will not work. (You can try a different device or a different friend.)
Step 3: Press the clicking device and then blow air gently toward your friend's eyes. Your friend should blink as a result of the puff of air.
Step 4: Repeat Step 3 ten times.
Step 5: Press the clicking device without blowing air and observe your friend. If your friend blinks, classical conditioning has occurred.
Step 6: To observe extinction, press the clicking device every 5 to 10 seconds until the blink response disappears.

great at the height of their popularity often baffle people 20 years later. Mere exposure effects are also responsible for people preferring the mirror image of their face to the perspective seen by other people; people are exposed to their mirror image more frequently. Mere exposure effects are also discussed in Chapter 10.

RELEVANT RESEARCH

BOX
5.7

The Link between Implicit Memory and the Impressionistic Canon

James Cutting of Cornell University suspected that mere exposure helps maintain artistic canons, or those works that a given culture holds in highest esteem. In 2003, Cutting tested this hypothesis using the canon of Impressionist paintings, which is comprised mainly of works formerly owned by an artist and art collector named Gustave Caillebotte, who donated his collection of 72 paintings by Paul Cézanne, Edgar Degas, Édouard Manet, Claude Monet, Camille Pissarro, Pierre-Auguste Renoir, and Alfred Sisley to the state of France after his death in 1894. Most of these paintings were hung in the Musée d'Orsay in Paris and have come to represent "the best" in Impressionism since that time. Cutting (2003) wondered if there was anything special about these paintings, or whether they were considered "the best" simply because they were reproduced more frequently in books as well as in souvenirs and prints. Cutting chose 64 of Caillebotte's paintings and matched each to another painting by the same artist, in the same general style and subject matter, and from the same general period. Cutting (2003) then determined the frequency with which each of the 132 appeared in 13 libraries on the campus of Cornell University. In a series of six experiments, Cutting assessed participants' recognition of each painting as well as whether they preferred the canonical painting or the matched control. Cutting's studies found that when adults viewed the images, the frequency with which an image appeared in print was correlated with preference for that image but not with recognition of that image. Thus preference for a painting could not be attributed to conscious recognition of a painting. When children viewed the images, however, frequency was not correlated with either recognition or preference. Cutting (2003) argues that frequency is correlated with preference because mere exposure to seeing the paintings more times makes the paintings more appealing. Cutting's (2003) argument is supported by the finding that children in his study did not show a frequency-based preference, suggesting that preference is built from experience and not to qualities innate to the Impressionist canon.

The results of Cutting (2003) suggest that implicit memory processes can significantly affect preferences.

Figure 5.8   Which painting do you prefer?

Above are two paintings by Pierre-Auguste Renoir used in Cutting (2003). On the left is *Madame Darras*; on the right is a painting known as *The Reader* (*La liseuse*). Both images are by the same artist and were painted around the same time. Both hang in the Musée d'Orsay in Paris. A similar small number of participants recognized each of these paintings; however, 80 per cent of adult participants preferred *The Reader* to *Madame Darras*. Cutting (2003) found *The Reader* to be represented in books about six times more frequently than *Madame Darras*. Cutting (2003) argues that findings like this suggest that art preference, and what is considered part of the Impressionist canon, is based largely on the effect of mere exposure.

DIY EXPERIMENT

BOX
5.8

Mere Exposure Part I

Step 1: List the letters of the alphabet on a piece of paper or in a document.
For example:

A

B

C

D

etc.

Step 2: List the digits 0 through 9 in a similar fashion.

Step 3: Rate each letter and number on a scale of 1 to 5, with 1 meaning you don't really like the letter/number and 5 meaning you really like the letter/number.

Step 4: Go to page 118 to interpret your results (in Box 5.9: Mere Exposure Part II).

Repetition Priming

Repetition priming occurs when previous exposure to a stimulus facilitates processing of that stimulus in some way. Repetition priming is thought to be the result of implicit memory mechanisms because it is observed across a wide variety of paradigms involving unintentional learning and indirect testing. The most widely used of these paradigms are word-stem completion (WSC) paradigms and word-fragment completion (WFC) paradigms.

repetition priming
when previous exposure to a stimulus facilitates processing in some way

Word-Stem Completion (WSC) Paradigms

Word-stem completion (WSC) paradigms have been used for decades to study the nature and extent of implicit memory mechanisms. When developing WSC experiments, researchers choose words that meet two criteria: first, the words must begin with three letters that could also be the first three letters of another word, and second, the word must not be the most common word that participants use to complete a word stem with those three letters. For example, researchers may choose the word STAKE for their study list because they know that when presented with the word stem STA___, most participants complete the word as STATE or STAY and not STAKE. After assembling a list of about 100 such words, the experimenter devises an incidental-learning task in which the participant performs some task related to the words without being explicitly instructed to remember them. For example, the researcher may have the participants rate each word based on its pleasantness, or indicate how many vowels are in the word. This is known as the incidental-learning phase. After a delay, participants

word-stem completion (WSC) paradigm
participants are presented with three letters and are asked to use the letters to complete a real word. The WSC can be used to assess implicit memory.

are presented with a list of word stems. Some of the stems will be the first three letters of words from the incidental-learning phase; these are known as the critical items. Researchers intentionally limit the number of stems that relate to the incidental-learning phase to help ensure that participants do not realize that they are participating in a memory experiment. A researcher can conclude that repetition priming has occurred if the participants complete the critical word stems with items from the incidental-learning phase at a higher rate than would be expected by chance alone. Because participants are not intentionally learning or recalling the words in the WSC paradigm experiments, evidence of repetition priming is attributed to implicit memory.

There have been thousands of published studies that have used the WSC paradigm. One well-replicated finding is that repetition priming is modality specific; seeing a picture of an object or hearing a word read aloud does not increase the rate at which that word is used for stem completion. This finding is consistent with the argument that neural circuit involved in implicit memory is perceptually driven, as the notion of a perceptually driven neural circuit predicts that only cues that match the perceptual features of the original stimulus will trigger implicit memory recall (Rajaram & Roediger, 1993). Repetition priming is found when people with profound amnesia participate in WSC experiments (Squire, Shimamura, & Graf, 1987), further supporting the argument that repetition priming results from implicit memory.

Word-Fragment Completion (WFC) Paradigms

word-fragment completion (WFC) paradigm

participants are presented with letters and blank spaces and are asked to fill in the blank spaces with letters to form a proper word. The WFC task is used to assess implicit memory.

Word-fragment completion (WFC) paradigms are similar to WSC paradigms in that experimenters have participants complete an incidental-learning activity involving a long list of words and then use an indirect test to see if participants use those words to complete the task at a higher rate than would be expected by chance. In WFC, researchers present a mix of letters and blanks together such as _Y S _ _R Y. Unlike with WSC, there is typically only one possible correct solution to the problems presented in WFC; for example, the fragment _ Y S T _ R Y can only be completed as the word MYSTERY. Individuals in control conditions are often unable to complete the word fragments. It is important that the word fragments be difficult to complete without prior exposure to the word so that researchers can be sure correct completions are the result of guessing. Try to solve the word fragments in Figure 5.9 before continuing.

Repetition priming is observed in the WFC; participants are more likely to complete the fragments if participants have seen the matching word recently. Unlike WSC effects, which last about two hours, WFC effects can last for more than a week. To demonstrate this try completing the words shown in Figure 5.10.

NO _ _ _ NE   _ E _ D _ L _ M   _ U _ R _ ET   _ E _ TUC _

Figure 5.9 Examples of word fragments from a typical word fragment task

Can you complete these word fragments? Chances are you found these difficult to complete. Difficult problems are presented in word-fragment completion experiments to ensure that participants who complete the words correctly are not simply guessing.

Source: Adapted from Tulving, Schacter, & Stark, 1982, p. 336

UFF A _   HO _ _ _ON   _ O _ _ UGH   K _ _ O _ _ NE

Figure 5.10 Examples of word fragments from a typical word fragment task

Can you complete these word fragments? If you've read this chapter carefully, then chances are you found most of them easy to complete because the correct solutions are all mentioned in the chapter. If you found them difficult, then it is likely that you didn't read Box 5.4 on page 110.

Source: Adapted from Tulving, Schacter, & Stark, 1982, p. 336

Repetition Priming and Nonverbal Stimuli

Not all repetition-priming experiments involve words. One nonverbal paradigm designed to study implicit memory was introduced by Gollin (1960). Gollin (1960) presented an image sequence in which a degraded object slowly became more complete as the image sequence progressed (see Figure 5.1 on p. 101). Participants were asked to indicate as soon as they recognized the object. Gollin (1960) found that participants were able to recognize familiar objects earlier in the image sequence; this was among the earliest experiments to exemplify implicit memory as learning was incidental and testing was indirect. Liu and Cooper (2001) presented participants with figures and had participants indicate whether the figure was possible (i.e., it could be built in three dimensions) or impossible (i.e., it could not be built in three dimensions). Later, participants were presented with some of the figures as well as new figures for 35 ms, which is too brief a presentation for conscious perception, and were asked to indicate whether they thought they saw a possible or impossible figure. Liu and Cooper (2001) found that participants were more likely to correctly identify a possible figure that they had seen before, while familiarity had no effect on the identification of impossible figures. Liu and Cooper (2001) suggest that their result shows that implicit memory includes an understanding of an object as a whole.

Lessons from Repetition Priming

Word-stem completion (WSC) and word-fragment completion (WFC) experiments show repetition-priming effects for different lengths of time. In a WSC task, priming effects last for about two hours, whereas in WFC tasks, priming effects can last for weeks. A critical question is which pattern best characterizes implicit memory. Participants usually complete word stems more quickly than word fragments, which has led some researchers, including Graf and Mandler (1984) and Squire et al. (1987) to argue that WSC is a better measure of implicit memory than WFC. Their logic is that word stems are completed too quickly to be influenced by explicit memory processes. These authors argue that it is thus best to characterize implicit memory based on data from WSC paradigm experiments, which show priming to last for two hours.

However, Suparna Rajaram and Henry Roediger wondered if WSC and WFC both reflect the same implicit memory process, but have different priming durations because the stimuli typically used in each paradigm are much different. In a typical WSC paradigm experiment, the words are high frequency and about 10 different words can be generated from each stem (e.g., STA _____ can be completed with *state, stay, stale, stall, stare, stamp, stallion*, etc.). In a typical WFC paradigm experiment, the words are very low frequency and the fragments can be used to generate one or two words (e.g., _R_E_D_H_P can only be completed as *friendship*). Because word frequency differs across typical WSC and WFC tasks (e.g., *state* has a higher frequency than *friendship*), Rajaram and Roediger (1993) suggested that word frequency

DIY EXPERIMENT

Mere Exposure Part II

Make sure you complete Box 5.8 Mere Exposure Part I on page 115 before you read the next part.

Step 1: After rating all the letters and numbers, circle your initials as well as the number associated with the month and day you were born (e.g., if you were born on July 23 circle 7, 2, and 3).

Step 2: Compare scores for your initials and dates associated with your birth to your other rankings. Most people prefer their initials and the numbers from their birthday over other letters and numbers because of mere exposure.

somehow creates shorter priming periods in WSC than WFC experiments. To test this hypothesis, Rajaram and Roediger (1993) used the same stimuli for both a WSC and a WFC task and looked at the duration of priming. The researchers found no difference in priming duration for each task and concluded that the difference in priming duration observed in other experiments is likely the result of the stimuli used, and not a characteristic of implicit memory per se. Rajaram and Roediger (1993) also found that performance on a variety of tests designed to test implicit memory, including WSC, WFC, degraded word identification, and anagram completion, were all similarly affected by whether the learning phase involved pictures or words, whether modality was the same during learning and test, and whether typeface was the same at learning and test. For all four implicit tasks tested, Rajaram and Roediger (1993) found priming to be greatest when a word was presented visually at learning and when typeface did not affect priming. The similarity in the results across all four tests of implicit memory led the researchers to conclude that a wide variety of implicit measures all utilize a single resource, implicit memory.

The Implicit-Association Test

One problem with studying many topics in social psychology is that individuals tend to choose responses that are socially acceptable even if those responses don't reflect their actual views. For example, if study participants are asked whether they agree with stereotypes about a particular group, participants will most likely say that they don't, not because they don't believe the stereotypes, but because they want to make the socially desirable response. One way to get around this problem is to use measures that tap implicit memory instead of explicit memory, because implicit memory is unconscious and automatic and is thus immune to social desirability effects. The best-known example of such a task is the implicit-association test (IAT) developed by Anthony Greenwald and his colleagues. The IAT is a computerized test in which participants categorize a word as quickly and accurately as possible by pressing one of two keys on a keyboard. In each experiment there are four categories of words and one key is used for two different categories. For example, an experiment may look at the stereotype that females are better at liberal arts and males are better at science. Participants are presented with words from each category (female, liberal arts, male, and science) and must press one of two keys depending on category membership. In stereotype-congruent blocks, one key would be used for both female words (like *aunt*) and liberal arts words (like *history*) and another key would be used for male words (like *uncle*) and science words (like *biology*). In stereotype-incongruent blocks, one key would be used for female and science words, and another key would be used for male and liberal arts words. The socially desirable response in the IAT is to have response times the same regardless of what the pairing of categories is. Differences in response times across conditions are argued to reflect true differences in the time it takes to process material in each condition. Researchers consistently find that participants are slower to categorize words when the categories grouped on one key conflict with widely held stereotypes than when the categories grouped on one key are consistent with widely held stereotypes, even among people who say they disagree with the stereotypes (Greenwald, McGhee, & Schwartz, 1998). These results are argued to reflect stubborn associations in implicit memory that develop through repeated exposure to stereotypes. For example, hearing that women dominate liberal arts while men dominate science over and over leads to implicit associations between females and liberal arts and males and science, even when a person has explicit knowledge that contradicts the stereotypes (like many male friends in liberal arts or many female friends in science). Results from the IAT also suggest that one way to combat stereotypes may be to repeatedly expose people to material that contradicts common stereotypes. For more information on the many ways that implicit memory is thought to influence social behaviour, see Chapter 10.

Negative-Priming Paradigm

Another paradigm that has been used to study implicit memory is known as the negative-priming paradigm. In a typical negative-priming experiment, the stimuli are two shapes of different colours such as red and green. Participants are instructed to attend to shapes of one colour (such as green) and ignore the shapes that appear in the other colour (such as red). On each trial, participants must indicate whether the shape presented in the to-be-attended-to colour presented on one side of the screen is the same or different as a white shape presented on the other side of the screen. On some trials, the to-be-attended-to-shape is a shape that was to-be-ignored on a previous trial. In these experiments, participants cannot recognize previously seen shapes using explicit tests of recognition but are typically slower at responding to previously ignored shapes than other shapes, a phenomenon known as **negative priming**. Figure 5.11 shows an example of two consecutive trials from a negative-priming experiment. Negative-priming paradigm experiments demonstrate that implicit memories for shapes are formed even when an individual is not attending to the stimulus. Negative-priming effects have been demonstrated for delays of up to one month, suggesting that these implicit memories are long-lasting (DeSchepper and Treisman, 1996).

negative priming
when response times are slowed for stimuli that have been ignored on previous trials

The Illusory-Truth Effect

In 1977, Lynn Hasher, David Goldstein, and Thomas Toppino found participants were more likely to rate a repeated statement as true than a new statement, a phenomenon labelled the **illusory-truth effect**. For example, if participants are asked to judge whether the statement "A giant oak tree can produce enough wood to create 300,000 pencils" is true or not, they will be more likely to indicate that it is true if they have seen it stated before. (In both cases, participants are unlikely to know how many pencils can be created from an oak tree.) Bacon (1979) tested whether the illusory-truth effect was the result of explicit or implicit memory for the previously

illusory-truth effect
when participants are more likely to rate a statement as being true when they have seen the statement before compared to when the statement is unfamiliar

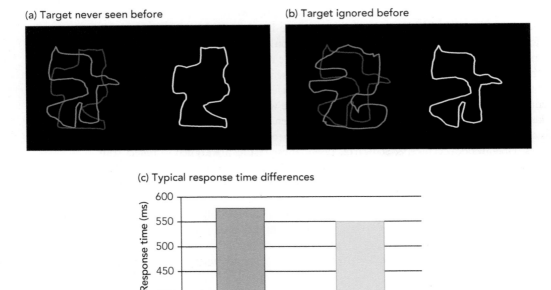

(a) Target never seen before   (b) Target ignored before

(c) Typical response time differences

Figure 5.11   Example of trial types in a negative-priming paradigm experiment

Participants must indicate whether the red shape matches the white shape (as in Figure 5.11.a). On some trials the shapes match; on other trials they do not. Participants are to ignore the green shape. On some trials, such as Figure 5.11.b, the target has been ignored on a previous trial. An example of negative priming is shown in Figure 5.11.c. Response times for same/different judgments are longer for previously ignored stimuli than novel stimuli. Negative priming is evidence that implicit memories are formed even when shapes are not attended to.

seen statement by telling participants that familiar statements were less likely to be true than unfamiliar statements. Bacon (1979) found that even when participants had explicit knowledge that familiar statements were unlikely to be true, truth ratings were still higher for familiar statements than unfamiliar ones, suggesting that implicit memory processes are fundamental to the illusory-truth effect.

Ian Begg and his colleagues at McMaster University also studied the contribution of explicit and implicit memory to the judgment of truth in a unique series of experiments. Begg, Anas, and Farinacci (1992) presented participants with statements read in a male or female voice. Participants were told ahead of time that the statements read by the female voice were true and the statements read by the male voice were false (or vice versa). Half of the statements were actually true and half were actually false, but because the statements were based on obscure facts, the participants were unlikely to know for certain whether a statement was true or false. After the statements had been read, participants were presented with new statements as well as previously presented statements that were true (familiar/true statements) and previously presented statements that were false (familiar/false statements) and asked to rate the truthfulness of each statement on a scale of one to seven. The experimenters wanted to see if previous explicit knowledge of truthfulness predicted truth ratings.

The results from this experiment are shown in Figure 5.12. Participants rated 45 per cent of unfamiliar statements as true. This result suggests that when participants have not seen

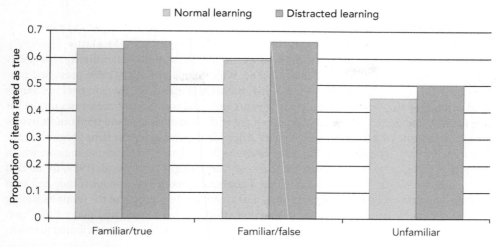

Figure 5.12   Results from Begg et al. (1992) showing the illusory-truth effect

Participants rated the truthfulness of familiar statements they had been told were true, familiar statements that they had been told were false, and unfamiliar statements. Participants were more likely to rate a familiar/false statement as true than they were to rate an unfamiliar statement as true, showing an illusory-truth effect. Further, the illusory-truth effect was observed even when participants were distracted during learning, suggesting that implicit, not explicit, processes generate the effect.

Source: Based on the results from Begg et al., 1992

a statement before, they simply guess about its truthfulness. Participants rated 63 per cent of familiar/true as true; however, this finding alone doesn't indicate which memory process contributes to ratings of truthfulness, as participants could be using either source recollection or familiarity as a basis for this truth rating. The critical finding was that participants rated 59 per cent of familiar/false statements as true. Participants could not have been using explicit memory when making these truth judgments; if they were, then very few familiar/false statements would be rated as true. Begg et al. (1992) computed the relative influence of explicit recollection and implicit familiarity in the truth judgments of their experiment and concluded that, while about 4 per cent of truth judgments were based on explicit knowledge of the truthfulness of a statement, about 63 per cent of judgments were based on implicit familiarity. The researchers concluded that simply having an implicit memory for an item results in that item being deemed true, and that implicit memory plays a greater role in truth judgments than explicit memory.

In a second experiment, Begg et al. (1992) had participants complete an arithmetic task while listening to the statements for the first time. Begg et al. (1992) argued that the arithmetic task would disrupt explicit but not implicit memory processes. Begg et al. (1992) found that when participants were distracted during the learning, there was no difference in the truthfulness ratings for familiar/true and familiar/false statements. Participants rated more familiar/true and familiar/false statements as true than new statements as true. This finding further confirms the suggestion that the illusory-truth effect results from implicit and not explicit memory processes.

The False-Fame Effect

In another type of experiment, Larry Jacoby and his colleagues at McMaster University demonstrated that implicit memory can produce an influential sense of familiarity that exerts its effect outside of conscious awareness. Jacoby, Woloshyn, and Kelley (1989) presented participants with a list of 40 nonfamous unfamiliar names and instructed them to read the names aloud. After they had read the names, participants were told that none of the names on the list were famous, and participants were then presented with a list of famous and nonfamous names and had to indicate which names were famous. After participants made the fame judgment, they were shown a final list including the names from the first list and were asked to indicate which names they recognized as being from that first list. Surprisingly, Jacoby et al. (1989) found that participants were more likely to indicate that a nonfamous name was famous if they had seen it before, and this effect occurred even when participants didn't recognize the name as having been on the study list. This so-called **false-fame effect** has been replicated many times and, because it shows the influence of familiarity outside of awareness, has been attributed to mechanisms related to implicit memory.

false-fame effect

participants being more likely to rate a nonfamous name as famous when they have seen the name before compared to when the name is unfamiliar

Implicit Memory and Anaesthesia

In the early 1950s, an anaesthesiologist named Bernie Levinson was concerned that his patients were able to hear negative remarks made by doctors while they were undergoing surgery. Levinson decided to test his hypothesis using an experiment that would be considered unethical by today's standards. While administering anaesthesia to 10 dental patients who were not experiencing any crisis, Levinson shouted, "Stop the operation! I don't like the patient's colour! His/her lips are turning blue. I'm going to give a little oxygen." One minute later Levinson spoke again, this time saying, "OK, everything is fine now." One month later Levinson interviewed the patients and claimed that none could explicitly recall any events from the operation, but that, once hypnotized by Levinson himself, four were able to recall, word for word, what Levinson had said during the fictitious crisis (Levinson, 1965). Levinson's research was not a true experiment because there was no control group, and in addition, Levinson (1965) offers only scant details about the hypnosis manipulation; nevertheless, his findings sparked a flurry of research investigating memory under anaesthesia (Wang, 2010).

For 30 years researchers claimed to have found evidence for both explicit and implicit learning under anaesthesia (see Merikle & Daneman, 1996, for a review); however, these studies did not objectively measure level of consciousness during anaesthesia, and there is now substantial evidence that many people who participated in these studies may have been conscious for part or all of their procedure. Until the 1990s, the most common type of anaesthesia was a mixture of benzodiazepines, nitrous oxide, and opioids. Some researchers were concerned that participants receiving this type of anaesthesia were experiencing pain or consciousness during medical procedures and set out to assess the problem. Doctors Michael Wang and Ian Russell developed the isolated forearm technique (IFT), which uses a tourniquet (that cuts off circulation) to prevent muscle relaxants from affecting one of the patients' hands during surgery. When the IFT paradigm is used, patients can use their hand to respond to questions during surgery if they are conscious. Research using the IFT technique has revealed that when given benzodiazepines, nitrous oxide, and opioids during surgery, many patients are able to respond to questions using their hands (indicating they are conscious) although they have no explicit memory of the procedure, or the questions, afterward because this particular form of anaesthesia has an amnesic effect. This finding suggests that research involving the use of benzodiazepines, nitrous oxide, and opioids cannot be used as evidence that memories could be formed while a person is unconscious simply because there is substantial evidence that this type of anaesthesia does not render every patient unconscious. The findings from IFT studies must be interpreted with some caution, however, as IFT can be implemented for only very brief periods of time to avoid brain damage.

In the 1990s, anaesthesiologists began to use volatile agents, such as propofol, as anaesthetics. When the IFT is used on patients anaesthetized with volatile agents, they cannot respond using their hands, indicating that patients are not conscious when receiving this type of anaesthesia. There have been no studies where patients have shown no conscious processing during anaesthesia but have later completed free recall, word stems, or priming tasks in a way that would indicate that they formed memories during the procedure (see Russell and Wang, 1997). Thus, implicit and explicit memories may be formed during anaesthesia, but only when that anaesthesia leaves the patient conscious.

One recent finding of note relates to emotional memories. Both Wang, Russell, and Logan (2004) and Wang, Russell, and Nicholson (2004) found that patients who showed signs of consciousness during surgery were more likely to exhibit signs of anxiety at follow-up appointments. Both studies suggest that this is because the patients developed implicit memories about emotional states experienced during the operation and these emotional states continue to trouble the patient long after. Because patients have no explicit memory of their operation, or the anxiety they felt, they can't pinpoint the source of anxiety.

Procedural Memory

Procedural memory is memory for how to do things. Procedural memories are fundamentally implicit; they are formed outside of awareness. Although you may be able to describe what you are doing when performing a procedure that you have learned, the implicit nature of memory for performing actions means the details are outside of conscious awareness. Consider climbing the stairs. You may say "To climb stairs I lift my left leg and place it on a stair and then lift my right leg and place it on the next stair" because you are aware of doing this as you climb stairs. However, this would be a gross oversimplification of the stair-climbing process. Stair climbing is actually a very complex skill that takes a great deal of practice to master. Engineers tasked with programming robots to use stairs have met a huge challenge; a specific and constantly changing body posture is needed to shift weight from one step to the next, even when a handrail is being used. As an individual attempts a movement, feedback from the body's senses are stored using the implicit memory system. The only way to access this type of implicit memory is to perform the action and have your brain record this feedback; explicit knowledge of the task is not a big help. You may be able to identify thousands of discrete movements needed to climb stairs (or perform a high dive, or perform a dance move), but unless you have practised, and encoded that perceptual information related to completing the task correctly, you will not be able to put those movements together and perform the task.

Richard Masters suspected that using explicit knowledge while performing a well-practised task could harm performance and might be responsible for many athletes "choking" under pressure. To test the notion that explicit knowledge can harm task performance under stress, Masters trained participants on a golf putting task. Participants were either provided with the rules (explicit group) or not provided with the rules (implicit group). At one point during the

procedural memory
a type of long-term memory comprised of knowledge of how to perform actions

experiment, participants were told that their subsequent putting performance would affect their compensation for participation; if they putted well, they would receive more money than expected; if they putted poorly, they would not receive any compensation at all. Masters (1992) found a decrease in performance for participants in the explicit group, but no effect of stress on participants in the implicit group. What's more, Masters (1992) found that if participants in the explicit group were distracted by a second task during learning, they were less likely to develop explicit strategies for putting the golf ball and performed better than non-distracted participants from the explicit group during stressful trials. The results of Masters (1992) suggest that stress can lead people to refer to explicitly known aspects of task performance, which can decrease their ability to perform the task as practised.

DIY EXPERIMENT

BOX 5.10

Test Your Procedural Memory

To experience the extent to which implicit knowledge guides your performance of procedures, try using a keyboard or cell phone that is different than the one you use most of the time. You will likely find it very difficult to type, but if you spend a few hours on the new device you will adapt to it. While experience on one type of keyboard affords you with knowledge of where different keys are located, and that knowledge can transfer from one keyboard to another, implicit aspects of the task, such as how much pressure is needed to type a letter, how high you must lift your hand in order to move it to another part of the keyboard, and the distance between the keys all involve implicit knowledge that can only be gained through practice.

CHAPTER REVIEW

- There are two main memory systems in the brain, implicit memory and explicit memory. Implicit and explicit memory evolved separately. Implicit memory operates outside of conscious awareness while explicit memory operates within conscious awareness.
- Individuals with anterograde amnesia have problems with explicit memory but retain the ability to use implicit memory. This observation supports the notion that explicit and implicit memory are distinct within the brain.
- Proponents of the processing account argue that it is the match between processing at the time of study and the time of test, and not separate memory systems, that produces dissociations in performance on explicit and implicit tests of memory.
- Mortimer Mishkin proposed that implicit and explicit memory involve different neural circuits. The neural circuit involved in implicit memory takes information in the neocortex and passes it through the

basal ganglia and ventral thalamus, eventually storing it in the premotor cortex. Damage to the basal ganglia, ventral thalamus, or premotor cortex will result in problems with implicit memory. Because the implicit memory circuit is unidirectional and does not send information back to the neocortex during retrieval, implicit memory resides outside of conscious awareness.

- The neural circuit involved in explicit memory is multidirectional and involves the prefrontal cortex, the thalamus, temporal lobe structures, and entorhinal areas at the base of the forebrain. Damage to any of these areas will result in problems with explicit memory. Because information within the explicit memory system can always be accessed by the neocortex, this information is within conscious awareness.

- Artificial grammars involve combining letters using a fixed set of rules and presenting those letters to participants. After being exposed to many examples of letter patterns that follow the grammar, participants are able to perform tasks that indicate they have learned the grammar even though they cannot explicitly state the grammatical rules. This suggests that language rules may be learned through implicit memory mechanisms.

- Pattern-learning paradigms replicate the findings of artificial grammars using patterns of dots in different areas of a computer screen. These paradigms reveal that participants are able to learn complex patterns simply by being exposed to them repeatedly. This learning is outside of awareness and is an example of implicit memory.

- Pattern-learning paradigm experiments conducted by Stadler (1995) demonstrated that attention is not required for implicit pattern learning, supporting the claim that implicit memory is independent of conscious awareness.

- Classical conditioning involves implicit memory.

- Implicit memory produces the mere exposure effect, which is a preference for things that an individual has seen before. The mere exposure effect can explain, for example, why people prefer famous paintings to paintings that are not famous.

- Repetition priming occurs when processing of a stimulus is facilitated by recent exposure to an identical stimulus. Repetition priming is studied using the word-stem completion (WSC) and word-fragment completion (WFC) paradigms. Both WSC and WFC have been shown to involve implicit memory.

- The study of stereotypes is hampered by participants' desire to make socially desirable responses. The implicit-association test (IAT) was designed to get around this problem. The IAT is a computerized test in which participants categorize a word as quickly and accurately as possible by pressing one of two keys on a keyboard. Faster responding when the words are grouped in ways that are congruent with stereotypes than when they are grouped in ways that are incongruent with stereotypes indicates implicit stereotypes. Results from the IAT also suggest that one way to combat stereotypes may be to repeatedly expose people to material that contradicts common stereotypes.

- In negative-priming experiments, researchers present participants with random shapes of different colours. The participant must ignore one of the shapes and decide if the other shape matches a sample shape on another part of the screen. Negative priming occurs when participants are slower to match a previously ignored stimulus than a stimulus that they have not seen before. Negative priming suggests that participants form implicit memories even when they are not attending to stimuli.

- The illusory-truth effect occurs when an individual is more likely to believe a statement is true because of having seen the statement before. The illusory-truth effect is observed even when participants are told that statements are actually false. Because the illusory-truth effect involves individuals ignoring explicit information about the truthfulness of statements, it can be said to be the result of implicit memory mechanisms.

- The false-fame effect occurs when participants rate familiar names as more famous than unfamiliar names even when people do not explicitly remember having seen the familiar names before. Because the false-fame effect occurs outside of awareness, it is attributed to implicit memory.
- Early research indicated that patients could form memories while under anaesthesia; however, more recent research suggests that these results likely occurred because patients were partially conscious during their procedures and not because it is possible to form memories while unconscious.
- Procedural memories are memories of how to do things and are fundamentally implicit; it is not possible to be consciously aware of how one rides a bicycle or climbs stairs. Research suggests that explicit instructions on how to perform a procedural task (like putting a golf ball) can actually decrease task performance.

MEMORY ACTIVITY

Using the Link Method to Memorize a Neural Circuit

The link method involves creating a story where the first letter of each word corresponds to the first letter of an item on the to-be-remembered list. The link method is an effective way to learn things in a prescribed order, so in this Memory Activity we will use the method to learn the neural circuits for implicit and explicit memory.

The neural circuit involved in implicit memory goes from the neocortex to the basal ganglia to the ventral thalamus to the premotor cortex. To use the link method to learn the neural circuit for implicit memory we first identify the four locations on the circuit:

    neocortex
    basal ganglia
    ventral thalamus
    premotor cortex

Next we need to develop a sentence with words starting with N, B, V, and P in that order such as "Now believe verbal primes." To see if the mnemonic is effective, test yourself on it frequently after developing it.

Finally, the circuit for explicit memory involves the prefrontal cortex, the temporal lobe, the medial thalamus, the hippocampus, and the entorhinal region at the base of the forebrain. Note the first letter for each of these locations and generate a link sentence that is easy to distinguish from the one you created for the implicit circuit.

Questions

1. Explain the link between consciousness, explicit memory, and implicit memory.
2. Suppose Patient M has anterograde amnesia. What types of memory tasks will Patient M do well, and what types of tasks will Patient M have difficulty with? Explain how the pattern of deficits is linked to explicit and implicit memory.

3. Using Mishkin's model as a reference, explain why implicit memories remain outside of awareness.
4. What is an artificial grammar? Why are artificial grammars a good method for studying implicit memory?
5. What aspect of classical conditioning suggests that this type of learning involves implicit memory?
6. Explain how implicit memory may play a role in people's choice of a particular laundry detergent.
7. Describe a typical experiment using word-stem completion. What aspects of the experiment lead researchers to argue that the task involves implicit memory?
8. Why might a researcher use an implicit memory task to study a topic such as stereotypes?
9. Explain how the illusory-truth effect may lend credence to the claim that "There is no such thing as bad publicity."
10. Anna has been experiencing anxiety and fear of her dentist ever since she had her wisdom teeth removed. During the procedure she was anaesthetized with benzodiazepines and nitrous oxide. She has no recollection of anything negative happening during the procedure and can't understand why she feels this fear. Explain what may be causing Anna's anxiety using what you know about the effects of anaesthesia on different types of memory.
11. Discuss the experiment that examined the influence of explicit instructions on a golf putting task.

Key Figures

Ian Begg p. 120
Teresa Blaxton p. 102
Francis Crick p. 100
James Cutting p. 113
Anthony Greenwald p. 118
Lynn Hasher p. 119
Larry Jacoby p. 122

Christof Koch p. 100
Bernie Levinson p. 122
Richard Masters p. 123
Mortimer Mishkin p. 106
Suparna Rajaram p. 117
Arthur Reber p. 108
Henry Roediger p. 117

Ian Russell p. 122
Michael Stadler p. 109
Michael Wang p. 122
Elizabeth Warrington p. 100
Lawrence Weiskrantz p. 100

6 Episodic Memory and Autobiographical Memory

LEARNING OBJECTIVES

Having read this chapter, you will be able to:

- Describe the characteristics of episodic memory.
- Differentiate between knowing and remembering.
- Explain how episodic memories are formed.
- Explain how state-dependent memory is connected to episodic memory.
- Differentiate between episodic memory and autobiographical memory.
- Discuss phenomena associated with autobiographical memory, including the reminiscence bump and nostalgia.
- Describe how cognitive bias can influence autobiographical memory.
- Define a flashbulb memory.
- Discuss unique attributes of flashbulb memories as well as attributes that are common to other episodic memories.
- Discuss the neuroscience of autobiographical memory.

EXTREME EPISODIC MEMORY: HYPERTHYMESIA

Marilu Henner (b. 1952) is a well-known actress and dancer who has starred in television and movies since the 1970s. In 2010, Henner revealed in an interview on *60 Minutes* that she has **hyperthymesia** and is able to remember, in detail, each day of her life, going back decades. This is an example of superior **episodic memory** or memory for personal events. To show the interviewer at *60 Minutes* just how detailed her memory is, Henner took them through her shoe closet and picked up different pairs of shoes and told the reporter when she got them, when she first wore them, and what day of the week it was. For example, she explained, "I first wore these shoes on October the 7th, 2007. These I wore on April the 21st of this year; it was Tuesday; and these I got in 1982, April 9th. It was a Friday." The next day

© Carrienelson1 | Dreamstime.com

Henner was interviewed on *The Early Show* and, during the interview, described the process of recalling these events using the analogy of a DVD with the "select a scene" feature on. Henner explains that when she recalls a year, for example, she "sees" each of the days of the year mapped out in a sequence and she is able to access whichever day she chooses. The interviewer asked Henner to talk about 1975, a year she has chosen at random. The first thing that Henner recalls is that her birthday was on Sunday, April 6, that Christmas was on a Thursday, and that Thanksgiving was on November 27. As she thinks more about the year, more details are filled in. She recalls a first date with a new boyfriend on August 12 and rehearsals for her first Broadway show. Henner tells an interviewer that the experience is like time travel. While she is explaining this experience she recalls what outfit she wore on that first date (which was a Tuesday), Henner explains that while she remembers exciting first dates and Broadway rehearsals, she also remembers mundane details. Her autobiographical memory is highly accurate for all events in her life. Hyperthymesia is an extremely rare condition that was first identified in 2006. Experts on the subject have only identified 25 people who are truly able to recall their lives day by day. Six of the people with hyperthymesia have been studied in depth by researchers and they all report vivid visual memories. Because people with hyperthymesia show typical patterns of recall for generic memories (like facts), this suggests that episodic memory is somehow distinct from other types of long-term memory. In this chapter, we will explore what makes episodic memory different from generic memory and attempt to explain exactly what causes hyperthymesia.

episodic memory

a type of long-term memory comprised of memories of specific situations, experiences, or events

hyperthymesia

a rare condition in which a person has exceptionally accurate episodic memory for events of personal relevance

Episodic memories are accompanied by a sense of remembering, while generic memories are not.

What Is Episodic Memory?

Episodic memory is the retrieval of personally experienced events accompanied by the feeling of *remembering*. For example, your memory of eating your breakfast this morning is an episodic memory. According to Endel Tulving, who coined the term *episodic memory* in 1972, episodic memories have three distinct features that make them different from generic memories. According to Tulving (1972), features of episodic memory include

- a subjective sense of time
- a connection to the self
- the presence of autonoetic consciousness

When one recalls an episodic memory, one recalls a feeling that the event took place at a certain point in time. When one recalls an episodic memory, one connects oneself to the event either as a viewer or as a participant. Finally, being conscious of one's conscious experiences in another point of time reflects **autonoetic consciousness** (Hassabis & Maguire, 2007). **Generic memory** (sometimes called semantic memory) is memory that is not connected to a specific point in time; generic memory is associated with a sense of *knowing*. For example, remembering the nickname of a one-dollar coin in Canada is a generic memory because the term *loonie* won't be associated with a specific experience. (Generic memory is discussed in Chapter 7.) Martin Conway expanded on Tulving's ideas and defined a total of nine characteristics of episodic memory (2009).

autonoetic consciousness

the ability for one to imagine oneself in past, future, or counterfactual situations

generic memory

memory for facts, concepts, and meanings that is context free and not associated with a particular point in time

Episodic memory:
- contains summary records of sensory-perceptual-conceptual-affective processing
- retains patterns of activation/inhibition in the form of (visual) images
- is often represented in the form of (visual) images
- always has a perspective (field or observer)
- represents short time slices of experience
- is represented on a temporal dimension roughly in order of occurrence
- is subject to rapid forgetting
- makes autobiographical remembering specific
- is recollectively experienced when accessed

Tulving's and Conway's ideas taken together describe episodic memory as a type of memory in which the rememberer recalls the sensations experienced during an event, a sense of the event happening across time, and a sense of witnessing the event first hand. Episodic memory is an example of **explicit memory**.

explicit memory

a memory that an individual can bring into conscious awareness

The most important difference between episodic memory and generic memory is that episodic memories are accompanied by a *sense of remembering* and feeling that does not accompany the retrieval of generic memories. When you recall an episodic memory, such as what you did on your last birthday, you will have a *sense of remembering* the celebration; however, when you recall a generic memory such as the year in which Canada was confederated, you will have a sense of knowing "1867" but likely not a sense remembering when you learned that fact. Episodic and generic memories are distinguished not so much by their content but by the experience the individual has when recalling the information. This feeling of remembering is separate from the memories themselves and occasionally occurs when retrieval has not taken place; when it does we experience déjà vu (Widner, Otani, & Winkelman, 2005). In this chapter, you will explore not only how episodic and autobiographical memories may be formed and remembered over time, but also how these memories provide contextual cues that can aid in the retrieval of factual information.

The Neuroscience of Episodic Memory

Episodic memories are formed in the hippocampus. György Buzsáki argues that a number of characteristics of the hippocampus appear to have evolved to quickly code arbitrary associations between experiences. First, cells in the CA3 layer of the hippocampus (shown in Figure 6.1) have very long axons that can be up to 440 mm in length (that's 4.4 cm!). Each of these axons synapses with between 25,000 and 50,000 other neurons. Thus the CA3 layer of the hippocampus is packed with connections and well equipped for the rapid formation of episodic memories posited by the complementation learning systems models (Buzsáki, 2006). The scientific literature suggests a number of hypotheses as to how the hippocampus records episodes. John Lisman argues that the hippocampus contains two recurrent neural circuits that are needed for representing the two main components of every episodic memory: the sequence in which events occurred and the context in which those events took place. The sequence of events is coded in the CA3 and CA1 regions of the hippocampus, which are densely packed with neurons that have NMDA receptors. NMDA receptors strengthen the synapse between neurons associated with one event and neurons associated with the next event. Thus, NMDA receptor neurons in the hippocampus record the temporal order of events, always creating synapses that lead from earlier events to later events, but not the reverse. This feature allows for the development of accurate episodic memories (Lisman, 1999). (For more on NMDA receptors, see Chapter 4.) According to Lisman (1999), the context of an event is coded by the EC to CA3 pathway of the hippocampus. The neurons that represent the first aspect of the context (such as the location) depolarize CA3 neurons at subthreshold level. Next, the subset of these CA3 neurons, that also receive input from the DG representing other aspects of the context (such as a specific event occurring), would be depolarized to their firing level and this pattern of activity would come to represent the context. This would be repeated for other contextual information. In the end, both the sequence of the events and the context are encoded by the hippocampus, creating an episodic memory. Because both temporal order and context are coded for each event, the individual can distinguish among discrete experiences. The individual may use multiple episodic memories of similar events to detect patterns (e.g., the individual may recall the reactions of people to attempts to hug them as a greeting and determine that, in general, strangers don't react well to hugs). This general information extracted from analyzing an episodic memory is referred to as a generic memory (Lisman, 1999). It should be noted that Lisman's (1999) theory is just one possible account of how the hippocampus codes episodic memories.

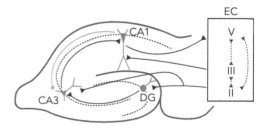

Figure 6.1   Basic circuit of the hippocampus

Source: Adapted from https://www.researchgate.net/figure/
Circuit-Schematic-representation-of-the-hippocampus-circuit-The-
connectivity-between_fig1_315901007

The prefrontal cortex is also essential for the formation of cohesive episodic memories; damage to the prefrontal cortex results in somewhat disorganized memories where the individual may be able to learn new information but is unable to link that learning to a specific episode (Janowsky, Shimamura, & Squire, 1989). Episodic memories rely on the neural circuit for explicit memory (Mishkin, 1982) that is described in detail in Chapter 5. The two-stage model of memory described in Chapter 4 provides one account of how episodic memories are consolidated.

cue-driven principle

a principle of memory that states that all memories are retrieved through cues

environmental cues

cues in the external world such as people, places, or things

Retrieving Episodic Memories

All memories are accessed the same way: a cue probes memory and if a match is found a memory is retrieved. This is known as the **cue-driven principle** (Surprenant & Neath, 2013). The cue used to probe memory will determine what memory is retrieved. Episodic memories are retrieved when the cue probing memory activates episodic information, often because the cue specifies some sort of contextual information such as a specific place, event, or experience. For example, when a person drives down a street in their old neighbourhood, the surroundings serve as a cue that probes memory and the person may become aware of a variety of episodic memories linked to that street.

Episodic memories are triggered by cues. Some cues are very common. Chances are you can retrieve an episodic memory associated with the picture above (although each person's memory will be different).

Two different types of contextual cues can probe for episodic memories. These are referred to as **environmental cues** and **internal cues**. Environmental cues include the physical surroundings that a person was in when an event occurred and internal cues include the mood and physiological state of the person at the time

---

DIY EXPERIMENT   **BOX 6.1**

The Role of Cues in Episodic Memory Retrieval Part I

Read the following dates and try to recall what you were doing on that day:

February 1, 2003
June 25, 2009
December 14, 2012
November 13, 2015
February 14, 2018
April 6, 2018
April 23, 2018

When you have finished, look for Box 6.8 on page 144.

of learning. Environmental cues give rise to a phenomenon known as **encoding/retrieval specificity** effects (such as remembering more items for a test when the test is taken in the study location than in another location) and internal memory cues give rise to **state-dependent memory effects** (such as being more likely to remember happy memories when in a good mood). In both cases matching contexts lead to improved episodic memory recall.

Encoding/Retrieval Specificity

One of the most widely studied phenomena related to episodic memory is known as **encoding/retrieval specificity**, the finding that memory performance is best when the context at the time of retrieval matches the context at the time of learning. The encoding/retrieval specificity effect was introduced as the *encoding-specificity principle* by Endel Tulving and Donald Thomson in 1973; however, because context at the time of retrieval is of critical importance to the phenomenon, *encoding/retrieval specificity* is a better descriptor (Nairne, 2002). In their experiments, Tulving and Thomson varied the context for target words at encoding and recall. For example, the word COLD could be learned either with a strong cue like "hot" or with a weak cue like "ground" (presented as "hot–COLD" or "ground–COLD" respectively). Each participant saw only one cue for each target word. Participants then needed to recall words from the list, which is an episodic memory task (because they must recall the learning episode to perform the task properly). Participants were provided with either a cue they had seen during encoding (same context) or the other cue (different context). For example, a participant who saw "hot–COLD" would see either "hot–_____" or "ground–_____." Tulving and Thomson observed better recall for congruent cues even in the weak cue condition. This was interesting because it showed that the semantic similarity between the cue and the target was not more important than the congruency of context between learning and test in a task involving episodic memory.

Many dramatic examples of encoding/retrieval specificity have been generated using a variety of experimental designs. In one well-known example, Duncan Godden and Alan Baddeley had participants learn a list of 36 words either on land or under water while scuba diving and then presented participants with 72 words either on land or while scuba diving and asked them to indicate whether each word was on the to-be-remembered list or not. Godden and Baddeley (1975) found that when the encoding and retrieval context was the same, either land–land or water–water, memory was better compared to when the context changed (land–water or water–land). This experimental result has since been used as evidence that contextual cues help memory; indeed, the results from Godden and Baddeley lend strong support to the cue-driven principle proposed by Surprenant and Neath (2013). The cue-driven principle states that in all situations the act of remembering begins with a cue, which initiates retrieval (Surprenant & Neath, 2013). The cue-driven principle is supported by the fact that when context could serve as a cue, more items were retrieved.

internal cues

cues that come from within a person, such as thoughts or other memories

encoding/retrieval specificity effects

an experimental finding in which similarity between conditions at encoding and retrieval predicts greater probability of memory retrieval

state-dependent memory effects

an experimental finding in which congruence between mood at the time of encoding and mood at the time of retrieval predicts a greater probability of memory retrieval

mihtiander/Thinkstock

Godden and Baddeley (1975) presented words to people on land or scuba diving and then tested their memory for the words either on land or scuba diving. Godden and Baddeley (1975) found that performance was best when the context was the same. The results support the cue-driven principle, which states that all remembering begins with a cue that initiates retrieval.

State-Dependent Memory

State-dependent memory is a phenomenon that is closely related to encoding/retrieval specificity, but in state-dependent memory the individual's state of consciousness provides the contextual cue. For example, a person who experiences an episode when intoxicated will be able
to better remember the events of that episode when intoxicated than when sober. Similarly, a
person who is depressed will better remember experiences during that depression when depressed again, rather than when in a more positive mood. State-dependent memory was first
uncovered in a lab in 1937 when Edward Girden and Elmer Culler administered the drug curare
to dogs when learning to, when they heard a buzzer, draw their paw away from a location to
avoid an electric shock. Girden and Culler found that dogs were more likely to remove their
paw when they heard the buzzer if curare was still in their system than if it was not. In addition,
they found that dogs that did not respond when curare had left their system responded when
the curare was reintroduced to their system. This result showed a connection between state of
consciousness and episodic memory. This result has been replicated many times with a variety
of substances; for example, in 1964 Donald Overton replicated the result using sodium pentobarbital in rats.

Alcohol has long been known to have state-dependent effects on people. For example, John
Elliotson writes in his 1835 book *Human Physiology*, "Dr Abel informed me . . . of an Irish
porter to a warehouse, who forgot, when sober, what he had done when drunk: but being drunk,
again recollected the transactions of his former state of intoxication" (Elliotson, 1835). Much of
modern research on state-dependent memory in humans has used alcohol to manipulate the
state of consciousness. For example, Weingartner, Adefris, Eich, and Murphy (1976) published a
widely cited study that demonstrated that when people learn material when they are intoxicated
and their recall for the material is tested later, they are better able to recall that material when
they are intoxicated than when they are sober.

People best remember material when their state of consciousness
matches their state at the time of encoding, a phenomenon known as
state-dependent memory. This means that when people learn material
while intoxicated, they tend to better remember that material when intoxicated than when sober.

Weingartner also linked mood to memory recall.
In a 1977 study, Weingartner and his colleagues
found that individuals with bipolar disorder, which
causes extremes in mood from depression to mania,
have been shown to better recall word associations
learned in the same mood state (Weingartner,
Miller, & Murphy, 1977). This effect has been more
difficult to replicate. Nutt and Lam (2011), for example, only found a mood-congruency effect for
memory of inkblots but not for verbal items.

Sherri-Lynn Pearce and her colleagues showed
that pain is also a state that can affect memory.
Pearce induced pain in participants by having them
submerge their hands in ice water. Pearce found
that memory recall for the words was better when
the pain condition at learning and recall was congruent (Pearce et al., 1990).

There are significant implications for state-
dependent memory. The success of a person asked
to recall any information from a given episode will

RELEVANT RESEARCH

BOX
6.2

The Link between Episodic Memory and Learning from Textbooks and Notes

Reading and re-reading a textbook will generate multiple episodic memory traces for the to-be-learned material, but this material may be very difficult to access due to the fact episodic memories are fleeting in nature. They are not meant to be particularly durable; they are meant to serve as the basis for the formation of more durable mental models. Generating the appropriate contextual cues to successfully probe memory for those episodic memories at the time of a test is difficult because the context for learning and test are so very different. Students can't rely on the external cues that give rise to the encoding/retrieval specificity effect or state-dependent effects. In order to get past this problem, students should strive to develop mental models of the to-be-remembered material by finding a personal link to the to-be-remembered material or linking it to other knowledge. Students who make information personal or connect it to other information consistently outperform students who simply read and re-read the text over and over. Tamara Ferguson and colleagues found that when students rated words in terms of how well the words described themselves and rated other words in terms of whether the word was easy to imagine, students were better at remembering the words that they had thought of in terms of themselves (Ferguson, Rule, & Carlson, 1983). This effect is known as the **self-reference effect** (Rogers, Kuiper, & Kirker, 1977). It has been replicated in labs hundreds of times, and is replicated by students who use it as a learning strategy every day.

DIY EXPERIMENT

BOX
6.3

The von Restorff Effect: The Experiment

Try this experiment before reading about the von Restorff effect. Cover all the lists except the one you are studying. Read the list trying to encode as many of the items as possible. Cover the studied items and write down as many items as you can remember.

List A	List B	List C
belt	kit	goose
trap	cat	mouse
hook	mat	camel
leaf	dog	horse
cape	tip	truck
bone	pet	raven
fork	lid	zebra
vase	mud	tiger
gate	dot	lemur
rice	fan	robin

See page 137 for an explanation of this experiment.

be affected by how closely their current state matches the state at the time of learning, which can have a significant impact on students who are tested frequently. State-dependent memory has also been shown to affect the treatment of phobias; individuals with a similar caffeine level in their systems during each treatment session have been found to show improvement more rapidly (Mystkowski, Mineka, Vernon, & Zinbarg, 2003). Children with attention deficit hyperactivity disorder (ADHD) who are taking methylphenidate (better known as Ritalin) show better recall when both learning and recall occur when Ritalin is in their system (Swanson & Kinsbourne, 1976) although people who have not been diagnosed with ADHD do not benefit significantly from Ritalin. This result suggests that Ritalin changes consciousness in children with ADHD in a way that promotes learning and has been used to justify the prescription of this medication for more than 40 years.

Phenomena Related to Episodic Memory

Déjà Vécu

When researchers talk about the phenomena of *remembering something that hasn't actually happened before* they use the term **déjà vécu**, which means already experienced, rather than déjà vu, which means already seen. Déjà vécu is preferred over déjà vu because the phenomenon involves all of the senses, not just vision. When one experiences déjà vécu, one experiences an episodic memory that has not really happened. People sometimes think they have experienced something before (although they have not) because the *feeling* of remembering can sometimes be activated without an accompanying memory. The exact cause of déjà vécu is not known; however, it is reported by people who cannot see, so it seems to have an endogenous cause, that is, a cause that comes from within a person, not from a trigger in the environment. In rare cases, individuals can experience persistent déjà vécu, believing that thoughts they have are memories of things that have actually happened (O'Connor, Lever, & Moulin, 2010). In these cases, individuals' lives are severely disrupted by déjà vécu; they are unable to know what they need to do to take care of themselves because they are not sure what they have already done. The impairment in people with disrupted episodic memory suggests that a primary purpose of episodic memory is to allow people to track experiences and to distinguish between daydreams and fantasies and thoughts representing events that have actually occurred. When people experience déjà vécu in everyday life, it is likely because the area of the brain associated with the feeling of remembering has been activated accidentally.

Hyperthymesia

The case study at the beginning of this chapter describes hyperthymesia, a condition in which individuals have unusually detailed and accurate memory for episodes in their lives. About 25 people have been identified as having hyperthymesia and thus it ranks among the rarest conditions on earth. Hyperthymesia cannot be attributed simply to superior memory because people with hyperthymesia do not excel at recalling non-episodic information, such as facts from generic memory. People with hyperthymesia would not do well on a game show like *Jeopardy!* nor do they outperform their peers when tested at school. People with hyperthymesia do one thing well: they remember events from their own lives. Hyperthymesia is sometimes labelled as exceptional autobiographical memory; however, this definition is incorrect. As you will see in

DIY EXPERIMENT

The von Restorff Effect: An Explanation

Most people remember distinctive items better than non-distinct items. In this DIY experiment, most participants recall "fork" from List A and "mat" from List B because they are different ink colours than the other items. For List C, most people recall "truck" because it is from a different semantic category than the other items. Recall of the other items on the list will be less predictable. Improved memory for distinct items is called the von Restorff effect.

the next section of this chapter, autobiographical memory includes much more than just events that have been personally experienced. It also includes facts and a sense of identity, which is information that people with hyperthymesia do not remember any better than the rest of the population. Many people with hyperthymesia find the condition a burden; A.J., one of the first people identified with the disorder, is often plagued by her memories, especially the bad ones. She reports recalling every negative thing ever said to her in a never-ending cycle and also has difficulty with anxiety and hoarding that appear to be linked to the disorder. Other individuals with hyperthymesia report similar experiences; they are weighed down by their memories to a point where they find it hard to function normally. It should be noted that many claims by people with hyperthymesia cannot be proven with certainty to be the result of highly detailed autobiographical memory. For example, if someone with hyperthymesia is asked what she or he was wearing on a randomly chosen day, and reports wearing a red sweater, there is no way to prove that this memory is accurate. The person with hyperthymesia may just be guessing, or may have a false memory. Further, if a person with hyperthymesia is asked about the weather on some random day, a fact that can be verified, there is no way of knowing for sure whether they recall the event from that day, or whether they memorized weather patterns after the fact. Thus, before the nature and extent of hyperthymesia can be fully understood, a systematic study of people with hyperthymesia that tests the accuracy and source of memories is needed.

Episodic Memory Is Distinct from Classical Conditioning

Recall from Chapter 1 that Henry Molaison (1926–2008) had a large part of his hippocampus removed to prevent epileptic seizures, which caused memory loss. One interesting aspect of Molaison's memory loss was that while he could not remember episodes that occurred just minutes before, he was able to gain new implicit memories through classical conditioning. For example, a researcher (whom Molaison had met dozens of times before but could not recognize) greeted Molaison with a handshake like he had in the past, but this time Molaison received a mild electric shock from the joy buzzer hidden in the researcher's hand. Molaison recoiled from the shock. A few hours later the researcher returned and extended his hand to Molaison, who refused to shake it, although he could not explain why. He did not recognize the researcher nor remember the episode where he had been shocked, yet he had learned from

Episodic Memory Is Linked to Taste Aversion

The brain has at least one specialized network for ensuring that an animal will recall details related to dangerous food. In 2014, Chinnakkaruppan, Wintzer, McHugh, and Rosenblum working at the University of Haifa uncovered a link between the brain area responsible for taste memory and the brain area responsible for recording time and place (episodic context). The researchers studied the links between the area of the temporal lobe that stores taste memories and three areas in the hippocampus: CA1, which stores spatial information (recall Figure 6.1 on p. 131); the dentate gyrus (DG), which stores time information; and CA3, which fills in missing episodic information. They conducted this study on mice by breeding mice with brains that functioned normally but lacked plasticity (the ability to create new memories) in these three areas of the hippocampus. The researchers gave a food that caused stomach pains and another food that did not to these specially bred mice as well as to neurotypical mice whose hippocampi could change with experience. The researchers found no difference between the two groups when the food was not accompanied by a negative feeling, but a clear difference when mice were given the food that caused stomach pains; mice who lacked plasticity in the area CA1, which is related to spatial memory, would return to the harmful food whereas other mice would not. Chinnakkaruppan et al. argued that the finding makes sense from an evolutionary point of view; it is beneficial, if not essential, for an animal to remember the location where they obtained a food that had negative consequences. This research also suggests that there is an episodic component to taste aversions.

the aversive handshake not to shake hands with that researcher again. This simple demonstration illustrates that conditioned responses and learning do not need to have an explicit episodic component to them. While an individual may remember an event of learning something (this is particularly likely when the experience was unusual), remembering the event is not necessary for learning. Recalling episodes is therefore not what makes classical and operant conditioning function.

Autobiographical Memory

Autobiographical memory is a collection of episodic and generic information that tells the story of a person's life. A good way to think of autobiographical memory is like a scrapbook where meaningful events and facts are recorded. Autobiographical memory is different from episodic memory in that autobiographical memory contains *both* events and factual information, whereas episodic memory consists *only* of events. While autobiographical memory may consist of some episodic memories, not all autobiographical memories are episodic (such as your birth date) and not all episodic memories are considered autobiographical (such as what you ate for dinner last night). Complete the DIY Experiment on page 140 to see for yourself how autobiographical memory differs from episodic memory.

Autobiographical memory changes as life changes, just as the scrapbook that a person would compile would be different if they compiled it when they were 5, 15, or 25 years old. Similar

CASE STUDY

BOX 6.6

Autobiographical Memory and *Forrest Gump*

The film *Forrest Gump* tells the story of a simple man living life in the mid-twentieth century completely unaware of the fact that he has influenced many significant historical events. Forrest Gump fails to see the importance of events from his life because his mind is focused on one thing, his love for Jenny and his desire to see her again. Although Forrest Gump's inability to see the relevance of these experiences may seem to depict a person with disrupted autobiographical memory, the movie actually portrays autobiographical memory extremely well. A person's autobiographical memory, and the significance that person ascribes to different life events, is not fixed. It is related to her or his self-concept, a belief in who she or he is. When people recall events from their lives that are not closely associated with their current self-concept, they tend to feel like a bystander, watching the events happening, but not really participating. For example, people recovering from addictions often recall events from when they were abusing substances as though they were happening to a different person. When Forrest recalls his life to a variety of people at the bus stop, he is not thinking of himself as a hero, or a businessman, or an inspiration, so when he recalls events in his life linked to these labels he views them as happening to someone else, as a third-party bystander. Forrest Gump's entire self-concept revolves around one thing: his love for Jenny. He sees himself as a man who has loved this girl his entire life and now gets to see her again. All the other events that have occurred lack meaning or substance to him. While audiences are bemused by Forrest's humility, what they are really seeing on the screen is a true rendering of the constructive and highly personal nature of autobiographical memory. While *Forrest Gump* is certainly not a scientific case study, the film portrays autobiographical memory in a thought-provoking and accurate way.

United Archives GmbH/Alamy Stock Photo

events are seen differently as a result of events that happen later. For example, a traumatic breakup may be recalled as heartbreaking a few weeks after it occurred, but may be recalled in a positive light a few years later when a person is in a new relationship that would have been impossible if the previous relationship had continued. Martin Conway developed a model that reflects the ever-changing nature of autobiographical memory.

Conway's Model of Autobiographical Memory

According to Martin Conway, autobiographical memory is constructed within a self-memory system (SMS) that is comprised of an **autobiographical knowledge base** and the **working self**. The autobiographical knowledge base contains knowledge of the self that can be used by the individual to determine what the self is, what the self was, and what the self can be (Conway, 2005). The working self is a set of personal goals and self-images that are organized in a hierarchy (see Figure 6.2).

autobiographical knowledge base

knowledge of the self that can be used by the individual to determine what the self is, what the self was, and what the self can be

working self

a set of personal goals and self-images that are organized in a hierarchy

BOX
6.7

DIY EXPERIMENT

The Difference between Autobiographical and Episodic Memory

Complete lists A and B on a separate piece of paper or in a notebook. You can also have a friend complete the lists; you should see the same effect.

Step 1: List A
Imagine you had to tell another person about your life. Using point form, list 15 things that you would like that other person to know about you.

Step 2: List B
List the first 15 events that you experienced that come to your mind.

Step 3: Review List A
Go through list A and put an "E" next to each item that was an event (an episodic memory) and an "F" next to each item that was a fact (which are generic memories).

Step 4: Compare List A and List B

When you compare lists A and B, you will see not everything in list A is episodic (chances are you included some facts, like when you were born) and not everything in list B is something that you would tell someone about if you had to describe your life. This is because not all autobiographical memory is episodic and not all episodic memory is autobiographical.

lifetime period

an aspect of the autobiographical knowledge base that contains information about activities, relationships, locations, and timeframes associated with various themes in one's life

general event

an aspect of the autobiographical knowledge base that is comprised of either multiple representations of repeated events or a sequence of related events that are related to achieving or failing at personal goals

The information in the autobiographical knowledge base is categorized into three areas: **lifetime periods, general events**, and **event-specific knowledge**. Lifetime periods contain thematic knowledge about specific periods of life, such that a person may have a school theme, a looking-for-work theme, a work theme, a parenting theme, etc. Lifetime periods contain information about activities, relationships, locations, and timeframes associated with each theme.

General events are more specific than lifetime periods and are comprised of either multiple representations of repeated events or a sequence of related events. General events are clustered around themes related to achieving personal goals or failing to achieve personal goals (Conway & Pleydell-Pearce, 2000). For example, a person's autobiographical knowledge base may include the general event of "buying my first car" or "getting fired from my job at the mall." According to Conway and Pleydell-Pearce (2000), general events representing "first-time" accomplishments, such as the first time driving a car or the first time kissing a romantic partner, are particularly vivid.

Event-specific knowledge (ESK) is highly detailed information about specific events gleaned from episodic memories. Most ESK fades quickly, however events that mark a new beginning, events related to turning points in life, anchoring events that affirm a person's beliefs, and analogous events that impact future behaviour all may resist memory decay (Pillemer, 2001).

As shown in Figure 6.2, lifetime periods, general events, and ESK form a hierarchy within the autobiographical knowledge base. Knowledge stored in lifetime periods contains cues for general events, and general events contain cues for ESK. According to the model, when a cue activates material in the autobiographical knowledge base that is linked to a lifetime period, a general event, and ESK, an autobiographical memory is retrieved. When the autobiographical

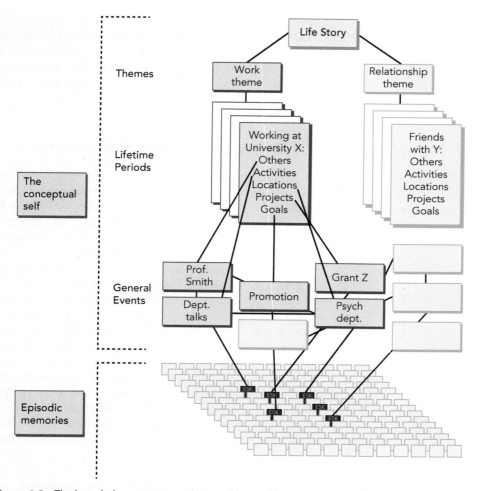

Figure 6.2   The knowledge structure within autobiographical memory according to Conway (2005)
Source: Conway, 2005 p. 609

memory includes an episodic memory, a person may experience autonoetic consciousness or **mental time travel**, which is a sense of one's self in the past and is typically accompanied by imagery featuring perceptual details related to the recollections. Conway (2005) argues that the autonoetic consciousness that accompanies the recollection of personally relevant episodic memory results from the integration of parts of the autobiographical knowledge base and the working self. The relationship between the autobiographical knowledge base and the working self is reciprocal. The working self manipulates the cues that activate the material in the autobiographical knowledge base while the autobiographical knowledge base determines the goals and self-images of the working self (Pillemer, 2001). Thus, according to the SMS theory, autobiographical memory is constructed based not as a series of personally experienced episodes in chronological order, but rather based on a person's current self-image and goals. Because a person's self-image and goals change over time, autobiographical memory also changes over time. For example, a student who takes developmental psychology in her or his second year at

event-specific knowledge

highly detailed information about specific life events

mental time travel

a sense of one's self in the past that is typically accompanied by imagery featuring perceptual details related to the recollections

university will look back on the significance of that course differently if later studying developmental psychology in grad school than if later studying microbiology in grad school. That second-year developmental course will feel like a "first" to the student who later specializes in that field and inconsequential to the person whose life has been unaffected by taking that course. Figure 6.2 illustrates how Conway's (2005) SMS model accounts for a person's autobiographical memory of her or his life.

The Neuroscience of Autobiographical Memory

Neuroscientists have found evidence justifying the distinction between episodic autobiographical memories (such as memories for personally experienced events) and generic autobiographical memories (such as memories for facts about one's life); different brain regions are associated with each of these types of recollections. Brian Levine and his colleagues (2004) had participants record episodes from their lives, repeated episodes, and world knowledge over the course of several months. Participants were then presented with these pieces of information while undergoing an fMRI scan. Levine found that both episodic and generic autobiographical information activated the anterior ventromedial prefrontal cortex (see Figure 6.3) associated with self-reference but episodic information activated this area to a greater degree. While the episodic autobiographical memories activated the right temporo-parietal and parietal-frontal systems (which are associated with the reconstruction of spatial information), the generic autobiographical information activated the left temporo-parietal and parieto-frontal systems associated with egocentric spatial processing. In addition, episodic autobiographical information also seemed to suppress processing in the emotion centres of the brain. Levine notes that these experimental findings are consistent with the finding from amnesic patients, who show different patterns of loss of episodic and generic autobiographical information depending on which area of the brain is damaged.

Through a variety of methods, researchers have generated evidence that episodic autobiographical memory is distinct from generic autobiographical memory. Martin Conway and his colleagues, and Narinder Kapur, have both reported case studies of individuals with retrograde amnesia (amnesia for events in the past but no difficulty learning new material) who in some cases lose access to episodic autobiographical memories but not generic autobiographical memories or vice versa (e.g., Conway & Fthenaki, 2000). (For more on retrograde amnesia, see Chapter 8.) Conway also conducted neuroimaging studies of neurotypical individuals (i.e., individuals with no brain damage) and established different neurological correlates for episodic and generic autobiographical memory (Conway, Pleydell-Pearce, & Whitecross, 2001). Brian Levine (Levine et al., 2004) of the University of Toronto led a research

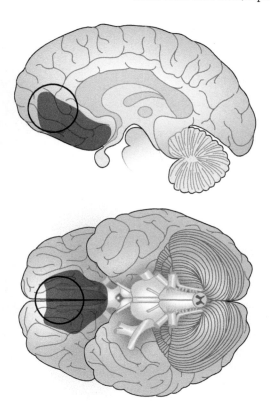

Figure 6.3   Ventromedial prefrontal area

The shaded cortical area shows the ventromedial prefrontal area. The area within the black circle shows the anterior ventromedial prefrontal area.

team that conducted autobiographical interviews with individuals with a variety of forms of amnesia and then coded recall as either generic or episodic. Levine found that neurotypical controls reported about twice as many episodic autobiographical memories as generic autobiographical memories during a well-structured interview. Individuals with damage to the ventral prefrontal regions (see Figure 6.3) reported fewer episodic autobiographical memories with no effect on the number of generic autobiographical memories. Individuals with damage to the dorsolateral prefrontal regions, on the other hand, reported the same number of episodic autobiographical memories and *more* generic autobiographical memories; individuals with frontal temporal dementia reported significantly fewer episodic autobiographical memories and significantly more generic autobiographical memories than controls. Taken together, this data suggests that episodic and generic autobiographical memory are distinct phenomena controlled by different neurological regions; episodic autobiographical memory relies on the frontal lobes whereas generic autobiographical memory does not. Levine speculates that frontal lobe damage can result in the inability to experience mental time travel, which impedes episodic autobiographical memory retrieval. Generic autobiographical memory is thought to be more closely associated with other generic memories.

Flashbulb Memories

The term **flashbulb memory**, first coined by Roger Brown and James Kulik in 1977, is used to describe an especially vivid memory of a highly emotional experience. Most flashbulb memories are related to hearing distressing news that can either be of personal or national significance. Thus, an individual may have an especially vivid memory of when they heard that their father had had a heart attack or when they heard that terrorists had attacked the United States on September 11, 2001.

Martin Conway identified six criteria that determine whether a memory can be labelled as a flashbulb memory. The memory must contain information about *where they were* when they heard the news, *what they were doing* when they heard the news, *who told them* the news, *the impact* of the news on the individual, *how they responded emotionally* to the news, and *what happened after* they heard the news. Because the event must have an emotional impact on the individual for a flashbulb memory to form, flashbulb memories are different for different cultures and for different generations. Most longitudinal research concerning flashbulb memories in North America concern the assassination of President John F. Kennedy on November 22, 1963, the assassination of John Lennon on December 8, 1980, the *Challenger* space shuttle disaster on January 28, 1986, and the attacks of September 11, 2001.

It's a flashbulb memory if:

- It was a highly emotional personal or national event.
- You remember where you were.
- You remember what you were doing.
- You remember who told you.
- You remember how the event impacted you.
- You remember the emotions you felt.
- You remember the aftermath of the event.

flashbulb memory
a highly detailed memory of a surprising event of personal significance

I remember where I was when I first heard about the attacks on 9/11 as though it was yesterday. I was in my car, in line for a coffee, listening to the CBC when the news anchor remarked that he had just seen the most astonishing thing, a fireball coming out of one of the World Trade Center towers. At first I thought it must have been an accident, but then the second plane hit and at that moment I knew America was under attack. I remember crying. I remember feeling like I was carrying a heavy weight on my shoulders for days after, as the news footage of the attacks, and the eventual collapse of the towers, played over and over in a relentless loop on CNN. Anyone who was an adult at the time will tell you, the world changed that day. We lost our innocence.

–C.P. Typical flashbulb memory for September 11, 2001

Are Flashbulb Memories More Accurate Than Other Episodic Memories?

There is no doubt that flashbulb memories are vivid, but there has been considerable debate as to whether this vividness translates to more accurate memories. Ulric Neisser, who was one of the best-known cognitive psychologists of the twentieth century, argued that flashbulb memories are largely constructed after the event after he discovered that his own flashbulb memory of the attack on Pearl Harbor contained several impossible facts that he had been certain were true for many decades (Neisser, 1982). One cognitive psychology professor loved to tell the story of how he recalled having been listening to a baseball game on the radio when he heard John F. Kennedy had been shot and that he carried that memory for years, until his wife pointed out that he couldn't have been listening to a baseball game because John F. Kennedy was shot in November (long after the end of baseball season).

BOX 6.8

DIY EXPERIMENT

The Role of Cues in Episodic Memory Retrieval Part II

Box 6.1 on page 132 lists a series of dates and asks you to recall what you were doing on those days. The dates listed all correspond to the dates of distressing news events (see below), which people tend to recall as flashbulb memories. You may have flashbulb memories of learning of many of the events listed below:

February 1, 2003	*Columbia* space shuttle disaster
June 25, 2009	Death of Michael Jackson
December 14, 2012	Sandy Hook elementary school shooting
November 13, 2015	Paris attacks
February 14, 2018	Parkland school shooting
April 6, 2018	Humboldt Broncos' bus crash
April 23, 2018	Toronto sidewalk attack

On September 12, 2001 (the day after 9/11), Jennifer Talarico and David Rubin of Duke University interviewed 54 university students, having them recall both memories about the attack from the day before and an event from the participant's life in the days prior to the attack. For the September 11 memory, participants were asked, "Who or what first told you the information?", "When did you first hear the news?", "Where were you when you first heard the news?", "What were you doing immediately before you heard the news?", and "Are there any other distinctive details from when you first heard the news?" For the everyday memory, participants were asked, "What was the event?", "When did it occur?", "Where were you, physically?", "Were there others present, and if so, who?", "What were you, personally, doing?", and "Are there any other distinctive details about the event?" Participants were also asked for a two-word descriptor that could serve as a cue for the event in the future. Most of the everyday memory events related to parties, sporting events, or studying. Participants then completed the Autobiographical Memory Questionnaire that measures key aspects of an autobiographical memory (Sheen, Kemp, & Rubin, 2001). The Autobiographical Questionnaire asks participants to rate the accuracy of statements such as "I feel as though I am reliving the experience," "I believe the event in my memory really occurred the way I remember it," "I can see the memory in my mind," and "I can hear the memory in my mind." Participants returned for a second session following a delay of 1, 6, or 32 weeks. During the second session, participants answered the same questions that they were asked during the first session. The researchers were primarily interested in seeing if flashbulb memories would be more consistent over time than everyday memories.

Talarico and Rubin (2003) found that there was no difference between flashbulb memories and everyday memories for their measure of recall consistency. The mean number of consistent and inconsistent details was similar for both memories. Memory was less consistent at longer delays for both the flashbulb memory of September 11 and the other event. However, participants tended to believe their flashbulb memory for September 11 was more accurate than their everyday memory. The researchers argue that flashbulb memories are not immune to forgetting, nor is it uncommon for them to be inconsistent over time; however, people have an exaggerated belief in the accuracy of the memory after long delays.

That participants tend to be confident but not accurate in their recall of flashbulb memories has been found in studies following the *Challenger* space shuttle disaster and the O.J. Simpson verdict (Bohannon, 1988; Schmolck, Buffalo, & Squire, 2000).

The Comprehensive Model of Flashbulb Memory

Martin Conway and his colleagues in Great Britain and the United States compared the extent of flashbulb memories for the resignation of British Prime Minister Margaret Thatcher on November 22, 1990, with people living in the United Kingdom and people living in the United States and found that people living in the United Kingdom had much more vivid and enduring flashbulb memories of this event than those in the United States. Because the vividness and accuracy was similar in people who reported rehearsing the event many times since it occurred and those who did not report rehearsing the event, Conway et al. suggested that flashbulb memories are formed almost immediately after the event and are the result of three interacting factors: a person's interest in a subject, the impact of the event, and the emotions evoked by the event. When interest, impact, and emotion are all high, recall of the event takes on flashbulb-memory characteristics; otherwise, the event is recalled without excessive detail. This is known as the comprehensive model of flashbulb memory (Conway et al., 1994). This model is most consistent with experimental findings because it doesn't make claims that flashbulb memories are more accurate; it simply implies that flashbulb memories are different from other episodic memories.

Phenomena Related to Autobiographical Memory

Not surprisingly, the way we think about ourselves is influenced by autobiographical memory. In the next section, we will discuss how autobiographical memory influences our self-concept and our recall of the important events in our lives. In addition, we will discuss the link between autobiographical memory and cognitive biases that affect how we view others and that, like episodic memory, autobiographical memory can be state dependent.

Self-Concept

Lisa Libby and Richard Eibach (2002) from Cornell University have used a variety of different experimental paradigms to demonstrate that the nature of a person's episodic autobiographical memory recall is tied to self-concept and whether the event being recalled is consistent or inconsistent with that current sense of self. For example, the researchers asked university students to list things about themselves that had changed since they started university and then list several events that occurred in high school. The participants were then asked to indicate whether their episodic recall of the past high school events was in the first person (i.e., they felt that they saw the event through their own eyes) or from the third person (i.e., they felt that they were a bystander watching the event happen). In this study, Libby and Eibach found that the participants were more likely to report feeling like they saw the event from the third-person perspective if the event was related to an aspect of their selves that they felt had changed since high school. This result supports Conway's assertion that autobiographical memory changes as one's working self changes. Libby and Eibach found similar results when they interviewed people who identified as religious and asked them to recall religious and non-religious experiences; they were more likely to recall religious experiences in the first person and non-religious experiences in the third person. Thus, the same autobiographical memory can be recalled differently depending on whether it is consistent or inconsistent with the current sense of self. This is evidenced in phenomena such as the reminiscence bump, nostalgia, cognitive bias, and the effect of mood on autobiographical memory recall, which are discussed next.

The Reminiscence Bump

At any point in life, a person is most likely to recall autobiographical memories that have happened recently (this is known as the **recency effect**); however, as people age their recall for memories that are not of recent events takes on a specific shape known as the **reminiscence bump** (see Figure 6.4). The reminiscent bump describes the tendency for older adults to recall events from adolescence and early adulthood more than other events from their past (Rathbone, Moulin, & Conway, 2008). Typical findings are shown in Figure 6.4. The reminiscence bump is found across cultures and, while the specific content of what is recalled differs, in all cultures there is a bias toward recalling positive life events (Wang & Conway, 2004). Because the

recency effect

recently acquired memories are more likely to be recalled than memories from further in the past

reminiscence bump

the tendency for older adults to recall autobiographical events from adolescence and early adulthood

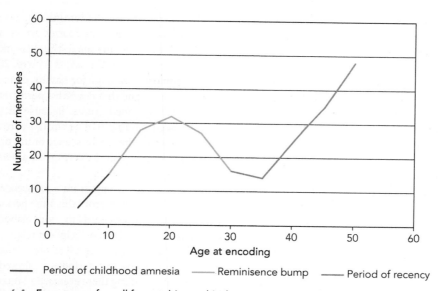

Figure 6.4 **Frequency of recall for autobiographical events across the lifespan**

An example of the reminiscence bump based on data from people in their fifties recalling autobiographical memories. Recency cannot explain all recall, as less recent events from the ages of 10 to 30 are more often recalled than more recent events from age 30 to 40. This is referred to as the reminiscence bump.

reminiscence bump seems to relate to how people tell the story of their lives, it is more closely associative with autobiographical memory than episodic memory.

Many researchers have found that the reminiscence bump tends to consist of positive life events rather than negative ones (e.g., Berntsen & Rubin, 2002). Anja Leist and colleagues studied the frequency of memories of positive life events in men and women and found that women remember more positive life events from their twenties while men remember more positive life events from their thirties. This corresponds to a slightly earlier reminiscence bump in women than in men (Janssen, Chessa, & Murre, 2005; Leist, Ferring, & Filipp, 2010).

When Martin Conway studied the reminiscence bump across cultures, he found the age of the reminiscence bump changes to reflect the age at which that culture considers a person an adult. Conway found that in Asian societies including China and Japan, where a person may not be considered an adult until they are established in a stable interdependent social network at about age 30, the reminiscence bump occurs later than in western cultures where adulthood is achieved earlier (Conway, Wang, Hanyu, & Haque, 2005). Thus cultural factors can shift the age range for the reminiscence bump. Cultural values also influence the autobiographical memories recalled; in individualistic cultures such as Canada, memories comprised within the reminiscence bump usually put the individual at the centre (e.g., a person would recall graduating from high school or getting married). In collectivistic cultures such as those of many parts of Asia, memories that form the reminiscence bump are less self-centred and more related to a person's affiliation within a group. This finding is consistent with other findings that show that autobiographical memory is strongly influenced by a person's sense of self; as the sense of self differs from individualistic to collectivistic cultures, so too does the nature of the content of the reminiscence bump (Conway et al., 2005).

There are biological, cognitive, and sociocultural explanations for the reminiscence bump. The biological account of the reminiscence bump suggests that more memories are recalled from adolescence and early adulthood because biological mechanisms make those memories easier to retrieve than other memories (Janssen et al., 2005; Janssen, Chessa, & Murre, 2007). Some researchers argue that this results from an evolutionary advantage for having memories from this era dominate autobiographical recall, while others argue that cognitive performance peaks during this age period and that this results in better encoded events. Because they are based on biology, these accounts predict that the reminiscence bump will be similar across all people regardless of gender or culture; however, the finding that the reminiscence bump occurs earlier for women than men, and contains different types of material depending on a person's culture, do not support the biological account (Berntsen & Rubin, 2002).

The cognitive account of the reminiscence bump suggests that events from adolescence and early adulthood are recalled more readily by older adults because events from this time period are more novel than events from other time periods and that this novelty leads to more elaborative rehearsal (e.g., Rubin, Rahhal, & Poon, 1998). This is consistent with the principle of relative distinctiveness (Surprenant & Neath, 2013) in which unusual events are better recalled. Some theorists also suggest that this effect is magnified by the fact that events in this time period are followed by a period of stability, which increases the stability of the cues for recalling these events, and increases the probability of recall (Rubin et al., 1998; Berntsen & Rubin, 2002). One weakness of this account, however, is that it cannot fully explain why the reminiscence bump tends to be comprised of positive but not negative life events, as many negative events can also be novel (Berntsen & Rubin, 2002).

Dorthe Berntsen and David Rubin propose a life-script account of the reminiscence bump. According to this account, each person's culture imposes a life script, which includes important transitional events that are viewed as positive, such as marriage, having a child, or buying a house. Events that deviate from the life script, such as divorce, infertility, or being unable to buy a house, are generally seen as negative. The life-script account suggests that, when recalling past life events, an individual uses the life script from her or his culture and the timing of the reminiscence bump will reflect the timing of transitional events in a given culture; thus, this model can account for

---

DIY EXPERIMENT   BOX 6.9

The Reminiscence Bump

Choose a friend or relative who is 50 years old or older and explain that you are doing some memory research, which you will explain at the end of the interview. Once they have consented, ask the individual to recall events from her or his life in any order she or he chooses. Note the event and the age the person was when the event occurred and whether it was a positive or negative experience. The interviewee should report about 20 life events. Once the interview is done, explain the reminiscence bump to the interviewee and how it tends to be associated with life scripts and positive emotions. You can then look over the interviewee's response and evaluate the extent to which that autobiographical memory report to you shows a reminiscence bump (bias toward ages 10 to 30). You can even create a simple frequency distribution, with age along the x-axis and number of events reported along the y-axis and see if you replicate the pattern shown in Figure 6.4.

differences in reminiscence bumps in men and women and across individualistic and collectivistic cultures. Further, because events that are consistent with the life script are viewed as positive and those that are not consistent are viewed as negative, this account can better explain the bias toward positive memories in the reminiscence bump (Berntsen & Rubin, 2002). This pattern of preferring positive memories over negative ones when accessing autobiographical memories generalizes from the very specific pattern of the reminiscence bump to the everyday experience of nostalgia.

Nostalgia

Nostalgia—it's delicate, but potent. . . . "Nostalgia" literally means "the pain from an old wound." It's a twinge in your heart far more powerful than memory alone. . . . It lets us travel the way a child travels—around and around, and back home again, to a place where we know we are loved.

  –Don Draper. *Mad Men*, Season 1, Episode 13, "The Wheel." Written by Matthew Weiner and Robin Veith. Courtesy of Lions Gate Entertainment Inc.

There was a time when being nostalgic, or wishing and longing for things from the past, was thought to be an indicator of illness caused by vibrations in the brain still connected to another place, or a change in altitude, or a neurological disorder of some sort. Regardless of the explanation, it was widely held that wanting to relive the past was pathological.

Today **nostalgia** is considered a normal and healthy part of life and *The New Oxford English Dictionary* defines nostalgia as "a sentimental longing or wistful affection for the past." Nostalgia is inextricably linked to autobiographical memory; our memories both provide the motivation for being nostalgic, and are the product of nostalgic reminiscing. In 2006, Tim Wildschut and colleagues studied the types of autobiographical memories that were most closely associated with the feeling of nostalgia by conducting a content analysis of nostalgic stories written by volunteers. The researchers found several characteristics that typify nostalgia. First, the researchers found that people engaging in nostalgia typically remember people who are close to them and personally treasured life events. Second, the researchers found that people tend to place themselves in the centre of these nostalgic events and rarely report events

nostalgia
a sentimental longing or wistful affection for the past

Craig Blankenhorn/AMC

where the self is an observer or bystander. Third, the narratives follow a predictable sequence in which negative feelings give way to positive outcomes. Finally, the narratives include indicators of positive emotions with far greater frequency than indicators of negative emotions. Wildschut, Sedikides, Arndt, and Routledge (2006) also looked at the frequency of nostalgic recollections in another study and found that 79 per cent of respondents experience nostalgia at least once a week. This finding has been replicated by researchers studying a variety of different cultures. Thus, nostalgia plays an important role in the lives of people all around the world (Wildschut et al., 2006).

Research indicates that nostalgia serves a purpose. When Wildschut et al. (2006) interviewed participants about what sorts of situations lead to feelings of nostalgia, the most commonly reported cause was negative mood associated with loneliness. Wildschut et al. (2006) then conducted an experiment to test the notion that nostalgia is triggered by negative affect. Wildschut induced various mood states in participants (positive, negative, and neutral) by manipulating the news story they read and then measured nostalgia in all participants using two scales. One measure was the **nostalgia inventory**, devised by Batcho (1995), where participants rate the extent to which they miss different parts of their past (friends, family, the way things were). The second measure was to ask participants to rate the statement "Right now I am feeling nostalgic." Wildschut et al. (2006) found that participants in the negative mood condition experienced more nostalgia after reading their news story than participants in the other two conditions. In a similar experiment, Wildschut induced feelings of loneliness in some participants and found that participants who felt the loneliest also reported the most feelings of nostalgia. In addition, Routledge et al. (2011) found that feeling meaningless could also induce feeling of nostalgia.

nostalgia inventory
a measure for assessing the extent to which an individual misses different parts of her or his past

Thus, there is a significant amount of experimental evidence suggesting that negative moods can lead to nostalgia and the selective recall of positive autobiographical memories. Wildschut et al. (2006) suggest that nostalgia serves at least three functions. First, nostalgia heightens positive mood. Second, nostalgia increases self-regard. Finally, nostalgia fosters a sense of connection to other people of importance to the person. Many experiments have confirmed this hypothesis (e.g., Routledge, Arndt, Sedikides, & Wildschut, 2008; Routledge et al., 2011; Turner, Wildschut, & Sedikides, 2012; Wildschut, Sedikides, Routledge, Arndt, & Cordaro, 2010; Vess, Arndt, Routledge, Sedikides, & Wildschut, 2012). This knowledge of how nostalgia can improve people's sense of well-being has been used successfully in a number of therapeutic settings.

RELEVANT RESEARCH

BOX 6.10

What *The Sound of Music* Can Teach about the Power of Nostalgia

In the 1967 film *The Sound of Music*, Maria, the governess, comforts the von Trapp children during a thunderstorm by singing the now famous song "My Favourite Things." It turns out that Maria's solution is validated by science. First, Wildschut et al. (2006) showed that negative feelings lead to increased feelings of nostalgia, suggesting that Maria's thoughts of "raindrops on roses and whiskers on kittens" during a scary thunderstorm were perfectly natural. Second, Wildschut et al. (2006) showed that thinking about nostalgic things improves mood and feelings of well-being, and thus singing about "cream-coloured ponies and crisp apple streudels" really could have lifted the spirits of Maria and the von Trapp children. The key, however, is to make recall personal. While "raindrops on roses and whiskers on kittens" were likely things that that song's author, Oscar Hammerstein, associated with a happy time in his life, these things won't evoke pleasant memories for someone who has been cut by thorns or who hates cats! Nostalgia needs to be generated from within. People can naturally recall events of personal distinction to themselves. That doesn't mean "My Favourite Things" will never improve mood, however, as watching this movie and singing this song is likely to make many people feel nostalgic regardless of their opinion of raindrops or kittens (or schnitzel, or mittens). The next time you or someone you are close to is feeling down, try to invoke a sense of nostalgia by thinking about "the good old days." Chances are mood will improve. Nostalgia is an effective and inexpensive mood enhancer that anyone can use.

Cognitive Bias and Autobiographical Memory

Anthony Greenwald (1980) is one of many researchers to argue that autobiographical memory recall is subject to a variety of cognitive biases, including **egocentricity**, **beneffectance**, and **conservatism**. Egocentricity describes the tendency to view ourselves as being more important than we really are. A number of experimental findings demonstrate how egocentricity can affect episodic autobiographical memory. In 1973, Brenner found that in group settings, people remember their own behaviours well, but do not have good recall of the behaviour of others. This may explain why, when people who complete group projects are asked about their own contributions, they tend to recall well what they did, and often complain that other people in the group did very little. In addition, it is well established that people are better able to remember information when it relates directly to themselves (e.g., Rogers et al., 1977) or when they have played an active role during the event (e.g., Erdelyi, Buschke, & Finkelstein, 1977). This may mean that episodic autobiographical memory is biased for events in which individuals played an active role even though they may experience many important events in which their role was less active.

Beneffectance refers to the tendency to assign responsibility for favourable events and deny responsibility for events that turned out poorly; beneffectance is also known as the self-serving bias. Beneffectance may affect whether a person recalls being involved in an event based on the outcome of that event, and not on really being involved. Beneffectance can also shape whether a person assesses a prior experience as fair or unfair; one well-known experiment showed that students who received high scores on a test were more likely to indicate that they thought the test was fair than students who received low scores (Greenwald, 1980). Thus, a person may develop memories of events that were "fair" or "unfair" based not on the event itself, but based on a bias that causes people to only take responsibility for events with good outcomes.

Finally, conservatism, sometimes known as confirmation bias, is the tendency to only seek information that supports existing belief systems. If people only look for information that is consistent with their beliefs, it is reasonable to assume they will tend to recall memories from their life that confirm their worldview and not those that conflict with it.

These examples further the argument that autobiographical memory is constructed by the individual, rather than being an objective recording of events.

State-Dependent Autobiographical Memory

A substantial body of research in the scientific literature demonstrates mood-congruency for free recall; that is, people experiencing a positive mood are more likely to recall positive words and events while people in a negative mood are more likely to recall negative words and events. This is known as the **negative memory bias**. However, both the reminiscence bump and the results from research on nostalgia suggest people favour positive autobiographical memories, a **positive memory bias**. This leaves the question as to which bias really affects people with depression, the negative memory bias or the positive one? In 2014, Jenny Lotterman and George Bonanno argued one problem with previous research on mood-congruency and memory is that it was based on participants' free recall of life events but had no way to independently verify whether those events occurred. To fix this, Lotterman and Bonanno conducted a longitudinal study in which participants were surveyed over the Internet at regular intervals over a four-year period and reported positive life events as well as emotional well-being. Later, they had

egocentricity

the tendency to remember one's own behaviours better than the behaviours of others

beneffectance

the tendency to take credit for events that have favourable outcomes and to blame other for events that have unfavourable outcomes

conservatism

the tendency to seek information that confirms existing beliefs

negative memory bias

the tendency to better recall events that are associated with negative emotions than those associated with positive emotions

positive memory bias

the tendency to better recall events that are associated with positive emotions than those associated with negative emotions

participants estimate how many positive and negative life events they had experienced in the past four years. The researchers found that while the number of positive and negative life events did not differ between depressed and non-depressed participants, depressed participants overestimated the number of positive life events while making more accurate estimates regarding the number of negative life events. This research supports the notion of positive memory bias for people with depression and is consistent with the research in nostalgia, which shows a tendency toward recalling positive autobiographical memories during times of loneliness and negative mood. These results suggest that, while mood may provide a cue for recall in some situations, negative mood is associated with a bias toward the recall of positive autobiographical memories. Once again, these results indicate that a person's autobiographical memory is affected by context and self-concept.

CHAPTER REVIEW

- Episodic memories are memories for experiences. Episodic memories differ from generic memories in that they are accompanied by a feeling of remembering when they are recalled.
- Phenomena associated with episodic memory include encoding/retrieval specificity (a tendency to better recall information when the environment is the same at learning and test), state-dependent memory (a tendency to better recall information when the state of consciousness is similar at the time of learning and test), and the von Restorff effect (a tendency to better remember unique events).
- The sequence and context that are characteristic of episodic memories are encoded by specialized cells in the hippocampus.
- Autobiographical memory is a collection of events and facts that a person assembles to tell her or his life story. Autobiographical memory differs from episodic memory in that autobiographical memory can consist of *both* event-related information and factual information while episodic memory only consists of event-related information.
- Episodic autobiographical memory seems to rely on the right temporo-parietal and parietal-frontal systems while generic autobiographical memory relies on the left temporo-parietal and parieto-frontal systems.
- Flashbulb memories are especially vivid autobiographical memories for the point in time when a person learns important news. Many people believe that flashbulb memories are more accurate than other episodic memories; however, research suggests that this is not true.
- Autobiographical memory is driven by a person's current self-concept; how individuals view themselves determines what facts and experiences they will recall when asked to describe their lives. When asked to recall autobiographical memories, people tend to recall events that occurred recently (recency effect) and events that occurred between the ages of about 10 and 30 (the reminiscence bump). The reminiscence bump likely occurs because many unique events related to a person's self-concept occur during this stage in life.
- Autobiographical memory is affected by cognitive biases including egocentricity, beneffectance, and conservatism.

MEMORY ACTIVITY

Make a Table to Aid Your Memory

In this chapter, you learned about the neuroscience of the episodic vs the generic components of autobiographical memory. Complete the chart below. Based on what you've read in this book so far, can you think of the reasons why developing this chart will aid in your memory for the information?

Here is the text excerpt that contains the relevant information:

> Levine found that both episodic and generic autobiographical information activated the anterior ventromedial prefrontal cortex (see Figure 6.3) associated with self-reference but episodic information activated this area to a greater degree. While the episodic autobiographical memories activated the right temporo-parietal and parietal-frontal systems (which are associated with the reconstruction of spatial information), the generic autobiographical information activated the left temporo-parietal and parieto-frontal systems associated with egocentric spatial processing. In addition, episodic autobiographical information also seemed to suppress processing in the emotion centres of the brain. Levine notes that these experimental findings are consistent with the finding from amnesic patients, who show different patterns of loss of episodic and generic autobiographical information depending on which area of the brain is damaged. Damage to the ventral prefrontal region leads to deficits in the episodic component of autobiographical memory whereas individuals with frontal temporal dementia tend to instead display deficits in generic autobiographical memory.

	Autobiographical Memory	
	Episodic Component	Generic Component
Associated brain area		
Impact on emotional processing		
Which type of amnesia is associated with an impairment in this type of memory?		

Questions

1. List three characteristics of episodic memory.
2. Explain how episodic memories are formed and why some episodic memories may be lost.
3. Describe encoding/retrieval specificity. Provide a real-life example where this phenomenon might be observed.
4. Describe state-dependent memory. Provide a real-life example where this phenomenon might be observed.
5. List the different brain areas associated with episodic memory. Indicate the specific role of each area.
6. Differentiate between episodic autobiographical memory and generic autobiographical memory. Provide an example of each.
7. List the defining characteristics of a flashbulb memory.

8. Describe an experiment that tested the consistency and accuracy of flashbulb memory. Explain what the results suggest about the nature of flashbulb memories.
9. Describe and evaluate three models of flashbulb memories.
10. Explain some way that self-concept is linked to autobiographical memory.
11. Describe the reminiscence bump. Describe two factors that influence the reminiscence bump.
12. Define nostalgia. Explain two ways in which nostalgia is linked to our emotional state.

Key Figures

Dorthe Berntsen p. 148
George Bonanno p. 151
Roger Brown p. 143
Martin Conway p. 130
Elmer Culler p. 134
Richard Eibach p. 146
Edward Girden p. 134

Anthony Greenwald p. 151
James Kulik p. 143
Anja Leist p. 147
Lisa Libby p. 146
Jenny Lotterman p. 151
Sherri-Lynn Pearce p. 134
David Rubin p. 145

Jennifer Talarico p. 145
Donald Thomson p. 133
Endel Tulving p. 130
Herbert Weingartner p. 134
Tim Wildschut p. 149

7 Generic Memory

LEARNING OBJECTIVES

Having read this chapter, you will be able to:

- Differentiate generic memory from other types of memory.
- Identify what type of information is stored in generic memory.
- Describe the hierarchical-network model and identify problems with this model.
- Describe the spreading-activation model and identify problems with this model.
- Describe the compound-cue model and explain how it can explain mediated priming.
- Explain how generic memories are formed.
- Identify the brain areas associated with generic memory.
- Discuss evidence that suggests concepts are modality specific, distributed, learned, and flexible.
- Explain how abstract concepts are coded.
- Describe the hub-and-spoke model.
- Differentiate among superordinate, subordinate, and basic category levels.

KEN JENNINGS: EXTRAORDINARY RECALL FOR ORDINARY THINGS

In 2004, Ken Jennings stunned North American TV audiences when he won a record 74 consecutive games of the popular game show *Jeopardy!*, winning more than $2,520,700 in the process. Mr Jennings answered questions about literature, geography, sports, science, politics, and popular culture, consistently outperforming his co-contestants for more than a year. During the last weeks of Jennings's amazing streak, *Jeopardy!*'s ratings skyrocketed by 22 per cent; each day millions of viewers tuned in to watch Jennings perform. The popularity of Ken's success speaks to people's obsession with maximizing memory, perhaps driven by the same urge that has led humans to develop written language, the printing press, photography, and computers—all human inventions that aid with memory. The popularity of shows like *Jeopardy!* and the proliferation of memory aids indicate that people *value* memory and constantly seek ways to improve it. In this chapter, we explore generic memory and will see that every day each person uses memory in just the same way that Ken Jennings did when he conquered *Jeopardy!*—just to a lesser extent!

Ben Hider/Getty Images

Introduction

generic memory

memory for facts, concepts, and meanings that is context free and not associated with a particular point in time

Generic memory refers to your knowledge of facts, such as your knowledge of the name of the capital city of Canada, the meaning of words you know, and what the characteristics of a cat are (it has four legs, fur, is a carnivore, etc.). Many researchers call this type of memory *semantic memory* (or the memory for meaning); however, not all knowledge is based on meaning. Indeed, you can know how to say "antidisestablishmentarianism" (once the longest word in the English language) and spell it without having the slightest clue what it means; this shows that you can have knowledge without meaning even when that knowledge is for a word. Other examples include the fact that people have knowledge of how things look, smell, feel, and taste, all of which are topics that are extrinsic to language and meaning. In this book, the term *generic memory*, instead of semantic memory, is used to refer to knowledge of facts, as generic memory better represents the scope of information stored and retrieved for the purposes of everyday life. Generic memory is a type of explicit memory.

Generic memory is comprised of **concepts**. A concept is a mental representation of something, like your mental representation of a desk, piece of fruit, dog, or verb. Concepts can often be labelled with words but concepts themselves aren't words; they are abstractions. Consider the example of someone who speaks English and French; that person may use the word *dog* in English and the word *chien* in French; however, the concept of "dog/*chien*" would be the same regardless of the language. Surprenant and Neath (2013, p. 224) state, "[A] concept is more than a word and does not have to be a verbal entity. An analogy might be that a concept is like the entry in a dictionary that follows a word, and not the word itself." Unlike episodic and autobiographical memory, generic memory is context free; where and when the concept was learned is not linked to the generic memory. In Chapter 6, we discussed Endel Tulving's view that there is a difference between *remembering* and *knowing*. Episodic and autobiographical memory involve *remembering*. For example, people *remember* episodes from their lives such as their last birthday and their high school graduation. Generic memory, on the other hand, involves *knowing*. For example, people *know* facts they have learned, such as how old they are and where they went to high school. Empirical evidence supports the notion that generic memory is distinct from episodic memory. First, people who acquire retrograde amnesia due to damage to the medial temporal lobe exhibit loss of

concept

A general idea derived or inferred from specific instances or occurrences

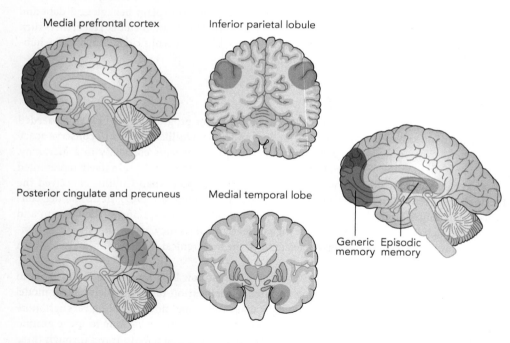

Medial prefrontal cortex

Inferior parietal lobule

Posterior cingulate and precuneus

Medial temporal lobe

Generic   Episodic
memory   memory

Figure 7.1   Brain regions associated with generic and episodic memory

Generic memory and episodic memory are considered distinct types of memory because each appears reliant on a different region of the brain. Damage to the anterior frontal lobe (shown in blue) affects generic memories but not episodic memories, while damage to the medial temporal lobe (shown in orange) affects episodic memories but not generic memories.

Source: Based on Eagleman & Downar, 2016, p. 283

"A rose by any other name would smell as sweet" . . . No matter what it is called, the concept remains the same.

episodic memories going back several years, but only exhibit loss of generic memories acquired shortly before the onset of amnesia (Manns, Hopkins, & Squire, 2003). This finding suggests that episodic memories are linked to the medial temporal lobe while generic memories are not. Second, people who develop **semantic dementia** due to damage in the anterior frontal lobe exhibit generic memory loss while their episodic memory remains intact (Rascovsky, Growdon, Pardo, Grossman, & Miller, 2009). This finding suggests that the anterior frontal lobe is linked to generic memories but not to episodic memories. Because generic and episodic memory involve different types of information and also rely on different brain regions, the notion that they should be considered distinct types of memory is supported.

Early Models of Generic Memory

semantic dementia

A condition associated with damage to the anterior temporal lobe where generic memory is lost while episodic memory remains intact

Models of generic memory attempt to explain how concepts in generic memories are represented and organized. Early models of generic memory, including the hierarchical-network model and the spreading-activation model, were developed to explain behavioural data and were highly influential from the 1960s through the 1990s. At present, memory researchers turn instead to models that can explain both behavioural and neuroscientific data, such as the hub-and-spoke model discussed later in this chapter.

hierarchical-network model

A model of generic memory in which concepts are organized from the most general at the top to the most specific at the bottom, with facts about a concept attached to the highest level of the hierarchy to which they apply

The Hierarchical-Network Model

In the late 1960s, Ross Quillian was developing a computer program to read text and needed the program to "know" facts in order to "understand" text. Quillian needed to conserve space on the hard drive, so he wrote a program that arranged concepts efficiently in a hierarchy. Once he had written the program, Quillian speculated that the human brain likely represented material in a similarly efficient way and thus, with the help of Allan Collins, conceived the **hierarchical-network model** of generic memory (Collins & Quillian, 1969). In this model, concepts are arranged from the most general at the top to the most specific at the bottom, and facts related to concepts are stored at the highest level to which they apply. This structure minimizes redundancy of information. An example of the hierarchical model for animals is shown in Figure 7.2.

sentence-verification task

A paradigm in which participants are presented with statements such as "A bird can fly" or "A fish eats rocks" and must indicate as quickly and accurately as possible whether the sentence is true or false

The hierarchical model makes clear predictions about how long it will take for a person to verify different types of sentences using a **sentence-verification task**. The hierarchical model stipulates that travelling through the hierarchy takes time, that more travelling through more levels takes more time, and that it will take about the same amount of time to move around the network no matter what level you start at. For example, if you have to travel through three concepts to get from "goldfish" to "has gills" (goldfish, fish, gills), it will take the same amount of time as travelling through three concepts to get from "minivan" to "powered by gasoline" (minivan, motor vehicle, powered by gasoline). Taken together, the model thus predicts that participants would verify the sentence "A salmon eats" more slowly than "A salmon is pink" because they would need to travel up the hierarchy to the animal node to verify that the salmon

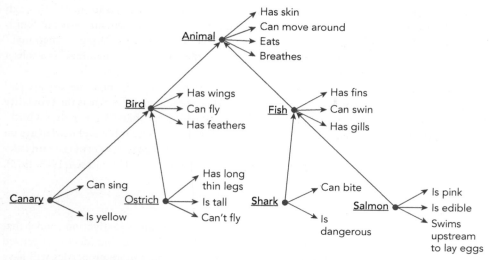

Figure 7.2 An illustration of the hierarchical model of generic memory

Source: Collins & Quillian, 1969, p. 24

eats, whereas they would not need to travel at all to verify that a salmon is pink (see Figure 7.2). Collins and Quillian presented participants with true and false statements about topics including games, animals, beverages, and trees. They found that when the participants had to traverse more levels in the hierarchy, they were slower to verify that a sentence was true.

Although Collins and Quillian created a model that withstood a basic prediction (that some sentences will be recognized more quickly than others), the model is problematic for several reasons. First, the hierarchical model does not really explain how participants are able to respond to a sentence as false; for example, consider the sentence "Salmon have fur." Participants quickly respond that this sentence is false; however, the model seems to predict that participants would need to consult the entire hierarchy before establishing a property was absent.

Second, the hierarchical model predicts that sentence verification will be related to a concept's hierarchy; however, Carol Conrad found that *frequency* of a property, not its level on the hierarchy, predicted verification times. Conrad (1972) first collected normative data, asking participants to name properties of categories she provided. If a property was named by at least 50 per cent of participants, it was considered high frequency; if was mentioned by fewer than 25 per cent of participants, it was considered low frequency; and if it was mentioned by between 25 and 50 per cent of participants, it was considered to be of moderate frequency. The hierarchical model predicts that participants will take longer to verify an item if it is further away in the hierarchy, regardless of frequency; however, Conrad (1972) found that response times for high-frequency items were not affected by hierarchy at all. Conrad (1972) also found that response times were linearly related to frequency such that high-frequency properties were verified more quickly than moderate-frequency properties, which were verified more quickly than low-frequency properties. Conrad (1972) concluded that the hierarchical model tends to put higher-frequency items at level 0 and lower-frequency items at lower levels, and that the familiarity of a property, rather than having to move through a network, could explain the response time differences for different levels of concepts.

Third, the hierarchical model also predicts that the further a person has to "move" through a hierarchy, the slower she or he will be, but Lance Rips, Edward Shoben, and Edward Smith demonstrated that participants are faster to verify "A pig is an animal" than "A pig is a mammal," even though a strictly hierarchical model would predict the opposite (as "mammal" is a subset of "animal"; Rips, Shoben, & Smith, 1973).

Finally, Michael Posner and Steve Keele showed that typical members of a category are recognized more quickly than atypical category members, a phenomenon known as the **typicality effect**. For example, "A robin is a bird" is recognized more quickly than "An ostrich is a bird." The typicality effect is problematic for the hierarchical model because robin and ostrich are on the same level in the hierarchy and therefore should be confirmed as members of the bird category in the same amount of time (e.g., Posner & Keele, 1968; Rips et al., 1973; Rosch, 1973, 1975).

The Spreading-Activation Model

In 1975, Allan Collins and Elizabeth Loftus developed the **spreading-activation model** that better fit the extant data. The spreading-activation model is based on the ideas that related concepts are connected in a network, and that concepts that share more properties will have more links between them (see Figure 7.3). According to the spreading-activation model, when a person thinks of a concept, activation spreads out along all paths connected to this concept. Activation is assumed to be limited, so when there are more paths, less activation goes to each path. For example, if you have a pitcher of water and need to divide it evenly among all the cups you have, you will have to put less water in each cup as the number of cups increases. When a concept has been activated by another concept, less additional activation is needed for that concept to reach a **decision criterion**. The spreading-activation model can account for the findings that were problematic for the hierarchical-network model. First, the model can explain why responses to false statements such as "A salmon has fur" are made relatively quickly—the model assumes that no activation will spread from salmon to fur. Second, the model can account for the fact that higher-frequency features such as "A salmon is a fish" are recognized more quickly than lower-frequency features such as "A salmon has skin" by assuming that connections between concepts and high-frequency features are closer than connections between concepts and low-frequency features. Third, the model can account for findings that seem to contradict a hierarchical structure, such as participants verifying "A pig is an animal" more quickly than "A pig is a mammal," if it is assumed that there is a closer connection between pig and animal than pig and mammal. Finally, spreading activation can account for the typicality effect by assuming that typical members of a category are more closely associated to a category than less typical members.

Spreading-activation models were also designed to account for **associative priming**, a phenomenon where a person recognizes an item more quickly when it follows a related concept than when it does not. Associative-priming effects support the spreading-activation model because they are consistent with the premise that activation spreads from a word to related nodes adding activation, thus reducing the amount of additional activation needed to reach the decision criterion, predicting that less activation (and time) will be needed to recognize "nurse" when it is preceded by "doctor." According to the spreading-activation model, "A robin is a bird" is recognized more quickly than "A robin is an animal" because the concepts of "robin" and "bird" share a closer association in the network than "robin" and "animal" do. Literally thousands of experiments have demonstrated associative priming.

typicality effect

The finding that response times in a sentence-verification task are faster for more typical instances of a category than less typical instances. For example, "A robin is a bird" is recognized more quickly than "An ostrich is a bird."

spreading-activation model

A model of the relationship among concepts in memory based on the ideas that related concepts are connected in a network, and that concepts that share more properties will have more links between them

decision criterion

A threshold of activation that must be met in order for an item to be retrieved from generic memory

associative priming

Faster recognition of a word when the word is preceded by a related word than when a word is preceded by an unrelated word

Soon after it was introduced, the spreading-activation model became the dominant view of generic memory. The model explains the results from sentence-verification tasks and the existence of semantic priming even when participants are not expecting to see words that are semantically related (Neely, 1977). The spreading-activation model is also supported by research showing greater associative priming for words that are closely related semantically than for those that are less closely related semantically. Rosa Sáchez-Casas and colleagues assembled a list of 80 words from a variety of categories and then linked each of these target words with four possible primes: the word itself (e.g., donkey–DONKEY), a prime that was very similar in meaning to the original word (e.g., horse–DONKEY), a prime from the same semantic category but that was less closely related (e.g., bear–DONKEY) and a prime that was unrelated (e.g., thimble–DONKEY). Participants completed a lexical decision task during which they had to indicate as quickly and accurately as possible, using the keyboard, if a letter string that was presented was a word such as DONKEY or a nonword such as HERLOP. Each participant saw each target word only once. Sánchez-Casas, Ferré, Garcia-Albea, and Guasch (2006) found that participants made a lexical decision for a target word (e.g., DONKEY) significantly faster when the prime was very closely related (e.g., horse–DONKEY) than when the prime was just closely related (e.g., bear–DONKEY). The researchers conducted an additional experiment with the same word stimuli, but in this

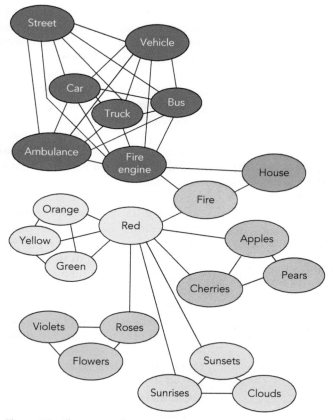

Figure 7.3 Illustration of concepts using a spreading-activation model

This image represents how related concepts may be connected in a spreading-activation model (Collins & Loftus, 1975). Note that closely related concepts and features are closer together on this concept map, and concepts that are not as closely related are farther away.

Source: Collins & Loftus, 1975, p. 412

Test the Connections in Your Own Generic Memory

Grab a piece of paper and write down the word PAPER. Next write down the first 10 words that come to mind. Now, grab another piece of paper and write down the word HOUSE. Write down 10 words but make sure that the words are NOT related to each other. Which task was more difficult? Was there a pattern in the first list of words generated? Chances are most words on the PAPER list were linked to the word PAPER and that it was difficult to generate words that are unrelated to one another. This is evidence that spreading activation does occur between concepts.

experiment participants saw the prime and target together (e.g., horse–DONKEY) and had to indicate if the word appearing in uppercase letters (e.g., DONKEY) was a concrete noun or not by pressing a key on the keyboard as quickly and accurately as possible. Once again, the participants responded more quickly when the prime and target were very closely related (e.g., horse–DONKEY) than when they were just closely related (e.g., bear–DONKEY). The results of Sánchez-Casas et al. (2006) support the spreading-activation model, as this model predicts that closer semantic relationships will result in greater semantic priming.

There are several weaknesses with the spreading-activation account. First, it is very difficult to disprove the spreading-activation model; how do you show that spreading activation is *not* taking place? A second weakness of the spreading-activation model is that it cannot explain the **mediated priming effect** and therefore can't give a good account of memory retrieval. Mediated priming is the finding that concepts that aren't directly linked to one another can still sometimes prime one another. For example, McNamara (1992) showed that the word *mane* can prime the word *stripe* even though the association between those words, according to the spreading-activation model, is quite remote (mane-lion-tiger-stripe). Mediated priming is problematic because in order for activation to spread from *mane* to *stripe*, thousands and thousands of other words would need to be activated in the system, which predicts that most words should prime most other words if there is even a remote association between them; but research has shown this is not the case. McNamara (1992) argues that each word has about 20 other words associated with it. Thus, McNamara argues, if *mane* were activated, 20 other words would also be activated, including *lion*. Next, for *lion* to activate *tiger*, 20 words associated with *lion* would need to be activated along with 20 words for each of the other words activated by *mane*; thus at this point 420 words would be active. Next activation would have to spread from *tiger* to *stripe*, activating 20 words related to *tiger* and also activating 20 words associated with each of the other 419 words that are current. At this point a staggering 8400 words would be active, meaning that a total of almost 10,000 words would be activated by the word *mane* and that each of these words could thus be primed by *mane* (see Figure 7.4). If an average person has a vocabulary of 30,000 words, this would mean that one-third of that vocabulary would be activated by *mane*, which McNamara (1992) argues would be highly inefficient. In addition, McNamara (1992) argues that, according to spreading activation, *mane* should not just prime *stripe* but also all words that are removed from *mane* by four or fewer degrees of association, such as *scissors* (mane-hair-haircut-scissors); however, *mane* is not likely to prime *scissors*. In fact, priming is a relatively rare occurrence. Even when participants are trained to associate two words through repeated exposure, priming effects aren't usually observed until about five weeks after learning.

A third problem with the spreading-activation model is that it predicts that priming effects will be very short in duration; after additional stimuli have been presented, new concepts will be active, and old items shouldn't produce priming. However, Joordens and Becker (1997) showed that semantic priming could occur over as many as eight intervening items. A fourth problem with the spreading-activation model is that the model assumes a single fixed representation for each concept in a network. Thus, the model predicts that a person reading the sentence "Amy painted the egg" and "Amy ate the egg" would activate the same nodes related to "egg." However, processing of the first sentence would likely focus on the exterior of the egg, while processing of the second sentence would focus on the interior of the egg, which are different concepts. Finally, the spreading-activation model represents concepts as individual

mediated priming effect

The finding that words that are associated by way of several other words can often prime each other. For example, *mane* can prime *stripe* even though they are not directly related concepts.

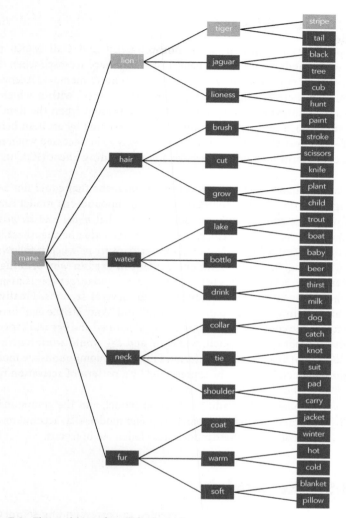

Figure 7.4 The problem of mediated priming

An illustration of how the spreading-activation account of how *mane* could prime *stripe* would also mean that many other words were also activated. Figure 7.4 shows what the network would look like if *mane* activated five additional words and each of those words activated three additional words, and each of those activated just two more words. Very quickly, 50 words have become activated by *mane* and yet most aren't primed by *mane*. Priming is actually quite rare. Mediated priming cannot easily be explained by a spreading-activation model.

nodes, implying localized representations in generic memory; however, there is substantial evidence in the literature dating back to the work of Lashley in the 1950s to suggest that generic memories are represented by patterns of activation distributed across neurons (Lashley, 1958). The compound-cue model was developed to offer an alternative to the spreading-activation model.

The Compound-Cue Model

The **compound-cue model** was first proposed by Roger Ratcliff and Gail McKoon of Northwestern University. The model suggests that generic memories are accessed when there is a match between cues in short-term memory and items in generic memory. According to the compound-cue model, there are three types of cues: the context within which the memory was learned (called **context cues**), the items that were present when the item was learned (called **inter-item cues**), and a sense of familiarity represented by an item being a cue for itself (called **self–self cues**). Generic memory is more likely to be accessed when more cues for an item are in short-term memory; cues have a compounding effect (Ratcliff and McKoon, 1988).

The compound-cue model can account for some of the phenomena that could not be explained by the spreading-activation model. For example, the compound-cue model can account for mediated priming. The compound-cue model assumes that *mane* and *stripe* have similar associations in memory, such as *large cat*, *claws*, *danger*, and *cubs* and that these associations are similar enough to significantly affect the familiarity of *stripe* when it follows the word *mane*, resulting in priming. The compound-cue model can explain why priming can sometimes occur when there are several items between the prime and target if it is assumed that the prime enters short-term memory and stays there for several seconds. Finally, the compound-cue model can explain why "Amy painted the egg" and "Amy ate the egg" bring to mind very different aspects of the concept "egg" if it is assumed *painted* and *egg* work together as inter-item cues for the concept of an eggshell, while *ate* and *egg* would work together as inter-item cues for the concept of an egg's edible interior. Finally, the compound-cue model is consistent with the notion that concepts may be represented by a pattern of activation rather than by a single node.

The hierarchical-network model, the spreading-activation model, and the compound-cue model are all based on behavioural data. Today, researchers prefer models that account for both behavioural and neuroscientific data; thus, these models have fallen out of favour.

The Hub-and-Spoke Model

Although it is clear that features of concepts are represented in corresponding sensory and motor areas of the brain, two lines of evidence suggest that various features of a concept are also integrated into a single supramodal concept. First, there is the fact that people can identify similarities in concepts that have very different perceptual or action-related features. For example, a hosta and a cactus have very different perceptual features but are both easily linked together as plants; a hammer and a saw have very different action-related features but are both easily grouped together as tools. This suggests that concepts don't rely entirely on perceptual or motor representations. Second, individuals with semantic dementia, which is caused by degeneration in the anterior temporal lobes, often lose knowledge of multiple features of a given concept; for example, they may not be able to identify a lemon by sight or by smell. This suggests that the frontotemporal area of the brain is involved in integrating multiple features of a given concept. Gorana Pobric, Elizabeth Jefferies, and Matthew Ralph (2010) used these observations as the basis for the **hub-and-spoke model of generic memory**. According to the hub-and-spoke model, six types of modality-specific representations (or spokes) all meet at a central hub in the anterior temporal lobe. The six types of modality-specific information are visual features, verbal descriptors, smells (olfaction), sounds, motor information (praxis), and information from the skin and internal organs (somatosensory). A depiction of the hub-and-spoke model can be seen in Figure 7.5a.

Pobric et al. (2010) used repetitive transcranial magnetic stimulation (rTMS) to test the hub-and-spoke model. When a brain region is stimulated with rTMS, it loses its functionality, and thus rTMS can be used to determine which specific brain regions are necessary for the completion of specific tasks. To test the hub-and-spoke model, Pobric et al. (2010) stimulated the anterior temporal lobe (ATL) and the inferior parietal lobule (IPL) while participants viewed images of living and nonliving objects (see Figure 7.5b). The hub-and-spoke model predicts that stimulation of the ATL will disrupt naming of both living and nonliving objects equally because all features of a concept are thought to be integrated in the ATL. The model also predicts that disrupting the IPL will only impact naming objects that can be manipulated by hand, because the IPL is associated with praxis but not with other features of a concept. The results of Pobric et al. (2010) support the hub-and-spoke model. Stimulating the ATL disrupted naming of all living and nonliving objects, supporting the notion that the ATL is linked to supramodal conceptual representations. Stimulating the IPL, on the other hand, only disrupted naming of nonliving objects that could be manipulated by hand, supporting the notion that concepts are represented in modality-specific regions of the brain as well. The hub-and-spoke model is a good model of generic memory because it not only explains behavioural data (such as patterns of deficits in people with semantic dementia), but it also explains how memories may be represented and interconnected within the brain.

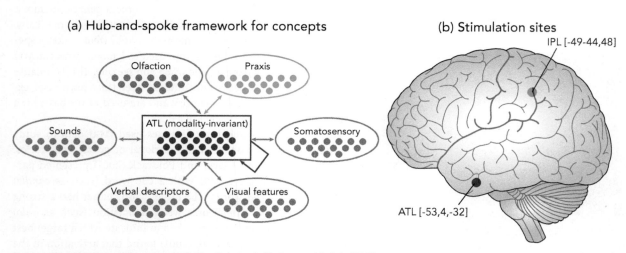

Figure 7.5   The hub-and-spoke model by Pobric, Jefferies, and Ralph (2010)

The model in part (a) shows six modality-specific inputs (visual features, sounds, olfaction, verbal descriptors, praxis, and somatosensory) connected to a single hub in the anterior temporal lobe. The hub integrates the modality-specific information into a single unified representation. Part (b) shows the brain regions that were stimulated using rTMS in Pobric et al. (2010). Stimulation of the left ATL, which is the hub in the model, slowed naming of living and nonliving objects. Stimulation of the IPL, which is associated with object manipulation, only slowed naming for nonliving objects. The results support the hub-and-spoke model.

Source: Pobric et al., 2010, p. 965

The Neuroscience of Generic Memory

Most researchers agree that generic memories are initially episodic memories stored in the hippocampus. Consider your knowledge about what animal is on the Canadian one-dollar coin. The first time you handled the coin, you may have noticed the distinct profile of a loon embossed on one side. Soon after, your parent may have asked you, "Why do you think this coin is called a loonie?" At this point you may have referred back to your episodic memory of seeing the loon on the coin and answered, "Because there is a loon on it." Over the coming months you would encounter the coin many more times. Recall from Chapter 4 that the two-stage model of memory suggests that, over time, features that overlap across episodic memories stored in the hippocampus are transferred to the neocortex (McClelland, McNaughton, & O'Reilly, 1995). This would have happened to your knowledge about the loon on the loonie. Once represented in the neocortex, you could recall that a loon is a feature on the one-dollar Canadian coin without remembering any particular episode during which you encountered the loon image.

Dagenbach, Horst, and Carr (1990) used associative priming to test the time course of the transfer of information from episodic to generic memory. Associative priming occurs when there is faster response to a word/nonword decision when a word is preceded by a related word (such as when DOCTOR is preceded by NURSE). Dagenbach et al. (1990) argued that associative priming is only observed for items that are part of generic memory; episodic memories do not produce priming. Dagenbach et al. (1990) ran their participants through an extensive study regimen that included learning novel nonword–word pairs such as DRUPE–CHERRY. After five weeks of intense study, DRUPE facilitated processing CHERRY. Dagenbach et al. (1990) concluded that the priming effect indicated that DRUPE had become part of generic memory and that, by extension, it takes at least five weeks for episodic information to become a generic memory.

Patterns are extracted from episodic information automatically. For example, you have probably never been told what makes a specific piece of furniture a desk (as opposed to a table); however, you can easily tell a desk from a table when you see one. This is because common features of desks encountered over time have been extracted from your episodic memory and are used as the basis for a generic memory of the concept of a desk.

Anthony Wagner and his colleagues used fMRI data to study the brain regions involved in the retrieval of generic memories. Wagner, Paré-Blagoev, Clark, and Poldrack (2001) presented participants undergoing an fMRI with a cue word (such as *candle*) above multiple target words. The target words either had a strong association (such as *flame*) or a weak association (such as *halo*) with the cue. Participants were asked to indicate which target best matched the cue. Wagner et al. (2001) found that activation in the left inferior prefrontal cortex (LIPC) was significantly greater in the weak associative strength condition than the strong associative strength condition and concluded that the left inferior prefrontal cortex is involved with controlled searches of generic memory, such as those involved with determining whether the word *candle* is more similar to the word *flame* or the word *halo*. Wagner et al. (2001) argue that some information in generic memory is retrieved

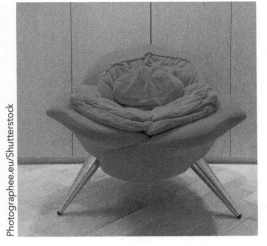

What is this object? Chances are you have never seen this exact image before, but you can immediately determine what it is. The ability to use existing knowledge to identify and classify novel items is made possible by generic memory.

automatically, such as the fact that candles produce flames. Other information, such as whether candles are more similar to a person's memory for the concept "flame" or the concept "halo," requires effort to retrieve, and effortful, controlled retrieval involves the LIPC.

Brains Areas Associated with Generic Memory

In the 1920s, Karl Lashley was convinced that, if he lesioned the correct part of the brain, he could eliminate a memory for a learned behaviour. Lashley was looking for localized engrams (Lashley, 1929). Despite years of trying, Lashley was never able to eliminate a learned behaviour and eventually concluded that generic memories were distributed across the brain and not localized after all. (For more on engrams, see Chapter 1. This topic will also be discussed in more detail later in this chapter).

Researchers have deduced which areas of the brain are critical for forming generic memories by observing people with anterograde amnesia (like H.M.) who have lost the ability to form new memories. Anterograde amnesia can be caused by damage to various brain structures, including the hippocampus, the mammillary body, the mammillothalamic tract, and the hippocampal gyrus (Butters & Cermak, 1980). The variety of causes of anterograde amnesia reinforces the notion that the creation of new generic memories involves many different brain regions. Figure 7.6 shows the general areas associated with the creation and maintenance of generic memories. When a person incurs damage to the anterior temporal lobe, she or he will

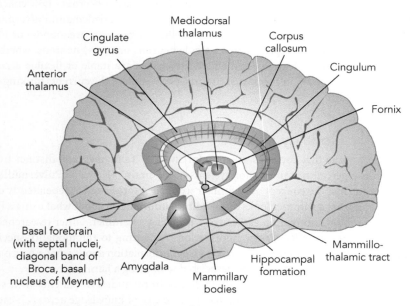

Figure 7.6   Brain regions associated with generic memory

This figure shows the location of the hippocampus, the mammillary bodies, the mammillothalamic tract, and the hippocampal formation, all of which are associated with the formation and maintenance of generic memory. Note that these areas are distributed in different areas of the brain rather than being localized. This distribution may have had evolutionary value, preventing most localized brain injuries from causing catastrophic memory impairment.

Source: Staniloiu & Markowitsch, 2012, pp. 5, Figure 2

develop semantic dementia and lose access to conceptual knowledge. When a person incurs damage to one of the sensory or motor areas, she or he may develop problems with concepts that revolve around that type of sensory or motor information. For example, a person who sustains damage to the visual cortex may have difficulty with highly visual generic memories, while someone who sustains damage to the motor areas may have difficulty with memories associated with actions.

We will now work toward a model of generic memory that takes into account these neuroscientific factors as well as the behavioural data from the literature. We begin by refining our definition of a concept.

The Neuroscience of Concepts

Concepts are fundamental to all cognitive tasks. Concepts are needed for object recognition, action planning, language, and thought because concepts indicate what objects, events, and abstract ideas mean (Kiefer & Pulvermüller, 2012). Researchers agree that concepts reflect our experiences in the world in a categorical fashion; our concept of "dog" includes all the information we have learned about a dog, such as dogs are animals, dogs have four legs, dogs have fur, dogs bark, dogs like to smell things, and dogs like to be petted. Concepts are extracted from specific episodes of experience and are, like all generic memories, context free. While most researchers agree that concepts are context free, there is considerable debate concerning how concepts are represented in the brain. In their 2012 paper, Markus Kiefer and Friedemann Pulvermüller explore the four issues that are central to this debate: whether concepts are amodal or modality specific, whether concepts are represented on single neurons or across neurons, whether concept categories are innate or learned, and whether concepts are stable or flexible across time (Kiefer & Pulvermüller, 2012). In the next sections, we will explore the current thinking on each of these issues.

Concepts Are Modality Specific

amodal

To be independent of perceptual and motor representations

Some researchers argue that concepts are **amodal** and are "fundamentally distinct from representations in the perceptual and motor systems of the brain" (Kiefer & Pulvermüller, 2012, p. 807). This means that the concept of a hammer would be represented independently of visual information about what a hammer looks like, auditory information about what using a hammer sounds like, and motor information associated with using a hammer. Other researchers argue that concepts contain *modality-specific* information. According to the modality-specific perspective, the concept of a hammer may include visual information about what a hammer looks like, and auditory and motor information associated with using a hammer.

The main evidence for the amodal position comes from studies of patients with semantic dementia. Patients with semantic dementia have severe loss of knowledge across all categories, including animals and objects made by humans, and across conceptual feature types, including all perceptual and action-related information (Kiefer & Pulvermüller, 2012). For example, individuals with semantic dementia may have no knowledge of what an apple looks like, smells like, tastes like, or is used for. They may also have no knowledge of what a hammer looks like, feels like, or is used for. Because semantic dementia generalizes across the senses and results in a loss of knowledge from all types of categories, some researchers have proposed that concepts must be represented in an amodal format, and that those representations are housed in the anterior temporal lobe (ATL), which is damaged in all people with semantic dementia (Kiefer & Pulvermüller, 2012; see also McClelland & Rogers, 2003; Patterson, Nestor, & Rogers, 2007; Rogers et al., 2004). However, one problem with this argument is that damage to other regions of the brain can impact conceptual processing as well, and the type of deficit observed can be predicted based on what area of the brain is damaged. Strokes that cause damage in the left cortex around the Sylvian fissure often result in difficulties with processing concepts of tools and small manipulative objects but not other concepts, while damage to the frontal cortex and motor areas tends to be associated with problems using action verbs (Kiefer & Pulvermüller, 2012; see also Bak, O'Donovan, Xuereb, Boniface, & Hodges, 2001; Cotelli et al., 2006; Daniele, Giustolisi, Silveri, Colosimo, & Gainotti, 1994). When researchers look at patients with aphasia (the loss of ability to use some aspect of language), those who have trouble with action-related words (like verbs) typically have lesions in the frontal and parietal/motor areas (Kiefer & Pulvermüller, 2012; see also Gainotti, 2004; Gainotti, Silveri, Daniele, & Giustolisi, 1995) while people with difficulty with words related to natural objects (like animal names) typically have lesions in the visual association cortex (Hart & Gordon, 1992; Kiefer & Pulvermüller, 2012; Tranel, Damasio, & Damasio, 1997; Tranel, Kemmerer, Adolphs, Damasio, & Damasio, 2003). Thus, it is possible to lose the ability to use some types of concepts without having any damage to the frontotemporal area, and the concepts that are disrupted vary depending on the region that is diseased. This supports the notion that concept representations contain modality-specific information.

Brain-imaging studies have shown activation in sensory and perceptual processing areas during the completion of conceptual tasks (Kiefer & Pulvermüller, 2012). For example, when study participants read words strongly associated with sounds, such as *telephone*, the left posterior superior and middle temporal gyri (pSTG/MTG) were highly active and the activity was similar to activity observed when participants were listening to actual sounds. However, Kiefer and Pulvermüller (2012) found that when the same participants read words that were not strongly linked to acoustic features (like *apple*), no such activity was observed. Kiefer and Pulvermüller argue that these results suggest that access to concepts involves partial reinstatement of the same perceptual processes that occurred during object perceptions (Kiefer & Pulvermüller, 2012). Other researchers have found that visual-processing areas are active when participants read words that are closely linked to visual stimuli (such as *apple*) and that odour-processing areas are active when participants read words that are closely linked to specific scents such as *cinnamon* (González et al., 2006). Hauk, Johnsrude, and Pulvermüller (2004) found that different motor areas are active when participants are listening to words that are associated with different body parts; the word *kick* activates foot-related areas, the word lick activates mouth-related areas, and the word *pick* activates hand-related areas. These results, taken together, suggest that the meaning of action words is embodied in the motor-related areas that would be needed to enact those actions (Kiefer & Pulvermüller, 2012). Further support for the notion that action-related concepts are embodied in the motor regions comes from studies in which transcranial magnetic stimulation (TMS) has been directed at different regions of the brain. These studies have found that TMS directed at the hand region of the motor cortex improved conceptual processing of arm-related words, while TMS to the foot region of the motor cortex improved conceptual processing of leg-related words (Kiefer & Pulvermüller, 2012).

Broad-reaching deficits in conceptual processing observed in patients with semantic dementia support the notion that concepts are amodal, while specific deficits observed in individuals with lesions in perceptual and motor-processing areas suggest that concept representations may be modality specific. Taken together, this suggests to researchers that concepts are represented by modality-specific systems that are linked to a conceptual hub that integrates the various modal information. The hub is located in the anterior temporal lobe, which is why people with damage to this area develop semantic dementia (Kiefer & Pulvermüller, 2012).

Concepts Are Distributed

Some single-cell recordings have revealed that there are neurons in temporal lobe structures that only respond to specific concepts, such as Halle Berry's face or name (Quiroga, Reddy, Kreiman, Koch, & Fried, 2005), suggesting that some concepts may be represented on individual neurons. However, there is also substantial evidence that concept representations are distributed throughout the brain. First, recall the evidence supporting the existence of modality-specific representations of concepts; these modality-specific representations are distributed in different parts of the sensory and motor cortices. Second, individuals with neurodegenerative diseases such as Alzheimer's disease or semantic dementia do not lose access to all aspects of a concept at once (Kiefer & Pulvermüller, 2012). For example, individuals with semantic dementia typically do not lose all information related to a concept at once; they may lose the concept "A canary can sing" in the early stages of the disease but may still know "A canary can move"; if concepts were localized, then all information about canaries should be lost at the same time (Rogers et al., 2004). Finally, different features of a concept are activated depending on the context (e.g., Barsalou, 1982), suggesting that concepts are comprised of many distinct features that are coded by different groups of cells (Kiefer & Pulvermüller, 2012). Thus, there is evidence that some individual neurons do respond selectively to very specific concepts, but there is also evidence that concept representations are distributed across many neurons in many regions of the brain (Bowers, 2009).

Researchers found neurons that respond only to pictures of Halle Berry's face (Quiroga et al., 2005).

Concepts Are Learned

In the 1980s, Elizabeth Warrington and Rosaleen McCarthy first described a patient known as V.E.R. who had severe language impairments following a left-hemisphere stroke. Despite impairments in speech and difficulty following many verbal instructions, when shown certain words, V.E.R. was able to point to the corresponding picture. What was unusual about V.E.R's performance is that she performed better when words related to living objects (such as flowers, animals, or natural foods) then when words referred to objects made by humans and nonliving things (such as tools or furniture; Warrington and McCarthy, 1983). Elizabeth Warrington and Tim Shallice soon identified four patients with the *opposite* problem with naming; in these four cases, all the patients had worse performance for living things than nonliving things (Warrington & Shallice, 1984). Warrington and Shallice (1984) studied object naming and knowledge in the two individuals in their group who were able to speak. J.B.R. (a 23-year-old male) and S.B.Y. (a 48-year-old male) were shown 96 colour pictures of animals, plants, and inanimate objects. First, they were asked to name or describe the objects they were shown. J.B.R. was able to name 90 per cent of nonliving objects he was shown, but was only able to name 6 per cent of the living objects. S.B.Y. was able to name 75 per cent of

Table 7.1   Examples of definitions given by J.B.R. and S.B.Y in Warrington and Shallice (1984)

Patient	Nonliving Objects – Response	Living Objects – Response
J.B.R.	tent – temporary outhouse, living home	parrot – don't know
	briefcase – small case used by students to carry papers	daffodil – plant
	compass – tools for telling direction you are going	snail – insect animal
	torch – handheld light	eel – not well
	dustbin – bin for putting rubbish in	ostrich – unusual
S.B.Y.	wheelbarrow – object used by people to take material about	duck – an animal
	towel – material used to dry people	wasp – bird that flies
	pram – used to carry people, with wheels and thing to sit on	crocus – rubbish material
	submarine – ship that goes underneath the sea	holly – what you drink
	umbrella – object used to protect you from water that comes	spider – person looking for things, he was a spider for a nation or country

Examples of definition responses from J.B.R. and S.B.Y. in Warrington and Shallice (1984) Experiment 2. While both individuals were able to define nonliving objects well, they were unable to correctly define any living objects.
Source: Adapted from Warrington & Shallice, 1984, p. 838

nonliving objects he was shown, but was unable to name any of the living objects he was shown. Next, they heard the names of each of the 96 objects they had just been shown and were asked to define each word. Table 7.1 shows some of the responses J.B.R. and S.B.Y. made to words they heard.

In several subsequent experiments, Warrington and Shallice (1984) replicated their general finding; they had identified a group of patients who seemed unable to locate generic memories for living things, but whose ability to locate generic memories for nonliving things seemed intact.

Alfonso Caramazza and Jennifer Shelton proposed the domain-specific knowledge hypothesis to explain this data. According to Caramazza and Shelton (1998), evolutionary pressures have led the human brain to develop specialized mechanisms for distinguishing between living and nonliving things; faster processing of animate information is argued to benefit survival. However the domain-specific hypothesis has difficulty explaining some of Warrington's other findings. For example, Warrington and Shallice (1984) found that J.B.R. had some deficits in naming objects from some nonliving categories, including metals, types of cloth, musical instruments, and precious stones. Warrington and McCarthy (1987) later found patient Y.O.T. with the *opposite* problem of J.B.R.; Y.O.T. could not match the names of most nonliving objects to their pictures, with the exception of metals, types of cloth, musical instruments, and precious stones. Warrington and Shallice (1984) argue that concepts related to living things rely on perceptual processing while concepts related to nonliving things rely on motor processing, and that damage to perceptual areas therefore results in problems with living concepts while damage to motor areas results in problems with nonliving concepts. This model is consistent with the observation that V.E.R. and

Y.O.T. sustained damage that primarily affected action planning but not visual perception, while J.B.R. and S.B.Y. sustained damage that primarily affected visual processing but not action planning. Consider the definitions in Table 7.1. Note that when J.B.R. and S.B.Y. were able to define nonliving objects, they only described the function of these objects, never their perceptual traits. For example, when S.B.Y. describes a submarine he states that it is "[a] ship that goes underneath the sea" but makes no reference to the fact that most submarines are long and cylindrical in shape and grey in colour. Thus, it may have appeared that J.B.R. and S.B.Y. were unable to define living concepts because of their conceptual category, when in reality it may have been because living things can only really be described with perceptual features, and J.B.R. and S.B.Y. had brain damage that limited their access to those features. To see how nonliving and living things tend to be described differently, try the DIY box below.

Martha Farah and James McClelland decided to run a computer simulation to see what effect limiting perceptual and action features would have on object recognition for living and nonliving objects respectively. First, Farah and McClelland looked at the proportion of visual descriptors and functional descriptors in the dictionary definitions of each stimulus used in Warrington and Shallice (1984). Farah and McClelland (1991) found a ratio of 7.7:1 visual descriptors to functional descriptors for living objects and a ratio of 1.4:1 visual descriptors to functional descriptors for nonliving objects. In other words, they found that living objects contained 7.7 times as many visual descriptors as functional descriptors while nonliving objects only contained 1.4 times as many visual descriptors as functional descriptors. Farah

---

DIY EXPERIMENT | BOX 7.2

Different Types of Knowledge

To complete this experiment, get a piece of paper. Write each word below and beside it write your own definition for that word.

car	scissors
donkey	axe
seaweed	desk
owl	shark
canoe	flamingo
acorn	stapler

Next, look at the types of words you used to define each object. You most likely described actions to define the words *car*, *canoe*, *scissors*, *axe*, *desk*, and *stapler* and perceptual features like colour, size, and texture to define *donkey*, *owl*, *acorn*, *flamingo*, *seaweed*, and *shark*. Warrington and Shallice (1984) argue that our generic memories for objects are generally divided into two broad categories: knowledge that is primarily related to what objects do and knowledge that is primarily related to what objects look like.

and McClelland's computational model was just like a human. It was given a ratio of 7.7:1 visual-to-functional inputs for each living object and 1.4:1 visual-to-functional inputs for each nonliving object. The model was trained to correctly identify 20 objects (10 living, 10 nonliving) based on these differing ratios of inputs. Once it was trained, researchers simulated brain damage by turning off 20 per cent, 40 per cent, 60 per cent, 80 per cent, and then 100 per cent of either the visual or the functional inputs and at each stage tested to see how well the model could identify the objects. Farah and McClelland (1991) found that as visual inputs were eliminated the model got progressively worse at identifying living objects, and as functional inputs were eliminated the model got progressively worse at identifying nonliving objects. While the results of Farah and McClelland (1991) don't prove that the modality-specific model is correct, they do demonstrate that the modality-specific model is neurally plausible.

Another study supporting the notion that learning plays a formidable role in concept development was conducted by Kiefer, Sim, Liebich, Hauk, and Tanaka. In this study, participants were shown a series of novel objects. Half the participants were instructed to pantomime interacting with each object (such as using part of it as a handle, or placing objects on top of it) while the other half were instructed to just point at the object. Later, the participants completed a categorization task that involved some of the novel objects while their brain activity was being monitored (see Figure 7.7). Kiefer et al. (2007) found that the pantomime group (but not the pointing group) showed increased activity in the frontotemporal lobes at the start of each trial and in the occipital parietal visual-motor regions later in the trial. Kiefer et al. (2007) concluded that the pantomime group showed this pattern of activity because they had learned an action-related concept of the object.

There is very little evidence to support the notion that concept categories are innate. Instead, evidence suggests that conceptual features are modality specific and coded from direct perceptual and action-based experiences.

Figure 7.7 Examples of pantomiming actions from Kiefer et al. (2007)

In Kiefer et al. (2007), participants were shown novel objects. Some participants were asked to pantomime interacting with the objects based on the instructions shown above. Other participants were instructed to just point at the objects. When the objects were shown again, participants who pantomimed interacting with the objects showed greater activation in the frontotemporal lobe and occipital parietal visual-motor regions than participants who had simply pointed at the objects. Kiefer et al. (2007) concluded that this activation reflected learning an action-related sequence as part of the concept for the object.

Source: Kiefer et al., 2007, p. 527; figure retrieved from Kiefer, M. and F. Pulvermüller (2012). Conceptual representations in mind and brain: Theoretical developments, current evidence and future directions. *Cortex, 48*(7), 805–25.

Concepts Are Flexible

Some researchers have argued that concepts are stable in that the same aspects of a concept are retrieved each time a concept is retrieved regardless of context, and that the same brain regions are activated each time a concept is retrieved. However, there is substantial evidence that different word meanings are recruited depending on the context (Barsalou, 1982; Kiefer, 2005). Lawrence Barsalou of Stanford University proposed that words contain context-independent conceptual properties, which are always activated when a word is activated, and context-dependent properties, which are activated by the context in which that word appears. Barsalou (1982) tested his hypothesis in two experiments. In the first experiment, Barsalou had participants read sentences that contained an underlined noun followed by a property. The participants had to indicate as quickly and accurately as possible whether the property applied to the underlined noun. Sometimes the sentence was related directly to the property and sometimes the sentence was unrelated. In addition, sometimes the property was considered context independent and sometimes the property was considered context dependent. Examples of the four types of sentences can be seen in Table 7.2.

Barsalou (1982) argued that when a concept is already active, then verifying that the concept is true of a noun will be faster than when it is not active. By extension, Barsalou (1982) argued that whether the sentence mentioned the property would not affect response times for context-independent properties (that were always activated by a word, such as the smell of a skunk) but that context would affect response times for context-dependent properties (such as whether a roof is stable); if the property were related to the sentence, response times should be faster. Barsalou (1982) confirmed his prediction and found response times were faster in the related condition for context-dependent properties but not context-independent properties; participants were faster at confirming that a roof can be walked on when shown the sentence

Table 7.2   Sample study and test items used in Barsalou (1982)

Item	Property	
Context-Independent "True" Items		
The skunk was under a large willow.	Has a smell	Unrelated
The skunk stank up the entire neighbourhood.	Has a smell	Related
The fire was easily visible through the trees.	Has a smell	Control
Context-Dependent "True" Items		
The roof had been renovated prior to the rainy season.	Can be walked upon	Unrelated
The roof creaked under the weight of the repairman.	Can be walked upon	Related
The tightrope was high off the ground.	Can be walked upon	Control
"False" Items		
The cheese was growing mouldy in the refrigerator.	Has gills	

Source: Adapted from Barsalou, 1982, p. 85

"The roof creaked under the weight of the repairman" than when shown the sentence "The roof had been renovated prior to the rainy season," but participants were just as quick to confirm that a skunk has a smell when shown the sentence "The skunk stank up the entire neighbourhood" as they were when shown the sentence "The skunk was under a large willow." The results of this experiment suggest that some conceptual properties are indeed activated by context and that concepts should be thought of as context dependent rather than as stable.

Neuroimaging studies have confirmed the notion that concepts are flexible. Klaus Hoenig, Eun-Jin Sim, Viktor Bochev, Bärbel Herrnberger, and Markus Kiefer had participants complete a semantic attribute verification task while activity was being monitored by an fMRI machine. Participants had to indicate whether an attribute fit a given word. Words were from either living or nonliving categories and the attributes either related to a perceptual property or an action-related property. Perceptual properties were assumed to be dominant for the living objects, while action-related properties were considered to be dominant for the nonliving objects. Sometimes the feature was dominant for the category ("An orange is round" or "A knife is sharp"); sometimes the feature was nondominant ("An orange can be cut" or "A knife is elongated"). The researchers found that when a dominant feature was mentioned (as with the sentence "An orange is round"), perceptual areas became active for living objects and motor areas became active for nonliving objects. However, if a nondominant feature was part of the sentence (as with the sentence "An orange can be cut"), modality-specific brain regions linked to the feature became active; the motor area became active for living objects and the visual area became active for nonliving objects. Thus, Hoenig et al. (2008) showed that different features of a concept are active in different contexts, and that concepts should be thought of as flexible and situationally dependent.

Abstract Concepts

Thus far, the discussion has focused on research related to concrete concepts, such as living objects (e.g., birds, skunks) and nonliving objects (e.g., roofs, balls). However, humans also work with abstract concepts, such as terms for social situations like *justice* and *freedom*, terms for scientific phenomena that can't be seen such as *gravitation*, and terms for inner emotional states such as *desire* and *pity*. If concepts are modality specific, then how are abstract concepts, which don't relate to objects or actions, represented? Markus Kiefer and Lawrence Barsalou both agree that abstract concepts may be grounded largely in their relationship with other words, but also suggest that abstract concepts may have modality-specific representations just like more concrete concepts (Kiefer & Barsalou, 2013). Some concepts, such as "beautiful," can be embedded in examples of things with specific perceptual traits, such as people, works of art, scenery, or events. At a neural level, then, the abstract concept "beautiful" would then be linked to visual representations. Other abstract concepts may be more closely linked to actions, such as the concept of "free," which may be linked to a variety of basic actions associated with freeing, such as releasing or the removal of constraints. (When you think of the word *justice*, you may also have a concrete image in mind.) At a neural level, these concepts would be linked to motor representations. Some abstract concepts such as "pity" may be linked to emotional states and represented in emotional centres of the brain. Recent neuroimaging studies have found that sensory and motor areas are active when participants are processing abstract concepts, suggesting that abstract concepts are in fact linked to concrete sensory and motor representations (Pexman, Hargreaves, Edwards, Henry, & Goodyear, 2007; Wilson-Mendenhall, Barrett, Simmons, & Barsalou, 2011).

RELEVANT RESEARCH

Solving the Mystery of Synesthesia

Synesthesia occurs when a stimulus triggers a perceptual experience that isn't actually associated with the stimulus. For example, synesthetes (the technical term for people with synesthesia) may taste flavours when they hear music, or experience colours when they think of individual letters from the alphabet. Synesthesia can occur across modalities (such as tasting music) or within a modality (such as seeing colours when reading plain black text). Some forms of synesthesia, such as seeing colours while reading black-and-white text, affect about 3 per cent of the population; other forms of synesthesia are far less common (Chiou & Rich, 2014). There is evidence that synesthesia has a genetic component, explaining why some people become synesthetes while others do not (Baron-Cohen, Burt, Smith-Laittan, Harrison, & Bolton, 1996).

Early models of synesthesia proposed that synesthesia is triggered very early in

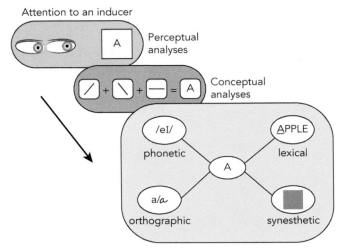

Figure 7.8   The role of conceptual knowledge in understanding synesthesia

An example of how a synesthete may come to perceive the concept of A as having the property red.

Source: Chiou & Rich, 2014, p. 8

processing, when incoming information is perceptual but still lacks meaning, for example when the letter A is represented as the features '/' '\' and '–' but is not yet known to be an "A" by the synesthete. Some of these models suggest that people with synesthesia are unable to inhibit other perceptual areas from being activated by these percepts, while other models suggest that there are excessive neural connections between certain cortical areas linked to perception. However, Rocco Chiou and Anina Rich were not satisfied with either of these views because they cannot account for the fact that synesthesia seems to rely on conceptual processing. For example, a person who sees colours surrounding text (grapheme-colour synesthesia) always experiences the same colour associated with the same letter (e.g., an A is always red) and this experience is independent of font. Thus synesthesia must be occurring late in processing, after the concept of the letter A has been activated. Further, there is substantial experimental evidence to suggest that the synesthetic features are not the same as perceptual features; for example, a synesthete experiencing red when seeing the letter A is not experiencing the colour red the same way that a person would if the letter A were printed in red ink. What synesthetes experience is the concept of red, not the sensation of red. Chiou and Rich (2014) used the hub-and-spoke model to develop their conceptual-mediation model of synesthesia. The hub-and-spoke model assumes that six different types of perceptual information can contribute to the supramodal representation of a concept: visual features, sounds, olfactory features, verbal descriptors, body movements, and skin sensations. According to this model, it is possible for virtually any feature to be associated with a concept.

While the supramodal (or hub) concept of the letter A is typically only linked to spokes conveying phonetic, lexical, and orthographic features, in a grapheme-colour synesthete there may also be a spoke linking the concept of A to the feature red. Similarly, the supramodal concept of jazz music may be linked to taste or olfactory features, or the concept of a specific shape may be associated with taste features, and so on. According to the conceptual-mediation model of synesthesia, virtually any combination of features can contribute to the supramodal representation of a concept. Thus, research into the dimensions of concepts hasn't just helped researchers better understand generic memory, it has also helped solve the mystery of synesthesia.

Concepts and Categorization

People have an innate ability to categorize objects based on their features. When you walk into a classroom you've never been in before, you easily identify chairs and desks; when you are searching your laundry for a clean pair of socks, you easily discern what is a sock and what is not. Knowing about categories saves us time and energy; it is easier to use previous experience with something to know how to respond to it than it is to learn about things every time we encounter them. So, if we develop a category for "chair" we will know what to look for when we need to sit down. Similarly, if we develop a category for "cat" we will know (more or less) what to expect that cat to do and how to treat that cat. The same goes for cars, boats, chairs, canoes, computers, and so on.

Some laboratory experiments have suggested that people use basic-level categories (such as "chair") more than other types of categories (such as the subordinate category "recliner" or the superordinate category "furniture"). For example, Rosch, Mervis, Gray, Johnson, and Boyes-Braem (1976) asked participants to name pictures of objects. Participants completed a total of just over 1600 trials and used basic-level categories (such as "chair") on 1595 trials. Basic-level categories are often the most practical choice because in many cases they inform a person of how to use an object; all chairs can be used in the same way, but different pieces of furniture are used in different ways. It many cases it isn't necessary to be more specific than to use the basic-level category, which likely explains the results from Rosch et al., (1976); however, researchers note that when it is *necessary* to use the subordinate, such as when people are experts in a field of knowledge, people do so. Tanaka and Taylor (1991) assembled a group of birdwatchers and dog experts and presented them with line drawings of birds and dogs embedded with distractors from both artifactual categories (such as musical instruments or cooking utensils) and natural categories (such as insects and flowers). Participants were asked to name the object in the picture as quickly and accurately as possible. The picture set included different types of birds and dogs (such as robins, jays, cardinals, beagles, collies, and poodles). Birdwatchers used the subordinate category name like "goldfinch" on 74 per cent of trials showing birds and dog experts used the subordinate category "beagle" on 40 per cent of trials showing dogs; however, birdwatchers only used the subordinate category 24 per cent of the time when naming dogs, and dog experts only used the subordinate category name 24 per cent of the time when naming birds. This result suggests that experts prefer the subordinate category name and that objects need not be organized based only on basic-level categories. In general, when people are highly familiar with the subordinate category they will use it instead of the basic-level category; category choice seems to depend entirely on experience.

While some categories have clear-cut criteria (such as birds, which must have feathers, beaks, and wings), many categories do not. In 1952, Ludwig Wittgenstein noted that "games" is an example of a category without clear boundaries. Wittgenstein argues that while we can list many features of games, these features are never exclusive to games or shared by all games. For example, the feature "has rules" is shared with the concept "prison" and thus one cannot determine that something is a game based on the fact that it has rules. The feature "played with teams," on the other hand, is only true of some games, and therefore one cannot determine that something is a game based on the fact that it is played with teams. Wittgenstein notes that even though games have no defining or characteristic features, we can easily judge the sentence "Writing a test is a game" as untrue, even though both tests and games have rules, and can judge the sentence "Hopscotch is a game" as true even though hopscotch shares few features with other games.

Researchers such as Douglas Medin (1989) have suggested that categorization revolves around the theories that people form about the world around them (e.g., Carey, 1988; Gelman & Markman, 1986; Keil & Kelly, 1987; Lakoff, 1987; Markman, 1987; Massey & Gelman, 1988; Murphy & Medin, 1985; Oden, 1987; Schank, Collins, & Hunter, 1986). Instead of directly matching an example to a sample or criteria represented in generic memory, people search memory for an explanatory relationship. Medin gives the example of someone jumping into a swimming pool while wearing clothes. What category that person falls into depends on the perceiver's *explanation* as to why the person jumped into the pool. The category might be "poor judgment" if the perceiver knew the person was intoxicated, but might be "hero" if the perceiver knew that someone who could not swim was in the pool. Research has demonstrated that theories about biology guide conceptual development in children. Gelman and Markman showed that children grouped animals based not on physical similarity, but on biological characteristics of the animal. When shown a picture of a flamingo and told "The flamingo feeds its baby mashed-up food" and shown a picture of a bat and told "The bat feeds its baby milk" as primes and then shown a picture of an owl (which was more physically similar to the bat than the flamingo) and asked how the owl feeds its baby, children as young as four correctly inferred that it was by mashing up food. This showed that biological characteristics are more salient than physical ones even when children are very young. Another example comes from Medin and Shoben (1988), who showed that white hair and grey hair are considered more similar than grey hair and black hair, but that white clouds and grey clouds were considered LESS similar than grey clouds and black clouds; this implies that concepts, like "Hair changes colour when a person ages" and "Clouds get dark

All of these pictures show a person in water wearing clothes, but most people would not categorize these people as the same; proponents of explanatory theories of categorization argue that this is because we categorize based on reasons, not physical features.
Sources: A3pfamily/Shutterstock; Steve Debenport/iStockphoto; mihtiander/Thinkstock

when it is about to rain," rather than perceptual characteristics guide judgments of similarity. It may be concluded, therefore, that connections in generic memory are more likely to be based on conceptual similarity than on similarity in physical form.

Schemas and Scripts

Another type of information contained within generic memory are schemas and scripts. **Schemas** are cognitive frameworks that help to organize and interpret information. Sometimes schemas relate to events and sometimes schemas relate to objects. Schemas are useful for many reasons, from telling us what we can and can't do while writing an exam, to telling us what we can and can't expect from a hotel room. Because schemas allow us to make predictions, they help us organize information so we can better remember it (see Box 7.4 below). Schemas also

schema

A cognitive framework that helps to organize and interpret information

---

DIY EXPERIMENT

BOX 7.4

Schemas and Memory

To complete this experiment, you will need at least two participants. If you are one of the participants, complete steps 1 and 2 without reading step 3.

1. Have the first participant read the following paragraph from Bransford and Johnson (1972, p. 722). Make sure the reader does not know the title of the paragraph while reading it:

   The procedure is quite simple. First, you arrange items into different groups. Of course, one pile may be sufficient depending on how much there is to do. If you have to go somewhere else due to lack of facilities, that is the next step; otherwise you are pretty well set. It is important not to overdo things. That is, it is better to do too few things at once than too many. In the short run this may not seem important, but complications can easily arise. A mistake can be expensive as well. The manipulation of the appropriate mechanisms should be self-explanatory, and we need not dwell on it here. At first, the whole procedure will seem complicated. Soon, however, it will become just another facet of life. It is difficult to foresee any end to the necessity for this task in the immediate future, but then one never can tell.

2. Ask the participant to recall as much as possible about the paragraph. Count how many facts were recalled.

3. You are now ready for your second participant. First you need to decode the title of the passage by subtracting one letter from each letter in the following phrase "xbtijoh dmpuift" (e.g., for the letter X you take away one letter and arrive at W). Once you know the title, repeat steps 1 and 2, but this time tell the participant the title of the paragraph before beginning step 1.

4. Compare the number of items recalled for Participant 1 and Participant 2. Chances are that Participant 2 remembered far more about the paragraph than Participant 1. This is because a schema helped Participant 2 organize the material. When Bransford and Johnson (1972) originally conducted this experiment, participants who were not given a title recalled 2.8 items from the passage while participants who were given a title recalled an average of 5.8 items from the passage.

help us to understand what people are saying in situations when it is hard to hear by allowing us to predict what a person is saying based on the general topic of the discussion.

scripts

Knowledge about the components of events and the order in which the components are to occur

Scripts are schemas that involve procedures for events. For example, people have scripts for how to order a meal at a restaurant, how to ride on an elevator, and how to greet people. Scripts are learned. In Canada there is a specific script related to how to behave when two people bump into each other. The person who is responsible for bumping into the other person must say "sorry" and then the person who was bumped into must also say "sorry." Failing to take part in this script is considered rude. Every culture has scripts to help people know what to do and when to do it. From a neuroscientific point of view, scripts are distinct from concepts. Elaine Funnell describes E.P., a patient with semantic dementia who had significant loss of conceptual knowledge (Funnell, 1996). E.P. was unable to match objects (e.g., pens and scissors) to their functions (e.g., writing and cutting) but was, however, able to follow scripts. When E.P. was told by the researcher that they needed to set up the next research appointment, E.P. got a calendar and pen from another room. E.P. was also able to sew a button onto a shirt when provided with a needle. This suggests that the brain areas involved with concepts (which was damaged in E.P.) is separate from the brain areas involved in following scripts (which seemed intact in E.P.).

In order for a script to be carried out successfully, the component actions must occur in a specific sequence. Think about different scripts you follow every day, such as getting dressed or brushing your teeth, and note that the order of operations is critical. Ordering actions requires planning and executive control, which are governed by the prefrontal cortex (see Chapter 3). Thus, patients with prefrontal damage often have difficulty with scripts. While Sirigu, Zalla, Pillon, Grafman, Agid, and Dubois (1995) found that patients with prefrontal damage were able to list the steps involved in completing a given task, they were not able to list the steps in the correct order. Similarly, Cosentino, Chute, Libon, Moore, and Grossman (2006) presented sequences of events related to commonly known scripts, such as catching a fish. Sometimes the sequences were in the correct order; sometimes steps were intentionally mixed up. The researchers found that patients with semantic dementia were able to identify scripts with incorrect sequences, while patients with prefrontal damage were not. This result suggests that scripts and concepts are independent from one another and involve different areas of the brain. Concepts seem to rely on the anterior temporal lobe, while scripts rely on the prefrontal cortex.

How Did Ken Jennings Conquer *Jeopardy!*?

The chapter began with a discussion of the amazing work of Ken Jennings, the all-time *Jeopardy!* champion and arguably someone with good control over his generic memory. Which model of generic memory can best account for Ken Jennings's feats? Interviews with Ken Jennings have revealed that he attributes his success to a lifelong love of learning and a strong associative memory; when Ken Jennings thinks about a topic, a huge amount of information comes to mind. Throughout Ken Jennings's life, he has been encountering new information and really *thinking* about it, drawing connections between new information and existing information resulting in a strong network of interconnected thoughts. Ken Jennings's superior memory is well explained by the compound-cue model, which predicts that recall will be best when there are many powerful inter-item associations to aid retrieval., His attention to detail and integration of new information with old creates inter-item associations that mean when presented with a *Jeorpardy!* answer like "This man served as the thirteenth prime minister of Canada," "thirteenth prime minister of Canada" serves as a powerful cue for information such as "John Diefenbaker," "Progressive Conservative," "served from 1957 to 1963," and so on, easily allowing Jennings to create the appropriate question "Who is John Diefenbaker?" Ken Jennings is not using any unique memory skills to be a *Jeopardy!* whiz; he is using the same skills as the rest of the population but to a greater extent.

CHAPTER REVIEW

- Generic memory is defined as an individual's knowledge about the world. Generic memory is context free, which distinguishes it from episodic memory.
- The first model of generic memory was the hierarchical-network model, which assumed that knowledge was represented on nodes and that nodes were arranged from the most general concepts at the top to the most specific at the bottom.
- Four key results from sentence-verification task experiments were inconsistent with the hierarchical-network model: people can quickly reject false statements, feature frequency affects verification time, distance needed to travel through the hierarchy is not a good predictor of sentence-verification time, and the typicality effect.
- The spreading-activation model was devised to explain data that could not be explained by the hierarchical-network model. The spreading-activation model assumes that related concepts are connected in a network, and that concepts that share more properties will have more links between them.
- There are four problems with the spreading-activation model: it is difficult to disprove, it cannot explain mediated priming, it cannot explain priming across multiple intervening words, and it predicts that the same aspects of a concept will be activated regardless of context.
- The compound-cue model suggests that generic memories are accessed when there is a match between a cue in short-term memory and an item in generic memory. There are three types of cues: the context within which the memory was learned (context cues), the items that were present when the item was learned (inter-item cues), and a sense of familiarity represented by an item being a cue for itself (self–self cues).
- Generic memories are formed when patterns are detected across multiple episodic memories.
- The formation of generic memories is closely linked to the hippocampus, the mammillary body, the mammillothalamic tract, and the hippocampal gyrus.
- Generic memories are stored in all sensory and motor areas in a systematic way that is consistent with the specific content of a given generic memory; visual memories are stored in visual areas, action-related memories are stored in motor areas, and so on.
- Concepts form the basis of generic memory. There are four debates concerning how concepts are represented in the brain: whether concepts are amodal or modality specific, whether concepts are represented on single neurons or across neurons, whether concept categories are innate or learned, and whether concepts are stable or flexible across time.
- Brain-imaging studies suggest that concept features are modality specific.

- Studies of patients with neurodegenerative diseases suggest that concepts are distributed rather than localized.
- Studies of individuals with difficulty naming objects, as well as brain-imaging studies that track brain activity as people learn concepts, suggest that concept categories are learned and not innate.
- Experimental evidence has shown that different aspects of a concept are active in different contexts. Concepts are flexible.
- Abstract concepts like "justice" are associated with perceptual and action-related traits and are stored in sensory and motor areas much like concrete concepts are.
- The hub-and-spoke model is based on the observation that concepts are modality specific, distributed, learned, and flexible. According to this model, six types of modality-specific representations (or spokes) all meet at a central hub in the anterior temporal lobe. The six types of modality-specific information are visual features, verbal descriptors, smells (olfaction), sounds, motor information (praxis), and information from the skin and internal organs (somatosensory). Each of these features is controlled by a different region of the brain.
- There are three types of categories: superordinate categories (like "furniture"), basic-level categories (like "chair"), and subordinate categories (like "armchair"). People use different levels of categories depending on the situation.
- Schemas help make predictions. Schemas assist with memory and making inferences while listening to speech. Scripts are schemas for events. Scripts are closely associated with goals and executive processing.

MEMORY ACTIVITY

Using a Rhyming Peg Word Mnemonic

The rhyming peg word mnemonic is one of many methods that can be used for learning lists of information (Bower, 1970). The rhyming peg word method involves developing cues for the to-be-remembered material that rhyme with an easy-to-remember peg word list (usually numbers). In this activity, you will see how to use the rhyming peg word mnemonic to memorize the six types of modality-specific information in the hub-and-spoke model discussed earlier in this chapter.

The first step in using the rhyming peg word method is to identify the to-be-remembered items. In this case, the items are visual features, verbal descriptors, smells (olfaction), sounds, motor information (praxis), and information from the skin and internal organs (somatosensory). Next, we look for a word representing each item to be remembered that also rhymes with one of the numbers from one to six such as what is shown below:

Word	Rhyme	Type of Information in Hub-and-Spoke Model
one	run	motor
two	stew	smell
three	see	visual features
four	snore	sounds
five	jive	verbal descriptors
six	pricks	skin and internal organs

Try to memorize the rhyming peg words to recall the types of modality-specific information in the hub-and-spoke model. Next see if you can apply this mnemonic to remember four features of concepts (concepts are flexible, learned, distributed, and modality specific).

	Word	Rhyme	Feature of Concept
one			
two			
three			
four			

Questions

1. What material is stored in generic memory? Why is the term *generic memory* a more accurate description of this material than the term *semantic memory*?
2. Give an example of a statement that could be used in a sentence-verification task. Explain how the statement would be validated based on the hierarchical-network model.
3. List four experimental findings that cannot be explained by the hierarchical-network model.
4. Explain how concepts are connected according to the spreading-activation model. Explain what is meant by a "decision criterion."
5. Explain how the spreading-activation model explains four experimental findings that cannot be explained by the hierarchical-network model.
6. Describe associative priming. Explain how the spreading-activation model accounts for this phenomenon.
7. Explain why mediated priming effects are problematic for the spreading-activation model.
8. Describe the compound-cue model. Explain how this model accounts for mediated priming effects.
9. Explain how generic memories are formed.
10. Identify brain structures associated with creating generic memories and brain structures associated with storing generic memories.
11. List four debates about how concepts are represented in the brain.
12. Describe semantic dementia.
13. Explain what evidence from people with semantic dementia suggests about whether concepts are amodal or modality specific.
14. Discuss research that relates to the question of whether concepts are localized or distributed.
15. Discuss evidence that relates to whether concepts are innate or learned.
16. Discuss evidence that demonstrates that concepts are flexible.
17. Generate an example of an abstract concept. Explain how it may be represented in a modality-specific way.
18. Describe the components of the hub-and-spoke model.
19. Explain why people use categories.
20. List three levels of categories and give an example of each.
21. Explain how situational factors may affect what level of category a person uses.
22. Discuss evidence that suggests that people use theories about the world to make categorical judgments.

23. Describe a schema. Explain how schemas affect memory.
24. Provide an example of a script.
25. Identify what type of brain damage leads to problems with script use.
26. Are scripts types of concepts? Defend your answer with evidence from studies of people with brain damage.

Key Figures

8   Forgetting

LEARNING OBJECTIVES

Having read this chapter, you will be able to:

- List the seven sins of memory.
- Recite John Wixted's definition of forgetting.
- Describe the forgetting curve.
- Describe the components of McGeoch's three-factor theory of forgetting.
- Explain how a paired-associate paradigm can be used to study proactive and retroactive interference.
- Explain why an organism may engage in promiscuous encoding.
- Describe the two components of an explicit memory and the regions of the brain associated with each component.
- Compare and contrast forgetting processes in the hippocampus and the neocortex.
- Describe infantile amnesia and provide an explanation for this phenomenon.
- Compare and contrast three different explanations of retrieval-induced forgetting.
- Compare and contrast incidental forgetting and motivated forgetting.
- Describe the item-method and the list-method directed-forgetting (DF) paradigms.
- Describe evidence that demonstrates that changes in mental context provide the best explanation for costs and benefits of forgetting observed in list-method DF paradigm experiments.
- Describe four different ways that people can achieve intentional forgetting.

FORGETTING IS A GOOD THING

Mecacci, L. (2013)

Dan Tuffs/Getty Images

Solomon Shereshevsky (1886–1958) and Jill Price (b. 1965) are examples of individuals who have been plagued by the inability to forget.

Solomon Shereshevsky (1886–1958) was born in Russia and from a young age was able to remember speeches, math problems, book passages, and conversations. Although Shereshevsky attempted to lead a normal life, and once was even a chair of a union, he was so overwhelmed with the connections between each new item he encountered that he could not make even the simplest decisions. Shereshevsky had to quit his job and make a living doing "feats of recollection" for audiences because his memory impeded his ability to do anything else (Luria & Solotaroff, 1987). The case of Shereshevsky demonstrates that exceptional memory isn't so much an ability to remember, it's a *failure* to forget. Although many people would like to have better memories, most individuals who are unable to forget report their memory is a burden, not a gift.

Jill Price is an American woman who can remember every day of her life since she was in her early teen years. Like Solomon Shereshevsky, Jill Price feels overwhelmed by her memories, describing each moment as occurring on two screens; one is the present, and the second is a playback of all the associated memories from the past (Parker, Cahill, & McGaugh, 2006). Solomon Shereshevsky and Jill Price are two of twenty individuals identified as having exceptional episodic memory or hyperthymesia (for more on hyperthymesia see Chapter 6). People with hyperthymesia don't remember anything particularly special; most of us can recall what we did a day earlier in great detail. What makes people with hyperthymesia different is that they do not forget that information over time like most people do. The cases of Solomon Shereshevsky and Jill Price suggest that forgetting is not only natural, but also beneficial, which may explain why people forget much more than they remember.

Introduction

A good place to begin this chapter is by exploring what it means to forget. Let's start with a simple exercise. First, try to answer this question: "In what year did Ivan Pavlov win the Nobel Prize?" Chances are you are unable to answer this question even though it is likely that you learned this fact sometime during your psychology studies. One might conclude that you have forgotten the answer; however, consider what happens when the question is reworded: "Did Ivan Pavlov win the Nobel Prize in 1900, 1904, 1914, or 1918?" When the question is worded this way, most people select the correct answer (the second alternative), indicating they have not actually forgotten the material at all. This is because **recall**, which involves retrieving a target from memory based on a cue that does not contain the target (such as "In what year did Ivan Pavlov win the Nobel Prize?") is typically more difficult than **recognition**, which involves retrieving a target from a cue that includes the target (such as "Did Ivan Pavlov win the Nobel Prize in 1900, 1904, 1914, or 1918?"). Hundreds of studies have demonstrated that recall is generally more difficult than recognition. For example, Meeter, Murre, and Janssen (2005) studied 14,000 participants' recall and recognition of news events from the Netherlands with **retention intervals** ranging from one day to two years and found that, while both recall and recognition accuracy decreased over time, at every retention interval participants' recognition was superior to their recall. The finding that people are often able to recognize material they cannot recall illustrates that when a person cannot recall a particular memory, it is possible that the memory is still available if the correct cues are given. Thus, we should only consider the complete loss of a memory trace as forgetting.

However, defining forgetting as a complete loss of a memory trace presents a major problem: How can a researcher determine the trace is truly gone? The researcher can't use the inability to recall information as a measure that the trace no longer exists, as there is ample evidence that people can recognize material they cannot recall. And recognition can also fail. All of us have had the experience where someone has asked, "Do you remember when so and so did such and such?" to which we initially answer, "No, I don't remember that" but, as the storyteller begins to recount the event, suddenly the memory returns. These experiences illustrate that recognition isn't a reliable measure of whether a memory trace is truly lost. Endel Tulving argues that forgetting is "the inability to recall something now that could be recalled on an earlier occasion" (Tulving, 1974). John Wixted refined Tulving's definition further and stipulates that forgetting may be defined as the inability to access information that was (a) successfully encoded and (b) could previously be retrieved by the same retrieval cue (Frankland, Köhler, & Josselyn, 2013). Thus, when we discuss forgetting in this chapter, we are referring to information that is inaccessible but not necessarily unavailable; forgetting can occur with or without the loss of the actual memory trace. This chapter also discusses two types of forgetting: *incidental forgetting*, which occurs without the intention to forget, and *motivated forgetting*, which occurs when an individual intentionally tries to suppress a memory. We begin with a discussion of the history of the study of incidental forgetting, followed by recent theories of the neuroscience of incidental forgetting. We begin with a summary of the most common causes of problems with recall, Daniel Schacter's *Seven Sins of Memory*.

recall

the act of retrieving a target based on a cue that does not include the target

recognition

the act of retrieving a target based on a cue that includes the target

retention interval

the period of time between a learning event and a test of memory for that event

The Seven Sins of Memory

In his 2002 book titled *The Seven Sins of Memory*, Daniel Schacter suggests that there are seven different ways that memory can fail: *transience*, *absent-mindedness*, *blocking*, *misattribution*, *suggestibility*, *bias*, and *persistence*. Schacter (2002) classified each sin as either one of omission (a failure to recall) or commission (a distortion in memory; Schacter, 2002).

sins of omission

memory failure that occurs because a process is not performed

transience

the loss of information over time

absent-mindedness

when inattention leads to the inability to recall information

blocking

when a person is unable to retrieve an item because of the unwanted recall of another item

sins of commission

when an error results in the failure to retrieve an item

misattribution

when a person recalls a piece of information but incorrectly recalls the source of that information

suggestibility

when a recollection is changed because an outside source indicates that the recollection is incorrect

bias

when a person's state of mind causes the recollection of some items but not others

persistence

the unwanted recall of distressing memories

Sins of Omission: Transience, Absent-Mindedness, and Blocking

Schacter (2002) argues that there are three reasons that people may fail to recall material, which he terms **sins of omission**. The first failure of omission is **transience**, which refers to the general loss of information over time. Transience can be caused by interference or decay (which we will discuss in detail later in this chapter). The second failure of omission is **absent-mindedness**. Absent-mindedness occurs when a person does not pay enough attention to the to-be-remembered material for the material to be recalled later. Forgetting where you placed your keys because you weren't paying attention when you put them down is an example of absent-mindedness. The third sin of omission is **blocking**. Blocking occurs when a person tries to retrieve an item from memory but another memory interferes, or "blocks," that retrieval. Blocking is responsible for the tip-of-the-tongue phenomenon where individuals know they know the information they want to retrieve but simply cannot retrieve it (Schacter, 2002).

Sins of Commission: Misattribution, Suggestibility, Bias, and Persistence

Schacter (2002) suggests that in addition to the failure to recall, there is the failure to recall *correctly*, which Schacter terms **sins of commission**. Sins of commission all involve an error of some type. The first sin of commission is **misattribution**, which occurs when a person correctly recalls a piece of information but incorrectly recalls the source of that information. For example, a person may recall reading that *vitamin X* cures cancer, but incorrectly recall that the information came from a medical journal rather than its true source, which was an advertisement on social media. Misattribution can be a significant problem for police investigations if speculation about a crime is released to the media before witnesses are questioned, because witnesses may produce information that they misattribute to their personal experience when really the information came from the media. (This is discussed in more detail in Chapter 11.) The second sin of commission is **suggestibility**, which involves changing a recollection because outside information suggests the original recollection is incorrect. For example, witness A may recall that the traffic light was green when an accident occurred; however, after hearing another witness insist that the light was red, witness A later "recalls" that the light was red. Like misattribution, suggestibility has serious implications for criminal justice. The third sin of commission is **bias**. Bias occurs when a person's present state of mind influences how she or he recalls the past. For example, a person who is depressed may tend to recall more negative events from the last year than a person who is not depressed, although both individuals experienced the same number of negative events. The final sin of commission is **persistence**, which involves the unwanted recall of distressing memories, ranging from embarrassing incidents to scary and traumatic experiences. Persistence can contribute to the development of phobias and is associated with post-traumatic stress disorder (Schacter, 2002). Keep an eye out for Schacter's (2002) seven sins of memory throughout this book.

The Time Course of Forgetting
The Forgetting Curve

The formal study of forgetting is one of the oldest in experimental psychology, dating back to a series of famous experiments conducted by Hermann Ebbinghaus in the late nineteenth century. In these experiments, Ebbinghaus (1885) created lists of nonsense syllables (such as hep, vax, and cru), memorized them, and then tested his memory for the syllables at different points in time. The results of these experiments led Ebbinghaus to propose the **forgetting curve** (depicted in Chapter 1, Figure 1.3b—do you remember what it looks like?). The forgetting curve shows that the rate of forgetting is very high soon after learning, but that the rate of forgetting slows with time, eventually levelling off such that retained material is much less likely to be lost than it was right after it was learned. The forgetting curve is reflected in **Jost's law**, which states that for memories of similar strength, older memories will decay more slowly than newer memories (Jost, 1897). Forgetting curves are one of the most reliable phenomena in psychology. Forgetting curves are observed for both recall and recognition and the rate of forgetting is the same regardless of the level of learning; people who learn material well forget at the same rate as people who know the information less well (Meeter, Murre, & Janssen, 2005).

The forgetting curve shows that forgetting occurs at different points in time after learning. The steep drop in recall at short time courses implies that much material is lost soon after learning. However, the curve shows that forgetting continues to occur at longer retention intervals as well. The shape of the forgetting curve suggests that there are different sources of forgetting. The steep drop soon after learning likely reflects the fact that much learning is never actually consolidated. The slower loss of information over time, on the other hand, seems to reflect processes that operate on consolidated memories.

Disruption in Consolidation as a Source of Forgetting

In the previous section we saw that a significant amount of forgetting occurs immediately after learning. In order for a memory to last over the long term, it must be consolidated; factors that prevent consolidation result in forgetting. The first theory about how consolidation affects memory was proposed in 1900 by Georg Müller and Alfons Pilzecker. Müller and Pilzecker suggested that after a learning event, such as being presented with a word list, a period of **perseveration** begins, and that the longer the perseveration period is, the more consolidated a memory will be. Because perseveration is a process that requires resources, Müller and Pilzecker's theory predicts that perseveration will be less effective following activities that demand cognitive resources than following inactivity. Indeed, many studies have shown more forgetting following wakeful activity than following a similar delay during which the individual slept (e.g., Cowan, Beschin, & Della Sala, 2004; Ebbinghaus, 1885; Jenkins & Dallenbach, 1924). The role of sleep in memory consolidation is explained in more detail in Chapter 4. In 1946, Minami and Dallenbach showed that roaches had more difficulty learning an avoidance response when they were allowed to move after trials than when they were prevented from moving, which led the researchers to conclude that physical activity can disrupt consolidation.

forgetting curve
a negatively accelerated function over time predicting that most forgetting occurs soon after learning, and that as time goes on less and less additional forgetting occurs

Jost's Law
when two memories are of similar strength, the older memory will decay at a slower rate than the newer memory

perseveration
the process by which memories are consolidated

The first biologically based consolidation theory was proposed by Donald Hebb in 1949. Hebb suggested that neurons require a period of perseveration during which time they create new connections. In Hebb's view, perseveration is a purely biological process and when this biological process is disrupted, memories are not consolidated and forgetting occurs. The best evidence for Hebb's theory that perseveration is biological is the occurrence of **retrograde amnesia** following traumatic head injuries. In these cases, individuals cannot recall events that happened just *before* the injury occurred, suggesting that the memories were not permanent at the time of experience, and that normal brain function was critical to their consolidation.

More recently, John Wixted has argued that new memories can produce forgetting of old memories if the new memories engage the same neural circuit as the old memory and if the old memory is not fully consolidated. Thus, recently learned material can be forgotten if new information is sufficiently similar to the old, unconsolidated information (Wixted, 2005). For example, you may have difficulty remembering brushing your teeth three nights ago because you have brushed your teeth several times since then. Wixted's (2005) argument is supported by the finding that inducing **long-term potentiation (LTP)** (the process that forms new memories) in the hippocampus weakens previously established LTP (Villarreal, Do, Haddad, & Derrick, 2002) and impacts hippocampal memory (Brun, Ytterbø, Morris, Moser, & Moser, 2001).

Consolidation theory can explain why some memories are never formed, but consolidation theory cannot explain retrieval failures for consolidated memories, that is, memories that *have* been successfully retrieved in the past. For example, consolidation theory can't explain why you were able to recall the first 40 elements in the periodic table two years ago but can't do so today. Next, we will explore sources of forgetting of consolidated memories.

Early Models of Forgetting: Decay Theory and Interference Theory

The first two explanations of forgetting proposed by cognitive psychologists were decay and interference. **Decay theories of forgetting**, such as the one described in 1913 by Edward Thorndike, proposed that unless a memory was retrieved, biological processes would lead it to simply vanish over time, although the exact biological mechanism that caused decay was never specified. Decay theories never really took hold in the scientific community; they were difficult to test and the inner workings of the brain were not well enough understood to provide a reason for decay. The first interference theory of forgetting was proposed by John McGeoch in 1932. McGeoch (1932) suggested that there are two types of interference that lead to forgetting, **proactive interference**, where existing memories affect one's ability to access newly formed memories, and **retroactive interference**, where learning new material makes it more difficult to access older memories. Having difficulty learning a new password because an old password is well learned is an example of proactive interference; old knowledge is affecting the acquisition of new knowledge. Having difficulty remembering an old postal code after moving to a new address is an example of retroactive interference. Interference is thought to be responsible for transience, which is one of Schacter's (2002) sins of omission discussed earlier in the chapter.

In the lab, proactive and retroactive interference have been studied extensively using a **paired-associate paradigm**. An illustration of how the paradigm works is shown in Table 8.1. Table 8.1a shows a set of words that may be used in a paired-associate paradigm and Table 8.1b

retrograde amnesia
the inability to remember facts learned in the past

long-term potentiation
a persistent strengthening of a synapse based on recent patterns of activity

decay theory of forgetting
forgetting occurs because of a decline in the memory trace due to some biological mechanism

interference theory of forgetting
forgetting occurs because of a conflict between new and old information

proactive interference
a reduction in the ability to create new memories because of existing memories

retroactive interference
a reduction in the ability to retrieve old memories because of newly learned information

paired-associate paradigm
a research paradigm where participants study word pairs (such as DOG–horse) and then later learn new word pairs that partially overlap with the old pairs (such as DOG–chair).

Table 8.1   An example of the structure of a paired-associate paradigm testing proactive and retroactive interference effects

(a) Sample of four word lists that could be combined in a pair-associate paradigm to produce either proactive or retroactive interference

A	B	C	D
DOG	horse	KITE	chair
CAR	bag	OVAL	key
LAMP	sail	FROG	otter
MANE	bowl	HASTE	rose
PAPER	flag	DRUM	vent
POINT	book	TENT	boat
JUMP	mouse	SUGAR	clamp

(b) How word lists are combined in a paired-associate paradigm to produce retroactive and proactive interference

	Learned First	Learned Second	Tested On	Type of Interference Observed
Control	A–B	C–D	A–B	
Experimental	A–B	A–D	A–B	Retroactive
Control	C–D	A–B	A–B	
Experimental	A–D	A–B	A–B	Proactive

shows how those word lists may be combined in different learning sessions to produce proactive and retroactive interference. When examining retroactive interference, the experimental group learns A–B pairs (e.g., DOG–horse) followed by A–D pairs (e.g., DOG–chair), while the control group learns A–B (e.g., DOG–horse) pairs and then C–D pairs (e.g., KITE–chair). In this condition, experimenters are testing whether learning the new association A–D will affect recall of the old association A–B. When examining proactive interference, the experimental group learns A–D (e.g., DOG–chair) pairs and then A–B pairs (e.g., DOG–horse) while the control group learns C–D pairs (e.g., KITE–chair) and then A–B pairs (e.g., DOG–horse). In this condition, experimenters are testing whether having learned the A–D associations will affect participants' ability to learn A–B associations. In every condition, participants in the experimental and control conditions are tested on their memory for the A–B pairs (e.g., DOG–horse).

Retroactive and proactive interference are calculated by comparing recall in the experimental condition to recall in the control condition. Note that participants are *always* tested on the A–B word list. If recall is worse in the experimental condition when participants first learn A–B pairs and then learn A–D pairs, then retroactive interference is indicated; learning the A–D pairs affected prior learning of A–B pairs (see Figure 8.1).

John McGeoch (1932) used the results from paired-associate paradigm experiments to propose the **three-factor theory of forgetting**. As the name suggests, McGeoch argued that there were three causes of forgetting: **response competition**, **altered stimulus conditions**, and **set**.

three-factor theory of forgetting

a theory that proposes that forgetting results from response competition, altered stimulus conditions, or set

response competition

when a query results in more than one item being retrieved in such a way that the correct response is not indicated

altered stimulus conditions

when the context at the time of test is different than the context at the time of learning

set

the portion of generic memory that is currently active

Response competition can affect retrieval if a query results in more than one item being retrieved. For example, in the paired-associate learning task outlined in Table 8.1, a participant may learn DOG–*chair* and then DOG–*horse* and then be given the query DOG–????? and instructed to complete it with the associate she or he learned first. The individual may recall both *chair* and *horse* but not which was learned first and thus has forgotten the correct answer to the query. Schacter (2002) has labelled this phenomenon as blocking. McGeoch also argues that altered stimulus conditions, or changing contexts, can cause retrieval failures. Researchers consistently find that when the context changes between learning and recall, performance is worse; for example, in 1940 Ethel Abernethy found that students who were tested in the classroom they learned in

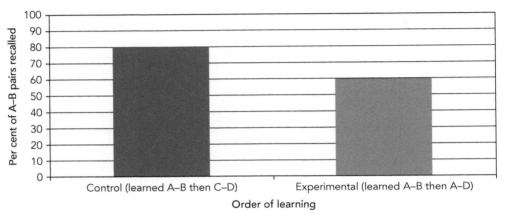

Figure 8.1   Example of retroactive interference

In this example, participants in the control condition learned A–B pairs then C–D pairs before being tested on A–B pairs, while participants in the experimental condition learned A–B then A–D pairs before being tested on A–B pairs. Here learning the A–D pairs after learning the A–B pairs produced retroactive interference.

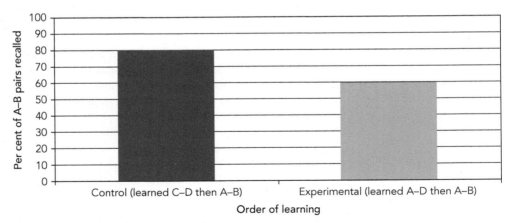

Figure 8.2   Example of proactive interference

In this example, participants in the control condition learned C–D pairs then A–B pairs before being tested on A–B pairs, while participants in the experimental condition learned A–D then A–B pairs before being tested on A–B pairs. Here learning the A–D pairs before the A–B pairs resulted in proactive interference.

performed better than students who were tested in another environment (Abernethy, 1940). In this case, like with the response competition explanation of forgetting, the retrieval error does not occur because the information is lost; it occurs because the appropriate retrieval cues are not available.

The final reason for forgetting stipulated by McGeoch is set (which is sometimes also referred to as mental set). In these cases, retrieval fails because context causes an individual to retrieve the wrong set of information. For example, suppose a person is watching a movie and trying to remember the name of an actor who seems familiar. The person will develop a set of possible names based on movies she or he has seen in the past. However, if the individual in the movie is not actually an actor but is instead a famous sports figure, the name may be more difficult to recall because the correct set has not been activated. Set reflects bias, one of Schacter's (2002) sins of commission discussed earlier in the chapter.

McGeoch's three-factor theory of forgetting is a good model of generic memory forgetting as it fits the preponderance of experimental data well. In recent years, McGeoch's basic idea that contextual cues are fundamental to forgetting have been repackaged in a series of models that explain forgetting as failure to discriminate among items in memory.

Interference theories fit experimental data well; researchers were able to produce proactive and retroactive interference in a variety of different learning situations. Beginning in the early 2000s, researchers began to provide neuroscientific support for interference theories. For example, research has shown that consolidated memories become plastic (or changeable), and that retrieval of multiple memories simultaneously can lead to changes in individual memories, including the integration of new information into each trace (Hupbach, Gomez, Hardt, & Nadel, 2007). So, for example, when individuals attempt to recall the location of the first psychology laboratory (a fact they know they once knew), they may recall "Leipzig" because they learned that Leipzig was the location of the first psychology lab earlier but also recall "Harvard" because they recently read William James and his work. Although only "Leipzig" is correct, both "Leipzig" and "Harvard" may be reconsolidated as the location of the first psychology laboratory because both were active while an individual was thinking about the location of the first psychology lab. The individual will no longer be able to remember which location was the location of the first psychology lab, and thus a consolidated long-term memory will appear forgotten through interference.

For almost 100 years, interference was thought to be the main source of forgetting of consolidated memories. At first, the neuroscientific evidence seemed to support interference but not decay as a source of forgetting. However, recent advances in the understanding of the cellular and molecular bases for long-term memory persistence suggest that decay is also a source of forgetting, and that this forgetting is highly adaptive. In the next section we will explore brain processes that lead to forgetting. Neurogenesis-dependent decay and molecular decay lead to the forgetting of episodic memories stored in the hippocampus, while interference leads to forgetting of generic memories, which are stored in the neocortex.

The Neuroscience of Forgetting

In Chapter 5, we explored the difference between implicit and explicit memory. Implicit memory is automatic and operates outside of consciousness while explicit memory is accessed deliberately and can be part of conscious awareness. Recall from Chapter 5 that implicit memory is thought to have evolved first to allow animals to learn adaptive responses in simple environments, while explicit memory is thought to have evolved later as an adaptive response to more complex environments where animals encountered a greater variety of foods and predators (Kolb & Whishaw, 2009). With explicit memory in place, an animal could deliberately use previous experiences to benefit its survival. However, animals with explicit memory systems are faced with an adaptive problem: their survival can benefit from memory, but they have no way of knowing ahead of time what elements of an event will be useful later and what elements can be ignored. For example, each time an animal eats, there is a possibility that the food it eats will be toxic and should be avoided in the future. Thus, in order for an animal to remember which foods had toxic effects, the animal would need to encode each meal and retain that information long enough to determine if the food was safe. Oliver Hardt, Karim Nader, and Lynn Nadel of McGill University argue that this adaptive problem has led to the evolution of a memory system that engages in **promiscuous encoding**, that is, encoding every event that is experienced. The main adaptive benefit of promiscuous encoding is that decisions about what information is useful and what can be discarded can be made later, when the usefulness of the encoded material has been evaluated. While promiscuous encoding has many benefits, such as allowing an animal to identify toxic foods, there is also a cost to promiscuous encoding; if left unchecked, the memory system would be overwhelmed very quickly. Thus Hardt and his colleagues argue that we have evolved a dedicated forgetting mechanism that removes old explicit memories and frees up space for subsequent encoding. According to Hardt et al. (2013), systematic forgetting occurs via either interference or decay depending on the location of the memory trace in the brain.

promiscuous encoding

the encoding of all events that are experienced by an organism

Two Codes, Two Forgetting Mechanisms

Explicit memories begin as episodic memories with two components. One component consists of the content of the memory and is largely dependent on the neocortex. An example of this component would be an apple that you ate as a snack. The other component consists of spatial-contextual information within which the content was acquired and is largely dependent on the hippocampus. An example of this component would be that you ate the apple as a snack at your desk on Wednesday morning. The two components are linked by an indexing function controlled by the hippocampus. The memory system is designed to encode as many episodes as possible and then to eliminate memories that don't turn out to be of any use (Hardt et al., 2013).

explicit memory

a memory that an individual can bring into conscious awareness

Distinguishing between episodes is essential; however, episodes can contain very similar information. For example, it's important to distinguish between what you ate for lunch today from what you ate yesterday (in case one of the meals is toxic); however, these two events will share many features, as you may eat lunch at your desk every day (like me), and/or you may eat similar foods each day. The hippocampus is able to produce distinct codes for distinct events (even if they are very similar) using a process called **pattern separation**. Pattern separation creates distinct neural codes for different episodic events. The two areas of the hippocampus that are key to pattern separation are the dentate gyrus (DG) and an area known as CA3 (see Figure 8.3).

pattern separation

ahe production of distinct neural codes for distinct episodic events

When the DG detects a pattern of neural activity that is similar to the neural activity associated with another memory in the hippocampus (such as another memory from the same location, or another memory involving the same objects), the CA3 uses a different population of neurons to code the new memory in the neocortex, a phenomenon known as **population coding** or **orthogonal coding**. A rough analogy would be choosing to use two different-coloured sticky notes to record the times of two different appointments that you have to go to

population coding/ orthogonal coding

when a unique set of neurons is used to form a memory

next week. When population coding occurs, two similar memories, such as the memory for two meals, or the memory for two attempts to accomplish a given goal, will not be represented by the same neurons. This means that these memories can be remembered separately, without activating each other, much like one sticky note can be read without reading any other sticky notes. The processes of pattern separation and population coding make hippocampal memories highly resistant to interference; similar memories are prevented from affecting each other just like the information on one sticky note doesn't affect the information on the other sticky note. Because hippocampal memories are **orthogonal** (meaning they don't use the same neurons), interference

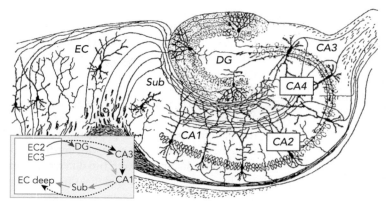

Figure 8.3   Hippocampus

Distinct neural codes for different episodes are created by the DG and CA3 areas of the hippocampus.

Source: Eagleman & Downar, 2016, p. 283

cannot account for forgetting of hippocampal memories; for interference to be involved, one memory must affect the neural coding of the other memory. Instead, forgetting in the hippocampus appears to result from at least two natural processes: the growth of new neurons, a process known as **neurogenesis**, and metabolic processes that can cause a loss of receptors.

orthogonal

when two representations do not overlap

neurogenesis

the growth of new neurons

Neurogenesis-Dependent Decay in the Hippocampus

In the 1960s, Joseph Altman was the first to demonstrate that neurogenesis occurs in the hippocampi of adult animals (Altman & Das, 1965). Beginning in the 1990s, new techniques allowed neurobiologists to establish that new neurons develop continually in the adult human, and that neurogenesis is particularly common in the hippocampus. When neurons are first formed, they are referred to as newborn **granule cells**. The granule cells migrate into the existing network of neurons in a process that can take several weeks. The introduction of these new granule cells into the neuronal network slowly changes connections between pre-existing neurons, just as introducing new roads changes the way that existing roads are connected to one another. One question concerns how this neurogenesis and subsequent changes in the neural circuitry in the hippocampus affect memory. To study this phenomenon, researchers have manipulated neurogenesis in adult rodents and then, following a delay, assessed whether the rodent is able to form new hippocampal memories, such as a conditioned eye-blink response, contextual learning (Shors et al., 2001), or spatial learning (Deng, Aimone, & Gage, 2010). Many of these experiments have shown that decreasing neurogenesis impairs hippocampal memory formation, while increasing neurogenesis sometimes facilitates hippocampal memory formation (Frankland et al., 2013). In some cases, there has been no effect of reducing neurogenesis on hippocampal memory formation. Researchers believe this is because existing neurons in the hippocampus can also be used to form memories (Frankland et al., 2013).

Recent studies suggest that neurogenesis increases the efficiency of pattern separation during encoding. In other words, the introduction of new neurons helps ensure that different sets of neurons are available for encoding similar events, much like introducing a new colour of sticky note enables

granule cells

cells that eventually develop into neurons

a person to create notes that are more distinct from one another. Yosuke Niibori, a neuroscientist working at the Hospital for Sick Children in Toronto, and his colleagues Sheena Josselyn and Paul Frankland from the University of Toronto, led a research team that demonstrated that reducing neurogenesis in adult mice (either using chemicals or through genetics) reduces the ability of the CA3 to perform pattern separation using population coding. Niibori et al. (2012) found that when hippocampal neurogenesis was reduced, similar CA3 neurons were active when the animals were in similar contexts, implying that the same neurons were being used to encode information in similar contexts (and that pattern separation and population coding were not occurring). Further evidence that pattern separation and population coding are impaired when neurogenesis is impaired comes from the observation that mice with impaired hippocampal neurogenesis also have increased difficulty discriminating between two different contexts in a fear-conditioning paradigm experiment.

The researchers concluded that this was because reducing neurogenesis impairs pattern separation and the mice were unable to remember the specific context where they had received the foot shock (Niibori et al., 2012). In addition, when Amar Sahay and his research colleagues at Columbia University increased neurogenesis in mice by promoting the survival of newborn granule cells, these mice were better able to perform spatial discrimination tasks than controls (Sahay et al., 2011). Taken together, these results suggest that neurogenesis facilitates pattern separation, which enables the hippocampus to form distinct episodic memories (Frankland et al., 2013). Next, we will discuss how neurogenesis can also lead to forgetting.

After it was well established that neurogenesis had a beneficial effect on the production of new memories, researchers began to wonder whether neurogenesis also impacted existing memories. The introduction of new neurons into the hippocampus always occurs the same way. The division of progenitor cells in the subgranular zone creates new cells that migrate into the innermost area of the granular cell layer. These new dentate granule cells (DGCs) integrate into existing dentate gyrus (DG) circuits and send mossy axons into pyramidal cells in the CA3. The new DGCs form new input and output patterns about two-and-a-half weeks after they migrate into the DG. Over time, neurogenesis-induced changes in the structure of the hippocampus begins to accumulate. The new DGCs compete with existing cells for inputs and outputs, sometimes replacing existing connections. This process is illustrated in panels (a), (b), and (c) of Figure 8.4 (Frankland et al., 2013). Neurogenesis does not just change the structure of the hippocampus; it may also change the synaptic strength of existing connections. Young neurons are more excitable than existing neurons; however, all neural networks aim to maintain a stable level of activation, meaning that the increased excitation brought into the system by new neurons results in decreased excitation in older neurons, which may eventually lead to some synapses being lost (Meltzer, Yabaluri, & Deisseroth, 2005). Paul Frankland and Sheena Josselyn of the University of Toronto and Stefan Köhler of the University of Western Ontario argue that the introduction of new neurons into the hippocampus may generate new synaptic connections, but may also alter the strength of existing synaptic connections, leading to forgetting.

pattern completion

matching an existing memory to a cue

neurogenesis-dependent decay

forgetting that is the result of impaired pattern completion following the integration of new neurons in the hippocampus

Recall that Tulving (1974) defined forgetting as the inability to retrieve a memory that could be retrieved on an earlier occasion. In the brain, retrieval occurs as a result of **pattern completion**, which involves the reactivation of the pattern of neural activity present at the time of encoding. Frankland et al. (2013) propose that because neurogenesis necessarily changes existing hippocampal circuits, neurogenesis reduces the probability that a previously effective retrieval cue will produce the same pattern of activation present during memory encoding and thus increases the probability that forgetting will occur. Forgetting that occurs through these mechanisms is known as **neurogenesis-dependent decay**.

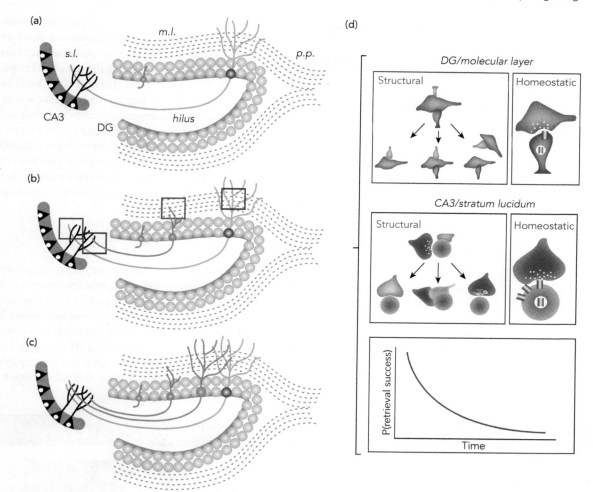

Figure 8.4   The integration of new neurons into the hippocampus

The integration of new neurons into the dentate gyrus induces forgetting of previously acquired (old) memories. (a) New dentate granule cells (DGCs, green) integrate into an establish DG circuit. (b) New DGCs form new input and output connections starting at ~2.5 weeks of age. (c) Neurogenesis-induced remodelling of hippocampal circuits accumulates over time.

Source: Adapted from Frankland et al., 2013, p. 499

It takes about two weeks for the axon of each new neuron to reach the CA3 region where it makes contact with 11 to 15 neurons, changing the connection network of each of these neurons (Acsády, Kamondi, Sik, Freund, & Buzsáki, 1998). Over time, more and more axons come in contact with neurons in CA3 and more and more connection networks are changed. Each change in the connection network in CA3 reduces the likelihood that pattern completion can occur. This is consistent with the observation that as the retention interval increases, forgetting is more likely. This is why you are more likely to have forgotten a conversation you had with your friend a month ago than a conversation you had with your friend yesterday.

To better understand the basic concept of neurogenesis-dependent decay, imagine that you are asked to match a picture in your hand to one of many similar pictures on a computer screen, where one image matches the one in your hand and the other images are similar but not identical to the image in your hand. Now imagine that, at a fairly constant rate, some pixels in the computer images change, making the pictures lose their distinctiveness. You can imagine that over time it will be more and more difficult to match the picture in your hand to an image on the computer screen. This is similar to what occurs in neurogenesis-dependent decay. Neurogenesis-dependent decay can explain Schacter's (2002) notion of transience, which is the general loss of information over time.

Further support for the notion that neurogenesis produces forgetting comes from **infantile amnesia**, which is the forgetting of most memories formed during the first three or four years of life. In the next section we will explore infantile amnesia in detail and review experimental evidence that many researchers believe demonstrates that infantile amnesia results from extremely high rates of neurogenesis in infants and young children.

infantile amnesia

the inability for adults to remember events from early in life

Infantile Amnesia

Think back as far as you can to your earliest childhood memory. This memory is probably from when you were about four years old. In addition, you probably have relatively few memories of your childhood from before you were seven years old, as compared to memories from after you were seven. The inability for adults to remember events from early in life is referred to as infantile amnesia. Infantile amnesia in humans has been studied extensively and a consistent two-phase pattern has emerged. Humans are unable to remember *any* events from the first three years of life. In addition, humans have relatively few memories from ages four through seven as compared to ages later in childhood (Peterson, 2002; Rubin, 1982; Rubin, 2000; Wetzler & Sweeney, 1986).

DIY EXPERIMENT

BOX 8.1

Childhood Memories

Create a list of memories you have from when you were a child. Try to generate at least 30 items. Review each item on the list and estimate your age at the time of the memory. When you have finished, create a table or chart depicting the number of memories for each age. What pattern do you see? Extensive research on childhood memories has found that people do not have episodic memories from the first three years of life and people remember relatively few memories from age four to seven compared to later in childhood. This phenomenon, known as *infantile amnesia*, was once thought to be linked to language development, but recent research suggests that a better explanation is that high rates of neurogenesis early in life result in the loss of early episodic memories.

kiankhoon/iStockphoto

There are four particularly interesting aspects of infantile amnesia in humans. First, infantile amnesia affects episodic memories (such as memories for events), but not semantic memories (such as language) or implicit memories (such as how to walk). Second, infantile amnesia is not an abrupt transition from "no memory" to "memory"; ages four through seven represent a stage where more memories are lost than are lost from later in childhood, but more memories are retained than are retained from earlier in childhood (Josselyn & Frankland, 2012). Third, older children remember information for longer than younger children. Carolyn Rovee-Collier and her colleagues demonstrated that memory retention increases steadily with age. While two-month-old infants could recall episodic information for about 24 hours, 18-month-old infants trained on a similar task could retain that information for up to 13 weeks (Rovee-Collier & Cuevas, 2009). Although infants of all ages eventually forget what they have learned, it takes longer for older children to experience forgetting. The final, and perhaps most interesting, aspect of infantile amnesia is that it is not unique to humans; young rodents and monkeys show the same pattern of forgetting as human children do. The finding that infantile amnesia occurs in nonhuman animals is important because it refutes early explanations of the phenomena that proposed that language development was responsible for the loss of early memories.

Byron Campbell of Princeton University began investigating infantile amnesia in rats in the 1960s. In his 1962 experiment, Campbell and his colleagues trained rats that were 18, 23, 38, 54, or 100 days old to avoid a shock by moving from one part of a cage to another. They then tested the rats' memory for this avoidance response after a delay of 0, 7, 21, or 42 days. While all the rats performed the avoidance manoeuvre at a delay of 0 days, as the delay increased, younger rats were less and less likely to exhibit the avoidance response. Thus, the results from Campbell and Campbell (1962) showed that younger rats forget avoidance responses faster than older rats, much like younger humans forget information more quickly than older humans. Age-related forgetting in rats has been replicated across a wide variety of learning paradigms for humans and rats, which demonstrates that the phenomenon is a robust, cross-species phenomenon.

Researchers have explored many explanations for infantile amnesia. As was mentioned earlier, one popular theory was that the emergence of the ability to use language changes the way memories are encoded (Harley & Reese, 1999; Nelson, 1993; Simcock & Hayne, 2002). Another theory was that the passage of time was responsible for infantile amnesia. To test this hypothesis, David Rubin of Duke University presented adults with a cue word, such as *bicycle*, and asked participants to recall memories associated with the word and estimate their age at the time of the memory. Rubin found no memories for ages zero through three, and fewer memories for ages three through seven than for older ages, and the number reported for ages three through seven was much smaller than would be predicted by the forgetting curve, indicating that the passage of time alone cannot explain

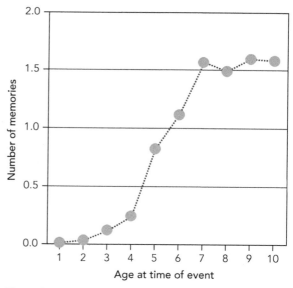

Figure 8.5 Number of memories recalled as a function of age from Rubin and Schulkind (1997)

The distribution of autobiographical memories from the first decade of life illustrates two phases of infantile amnesia. Values (mean number of memories per year) are approximate and are based on Rubin and Schulkind (1997). Participants were 20, 34, and 70 years of age. Few participants reported memories before the age of three. The number of memories recalled from the ages of three to seven appear to increase linearly and then level off at age 10.

Source: Josselyn & Frankland, 2012, p. 424

infantile amnesia. Indeed, no purely psychological account of infantile amnesia has been able to explain the phenomenon. This, coupled with the fact that infantile amnesia is also observed in nonhuman animals, suggests that the brain, rather than psychology per se, causes the effect (Rubin & Schulkind, 1997).

Some neuroscientists have proposed that infantile amnesia results from the fact that young individuals have brains that are not fully developed. These theories suggest that immature brains cannot form lasting memories very well. Indeed, the brains of animals that show infantile amnesia are not fully developed at first. Neurons in the cortex undergo myelination during the first year of life, which affects processing speed (Huttenlocher & Dabholkar, 1997), and neurons continue to be added to the DG region of the hippocampus, which may affect episodic memory formation (e.g., Sierra, Encinas, & Maletic-Savatic, 2011). Support for immature brain hypotheses comes from the observation that memory retention increases with age. However, these theories don't fully explain the phenomenon; they don't explain why memories are retained in the very short term but are completely forgotten over time. In addition, the structures of the hippocampus are fully developed by about 18 months of age; if hippocampal immaturity were responsible for infantile amnesia, then the amnesia should only affect memories for experiences prior to this age. The cortex, on the other hand, continues to change and mature well into puberty; if cortical immaturity were responsible for infantile amnesia, then the amnesia should affect memories right through puberty. Thus, neither phase of infantile amnesia is well explained by an immature brain account.

A biological explanation that can account for both the nature and time course of infantile amnesia across species is the neurogenic hypothesis of infantile amnesia.

The Neurogenic Hypothesis of Infantile Amnesia

Sheena Josselyn and Paul Frankland from the University of Toronto present support for what they term the *neurogenic hypothesis of infantile amnesia*. According to this hypothesis, infantile amnesia is related to neurogenesis in the hippocampus. The authors note that neurogenesis in the hippocampus and memory stability over time are inversely related. Early in life, when the rate of neurogenesis is at its highest, memory stability is at its lowest and infantile amnesia is observed. It is not until neurogenesis slows down that infantile amnesia disappears and an individual is able to recall memories from early in life. Josselyn and Frankland (2012) propose that forgetting that results in infantile amnesia occurs through neurogenesis-dependent decay; however, because neurogenesis is rampant in young individuals, the forgetting is extensive and affects all hippocampal-based memories.

At birth, neurogenesis is largely complete in most brain areas; however, two brain areas continue to produce neurons throughout life. One is the subventricular zone of the lateral ventricle, which provides new neurons for the olfactory bulb. The second is the subgranular zone of the hippocampus, which provides new neurons for the dentate gyrus (DG). The factor that *most* affects the rate of neurogenesis in the hippocampus is age; in most species, production of new neurons in the hippocampus peaks soon after birth and then begins to decline. In rats, for example, the rate of neurogenesis decreases by half between one and two months of age. By the time a rat is 18 months of age (old age for a rat), neurogenesis occurs at 1/100th of the rate that it did when the rat was first born (Seki & Arai, 1993). Jabès, Lavenex, Amaral, and Lavenex (2010) found the same pattern in macaques (who also show infantile amnesia); high levels of neurogenesis from birth to three months of age, followed by a lower rate of neurogenesis beyond three months of age. Post-mortem studies of human brains have allowed researchers to estimate the rate of neurogenesis in humans across the lifespan. Newly formed neurons are stained when they come in contact with a chemical called doublecortin. Using this technique on brains from individuals of varying ages, Knoth and his colleagues estimate that neurogenesis is 100 times greater in newborn humans than in humans who are 100 years old, which mirrors what is found across the lifespan of rats (Knoth et al., 2010). Further, changes in neurogenesis are similar across rats, macaques, and humans. Cameron and McKay (2001) report that adult rats increase the number of neurons in the DG cell granule cell layer by about 0.2 per cent per day, and that five- to ten-year-old adult macaques produce about 0.02 per cent more neurons per day in the DG. Given that macaques live about 10 times longer than rats, researchers suggest that these two rates should be considered as roughly equivalent.

Rats are **altricial** rodents, meaning they have brief gestation periods and are born relatively helpless (humans are also altricial). Rat pups gestate for just 21 days and their brain weight increases 600 per cent over their lifespan. Guinea pigs, on the other hand, are **precocial** rodents, meaning they have a longer gestation period and are born with the ability to see and walk. Guinea pigs gestate for 65 days and their brain weight only increases by 60 per cent over their lifespan. When researchers compare memory over time in rats and guinea pigs, they observe an effect of age for rats but not for guinea pigs. Five-week-old rats are better able to remember context information over a two-week period than two-week-old rats; however, five-day-old guinea pigs retain context information just as well as adult guinea pigs (Campbell, Misanin, White, & Lytle, 1974). This difference is consistent with the amount of neurogenesis each species experiences in the DG after birth. While rats experience an 80 per cent increase in DG neurons in the first two weeks of life, guinea pigs have only a 20 per cent increase over the first month of life. The fact that newborn rats are more susceptible to forgetting than newborn guinea pigs is thus consistent with the hypothesis that infantile amnesia is caused by neurogenesis in the DG (Josselyn & Frankland, 2012).

The neurogenic hypothesis of infantile amnesia proposed by Josselyn and Frankland (2012) suggests that infantile amnesia occurs because rampant neurogenesis leads to rampant neurogenesis-dependent decay. The decay may occur either because new neurons alter the wiring of existing hippocampal networks or because newborn DG cells are more excitable than older cells, and when they are introduced into the network, homeostatic mechanisms decrease activation in existing neurons, leading to synaptic loss.

altricial

a term describing an animal born in an undeveloped state that requires care and feeding by the parents

precocial

a term describing an animal born in an advanced state that is able to feed itself almost immediately

Guinea pigs (left, shown here at five days old) are an example of a precocial rodent. Guinea pigs are born with the ability to care for themselves, have less neurogenesis during infancy, and show less infantile amnesia. Rats (right, shown here at five days old) are an example of an altricial rodent. Rats are dependent on their mothers for several weeks after birth, have more neurogenesis during infancy, and show more infantile amnesia.

High rates of neurogenesis in young animals are adaptive for two reasons. First, neurogenesis accelerates the transfer of memories from being hippocampus-dependent to being hippocampus-independent (Kitamura et al., 2009), allowing the animal to generalize across a series of individual episodes. Second, neurogenesis clears existing hippocampal representations, making way for new learning, and new learning is arguably most important early in life (Inokuchi, 2011).

Recall that research consistently shows two phases of infantile amnesia in humans. First there is an initial phase of frank amnesia where essentially no information learned prior to the age of three is retained. Next there is a second phase of moderate amnesia where some information is recalled, but this is less than is predicted by the standard forgetting curve. The second phase spans ages four through seven. The neurogenic hypothesis of infantile amnesia necessarily stipulates that neurogenesis in the DG is at its highest prior to the age of three, and then decreases over the next four years until it finally reaches a level that is similar to rates of neurogenesis experienced throughout adulthood. Thus, the amount of forgetting reflects the rate of neurogenesis, supporting the neurogenic hypothesis for infantile amnesia.

Memory-Trace Consolidation

memory-trace consolidation

a strengthening of the connection between neurons comprising a given memory

Although forgetting appears to be a natural consequence of neurogenesis, not all memories are forgotten. Some memories persist for many decades. Frankland et al. (2013) suggest that whether a memory is retained or lost through neurogenesis-dependent decay depends on the outcome of a struggle between two competing processes: neurogenesis-dependent decay, described in the preceding section, and **memory-trace consolidation**. Memory-trace consolidation occurs when the memory is reactivated through wakeful retrieval or during sleep. The reactivation causes the trace to be proliferated and stabilized in the hippocampus and/or in the neocortex (Winocur & Moscovitch, 2011). Because retrieval triggers consolidation, memories that are retrieved more often have stronger traces. Frankland et al. (2013) suggest that memories are retained if consolidation processes overpower neurogenesis-dependent decay. In other words, when the trace is strengthened more by memory-trace consolidation than it is weakened by neurogenesis-dependent decay, the memory will persist. Thus, memories that are activated frequently (such as events that are talked about often, facts that are considered often, etc.) are less vulnerable to neurogenesis-dependent decay because these memories benefit from memory-trace consolidation, which counters the effect of neurogenesis-dependent decay. This can help explain why people can remember an often-discussed party from two years ago but not what they did the day before or after that party.

Factors that influence neurogenesis will also impact neurogenesis-related forgetting. For example, when neurogenesis is slowed, forgetting due to neurogenesis-dependent decay is less likely to occur (because neurogenesis has less of an impact on the connections between neurons in the hippocampus). Research suggests that stress, drugs of abuse, and diet can reduce neurogenesis, thus reducing the threat of forgetting due to neurogenesis-dependent decay. Other factors tend to increase neurogenesis, including exercise, environmental enrichment, and serotonin-specific reuptake inhibitors (SSRIs). SSRIs may increase the possibility of hippocampal memories being lost due to neurogenesis-dependent decay. In these cases, neurogenesis has a more significant impact on the connections between neurons in the hippocampus.

Frankland et al. (2013) also speculate that learning new material that conflicts with previously learned material will be affected by neurogenesis. If neurogenesis is occurring, it will facilitate the forgetting of old material and favour the retention of new conflicting information.

If neurogenesis is impeded, however, it may be difficult to learn new conflicting information because neurogenesis-dependent forgetting is not occurring. This means that people under stress, who abuse drugs, or who have a poor diet may have difficulty forming new memories because their lifestyle impedes neurogenesis. When neurogenesis is not occurring, an individual will be more likely to experience misattribution and suggestibility as old memories conflict with new information.

Neurogenesis-dependent decay is consistent with arguments that suggest that forgetting is critical for healthy memory function for at least three reasons. First, as we saw in the chapter-opening case study, many people with hyperthymesia have difficulty functioning normally as a result of their inability to forget episodic memories. Second, maintaining memories over time requires an animal to expend energy; forgetting conserves this energy for only the most pertinent information. Finally, neurogenesis-dependent forgetting makes recalling pertinent information easier and more accurate by eliminating other similar (redundant) memories.

Molecular Decay in the Hippocampus

Molecular mechanisms may also result in decay of hippocampal memories. In order for a neuron to sustain long-term potentiation, it must possess the constitutionally active, atypical protein kinase C isoform M-zeta (PKMζ; pronounced pee-kay-em-zeta). PKMζ is synthesized during memory formation (Osten, Valsamis, Harris, & Sacktor, 1996). Research has found that inhibiting PKMζ activity can impair and even abolish consolidated memories (Serrano et al., 2008) and that overexpressing PKMζ can help enhance weak memories. PKMζ is to neurons like air is to humans; without it, the neuron cannot survive. Hippocampal neurons contain GluA2-containing AMPA receptors which, while crucial to maintaining connections between hippocampal neurons, have a natural tendency to degrade over time. If there is no PKMζ present, the GluA2-containing AMPA receptors will be absorbed into the neuron and the neuron will lose its potentiation, or ability to fire (Migues et al., 2010). PKMζ also degrades over time and must be replenished for GluA2-containing AMPA receptors to remain active. PKMζ is synthesized when a memory is activated, and thus neurons associated with memories that are recalled often are more likely to maintain their connections than those associated with memories that are not recalled often. Thus, there is a neuroscientific explanation for why people tend to better remember memories they recall often.

Hippocampal neurons also contain Glu2NB-containing NMDA receptors. Glu2NB-containing NMDA receptors occasionally allow a small amount of calcium into a neuron. The calcium ions are positively charged and as a result they depolarize the neuron, which is negatively charged in its resting state. Researchers believe that occasionally this depolarization makes the neuron appear to be in a state of **long-term depotentiation (LTD)** in which it has lost its ability to generate action potentials. This LTD may signal the GluA2-containing AMPA receptors to degrade and lose potentiation, leading to memory loss (transience).

Hardt et al. (2013) argue that the active regulation of GluA2-containing AMPA receptors is central to whether a memory decays. GluA2-containing AMPA receptors are protected by the reactivation of memories through the manufacture of additional PKMζ, which ensures that important information is preserved. However, these receptors are lost if a memory is not reactivated or if nearby Glu2NB-containing NMDA receptors lose potentiation. These two molecular mechanisms could lead to rapid forgetting in the hippocampus, thus explaining why episodic memories (which are initially stored in the hippocampus) are sometimes lost soon after learning,

long-term depotentiation (LTD)

when a cell loses its ability to create an action potential

long before neurogenesis-dependent forgetting, which takes about two weeks, could occur. This forgetting may be reflected in the steepness of the forgetting curve soon after learning.

Thus there are two possible mechanisms for decay in the hippocampus: neurogenesis-dependent decay and molecular decay. Recall that an explicit memory initially generates two codes, one in the hippocampus and one in the neocortex. In a normal brain, forgetting of hippocampal memories will occur due to decay; because neurogenesis helps with pattern separation, the hippocampal memories will be resistant to interference. The converse is true for neocortical representations. Neocortical representations are not affected by decay; instead, they are primarily affected by interference.

Interference as a Source of Forgetting of Neocortical Memories

As we saw in Chapter 7, unlike hippocampal memories, neocortical memories are encoded by the medial temporal lobe (MTL) and perirhinal cortex (PRc). To create a neocortical memory, the MTL and PRc process fine details of a single item in hippocampal memory (Deng et al., 2010; Ko et al., 2009) and then merge that information with similar information stored in neocortical regions using a similar set of neurons, while maintaining a link between the neocortical representation and the hippocampal representation it originated from. The memory can be distinguished from other similar memories, as long as the link to the hippocampal memory remains strong, because the hippocampal memory provides the specific context for that memory. While hippocampal memories appear to be susceptible to forgetting through decay but not interference, neocortical memories appear to be susceptible to forgetting through interference but not decay.

Talya Sadeh, Jason Ozubko, Gordon Winocur, and Morris Moscovitch of the Rotman Research Institute in Toronto have demonstrated that neocortical memories are susceptible to interference but not decay, while the reverse is true for hippocampal memories, by comparing the effects of interference on recollection-based memory and familiarity judgments across a variety of experiments. **Recollection** is "a conscious process involving the reinstatement of an event from memory along with contextual details and an accompanying sense of self" (Sadeh et al., 2014, p. 26). For example, when you remember being at a holiday gathering, you are recollecting that event. Recollection is linked to hippocampal memories. **Familiarity**, on the other hand, does not involve the reinstatement of context but, as the name suggests, is characterized by the feeling the item has been encountered on a previous occasion. For example, when you remember that Margaret Atwood is the author of *A Handmaid's Tale* but you don't recall when you learned this fact, you are experiencing familiarity. Familiarity is associated with neocortical memories. Sadeh et al. (2014) present a number of experiments that demonstrate that recollection is affected by decay but not interference, while familiarity is affected by interference but not decay. Sadeh et al. (2014) argue that these results indicate that interference is the main source of forgetting for neocortical memories.

In 1992, William Hockley of Wilfrid Laurier University conducted a series of experiments that assessed the effect of interference on participants' ability to make correct old/new judgments on both individual items and word pairs. Hockley (1992) used a continuous-recognition paradigm in which word pairs were intermixed with probes consisting of old or new individual items or word pairs (see Figure 8.6). Hockley (1992) reasoned that familiarity-based memory would be sufficient to make a correct old/new judgment for an individual item, whereas recollection would be required to indicate whether a given word pair had been seen before. This is because a word pair could potentially consist of two words that were presented before but

recollection

the reinstatement of an event from memory that includes contextual details and an accompanying sense of self

familiarity

a feeling that an item has been encountered before

Trial#	Word Pair/Prope	Old/New
1	HUNTER–MUSIC	
2	RABBIT–APPLE	
3	? HUNTER ?	Old
4	OLIVE–VISION	
5	MIRROR–COBRA	
6	CHISEL–UNDER	
7	WATER–HOTEL	
8	? OLIVE– COBRA ?	New
9	YELLOW–BAKER	
10	PILOT–MEADOW	
11	IGLOO–FUNNEL	
12	CHERRY–DRAWING	
13	MANTLE–DUCKLING	
14	POPPY–JESTER	
15	GIRAFFE–FANCY	
16	TRAINER–BAGEL	
17	? PURPLE ?	New

Figure 8.6 Example of word pairs and probes from a continuous-recognition paradigm

In a continuous-recognition paradigm experiment, word pairs are presented. Probes are presented following various intervals and are signalled by the presentation of question marks on either side of the word. The participant must indicate whether the individual word or word pair is old (meaning it was presented earlier in the experiment) or is new (has not been presented earlier in the experiment). Interference can be increased by increasing the number of intervening items between a word and its probe. Hockley (1992) used a continuous-recognition paradigm and found that the number of intervening items affected the accuracy of old/new judgments for words but not for word pairs, and concluded that familiarity-based memory is vulnerable to interference but that recollective memory is not.

not as part of the same pair. Words that were not presented previously were also sometimes used as probes. Hockley (1992) manipulated interference by having 2, 4, 6, 8, or 16 word pairs intervene between the presentation of a word or word pair and its item or word-pair probe. Hockley (1992) found that as the number of intervening items increased, the accuracy of old/new judgments decreased for probes consisting of individual items but not for probes consisting of word pairs (see Figure 8.7). Hockley's (1992) result demonstrates that familiarity-based memory is subject to forgetting through interference while recollection-based memory is not. Because familiarity is associated with neocortical memories and recollection is associated with hippocampal memories, Hockley's (1992) result suggests that neocortical memories are more susceptible to forgetting through interference than hippocampal memories, which supports Sadeh et al.'s (2014) claim that hippocampal-based memories are more resistant to interference than memories coded through the MTL and PRc.

Additional support for the notion that forgetting in the neocortex is due to interference, rather than decay, comes from observing individuals who have sustained hippocampal damage. These individuals cannot encode information in the hippocampus and thus any memories that are retained must reflect neocortical representations. A consistent observation of people with hippocampal damage is that they are highly susceptible to interference. Under conditions where the presentation of new information is followed by activities that make demands on perceptual and cognitive systems, individuals with hippocampal damage forget

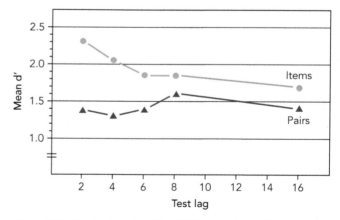

Figure 8.7 Results from Hockley (1992, experiment 1)
Source: Hockley, 1992, p. 1323

new information almost immediately. However, if the presentation of new information is followed by a period of rest, information can be retained for much longer (Cowan et al., 2004; Dewar, Garcia, Cowan, & Sala, 2009). Because the level of perceptual and cognitive activity is directly linked to the retention of material that must be coded in the neocortex, this provides support for the claim that interference is the main source of forgetting for neocortical representations.

Memories that have representations in both the hippocampus and the neocortex are relatively immune to interference because the hippocampus will ensure that new, similar memories receive orthogonal coding. However, when a neocortical representation is not supported by a hippocampal representation, interference may cause forgetting.

Retrieval-Induced Forgetting

retrieval-induced forgetting (RIF)

forgetting that occurs because in order to retrieve one item accurately, similar items must be inhibited

competition-induced interference

when having to inhibit retrieval of an item results in later forgetting of that same item

In the 1990s, Michael Anderson and his colleagues began to examine how retrieving some items from a learned list impacted memory for the other items on that list using what came to be known as the retrieval-induced forgetting (RIF) paradigm, shown in Figure 8.8. The RIF paradigm involves a study phase, a retrieval practice phase, and a final test. In the study phase, each participant is presented with paired associates. The first item in the pair is a general category (such as FRUIT) and the second item is an example from that category (such as *peach*). Each study list includes pairs from two different categories (such as FRUIT and SPORT). During the retrieval practice phase, participants practise retrieving *half* of the items from *one* of the categories, such as FRUIT, by completing paired-associate word stems such as FRUIT–*pe___*; these practiced items are referred to as RP+ items. The participants do not practise retrieving the other half of the items from the practiced category such as FRUIT–*cherry*; these are referred to as RP– items. Participants do not practise any of the items from the second category, in our example, SPORTS; these are referred to as no repeated practice (NRP) items. Following a delay, participants are asked to recall as many items from the study list as possible. Two consistent findings from experiments employing the RIF paradigm are illustrated in Figure 8.9. The first is that RP+ items are more likely to be recalled than NRP items, suggesting that retrieval practice aids recall. The second, more surprising, finding is that RP– items are less likely to be recalled than NRP items. Thus, if a participant practises FRUIT–*ch___*, that participant is less likely to recall other items from the FRUIT category that were not practised; this phenomenon is known as **retrieval-induced forgetting (RIF)**.

There are several explanations for retrieval-induced forgetting in the literature. Michael Anderson, Robert Bjork, and Elizabeth Bjork asserted that retrieval-induced forgetting results from a type of inhibition called **competition-induced interference**, or forgetting that results from having to suppress items that are similar to a target item. According to Anderson, Bjork, and Bjork (1994), when FRUIT–*pe___* is presented during retrieval practice, many items strongly associated with FRUIT

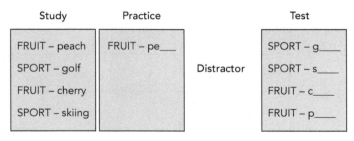

Figure 8.8 The three-phase procedure of a typical retrieval-induced forgetting (RIF) experiment

In the study phase of the RIF paradigm, participants are shown paired associates from two different categories. In the practice phase, participants practise retrieving one-half of the items from one category of the study phase. After a distractor task, participants are tested on their ability to recall items from the study phase.
Source: Jonker, Seli, & MacLeod, 2013, p. 203

(such as cherry, banana, and orange) are activated and compete for retrieval. In order for the participant to retrieve the correct response, *peach*, the participant must suppress, or inhibit, these other activated fruits. This suppression is argued to have a lasting effect, making these suppressed items more difficult to retrieve in the future. Importantly, this explanation for RIF suggests that the memory representation for RP– items is inhibited and thus predicts that suppressed items will be difficult to retrieve during the final test. Thus, if *cherry* is inhibited during retrieval practice of FRUIT–*pe___*, then *cherry* will be more difficult to retrieve during all subsequent memory tasks. This prediction is supported by the results from several experiments (e.g., Anderson & Spellman, 1995; Johnson & Anderson, 2004; Saunders & MacLeod, 2006). This account suggests that RIF results from blocking, one of Schacter's (2002) sins of omission.

Tanya Jonker, Paul Seli, and Colin MacLeod of the University of Waterloo instead argue

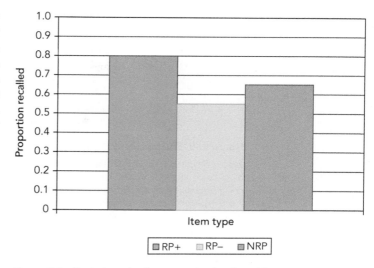

Figure 8.9 Typical results from a retrieval-induced forgetting (RIF) paradigm experiment

The NRP items serve as a baseline. The RP+ items receive retrieval practice and recall is higher than baseline for those items. The RP– items do not receive retrieval practice and recall is lower than baseline for those items.

Source: Based on Jonker, Seli, & MacLeod, 2013, p. 852

that retrieval-induced forgetting effects are the result of context. Jonker et al. (2013) argue that mental context is established by the sorts of cognitive activities that are taking place at a given time and that this mental context can serve as a memory cue. Jonker et al. (2013) argue that studying words creates a different mental context than attempting to retrieve words, and thus that the mental context of the study phase of a RIF paradigm experiment is different than the mental context of the retrieval practice phase of a RIF paradigm experiment. According to the context account of RIF, all items are associated with the study context, but only RP+ items are associated with the retrieval practice context. Jonker et al. (2013) suggest that, during the test phase, both the mental activity of retrieval and the category words serve as contextual cues. When the participant sees a category name that was only present in the study phase, the study phase context is reinstated; the fact that the mental context is different is of no consequence. However, the authors argue that when the participant sees a context word presented during the retrieval practice phase, the retrieval practice context is instead reinstated because this is more similar to the current context than the study context. Because the retrieval practice context is not associated with RP– items, RP– items are less likely to be recalled, leading to the RIF effect. An illustration of the argument by Jonker et al. (2013) is shown in Figure 8.10.

Jonker et al. (2013) tested the context account of the RIF effect. In a RIF-like experiment, Jonker et al. (2013) had participants learn a list of word pairs from four different categories. Next, participants imagined their parents' house in as much detail as possible for one minute. Participants were given extra study time for half the word pairs from half of the categories by reading the word pairs aloud. (These were the RP+ items; the non-practiced items from the practiced categories were the RP– items; the remaining were NRP items.) Because the extra study phase in this experiment does not involve retrieval, the inhibition account predicts no difference in recall for the RP– and

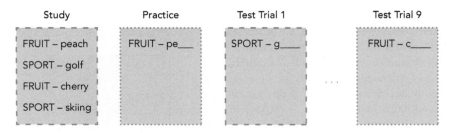

Figure 8.10   The possible effect of context on recall in a RIF paradigm experiment

Jonker, Seli, and MacLeod (2013) suggest that the Study and Practice phases of a RIF paradigm experiment produce distinct mental contexts. The different contexts are represented by different borders around Study and Practice items. When the NRP category is presented on Test Trial 1, the Study context is activated because this is the only previous context where SPORT items appeared. On Test Trial 9, however, the Practice context is activated because there is more overlap with the Practice contexts than with the Test Trial and Study contexts. Because RP– items are not associated with the Practice context, RP– items are unlikely to be retrieved.

Source: Jonker, Seli, & McLeod, 2013, p. 856

the NRP items. However, because the imagination task creates a highly salient context for the RP+ items right before the test phase, the context account predicts that the RP+ items will be better recalled than the NRP items. Jonker et al. (2013) found worse recall for RP– items than NRP items, supporting Jonker et al.'s (2013) argument that retrieval-induced forgetting is the result of a more similar context between the test phase and the context associated with RP+ items than between the test phase and the context associated with the RP– items. In a second experiment, Jonker et al. (2013) reinstated the study context just before the test phase by having participants answer questions that referred to their experiences leading up to and during the study session. When Jonker et al. (2013) had participants think about the study phase just prior to the test phase, the RIF effect was eliminated. Thus, the results of Jonker et al. (2013) strongly suggest that retrieval-induced forgetting is the result of mental context effects and not the inhibition of RP– items. This account of RIF suggests that RIF is due to bias, one of Schacter's (2002) sins of commission.

Forgetting that occurs due to neurogenesis, molecular decay, or interference are all examples of *incidental forgetting*. Incidental forgetting occurs without the intention to forget. However, people can also experience *motivated forgetting*. Unlike incidental forgetting, motivated forgetting relies on deliberate psychological processes, which we will explore next.

Motivated Forgetting

Thus far our discussion on forgetting has focused on **incidental forgetting**, or forgetting that occurs without cognitive activity related to suppressing encoding or retrieval. There is, however, ample evidence of **motivated forgetting** as a result of cognitive processes initiated either intentionally or unintentionally by the rememberer. For example, an individual may engage in **intentional forgetting**, deliberately trying to limit encoding or retrieval of certain memories. Reasons for this may include the information being no long relevant (like an obsolete phone number) or the fact that the memory was unpleasant (like failing an exam). Intentional forgetting isn't the only way that forgetting occurs through cognitive mechanisms. Individuals may experience **psychogenic amnesia**, where they are unable to remember aspects of their personal

incidental forgetting

forgetting that occurs without cognitive activity related to suppressing encoding or retrieval

motivated forgetting

forgetting that occurs because of conscious strategies to forget, or because of cognitive processes whose by-product is forgetting

intentional forgetting

forgetting that results from deliberate attempts to suppress certain memories

psychogenic amnesia

significant memory loss resulting from psychological factors

history or event because of psychological mechanisms. Both intentional forgetting and psychogenic amnesia are examples of motivated forgetting—forgetting that is the result of cognitive activity that either directly or indirectly makes retrieval less likely.

The Directed-Forgetting Paradigm

Intentional forgetting has been studied extensively in the lab using what are known as directed-forgetting (DF) paradigms. There are two main types of DF paradigms: the item-method and the list-method. In an **item-method DF paradigm**, participants are presented with items and told to forget certain items immediately after the item is presented. For example, in an item-method DF paradigm experiment, a participant may be presented with words on a computer screen and be shown the word *remember* or the word *forget* immediately following the presentation of each word. The participant's memory for the items is then tested. Barbara and David Basden compared recall for pictures, words, and words that were imagined as images by the participants using an item-method paradigm. Basden and Basden (1996) found similar results across all three stimulus types. Participants recalled about 75 per cent of to-be-remembered items and recalled about 40 per cent of to-be-forgotten items, indicating that memory is significantly worse when following instructions to forget. When performance is worse in the forget condition than the remember condition in a DF paradigm experiment, there is said to be a **cost of forgetting**. A cost of forgetting is also observed for to-be-forgotten items when recognition, rather than recall, is used as a dependent measure (e.g., Basden, Basden, & Gargano, 1993).

In a typical **list-method DF paradigm** experiment, participants are presented with one list of words (L1), then given a set of instructions, and then presented with a second list of words (L2). Participants in the forget condition are instructed to disregard L1, while participants in the remember condition are instructed to continue to remember L1 as they proceed through L2. Participants' memory for L1 and L2 items is then tested. There are two consistent findings from list-method DF paradigm experiments. First, like with the item-method DF paradigm, participants show a cost of forgetting; participants in the forget condition tend to remember fewer L1 items than participants in the remember condition. The list-method DF paradigm also typically produces a **benefit of forgetting**, where participants in the forget condition are better able to recall L2 items than participants in the remember condition (see Bjork, Bjork, & Anderson, 1998 for a review). The cost of forgetting has been replicated dozens of times using variants of this basic paradigm. Unlike the item-method DF paradigm, the list-method DF paradigm does not typically lead to deficits in recognition or other implicit tests of memory (Sahakyan, Delaney, Foster, & Abushanab, 2013).

Lili Sahakyan and her colleagues at the University of North Carolina propose a two-factor account of directed forgetting. The cost of forgetting is attributed to a change in context between L1 and L2. The benefit of forgetting is attributed to improved strategies for remembering that are adopted by participants after they are told that they no longer have to remember L1. The basic architecture of the two-factor process-based model of directed forgetting is shown in Figure 8.11.

The two-factor process-based framework for list-method directed forgetting presented by Sahakyan et al. (2013) suggests that the directed-forgetting cue first leads to a strategic decision on how to best forget the preceding items, which changes the mental context that the L2 items are encoded in. At the time of test, the participant's mental context is similar to the context experienced when learning L2 items, but different from the mental context experienced when learning the L1 items. The similarity between L2 learning and test contexts facilitates retrieval of

item-method DF paradigm

a paradigm in which participants are instructed to forget specific items from a single list immediately after the item is presented

cost of forgetting

in a directed-forgetting paradigm, worse memory performance for to-be-forgotten items than to-be-remembered items

list-method DF paradigm

a paradigm in which participants are instructed to forget an entire list of items after it has been presented

benefit of forgetting

in a directed-forgetting paradigm, better memory performance in the forget condition than the remember condition

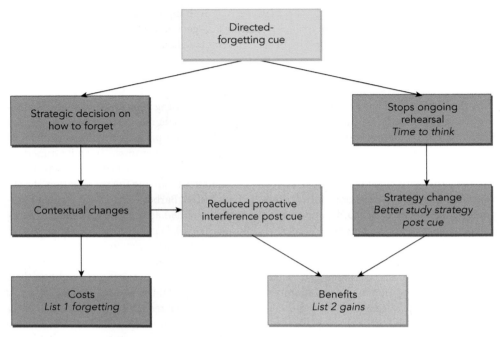

Figure 8.11   A two-factor process-based framework for list-method directed forgetting

The two-factor process-based framework for list-method directed forgetting presented by Sahakyan et al. (2013) suggests that the directed- forgetting cue leads to a strategic decision on how to best forget the preceding items, which changes the mental context that the L2 items are encoded in, leading to a cost of forgetting for L1. In addition, the retrieval cue also gives the participant time to consider the best strategy for remembering L2 items. This, combined with a reduction in proactive interference from L1 due to the opportunity to forget L1, results in a benefit of forgetting for L2 items.

Source: Sahakyan et al., 2013, p. 140

L2 items; however, the difference between L1 learning and test contexts makes it more difficult to retrieve L1 items, leading to a cost of forgetting. In addition, participants in the forget condition have a chance to consider their learning strategy for the upcoming L2 items when they are told they can forget the L1 items. This opportunity is not afforded to participants learning L1 or participants in the remember condition, and is argued to lead to more effective mnemonic strategies and a subsequent benefit of forgetting. Sahakyan et al. (2013) also speculate that participants in the remember condition will experience less proactive interference from L1 items when learning L2 items and that this may also contribute to the benefit of forgetting.

Nathan Foster and Lili Sahakyan examined the reports of 290 individuals who participated in list-method DF forgetting experiments. (Half were in the forget condition; half were in the remember condition.) The researchers found five common strategies among participants: stopping rehearsal of L1 items, stopping thinking about L1 item, focusing on upcoming L2 items, diverting their thoughts away from L1 items, and clearing their head. Diversionary thoughts resulted in the largest cost of forgetting. Participants in the forget condition who reported using this strategy recalled about 12 per cent of L1 items while participants who did not receive a forget cue recalled about 40 per cent of L1 items. Participants who stopped rehearsing recalled about 22 per cent of L1 items. Participants who stopped thinking about L1 items recalled about

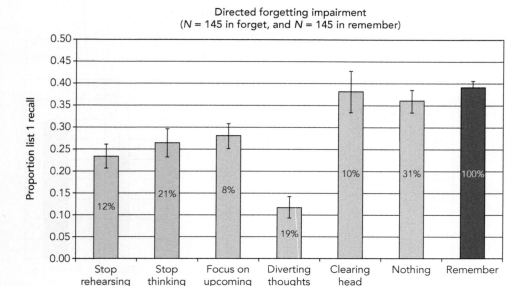

Figure 8.12   Recall of L1 items as a function of forgetting strategy

This graph shows directed-forgetting L1 recall costs as a function of forgetting strategies reported by for-get-group participants. The blue bar represents the remember condition. The pink bars represent the subgroups of the forget condition. The numbers inside the bars indicate the percentage of participants in each condition.
Source: Sahakyan et al., 2013, p. 147

26 per cent of L1 items. Participants who tried to focus on L2 items recalled about 28 per cent of L1 items. Participants who cleared their heads or did not engage in a strategy to forget recalled about the same proportion recalled by participants in the remember condition (see Figure 8.12).

Nathan Foster and Lili Sahakyan also looked at the benefits of forgetting as a function of forgetting strategy (see Figure 8.13). Participants in the forget condition recalled significantly more L2 items than participants in the remember condition. The largest benefit was seen among participants who reported that their forgetting strategy was to stop thinking about L1 items; this group recalled about 50 per cent of L2 items compared to 35 per cent recalled by participants in the remember condition. Sahakyan et al. (2013) argue that the forget cue causes many participants to switch their coding strategies and that this results in both a cost of forgetting for L1 and a benefit of forgetting for L2. Sahakyan et al. (2013) argue that the effect of the change in strategy has an effect that is independent from change in context, because participants who change strategies between L1 and L2 show a benefit in recalling L2 items even if they are not instructed to forget L1 items. The change in strategy is argued to reduce proactive interference. The independent effects of strategy change and mental context change on performance in DF experiments are fundamental to the dual-process account (Sahakyan et al., 2013).

Studies examining neural activity during list-method DF paradigm experiments provide support for the dual-process account. Karl-Heinz Bäuml, Simon Hanslmayr, Bernhard Pastötter, and Wolfgang Klimesch studied patterns in brain oscillation in participants participating in a list-method DF paradigm experiment. Brain oscillations were measured using an electroencephalogram (EEG) and were categorized according to their frequency. Waves categories included

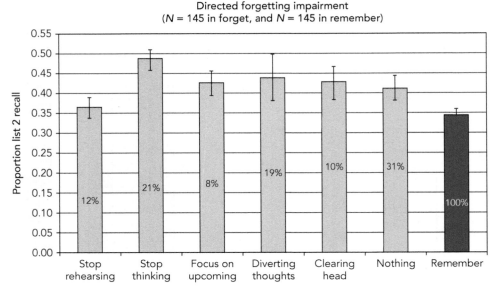

Figure 8.13   Recall of L2 items as a function of forgetting strategy

This graph shows directed-forgetting L2 recall benefits as a function of forgetting strategies reported by forget-group participants. The blue bar represents the remember condition. The pink bars represent the subgroups of the forget condition. The numbers inside the bars indicate the percentage of participants in each condition.
Source: Sahakyan et al., 2013, p. 147

delta (2–4 Hz), theta (4–7 Hz), alpha (7–13 Hz), beta (13–30 Hz), and gamma (above 30 Hz). There are two main features of brain oscillations: power and phase. Power is regarded as a measure of local synchrony (the extent to which neurons in a given area are firing together), while phase is considered a measure of distant synchrony (the extent to which two separate regions are firing at the same time). Bäuml et al. (2008) found greater alpha oscillation power and reduced alpha oscillation phase coupling in the forget condition than in the remember condition. The researchers found that these two differences were related to two different behavioural effects. The increase in alpha power was associated with benefits of forgetting while the reduction in alpha phase coupling was associated with costs of forgetting. The authors concluded that the costs and benefits of forgetting resulted from two separate neural mechanisms (Bäuml et al., 2008). The notion that costs and benefits of forgetting are produced by two distinct processes is consistent with the dual-process account but difficult to reconcile with either the selective rehearsal or retrieval inhibition accounts of DF effects.

Motivated Forgetting of Personal Experiences

Everyone experiences unpleasant personal events that they would like to forget. The event may be as innocuous as failing a test, or as serious as losing a loved one or being in a life-threatening accident. In each case, individuals are motivated to forget these incidents in order to save themselves the emotional pain that comes with recalling them. There are several ways that people can intentionally forget experiences: the person can engage in activities that prevent encoding, avoid reminders, or engage in activities that prevent retrieval.

Encoding Suppression

If individuals experience an event and know immediately that they wish to forget the event, they can engage in **encoding suppression**, or processes that make encoding less likely to be successful. Encoding suppression has been studied in the laboratory by recording brain activity while participants participate in item-method DF experiments. In these studies, participants are presented with a series of items and after each item are presented with a cue indicating whether they should forget or remember the item. Multiple studies have shown that the right and middle frontal gyrus and the right inferior parietal lobe are more active following a forget instruction than following a remember instruction (Rizio & Dennis, 2013; see Figure 8.14). In addition, several behavioural studies have found that participants are slower at completing simple response-time tasks following forget instructions than when following remember instructions, suggesting that, after receiving the instruction to forget, an individual engages in effortful processing. Avery Rizio and Nancy Dennis found that when the right dorsolateral prefrontal cortex (DL) is more active following a forget instruction, activity in the left hippocampus is reduced (Rizio & Dennis, 2013). Taken together, these results suggest that a forget cue engages the right prefrontal-hippocampal network that suppresses encoding processes (Anderson & Hanslmayr, 2014). Thus, in a real-world

> **encoding suppression**
>
> any process that makes encoding less likely to be successful

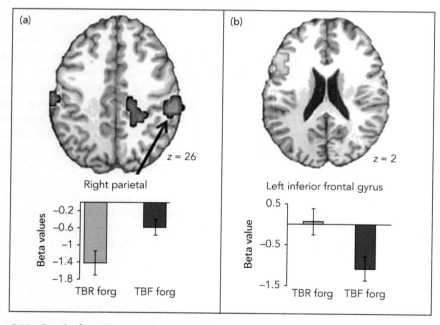

Figure 8.14   Results from Rizio and Dennis (2013)

In Rizio and Dennis (2013), (a) the right parietal cortex was significantly more active for intentional forgetting than incidental forgetting, whereas (b) the left inferior frontal gyrus was more active for incidental forgetting than intentional forgetting.

Source: Rizio & Dennis, 2013, p. 306

setting, it is reasonable to assume that a person could utilize a forget cue and engage similar brain areas to stop an event from being encoded.

Changing Context

Sometimes people who have encoded events that they wish to forget will avoid the context that the event occurred in. For example, a person who was in a car accident may avoid the roads where the accident occurred. Avoiding the context related to an unpleasant memory can aid in forgetting in many ways. First, by avoiding the context, the individual is avoiding retrieval cues that can trigger recall. Second, by avoiding recall, the individual prevents reactivation of the memory and consequent strengthening of the memory trace. Third, by avoiding the context and thereby not retrieving the memory, the individual is more likely to develop a positive mood state. The positive mood state then creates a difference in mental context that makes retrieval of the unpleasant memory less likely. The link between changes in mental context and forgetting is well supported in the literature (see Sahakyan et al., 2013 for a review).

Retrieval Suppression

retrieval suppression

a process by which a person stops an encoded memory from entering conscious awareness

Sometimes people have encoded events they wish to forget but they cannot avoid context or retrieval cues associated with that event. For example, a person may have failed a test at school but must return to the same classroom and be taught by the same teacher. However, an individual can still exclude the unwanted memory from awareness through **retrieval suppression**. Michael Anderson and Collin Green developed the think/no think (TNT) paradigm to examine the extent to which individuals can control what they think about, and what they do not think about. In a TNT paradigm experiment, participants first learn to associate cues with specific items; for example, they may learn to associate the cue *ocean* with the word *WHALE*. At some point after learning, participants are presented with some of the cues and are told to suppress any items they recall; for example, if they are presented with *ocean* they are to suppress thinking about the word *WHALE*. Later, participants are presented with all of the cues and their memory for the words is tested. Many experiments that have used TNT procedures have produced forgetting (see Anderson & Hanslmayr, 2014 for a review). The TNT procedure has produced forgetting with numerous different types of stimuli, including word pairs, face–scene pairs, and pictures and autobiographical experiences (Anderson & Hanslmayr, 2014). Forgetting increases as the number of suppression attempts increases (e.g., Lambert, Good, and Kirk, 2010); an individual who has suppressed retrieval of an item 16 times will be less likely to recall that item than someone who has only suppressed retrieval of an item four times.

Michael Anderson and his colleagues speculated that the mechanisms used to suppress retrieval were similar to the mechanisms used to suppress reflexive actions. To test this hypothesis, Anderson et al. (2004) collected fMRI data while participants completed a TNT experiment. Anderson et al. (2004) found that the right lateral prefrontal cortex and the angular cingulate gyrus were more active during suppression trials than retrieval trials; these are the same areas that are believed to be involved in stopping reflexive motor actions. In addition, Anderson et al. (2004) found that the hippocampus was less active during suppress trials than when participants were engaged in retrieval. Anderson et al. (2004) argue that retrieval suppression initiated by instructions given in the TNT paradigm triggers activity in the brain that is consistent with first stopping reflexive retrieval of hippocampal memories.

RELEVANT RESEARCH

BOX
8.2

Intentionally Forgetting Autobiographical Memories

Directed-forgetting experiments have been used to show that individuals can intentionally forget a variety of arbitrary stimuli, including words (Sahakyan et al., 2013), sentences (Geiselman, 1974), and pictures (Basden & Basden, 1996). Susan Joslyn and Mark Oakes decided to test whether directed-forgetting instructions could also produce forgetting of autobiographical memories. The experiment took place over a two-week period. On five pre-specified days during week one, participants recorded two events that they deemed to be memorable. At the end of week one, all participants met with the experimenter and submitted their memories from week one. Participants in the forget condition were told that the events from the first week were not going to be used as part of this experiment and that they should actively try to forget those events. The participants in the remember condition were told that they would eventually be asked to recall all events from the study. At the end of the second week, participants submitted their week two memories and were immediately given a recall test. Joslyn and Oakes (2005) found participants in both the forget and the remember conditions recalled a similar number of week two events, but participants in the forget condition remembered significantly fewer week one events than participants in the remember condition. Joslyn and Oakes (2005) concluded that individuals can indeed intentionally forget autobiographical memories. The results from Joslyn and Oakes (2005) suggest that it is possible for individuals to intentionally forget unpleasant life experiences, providing an explanation for why people tend to remember more positive life experiences than negative life experiences.

Thought Substitution

When participants in the forget condition of a list-method DF paradigm experiment are asked what actions they took to try to forget the preceding items, participants who are most successful at forgetting tend to report that they intentionally thought about other things when items from the to-be-forgotten list came to mind (Sahakyan et al., 2013). Many people who have recently experienced trauma or loss report that keeping themselves busy has helped them to cope, suggesting that having other things to think about when unpleasant memories arise aids in forgetting. For example, in *The Sound of Music*, Maria teaches the von Trapp children that thinking about their favourite things (like "raindrops on roses" or "whiskers on kittens") is an effective way of dealing with trauma (like "when the dog bites" or "when the bee stings"). Because thought substitution involves retrieving memories to replace unwanted memories in conscious awareness, a person cannot engage in both retrieval suppression and thought substitution at the same time; retrieval suppression would stop thought substitution. Roland Benoit and Michael Anderson examined the fMRI data of participants who were engaging in thought substitution. In the experiment reported by Benoit and Anderson (2012), participants learned to associated one cue with two different words, e.g., BEACH–AFRICA and BEACH–SNORKEL. During critical trials, participants were presented with the cue. If the cue was presented in green, the participant was to recall the *first* word they learned to associate with that cue (in this example, AFRICA). When the cue was presented in red, the participant was instructed to substitute any thoughts regarding the first word they learned to associate with the cue (e.g., AFRICA) with the second word they learned to associate with the cue (e.g., SNORKEL). Benoit and Anderson (2012) found that participants performing thought substitution showed increased activity in the left caudal prefrontal cortex (cPFC) and ventrolateral prefrontal cortex (VLPFC) compared to a baseline group that was just required to recall words. These areas are thought to be involved in post-retrieval selection of memories (Badre & Wagner, 2007; Kuhl & Rivera-Gaxiola, 2008). Benoit and Anderson (2013) suggest that the activation of two memories during thought substitution may lead to forgetting in two ways. First, the unwanted memory may be selectively weakened, making it less accessible in subsequent retrieval attempts (Storm & Nestojko, 2010). Second, it is possible that the preferred thought may be strengthened during thought substitution, making this substitute memory easier to access later on. The strengthening of the preferred memory may lead to weakening of all competing memories, including the unwanted memory (Levy & Anderson, 2002).

Benoit and Anderson (2012) argue that, regardless of which mechanism leads to forgetting, less forgetting is predicted when the unwanted memory and the substitute memory are more

RELEVANT RESEARCH

BOX 8.3

Is Psychogenic Amnesia Caused by Retrieval Suppression?

Psychogenic amnesia is a rare form of retrograde amnesia caused by psychological, rather than biological, mechanisms, and typically develops following a traumatic or stressful life event. Individuals with psychogenic amnesia are unable to remember memories from their past but are usually able to develop new memories. Symptoms can last anywhere from a few days to many years. Hirokazu Kikuchi and his colleagues at Tohoku University Graduate School of Medicine in Sendai, Japan conducted fMRI studies on two individuals with psychogenic amnesia to see what parts of their brains were active when they viewed pictures from a time in their lives that they cannot overtly recall. Patient 1 in the study was a 27-year-old businessman from Japan who woke up one day unable to recognize where he was or remember where he worked. Further examination revealed he had no memory for any events that occurred after the last half of his last year of university, four-and-a-half years earlier. Patient 1 was under stress at work and possibly anxious about his upcoming marriage. Patient 2 was a 52-year-old businessman, also from Japan, who was put on a leave of absence from work after he accidentally drove into a guard rail one day. Although he did not sustain any head injuries, soon after the accident Patient 2 could remember nothing that occurred after he started university about 34 years earlier. Both patients had normal IQs and otherwise normal cognitive abilities. Both men could form new memories of events that happened after the onset of their psychogenic amnesia. Kikuchi et al. (2010) assembled three types of names and faces for each patient that would be presented during the fMRI. The first were names and faces of people the patients went to high school with. These were recognized by the patients before the fMRI. The second were names and faces of people that the patients worked with. These were not recognized by the patients before the fMRI. The third were names and faces of people the patients had never met, which served as controls. While undergoing an fMRI, each patient was presented with each face and name separately. Patients were to press a button if they recognized a face or name. Both patients showed increased activity in the prefrontal cortex and decreased activity in the hippocampus when presented with the unrecognizable faces compared to when they were presented with the recognizable faces. This pattern of activity is the same as what is observed when patients are deliberately performing retrieval suppression (see, e.g., Anderson et al., 2004). The results from Kikuchi et al. (2010) are consistent with the hypothesis that at least some cases of psychogenic amnesia are caused by retrieval suppression, rather than an actual loss of memory traces.

similar than when they are more different. This is because two similar memories will be coded with overlapping neurons; thus weakening one will weaken the other, and strengthening one will strengthen the other, making it less likely for the substitute to become more accessible than the unwanted memory. This means that if thought substitution is to be used as a means of forgetting, it is essential that the unwanted memory and the substitute memory be very different. Once again, people seem to know this intuitively; typically, people attempt to replace unwanted negative thoughts with positive thoughts. The difference in emotional valence means the two thoughts are unlikely to have overlapping neuronal representations, thus making thought substitution possible.

Summary

We began this chapter with a review of Schacter's (2002) seven sins of memory: transience, absent-mindedness, blocking, misattribution, suggestibility, bias, and persistence. Each of the topics discussed in this chapter reflects at least one of these sins.

For example, the chapter-opening case study on the problems associated with being unable to forget demonstrated persistence. The loss of hippocampal memories due to neurogenesis or molecular decay and the loss of neocortical memories due to interference reflect transience. Retrieval-induced forgetting appears to result from changes in context, which aligns with Schacter's sin of bias.

Further, we found a possible cause for many sins of forgetting. Transience can be produced by neurogenesis, molecular decay, or interference in the neocortex. Blocking can result from thought substitution, which weakens one memory trace while strengthening the other. Blocking can also result from retrieval suppression and may involve similar parts of the brain that are involved in stopping reflexive motor actions. Absent-mindedness can occur when the hippocampus is less active. Finally, misattribution, suggestibility, and persistence can all result from reduced neurogenesis.

CHAPTER REVIEW

- Forgetting is defined as the inability to access information that was (a) successfully encoded and (b) could previously be retrieved by the same retrieval cue.
- Daniel Schacter proposes that there are seven sins of memory: transience, absent-mindedness, and blocking are considered sins of omission; misattribution, suggestibility, bias, and persistence are considered sins of commission. Each of the seven sins leads to forgetting.
- The forgetting curve demonstrates that most forgetting happens soon after learning.
- The first two models of forgetting were the decay theory of forgetting proposed by Edward Thorndike in 1913 and the three-factor model of forgetting proposed by John McGeoch in 1932. The decay theory of forgetting suggested that biological processes result in the loss of memory traces, while the three-factor model of forgetting proposed that response competition, altered stimulus conditions, and set cause memory loss.

- Explicit memories begin as episodic memories with two components: the content of the memory, which is coded in the neocortex, and the context of the memory, which is coded in the hippocampus. The two components are linked by an indexing function controlled by the hippocampus.
- Hippocampal memories may be lost through neurogenesis-dependent decay or processes that cause a loss of receptors. Neurogenesis-dependent decay occurs when the introduction of new neurons makes it more difficult for pattern completion to occur and a given memory to be retrieved. Receptors can be lost when there is insufficient protein kinase C isoform M-zeta (PKMζ; pronounced pee-kay-em-zeta) at the receptor site.
- Hippocampal memories are not susceptible to interference because the hippocampus automatically codes similar memories with different populations of neurons.
- Neocortical memories may be lost through interference because similar information may be coded using a similar set of neurons in the neocortex. Evidence that neocortical memories are susceptible to interference but not decay comes from studies that show that recollection (which is associated with the neocortex) is susceptible to retroactive interference.
- Retrieval can impair retrieval; when this happens the memory loss is called retrieval-induced forgetting (RIF). The preponderance of evidence suggests that RIF is caused by a mismatch in mental context between the time of learning and the time of test.
- Infantile amnesia is observed in all people. It is characterized by the inability to remember events that occurred before about three years of age, and fewer memories from ages four through seven than would be expected through normal forgetting processes. The neurogenic hypothesis of infantile amnesia suggests that infantile amnesia results from high rates of neurogenesis early in life, which causes forgetting through neurogenesis-dependent decay. This hypothesis is supported by the fact that animals that experience more neurogenesis display more infantile amnesia.
- Motivated forgetting is forgetting that is the result of cognitive activity that either directly or indirectly makes retrieval less likely. Two examples of motivated forgetting are intentional forgetting and psychogenic amnesia.
- Intentional forgetting has been studied extensively with the list-method DF paradigm, in which participants see a list of stimuli and are then told to either forget that first list (L1) or remember that list, and then see a second list of stimuli (L2). The list-method DF paradigm produces costs and benefits of being in the forgetting condition. The preponderance of experimental evidence supports the two-factor account of list-method directed forgetting. This account suggests that, when given the instruction to forget, participants make a strategic decision about how to forget, and they stop rehearsing L1 items. The change in strategy creates a difference in mental context between learning and test, which produces costs of forgetting. Stopping rehearsal of L1 items reduces proactive interference and gives participants an opportunity to use a better study strategy for L2 items, which combine to result in a benefit of forgetting. The two-process model is consistent with two changes in brain activity that accompany the forget instruction.
- There are four strategies that a person can use to avoid remembering a painful experience: encoding suppression, changing context, retrieval suppression, and thought substitution.
- Encoding suppression may be achieved through the activation of the right prefrontal-hippocampal network. Context changes may result in forgetting by reducing retrieval cues, by reducing reactivations that would otherwise strengthen the trace, or by producing a positive change in mood that leads to a mismatch between current mental context and the mental context at the time of encoding. Retrieval suppression is associated with increased activity in the prefrontal cortex and decreased activity in the hippocampus. Thought substitution may result in forgetting by either weakening the to-be-forgotten memory or by strengthening a competing memory.

MEMORY ACTIVITY

Remembering the Seven Sins of Memory

At the beginning of this chapter, you read about Daniel Schacter's (2002) so-called seven sins of memory, which are transience, absent-mindedness, blocking, misattribution, suggestibility, bias, and persistence. Research suggests that the more personal associations an individual has with an item, the better the item will be remembered (Rogers, Kuiper, & Kirker, 1977). In this activity, you will think of each of the seven sins of memory in terms of yourself in order to commit them to memory. Below is a table listing each sin of memory. First, review each sin and generate a definition. Then, generate an example from your own life. (An example is provided.) The list itself can be memorized using the anagram TAB for MS BoP.

Sin	Definition	Personal Example
Transience	Loss of memory over time	I have forgotten my postal code from my old apartment because of transience.
Absent-mindedness		
Blocking		
Misattribution		
Suggestibility		
Bias		
Persistence		

Questions

1. List the seven sins of memory, separating them into sins of omission and sins of commission.
2. Explain the origins of John Wixted's definition of forgetting.
3. Describe the forgetting curve. How might the forgetting curve be used to determine if a person has a problem with forgetting?
4. Describe each of the components of McGeoch's three-factor theory of forgetting.
5. Describe a paired-associate memory paradigm. Describe in detail how the paradigm can be used to study proactive and retroactive interference.
6. Explain why an animal may engage in promiscuous encoding.
7. Explain how explicit memories are formed, including a description of each component of the memory and the region of the brain where that component is stored.
8. Explain how the hippocampus encodes two similar episodes.
9. Provide a detailed description of the processes that lead to the forgetting of hippocampal memories.
10. Explain why drugs of abuse can lead to difficulty in forming new memories.
11. Identify factors that help people learn. Explain how these factors affect neurogenesis.
12. Provide a detailed description of the processes that lead to the forgetting of neocortical memories.
13. Describe in detail an experimental paradigm and an experimental result that have been used to hypothesize about the effect of interference on hippocampal and neocortical memories.

14. Identify the two stages of infantile amnesia.
15. Describe the neurogenic hypothesis of infantile amnesia and provide experimental evidence that supports this hypothesis.
16. Some birds imprint on the first moving animal that they see and will follow that specific animal throughout their development. Would you expect the bird to be precocial or altricial? Explain your answer.
17. What is the difference between incidental forgetting and motivated forgetting? What are two examples of each type of forgetting?
18. Describe in detail the list-method directed-forgetting (DF) paradigm and a typical result generated by this paradigm.
19. Identify three explanations for costs and benefits of forgetting. Which explanation is the best and why?
20. Describe some experiments that have shown that mental context affects forgetting.
21. Identify four different ways that people can intentionally forget an unpleasant memory. Provide an example for each method.

Key Figures

Joseph Altman p. 195
Michael Anderson p. 206
Robert Bjork p. 206
Hermann Ebbinghaus p. 189
Nathan Foster p. 210
Paul Frankland p. 196
William Hockley p. 204

Tanya Jonker p. 207
Sheena Josselyn p. 196
Stefan Köhler p. 196
John McGeoch p. 190
Colin MacLeod p. 207
Morris Moscovitch p. 204
Jason Ozubko p. 204

Talya Sadeh p. 204
Lili Sahakyan p. 209
Paul Seli p. 207
Endel Tulving p. 187
Gordon Winocur p. 204
John Wixted p. 187

9 Memory across the Lifespan

LEARNING OBJECTIVES

Having read this chapter, you will be able to:

- Describe what habituation, exposure learning, and high-amplitude sucking paradigms have revealed about the memories of fetuses and newborns.
- Explain how associative-chain experiments have been used to demonstrate transitivity in infants.
- Summarize what research has revealed about the nature and duration of memory in infants.
- Define fast mapping and explain how exuberant learning changes as infants age.
- Compare and contrast the neuroanatomical model of memory development with the ecological model of memory development.
- Explain how memory span, retrieval strategies, and organization of memory change over childhood.
- Explain how memory span, working memory, long-term memory, prospective memory, and implicit memory are affected by age.
- Discuss how the aging brain affects memory.

JAKE HAUSLER

Jake Hausler (b. 2003) has always demonstrated exceptional memory. When he was three years old, he knew the inspection-sticker numbers for every car in his neighbourhood and could memorize iTunes playlists with ease. When he was four, he memorized the location of every item in the grocery store. At five, he could easily report the weather from the preceding 30 days.

If you suspect that Jake has hyperthymesia (exceptional autobiographical memory), you are correct. Jake's case demonstrates two important aspects of childrens' memories. First, it shows that even very young children can encode very detailed information, much like adults do, as evidenced by Jake's detailed memories from when he was three. Second, because Jake's case is so rare (he is the only child ever to be identified with hyperthymesia), it suggests that rapid forgetting may be adaptive in children just like it is in adults, and that poor memory retention in children may help rather than hinder them.

Photo by KEVIN A. ROBERTS

Introduction

The human mind, and its control over the body, changes a great deal over the lifespan. Our movements begin as random flails and kicks and slowly become more refined and controlled. Language begins as coos and babbles and expands to include single words, then two-word sentences, and then slowly but surely full language emerges. Social interactions begin with gazes and smiles and develop into complex bonds. Knowledge does not exist at birth but increases throughout life. Movement, language, social behaviour, and knowledge all involve memory. This chapter explores memory across the lifespan, beginning with memory for experiences in the womb and ending with a discussion of how aging affects memory. One surprising finding is that despite the physical differences between newborns and adults, their memory capabilities are remarkably similar.

Memory before Birth and Memory in Newborns

Most memory paradigms used to study children and adults rely on language; the instructions are spoken or written, the stimuli are often words, and memory tests involve written or spoken language. These language-based paradigms cannot be used to study the memory of preverbal humans, so researchers have devised a number of clever tasks that allow memory to be inferred without using language.

One method used to study memory in fetuses is **habituation**. Habituation is defined as a decrement in response to a stimulus following repeated presentation of the same stimulus. In a typical fetal auditory habituation paradigm, the researchers first acquire a baseline level of movement for the fetus. Next the fetus is presented with a specific frequency of tone. Fetuses respond to unfamiliar stimuli by moving, so when the tone is first presented, the fetus will move. Researchers present the same tone repeatedly until the fetus habituates to the tone and the movement returns to baseline levels. The researchers then present a different tone to the fetus. If the fetus increases movement in response to the new tone, it implies that the fetus can recall the previous tone. Research has shown that fetuses as young as 22 weeks of gestation (that's about halfway through a typical pregnancy) can habituate to an auditory stimulus (Leader & Baillie, 1991). Other studies have looked at changes in heart rate instead of physical movement and have also found habituation to tones from about 22 weeks gestation onward (Goldkrand & Litvack, 1991; Leader, Baillie, Martin, Molteno, & Wynchank, 1984).

Another method for studying memory in fetuses is **exposure learning**. In this method a fetus is exposed to a stimulus, such as a specific song, and then response to this song is compared to response to an unfamiliar song. A difference in behaviour in the two conditions is inferred to indicate memory for the familiar song. In one study conducted by Peter Hepper, the movement of fetuses in response to a theme song from a popular Australian television show called *Neighbours* was observed via ultrasound at both 30 and 37 weeks gestation. Half of the fetuses had heard the song previously (because their mother watched the show), while the other half did not. None of the fetuses changed their behaviour in response to the song at 30 weeks. However, at 37 weeks those familiar with the song stopped moving, oriented toward the sound, and displayed a decreased heart rate when the song was presented; the behaviour of those not familiar with the song did not change. This result suggests that sometime between 30 and 37 weeks gestation, fetuses develop the ability to remember sensory events (Hepper, 1991).

Researchers can also present a stimulus in utero and then look for evidence of memory for that stimulus after the individual is born. In one experiment, Hepper gave a pregnant woman cumin to eat during the last 12 days of her pregnancy. After the infant was born, Hepper presented the infant with cumin as well as a citric compound. The infant's heart rate decreased

habituation

a decrement in response to a stimulus following repeated presentation of the same stimulus

exposure learning

a method for studying memory in which the individual is exposed to stimuli, such as a specific song, and then response to this song is compared to response to an unfamiliar song. A difference in behaviour in the two conditions is inferred to indicate memory for the familiar song.

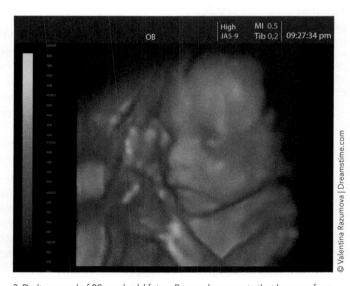

3-D ultrasound of 22-week-old fetus. Research suggests that humans form memories while still in the womb.

Enzo Nguyen@Tercer Ojo Photography/iStockphoto

Newborns show evidence of memory for events they experienced before they were born.

high-amplitude sucking paradigm

an experimental method in which an infant's rate of sucking on a pressure-sensitive pacifier is used to assess an infant's interest or disinterest in a stimulus

pressure-sensitive pacifier

a tool used by infant researchers to record sucking rates of infants in high-amplitude sucking paradigm experiments

when cumin was presented but not when the citric compound was presented, suggesting that the cumin scent was familiar. In a second study, Hepper asked a group of pregnant women to eat garlic while pregnant, while another group was asked not to eat garlic. When tested 20 hours after birth, infants who had not been exposed to garlic avoided the garlic smell, whereas those who had been exposed to garlic did not, again suggesting scent memory from before birth (Hepper, 1997).

The **high-amplitude sucking paradigm** is also used to test for memories acquired before birth. The high-amplitude sucking paradigm allows infants to control what they see, hear, or taste using a **pressure-sensitive pacifier** that changes the presentation of stimuli in response to increases or decreases in sucking rates. In a well-known study by DeCasper and Fifer (1980), newborn infants were given a pressure-sensitive pacifier and then presented with a recording that changed from their own mother's voice to the voice of another infant's mother depending on their sucking rate; thus, infants sometimes had to increase or decrease the pause between sucks to get the recording to switch to their own mother's voice. DeCasper and Fifer (1980) found that newborn infants who were three days old were able to alter their sucking in order to hear their own mother's voice. Because the infants were newborns who had had little time outside of the womb to learn, DeCasper and Fifer (1980) concluded that a preference for the mother's voice was likely learned *before* the infant was born. DeCasper and Spence (1986) later asked mothers to read a specific passage of prose for the last six weeks of pregnancy. Newborns were then given the pressure-sensitive pacifier and their sucking pattern determined whether they listened to the passage they had heard before birth or another passage. Infants developed a sucking pattern that triggered the presentation of the passage they had heard before birth (rather than the unfamiliar passage) but showed no preference for who was reading it, whether it be their own mother or another infant's mother. Newborns who had not heard the prose passages before birth showed no preference for which passage was read. When considered together, the work of DeCasper and Fifer (1980) and DeCasper and Spence (1986) suggests that infants can encode speech sounds before birth and retain that information until after they are born.

The preceding studies all examined whether newborns have memory for stimuli presented before birth. Researchers have also examined newborns' ability to recall stimuli presented to them after birth. Irina Swain of the University of Massachusetts and Philip Zelazo of McGill University studied newborn memory using a habituation paradigm. On Day 1 of the experiment, each of the newborns in the study was presented with a recording of a woman repeating either the word *beagle* or the word *tinder* either to their right or left ear for 30 seconds. The experimenters recorded the extent to which the newborns turned their heads toward or away from the sound source on each trial. On Day 2 of the experiment, the same basic procedure was repeated except half of the infants heard the same word they heard on the first day (this was the "no change" group) while the other half heard the word not heard on the first day (this was the "change" group). In addition, all infants heard the word *papa* repeatedly at the end of the sixth block of trials. The researchers found that, on Day 1, all infants initially looked in the direction of the recording but did so less and less as the blocks progressed, indicating that the infants had habituated to the recorded word. Twenty-four hours later, newborns in the "no change" group made fewer head turns toward the sound source than newborns in the "change" group, indicating that the habituation from the day before lasted at least 24 hours. In addition, newborns in both the "no change" and the "change" groups turned their heads toward the novel stimulus *papa* when it was presented. The observation that infants in the "no change" group did not turn their heads toward the word they had heard on Day 1 but did turn their heads toward the novel stimulus is good evidence that the newborns were able to remember the word that they heard on Day 1 (Swain, Zelazo, & Clifton, 1993). Thus, newborns appear to be able to form memories that last at least one day for speech sounds.

Infant Memory

Most research on infant memory has involved children who are at least three months old because infants who are this age or older have better visual acuity and motor control than younger infants. Next, we explore some of the more popular paradigms for studying infant memory including sensory preconditioning, potentiation, and associative chains.

Sensory Preconditioning

Sensory preconditioning (SPC) occurs when an association is formed between two neutral stimuli in the absence of reinforcement. The SPC paradigm consists of three phases. In the pre-exposure phase, individuals are exposed to a pair of stimuli, S1 and S2 (e.g., a red cloth and a blue cloth). In the training phase, the individual learns to associate S1 (the red cloth) with a source of reinforcement (e.g., kicking results in a moving mobile). In the transfer test phase, individuals are presented with S2 (the blue cloth) and their behaviour is observed. If individuals respond to S2 (the blue cloth) like they have learned to respond to S1 (the red cloth), then it can be concluded that an association between S1 and S2 (the red cloth and the blue cloth) was learned in the pre-exposure phase and that individuals have a memory for that association (Rovee-Collier & Giles, 2010).

Researchers have found SPC in newborn rats (Cheslock, Varlinskaya, High, & Spear, 2003), 8-day-old rats, and 12-day-old rats but *not* in 21-day-old rats, suggesting that SPC ends after a rat is about two weeks old (Chen, Lariviere, Heyser, Spear, & Spear, 1991). In 1997, Kimberly Boller was the first researcher to study sensory preconditioning in human infants. In the pre-exposure phase of Boller's experiment, six-month-old infants in the experimental group were presented with two different cloth panels (panel 1 and panel 2)

sensory preconditioning (SPC)

an association that is developed in the absence of reinforcement

Tatiana Chekryzhova/123RF

At about three months of age, children can focus their eyes around a room and control basic movements with their arms and legs. At this point, a child is considered an infant.

together for a total of one hour per day on seven consecutive days. A control group was presented with the same panels separately but for the same amount of time. The next day, in the training phase, all the infants learned that if they kicked their feet in the presence of panel 1, a mobile would move. One day later, all the infants were presented with panel 2 and their kicking behaviour was measured. Infants in the experimental group kicked in the presence of the second panel much more than the infants in the control group, suggesting that these infants had developed an association between panel 1 and panel 2 during the pre-exposure phase (Boller, 1997).

Rachel Barr, Heidi Marrott, and Carolyn Rovee-Collier studied SPC using a deferred imitation paradigm that is shown in Figure 9.1. In the pre-exposure phase of their experiment, six-month-olds were shown two hand puppets (puppet A and puppet B) for one hour per day on seven consecutive days. One day later, during the training phase, the infants saw a series of actions being modelled on puppet A. On a later day, the infants were presented with puppet B and were given the opportunity to replicate the actions they had seen modelled by puppet A. The experimenters measured how often the infant reproduced the target action on puppet B over a 120-second test period. There were two control groups: the unpaired control group never saw puppet A and puppet B together, and the baseline control group never saw the puppets before interacting with puppet B for the first time. The experimental group was significantly more likely to imitate actions observed in the training phase during the transfer test phase than the unpaired control group. Further, when infants in the experimental condition were given the opportunity to interact with a new puppet, puppet C, the infants did not imitate the behaviour observed during the training phase. Barr, Marrott, and Rovee-Collier (2003) found the same results when they replicated the experiment with only two days of pre-exposure.

Reynolds and Rovee-Collier (2005) replicated Barr et al. (2003) but included older infants in their experiments and extended the delay between the pre-exposure and training phases to one, two, or three weeks, and then conducted the transfer test one day after the training phase. Reynolds and Rovee-Collier (2005) predicted that the older infants would retain the association for a longer time, but found the opposite; the 12-month-old infants showed no sign of ever developing the association between the puppets. Even when the transfer test occurred one day after the pre-exposure, the 12-month-old infants did not show any signs of imitation, suggesting that the pre-exposure did not result in an association being formed in this older group.

Figure 9.1 The deferred imitation sensory preconditioning paradigm used by Barr, Marrott, and Rovee-Collier (2003)

This figure shows a six-month-old infant in the sensory preconditioning (SPC) procedure. *Left panel*: Pre-exposure phase where puppet A and puppet B are shown together. *Middle panel*: Training phase where the infant watches puppet A perform an action. *Right panel*: Transfer test phase where the infant is presented with puppet B and the extent to which the actions from the training phase are imitated is measured.

Source: Barr, Marrott, & Rovee-Collier, 2003, p. 19

In contrast, the six- and nine-month-old infants showed deferred imitation at delays up to two weeks, indicating that they had developed an association between the two puppets and that they remembered that association for two weeks. Cuevas, Giles, and Rovee-Collier (2009) replicated Reynolds and Rovee-Collier (2005) and extended the age range to include 15- and 18-month-old infants as well as 6-, 9- and 12-month-olds. Cuevas et al. (2009) found no deferred imitation in any of the infants that were older than nine months; the 12-, 15-, and 18-month-olds did not develop an association between the two puppets during pre-exposure. Recall that research has shown that rats only show SPC early in infancy. The results of Reynolds and Rovee-Collier (2005) and Cuevas et al. (2009) suggest that the same is true for humans; after about nine months of age, SPC is no longer observed.

Jennifer Campanella and Carolyn Rovee-Collier (2005) modified the SPC puppet paradigm to study SPC in infants younger than six months of age. Three-month-old infants in the experimental group were presented with a pair of puppets (puppet A and puppet B) for one hour on each of seven consecutive days. Age-matched controls saw puppet A and puppet B separately but for the same amount of time across the seven days. Because three-month-old infants cannot imitate the motor actions shown with the puppets, the rest of the experiment (training and transfer testing) was delayed for three months. Memory for the puppets was maintained in the interim by showing the infant puppet A for 30 seconds six times over the three-month period, with the sixth reminder occurring one day before training. The training occurred when the infant was six months old and consisted of puppet A performing a target action. One day later, the infant was given puppet B and allowed to use it any way she or he wished. Infants in the experimental group imitated the target action; infants in the control group did not. The results of Campanella and Rovee-Collier (2005) suggest that three-month-olds formed associations between paired stimuli much like six- and nine-month-olds did in other experiments.

Campanella and Rovee-Collier (2005) also conducted an experiment to see if the infant could remember the target action, as well as the association, over the three-month period between three and six months of age. In this experiment, three-month-olds in the experimental group saw puppet A and puppet B together during a pre-exposure phase. On the next day, infants were shown puppet A performing the target action. The experimenter then delayed the transfer test for three months, but periodically showed the infants puppet A for 60 seconds as a reminder. When the infants were six months old, they were given puppet B. Infants in the experimental group imitated the target action on puppet B even though they had not seen this puppet for three months. This result demonstrates that young infants can learn associations between stimuli very quickly and maintain that association for at least three months.

Ramesh Bhatt and Carolyn Rovee-Collier conducted a series of experiments that assessed the amount of detail retained in the memory representations of three-month-olds using mobiles with six blocks hanging from them. There were two sets of three identical blocks on each mobile. The blocks were each either yellow, black, green, or red, and each block had either letter As or number 2s in a different colour (black, red, green, or yellow) on all sides. Infants were trained with three blocks of one colour with the letter A on all sides and three blocks of a different colour with 2s on all sides. At the time of test, the experimenter changed the blocks in one of four ways shown in Figure 9.2. In one condition, the figure shape was changed but the colour combination stayed the same. In a second condition, the figure colour was changed but the shape and block colour stayed the same. In a third condition, the block colour was changed but the figure colour and shape stayed the same. In a fourth condition, both the figure and the block colour were switched.

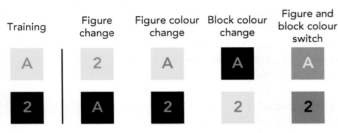

Figure 9.2 Examples of mobile block stimuli from Bhatt and Rrovee-Collier (1994)

In this figure, the first column shows the pair of blocks that the infant saw during training and the subsequent blocks show the stimuli in the four experimental conditions. Infants detected change when one stimulus property was changed, but not when two properties were changed, while adults showed the opposite pattern.

Source: Based on Bhatt & Rovee-Collier, 1994

The experimenters measured the kicking rate for the first three minutes during the test phase and compared it to the kicking rate during the first three minutes of the training phase. If the infant is able to remember the features of the training mobile and discriminate that mobile from the new mobile, the kicking rate should decrease because the infant will not expect kicking to produce movement. If, on the other hand, the infant believes the training and test mobiles are the same, the kicking rate should stay the same because the infant will expect the mobile to move by kicking.

Bhatt and Rovee-Collier (1994, 1996) consistently found that infants had reduced kicking rates for the figure change, colour change, and block colour change conditions, indicating that the infants could remember the features of the training blocks in great detail. Infants did not, however, reduce kicking for the figure and block colour switch condition, which was the only condition where the change occurred entirely within a block (all other changes occurred across blocks). In addition, when adults were tested with an age-appropriate paradigm using the same stimuli, the only change that adults detected was the one that infants did not detect, the figure and block colour switch. Bhatt and Rovee-Collier (1994, 1996) suggest that these results show that infants spontaneously form many associations among components of a multi-element event, select to encode different information from the event than adults, and actually learn more about the same multi-element event than adults.

Researchers also use the mobile conjugate reinforcement paradigm, a sensory preconditioning paradigm first devised by Carolyn Rovee-Collier in the late 1960s, to study the memory of young infants. In this paradigm, infants learn to kick their legs to produce movement in a mobile. In the first phase, infants have a ribbon attached to their leg and to the base of a mobile and can see an appealing mobile overhead, but their movements do not affect the mobile's movements. In the second phase, the ribbon is attached to the mobile such that kicking makes the mobile move; infants find the novel movement of the mobile reinforcing and kick enthusiastically. The more an infant kicks, the more the mobile moves (which is why it is called conjugate reinforcement). The final test session occurs after a delay (to test memory duration). During the test session, a ribbon is tied to the infant's leg but it does not affect the movement of the mobile. If the infant kicks at the kick rate that is similar to the conjugate reinforcement phase, then memory for the session can be inferred. When infants are two months old they are able to remember the connection between the ribbon and the novel stimulus for about two days (Greco, Rovee-Collier, Hayne, Griesler, & Earley, 1986) but the retention interval extends to as much as six weeks by the time the infant is six months old (Hill, Borovsky, & Rovee-Collier, 1988; Rovee-Collier, Schechter, Shyi, & Shields, 1992). In one experiment, Butler and Rovee-Collier (1989) kept the crib liner the same in both sessions for some infants and changed it for others and found that infants kicked more if the crib liner was the same in the second session than if it was different, leading the researchers to conclude that these young infants were encoding the context and used that memory to guide their behaviour.

Figure 9.3   A six-month-old infant performing the train task used in Hartshorn and Rovee-Collier (1997)

During the reinforcement phase of the train task used by Hartshorn and Rovee-Collier (1997), a six-month-old infant presses a lever that makes the train move for two seconds and causes lights to come on for one cycle.

Source: Hartshorn & Rovee-Collier, 1997, p. 74

Kristin Hartshorn and Carolyn Rovee-Collier developed a train task that was similar to the mobile task but appropriate for older infants. In the train task, a train that lights up is on a circular track that can be seen by the infant but is out of reach (see Figure 9.3). When the infant presses a large button, the train moves for two seconds and the lights turn on for one cycle. Hartshorn and Rovee-Collier (1997) found that six-month-old infants can remember what to do in the train task for about two weeks, which mirrors the duration of retention for the mobile task at this age. Hartshorn et al. (1998) report the results from several experiments that used the mobile task or the train task to measure memory in infants and toddlers. The mobile task was used for infants six months of age and younger; the train task was used for infants and toddlers six months of age and older. (Six-month-old infants completed both tasks.) Hartshorn et al. (1998) found that the duration of memory for the conditioned task increased steadily with age (see Figure 9.4). Hartshorn et al. (1998) concluded that memory improves at a fairly constant rate during infancy and toddlerhood.

The results from sensory preconditioning experiments show that young infants form detailed memories spontaneously and that these memories can be maintained for long periods of time. Further, the results show that young infants actually remember more than older counterparts, including toddlers, when the SPC paradigm is employed.

Potentiation

Researchers have also studied **potentiation** in order to assess infant memory. Potentiation occurs when, compared to a weak stimulus presented alone, learning of a weaker (less salient) stimulus is improved when it is presented alongside a stronger (more salient) stimulus.

potentiation

when a stimulus is better learned when presented along with a stronger, more salient stimulus than when it is presented alone

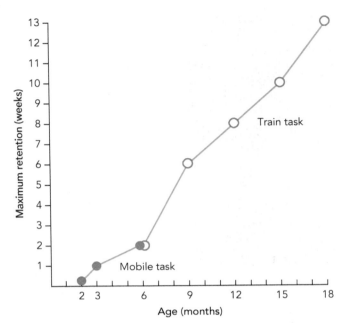

Figure 9.4   Duration of memory retention for infants aged 2 to 18 months

Six-month-olds were trained and tested in both the mobile and the train tasks. [Data for two-month-olds are from Vander Linde, Morrongiello, & Rovee-Collier, 1985; data for three-month-olds are from Greco et al., 1986; data for six-month-olds are from Hill et al., 1988 (*mobile task*) and Hartshorn & Rovee-Collier, 1997 (*train task*).]

Source: Hartshorn et al., 1998, p. 83

overshadowing

when a stimulus is less well learned when presented along with a stronger, more salient stimulus than when it is presented alone

Potentiation is thought to occur because the stronger, more salient stimulus already has more associative strength, and this strength is transferred to the weak stimulus when the stimuli are presented together. Potentiation does not typically occur in adults; instead adults experience **overshadowing**, which is worse learning of a weaker stimulus when presented with a strong stimulus than when the weak stimulus is presented alone.

Rachel Barr, Aurora Vieira, and Carolyn Rovee-Collier (2001) examined potentiation in six-month-old infants. The infants first learned how to move a train around a track (see Figure 9.5). The train served as the strong potentiating stimulus because infants reliably show great interest in the train. Once the infants had learned how to use the train, an experimenter modelled target actions using a hand puppet, which served as the weaker stimulus. Half of infants saw the puppet perform the target actions in front of the train; half saw the target action in a neutral setting. After a delay, infants were given the hand puppet and the researchers observed to see if the infant would mimic the target action. While all infants mimicked the puppet's actions following a one-day delay, only the infants who saw the puppet perform the target action in front of the train mimicked the target action two weeks later. This result indicates potentiation; *the train stimulus facilitated learning of puppet stimulus.*

In 2011, Rachel Barr and Carolyn Rovee-Collier replicated the train/puppet paradigm but tested to see if they could extend memory for the puppet action by reminding the infants of the train task. When they simply placed the train within view of the infant two weeks after learning the train task, Barr and Rovee-Collier (2011) found that infants could mimic the puppet action after only seeing the action once, for 60 seconds four weeks earlier!

The Paired-Comparison Task

The **paired-comparison task**, also known as the novelty-preference task, is also used frequently to study infant memory. The paired-comparison task uses looking time as the main dependent measure. In the familiarization phase of this experiment, infants are exposed to a visual stimulus until they have spent a predetermined amount of time looking directly at the stimulus. In the test phase, the infant is presented with the now-familiar stimulus as well as a novel stimulus; the amount of time the infant spends looking at each stimulus is measured. As a rule, infants prefer novel stimuli, and thus, if they remember the stimulus from the familiarization phase, they will spend longer looking at the unfamiliar stimulus than the familiarized stimulus during the test phase. If, on the other hand, an infant doesn't remember the stimulus from the familiarization phase, then the infant should spend the same amount of time looking at each stimulus

Figure 9.5   The moving model train that was used as the strong stimulus in the potentiation experiment conducted by Barr et al. (2001)

Source: Barr et al., 2001, p. 236

during the test phase because both will be equally novel to the infant. Researchers vary the age at familiarization and the delay between familiarization and test to assess the duration of infant memory. Bahrick and Pickens (1995) used this method and found that three-month-old infants can retain information for as long as three months.

Associative-Chain Paradigms

Associative-chain paradigms test to see whether an individual will form an association between two stimuli that have never been presented before, but that are connected through a series of associations. For example, stimulus A and stimulus B are presented together, then stimulus B and stimulus C are presented together, and then stimulus C and stimulus D are presented together. Then the researcher will test to see if an association has been made between stimulus A and stimulus D (which were never presented together). Barr, Vieira, and Rovee-Collier (2002) discovered that infants could perform delayed imitation on a puppet when the delay was one day but not longer. However, Barr et al. (2002) also found that delayed imitation could extend to two weeks if the puppet was associated with a novel train task.

In 2006, Kimberly Cuevas, Carolyn Rovee-Collier, and Amy Learmonth conducted an associative-chain experiment to see if deferred imitation on a puppet would again be extended from a day to two weeks if a novel mobile task was incorporated into the paradigm. In their experiment, Cuevas, Rovee-Collier, and Learmonth (2006) first pre-exposed six-month-old infants to two puppets (puppet A and puppet B) for one hour on two consecutive days in order to build an association between puppet A and puppet B. Over the next two days, the infant learned to kick in order for a mobile to move. After two days of training, puppet A was placed where the mobile had been. At this point the infant would develop an association between the mobile and puppet A. Researchers

paired-comparison task

an experimental paradigm in which an individual is familiarized with a stimulus and then, following a delay, presented with that stimulus and a novel stimulus during a test phase. Researchers measure the amount of time spent looking at each stimulus during the test phase.

modelled a target action using puppet B and then tested infants' ability to mimic the puppet after varying delays. Cuevas et al. (2006) found that the infants who had developed an association between puppet A and the mobile, and puppet A and puppet B, were able to imitate puppet B after a two-week delay, while infants in control groups where these associations were not developed could only imitate the puppet after a delay of one day. The results of Cuevas et al. (2006) indicate that the infants established an association between puppet B and the mobile without ever having seen the two objects together. This phenomenon is known as **transitivity**. Transitivity involves explicit memory. Suppose an individual is shown A and B together and then B and C together. In order to associate A and C through transitivity, the individual must consciously recall the A–B association while thinking about the A–C association. In the experiment by Cuevas et al. (2006), the infants could only have benefited from the mobile memory associated with puppet A if they remembered seeing the mobile with puppet A and they remembered seeing puppet A with puppet B.

transitivity

when stimuli become associated because they are each independently associated with the same stimulus

Summary

The research reviewed so far has shown that infants can encode and retain very detailed information and that young infants have good explicit memory with a retention interval of at least two weeks. In the next section, we will explore research examining the speed with which infants can form new associations at different points in infancy.

Fast Mapping

In 2009, Kimberly Cuevas presented two puppets (puppet A and puppet B) to 6-, 9-, and 12-month-old infants either simultaneously or sequentially in a sensory preconditioning (SPC) paradigm experiment. Cuevas (2009) reasoned that if the infant later mimicked puppet A's target action using puppet B, then the infant had formed an association between the puppets. Cuevas (2009) found six-month-olds associated puppets when the puppets were presented simultaneously but not when the puppets were presented sequentially, nine-month-old infants associated puppets that were presented either simultaneously or sequentially, and 12-month-old infants associated puppets that were presented sequentially but not when they were presented simultaneously. The results from Cuevas (2009) suggest that young infants form associations very quickly, but this exuberant learning ends around nine months of age. Carolyn Rovee-Collier argues that the onset and eventual decline of exuberant learning in infants reflects a general learning mechanism commonly referred to as **fast mapping**. Fast mapping was first described by Carey and Bartlett (1978) to describe the way in which two-year-olds can learn a new word following a single brief exposure to the words. Fast mapping is a good way to explain how very young infants learn correlated attributes, as in the mobile memory experiments conducted by Bhatt and Rovee-Collier (1994, 1996). Fast mapping can also account for stimulus preconditioning (SPC) in three-month-olds that was observed in Barr et al. (2011) and the ability of infants to rapidly form associations between chains of stimulus, as was observed in Cuevas et al. (2006).

fast mapping

when learning can occur with a single brief exposure to the stimulus

Forgetting in Infancy

Hsu and Rovee-Collier (2009) found that retrieving a memory at the end of the forgetting function (in other words, right before a point in time when researchers typically observe forgetting) prolongs retention 136 per cent in six-month-old infants, 67 per cent in nine-month-old infants,

62 per cent in 12-month-old infants, and 40 per cent in 15-month-old infants; the benefit is three times greater in six-month-olds than 15-month-olds. However, young infants also forget information more quickly. The retention interval for six-month-olds is about five weeks, and this time window increases at a steady rate to nine weeks in 24-month-olds. Because young infants forget information more quickly, Hsu and Rovee-Collier (2009) suggest that their result, showing younger infants benefit more from reminders than older infants, is evidence for an evolutionary mechanism intended to offset rapid forgetting in very young infants. More rapid forgetting in the early stages of life has also been observed in rats (Campbell & Campbell, 1962), monkeys (Green, 1962), puppies (Fox, 1971), mice (Nagy, 1979), chicks (Peters & Isaacson, 1963), and frogs (Miller & Berk, 1977).

Models of Memory Development

Our review of encoding, retention, and forgetting in infants suggests that while infant memory is sophisticated, it differs from adult memory in many ways. Infants encode more associations than older individuals, and retain those associations for less time than older individuals. There are two explanations for these differences in the memory literature. Proponents of the **neuroanatomical model of memory development** assert that infant memory processes are qualitatively different than the memory processes of older individuals because the hippocampus is not fully mature until a person is about nine months old. Proponents of the **ecological model of memory development**, on the other hand, assert that infant memory processes are essentially the same as those of older individuals; however, the demands of different ecological niches lead infants to attend to and encode different information than older individuals.

neuroanatomical model of memory development

explains changes in memory performance across infancy as resulting from maturation of the hippocampus

ecological model of memory development

explains changes in memory performance across infancy as resulting from changes in the ecological niche occupied by infants of different ages

The Neuroanatomical Model of Memory Development

The neuroanatomical model of infant memory finds its roots in the case of H.M. Recall that H.M. developed anterograde amnesia following surgery that removed his medial temporal lobe (MTL) and most of his hippocampi in an attempt to control his epilepsy. Subsequent research revealed that while H.M. could not consciously recall new facts or events, he could learn to perform new tasks. Researchers concluded that the case of H.M. implied that humans must possess two independent memory systems: one that is governed by the MTL and hippocampus (which was damaged in H.M.) that allows explicit memories to be formed and another, operated by other brain structures, that allows implicit memories (like how to trace a star in a mirror and conditioned responses) to be formed. It was later determined that implicit memory relied on a neural circuit that was dependent on the striatum, cerebellum, and the brain stem (Richmond & Nelson, 2007).

In 1984, Daniel Schacter and Morris Moscovitch from the University of Toronto argued that the pattern of data observed in people with amnesia reflected how memory developed in **neurotypical** humans. Schacter and Moscovitch (1984) refer to a logical framework first put forth by J. Hughlings Jackson in 1884. According to Jackson (1884), the *first* system that an animal loses when the animal is injured will be *last* system that developed in that animal. Schacter and Moscovitch (1984) note that individuals with amnesia, such as H.M., consistently show deficits in explicit memory but few issues with implicit memory and that, according to Jacksonian logic, indicates that explicit memory develops *after* implicit memory

neurotypical

a nervous system that is functioning normally

in human development. Research suggests that areas that control implicit memory, including the striatum, the cerebellum, and the brain stem are fully developed at birth while areas of the brain that are involved with explicit memory, such as the dentate gyrus (DG) in the hippocampus, are not fully developed until the end of the first postnatal year (Nelson, 1995). Schacter and Moscovitch (1984) and Nelson (1995) propose a neuroanatomical model of memory development that suggests that humans possess an early-maturing system and a late-maturing system. The early-maturing system is likely present at birth and controls implicit memory; the late-maturing system emerges around eight or nine months of age and controls explicit memory (Richmond & Nelson, 2007). According to the neuroanatomical model, the early-maturing system mediates memories of simple learned procedures and perceptual and motor skills but does not allow for complex encoding. The neuroanatomical model predicts that infants younger than nine months of age will have unstable memory traces that lack detail because of the immaturity of their explicit memory system (Bauer, 2008, 2009).

The Ecological Model of Memory Development

The ecological model of memory development was developed by Carolyn Rovee-Collier and Kimberly Cuevas and is based on two assertions. First, infants are born fully capable of forming explicit and implicit memories, and second, individuals of every age are perfectly adapted to use these memory processes in a way that best serves their current needs. According to the ecological model, young infants are best served by encoding as much information about their environment as possible because they have no way of knowing what information will turn out to be useful. Older infants, on the other hand, can move around independently and thus need to focus attention on remembering information related to completing tasks. The ecological model predicts that young infants will be exuberant encoders and that any differences observed between young infants and older children are the result of differences in the ecological niche occupied by each group, and not the result of differences in neuroanatomical development (Rovee-Collier & Cuevas, 2009).

The neuroanatomical model and the ecological model make very different predictions about infant memory and are summarized in Table 9.1. While the neuroanatomical model suggests that the explicit memory of young infants will be poor, the ecological model predicts that the explicit memory of young infants will be exuberant. While the neuroanatomical model predicts that memory of older infants will always be superior to memory of younger infants, the ecological model predicts that younger infants may sometimes have memory that is superior to older individuals due to exuberant encoding. The two models also make different predictions about forgetting. Because the neuroanatomical model predicts that young infants do not encode very much information, it also predicts that young infants will not possess any mechanisms that enhance forgetting. The ecological model, on the other hand, predicts that infants will possess mechanisms that enhance forgetting in order to compensate for exuberant encoding. Thus, the ecological model of memory development is consistent with the neurogenic hypothesis of infantile amnesia discussed in Chapter 8, which suggests that infants have adapted rapid neurogenesis in the hippocampus to cope with the need to encode, and then forget, large amounts of information early in life. In the next sections, we will evaluate the predictions of each of these models using data from the infant memory literature.

Table 9.1   Neuroanatomical vs ecological model of infant memory

Neuroanatomical Model	Ecological Model
Early-maturing implicit memory system; late-maturing hippocampal-dependent explicit memory system	All systems functional at birth
Memory in infants determined by maturity of hippocampus	Memory in infants determined by demands of their ecological niche
Infants younger than nine months of age cannot form detailed, lasting episodic memories.	Infants younger than nine months of age can form detailed, lasting, episodic memories.
Memory performance of an older individual will always be better than memory performance of a younger individual.	Memory performance is determined not by age but by the demands of an individual's ecological niche.
Older infants perform differently on memory tasks than younger infants because their hippocampus is more mature.	Older infants perform differently on memory tasks than younger infants because mobile infants occupy a different ecological niche than immobile infants.

Evaluating Models of Memory Development

The results from experiments discussed earlier in the chapter can be used to evaluate the validity of the predictions made by the neuroanatomical and ecological models of memory development.

The results from sensory preconditioning (SPC), potentiation, paired-comparison, and associative-chain experiments show that young infants form detailed memories spontaneously and that these memories can be maintained for long periods of time. Further, the results show that young infants remember more than older counterparts, including toddlers, when the SPC paradigm is employed. These results cannot be reconciled with the neuroanatomical model for two reasons. First, the neuroanatomical model stipulates that young infants are unable to form episodic memories because of a late-maturing hippocampus. Second, the neuroanatomical model predicts that older individuals will always outperform younger individuals on tests of memory because they will have a more developed memory system. The results are, however, consistent with the ecological model of memory development. The ecological model predicts exuberant encoding in young infants, which is demonstrated from the results of the various SPC tasks. In addition, the ecological model predicts that younger infants will be less selective with what they encode and thus will be able to remember more details about a situation than older individuals, which is exactly what was found when performance in SPC paradigms was compared across age groups.

The results of a variety of experiments show that young infants exhibit fast mapping, but that this phenomenon begins to disappear around nine months of age. While the neuroanatomical model suggests that there is a shift in memory at nine months of age, this model fails to explain exuberant learning *prior* to nine months of age. The ecological model suggests that, when infants are immobile, their ecological niche changes quickly and that fast mapping is adapted to this fast rate of change. According to the ecological model, once an infant is mobile, around nine months of age, their ecological niche changes more slowly and more selective attention and encoding are adaptations that meet the needs of individuals in this slower-changing niche. Proponents of the ecological model of infant memory suggest that fast mapping disappears when infants enter an ecological niche that changes more slowly.

Proponents of the neuroanatomical model have argued that rapid forgetting results from having an explicit memory system that isn't fully mature (Carver & Bauer, 2001). Proponents of the ecological models suggest that the observation of this pattern of forgetting in a wide variety of species, including amphibians, birds, and mammals, implies that rapid forgetting has adaptive value; however, rapid forgetting would hardly be adaptive if an animal were having a great dealing of difficulty forming memories in the first place, as suggested by the neuroanatomical model. According to the ecological model, rapid forgetting exists so that young animals can form large numbers of associations in their rapidly changing ecological niche, and then discard the memories that turn out to have no use. According to this model, rapid forgetting ends at the point when infants start moving in their environment and encoding cause-and-effect relationships that need to be maintained. Changes in the neuroscientific mechanisms related to forgetting as a function of age are discussed in more detail in Chapter 8.

Summary of Infant Memory

The results from infant memory research show that infants are exuberant learners and that this exuberance is most pronounced when infants are younger than nine months of age (Rovee-Collier & Giles, 2010). In addition, research seems to suggest that young infants are also more prone to forgetting (Hsu & Rovee-Collier, 2009). Rapid forgetting is observed in a variety of nonhuman species as well (see Chapter 8), suggesting that this forgetting has adaptive value (Rovee-Collier & Giles, 2010). These results contradict the assertions of the neuroanatomical model and support the ecological model of memory development.

The neuroanatomical changes in the hippocampus that take place during the first year in life do not seem to impede infants in their ability to form long-lasting episodic memories. This does not necessarily mean that these changes in neuroanatomy have no impact. The results simply indicate that the impact of changes in the hippocampus on the memory of infants has yet to be uncovered.

Memory in Childhood

Memory changes throughout the lifespan and childhood memories are, of course, no exception. During childhood memory span, retrieval strategies and the organization of memory all change dramatically. Key to these improvements is metamemory development. As children develop more knowledge about how their memory operates, they can use that knowledge to improve their memory performance.

Working Memory

In 2004, Susan Gathercole and her colleagues investigated working memory in children between the ages of 4 and 15. The researchers assembled a battery of tests from the working memory literature and administered them to 700 children in England. The tests reflected three aspects of working memory from Baddeley's (2012) model: the phonological loop, the visuospatial sketchpad, and the central executive. These are listed in Figure 9.6. Gathercole, Pickering, Ambridge, and Wearing (2004) argue that the digit, word, and nonword test performances reflect the functionality of the phonological loop because successful completion of these tests relies on the participant's ability to maintain verbal material that has recently been said to them. The authors argue that the counting task, mazes test, block-recall test, and visual-pattern test reflect the functionality of the visuospatial sketchpad, as these tests rely on maintaining a visual image

BOX
9.1

RELEVANT RESEARCH

Verbal Labels and Memory in Toddlers

Jane Herbert and Harlene Hayne were interested in the role that verbal labels played in young children's ability to perform deferred imitation. In their experiment, 18- and 24-month-olds were given a unique verbal label for an object used during a demonstration. Twenty-four hours later, they were presented with the same object or a new object that could achieve the same task. The researchers found that all of the infants were able to recall how the object was used the day before and imitate it; however, the 24-month-old infants were able to generalize to a new object much more readily when the earlier object had been given a verbal label than when it had not. (No such influence of verbal labels was seen for the 18-month-olds.) Thus, imitation paradigms have shown that infants can learn simply by observing, but that they can retain that information for longer if given verbal cues. Further, practice helps infants as young as 18 months better retain learned tasks, and verbal cues facilitate the generalization of information learned through imitation in children beginning around 24 months of age (Herbert & Hayne, 2000).

from trial to trial. Finally, the authors argue that the backward-counting, listening-recall, and counting-recall tasks reflect the combined functionality of the central executive and phonological loop because these tasks rely on the ability to shift attention from one task to another while maintaining material that was heard on an earlier trial.

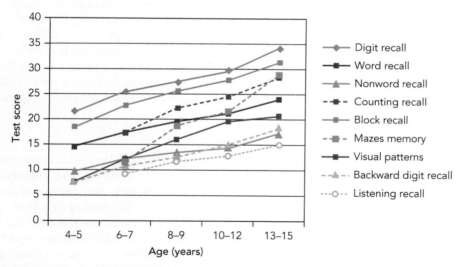

Figure 9.6 Working-memory task performance of children aged 4 through 15

The results from the nine working-memory tests administered by Gathercole et al. (2004) show a linear increase in performance from age four through adolescence.

Source: Based on data from Gathercole et al., 2004, p. 177

The results from Gathercole et al. (2004) can be seen in Figure 9.6. Gathercole et al. (2004) found a linear increase in performance for all the working-memory tests in their experiment, which they argue reflects a linear increase in performance in the capacity of the phonological loop, central executive, and visuospatial sketchpad as children age. A detailed statistical analysis of the data led Gathercole et al. (2004) to conclude that the central executive, phonological loop, and visuospatial sketchpad resemble the adult system by six years of age. (For a full explanation of each task and the analysis that led to this conclusion, see Gathercole et al., 2004.)

Michalczyk, Malstädt, Worgt, Könen, and Hasselhorn (2013) also assessed working memory in children aged 5 through 12 and found the same result as Gathercole et al. (2004); working-memory performance increases steadily throughout childhood and the components of working memory appear to remain constant throughout childhood. Similar changes in working memory across childhood have also been reported by Conklin, Luciana, Hooper, and Yarger (2007) and Luna, Garver, Urban, Lazar, and Sweeney (2004).

The changes in working memory performance across childhood are likely the result of structural changes in the brain (Tamnes et al., 2013). It is well established that working memory is supported by a distributed network of brain regions, including prefrontal and posterior parietal cortices as well as primary cortical areas in both adults (Burzynska et al., 2011; Cabeza & Nyberg, 2000; Gerton et al., 2004; Owen, McMillan, Laird, & Bullmore, 2005; Wager & Smith, 2003) and children (Crone, Wendelken, Donohue, van Leijenhorst, & Bunge, 2006; Klingberg, 2006; Klingberg, Forssberg, & Westerberg, 2002; Kwon, Reiss, & Menon, 2002; Olesen, Nagy, Westerberg, & Klingberg, 2003; Scherf, Sweeney, & Luna, 2006). It is also well established that the cerebral cortex and subcortical and cerebellar structures undergo changes throughout childhood and adolescence (Brown et al., 2012; Lenroot et al., 2007; Tamnes et al., 2013; Tiemeier et al., 2010; van Soelen et al., 2012).

Christian Tamnes and his colleagues decided to conduct a longitudinal MRI study to see if they could establish a correlation between improvements in working memory and changes in cortical structure. Tamnes et al. (2013) assessed verbal working memory and brain structure in 79 adolescents at two points in time roughly two-and-a-half years apart. The researchers found that improvements in working memory were correlated with volume reductions in many frontal and parietal regions, including the frontoparietal region associated with working memory. Thus, the results of Tamnes et al. (2013) support the notion that changes in the frontoparietal cortical network that occur during childhood and adolescence support working memory development.

The Development of Rehearsal Strategies

The rehearsal of information helps an individual maintain material in short-term memory and also helps form sufficiently durable traces for recall following a delay. For example, you may use rehearsal to remember a postal code as you write it on an envelope, or you may use rehearsal before entering a grocery store to ensure you remember a few key items missing from your cupboards. Children learn to rehearse quite young, but their approach to rehearsal changes significantly as they age. The precursor to rehearsal strategies can be seen in children as young as two years. In one experiment conducted by DeLoache, Cassidy, and Brown in 1985, children aged 18 to 24 months were shown that there was an appealing toy hidden behind a pillow and then attempts were made to distract the child for several minutes before she or he was allowed to retrieve the toy. During this time, the children pointed at the pillow, looked in the direction of the pillow, or repeated the name of the toy. DeLoache concluded that this was a rehearsal strategy and not an attempt to get the toy because, when the toy was placed on top of the pillow instead of underneath it, the children rarely pointed, named the object, or looked at the object, suggesting that presence of these behaviours when the toy was hidden served to help the child remember where the toy was hidden. By about age five, most children use rehearsal strategies (Flavell, Beach, & Chinsky, 1966); however, rehearsal techniques differ with age. In 1975, Ornstein, Naus, and Liberty asked 8-, 12- and 14-year-old children to rehearse out loud while retaining items for a recall task. The researchers found no significant difference in the amount of rehearsal for children of different ages; however, older children recalled significantly more items than younger children. The authors concluded that this was because the nature of the rehearsal differed across age; younger children tended to repeat the same item over and over, while children aged 10 or older repeated groups of items over and over. In general, children adopt rehearsal strategies slowly and don't use them as well or as frequently when they first discover them as they do later on. Failing to rehearse likely impacts the recall capacity for younger children significantly more than an actual capacity to recall does.

The Development of Memory Strategies

In addition to rehearsal, adults use organizational strategies to help them remember items. Organization can help rehearsal and organization can also help retrieval following a delay. For example, if you need to remember to buy lettuce, milk, bread, cream, tomatoes, and bagels you might organize this list by type of food, such as lettuce and tomatoes, bread and bagels, and milk and cream. In the lab, adults who organize material recall more items (Schleepen & Jonkman, 2012).

Young children don't spontaneously organize material in order to help them remember it. For example, Schleepen and Jonkman (2012) presented children between the ages of 6 and 12 with 12 pictures selected from three categories (fruit, animals, and clothes) and then had children recall as many items as they could. The number of items recalled increased steadily with age; however, only the 12-year-old children organized the material into categories to aid with rehearsal. Schleepen and Jonkman (2012) hypothesized that the ability to organize material while rehearsing it is dependent on working-memory capacity. Schleepen and Jonkman (2012) also assessed working-memory capacity and found that as working-memory capacity increased, so too did the likelihood that the child would use organizational strategies in the list recall task.

Schneider, Knopf, and Stefanek (2002) analyzed longitudinal data from 186 German children aged 4 through 17. Schneider et al. (2002) looked at data from a battery of tests, including a sort recall test (that assessed memory strategy use) and several tests of short-term memory capacity. The researchers found that most children employed memory strategies that benefited performance on the sort recall task by about age 12. The researchers also examined sort recall across various educational environments; some children in the German sample were in much more demanding educational streams than others. The researchers found no effect of educational stream on memory strategy development, suggesting that memory strategies develop in a similar way in children in a variety of educational contexts.

Changes in Processing Speed and Memory

In general, younger children perform cognitive tasks more slowly than older children (Kail & Salthouse, 1994). One possibility is that a change in speaking rates results in better memory as children age; a child who can speak more quickly can also rehearse more information and provide more elaboration to help solidify memories. Hulme, Thompson, Muir, and Lawrence (1984) support this view by showing that memory span is correlated with the rate at which a child can articulate words, and suggest that speaking rate is largely responsible for improvements in memory span with age; children can rehearse more times because they can speak faster and this directly impacts memory span. However, Cowan (1992) found older children have faster speaking rates not because they speak faster but because they take shorter pauses between words. Cowan (1992) argues that older children don't have better recall because they are talking faster, but rather because they have more time to rehearse due to needing less time to perform memory searches.

The Development of Retrieval Strategies

As children develop, their retrieval strategies also change, resulting in improved recall ability. In one study, Samuel (1978) looked at recall performance for 6-, 8-, and 11-year-old children compared to 19-year-old adults. Samuel (1978) suggested that the optimal retrieval strategy is to report a word that is likely to be correct before reporting words that are less likely to be correct simply because if a word that is likely to be correct is not reported immediately it could be lost, reducing performance. Samuel (1978) assessed the extent to which individuals of different ages use this strategy by computing the correlation between the output position (first word reported, second word reported, etc.) and the accuracy of the recall. If an individual is using optimal retrieval strategies, then the correlation between output position and recall will approach 1.0; correct words will always be reported before incorrect words. Samuel (1978) found that as children age, the correlation between output position and recall accuracy increases significantly; six-year-old children show a correlation of just .48 while 11-year-olds show a correlation of .72. Nineteen-year-olds in the study showed a correlation of .88, indicating mastery of this strategy. These results are good evidence that improvements in retrieval strategies occur as children mature, and that these contribute to better memory performance with age.

Implicit Memory in Children

Implicit memory does not appear to change over the course of development. Researchers using a variety of implicit memory measures have found no difference between children of different ages (e.g., Parkin and Streete, 1988; Perez, Peynicioğlu, & Blaxton, 1998) and no difference in implicit memory performance between children and adults (Finn et al., 2016).

Alan Parkin and Sarah Streete presented three-, five-, and seven-year-olds with a picture-naming task where fragments of pictures were added in eight stages until the participant could name the subject of the picture. (This is similar to the Gollin figures discussed in Chapter 5). Following a delay of one hour or two weeks, participants were again presented with the picture-fragment sequences, some of which they had seen before, and some of which were new. Participants had to name the picture and also indicate if it was old or new. Parkin and Streete (1988) found no effect of age on the picture-naming task. All groups named the pictures more quickly when the pictures had been seen before. (This is known as savings and is a measure of implicit memory.) However, there was a significant effect of age on the recognition task; older children performed better than younger children.

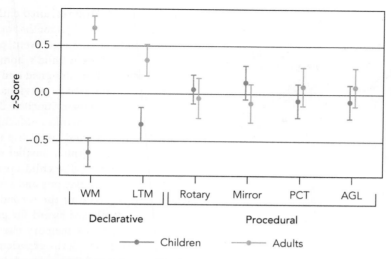

Figure 9.7 Declarative/Explicit and procedural/implicit memory in children and adults

The results from the six tests administered by Finn et al. (2016) show that children perform worse than adults on tests of declarative/explicit memory but perform the same as adults on tests of procedural/implicit memory.

Source: Finn et al., 2016, p. 217

Amy Finn of the University of Toronto and her colleagues compared the performance of children and adults in two tasks involving explicit memory and four tasks involving implicit memory. The results from the six tests administered by Finn et al. (2016) are shown in Figure 9.7 and show that children perform worse than adults on tests of declarative/explicit memory but perform the same as adults on tests of procedural/implicit memory.

Long-Term Memory in Children

Recall from Chapter 8 that when adults are asked to recall their earliest memory, it typically dates back to when they were about three-and-a-half or four years old (e.g., Jack & Hayne, 2007; Kihlstrom & Harackiewicz, 1982; MacDonald, Uesiliana, & Hayne, 2000). The absence of memories prior to this age is typically referred to as **infantile amnesia**. However, the presence of infantile amnesia in adults does not necessarily mean that children do not form long-lasting memories from an early age. As discussed in Chapter 8, infantile amnesia appears to be facilitated by high rates of hippocampal neurogenesis in young children.

Hippocampal neurogenesis can account for the general finding that more memories are forgotten from childhood than from other periods in life; however, this does not mean that *all* early memories will be erased in all people. The process simply means that memories are less likely to be preserved than if they were formed later in life. Indeed, Tustin and Hayne (2010) found that 40 per cent of individuals in their study on earliest childhood memories had early memories from their first two years of life, suggesting that not all memories are lost from early childhood and that in some cases people are able to maintain memories from earlier than four years of age.

Fiona Jack, Gabrielle Simcock, and Harlene Hayne decided to conduct a longitudinal study to see if very young children would remember a unique event six years after it

infantile amnesia

the inability for adults to remember events from early in life

Figure 9.8   The magic shrinking machine

Source: Simcock & Hayne, 2002, p. 277

occurred. Jack et al. (2012) recruited children between the ages of 27 and 51 months for the first phase of their study. In the target event, phase two experimenters visited each child's home with a Magic Shrinking Machine designed and made by the experimenters and used in previous memory research with children (see Simcock & Hayne, 2002, 2003). The Magic Shrinking Machine was a large black box that a child could use to "magically" change a large toy into a smaller version of that toy (see Figure 9.8). The child operated the machine seven times on day one and seven times the next day. At the end of the second day, the child received a cardboard award for participating, which was used as a memory cue during a subsequent interview about the experience.

Twenty-four hours after the second demonstration, the experimenters returned to the house to test the child's memory for the event. The children's memories for the machine were probed using photographs of the machine, questions about the machine, and finally with a test of how to use the machine. Six years later, a similar interview was conducted with each child, except this time in the researcher's laboratory. All the children remembered some aspect of the Magic Shrinking Machine following the 24-hour delay. Older children recognized more photographs and were more successful at using the machine on their own following this delay. Although older children showed better recall after the 24-hour delay, age did not affect the probability that a child would recall the event six years later. Two of the nine participants with good memories of the Magic Shrinking Machine were only two years old during the target event. Thus, the results of Jack et al. (2012) demonstrate that, while it is rare, children as young as two years of age are able to retain memories for events for at least six years. This result, combined with the results of Tustin and Hayne (2010), suggests that while most people may not recall events prior to three-and-a-half years of age, some people are indeed able to form and maintain memories from much earlier. Jack et al. (2012) provide anecdotal evidence

---

BOX 9.2

DIY EXPERIMENT

Strategies to Aid in Recall

All you need for this demonstration is a timer, a paper, and a pen.

Part A: Set the timer for 60 seconds and study the list below. After 30 seconds, cover the list and wait for the timer to reach 60 seconds. Then record as many of the items as possible in whatever order you wish. When you have finished, move on to part B.

L   T   S   R   N   C   F   K   B   K   J   M

Part B: Set the timer for 60 seconds and study the list below. After 30 seconds, cover the list and wait for the timer to reach 60 seconds. Recall as many items as possible in whatever order you wish.

red
cow
two
blue
horse
nine
yellow
sheep
five
green
pig
seven

Discussion: How did your performance on Part A compare to your performance on Part B? You may have noticed that Part A was more difficult than Part B because you needed to rely on maintenance rehearsal to recall unrelated letters, but that for Part B you were able to organize the information into colours, animals, and numbers, making rehearsal more manageable. As an adult you have no trouble making the most of different rehearsal strategies, but children learn and perfect these strategies over time. Differences in their ability to use different strategies dramatically affects their recall at different ages.

to suggest that a child's involvement in conversation during the target event may be a good predictor of whether the early memory is retained in the long term.

Memory and Aging

Most people believe that memory naturally declines with age. Indeed, memory lapses in people over 65 are frequently depicted in books, movies, and television shows. When older people can't remember where they put their keys, or someone's name, they are quick to assume the lapse is due to age, but this may not always be the case. All people, regardless of age, forget things from time to time. It is thus plausible that older people believe they are more forgetful because of ageist stereotypes and not because their memory has actually declined. In this section, we will explore research examining the effect of age of memory. This research reveals that while some aspects of memory change with age, these changes are relatively slight for most people, and are only observed in a narrow range of situations.

In the popular 1980s sitcom *The Golden Girls*, the eldest character, Sophia (far right), was depicted as being prone to profound lapses in memory. This is a common stereotype about older people; however, it is not accurate. Normal aging involves only minor losses in memory.

NBC/NBCU Photo Bank/Getty Images

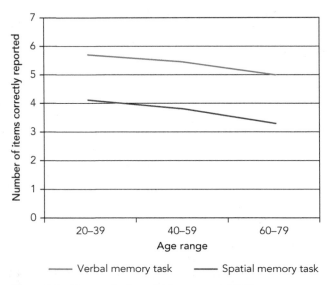

Figure 9.9 · The results from Salthouse et al. (1988)

Performance on a verbal memory task and a spatial memory task for three groups aged 20–39 (mean age = 27), 40–59 (mean age = 50) and 60–79 (mean age = 68). Performance is worse on the spatial memory task than on the verbal memory task for all ages; however, performance on both tasks appears to decline at approximately the same rate.

Source: Based on data from Salthouse et al., 1998, p. 158

Memory Span

Timothy Salthouse and his colleagues have been investigating memory and aging for more than 30 years. Salthouse examined verbal and spatial short-term memory in 362 adults between the ages of 20 and 79. All participants had approximately 13 years of education and reported that they were in good health. Salthouse (1994) used the same stimuli for a verbal memory task and a spatial memory task. The stimuli consisted of a 5 × 5 matrix of squares with a letter inside of each square. Seven spaces on the matrix were shaded grey, the remainder were white, and each matrix was presented for three seconds. In the verbal memory task, participants were asked to report the letters that had occupied the grey squares. Salthouse, Kausler, and Saults (1988) found that participants in all age groups performed better on the verbal memory task than on the spatial memory task, and that performance on both tasks appeared to decline at roughly the same rate (see Figure 9.9).

Parkinson, Inman, and Dannenbaum (1985) found a memory span for letters to be 6.6 at age 20 and 5.8 at age 75, again showing a small but significant decline. Spinnler, Della Sala, Bandera, and Baddeley (1988) tested participants' ability to tap out a sequence on patterned blocks and found a decrease from a mean of 5.1 blocks to 4.7 blocks over the course of adult life. Numerous other studies examining the effect of age on short-term memory span have found similar results (e.g., Craik, 1985; Parkinson, 1985; Salthouse & Babcock, 1991).

Working Memory

Working-memory tasks require the individual to hold material in short-term memory while simultaneously manipulating information in some way. For example, in one working memory-span paradigm devised by Daneman and Carpenter (1980), participants read sentences while holding the final word from the previous sentence in memory. Span was defined as the largest number of words that could be accurately reported on at least 50 per cent of trials while completing this task. Sentence-span paradigm experiments demonstrate small but significant effects of age on performance (Verhaeghen, Marcoen, & Goossens, 1993).

In the Brown-Peterson paradigm, participants are given an item that needs to be reported later (e.g., a trigram like *HRX*) and are then instructed to perform a distracting task, such as counting backwards from 1000 by 7s, for a certain amount of time. The counting task is intended to prevent rehearsal. At the end of the counting task, participants are asked to recall the trigram and the dependent measure is the number of letters recalled. The length of the counting interval is varied across trials. When Parkinson et al. (1985) conducted an experiment using the

Brown-Peterson paradigm, they found that young people recalled more letters than older individuals and that this difference was greater at longer delays. However, this difference was found to be entirely due to differences in immediate recall; the young participants needed about 2.25 repetitions of a trigram to recall it perfectly 90 per cent of the time with no delay while older participants needed 2.8 repetitions to achieve the same performance. When the participants were given an opportunity to repeat the to-be-remembered sequences before performing the counting task, there were no age differences in performance.

In another experiment, Fergus Craik of the University of Toronto presented young and old participants with a list of three-letter words such as *dog, zoo, hat, pen*. In one condition, participants were asked to report the words in any order; in another condition, participants were asked to report the items in alphabetic order (alphabetizing involves the use of working memory). Young and old participants recalled the same words when they could report them in any order; however, young participants outperformed the older participants when the words had to be reported alphabetically (Craik, 1986).

RELEVANT RESEARCH

BOX 9.3

Can *Ginkgo biloba* Prevent Cognitive Decline in Older Adults?

One of the greatest worries of people as they age is that their memory and cognitive function will decline. As a result, there has been great interest in treatments that may stave off such declines. One of the most popular is *Ginkgo biloba* (*G biloba*), a herbal supplement made from the leaves of a *Ginkgo biloba* tree. *G biloba* has been used in Asian cultures for thousands of years with the intention of maintaining cognitive health in aging. Recently, researchers have conducted carefully controlled clinical trials examining the effects of the supplement on memory and cognitive function. Beth Snitz and her colleagues conducted the Ginkgo Evaluation of Memory (GEM) study to determine whether *G biloba* slows the rate of cognitive decline in older adults. The study was a randomized, double-blind, placebo-controlled clinical trial involving 3069 community-dwelling participants between the ages of 72 and 96 over the course of six years. Participants received a twice-daily dose of 120 mg of *G biloba* or an identical-appearing placebo. The researchers assessed memory and other cognitive skills in all participants every six months. Compared with placebo, the use of *G biloba* did not result in less cognitive decline in older adults with normal cognition, nor did it reduce the rate of decline in adults with mild cognitive impairment (Snitz et al., 2009). A similar study conducted by Bruno Vellas and his colleagues found identical results; *G biloba* had no effect on memory in older adults compared to a placebo (Vellas et al., 2012). Because *G biloba* often produces unpleasant, sometimes serious, side effects, older adults are likely best off avoiding this supplement altogether.

© Mzagajewska | Dreamstime.com

Thus, different working-memory paradigms generate different age effects; Craik's alphabetized recall task generated large age effects, sentence-span tasks generate moderate age effects, and the Brown-Peterson paradigm produced no age effects. One explanation for these differences offered by Cynthia May, Lynn Hasher, and Michael Kane is that older individuals are less able to inhibit irrelevant information, such as material learned on earlier trials, when performing these tasks. This argument predicts that when an experiment consists of many trials with large numbers of similar stimuli, older individuals will have trouble inhibiting material from earlier trials as the experiment progresses and their performance declines. The decline in performance near the end of the experiment will reduce average memory performance scores for older adults making it appear as though there is a working-memory deficit when the problem is actually proactive interference (May et al., 1999). May et al.'s (1999) argument is consistent with the pattern in the data reviewed here. The Brown-Peterson task, which does not use a lot of stimuli in a given experiment, shows the smallest age effect. The sentence-span task analyzed by Verhaeghen et al. (1993) uses more stimuli than the Brown-Peterson task and there is a greater effect of age, although it is still slight. Finally, the word-alphabetization task utilized by Craik (1986) uses the most stimuli and the age differences are greatest.

Long-Term Memory

Many experimental paradigms show a decline in long-term memory with advancing age. In one experiment, Eileen Simon (1979) had young, middle-aged, and older participants learn sentences in which one word was underlined (e.g., "The farmer drove his truck.") Half of the participants were given a free-recall test, in which they had to recall as many of the underlined words as possible, while the other half were given a cued-recall test, in which they were given the rest of the sentence as a cue (e.g., "The farmer drove his ____.") The results from the experiment are shown in Figure 9.10.

The results from Simon (1979) suggest that older individuals are less able to use cues than younger individuals. This may reflect a general tendency to encode less information about a stimulus. For example, Kausler and Puckett (1980) presented young and old participants with a study list of words that were presented in upper or lower case and found that older participants were less likely to recall which case a given word had been presented in. Similarly, Kausler and Puckett (1981) presented lists of words auditorially using two different voices and found that older participants were less able to recall which voice had spoken a given word. Johnson, De Leonardis, Hashtroudi, and Ferguson (1995) also found older adults had more difficulty identifying the speaker of words presented to them. Micco and Masson (1992) examined the ability of younger and older individuals to generate useful word cues. In the first phase of the experiment, Micco and Masson asked young and old participants to generate cues for a target word. In the second phase of the experiment, young and old

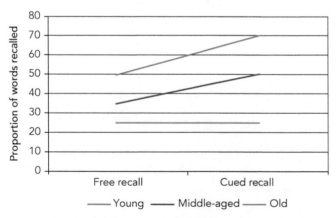

Figure 9.10   The effect of age on free recall and cued recall

The results from Simon (1979) suggest that older individuals are less able to use cues to recall words.

Source: Based on the results of Simon, 1979

participants were given the cues generated in the first phase and were asked to come up with the associated word. Micco and Masson (1992) found that older adults generated less effective cues and were less able to generate the target word regardless of whose cue they were given. The notion that older individuals have specific deficits in the use of cues is consistent with the results of Craik and McDowd (1987), who found that older individuals performed significantly worse than younger individuals on a recall task, where there are no retrieval cues at the time of test, but not on a recognition task, where each item is a retrieval cue for itself.

Fergus Craik, Mark Byrd, and James Swanson were interested in examining the extent to which environmental factors, such as education, socioeconomic status, and involvement in the community, may influence performance on cued-recall tasks. To achieve this, they examined recall performance of three different populations of older adults. Using verbal intelligence scores, socioeconomic status, and involvement in community activities as a guide, Craik et al. (1987) created three samples of older adults. One group (Old 1) had relatively low socioeconomic status, relatively low verbal intelligence scores, and were not very active. A second group (Old 2) were similar to Old 1 except they were involved in community activities. A third group (Old 3) had activity levels that were similar to Old 2 but were wealthier and had higher average verbal intelligence scores. All groups had an average age of about 74 years. Craik et al. (1987) examined recall for a list of 10 words across two learning conditions (free learning and cued learning) and two testing conditions (free recall and cued recall). In the free learning condition, participants were given a list of 10 words and were instructed to learn the list as best they could. In the cued learning, condition participants were given a cue before each to-be-remembered word, such as "a protector–SOLDIER" or "a covering–CURTAIN." In the free-recall condition, participants were asked to recall as many of the studied items as possible. In the cued-recall condition, participants were presented with a cue for the word, such as "What was the type of protector?" or "What was the types of covering?" Each of the four learning × test conditions was examined across the three older populations and a young population of university students. The results are shown in Table 9.2.

All groups recalled the most items in the cued-learning/cued-recall condition, indicating that people of all ages can benefit from cues. Note that Old 2 outperformed Old 3 in every condition, even though the only difference between these groups was the level of activity in the community. The results from this experiment suggest that environmental variables such as community activity and socioeconomic status can significantly affect memory performance in

Table 9.2   The results from Craik, Byrd, and Swanson, 1987

Condition	Group Number of Items Recalled			
	Old 1	Old 2	Old 3	Young
Cued learning/cued recall	5.5	7.3	8.1	7.8
Cued learning/free recall	2.2	5.4	5.8	5.6
Free learning/cued recall	2.2	4.5	5.4	5.8
Free learning/free recall	2.4	4.6	4.7	6.0

Source: Craik et al. 1987, p. 82

older people. There were no significant differences in recall between the Old 3 group and the young group except in the free-learning/free-recall condition. This result suggests that, even when socioeconomic and community activity are controlled for, older adults have difficulty with tasks where they are required to generate their own cues.

Claudia de Wall, Barbara Wilson, and Alan Baddeley developed the Extended Rivermead Behavioural Memory Test (ERBMT) to assess older individuals' memory for the sorts of material they may need to recall to function day to day (de Wall, Wilson, & Baddeley, 1994). The ERBMT is comprised of nine components: remembering the names of two people, remembering the location of two hidden objects, remembering an appointment, recognizing a picture, remembering a newspaper article (immediate and delayed recall), recognizing a face, remembering a new route with immediate and delayed recall, delivering two messages, and remembering the current date, as well as 11 orientation questions (year, month, day, time, place, city, year of birth, present prime minister, previous prime minister, present president of the United States, and previous president of the United States). de Wall, Wilson, and Baddeley examined performance on each item of the ERBMT for middle-aged individuals (mean age = 46) and older adults (mean age = 70) and found that older adults performed significantly worse on every item on the test except for remembering the newspaper story. When scores for all items were combined, there was a large significant difference between the age groups. The highest-scoring older adults performed worse than the lowest-scoring middle-aged adults.

The Positive Memory Bias

Older adults often demonstrate a positive memory bias (a tendency to recall positive life experiences better than negative life experiences; for more see Chapter 6). The positive memory bias reveals itself in two ways. First, older adults seem to selectively remember a higher proportion of positive stimuli (such as pleasant pictures) and a lower proportion of negative stimuli (such as unpleasant pictures) than younger adults (Charles, Mather, & Carstensen, 2003; Knight, Maines, & Robinson, 2002; Mather & Carstensen, 2005; Mather, Knight, & McCaffrey, 2005). Second, older adults tend to reconstruct autobiographical memories so that they seem more positive than they actually were (Mather & Johnson, 2000). For example, an older adult may recall a car accident, being fired from a job, or a personal loss as being less distressing than it really was at the time. Researchers believe that older adults engage in more emotional regulation than younger adults, and that positive memory bias helps keeps an older adult feeling content (Kennedy, Mather, & Carstensen, 2004).

Prospective Memory

Prospective memory is the ability to remember to do something in the future. For example, when you remember to go to an appointment, give a message to a friend when you see her or him, or take a medication at a specific time, you are using prospective memory. Prospective memory is crucial for independent living and for this reason many researchers have studied how it is affected by age. Early studies of prospective memory, including Moscovitch (1982) and Poon and Schaffer (1982), found no age difference or, in the case of Rendell and Thomson (1993), found better prospective memory in older participants, which is in marked contrast to other studies of memory and aging. Many later studies, however, found the reverse; younger participants performed better than older participants (see Cockburn & Smith, 1988, 1991; Einstein, Holland, McDaniel, & Guynn, 1992; Maylor 1993, 1996; Park, Hertzog, Kidder, Morrell, & Mayhorn, 1997). Peter

Rendell and Donald Thomson noted that the early studies, in which older people outperformed their younger counterparts, used very naturalistic research paradigms, whereas the later studies, where younger participants outperformed their older counterparts, used laboratory paradigms. Rendell and Thomson conducted both naturalistic and laboratory experiments using the same participants in order to get a better understanding of why there had been such variable results in previous research. In their first experiment, young adults in their twenties and older adults in their sixties and eighties were required to enter the time and date into a device called a Sharp Organizer (somewhat like an iPod touch but much more basic) at set regular times over the course of a week. There were four conditions in the experiment that varied in complexity. An earlier laboratory experiment conducted by Einstein et al. (1992) revealed that older adults' performance was much worse when the task was more complex. (Young adults were not affected by the manipulation.) Thus, the researchers expected that increasing the complexity would eliminate or even reverse the older-adult advantage observed in Rendell and Thomson (1993). The four levels of complexity varied in whether the times were on the hour or half-hour (regular) or not (irregular) and whether it was the same regimen each day (same) or not (change). The same/regular condition was thought to be the least complex followed by the same/irregular, different/regular, and different/irregular conditions. The dependent variable was whether the required log entry was on time, late, or missed. In this experiment, older adults consistently outperformed younger adults and the complexity manipulation had no impact on this age effect.

In the second experiment, Rendell and Thomson (1999) found that, even when participants had access to external cues to help them remember to log their times, older adults still performed significantly better than younger adults.

In their third experiment, Rendell and Thomson (1999) used the same participants as in the first and second experiments to study retrospective memory (memory for things that already happened) and prospective memory in a laboratory setting. Participants completed two recall tests: a recognition test and a questionnaire about themselves. When the testing session began, participants were given two prospective memory tasks; they were instructed to stop the clock after seven minutes (stop-clock task) and to note the time that they completed the questionnaire (note-finish task; Rendell & Thomson, 1999). The typical age-related decline was observed for the free-recall and recognition tasks; younger participants remembered more items than older participants. Older adults also performed worse on the stop-clock and note-finish tasks than the younger participants. This result replicates the results from other laboratory-based prospective memory experiments.

Research suggests that older adults perform better than younger adults in naturalistic prospective memory tasks, but worse on laboratory-based prospective memory tasks. Rendell and Thomson (1999) speculate that multiple factors likely contribute to this paradoxical finding. First, they suggest that because older adults are more likely to take medications, they may have more practice with completing prospective memory tasks in the real world; however, because the laboratory tasks were somewhat arbitrary and artificial, this practice did not benefit those tasks. The researchers also suggest that older adults may develop compensatory strategies for dealing with losses in memory function, and that having a very organized life may be one of those strategies.

Implicit Memory

There are many different measures of implicit memory, including stem-completion tasks, priming tasks, recognition tasks, serial pattern learning, picture-completion tasks, and motor learning. (For more on these tasks, please see Chapter 5.) Light and Singh (1987) and Java and

Gardiner (1991) report no age effects of stem-completion tasks. Parkin and Walter (1992) studied picture recognition in old and young participants. When participants identified familiar pictures, they were asked to indicate whether they remembered seeing the picture before, or if they simply knew they had seen the picture before. Although there was no age effect on the accuracy of picture recognition, older adults were far more likely to give a "know" response than a "remember" response. This latter result suggests that implicit processes may be intact but that episodic memory may be weaker in older individuals.

Howard and Howard (1992) studied pattern recognition in young and old adults. In the first phase of the experiment, participants were instructed to press one of four keys on a keyboard based on the location of an asterisk on the computer screen. The target pattern was DBCACBDCBA. The first two blocks followed the target pattern, the third block followed a random pattern, and the fourth block again followed the target pattern. Although the older participants (mean age = 73) were slower than the younger participants (mean age = 19), the older participants were more accurate. The researchers compared response times in blocks 3 and 4; if the participant were faster in block 4 than block 3, this would indicate that they had learned the pattern during blocks 1 and 2. Both the young and old groups were slower in block 3 than block 4 and there was no age difference for this implicit measure. However, when the researchers asked the participants to predict where the asterisk would be on the next trial, the young participants were more accurate than the older participants. Thus, the results of the serial pattern–learning experiment suggest that implicit memory is unaffected by age, but that explicit memory processes do decline as one gets older. Although movement slows with age, the ability to learn new movements does not seems to decline. Willingham and Winter (1995) found that older adults learned to complete a maze on a computer just as quickly as their younger counterparts. Howard, Shaw, and Heisey (1986) found that older adults needed a 500 ms gap between the prime and the target in order for priming effects to be observed.

The Victoria Longitudinal Study

The Victoria Longitudinal Study (VLS) is an ongoing research project being conducted at the University of Alberta and tests the same individuals at different ages. The VLS tracks older adults across a wide variety of dimensions related to memory, cognition, and health. David Hultsch used data from the VLS to study the memory of 487 individuals ranging in age from 57 to 86 over the course of six years. Each of the participants was given a battery of tests related to memory, cognition, and health at least three times in the six-year period. The tests evaluated episodic, semantic, and implicit memory; verbal fluency; reading comprehension; and activity levels. Hultsch, Hertzog, Small, and Dixon (1999) found significant differences between younger and older adults. Hultsch et al. (1999) found that fact recall, working memory, and comprehension speed all decline with age and that the declines accelerate from one year to the next up to about the age of 75. Consistent with other research involving older adults, Hultsch et al. (1999) found implicit memory performance and text recall were relatively unaffected by age. Hultsch et al. (1999) concluded that a decline in working memory was the best predictor of declines in other cognitive tasks, noting that when working memory goes, a lot goes with it (Hultsch et al. 1999). Because working memory and implicit memory involve distinct memory circuits, declines in working memory performance have no effect on implicit memory performance.

The Neuroscience of the Aging Brain

This section explores normal changes in the brain during aging. Age-related memory disorders such as Alzheimer's disease (which aren't the result of normal aging) are discussed in Chapter 13.

As people get older, the structure of the brain itself changes as the brain shrinks in size and the ventricles become larger; however, different parts of the brain shrink at different rates. The frontal lobes shrink more quickly; the temporal and occipital lobes shrink more slowly (Anderson & Craik, 2000; Raz, 2000). This may be why the memory deficits observed in neurotypical older people resemble memory deficits in people with frontal lobe damage, although memory deficits in neurotypical older people are much less severe. The frontal lobes are involved in controlling attention, which in turn may make it more difficult to select and encode information. Cabeza et al. (2004) scanned young and old adults while they completed working-memory, visual-attention, and episodic-retrieval tasks. Cabeza et al. (2004) found that older adults showed more bilateral patterns of prefrontal activity than younger adults during working-memory and visual-attention tasks. This finding has been replicated using many different memory paradigms and has led to the development of the Hemispheric Asymmetry Reduction in Older Adults (HAROLD) model (for a review, see Cabeza, 2002). Many researchers believe that when increased brain activation is observed in older individuals, it reflects deliberate compensatory activities.

The chemistry inside the brain also changes with age. It is estimated that individuals lose 5 to 10 per cent of the dopamine in their brains every decade (Antonini et al., 1993). Both Parkinson's disease and Huntington's disease involve cognitive impairment and decreases in dopamine (Bäckman et al., 1997; Brown and Marsden, 1990). It is possible to approximate the amount of dopamine in the brain by measuring D_2 receptor binding using a PET scan. In one study, Bäckman et al. (2000) first had 11 healthy participants ranging in age from 21 to 68 years old complete tasks that assessed both their perceptual speed and episodic memory. Next Bäckman et al. (2000) used a PET scan to measure D_2 receptor–binding activity in the caudate and putamen. The researchers looked for correlations between the cognitive tasks and dopamine activity. The researchers found a significant correlation between dopamine levels and episodic memory. These correlations accounted for 38 per cent of the variance in word recognition and 48 per cent of the variance in face recognition. The researchers then used statistical regression to remove dopamine from the equation. When dopamine was no longer a factor, age had very little impact on memory performance, suggesting that decreases in dopamine that occur with age drive some age-related declines in memory functioning.

Conclusions

The human body changes a great deal over a normal lifespan, as does that human's roles and responsibilities in the world around them. However, despite these dramatic changes in the body and lifestyle, memory changes remarkably little. Infants encode complex information easily long before they can speak, and despite stereotypes that older adults are highly forgetful, most aspects of memory change very little with age, and prospective memory may actually improve. Of all the aspects of memory, working memory shows the most significant age effects; working memory develops over the first decade of life, and declines at a fairly steady rate in many people over the age of 65. Working memory is highly dependent on the prefrontal cortex, which develops slowly in children and shrinks as we age. Age effects in episodic memory performance may be more closely linked to dopamine levels in the brain than aging per se.

CHAPTER REVIEW

- Newborns demonstrate memories for things they experienced before they were born, including tastes, the sound of their mother's voice, and specific passages of prose.
- Sensory preconditioning (SPC), potentiation, and paired-comparison experiments have shown that even very young infants can remember detailed information for long periods of time.
- The neuroanatomical model of infant memory development suggests that infants are born with poor memories because their hippocampus is not fully mature until about nine months of age. The ecological model of memory development suggests that an individual's memory processes are perfectly adapted to their ecological niche. This model predicts that young infants will be exuberant encoders because rapid learning is highly adaptive for infants who have no pre-existing knowledge about their environment. Researchers have found that infants engage in exuberant encoding and rapid forgetting. These results are inconsistent with the neuroanatomical model and are consistent with the ecological model.
- During childhood, memory span, retrieval strategies, the organization of memory, and retrieval strategies all change dramatically. As children develop more knowledge about how their memory operates, they can use that knowledge to improve their memory performance.
- Implicit memory does not appear to change over the course of childhood.
- Although most people believe memory loss is a natural part of aging, research instead suggests that memory is only modestly affected by age, and many aspects of memory are not negatively impacted by age at all.
- Performance on some working-memory tasks declines with age; some tasks show no age effects. It is possible that older adults are less able to inhibit irrelevant information, which affects tasks with a lot of stimuli more than tasks with fewer stimuli.
- Research suggests that both socioeconomic status and level of activity in the community can affect recall performance in older individuals.
- Older adults outperform younger adults in naturalistic prospective memory tasks while the reverse is true for laboratory prospective memory tasks. Older adults may be more organized in day-to-day life, giving them an advantage in real-life prospective memory tasks.
- Implicit memory is not affected by normal aging.
- The brain shrinks with age, with the frontal lobes shrinking most rapidly. The frontal lobes are associated with working memory.
- Older adults often use both hemispheres of the brain on tasks where younger adults use only one hemisphere. This most likely reflects deliberate compensatory activities.
- The chemistry of the brain changes with age. Individuals lose 5 to 10 per cent of dopamine in their brain during each decade of life. Dopamine levels are highly correlated with episodic memory. One study of older and younger adults found that most of the age effect could be explained by lower levels of dopamine in older adults.

MEMORY ACTIVITY

Using Chunking to Help Remember Long Lists

In this chapter, you read about the neuroanatomical model of memory development and the ecological model of memory development and were provided with this table summarizing both models. In this activity you will review the table and add to it, creating cues that will help you remember the material later.

First, review the table. Next, consider the main topic in each row of the table and come up with a word or short phrase describing that topic (e.g., "maturation" is one possible main topic of the first row).

Neuroanatomical Model	Ecological Model	Topic (this is your memory cue)
Early-maturing implicit memory system; late-maturing hippocampal-dependent explicit memory system	All systems functional at birth	maturation
Memory in infants is determined by maturity of hippocampus.	Memory of infants is determined by demands of their ecological niche.	
Infants younger than nine months of age cannot form detailed, lasting episodic memories.	Infants younger than nine months of age can form detailed, lasting, episodic memories.	
Memory performance of an older individual will always be better than memory performance of a younger individual	Memory performance is not determined by age but by the demands of an individual's ecological niche.	
Older infants perform differently on memory tasks than younger infants because their hippocampus is more mature.	Older infants perform differently than younger infants because mobile infants occupy a different ecological niche than immobile infants.	

Finally, list the five topics that you have created and then choose a mnemonic from earlier in the book to help you memorize the items.

Questions

1. How can researchers use habituation to infer memory in very young infants?
2. Imagine you have been asked to conduct a sensory preconditioning experiment to test the memory of infants. Describe your study plan in detail, including the population of infants you would study and the procedure you would use. Also explain what results you expect to see.
3. Explain potentiation and how it can be used to study memory in infants.
4. Compare and contrast the neuroanatomical model and the ecological model of memory development. Which model is supported by extant data in the literature?
5. Describe the changes in memory that are observed in children between the ages of 4 and 15.
6. What aspects of metamemory change over the course of childhood?
7. Evaluate the stereotype that older people are highly forgetful.
8. Describe the cross-sectional and longitudinal research paradigms. List possible problems associated with each as well as ways that researchers can minimize these problems.

9. Describe the aspects of memory that show age effects and aspects of memory that do not seem to decline with age.
10. Describe the age effects found in naturalistic and laboratory prospective memory experiments. Offer an explanation for the pattern of results that is typically observed.
11. Describe two ways that the brain changes with age and explain how these changes may impact memory.

Key Figures

10 Memory and Our Social Selves

LEARNING OBJECTIVES

Having read this chapter, you will be able to:

- Define transactive memory.
- Describe benefits and costs of collaborative remembering.
- Describe the generation effect.
- Explain how retrieval can be used to help people forget painful memories.
- Discuss how a social network influences memory.
- Define collective memory.
- Explain how illusory correlations can give rise to stereotypes.
- Describe the mere exposure effect, the propinquity effect, and the illusory-truth effect.
- Describe the implicit-association test (IAT) and explain what the IAT is used to measure.
- Explain how cognitive dissonance can affect autobiographical memory.

THE SEARCH FOR BRIDEY MURPHY

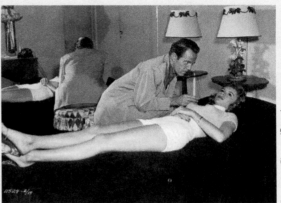

Paramount Pictures/Getty Images

In 1952, an American woman named Virginia Tighe (1923–95) was hypnotized by an amateur hypnotist named Morey Bernstein in Pueblo, Colorado. According to Bernstein, while Tighe was hypnotized she spoke with an Irish accent, claimed her name was Bridey Murphy, and claimed that she had been born in Cork, Ireland, in 1798. Through the voice of Bridey Murphy, Tighe provided Bernstein with many details about Bridey's life in Ireland, including her marriage to Sean Brian Joseph McCarthy and her own death and burial in Belfast in 1864. As Bridey, Tighe sang Irish songs and told traditional Irish folk tales. Tighe and Bernstein became convinced that the *only* way Tighe could have come to this knowledge was if she was the reincarnation of Bridey Murphy. In 1956, Bernstein published a wildly popular book titled *The Search for Bridey Murphy* and sold recordings of the hypnosis sessions in 12 languages. The story was also turned into a popular feature film by the same name. For a moment in the late 1950s, there seemed to finally be "proof" of life after death in the story of Bridey Murphy. Looking to ride on Bernstein's success, many reporters travelled to Ireland to find records of Bridey Murphy but, much to their dismay, no matching records could be found. Reporters at the *Chicago American* did, however, find records of a Bridie Murphy Corkell who had lived in the house across the street from where Virginia Tighe had grown up in Chicago, Illinois. When presented with this information, Virginia Tighe claimed she could never have known the maiden name of Bridie Corkell; however, the 1930 U.S. census shows Bridie Corkell's unmarried sister, Margaret Murphy, living with Bridie at the time that she and Tighe were neighbours, explaining the connection. All along, what Tighe had assumed were memories of things that happened to her were actually memories of stories from her early childhood, a clear case of source confusion. In the mid-twentieth century, little research had been conducted on the concepts of source confusion, false memory, and confabulation. Memory was seen as indelible and not modifiable, like a photograph or tape recording. When Bridey Murphy's story came out, the assumption was that the only way to *remember* being Bridey Murphy was to actually have *been* Bridey Murphy. However, since the time of the story of Bridey Murphy, researchers have learned a great deal about social influences on memory that can affect the nature of memories and how they are recalled. In this chapter, we will explore the many ways in which memory interacts with social factors.

Introduction

There have always been psychologists who recognized the importance of social context on understanding memory processes. Hermann Ebbinghaus, the first researcher to study memory experimentally, used nonsense syllables, instead of words, to study his memory because he didn't want his memory to be biased for some items more than others as a result of his own personal experience with those words. Frederic Bartlett, who introduced us to memory schemas, argued that the act of remembering was inextricably linked with a person's current attitudes. Lev Vygotsky, an influential developmental psychologist, believed that it was not possible to understand people without looking at what they remembered in a broader social context. Despite the fact that these researchers all had valid arguments for considering social factors when modelling memory, their views were ignored by psychologists who developed the purely cognitive models of memory. While the cognitive psychologists were busy in their labs, carefully recording recall and recognition for arbitrary word pairs and nonsense syllables, social psychologists were conducting research into the ways in which social process and memory interact.

In this chapter, we will explore the effect that social interaction has an effect on memory, as well as memory biases that develop as a result of social interaction. In the first section, we will investigate how collaborating with others can help recall in some situations but hinder recall in other situations. In the second section, we will discuss the effect that conversation has on our memory. We will see that sometimes misinformation that is introduced during conversation alters our existing memory for events, while other times the choice *not* to recall a topic in a conversation can make that information harder to access later on. We will also discuss the concept of collective memory. In the third section, we will explore the many ways that implicit memory influences social behaviour, from influencing the development of stereotypes, to influencing who we find attractive and, in some cases, leading us to believe things that aren't true. In the final section, we will review evidence suggesting that our current attitude can influence our autobiographical memory. We begin by discussing how collaborating with others influences recall.

DIY EXPERIMENT   BOX
                                                                     10.1

Fact Experiment Part I

Read the following statements several times. You will do the second part of this experiment at the end of the chapter.

French horn players get a bonus to stay in the Canadian Army.
Israel has the twenty-ninth largest economy in the world.
The emu is the largest bird on earth.
Toronto, Ontario, has a larger population than Boston, Massachusetts.
Argon is the densest gas.
The number of teen pregnancies in Canada has increased 300 per cent since 1990.

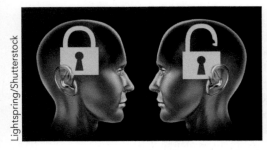

There are both costs and benefits associated with groups of people working together to try to recall the same information.

The Impact of Collaboration on Recall

People have a natural tendency to talk about events they experienced together. A couple may go to a party together and, while driving home, talk about things people said and did. Former classmates at a high school reunion may get together to reminisce about the good old days. A group of strangers may discuss an accident that they just witnessed. In each of these examples, memory is collaborative; that is, it is the task of the group to help each other remember. In the next section, we will see that collaborating with others can benefit memory in some situations, but can have a negative impact, or cost, on memory in other situations.

Benefits of Collaborative Remembering

transactive memory

when people share a memory task and fill in the gaps of each other's recall

Some research has found a clear benefit to memory when people work as a group on a memory task, a phenomenon known as **transactive memory**. The theory of transactive memory suggests that when a group of people is tasked with remembering material, if they divide the tasks among themselves, and each help others fill in missing parts of recall, they will recall more information than if any individual had taken on the task alone (Kerr & Tindale, 2004). A facilitative effect of collaboration has been found for a wide variety of to-be-remembered information, from word lists, to stories, to how to perform tasks (Hirst & Echterhoff, 2012). During collaboration, other people serve as external aids to memory, like reference books or notes.

Studies of transactive memory typically involve participants recalling recently learned information from a specific domain, such as history or science. In the first phase of the experiment, participants estimate their own expertise and the expertise of the other rememberers. In the next phase, participants study the to-be-remembered material individually and then are asked to recall the learned information as a group. Researchers include a test between study and recall, or during collaborative recall, in order to compare individual to group performance. Benefits from collaborative recall have been found when the participants are close friends, romantic partners, or involved in work teams and professional relationships (Hollingshead & Brandon, 2003) as well as when the participants don't know each other (Weldon, 2000). Transactive memory is thought to occur because different people find different material more memorable. If tasked with recalling facts A, B, and C, one person may find A and B easy to remember and find C difficult to remember, while the other person may find B and C easy to remember but find A particularly challenging to recall. Alone, each person would only recall facts A and B or facts B and C, but

Here a family gets together to look at photographs. The adults will use transactive memory in a real-world setting to help generate memories from the photographs.

together they recall facts A, B, and C because the first person fills in fact A for the second person, and the second person fills in fact C for the first person (Hirst & Echterhoff, 2012).

Costs of Collaborative Remembering

Research suggests that the group may remember more than an individual would remember alone; however, the group does not necessarily remember everything that an individual is capable of recalling. In other words, the sum of what is remembered as a group is less than the sum of all the individual memories. Researchers have identified three reasons for this finding: *collaborative inhibition*, *information-sampling bias*, and *audience tuning* (Hirst & Echterhoff, 2012).

Collaborative Inhibition

Collaborative inhibition occurs when the act of collaboration inhibits recall among group members. Researchers interested in collaborative inhibition have participants study material and test participants individually during a control phase. During this phase, researchers derive a nominal recall score. The **nominal recall score** reflects the *total number of different items recalled when participants are quizzed separately*. For example, suppose Anne and Mark study facts A, B, C, D, E, and F. Anne may recall items A, C, and D and Mark may recall items A, B, C, and E. The nominal recall score in this case is five because together Anne and Mark recalled five different items (A, B, C, D, and E). During the collaborative recall phase, researchers note the total number of facts recalled and label this measure the **group recall score**. In our present example, researchers may find Anne and Mark jointly recall facts A, C, and E, in which case the group recall score is three. In this example, the group recall score of three is *less* than the nominal recall score of five, suggesting that Anne and Mark remembered less when working together than they did individually. Many experiments looking at collaboration find group scores are less than nominal scores, reflecting a cost associated with collaboration known as *collaborative inhibition* (Rajaram & Pereira-Pasarin, 2010). Anne and Mark should have remembered five items but collaborative inhibition reduced that to three.

Early theories explaining collaborative inhibition suggested that social loafing, or reduced motivation to recall when in a group as compared to when working alone, was responsible for collaborative inhibition. However, Weldon (2000) manipulated personal accountability and motivation, effectively eliminating the desire for social loafing, and still found collaborative inhibition. A better-supported explanation for collaborative inhibition is the **retrieval-disruption hypothesis** (Basden, Basden, Bryner, & Thomas, 1997). The retrieval-disruption hypothesis asserts that collaborative inhibition occurs because one group member's retrieval strategy disrupts retrieval strategies that would lead to better recall by other group members. Retrieval disruption primarily occurs when different members of the group organize the to-be-remembered material differently. In other words, different people create different cues for recalling items. For example, some people may group items by their function, some by colour, some by the first letter in the item's name, and for each the retrieval cues (function, colour, or first letter) would be specific to the individual. Because different rememberers in the group have different retrieval cues, one person's retrieval will not help another person retrieve additional items. The retrieval-disruption hypothesis is supported by the results of experiments that show that when organizational structure is controlled (so all participants group to-be-remembered items by the same feature), collaborative inhibition disappears (Finlay, Hitch, & Meudell, 2000).

collaborative inhibition

when nominal recall is greater than group recall, indicating that the act of collaboration inhibited recall in one or more group members

nominal recall score

the number of items that an individual recalls on her or his own during the control phase of a collaborative learning experiment

group recall score

the number of items that a group jointly recalls during collaborative recall

retrieval-disruption hypothesis

the claim that collaborative inhibition occurs because one group member's retrieval strategy disrupts retrieval strategies that would lead to better recall in other group members

The retrieval-disruption hypothesis predicts that the larger the category, the larger the variability in organization and thus the greater the disruption. This prediction was confirmed in experiments conducted by Basden et al. (1997). Basden et al. (1997) also found that forcing participants to recall one category at a time eliminated collaborative inhibition.

partial-list cueing effect

when participants study a list and are given some items as cues at recall, participants recall fewer items than when not given part of the list as a cue

Collaborative inhibition is similar to the **partial-list cueing effect** that is often found in tests of individual memory. In partial-list cueing experiments, participants study lists of items that they know they will need to recall later. At the time of recall, some of the participants are provided with some items from the list (partial-list cueing condition) while other participants are not (control condition). Rather than helping performance, participants in the partial-list cueing condition recall fewer items than controls; the partial list inhibits recall. Like collaborative inhibition, the partial-list cueing effect is attributed to retrieval disruption due to the partial list being organized in a different way than the participant's own mnemonic organization. Because of this difference in organization, participants may be forced to engage in ineffective retrieval strategies and recall less. In collaborative recall, as each member recalls an item, each is creating a partial list of items for the rest of the group. This partial list serves as a cue for other group members; however, because different people have organized material differently, the cues won't be as effective as if individuals recalled material on their own. As a result, collaborative inhibition is observed.

Researchers have found evidence of collaborative inhibition using a wide range of materials, including related words, unrelated words, word pairs, stories, semantic memories, episodic memories, pictures, short video clips, and emotionally charged events (Hirst & Echterhoff, 2012; see also Rajaram & Pereira-Pasarin, 2010). Collaborative inhibition increases with group size because as the group size grows, so does the variability in the organization of the to-be-remembered items. Collaborative inhibition has not been observed in experiments where the group is comprised of a pair of close friends or married couples, presumably because people who are close to one another understand how each other think and organize materials. Collaborative inhibition is also affected by expertise; while novice pilots showed collaborative inhibition on a navigation task with other novice pilots, expert pilots produced a group recall score that was greater than the nominal recall score, showing a benefit of collaboration and suggesting that expert pilots shared the same style of organization and knowledge about flying (Meade & Roediger, 2009). The variability in the incidence of collaborative inhibition predicts that the way people study should affect whether collaborative inhibition is observed. Pereira-Pasarin and Rajaram (2011) presented groups of three participants with lists of target words either once or repeatedly before asking the group of three to recall the words together. When words were repeated, collaborative inhibition was reduced. Congleton and Rajaram (2011) had two groups of participants work with material before a collaborative recall test. There were a total of three sessions and what occurred in the sessions varied between groups. One group studied for all three sessions (i.e., study, study, study); the other studied for one session and then attempted individual recall for the other two sessions (i.e., study, recall, recall). Thus, one group repeated studying; the other repeated recall. Congleton and Rajaram (2011) found less collaborative inhibition in participants in the repeated recall condition than in participants in the repeated study group. Congleton and Rajaram (2011) concluded that repeated recall solidified retrieval strategies and subsequently reduced collaborative inhibition. The retrieval-disruption hypothesis is also supported by the effect of divided attention on collaborative inhibition. Dividing attention during learning will reduce the organization of the material and, as a result, more collaborative inhibition will be observed. Retrieval disruption can thus explain collaborative interference in a wide range of settings.

RELEVANT RESEARCH

BOX
10.2

The Pros and Cons of Studying in Groups

Students are often faced with the opportunity to study in groups; however, it is important to balance the potential benefits of this approach with the potential costs. In Chapter 9, we saw that people who talk about to-be-remembered material are more likely to remember that material, and thus that study groups where there is a lot of discussion can benefit memory. However, collaborative inhibition and informational-sampling bias may lead to some topics covered in the course not being discussed in study sessions. By discussing some topics but not others, students may experience retrieval inhibition,

StockSnap from Pixabay

or more difficulty remembering material NOT discussed in the group, later on. In order to combat these problems, students studying together should use one common system for organization, ideally the course textbook, and should make sure that each topic in the text is covered in discussion. Similarly, it may not be such a great idea to study from someone else's notes; reading other people's notes may result in partial list-cueing effects, making it more difficult to recall material from the course. In addition, because the notes may not be complete, using someone else's notes may result in retrieval inhibition.

Information-Sampling Bias

Another explanation for collaborative inhibition is **information-sampling bias**, a phenomenon where members of a group will not discuss an item if no one else in the group mentions it (Hirst & Echterhoff, 2012; Wittenbaum, Hollingshead, & Botero, 2004; Wittenbaum & Park, 2001). Support for the influence of information-sampling bias on collaborative inhibition comes from research conducted by Gwen Wittenbaum and her colleagues. In one experiment, Wittenbaum taught individual participants about a political candidate and then placed participants in small groups to talk about what they had learned. Each participant knew unique facts and facts known by other participants. Wittenbaum found that participants were more likely to recall shared information than uniquely held information. Wittenbaum argues that when memories are shared, there is a greater probability that those memories will be recalled than if the memory is uniquely held. For example, suppose five people each learn two facts: one shared fact (fact A) and one unique fact (fact B, C, D, E, or F depending on the person). Thus, person 1 knows facts A and B, person 2 knows facts A and C, person 3 knows facts A and D, and so on. Now suppose each person can remember only one fact and there is an equal probability of remembering shared fact A or the unique fact. The odds are almost certain that at least one person will recall fact A, but the odds that any of the unique facts will be recalled is much less (Wittenbaum et al., 2004; Wittenbaum & Park, 2001). Thus, some collaborative inhibition may be due to the fact that different people have different memories and that it is statistically less probable that a unique memory will be recalled than a shared one.

information-sampling bias

a phenomenon where members of a group will not discuss an item if no one else in the group mentions it

© Wideonet | Dreamstime.com

Audience Tuning

Collaborative inhibition may also occur because each member of the group may take into account their audience when recalling information, a phenomenon known as **audience tuning**. Depending on the audience and whether they are recalling or retelling information, some people may exclude information, resulting in collaborative inhibition (Marsh, 2007). Suppose, for example, a person is given a story to learn. If the person is asked to *recall* the story to an audience, the narrator will attempt to remember all the elements of the story as accurately as possible. If asked to *retell* the story to an audience, on the other hand, the person will recount the story without attempting to be either accurate or complete. Marsh (2007) notes that retelling is shaped by goals and retelling will be different if the goal is to teach rather than if the goal is to entertain.

audience tuning

when speakers recall events based on the nature of the audience they are speaking to

Nicole Dudukovic had participants learn stories and compared the retelling of the stories. Some people were instructed to describe the material, while others were instructed to entertain. Dudukovic found that people with the goal of entertaining recalled fewer of the events in the story, included fewer references to sensations, and included more intrusions (information not in the story) than people who were recalling an event with the goal of describing facts. The entertaining stories contained more errors, were more likely to be told in the present tense, and were more emotional than the factual retellings (Dudukovic, Marsh, & Tversky, 2004). Thus, collaborative inhibition may occur because the rememberer is retelling, not recalling, the information and has a goal of entertaining, rather than teaching, the audience. Imagine, for example, that one person learns a story of how to make a nutritious smoothie in a blender and that this story includes details about the correct ingredients to use, the order in which to incorporate the ingredients, and a description of the very messy consequences of not securing the lid on the blender before turning it on. If rememberers are asked to recall this information, they will likely include all the information they can. However, if rememberers are instead asked to retell the story with a goal of entertaining their audience, they will likely skip many details about the ingredients and the order of incorporation and focus on the mess that will be made if the lid is not secure. In the latter case, the audience will not have learned much of the information in the story, and collaborative inhibition will have occurred.

Speakers not only adjust what they say to whether they are recalling or retelling a story; they also adjust what they say based on what they think the listener expects to hear. For example, in research conducted by André Vandierendonck and Rita Van Damme, speakers included less detail when listeners seemed bored than when they seemed interested. In a similar study, Vandierendonck and Van Damme (1988) found that participants recalled more details about a doctor's visit when talking to someone who did not know much about a subject (in one experiment it was a hypothetical Martian) than when speaking to someone whom the teller knew was knowledgeable about the subject (Vandierendonck & Van Damme, 1988). Participants have also been shown to tune into the attitudes of the listener, recalling positive attributes of people he knows the listener likes and negative attributes of people he knows the listener dislikes (Echterhoff, Higgins, & Levine, 2009). The rules of conversation may also determine what people say when in groups. It is well established that speakers conform to general conversational rules when retelling information, which includes not saying more than is necessary and staying on topic (Grice, Cole, & Morgan, 1975). As a result of retrieval disruption, sampling biases, audience tuning, and the rules of conversation, retelling tends to convey less information than might be reported in a formal laboratory setting. The rules of conversation can constrain what is said, and consequently decrease what can be remembered. In addition, the act of conversing itself has many effects on memory, which we will discuss in the next section.

The Effect of Conversational Remembering on Subsequent Memory

During a conversation, thousands of past experiences may be relevant, and yet people selectively remember a small subset of this material because of factors specific to the social interaction. What's more, this selective recall affects subsequent recall of the conversation. To understand the impact that recall has on memory, we must understand **social contagion**, which is the spread of ideas, information, and practices through interpersonal contact or communication.

Social Contagion

Social contagion involves the spread of memories from person to person. Through interactions with others, people can both acquire new memories and have their existing memories changed. Elizabeth Loftus conducted a series of well-known experiments on the effect of social contagion on subsequent memory. In Loftus's social contagion experiments, participants witnessed an event and then received information about the event that was not true, which was termed **post-event misinformation**. If participants witnessed a traffic accident, for example, they might be told there was a stop sign when there wasn't, or told that there was broken glass when there wasn't. Participants' memory for the witnessed event was then tested. In Loftus's experiments, participants often reported the misinformation rather than aspects of the event that they actually witnessed, a phenomenon Loftus referred is as the **misinformation effect**. For example, participants reported stop signs and broken glass that they never actually witnessed. In other experiments, Loftus also showed that about 30 per cent could be made to falsely remember entire events, such as being lost in a shopping mall as a child or taking a hot-air balloon ride. Loftus's findings have significant implications for the interpretation of eyewitness testimony, which is explored in more detail in Chapter 11.

Loftus found the misinformation effect for eyewitness memory, but the misinformation effect can also be found in conversational settings. In one type of experiment, a participant learns information and then engages in collaborative recall with an experimental **confederate** who intentionally provides incorrect information. The participant's recall is then tested (e.g., Meade & Roediger, 2002). In another type of experiment, researchers look at individual memories for events before and after collaborative recall of the event (e.g., Cuc, Koppel, & Hirst, 2007). In both of these paradigms, participants' recall has been shown to be significantly impacted by what is said by others during collaborative recall. The results from these studies reflect **social conformity**, which was famously demonstrated in experiments by Solomon Asch in the 1950s.

social contagion
the spread of ideas through interpersonal contact, interaction, or communication

post-event misinformation
inaccurate facts about an event that was witnessed by a person that are sometimes deliberately created for experimental purposes, but can also occur naturally

misinformation effect
the observation that people often recall post-event misinformation when recalling a witnessed event

confederate
a person who is working on behalf of the experimenter to say and do specific things during an experiment. Other participants are not aware that the confederate is playing a role.

social conformity
changing one's beliefs or behaviours in order to fit in with the group

Asch asked participants to indicate which line (A, B, or C) a sample line matched in length. When confederates who participated lied and chose an answer that was clearly incorrect, 75 per cent of participants conformed and matched their response to the confederate's response at least some of the time (Asch, 1956). Thus, some researchers argue that misinformation effects result from a desire to conform. Other researchers suggest that social contagion can result from **source confusion**, or the participant's inability to recall whether the source of a piece of information was the original witnessed event or information provided after the event.

source confusion

a phenomenon in which a person cannot recall the original source of a memory

If participants cannot recall if they learned a piece of information from the to-be-studied material, or later during a collaborative session, they will be unable to know whether it is possible that this information could be incorrect (Mitchell & Johnston, 2009). Recall that in the chapter-opening case study it was determined that the case of Bridey Murphy was an example of source confusion.

Still other researchers suggest that **normative influences** produce social contagion. Normative influences are a type of social conformity that occurs when a person conforms to the speaker's view for social reasons, such as to be liked or to remain in a group. Baron, Vandello, and Brunsman (1996) found that when a memory task is easy and participants are motivated to be accurate, normative influences can result in social contagion.

normative influence

when a person conforms with another person in order to avoid social costs

Moderators of Social Contagion: How Is the Effect Altered?

Cognitive moderators, or factors that heighten or lessen the observation of social contagion, may include whether the information (or contagion) is consistent with a person's existing cognitive schemas, how much time a person has to learn the information, whether the information is new or old, and whether the person providing the information is perceived as an expert (Hirst & Echterhoff, 2012). The effect of expertise on social contagion may occur because source monitoring is a cognitively demanding task. A person may choose not to put effort into source monitoring when an expert is speaking. Without source monitoring, information from the speaker is more likely to be recalled as "fact" rather than "information provided by this person."

Participants are also more likely to show social contagion when the speaker has more power than the listener, when the listener is anxious about negative evaluation, when more than one speaker states the same facts, and when the information is being provided face to face (Hirst & Echterhoff, 2012). For example, a person would be more likely to believe that astronauts found life on the moon if it were told to them by a panel of astrophysicists at a university lecture than if told by a dishevelled stranger in a coffee shop.

People whose job is to influence the ideas of other people are well aware of these moderators of social contagion and use them to their advantage. Consider a cult as an extreme example. The most successful cult leaders (the ones who get their flock to abandon their lives, their money, and their loved ones) appear to be experts, exert power over the people hearing their message, make their flock fear negative evaluation, encourage other believers to repeat their beliefs without dissent, and present the information face to face. These are perfect conditions for social contagion, even if the message is something as "unbelievable" as the fact that the world is about to end and that only by committing suicide can you be saved.

Participants' social contagion can be influenced by warnings that a speaker may not be a good source of information. Warnings can sometimes make participants less likely to recall misinformation, but the timing of the warning is important. Warnings are most effective if they occur *before* the presentation of the erroneous material, and warnings are only effective

RELEVANT RESEARCH

BOX
10.3

The Effect of Retrieval and Re-Exposure on Subsequent Memory

Recalling a conversation once can influence subsequent recall of the same conversation. Conversational participants can add new correct or incorrect information, and facts that are recalled during conversation are reinforced, making them more likely to be recalled in the future. Generally, the effect of retrieval is greater for the speaker than the listener. For example, someone who has told a story many times is likely to better remember it than someone who has listened to it over and over. Better memory for material that has been brought up in conversation is related to the **generation effect**, a phenomenon found in many memory paradigms where material that has been generated by the participants is better recalled than material provided by an outside source (Slamecka & Graf, 1978). Thus, a student who engages in discussions about test material in class, in a study group, or in a lab will better remember that material at the time of test.

if given after the presentation of the erroneous material *if* the participant is highly motivated to be accurate or fears appearing gullible (Boon & Baxter, 2000). Even though warnings can reduce social contagion, they do not eliminate it; social contagion is a highly robust effect. Some researchers have even found increased social contagion following pre-warnings that information may be incorrect; this is likely due to the fact that a pre-warning makes participants pay closer attention to the speaker, and paying closer attention leads to a stronger memory trace despite the inaccuracy of the information. Post-warnings that information that has already been heard may be incorrect sometimes reduces social contagion, presumably because the post-warning makes participants check source information more closely before reporting recall. This can lead to the correct rejection of incorrect information, but also the incorrect rejection of correct information out of concern for accuracy. In general, post-warnings lead to less information being reported.

generation effect

material that is generated by the participant is better remembered than material that is provided to the participant by an outside source

Retrieval-Induced Forgetting

During conversation, people must discuss some information while intentionally *not* discussing other information. Charles Stone and his colleagues refer to these unmentioned memories as **mnemonic silences** (Stone, Coman, Brown, Koppel, & Hirst, 2012). John Wixted has argued that the silence leads to memory decay (see Wixted, 2004), but this theory isn't consistent with the evidence in the literature, which suggests that decay is the result of neurogenesis (i.e., the growth of new neurons), not the passage of time per se. (See Chapter 8 for more on this type of forgetting.) An alternative explanation that is more consistent with the memory literature is that a problem with cueing produces the mnemonic silences. This logic suggests that discussing a memory during a conversation strengthens cues for that memory, making it more likely to be recalled in the future, while material that is not mentioned does not benefit from increases in cue strength. In addition, mnemonic silences may occur because in order to retrieve the set of information that is part of the conversation, other information that is related but not part of the conversation must be inhibited; this is referred to as **retrieval-induced forgetting**. For example, to recall details from your trip to Walt Disney World, you may need to inhibit recall of your similar trip to Universal Studios. The inhibition of details related to Universal Studios as part

mnemonic silences

memories related to conversational topics that are not retrieved as part of the conversation

retrieval-induced forgetting

forgetting that occurs because in order to retrieve one item accurately, similar items must be inhibited

of recalling details from Walt Disney World may make it more difficult to activate those details from Universal Studios later on. Retrieval-induced forgetting can be measured by seeing what details a person recalls about an event before and after conversing about the event.

Retrieval-induced forgetting has been found in studies that have looked at the memory of the listener as well as the speaker. One interesting result is that the more attention the listener pays to details, the more likely the listener is to retrieve the memory being mentioned and inhibit similar memories. This means that an attentive jury member, for example, may be more likely than an inattentive juror to forget other details related to the case because of a dramatic speech by an attorney. Retrieval-induced forgetting is also reduced when the speaker is perceived as an expert. In this situation, listeners do less source monitoring and therefore are less likely to recall related material that they must subsequently inhibit in order to follow what the speaker is saying.

The Impact of the Social Network on Memory

Thus far, the discussion has focused on how social contagion, reinforcement, and retrieval-induced forgetting impact subsequent recall of a person engaged in single two-way conversation. However, social interactions typically involve several exchanges and can involve multiple sources. For example, many people's conversations revolve around news events. Initially a person may gain information from reading the news, seeing a news broadcast, seeing information posted on social media, and/or hearing a politician speaking on an issue. People then talk to other people and information spreads through social networks. "Fake news" spreads through social contagion, which is what makes it so harmful. You may think that researchers would have first started studying "social networks" after the Internet came to the forefront in the 1990s, but in truth social networks exist even in the absence of technology. In 1932, Frederic Bartlett was the first psychologist to publish work on social networks and memory. Bartlett created a serial repetition task where one person tells another a story and changes are observed over time (just like the party game "broken telephone"). Bartlett observed that when changes occurred in the message, the changes were consistent with the listener's schemas; listeners apparently modify stories so they can be retold from their own perspective.

Social networks transmit information very well. Research by Coman and Hirst (2012) found that the memory of people who heard a speech and the memory of people who learned the content of the speech through conversation were very similar. This result may help explain why politicians make such an effort to make speeches; they know that people will talk about their speeches and, when they do, their memory for the information in the speech will improve.

Gerald Echterhoff and his colleagues demonstrated that audience tuning can affect the memory of the speaker (Echterhoff, Higgins, & Levine, 2009; Echterhoff, Hirst, & Hussy, 2005). In one experiment, participants were given a description of Donald, who was described as liking coupons, disliking giving gifts, and liking buying things on sale; Donald could be perceived as either thrifty (a positive attribute) or stingy (a negative attribute). At this point, the participant should have had neither a positive or negative view of Donald.

Created at https://www.fakewhats.com/generator

Next, the participant was asked to describe Donald to an audience that the participant believed either liked or disliked Donald. The participants tuned their description to the audience, highlighting thriftiness to the audience that liked Donald and highlighting stinginess to the audience that disliked Donald. When the memory of the participants was tested later, their recall of Donald reflected how they described the person to the audience. Echterhoff argues that this phenomenon occurs because people are motivated to create a shared reality with other people. Echterhoff had participants make speeches to people they considered to be members of their **in-group** (in this case, fellow Germans) or people they considered members of an **out-group** (in this case, people from Turkey). Echterhoff varied whether the speaker believed the listeners liked or disliked the message. While speakers were more likely to audience tune the message when speaking to the out-group, participants' memories were not affected by speaking to this group. (They remembered the same information whether they audience tuned to the group who liked the message or didn't like the message.) Speakers who spoke to members of their in-group, on the other hand, tuned the message less but were much more likely to have their memory shaped by what they said in their speech. Echterhoff argues that this difference occurs because speakers want to create a shared reality with their in-group but not with an out-group.

in-group

a social group that a person feels she or he belongs to

out-group

A social group that a person feels she or he does not belong to

Collective Memory

The term **collective memory** refers to memories that are common to a group of people who share a similar social identity. When Canadians are asked about what comprises their identity as Canadian, frequent responses include the Canadian flag, the healthcare system, and being decidedly un-American. It follows that the collective memory for Canadians would include the memory for the Canadian flag, the healthcare system, and examples of how Canada is distinct from the United States. These memories differ from **shared memories**, or memories that many Canadian may hold but that have no bearing on cultural identity. For example, many Canadians may recall Hurricane Irma in 2017; however, this is a shared memory, not a collective memory, because Hurricane Irma was not directly linked to Canadian identity. The distinction between collective memory and shared memory is much like the distinction between autobiographical memory and episodic memory discussed in Chapter 6. Autobiographical memories are the

collective memory

memories shared by members of the same social group that relate to their group identity

shared memory

memories that many people possess but that are not linked to a social identity

An image of a Canadian flag (left) is part of the collective memory of Canadians because it is part of Canadian identity, whereas Hurricane Irma in 2017 (right) would be a shared memory, not a collective memory, because it is not linked to Canadian identity.

subset of episodic memories that a person relates to their personal identity, just as collective memories are a subset of shared memories that relate to a culture's identity.

Mechanisms such as social contagion, reinforcement, and retrieval-induced forgetting all work to shape collective memories across people from the same social group. Speakers and listeners interact to develop a shared representation of the past. The act of retrieval in conversation may serve to inhibit the recall of events not discussed. Some theorists argue that this make sense from an evolutionary perspective; by suppressing similar memories, the memories of group members become more similar, making groups more cohesive and more likely to work together toward a common goal.

Collective and Shared Memories of Indigenous People in Canada

From the 1800s until 1996, the Canadian government regularly took Indigenous children away from their families and placed them in residential schools, insisting that this displacement was for the children's own good because their parents were incapable of caring for them. In fact, it is now known residential schools inflicted harm that extended across generations and is a source of extensive social problems among Indigenous people today (Truth and Reconciliation Commission of Canada, 2015). Until recently the truth about the residential school program and its impact was not part of Canadian collective memory, because the two groups shared different versions of the past they could not reconcile.

The Truth and Reconciliation Commission (TRC) has a mandate to inform all Canadians of the truth about what happened in residential schools in the hope that the truth can lead to reconciliation. (For more on Truth and Reconciliation, please visit http://www.trc.ca.) In 2015, the TRC published a report with more than 90 calls to action for Canada in order "to redress the legacy of residential schools and advance the process of Canadian reconciliation" (TRC, 2015, p. 1). Many calls to actions in the TRC Report are aimed at changing Canadians' collective memory of Indigenous history by educating all Canadians about residential schools, treaties, and the contributions of Indigenous peoples to Canada. An accurate collective memory of Indigenous history shared by Canadians and Indigenous people alike is hoped to help reconciliation and to help Indigenous people maintain a positive image of their culture (TRC, 2015, p. 3).

Take a moment to consider another marginalized group. What collective memories for this group exist and what is the source of those memories? What change in collective memory could help improve equity and justice in that group?

stereotype
a widely held but fixed and oversimplified image or idea of a particular type of person or thing

Canada. Dept. Indian and Northern Affairs/Library and Archives Canada/e011080274

A group of students in class at Cross Lake Indian Residential School, Manitoba, 1940. The Truth and Reconciliation Commission (TRC) calls us to change the collective memory of Canadians by insisting that all people living in Canada be educated about this history.

Stereotype Maintenance through Conversation

Anthony Lyons and Yoshihisa Kashima (2003) have studied the link between memory and the formation of **stereotypes**. In one study, participants were taught about what was typical of a

Jamavan, a fictitious group of people. Participants were then presented with information about the Jamavans that was either consistent or inconsistent with the stereotypical Jamavan. Next, the researchers looked to see what type of information about the Jamavans participants were most likely to share with others. Perhaps not surprisingly, given the prevalence of stereotypes in society, stereotypical information was transmitted much more readily than information that did not support the stereotypes.

Thus, stereotypes may persist, in part, because stereotypical information is more likely than non-stereotypical information to be shared among people, which enhances memory for the stereotype, *and* because every time a stereotype is relayed to another person, information that may disprove the stereotype must be suppressed, and retrieval inhibition occurs. For example, suppose Jim believes the untrue stereotype that all people from a fictitious city we'll call Driverville are bad drivers. Next, suppose Jim vacations in Driverville and has a lovely time, although one day the taxi he is in is cut off by a Driverville driver. When Jim returns home he is likely to tell Mary about the one bad driving incident because it is consistent with his stereotype about people from Driverville. Telling about the bad driving incident will increase the memory trace for the stereotype "people from Driverville are bad drivers" in both Jim and Mary, and will also inhibit any memories that either of them has about Drivervillians who drove well. Both Jim and Mary will be better able to access examples that are consistent with the stereotype than ones that are not, making them believe the stereotype to be true.

Implicit Memory and Social Behaviour

Implicit memory is memory that operates outside of awareness. As discussed in Chapter 5, implicit memory is experienced as a sense of knowing without a sense of remembering. The sense of familiarity generated by implicit memory influences our beliefs and affects our social behaviour in a variety of ways. In this section, we will see how implicit memory can lead to the development of illusory correlations that serve as the basis for many stereotypes. We will also see that implicit memory is responsible for our preference for familiar people (the propinquity effect) and our preference for familiar facts (the illusory-truth effect).

Distinctiveness-Based Illusory Correlations

When two stimuli are distinct from other stimuli, people have a tendency to overestimate the frequency with which the two stimuli co-occur. This is known as a **distinctiveness-based illusory correlation**. For example, a person may believe that all people over seven feet tall play basketball when this is not the case; the person is overestimating the frequency with which being very tall and playing basketball occur together. Loren Chapman employed a simple paradigm to demonstrate how easy it is to generate a distinctiveness-based illusory correlation. In his experiment, participants were presented with pairs of words; 12 words appeared on the left-hand screen, each paired once with each of nine other words. Most words were short (e.g., *lion, boat, tiger*), but some words were long (*magazine, notebook, blossoms*). After the words were presented, Chapman asked each participant to estimate the number of times each of the words from the left-hand side of the screen appeared with each of the words on the right. Although the actual probability of any two words being paired together was always the same, Chapman (1967) found participants consistently overestimated the frequency with which long words appeared together.

distinctiveness-based illusory correlation
incorrect judgments about the relationship between two variables based on the co-occurrence of distinctive stimulus events

For example, participants predicted that *blossoms-notebook* appeared more frequently together than *boat-notebook*, even though they had appeared together exactly the same number of times. The notion that *blossom* was a better predictor of *notebook* than *boat* is an example of an **illusory correlation** because in reality both words were equally good predictors of *notebook*; the belief that *blossom* was a better predictor was an illusion. Because the only difference between *boat* and *blossom* was how distinctive the word looked compared to the other words, Chapman concluded that the illusory correlation was based on distinctiveness. Thus, if stimuli are distinctive in memory, people can make incorrect judgments about those stimuli.

David Hamilton and Robert Gifford of Yale University were the first to look at whether distinctiveness-based illusory correlations may contribute to the development of stereotypes. Hamilton and Gifford (1976) noted that minority groups are by definition distinctive and most distinctive behaviours are perceived as negative; thus, if illusory correlations are formed when two distinctive events co-occur, a small number of incidences associating minority groups with unusual negative behaviours may lead people to conclude that all members of that group have a propensity for that behaviour, an illusory correlation based on distinctiveness. To test this hypothesis, the researchers developed a list of statements reflecting 27 moderately desirable behaviours (e.g., "Bill helps his friends when they are in need") and 12 moderately undesirable behaviours (e.g., "Brian take sides when his friends argue") and presented these statements, along with the individual's supposed membership in Group A or Group B. Two-thirds of the statements were associated with Group A, the majority, and one-third were associated with Group B, the minority. Participants then completed three tasks to assess the existence of illusory correlations. First, participants rated how well a variety of traits such as *popular, foolish, intelligent,* and *lazy* described each group. Second, participants were asked to use memory to assign group membership to a series of statements describing positive and negative traits such "A member of Group ____ takes sides when his friends argue." Finally, participants were asked to estimate the frequency of the presentation of statements related to each group as well as the frequency of desirable and undesirable behaviours for each group.

The results of the experiment showed the creation of illusory correlations. For the traits task, participants associated desirable traits (e.g., generosity) with the majority group and undesirable traits (e.g., selfishness) with the minority group. In the attributions tasks, where participants had to recall which behaviour had been presented in association with which group, participants correctly attributed two-thirds of desirable behaviours to the majority group and one-third to the minority group, but attributed less than half of the undesirable behaviours to the majority group and more than half to the minority group. If memory were solely responsible for performance on this task, then participants should have attributed two-thirds of the undesirable behaviours to the majority group and one-third to the minority group. Participants also estimated that a larger number of the undesirable behaviours had been associated with the minority group even though, in reality, fewer undesirable traits were shown for this group because there were fewer statements about the minority group overall. Hamilton and Gifford replicated their experiment but changed the proportions of desirable and undesirable behaviours such that the most distinct condition was desirable behaviours observed for members of the minority group. In this case, they also found distinctiveness-based illusory correlations; the participants overestimated the desirable traits among the minority group (Hamilton & Gifford, 1976). Their results showed that stereotypes can be produced with relative ease because distinctiveness-based illusory correlations may not reflect true representativeness of events in memory, but rather the relative distinctiveness of the person and the event in memory.

When Brian Mullen and Craig Johnson conducted a meta-analysis of dozens of distinctiveness-based illusory correlation studies, they found the effect to be highly significant and of moderate magnitude. Mullen and Johnson (1990) found that distinctiveness-based illusory correlations were stronger for behaviours that were negative than for those that were positive, and greater when a person had a greater number of exemplars in memory. This implies that the more people that one encounters, the more likely one is to develop a distinctiveness-based illusory correlation. One is also more likely to develop an illusory correlation for a negative behaviour than a positive one (Mullen & Johnson, 1990). Thus, if Person A observes Person B, whom Person A considers a minority, displaying a distinctive negative behaviour, that behaviour is more likely to be seen as typical for the minority group than if someone who was not in the minority displayed the same behaviour. Further, if the same Person A observes the same Person B from a minority group displaying a positive behaviour, that behaviour is less likely to be remembered as typical for the minority group. This may explain why more stereotypes tend to be held for minority groups, and why the stereotypes tend to be negative. The take-away message from this lesson is that stereotypes are persistent but do not reflect actual memory or reality. It is our personal responsibility to ignore stereotypes when making our own judgments and to openly critique people who perpetuate them.

This section has shown two ways in which social experiences can override actual memories in the creation of stereotypes. The first is through biased communication that has the tendency to reinforce memories for stereotype-consistent information and inhibit memories that are stereotype-inconsistent. The second is the formation of stereotypes based on the co-occurrence of events that are, compared to other memories, distinct.

CASE STUDY

BOX 10.4

Horoscopes and Illusory Correlations

Horoscopes place a person in a distinctive context; everyone knows that there is only a 1/12 chance of belonging to a given zodiacal sign. Even though they are extremely vague ("Something very good will happen" or "People are talking about you" occur a lot), horoscopes are still rarely very accurate. So why do some people believe them? Because occasionally, by chance, the horoscope is correct. The horoscope says, "You will get into a fight with your significant other" the day you get into a fight with your significant other. The horoscope says, "You will have to spend money on something unexpected" the day you drop your phone and crack it. The co-occurrence of the distinctiveness of being a member of a small group (one's zodiac sign) and a distinct event (such as the accurate prediction about a disagreement) can lead to a

TatianaKost94/Shutterstock

distinctiveness-based illusory correlation, which makes some people believe that their life experiences are somehow linked to the day of the year they happen to have born on.

DIY EXPERIMENT

Fact Experiment Part II

Before reading further, make sure you have completed Fact Experiment Part I in Box 10.1 at the start of this chapter.

Indicate whether you believe the following statements are true or false:

1. French horn players get a bonus to stay in the Canadian Army.
2. Manitoba is 847,797 square kilometres in size.
3. Israel has the twenty-ninth largest economy in the world.
4. John Diefenbaker was the tenth prime minister of Canada.
5. The emu is the largest bird on earth.
6. It takes 12.4 hours for light from the Sun to reach Neptune.
7. Toronto, Ontario, has a larger population than Boston, Massachusetts.
8. A mother rat produces an average of 500 pups in her first year of life.
9. Argon is the densest gas.
10. "Almost" is the longest English word in which the letters appear in alphabetical order.

Debriefing: Chances are that you weren't sure what the correct answer was to most of the statements (they are obscure on purpose); however, you likely marked more odd-numbered questions as true than even-numbered questions even though all of the statements were actually false. This is because the odd-numbered questions appeared earlier in this chapter and you are more likely to believe familiar facts than unfamiliar facts, a phenomenon known as the illusion of truth. The illusion of truth is discussed in the next section.

Mere Exposure Effects

The **mere exposure effect** is a term used in social psychology to describe an increase in positive affect that follows from repeated exposure to a previously unfamiliar stimulus. For example, a

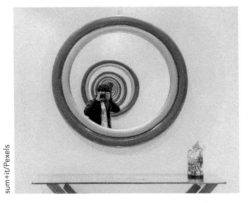

sum+it/Pexels

People tend to prefer their face when viewed in a mirror rather than when viewed in a photograph because of the mere exposure effect.

person's ratings of her or his feelings toward the unfamiliar Finnish word *talo*, meaning "house," would increase if *talo* were presented to a person many times, even if the person never knew what the word *talo* meant. The mere exposure effect has been demonstrated for words, shapes, and people in social situations and the evidence is clear; people prefer stimuli they have seen before over novel stimuli (Bornstein, 1989). In 1980, Robert Zajonc presented participants with irregular polygons repeatedly for just 1 ms (that's 1/1000 of a second and well below the threshold of awareness). Participants were then presented with previously presented polygons paired with new polygons and were asked which one they recognized and which polygon they liked better. Although participants were not able to recognize the previously presented polygons (they performed this task at the rate of chance), they were more likely to say they liked a polygon that they had seen before. Because participants demonstrated a change in liking for a stimulus without explicitly recognizing the stimulus, researchers concluded that the mere exposure effect is an example of implicit memory (Schacter, 1987).

The mere exposure effect has led to the saying "familiarity breeds liking"; in other words, the more familiar something is, the more we like it. The mere exposure effect is closely related to the **propinquity effect**, which is the general finding that people who are around each other more like each other better. People who share a stairway in an apartment building, for example, will rank their liking for each other as higher than their liking for other people who live in the building who use a different stairway. Propinquity effects can also explain why people are more likely to become friends with their roommates than with other people living in their residence and why so many people wind up in romantic relationships with people they work with on a daily basis.

Another effect related to the mere exposure effect is the **illusory-truth effect** first identified by Hasher, Goldstein, and Toppino in 1977. In their experiment, Hasher et al. (1977) had participants rate the validity of "factoids" related to politics, sports, and the arts on three occasions over a six-week period. While some factoids were true and some were false, the topics chosen were obscure and the participants were unlikely to know if the fact was actually true or not. Some of the factoids were repeated across sessions while others were not. Hasher et al. (1977) found that participants were more likely to rate a repeated item than a non-repeated item as valid, regardless of whether it was actually true. Thus, whether or not a fact has been seen before appears to be an important criterion determining whether it is believed to be true. Examples from Hasher et al. (1977) appear in Table 10.1.

Thus, what we like, who we like, and what we believe all appear to be influenced by implicit memory. Specifically, repeated exposure to a stimulus increases the positive emotional associations we have for that stimulus through the phenomenon of mere exposure. When we see a more familiar stimulus, implicit memory triggers a more positive emotional response resulting in the propinquity effect and the illusory-truth effect.

Implicit memory is also closely associated with stereotypes. Research has demonstrated that people will often show stereotypical beliefs in implicit memory tasks while denying holding stereotypical beliefs in explicit tasks. A well-known way this effect has been demonstrated is through the implicit-association test (IAT), which is a specific experimental paradigm developed at Harvard that demonstrates that people are slower at associating positive concepts with groups that are generally associated with negative stereotypes, including people of colour, people who are old, people who are gay, and people who are obese.

mere exposure effect
when a person comes to prefer stimuli merely because she or he has been exposed to the stimulus repeatedly

propinquity effect
a finding that people who spend time together tend to like each other

illusory-truth effect
when participants are more likely to rate a statement as being true when they have seen the statement before compared to when the statement is unfamiliar

Table 10.1   Examples of true and false statements from Hasher, Goldstein, and Toppino (1977)

True Statements	False Statements
Australia is approximately equal in area to the United States.	The capybara is the largest of the marsupials.
In Malaya, if a man goes to jail for being drunk, his wife goes too.	The largest museum in the world is the Louvre in Paris.
French horn players get cash bonuses to stay in the U.S. Army.	In the United States, divorced people outnumber those who are widowed.
Lithium is the lightest of all metals.	The People's Republic of China was founded in 1947.

Source: Hasher et al., 1977, p. 109

DIY EXPERIMENT

Take an Implicit-Association Test

After going to https://implicit.harvard.edu/implicit/takeatest.html, choose a group or topic that you don't believe you hold a strong stereotype against. For example, you may not feel you have a stereotypical view of people with disabilities, so try that test. Follow the instructions on the screen.

When the test is done, note what your results were. If you showed stereotypical thinking, make a plan for how you can reduce your stereotype.

The Implicit-Association Test

The notion that implicit memory could affect social cognition was first suggested by Anthony Greenwald and Mahzarin Banaji in 1995. In 1998, the first article using a procedure now known as the implicit-association test (IAT) was published by Greenwald, McGhee, and Schwartz. The Greenwald et al. (1998) article has been cited more than 6000 times; its influence has been enormous. Harvard University now hosts a website called Project Implicit, which makes implicit-association tests available to anyone who wishes to take one. You can learn more about the IAT at https://implicit.harvard.edu/implicit/iatdetails.html and you can take the test at https://implicit.harvard.edu/implicit/takeatest.html.

The IAT is a computerized test in which participants categorize a word as quickly and accurately as possible. Participants complete six blocks of trials in random order. In two blocks of trials, the words all come from one of two groups. For example, one group might be "male" (e.g., man, boy, husband) or "female" (e.g., woman, girl, wife), and a second group might be "science" (e.g., biology, chemistry, math) or "liberal arts" (e.g., philosophy, literature, music). The participant responds by pressing a button on the same side of the keyboard as the corresponding category (see Figure 10.1a and b). These trials serve as a baseline measure. There are also experimental trials in which participants are presented with a word to be categorized and must press the button corresponding to the side of the computer screen where the appropriate group appears, but in these trials TWO categories are present and the word may come from either category. For example, a participant may need to use one key to categorize a word as belonging to "male" or "science" and another key for a word belonging to "female" or "liberal arts" (see Figure 10.1c and d). On other blocks of trials, participants use one key for "female" or "science" and another key for "male" or "liberal arts" (see Figure 10.1e and f).

After all the possible combinations of groups have been presented, the response times for trials in which the participant made a correct response are compared. The results from the IAT are very consistent; when a stereotype exists in a population, response times are faster when group pairings match the stereotype than when they do not. For example, in a population that holds a stereotype that associates men with science and women with the liberal arts, responses to categorizing both gender words and academic words will be faster when "male" and "science" are paired together and "female" and "liberal arts" are paired together, as in Figure 10.1c and d.

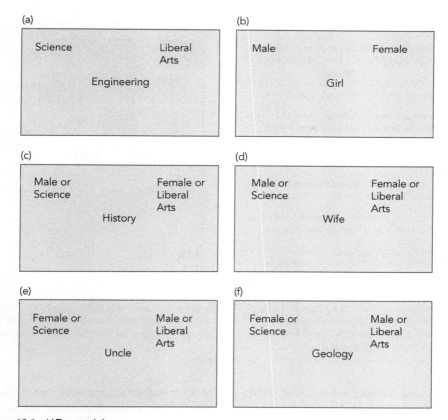

Figure 10.1   IAT test trials

Panels (a) and (b) show examples of practice trials from an IAT test examining gender and academics. Panels (c) through (f) show examples from blocks of experimental trials examining gender and academics. On each trial, the participant presses the E key if the word in the centre falls into the category shown in the upper left-hand corner and the I key if the word in the centre falls into the category shown in the upper right-hand corner. There would also be four more blocks of trials that were mirror images of panels (c) through (f) to help counter any effects of handedness on responding.

Responses will be slower when the grouping is inconsistent with a stereotype, such as when "male" and "liberal arts" are paired together and "female" and "science" are paired together such as in Figure 10.1e and f. People who take the IAT test through the Project Implicit website will be able to see what per cent of their responses reflect different degrees of automatic associations between the groups. An example is shown in Figure 10.2.

The IAT has been used to examine implicit stereotypes related to race, age, weight, romantic affiliation, ethnicity, and gender as well as many others. In many cases, people who take the IAT will explicitly deny holding stereotypical views but will still show a tendency to make stereotype-consistent responses more quickly than responses that are inconsistent with a stereotype. Proponents of the IAT argue that this is because stereotypes are held in implicit memory beyond awareness and activated automatically, explaining, for example, how a female

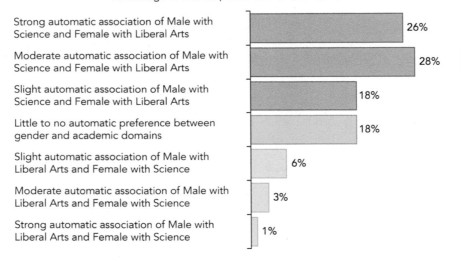

Figure 10.2   Sample results for IAT test

This figure shows sample data from the Project Implicit IAT for gender and science as of February 2016. The greatest percentage of web respondents show the most responses in the "Moderate automatic association of Male with Science and Female with Liberal Arts" category, indicating they have a tendency to associate males with science and females with liberal arts.

Source: https://implicit.harvard.edu/implicit/Study?tid=-1, retrieved February 2016

scientist who knows for a fact that women can perform well in science (and men in liberal arts) may still categorize more quickly when the task involves a stereotype-consistent pairing. Thousands of people have taken the IAT and the results are highly reliable; regardless of age, race, gender, ethnicity, and explicit attitude toward a group, people still seem to automatically activate stereotypes that are common within a culture.

Sentence-completion tasks can also reveal the influence of implicit memory. Lisa Sinclair and Ziva Kunda at the University of Waterloo found that White participants completed sentences in a way that confirmed stereotypes about Blacks more often after negative feedback from a Black confederate and less often after positive feedback from a Black confederate (Sinclair & Kunda, 1999).

Reducing Automatic Stereotypes

Paradigms like the IAT have allowed researchers to see how implicit stereotypes are activated, but researchers have also investigated factors that reduce stereotypes. Implicit stereotypes can also be reduced by presenting counterstereotypes. For example, Dasgupta and Asgari (2004) found that reading biographies about successful women reduced implicit gender stereotypes measured using the IAT. Blair, Ma, and Lenton (2001) found that imagining strong women reduced implicit gender stereotypes measured using the IAT while imagining storybook princesses increased implicit gender stereotypes.

We turn now to the final section in this chapter, in which we will discuss how our current social attitudes influence the way in which we remember past experiences.

Cognitive Dissonance and Its Influence on Autobiographical Memory

Cognitive dissonance (a term first coined by Leon Festinger in 1957) refers to a mental state of conflict in which a person holds two opposing views or is presented with new information that contradicts an existing belief. According to cognitive dissonance theory, people are motivated to reduce cognitive dissonance (Festinger, 1962). For example, if a person has a negative view of a certain university but is then offered a full scholarship to that university (and only that university), the person would be motivated to change her or his opinion about the university because of cognitive dissonance. Recently, researchers have begun to wonder whether cognitive dissonance may underlie memory distortions, as memories can be changed while real events cannot.

Rodriguez and Strange (2014a) used an induced-compliance paradigm related to tuition increases to study the link between cognitive dissonance and memory distortions. Participants' attitude toward a tuition increase was obtained through an online questionnaire a few days before the experiment. When participants arrived at the experiment, they were told that the university was considering a 10 per cent tuition hike and was looking for arguments on both sides of the issue. Participants were randomly assigned to one of two choice conditions. In the low-choice condition, participants were told that they had been randomly assigned to write a paper supporting the tuition increase. In the high-choice condition, participants were told that the university already had many submissions against the tuition increase and would prefer to collect essays supporting the increase but that writing in support of the increase would be completely voluntary. After participants had written their essay, the experimenter collected data on the participants' attitudes about tuition increases. Finally, the experimenter gave each participant a memory questionnaire that contained the same items as the online questionnaire.

As predicted by cognitive dissonance theory, participants who felt they chose to write an essay supporting tuition increases (high-choice condition) showed greater shifts in favour of tuition increases than those who were forced to write in support of the increase (low-choice condition). The researchers suggested that participants had to change their attitude about tuition in order to be consistent with a social behaviour that could not be changed. In addition, participants who showed the greatest shift in attitudes (those in the high-choice condition) were also significantly more likely to misremember their original attitude toward tuition increases than those in the low-choice condition, although their memory for other items on the online questionnaire was not affected by the experimental manipulation. Rodriguez and Strange (2014a) thus showed that cognitive dissonance can lead to memory distortions, and that those distortions favour currently held views.

Rodriguez and Strange (2014b) further investigated the effect of cognitive dissonance on memory using a free-choice paradigm. In this experiment, participants were first given what they thought was a marketing survey assessing their attitudes about various cell phones. Next, the experimenter told all the participants that the cell-phone provider had given them some cell phones to give away in a lottery. Participants were randomly assigned to one of two conditions. In the difficult-decision condition, participants were asked to choose which of two cell phones they preferred out of the phones they ranked most highly in the survey. In the easy-decision condition, participants were asked which of two cell phones they preferred, choosing between one they had rated poorly on the survey and another they rated high on the survey.

cognitive dissonance
a mental state in which a person holds two contradictory beliefs or values at the same time

Once participants made their choice, they were asked to rank the difficulty of their decision on a 10-point scale and were asked how satisfied they were with their decision and how confident they were with their decision. It would be these responses that the participant would need to remember later. Rodriguez and Strange (2014b) then presented participants with reviews of the cell phones and, after a delay, asked participants to try to remember their initial review of each cell phone. Rodriguez and Strange (2014b) found that participants in the difficult-decision condition tended to devalue the phone they rejected after they rejected it, indicating that they had experienced cognitive dissonance while making the decision. Participants in the easy-decision group did not show this effect. Participants in the difficult-decision group also misremembered their initial decision, recalling the experience more favourably than those in the easy-decision group. Once again, the researchers found that a manipulation that induced cognitive dissonance resulted in a memory distortion.

The Neuroscience of Cognitive Dissonance

Vincent Van Veen and his colleagues studied the neural correlates of cognitive dissonance. In their experiment, Van Veen, Krug, Schooler, and Carter (2009) scanned participants in an uncomfortable fMRI and then asked the participants to pretend they were enjoying the fMRI to help a (fictitious) nervous patient who was waiting for the next turn. Van Veen et al. (2009) measured participants' and controls' attitudes toward the fMRI scan before and after the scan. Van Veen et al. (2009) found that activation of the dorsal angular cingulate cortex and anterior insula occurred in participants who changed their attitude about the fMRI from unpleasant to pleasant but saw no such activation in controls or participants whose attitudes did not change.

Cognitive dissonance can happen in almost any social situation, and this research suggests that memory is distorted as a result. Much of the time, a distortion in memory is harmless; for example, the accuracy of a person's memory for her or his past attitudes is probably inconsequential, but there are also some situations where these memory distortions could have significant impact. We will discuss the effect that cognitive dissonance may have on eyewitnesses and jurors in Chapter 11.

CHAPTER REVIEW

- When people divide a memory task among themselves and fill in the gaps of each other's recall, the process is referred to as transactive memory.
- When groups work to remember things, the process is referred to as collaborative memory. Research suggests that collaborative memory is less than the sum of individual memory for three reasons: collaborative inhibition, information-sampling bias, and audience tuning.
- Interacting with others can affect memory through social contagion, retrieval-induced forgetting, and the nature of social networking.
- Collective memory contains memories that are shared by members of the same social group and that relate to their social identity.

- There is substantial evidence in the literature that distinctiveness-based illusory correlations lead to the development of stereotypes.
- Mere exposure can influence social behaviour as evidenced in the propinquity effect and the illusory-truth effect.
- The implicit-association test (IAT) has demonstrated that implicit memory can influence stereotypical beliefs. Exposure to information that contradicts a stereotype may help reduce that stereotype.
- Cognitive dissonance occurs when a person holds two or more conflicting beliefs. People are highly motivated to reduce cognitive dissonance. Substantial research evidence suggests that people may alter their memories to reduce cognitive dissonance.

MEMORY ACTIVITY

Remembering What Can Make Fake News Seem Believable

In this chapter, you learned about social contagion as well as about the cognitive moderators that heighten or lessen the observation of social contagion. These moderators are whether the information (or contagion) is consistent with a person's existing cognitive schemas, how much time a person has to learn the information, whether the information is new or old, and whether the person providing the information is perceived as an expert.

Consider all the factors that influence social contagion and identify the type of fake news that is MOST likely to travel by social contagion and the type of fake news LEAST likely to travel by social contagion. Also identify steps people may be able to take to ensure that they themselves do not come to believe fake news.

Questions

1. Define collaborative remembering. Identify one factor that may make collaborative remembering more effective than individual remembering.
2. Define collaborative inhibition. Describe an experiment that demonstrates this effect.
3. Identify and briefly describe three possible causes of collaborative inhibition.
4. Explain the relationship between collaborative inhibition and group size.
5. Define social contagion. Describe an experiment by Elizabeth Loftus that demonstrated this effect.
6. Describe three possible causes for social contagion.
7. Identify some cognitive moderators of social contagion.
8. Define retrieval-induced forgetting. Identify two ways that this type of forgetting can occur.
9. Describe an experiment that demonstrated that audience tuning can impact the memory of the speaker.
10. Compare and contrast collective memory and shared memory. Provide an example of each.
11. Explain what an illusory correlation is. Describe the experiment that led Loren Chapman to conclude that illusory correlations are related to how distinctive a memory is.
12. Describe an experiment that demonstrated that distinctiveness-based illusory correlations can lead to the development of stereotypes.
13. Based on the information in this chapter, explain why so many stereotypes are negative and relate to minority groups.

14. Explain the nature of the mere exposure effect. Describe two effects discussed in the text that are the result of mere exposure.
15. Briefly describe the implicit-association test (IAT) paradigm.
16. Briefly describe the results of a typical IAT experiment. Explain how the results of an IAT experiment may be used to find ways to combat stereotypes.
17. Define and provide an example of cognitive dissonance.
18. Describe an experiment that examined how cognitive dissonance can influence memory.

Key Figures

Frederic Bartlett p. 257
Loren Chapman p. 269
Gerald Echterhoff p. 266

Hermann Ebbinghaus p. 257
Robert Gifford p. 270
David Hamilton p. 270

Elizabeth Loftus p. 263
Anthony Lyons p. 268
Gwen Wittenbaum p. 261

11   Memory and the Law

LEARNING OBJECTIVES

Having read this chapter, you will be able to:

- Explain the misinformation effect and provide an example of an experiment that demonstrates this effect.
- Describe how experimenters were able to implant false memories and the implications this has for psychotherapy.
- Describe the different types of identification procedures.
- Discuss what social factors can lead to less reliable eyewitness identifications.
- Explain how an investigator may use confidence ratings to assess the accuracy of an eyewitness identification.
- Describe the memory war and its outcome.
- Explain how normal memory processes can lead a person to make a false confession.
- Explain how pre-trial publicity and note taking may influence jurors' memories.
- Describe how emotional testimony influences jurors' memories.
- Describe and critique brain fingerprinting.
- Identify memory theories that underlie the cognitive interview.

THOMAS SOPHONOW

Thomas Sophonow was accused of murdering a young woman who worked at a doughnut shop in Winnipeg, Manitoba. Several eyewitnesses identified Sophonow, but the procedures used for the identification were problematic (Harland-Logan, 2019). For one, many eyewitnesses were shown an array of pictures in which only the picture of Sophonow was taken outside, and only Sophonow was wearing a cowboy hat. In addition, Sophonow was the only person who was presented in both the photo lineup and the physical lineup, making it possible that

Thomas Sophonow (above) was wrongly convicted of murder due to inaccurate eyewitness identification. This photo was taken at the judicial inquiry to determine his compensation in 2000.

some eyewitnesses who had seen both identified Sophonow because he was familiar, and not because they associated him with the crime. Also, Sophonow was the tallest man in the physical lineup and it was widely publicized that the suspect was a tall man (Harland-Logan, 2019). Sophonow was convicted of the murder and spent four years in prison before being declared factually innocent (Harland-Logan, 2019). Sophonow's case is just one of thousands of cases in which eyewitness testimony has been proven to be inaccurate. In this chapter, we will explore the many ways that the legal system depends on memory, and highlight ways in which the legal system can be made more just by acknowledging known patterns in human remembering.

Eyewitness Memory

The first psychologist to suggest that eyewitness memory may be unreliable was Hugo Münsterberg, a German-American psychology who wrote *On the Witness Stand* in 1908. Because of Münsterberg's open allegiance to Germany during World War I (Münsterberg was living in the United States at the time) and the fact that he died in 1916, which was very soon after publishing most of his work, Münsterberg's theories were largely ignored by American psychologists in the twentieth century. However, recent reviews of Münsterberg's work have found the work was valid and in many cases decades ahead of its time. In 1932, Yale law professor Edwin Borchand would write *Convicting the Innocent*, which also called eyewitness testimony into question. Borchand claimed, based on his analysis of 65 cases, that eyewitness misidentification was the single leading cause of wrongful convictions. Despite the assertions of these authors, it would be 70 years before experimental psychologists would methodically test the veracity of eyewitness accounts. The examination of eyewitness memory grew out of research into the extent to which leading questions can create bias in the courtroom.

In the vast majority of situations, the accuracy of our memory is inconsequential. If we misremember a conversation with a classmate, or recall an event that never really happened, it doesn't matter. Life goes on. One exception to the inconsequentiality of memory relates to the law. When individuals use memory to identify perpetrators of crime, report criminal events, or make decisions as a juror, accuracy clearly matters. Justice is at stake. For most of human history, eyewitnesses were taken at their word. A positive identification in a police lineup was regarded as proof that a person was the perpetrator, and recounts by eyewitnesses in courtroom testimony were generally believed to represent what really occurred. However, beginning in the 1970s, research began to reveal that people are not very good eyewitnesses at all. Our memories are often incomplete and can be shaped and shifted without our awareness.

Hugo Münsterberg (1868–1916)

In this chapter, we will explore research on eyewitness memory and will see that after-the-fact information can change our memories, and recollection can actually make us believe we have a memory for something that didn't occur. We will see that once it was clear that memories could be implanted in people, the notion of repressed memories was turned on its head and a long, angry dispute erupted between therapists who thought they could tease forgotten memories out of their clients, and researchers who believed that therapists were, likely unknowingly, creating upsetting false memories in their clients. We will also discuss how the nature of human memory affects other aspects of the legal system, such as the reliability of confessions, the identification of individuals from police lineups, and jury deliberation. Finally, we will discuss neuroscientific methods for identifying individuals with memories for crime-related events. We will see that, while often used successfully to identify guilty knowledge in the lab, these methods assume that perpetrators' memories of crimes they committed are accurate, when we know that perpetrators, like all people, often possess inaccurate and/or incomplete memories for events that they have experienced.

Leading Questions: Early Research on the Malleability of Eyewitness Memory

In the early 1970s, American psychologists Elizabeth Loftus and John Palmer conducted a series of simple experiments that would change the way that eyewitness memory was viewed forever. The authors were specifically interested in whether peoples' memories for traffic accidents actually operated like a camera, creating a permanent and immutable trace as asserted by the computer model of memory that was dominant at the time of their research, and whether **leading questions** could influence recall. In their 1974 study, Loftus and Palmer showed participants films of traffic accidents and then asked the participants to answer a series of questions about the speed of the vehicle.

The only difference between the questions asked of participants was the verb used in the question. The five different questions asked and the mean estimated speed for the crash are shown in Table 11.1.

leading question

a question that by its form or content suggests the desired answer to the witness, or leads the witness to the desired answer

Table 11.1   Results from Loftus and Palmer (1974) Experiment 1

Leading Question Asked after Viewing the Film in Loftus and Palmer (1974) Experiment 1	Estimated Speed of Crash in Miles per Hour
"About how fast were the cars going when they smashed into each other?"	40.8
"About how fast were the cars going when they collided with each other?"	39.3
"About how fast were the cars going when they bumped each other?"	38.1
"About how fast were the cars going when they hit each other?"	34.0
"About how fast were the cars going when they contacted each other?"	31.8

Loftus and Palmer (1974) demonstrated that participants "remembered" cars as having been travelling at different speeds depending on what words were used to describe the accident. Participants who heard the word *smashed* estimated the speed as 10 miles an hour faster than participants who heard the word *contacted*.
Source: Loftus & Palmer, 1974, p. 586

Loftus and Palmer (1974) found that mean estimates for the speed the vehicles were travelling were significantly affected by the type of question asked. (All participants saw exactly the same film.) The more the sentence *implied* a fast crash, the faster the estimates of the witnesses. This experiment showed that leading questions (questions that suggest that a certain response is correct) can affect eyewitness responses.

To see if the leading questions changed the memories (and not just the responses) of the witnesses, Loftus and Palmer conducted a second experiment. In this experiment, participants were again shown a film depicting a car accident. Participants were then given a questionnaire that first asked them to describe the accident in their own words and then asked them to answer a series of questions about the accident. One-third of the participants were asked, "About how fast were the cars going when they smashed into one another?" One-third were asked, "About how fast were the cars going when they hit each other?" One-third of the participants were not asked any questions related to the speed of the cars. A week later, the participants returned to the lab and were asked a series of questions about the accident they had seen a week earlier. All participants were asked, "Did you see any broken glass?" although there was no broken glass in the accident they had seen. Loftus and Palmer (1974) found that participants who were asked "About how fast were the cars going when they smashed into each other?" were more than twice as likely to recall seeing broken glass than either participants who were asked "About how fast were the cars going when they hit each other?" or participants who were not asked about the speed of the cars at all. This indicated that leading questions affected participants' memories

Robert Crum/Shutterstock

Loftus and Palmer (1974) showed participants films of traffic accidents and then asked them questions about what they had seen. The researchers found that participants reported having seen different things depending on the questions they were asked.

for scenes. The researchers concluded that post-event information, including leading questions, has the potential to taint eyewitness testimony, and spurred dozens of researchers to further explore the malleability of eyewitness memory.

Misinformation Effects

In 1978, Elizabeth Loftus, Helen Miller, and David Burns collaborated on a large-scale study exploring this newfound influence of post-event information on memory. While Loftus and Palmer (1974) presented visual information to be remembered and then used verbal means to introduce new information and test participants' memory, Loftus, Miller, and Burns (1978) used a recognition procedure in order to reduce possible confounds introduced by utilizing different modalities during different phases of the experiment. In Loftus et al. (1978), participants were presented with a series of 30 colour slides, each presented for about three seconds. Half of the participants saw a distinctive red car (called a Datsun) stopped at a stop sign, while the other half saw the same car stopped at a yield sign. All participants also saw the same red car turning right and then knocking down a pedestrian who was crossing the road at a crosswalk. Participants were then given a questionnaire containing 20 questions about the slides that had been shown. For half the participants question 17 was "Did another car pass the red Datsun while it was stopped at the stop sign?" and for the other half of the participants question 17 read "Did another car pass the red Datsun when it was stopped at the yield sign?" Some participants who had seen a stop sign were asked a question about a yield sign and vice versa. After a delay, participants were presented with 15 pairs of slides side by side, and had to indicate which they had seen before. The critical pair was the slide depicting the red Datsun at a stop sign and the red Datsun stopped at a yield sign. Participants correctly identified the slide they had seen earlier 75 per cent of the time when question 17 contained consistent information; however, only 41 per cent of participants chose the slide they had actually seen earlier when the questionnaire contained misleading information. Thus, both Loftus and Palmer (1974) and Loftus et al. (1978) showed that post-event information doesn't just bias responses, but can affect memory for events that have been witnessed. The impact of these articles cannot be overstated. This paradigm is described in most introductory psychology textbooks and memory textbooks. Together, these two articles have been cited in more than 3000 journal articles since their publication.

Once it was well established that it was possible to change memories with post-event misinformation, Elizabeth Loftus and her colleagues wanted to determine how the new misinformation was integrated into memory. In 1979, Elizabeth Loftus published a series of experiments that were designed to determine whether misinformation is integrated the moment that it is introduced, or whether this integration takes place later when the person is asked to recollect the original experience. In Experiment 1, participants were shown 24 slides depicting a red wallet being snatched. Participants then completed a questionnaire that assessed their memory for the slides they had seen as well as their confidence in their memories. The next day, participants were given a one-page narrative about a wallet-snatching incident apparently written by a professor in the department. Participants were asked to rate the clarity and writing style of the narrative in order to disguise the true purpose of presenting the narrative. Each narrative contained erroneous information about four critical items that were relatively peripheral to the scene, such as descriptions of items that could be seen in the windows above the street. Half of the participants' narratives also contained a blatant error about the colour of the wallet. Participants were then given a 20-item questionnaire that asked them to correctly complete sentences using one of

Table 11.2   Results from Loftus (1979) Experiments 1 and 2

| Item seen in Loftus (1979) | Loftus (1979) Experiment 1, No Delay | | | | Experiment 2 | | | |
	Blatant group's narrative content	Recall	Subtle group's narrative content	Recall	Blatant info delay, group's narrative content	Recall	Subtle group's narrative content	Recall
Red wallet	brown wallet	good	red wallet	good	brown wallet	good	red wallet	good
Shirt in window	different	good	different	poor	different	poor	different	poor
Overhanging sign	different	good	different	poor	different	poor	different	poor
Person passing by	different	good	different	poor	different	poor	different	poor
Object in friend's hand	different	good	different	poor	different	poor	different	poor

The results from Loftus (1979) show that blatantly inaccurate information can help inoculate participants from encoding more subtle misinformation, but only if the blatantly false information is presented at the same time as the other misinformation. Loftus (1979) suggests that this pattern occurs because a person only maintains one representation of an event at a time.
Source: Loftus, 1979, p. 371

three words provided to them by the experimenter, and they were asked to remember the slide show, not the narrative, when completing the questionnaire. Participants also rated their confidence. Loftus (1979) found that 98 per cent of participants correctly identified the colour of the wallet even when they had been given misinformation about the wallet's colour in the narrative, and that those participants who read the narrative with the blatant error were less likely to be misled by the more subtle errors in the narrative.

Loftus (1979) wondered why being presented with blatantly false information seemed to inoculate participants from more subtle types of misinformation. One alternative was that the blatantly false information caused the participants to scrutinize the material more closely. If this is the case, then delaying the blatantly false information should eliminate the protective effect. Alternatively, it is possible that participants encoded the information from the slides and the information from the narrative but, because of the blatantly false information, chose to use one source of information (the slides) over the other (the narrative) when answering the questions. If this is true, then even delayed blatantly false information should still have a protective effect as it will cue the learner to use the original and not the new information when answering questions. In order to determine which of these two hypotheses was accurate, Loftus (1979) conducted a second experiment in which the presentation of the blatantly false information was delayed for some participants. Loftus (1979) found that when the blatantly false information was delayed, participants were much more likely to recall the subtle misinformation. Loftus (1979) concludes that a person maintains a single representation of an event and that the representation can be updated with new (possibly erroneous) information as the information become available. A person does not maintain two representations, one original and one new, but rather a single integrated point of reference. This finding is very important when one considers eyewitness testimony, as it suggests that if eyewitnesses are presented with misinformation that they believe could be true, that misinformation could permanently change their representation of the events they have witnessed and they may report false information consistently and with confidence.

Implanting False Memories: The "Lost in the Mall" Paradigm

After discovering the influence that post-event information could have on the recall of details of an actual event, Elizabeth Loftus and her colleagues wanted to know if it was possible to implant a memory for an entire event that did not occur. In one experiment, Elizabeth Loftus and Jacquie Pickrell tested to see if they could get participants to believe that they had been lost in a shopping mall as a child (when in fact the researchers knew from interviewing the participants' families that they had not). The approach was simple. Loftus and Pickrell simply told participants that their families had told them that they had been lost in a mall as a child. About one-quarter of their subjects subsequently came to believe they had been lost in a mall (Loftus & Pickrell, 1995). Loftus and Pickrell's "lost in the mall" paradigm started a flurry of research into memory distortion. One research group at the University of British Columbia was able to implant memories of serious childhood injuries in 26 per cent of participants. Another group at the University of Tennessee had participants repeatedly imagine events that did not actually occur. In that experiment, 37 per cent of participants came to believe the events had actually happened to them. In many cases, participants in these experiments developed extremely detailed "memories." Some small differences between real and implanted memories did emerge. Researchers found that true memories were more emotional and more likely to be recalled from the first-person perspective, while implanted memories held less emotional content and were more likely to be recalled from the perspective of an observer; however, these differences were eliminated when the false memories were rehearsed or retold numerous times (Loftus, 1999). The more a person imagines a fictitious event, the more likely the person is to develop a **false memory** that the event actually occurred.

> **false memory**
>
> a psychological phenomenon in which a person recalls information that did not actually occur

To date, Loftus's experiments had all taken place in laboratories, but she was interested to see if similar misinformation could develop in a more realistic therapeutic setting and thus might explain many cases of repressed memories revealed by therapists that turned out to be untrue or impossible. Dream analysis was a popular therapeutic tool at the time, so Loftus devised an experiment to see whether dream analysis could influence a person's memories. Loftus and her colleagues surveyed undergraduates about their childhoods to compose a sample of individuals who were unlikely to actually have experienced specific traumatic events in childhood, including being lost or separated from their parents or feeling abandoned before the age of three. Half of the chosen sample were told they were participating in a study about sleep and dreams, while the other half served as a control and did not receive any dream analysis. The participants in the sleep-and-dream study group related their dreams to a trained clinician who gave the same analysis to each subject; in every case he said that the individual had some unhappiness related to a past experience that happened when the person was very young and might not be remembered. The clinician suggested that the dream was consistent with the individual having been lost in a public place for an extended

© Phuttaphat Tipsana | Dreamstime.com

Loftus and her colleagues found that a therapist suggesting that a person was lost in the mall as a child once during one 30-minute therapy session was sufficient for many people to develop a false memory of being lost in a mall.

period of time before the age of three. (Note that most people cannot accurately report events that occurred before age three.) All of the participants returned two weeks later and completed the same survey they had completed two weeks earlier. The majority of participants in the sleep-and-dream study group were now confident that they had been lost in a public place before age three (even though they did not believe they had been lost in a mall before the dream analysis took place), while participants in the control group (who did not receive the dream analysis) did not change their responses significantly. Loftus was astounded that such significant changes in memory could be made so easily. Participants had each spent only half an hour with a clinician. Loftus notes that the extensive dream analysis that is part of many types of psychotherapy is thus a potential source for distortions in a person's memories of her or his personal past.

RELEVANT RESEARCH

BOX
11.1

French Scientists Implant False Memories in Sleeping Mice

Neuroscientists in France successfully implanted false memories in mice while they slept. To achieve this odd (but remarkable) feat, researchers first implanted special electrodes in the medial forebrain bundle (MFB), which is stimulated when an animal experiences something rewarding, and the CA1 region of the hippocampus, which contains cells related to spatial navigation. Researchers then observed which neurons were active when the mice were in a specific location. Researchers knew that stimulating the MFB while an alert mouse is in a specific location causes the mouse to prefer that location over others. The re-

searchers wanted to see if the same effect could be achieved while the mouse was asleep. The researchers monitored brain activity in sleeping mice and, when the neuron associated with a specific location fired, they stimulated the MFB. After these mice awoke, many went directly to the location associated with the neuron that was paired with MFB stimulation, indicating that the mice "remembered" that this location was rewarding. Not only did this experiment demonstrate that it is possible to implant false memories, but it also showed the important role that sleep plays in memory consolidation. The researchers found that stimulating the MFB was most likely to produce a false memory if the mouse was in a slow-wave sleep state, bolstering a theory that a brain pattern called sharp-wave ripples is necessary for memory consolidation during sleep.

Now that we have established that a person's memory can be affected by post-event information, we will explore in more detail special instances where eyewitness memory is called upon in legal settings, including police identification procedures, testimony of witnesses in court, and testimony of victims in court.

Repressed Memory

Michael Kliman was a vice-principal at James McKinney Elementary School in Richmond, British Columbia. In 1992, he was accused of having molested a sixth-grade student 20 years earlier. The student claimed to have recovered memories of abuse by Kliman while in therapy and was encouraged by the police department to press charges. The student recalled many details of abuse, including Kliman taking her into a private room at the school and torturing her sexually. Soon a second student came forward who stated that, while initially having no memory of the abuse, through therapy that student recovered memories of regular abuse that took place three times a week for the entire school year. Kliman was convicted of sexual assault in 1994, had a hung jury in a retrial that took place in 1996, and was eventually acquitted in 1997 (Loftus, 2003).

At the time of Michael Kliman's initial arrest, there was a widely held belief among psychotherapists and the general public that painful memories could be "repressed" in order to protect the individual from having to think about them, but that these memories could be recovered through hypnosis and other types of therapy. However, researchers at that time were beginning to argue that there was little or no support for the notion of repressed memories. Elizabeth Loftus and her colleagues had successfully shown, over and over, that it was possible to create false memories in a therapeutic setting (e.g., Loftus, 1993). Other researchers were demonstrating that participants in laboratory studies were no more likely to forget distressing information than mundane information, which countered the claim that repression occurred because distressing memories were too painful to recall (e.g., Holmes, 1990). Many therapists and survivors of sexual abuse were angered by the suggestion that recovered memories could be false and what followed was "a controversy that has been among the most vitriolic and emotionally charged in the history of psychology" (Loftus & Davis, 2006, p. 470) known as **the memory war**. On one side of the memory war were practicing therapists who claimed that, despite this research, there was still overwhelming research in support of the notion of repressed memories, and that laboratory research cannot be applied to memories of sexual abuse because traumatic memories are fundamentally different from other types of memories. On the other side of the memory war were psychologists who had studied the malleability and suggestibility of memory. These researchers argued that traumatic memories are more likely to be recalled than other memories; that traumatic memories can be created, distorted, and confabulated just as easily as other types of memories; and that many therapeutic techniques (such as hypnosis, guided imagery, or dream analysis) may encourage the development of false memories.

the memory war

a scholarly debate over whether or not traumatic memories could be repressed and later recovered

Evidence for the Repression and Recovery of Traumatic Memories

Some researchers have used the results from **retrospective studies** as evidence for the notion of memory repression. In retrospective studies, a person who has been abused is asked whether there was ever a time when they forgot about their abuse (e.g., Briere & Conte, 1993). One problem with these studies is that they do not allow researchers to differentiate between forgetting

retrospective studies

a method of gathering data where researchers look for evidence related to their hypothesis by looking at events that have already happened (which occurs for many life events) and repression (which is argued to be specific to traumatic life events). A person's forgetting of abuse may reflect normal memory processes and not repression per se; retrospective studies cannot make this distinction. Another problem with retrospective studies is that it is possible that a person thinks she or he forgot the abuse but did not forget. This is not unheard of. Many cases have been reported where a person has discussed an event with other people and then forgets having had that conversation (Fivush & Edwards, 2004).

prospective studies
a method of gathering data where researchers identify a group and then look for evidence related to their hypothesis as time passes

Other researchers have cited the results from **prospective studies** as evidence for repressed memories. Williams (1994) reports on the memories of girls who, between the ages of 10 months and 12 years, were brought into a hospital because they had been sexually abused. Williams reports on their memories 17 years after the hospital visit. In this study, 38 per cent of girls had no recollection of the hospital visit. This result has often been used to support the argument that sexual abuse is often repressed; however, critics note that a myriad of other factors could have led to this result. Very young children may not remember abuse because of infantile amnesia (see Chapter 8) and not because of repression per se. In addition, some may not have reported the abuse because they didn't feel comfortable with the interviewer or because they were not directly asked about the abuse. Some may also have forgotten the incident through normal forgetting (Loftus & Davis, 2006). Goodman-Brown, Edelstein, Goodman, Jones, and Gordon (2003) interviewed girls who had been victims of sexual abuse between the ages of 3 and 17 ten years after the abuse. In this sample, only 8 per cent did not report the abuse to the interviewer, suggesting that the claim that large numbers of victims of sexual abuse have repressed their memories of their abuse was probably not realistic.

case studies
a research report style in which an individual researcher reports the details of an individual case

Proponents who argue for the existence of repressed memories also sometimes use **case studies** to bolster their claims. A case study includes a case history of an individual as well as an interpretation by the therapist that the patient has repressed and then recovered a memory. Case studies are very difficult to verify and there have been instances cited as "verified" examples of repression that have turned out to be completely fabricated by the author. For example, Loftus and Guyer (2002) delved deeper into a case study of a girl named "Jane Doe" who was apparently abused, forgot about the abuse, and then recovered her memories of abuse with the help of her therapist. Loftus and Guyer (2002) reviewed newspaper articles and court records and eventually found Jane Doe's family. They learned that not only was it not likely that Jane Doe was abused, but that the family believed that the abuse story had been created in order to remove Jane Doe from her mother's custody.

There are a small number of case studies where a victim has forgotten a verifiable instance of sexual abuse for some time and then later recalled it, which are reported by Schooler, Bendiksen, and Ambadar (1997). What is interesting about these cases is that they follow a pattern that is distinctly different from what is reported in the unverified case studies related to repressed and recovered memory. According to Schooler et al. (1997), in all but one case the recollection of the abuse occurred without the help of a therapist, the memory came back clearly without the need of prodding or deciphering, the memory was for a single event committed by a non-family member, and the victim was at least nine years old at the time of the abuse. In every verified case, the victim may have claimed amnesia for the event, but had discussed the event at some time with someone else. Not one of the verified cases involved the recovery of memory in therapy; none involved abuse that began in early childhood, repeated abuse, abuse by a family member, or sexual intercourse. In other words, none of the verified cases resembled the typical cases used to support the argument that traumatic memories are often repressed and then recovered in therapy. In sum, there is very little empirical evidence to indicate that victims of abuse systematically repress memory of abuse.

Evidence for False Memories of Abuse

Unlike evidence for repressed and then recovered memories of abuse, there is a substantial amount of evidence supporting the notion that people can hold **false memories of abuse**. Some evidence for false memories of real-life trauma comes from case studies of repressed and recovered memories that have proven to be impossible. For example, one case study claims that a girl had been repeatedly raped by members of a satanic cult, yet her hymen was intact, making this claim biologically impossible. One case study reported the recovered memory of witnessing the sacrificial killing of someone who was later found to be alive, making this claim factually impossible. In another case, the victim was living several states away from the alleged attacker, making the recovered memory geographically impossible. There have also been claims of repressed and recovered memory from infancy which, because of infantile amnesia, are psychologically impossible. (See Chapter 8 for more on infantile amnesia.) Each of these cases was originally brought forward as evidence for repressed and recovered memories, but is actually evidence supporting the possible existence of false memories of abuse. In sum, there is little evidence for repressed and recovered false memories, but plenty of evidence that false memories of abuse can be developed (Loftus & Davis, 2006).

false memory of abuse

a memory of being abused that is not based on events that actually happened

Conclusions Regarding Repressed and Recovered Memories

There is no evidence to suggest that people repress traumatic memories in any way that is different from normal forgetting of autobiographical events (Loftus & Davis, 2006). The prevalence of claims of repressed and recovered memories was likely the result of many patients and therapists believing in the possible existence of repressed memories because of extensive media coverage on the subject. If a therapist and client both believe that repressed memories could exist, they are more likely to search for them, engaging in activities such as hypnosis and dream analysis, which are just the sort of activities that have been shown to lead to the development of false memories (Loftus & Davis, 2006).

The memory war is now essentially over; the majority of practicing clinicians refute the possibility of repressed and recovered memories and avoid engaging in therapeutic activities that may lead to the development of false memories (Loftus & Davis, 2006). False memories of abuse can have harmful consequences both by making people believe they have been victimized when they have not, and by bringing forward allegations of abuse against people who are in fact innocent. The danger of false memories of abuse is reflected in the current policies of the majority of medical and psychiatric associations around the world, including the Canadian Psychiatric Association, that actively discourage therapeutic activities that could give rise to false memories (Loftus & Davis, 2006).

Memory and False Confessions

Research conducted by Elizabeth Loftus and other false memory researchers has shown that it is relatively easy to implant false memories. Researchers have shown it is possible to get people to falsely remember being lost in the mall, being saved by a lifeguard, and even meeting Bugs Bunny at Disneyland (which is impossible because Bugs Bunny is not a Disney character;

CASE STUDY

BOX
11.2

The False Confession of Frank Sterling

In 1991, Frank Sterling confessed to the 1988 killing of an elderly woman. Sterling was interrogated for 12 hours without an attorney. Only the last half-hour of his interrogation was videotaped. During this time Sterling provided key details related to the crime, including the location of the murder, the colour of the victim's clothing, and the fact that a BB gun was used as the weapon (Innocence Project, n.d.). Thanks largely to his confession, Frank Sterling was convicted of the crime. The problem was that Sterling was innocent. He had provided a **false confession** and served almost 19 years in prison before DNA evidence proved he was innocent. Although false confessions may seem completely irrational, they are actually quite common. According to the Innocence Project, about one in four people who has been exonerated by DNA evidence made a false confession or incriminating statement that led to imprisonment (Innocence Project, n.d). One reason false confessions are so prevalent is that in many places police interrogation techniques can lead innocent suspects to falsely remember committing crimes, and these false memories, combined with heavy police pressure to admit their role in the crime, lead to confessions.

false confession

when a person takes responsibility for a crime that she or he did not commit

Loftus, 1993). The same processes that allowed false memories to be created in participants in these experiments can lead innocent suspects to come to believe they committed crimes during interrogations. Most interrogations involve the interrogator suggesting a plausible scenario that gives the suspect means, motive, and opportunity to commit the crime. The interrogator repeats this scenario over and over, hoping the suspect will admit that yes, that is how the crime occurred. For example, the interviewer may say, "Come on, admit it. You were angry because the victim was dating your ex-girlfriend. You left the bar that night having had a lot to drink and walked over to the victim's house, where you assaulted him with a brick that you found outside his house. You then cleaned yourself up at a coffee shop and made your way home to bed." In truth, the suspect may have been angry at the victim, and may have been at that bar that night, but did not actually commit the crime. However, each time the interviewer repeats this scenario and demands that the suspect admit that this is what happened, the suspect must imagine the scenario of committing the crime in order to probe her or his memory for what really occurred. In addition, in many locations including parts of the United States, police are allowed to claim they have evidence proving the guilt of a suspect even when no such evidence exists. So, for example, the interviewer may lie and tell the innocent suspect that the police found a brick at the scene of the crime with the suspect's blood on it, or tell the innocent suspect that there is video surveillance showing the suspect cleaning himself up at the coffee shop after the crime. This false evidence will also be imagined by the suspect while hearing it repeated by the interrogator over and over again. After being made to repeatedly imagine themselves committing the crime, and after being given what they believe is evidence to validate the story told by the interrogator, innocent suspects may come to believe that they did in fact perpetrate the crime through **imagination inflation** and confess. If the confession involves information that is not public knowledge (called **confession contamination**), information that only the culprit could know, the confession can carry a great deal of weight in court and lead to the conviction of someone who did not commit the crime. The Innocence

imagination inflation

when a person comes to believe that her or his memory of an imagined event represents a memory for an event that occurred

confession contamination

when police provide a suspect of a crime information that only the culprit would know and that information is later included in a confession

---

DIY EXPERIMENT

BOX 11.3

Misinformation Effects

Select six people and show each of them the picture of the car crash printed on page 284. Ask three of the people "How fast do you think the cars were going when they contacted each other?" and record the speed they guess. Ask the other three "How fast do you think the cars were going when they smashed into each other?" and record the speed. About a week later, ask all six participants three questions in random order: "What colour were the cars in the accident?" "At what time of day did the accident occur?" "Did you see any broken glass?" Participants in the "smashed" condition are more likely to recall seeing broken glass than participants in the "contacted" condition because of the misinformation effect.

Project in the United States has many suggestions for how to prevent false confessions. The first is to implement mandatory recording of all interrogations so that there will be evidence of any confession contamination should the suspect confess. Second, it is recommended that judges conduct hearings to evaluate the reliability of any recorded confessions before allowing them in court.

Identification Procedures

The most common form of suggestive post-event information that witnesses are exposed to is provided by the identification procedure. Most identification procedures are either **showup procedures** or **lineup procedures**. In a showup procedure, a witness is presented with an image of a single suspect and is asked, "Is this the person you saw commit the crime?" (see Figure 11.1). In a lineup procedure, the suspect's picture is mixed with pictures of similar individuals (called **fillers**) not associated with the crime. The witness is asked if anyone in the lineup is the person who committed the crime. Showup procedures are problematic for several reasons. First, seeing a single person in a showup can cause a witness with a hazy recollection of the perpetrator to replace that recollection with the person in the showup, even if the person in the showup was not the actual perpetrator. This problem is confounded by the fact that the witness, when shown a showup, is likely to be somewhat biased. The witness may suspect that the police know that the person in the showup is the actual perpetrator and feel compelled to identify that person (lest they be set free) even if the

showup procedure

an identification procedure wherein the witness is shown a single picture of a suspect and asked if the person in the picture was the person who committed the crime

This iconic image from *The Usual Suspects* (1995) shows what most people imagine a police lineup to be like.

AF archive/Alamy Stock Photo

(a) Showup

Is this the person who commited the crime?

(b) Lineup

Is one of these people the person who committed the crime?

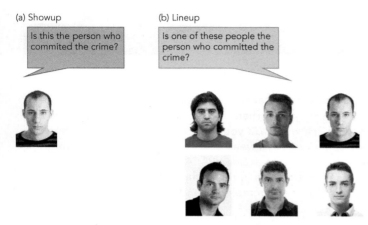

Figure 11.1   The Difference between a showup and a lineup

In a showup procedure (part (a) above), a witness is asked, "Is this the person who committed the crime?" whereas in a lineup procedure (part (b) above) the witness is asked, "Is one of these people the person who committed the crime?" When lineup procedures are done correctly, they are less biased than showup procedures.

Sources: © Erik Reis | Dreamstime.com; © Soleilc | Dreamstime.com; © Artofphoto | Dreamstime.com; © Erik Reis | Dreamstime.com; © Ant Clausen | Dreamstime.com; © Simon Greig | Dreamstime.com; © Lenanet | Dreamstime.com

lineup procedure

an identification procedure wherein the suspect's picture is mixed in with pictures of similar-looking individuals who are not associated with the crime. The witness is asked if anyone in the picture array committed the crime.

filler

an individual presented in a lineup who is not associated with the crime

double-blind procedure

when neither the police officer administering the lineup nor the witness knows who is the suspect in the lineup

witness is not sure. The uncertain witness may make a positive identification to comply with police pressure. Witnesses may also make a positive identification of the showup because of their desire to have someone arrested for the crime. Thus, there are many reasons why a positive identification may be made even when the witness is unsure. When added to the bias produced by showing a witness the picture of a suspect, experts agree that showups are a problematic form of identification.

Lineup procedures, when they are unbiased, are better than showup procedures to see if there is a match between the memory of the witness and the image of the suspect. However, there are at least four types of potential bias in a lineup. The first is if the fillers do not meet the description of the witness. For example, if the witness described the perpetrator as "a White male with a scar on his chin," all the fillers should be White males with scars on their chins or else the witness can immediately discount some of the fillers. A second problem can occur if the suspect's picture is physically different from the fillers, for example, if the suspect's picture is colour and the fillers are black and white. Size and background differences can also make the suspect's picture stand out and bias the witness. A third problem occurs when the lineup is not a **double-blind procedure** in which neither the police officer who administers the lineup nor the witness knows who is the suspect in the array. A double-blind procedure prevents bias that may come from the police officer giving cues to the suspect (even unintentionally) that lead witnesses to an identification they are unsure of. For example, if the witness focuses on what the police officer knows is a filler, the police officer may say, "Is there anyone else in the lineup you think may have done it?" (Busey & Loftus, 2007). The final type of bias is referred to as **unconscious transference** and occurs when the witness has seen the suspect at some other time other than at the time of the crime or during the lineup. For example, the witness may have seen the suspect in the neighbourhood or on television. Previous exposure to the suspect makes the suspect appear more familiar than the other members of the lineup, and the feeling of familiarity can lead to an identification even when the suspect does not match the memory trace of the person who perpetrated the crime.

In-Group and Out-Group Eyewitness Identifications

More than 50 years ago, researchers discovered that eyewitnesses are less accurate at making identifications when the suspects are of a different race. This phenomenon was labelled the **cross-race effect (CRE)**. The CRE has been empirically demonstrated by nearly every racial group in our society, and across many cultures around the world. The CRE has been observed in controlled laboratory settings as well as in naturalistic settings (Wilson, Hugenberg, & Bernstein, 2013).

CASE STUDY

The Mistaken Identity of John Jerome White

In 1979, a man broke into the home of a 74-year-old woman in Georgia, raped her, beat her, and demanded all her money. While no rape kit was collected at the hospital because of the extent of the woman's injuries, a police search of the house found a pubic hair and piece of skin that they believed belonged to the perpetrator. Six weeks after the crime, the police compiled a photo lineup that included John Jerome White and four other men. The victim chose White out of a live lineup, saying she was certain he was the perpetrator. White served 22 years for the assault before a DNA test on the hair and skin samples was conducted, exonerating White (and was matched to James Parham). What was unique about this case is that the actual perpetrator, James Parham, was a "filler" in the live lineup with White when the victim made her identifica-

https://harvardpress.typepad.com/hup_publicity/2011/03/understanding-eyewitness-misidentifications.html

John Jerome White is the third individual in this lineup. He was mistakenly identified by the victim even though the actual perpetrator, James Parham, is the fifth person in this lineup. White was likely mistakenly identified because he was the only person in this lineup to have also appeared in an earlier photo lineup.

tion, and yet the victim chose White, who did not look like Parham at all. Gary Wells, an American expert on eyewitness testimony and identification, believes that the victim misidentified White because he was the only person to appear in both the photo lineup and the live lineup and that White seemed familiar to the victim for that reason, leading to an identification. This case demonstrates that witnesses may falsely identify a suspect simply because they appear familiar, and that in at least one known case, this feeling of familiarity was so persuasive that it caused a misidentification even when the actual perpetrator was also in the lineup.

In 2008, Luke Jackiw and his colleagues at the University of Regina looked at cross-race eyewitness identification accuracy among White Canadians and Indigenous people. Jackiw, Arbuthnott, Pfeifer, Marcon, and Meissner (2008) found a significant CRE such that both groups were better at identifying individuals from their own racial group. Jackiw et al. (2008) also found that participants in both groups were, on average, 1.25 times more likely to falsely identify an Indigenous person in a lineup than a White person in a lineup.

One popular explanation for this effect claims that different experience with same-race and cross-race individuals is responsible for the effect. However, a meta-analysis conducted by Meissner and Brigham (2001) showed that past experience with cross-race faces only accounted for a small amount of variance in false memory. There is much more compelling experimental evidence suggesting that the CRE is linked to better encoding of facial information for people perceived as members of a person's **in-group** than people perceived as members of their **out-group**. An in-group is any social group that a person feels a member of. This can include sex, race, age, and religion as well as school, political parties, or even sports teams. An

unconscious transference

when previous exposure to a suspect leads to a feeling of familiarity that provides the sole basis for the identification of the suspect

cross-race effect (CRE)

eyewitnesses are less accurate at making identifications when the suspects are of a different race

BOX
11.5

CASE STUDY

Was the Lockerbie Bombing Suspect a Real Case of Eyewitness Misidentification?

On December 21, 1988, Pan Am Flight 103 originating from Libya exploded in mid-air, crashing down on the town of Lockerbie, Scotland, and killing a total of 270 people, 259 on the plane and 11 on the ground. Investigators traced the bomb to a transistor radio packed with some clothes inside a Samsonite suitcase, and then traced those clothes to a shop in Malta. On September 1, 1989, nine months after the crash of Flight 103, a Maltese shopkeeper named Mr Gauci was interviewed by investigators who believed that the clothes packed with the bomb might have been purchased at his store (Loftus, 2013). Gauci revealed that he did in fact recall a man purchasing some trousers as well as pajamas similar to those found in the wreckage of the di-

Pan Am Flight 103 crashed in Lockerbie, Scotland, on December 21, 1988. Abdelbaset al-Megrahi was convicted of planting the bomb that brought down the plane based on the evidence of one eyewitness whose story changed considerably over time (Loftus, 2013).

Press Association via AP Images

saster in the winter of 1988. At the time of the interview, Gauci described the man as over six feet tall and about 50 years of age and he recalled that, as it was raining, the man carried an umbrella. Gauci worked with police on creating a sketch of the man who bought the clothes and was very satisfied with the resulting image of a tall, distinctive-looking man in his early fifties. Gauci was shown several photo lineups and consistently said that the man who bought the clothes was not in the lineup and that everyone in the lineup was too young to be the suspect. When pressed, Gauci said that a man named Abdelbaset al-Megrahi looked similar to the suspect, but was too young. At this point in time, al-Megrahi became a suspect and wanted posters for al-Megrahi were circulated widely (Loftus, 2013).

In April 1999, 10 years after the bombing and after images of al-Megrahi were released, Gauci made his first identification of al-Megrahi from a photo lineup. During al-Megrahi's trial, Gauci's testimony changed to fit al-Megrahi. While Gauci originally stated that the mystery shopper was over six feet tall, at al-Megrahi's trial Gauci said the shopper was less than six feet tall. (al-Megrahi was well under six feet tall.) While at the time of his initial interview Gauci claimed not to recall the specific date of the incident, at the time of al-Megrahi's trial the date became crucial because al-Megrahi was only in Malta on December 7 , 1988. Gauci had originally testified that there were no Christmas decorations up when the shopper visited (suggesting that the date could not have been December 7) but at the trial testified that "there were Christmas lights on already, I'm sure." In addition, in his original interview Gauci recalled that it was raining heavily when the shopper came in, because he remembered the shopper's wet umbrella, but at the time of al-Megrahi's trial Gauci's memory had changed and he reported that it was only dribbling and possibly not raining at all; once again Gauci's new testimony conflicted with his original testimony but fit with the weather on December 7, 1988 (when there was not rain; Loftus, 2013).

Abdelbaset al-Megrahi was eventually convicted of the Lockerbie bombing. His conviction brought relief to hundreds of families who wanted justice for their lost loved ones, and to a nervous public who wanted to know that the person who had committed such a horrible crime was not free to kill again. However, the Scottish Criminal Cases Review Commission concluded that it was likely that a miscarriage of justice had occurred in the conviction of al-Megrahi, and that he should not have been convicted solely on an eyewitness identification that occurred after it was known that he was the main suspect in such a horrendous crime. al-Megrahi died of cancer in 2012 after being released to his family home on compassionate grounds when it was learned that he had terminal cancer. Many members of the public were outraged when al-Megrahi was released and allowed to die at home. A careful examination of the changing testimony of the only eyewitness, Mr Gauci, suggests that there was no reliable evidence that al-Megrahi actually purchased those clothes on that fateful day in 1988, and that it is very possible that the Lockerbie bomber is still at large today (Loftus, 2013).

out-group is a group to which a person does not feel a sense of belonging. Research suggests that the CRE is not so much about remembering the faces of people of a different race as it is about remembering the faces of people from our in-groups. In a study conducted by Van Bavel, Packer, and Cunningham (2011), Black and White participants were assigned to one of two teams, the Leopards or the Tigers. They were then presented with pictures of Black and White faces that were labelled as Leopards or Tigers. Participants were better able to recognize faces from the team they were assigned to regardless of the person's race. Other research has shown that memory for faces is better when the perceiver believes the person goes to the same university as the perceiver, or has similar personality characteristics (Bernstein, Young, & Hugenberg, 2007). It is argued that a person who is a member of an in-group receives more attention, and more attention leads to better encoding and recall of details about that person, including their facial features. Similarly, a person who is believed to be a member of an out-group receives less attention and that person's specific facial features are less likely to be encoded and later remembered. Thus, whether eyewitnesses view a suspect as part of their in-group or out-group may have a significant effect on their ability to recognize the suspect. The implication of this finding is clear: Victims may make poor witnesses because they will see perpetrators as belonging to a different social group. This finding may explain why eyewitnesses make so many errors, and gives added credence to the argument that eyewitness identification procedures should be designed to reduce errors whenever possible (Wilson et al., 2013).

in-group
a social group that a person feels she or he belongs to

out-group
a social group that a person does not feel she or he belongs to

New Approaches to Suspect Identification
Using Confidence Ratings to Predict the Accuracy of Eyewitness Identification

One problem with eyewitness identification is that eyewitnesses' memories of the culprit are often poor because of either only having seen the culprit for a brief period of time, or because a long period of time has elapsed between witnessing the event and being shown a lineup (Brewer & Wells, 2011). In addition to problems with memory, a given witness may have any number of decision criteria to use when evaluating a possible perpetrator that may affect their identification (or lack of identification). For example, witnesses may be overly concerned with misidentification and be cautious about selecting someone they think may be guilty. On the other hand, witnesses may instead be overly concerned with a guilty person going free, making them more likely to identify a person in a lineup who they are not sure was the actual perpetrator.

Australian psychologist Neil Brewer and his colleagues developed a procedure that they hoped would access eyewitness memory while minimizing the influence of strategies that affect response criteria. In this procedure, witnesses rate the degree of match between the culprit and each lineup while under significant time pressure (a decision must be made within three seconds). In this procedure, confidence is used as an index of memory strength; higher degrees of confidence are assumed to reflect a greater contribution of memory, either helping to identify a true culprit, or helping to determine that a filler was in fact not the culprit. Confidence judgments have been used successfully as indices of recognition memory in numerous experiments such as Bernbach (1973) and Cleary and Greene (2000). Under this paradigm, Brewer and his colleagues argue that a large difference between the confidence rating for one face over others in a lineup could serve as a means of eyewitness identification that is less fraught with bias than traditional lineups. Brewer and Wells (2011) found that when the discrepancies between confidence ratings across suspects exceeded 60 per cent (e.g., when the confidence rating for one suspect was at least 60 per cent higher than the confidence rating for the other suspects), accuracy at identifying the suspect was very high. When the discrepancy was very low, accuracy was also very low. Thus, in a real-world setting, an investigator could take a high confidence discrepancy between a suspect and similar-looking fillers as an indicator that the eyewitness recognized the culprit, and similarly could take a low discrepancy between confidence ratings to indicate that the eyewitness did not recognize any of the faces as being that of the culprit (Brewer & Wells, 2011).

Allowing Eyewitnesses to Say "I Don't Know"

Australian researcher Nathan Weber and his colleague Timothy Perfect, who conducts research in England, also felt that eyewitness identification was closely tied to the confidence of the eyewitness. Instead of asking participants for confidence ratings, however, Weber and Perfect (2012) implemented a paradigm in which some participants had the option of saying "I don't know" when presented with a possible culprit. Weber and Perfect (2012) presented more than 400 participants with a mock crime and then had them complete a showup procedure either three minutes or three weeks after seeing the videos. The research varied the instructions slightly across groups. Participants in the forced-report conditions were instructed to indicate "Yes" if the image was of the culprit and "No" otherwise. Participants in the explicit free-report condition were told to click "Yes" if the image was of the culprit, "No" if the image was not the culprit, and "I don't know" if they were not sure. Finally, participants in the spontaneous free-report condition were shown the image and asked to type their yes/no response below the image and click "Done" when they were finished. Weber and Perfect (2012) found that participants in the explicit free-report procedure had fewer false positives and misses in their responses than participants in the other groups, suggesting that an explicit free-report procedure can produce the most accurate responses.

Summing Up Eyewitness Memory

Research has demonstrated that eyewitness memory is malleable and can be influenced by post-event information and may be unreliable for that reason. When combined with research that has shown that many aspects of the identification procedures themselves (such as the fillers chosen

CASE STUDY

BOX 11.6

Hands Up, Don't Shoot: Eyewitness Accounts of the Shooting of Michael Brown

Eyewitness memory can be influenced by post-event information. On August 9, 2014, witnesses saw 18-year-old Michael Brown shot and killed by Ferguson, Missouri police officer Darren Wilson. Initial reports were that Michael Brown had his hands up and was surrendering when he was shot, which led protestors to take to the streets of Ferguson chanting, "Hands up, don't shoot!" When a grand jury was convened many months after the shooting, several witnesses were convinced that Michael Brown was retreating with his hands up when he was shot by Wilson, although a blood trail and other forensic evidence strongly suggest that this was impossible. Several witnesses changed their testimony between the time they were first interviewed and the time of the grand jury. Shortly after Michael Brown was shot by police, protestors in Ferguson chose "Hands up, don't shoot" as their mantra, which likely affected the memories of these witnesses. Prosecutors were sympathetic to the influence that the publicity of this case may have had on the recall of eyewitnesses and chose not to prosecute the witnesses who perjured themselves. In March 2015, the U.S. Department of Justice announced that it would not indict Darren Wilson for the shooting of Michael Brown; however, so many people were convinced that Wilson actually shot Brown while Brown was trying to surrender that Wilson resigned from police work citing fears for his own safety.

for the lineup and instructions that force witnesses to say "yes" or "no" to each possible suspect) can lead the eyewitness to make a misidentification, it really is no surprise that so many errors in identification are made. (Recall that the Innocence Project reports that 75 per cent of convictions later overturned by DNA evidence have been based on eyewitness identifications.)

Researchers have identified two new methods for eyewitness identification that may reduce the rate of misidentifications. Both methods are based on the assumption that the strength of eyewitnesses' memory for a culprit is positively correlated with their confidence in making an identification, a finding that has been established in the memory literature for some time (see, e.g., Bernbach, 1971). In Brewer's method, a comparison of confidence ratings is used to determine which responses made by the subject most likely represent recognition of the culprit. In Weber's method, including instructions to say "I don't know" allows eyewitnesses to admit low confidence when viewing a suspect. Both methods have been found to significantly decrease eyewitness misidentifications and perhaps will someday be adopted by law enforcement agencies.

Juries

While eyewitness identification can result in an accused person going to trial, in most cases the jury decides the accused's fate. Many factors related to memory can influence juries, including a juror's memory for pre-trial publicity, a juror's memory

© Photographerlondon | Dreamstime.com

for testimony, and a juror's beliefs about the credibility of the memory of eyewitnesses. This section explores research related to memory and juries and offers recommendations as to how the legal system can prevent jurors' memories from leading them to erroneous convictions.

Pre-Trial Publicity

Most criminal trials occur without little or no media coverage; however, those that are unique because of the severity of the crime or the status of the defendant or victim may receive extensive media coverage or **pre-trial publicity (PTP)**. PTP has the potential to affect juries significantly. Although there are strict rules about what information can be presented during a trial, the same rules don't usually apply to the media. The media may release information about the life of the defendant or the victim that wouldn't be allowed in the court (such as their criminal record); the media can also release unsubstantiated details about the crime itself, such as possible recreations of the crime. A question that concerns legal experts is the extent to which this PTP influences the memory and subsequent decisions of juries. Christine Ruva and her colleagues have studied this topic extensively for over a decade and have found evidence demonstrating that PTP can impact the memories of jurors and the deliberation process.

pre-trial publicity (PTP)

media coverage of a crime that occurs before the case is brought to trial

Pre-Trial Publicity and Juror Memory

Christine Ruva and her colleague Cathy McEvoy at the University of South Florida were interested in determining the extent to which jurors may confuse PTP with trial testimony and make **source attribution errors** when making verdict decisions. Ruva and McEvoy (2008) chose an actual murder case where a man named Dan Bias was accused of shooting his wife Lise but pled not guilty and claimed that his wife actually shot herself. This case was chosen because previous research had indicated that the defendant's guilt was ambiguous (Ruva, McEvoy, & Bryant, 2007). The researchers then assembled a mock jury and had them read one of three news articles. One group read an article that was **positive PTP** and included information such as "Dan and Lise were planning a second honeymoon. The second honeymoon had been Dan's idea" and "Dan never wanted a gun in the house, but Lise insisted on having it for self-defence." Another group read **negative PTP** that included information such as "Lise Bias's body was found in the doorway of the couple's bedroom" and "Lise did not know how to use guns and disliked guns." The third group read unrelated news material. At this point, jurors were told that they might have read PTP related to the trial and if they had that they should disregard that information when deciding their verdict. Next, the participants viewed an edited version of the trial of Dan Bias, which lasted about 30 minutes. During the trial, they heard other information about the case that conflicted with the negative PTP. For example, the jurors heard "Lise was standing by the mirror when the gun went off," which conflicted with the negative PTP "Lise Bias's body was found in the doorway of the couple's bedroom." Five days later, the mock jurors came back and rendered a verdict of guilty or innocent. After the verdict was given, each juror was presented with a series of statements to test her or his source monitoring. For each statement, the juror had to indicate the source (trial, PTP, or new) and rate her or his confidence in that source attribution. Jurors then rated Dan Bias's guilt, as well as the credibility of the defendant and the attorneys, on a scale of 1 to 7.

Ruva and McEvoy (2008) found that jurors who saw negative PTP were nearly twice as likely to find the defendant guilty as participants who did not see any PTP, and that jurors exposed

source attribution error

a memory error wherein an individual believes that a piece of information came from one source when really it came from a different source

positive PTP

pre-trial publicity that depicts the defendant in a way that suggests the defendant would not or could not commit the crime he or she is accused of committing

negative PTP

pre-trial publicity that depicts the defendant in a way that suggests the defendant committed the crime or was capable of committing the crime she or he is accused of committing

to positive PTP were less likely to render a guilty verdict than jurors who did not see any PTP. Finally, Ruva and McEvoy (2008) found significant source memory errors for all types of information presented to the jurors, including the PTP and statements from the trial, and that when errors were made, jurors were confident that they were in fact correctly attributing the source of the information. This finding strongly suggests that, even if instructed to disregard PTP when deciding guilt, jurors may be unable to distinguish PTP from information from the trial and are thus unable to follow the instruction.

When it was clear that juror memory was influenced by PTP, in 2015 Christine Ruva and Christina Guenther decided to examine how PTP affects jury deliberations. Ruva and Guenther (2015) had half of their participants view negative PTP related to the Daniel Bias trial and half view unrelated crime stories. One week after viewing the PTP, participants viewed the 30-minute edited trial of Daniel Bias used in Ruva and McEvoy (2008). Two days after viewing the trial, the mock jurors were assembled and were instructed that they might have been shown PTP related to the trial that they saw, but that they were to ignore that information when making decisions about the defendant's guilt. Each juror then gave a pre-deliberation verdict and confidence rating related to the guilt of the suspect. Mock jurors were then randomly assigned to either a deliberating condition or a nominal condition. Jurors in the deliberating condition were taken to a mock deliberation room and given 30 minutes to come up with a verdict for the trial. At the end of the 30 minutes, the juries completed a form indicating whether they found the defendant guilty or not guilty, or whether the jury was hung. Jurors in the nominal condition sat in a separate room and were instructed not to speak to each other and read magazines for 25 minutes and then completed the same verdict form but without the "hung" option. After the verdict forms were collected, all mock jurors completed a source memory test and rated the credibility of the defendant and the effectiveness of the attorneys, just like jurors had done in Ruva and McEvoy (2008). Ruva and Guenther (2015) found that jurors exposed to negative PTP were significantly more likely than no-PTP jurors to find the defendant guilty. Negative-PTP jurors also perceived the defendant as less credible and made more source memory errors; they were less likely to attribute information presented in the trial to the trial, and significantly more likely to attribute information presented in the PTP to the trial. Jurors in the deliberation condition made even more memory errors than jurors in the nominal condition.

Next, Ruva and Guenther (2015) did a content analysis on transcripts of the jury deliberations. The researchers found that, despite being instructed to ignore PTP, PTP was discussed during deliberation. Ruva and Guenther (2015) speculate that some of the jurors' discussions of PTP during deliberation may have been the result of source memory errors; the jurors did not remember the information came from the PTP instead of the trial, so they included the PTP information in the deliberation accidentally. Other times, though, PTP was mentioned with acknowledgment that the information was not presented in trial, despite the fact that jurors were instructed not to include this information in the deliberations. The authors conclude that the inclusion of PTP into deliberations because of source memory errors is one reason for jury bias, and that jurors knowingly considering PTP also likely influences verdicts in cases where the guilt or innocence of the suspect is not obvious (as in the Daniel Bias case). This phenomenon of using the PTP when the correct verdict is ambiguous is referred to as coming to a "just" verdict; the jurors want to make the right decision but, with little evidence from the trial directing them to that decision, they may use PTP intentionally to arrive at what they think is the correct conclusion. In cases where most PTP is negative, this may lead to substantial bias against the defendant.

Jurors' Memories during Trials

During a typical trial, a jury is presented with a large amount of information over a series of days or even weeks. Because witnesses are not allowed to speculate while testifying, the temporal sequence of events presented to jurors is often not specified. How do juries remember all that information when it is time to deliberate? Research by Nancy Pennington and Reid Hastie suggest jurors cope by developing a story that combines three types of information together into a narrative. The first source is case-specific information acquired during the trial, such as statements made by witnesses. The second is jurors' own knowledge about similar crimes, such as crimes they have read about in the past, or even previous criminal cases they have been involved with. The third component is the jurors' generic expectations about what makes a complete story, such as the knowledge that human behaviour is usually motivated by goals. Because all these sources of information may vary from juror to juror, when complete each juror possesses one of many possible interpretations of the evidence in story form (Pennington & Hastie, 1992). The story is then matched against the available verdicts during deliberation. A juror whose story suggests that the suspect committed the crime will match to a guilty verdict whereas a juror whose story suggests that there is reasonable doubt that the suspect committed the crime will match to a not guilty verdict. The story model suggests that the memory of trial evidence contributes to the story developed by jurors but that the verdict can be influenced by factors other than evidence, such as the juror's own experiences and the narratives provided by the attorneys that suggest a sequence of events. Pennington and Hastie (1992) demonstrated that jurors also tend to rely on the story that is easiest to construe, not necessarily the story that is most just. Thus, if it easier to create a story in which the defendant is guilty than one in which the defendant is innocent, the juror will develop that story and render the guilty verdict.

The Impact of Note Taking on Jurors' Memories

Jurors are encouraged to take notes during most trials in an attempt to help boost their memory when it is time to deliberate. One question concerns whether note taking is really helpful or whether, as Pennington and Hastie (1992) found, it can actually interfere with recall. To test this hypothesis, David Rosenhan and his colleagues recruited university students into a realistic court setting and presented them with a 75-minute trial depicting the judge's instructions and the opening statements from a complicated fraud scenario in which several individuals and banks were involved in writing bad cheques. Half of the groups of jurors who viewed the trial were allowed to take notes and half were not. Jurors who were allowed to take notes were also allowed to decline taking notes if they wished. Thus, there were three groups, non–note-taking jurors, note-taking jurors, and note-decliners. After viewing the trial, each juror completed a questionnaire that included 11 open-ended questions. Note-taking jurors were allowed to consult their notes when completing the questionnaire. Note-decliners and non–note-takers completed the questionnaire without notes. Jurors were given more points if their responses to the open-ended questions contained more information and showed a better understanding of the allegations and evidence presented during the trial. The questionnaire also asked all jurors how engaged they were during the trial, how useful they felt their notes were, or, if they did not take notes, how useful notes would have been for their verdict (Rosenhan, Eisner, & Robinson, 1994).

Rosenhan et al. (1994) found that note-taking jurors remembered significantly more than those who did not take notes (non–note-takers and note-decliners). This result suggests that juror notes can help recall of trial-related information. Rosenhan also looked at the quantity and quality of the notes taken. For those who took notes, Rosenhan found a moderate correlation between the amount of words written and recall scores; note-takers who wrote more tended to recall more. In addition, Rosenhan found that for note-takers, note-decliners, and non–note-takers, the distribution of verdicts was about the same; about 54 per cent found the defendant guilty, 32 per cent found the defendant not guilty, and 14 per cent were undecided (Rosenhan et al., 1994). Note-takers reported being slightly more attentive during the trial than non–note-takers and note-decliners. All groups reported that they thought note taking was helpful; however, of all three groups, more of those who were not allowed to take notes reported thinking note taking would be helpful. The results from this study suggest, perhaps not surprisingly, that note taking should be encouraged during trials where jurors need to remember large amounts of complex information.

Jurors construct stories to manage all the evidence presented during a trial. Sometimes these stories may include inferences based on juror experience or suggestion by an attorney, but not on fact. Reviewing notes from the entire trial prior to deliberation may also help jurors construct a story model that is based more on evidence and less on assumption.

The Impact of Emotional Testimony and Personal Relevance on Jurors' Memories

You can probably remember seeing a trial (either real or fictional) in which the attorneys for both sides seem to carefully manipulate the emotions in the courtroom, but in different ways. The prosecution likely tried to ensure that the description of the victim was graphic, perhaps apologizing for the graphic nature of the testimony but suggesting it was necessary in order to connect the accused to the attack. The defence, on the other hand, likely kept questions related to the victim subdued and brief, but when it came time for the defence witnesses to take the stand, made sure their testimony was filled with emotion. Both attorneys likely gave closing statements in which their argument, their narrative, was presented in such a way that those watching felt their passion, their sense of injustice, and empathy for those whom they were arguing were victimized.

None of this was accidental, of course. Attorneys know a fair bit about juror memory and their use of emotional testimony is an attempt to harness that knowledge. Dozens of studies have shown that jurors better remember testimony associated with negative emotions than testimony associated with positive emotions or no emotions at all (e.g., Burke, Heuer, & Reisberg, 1992; Harris & Pashler, 2005; Kensinger & Corkin, 2003). For this reason, attorneys want the key points of their narratives to be associated with those negative emotions, leading to graphic descriptions of victims, sobbing witnesses on both sides, and cold, emotionless cross-examinations when the witness is presenting evidence that is inconsistent with the attorney's narrative.

Research suggests that emotional testimony evokes neural mechanisms that enhance memory (see, e.g., Phelps, 2004). Trial attorneys also often try to include testimony that relates to jurors in order to get them to better remember it. The attorneys may be strategic in jury selection and try to select jurors who will relate to their narrative (if they have a strong case) or who will be unable to relate to the narrative of the opposing side. For example, when selecting jurors for a trial where a 50-year-old man is accused of murdering a 30-year-old woman, the prosecution may want jurors who can relate to the victim and select jurors who are 30-year-old women or who have daughters who are 30-year-old women. The defence may want jurors who cannot relate to the victim (e.g., have no connection to 30-year-old women) and who are older men who may be able to relate to the accused.

Stephanie Block and her colleagues Seth Greenberg and Gail Goodman put the notion that emotional content and self-reference can influence juror memory to the test when they conducted an experiment in which emotional tone and personal relevance were varied. Eighty-one college students were presented with one of four narratives and then given a surprise memory test. The first narrative described a campus rape, which was both highly emotional and highly self-relevant to the participants. The second described a rape that occurred in prison, which was highly emotional but not self-relevant. The third narrative described the process of registering for class on a college campus, which was not emotional but was self-relevant to the college students participating in the study. The fourth narrative described the process of registering to vote in a foreign country, which was neither emotional nor self-relevant to the study's participants. The researchers presented participants with one of these narratives and then administered a memory questionnaire related to the narrative that posed 22 open-ended questions (such as "How many friends did she go with?") and 22 multiple-choice questions (such as "What are the names of the friends she went with?" with three response options). The researchers found that memory was better for emotional narratives than non-emotional narratives and that memory was better when the material was personally relevant than when it was not (Block, Greenberg, & Goodman, 2009).

The findings of Block et al. (2009) support the strategies commonly used by attorneys and suggest that if an attorney wants a jury to remember material, it should be as emotional and personally relevant as possible. This finding also substantiates arguments sometimes made by attorneys to limit graphic testimony (which may bias the jury to remember the prosecution's narrative) and to move a trial to a different location in high-profile cases (because jurors may find the elements of the crime personally relevant). This also can explain why people accused of crimes often have such a hard time deciding whether to take the stand in their own defence. While taking the stand may make some jurors relate to the accused better (and remember the defence better), a highly charged and emotional cross-examination by the prosecution may also be well remembered and hurt the defendant's case.

The Impact of Deliberation on Jurors' Memories for Trial Evidence

jury deliberation process

when the jurors from a trial convene to decide on a verdict

memory pooling

the sharing of memories of many individual experiences of a single event, such as the proceedings of a trial

error correction

when incorrect memories are identified and corrected through the process of gathering new information

There is substantial evidence that jurors do not have perfect memory for evidence presented in trial (see, e.g., Rosenhan et al., 1994); however, these memory problems are often downplayed because of a general assumption that errors in memory will be corrected during the **jury deliberation process** when all the jurors convene to decide on a verdict for the trial based on the evidence. Two aspects of deliberation are assumed to improve memory of jurors. The first is **memory pooling**, which assumes jurors share all their individual memories, filling in gaps for jurors who missed information. The second is **error correction**, which assumes any erroneous memories will be corrected through discussion of the evidence with other jurors.

Mary Pritchard and Janice Keenan designed a mock jury experiment that tracked performance on trial-related items throughout the deliberation process to see if deliberation does in fact improve memory. In their experiment, groups of five or six mock jurors viewed the 30-minute edited video of *New Jersey vs Bias* that depicted a crime where the correct verdict was ambiguous. After the video ended, participants rated their confidence in their memory for the trial, indicated what verdict they thought was correct, and rated their confidence in that verdict on a scale of one to five. Participants then completed a 24-item short-answer memory test related to the evidence presented at trial. Some of the items related to details that were central to the case (e.g., "Had Lise Bias threatened to kill herself before the night she died?") while other items related to peripheral details (e.g., "What type of gun was used in the shooting?"). After the test had been completed, the mock jurors were told that they now needed to deliberate for 30 minutes and come to a unanimous verdict. After the deliberation was over, the verdicts were recorded and participants took the same 24-item memory test again. Pritchard and Keenan (2002) found a slight but significant improvement in memory performance on the post-deliberation test; scores were 3.4 per cent higher than they were for the pre-deliberation test. The improvement was the same for central and peripheral details related to the case.

When Pritchard and Keenan (2002) examined the mistakes that mock jurors made on the memory test, they found more errors of omission (leaving an item blank) than errors of distortion (entering an incorrect answer). Pritchard and Keenan (2002) also found that deliberations helped to correct distortions in memory and did not result in new errors being made by the participants in this study, supporting the general rationale behind having jurors deliberate. However, Pritchard and Keenan (2002) also uncovered some aspects of the deliberation process related to memory that may be problematic. First, Pritchard and Keenan (2002) only found a weak correlation between juror memory accuracy and juror memory confidence. Second, the researchers found that the more confident jurors tended to lead jury deliberations. By extension, this means that jurors with less accurate memories tended to be more influential during deliberation. Finally, the researchers found that jurors who were less confident (and who actually had better memories) were more likely to change their verdicts in order to match the verdict of those leading the deliberation; in other words, verdicts are more likely to be determined by jurors with less accurate memories. The results from this study strongly suggest that while juror deliberation can lead to slight improvement in juror memory, with that comes the potential problem of memory confidence, rather than memory accuracy, influencing the outcome of the trial. One possible solution may be to inform jurors that memory confidence is not necessarily a marker of memory accuracy, and that they should not come to a verdict simply because another juror seems very sure of the facts of the trial.

brain fingerprinting
a process that attempts to detect a match between criminal evidence and the memory of a suspect

electroencephalogram (EEG)
a method for measuring the electrical activity occurring in the brain in real time using conductors applied to the scalp

Brain Fingerprinting

Lawrence Farwell developed a highly controversial investigative method known as **brain fingerprinting** and claims that this technique makes it possible to detect whether a suspect possesses memories of committing a specific crime by monitoring brain activity while the suspect is being questioned. In the brain fingerprinting procedure, the electrical activity in the brain is monitored in real time using an **electroencephalogram (EEG)** while the subject is presented with probes consisting of words, phrases, or pictures containing details salient to a crime or criminal investigation along with irrelevant information (Farwell, 2012). Farwell claims that when a

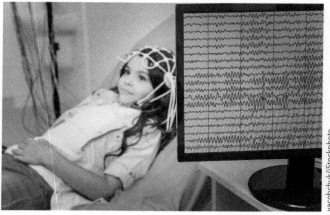

An example of the raw output of an electroencephalogram (EEG), which is used in brain fingerprinting

stimulus matches a stimulus in the examinee's memory, the examinee will automatically produce a distinctive brainwave pattern known as a P300 memory and encode related multifaceted electroencephalographic response (or P300-MERMER). The P300-MERMER response begins with a peak of positive electrical activity about 300 to 800 ms after the presentation of the stimulus and is followed by negative electrical activity a few hundred milliseconds later; the whole P300-MERMER lasts about 1200 ms. According to Farwell (2012), if a person is guilty of a crime, she or he will produce a P300-MERMER pattern when presented with details only the perpetrator would know, and if a person is innocent the P300-MERMER pattern will not be produced (Farwell, 2012).

Cases in Which Brain Fingerprinting Has Been Used

In 1999, Lawrence Farwell administered a brain fingerprinting test on James B. Grinder, who was a suspect in the rape and murder of Julie Helton. The test was administered to see if James B. Grinder had memories of the specific details of the crime. The test revealed P300-MERMERs for the probes, indicating that James B. Grinder had knowledge of the case not revealed to the investigators. Grinder had entered a not guilty plea when he was first arraigned but, after the brain fingerprinting test, he changed his plea to guilty and is currently serving a life sentence. Grinder also subsequently confessed to the rape and murder of three other women (Farwell, 2012).

In 1977, an alleged witness accused Terry Harrington of murdering John Schweer in Council Bluffs, Iowa. In 1978, Harrington was convicted by a jury and sentenced to life in prison with no possibility of being released. In 2000, Lawrence Farwell administered a brain fingerprinting test to Harrington. The brain fingerprinting test showed that Harrington had no specific memories for details pertinent to the murder. A subsequent brain fingerprinting test showed Harrington did have memories related to his alibi. Farwell confronted the alleged witness with the brain fingerprinting results. The witness recanted his testimony and admitted that he had accused Harrington to avoid being prosecuted himself. Harrington sought to have his conviction overturned based on the brain fingerprinting evidence. However, because the only witness in the case had recanted, the prosecution dismissed the case entirely and Harrington was set free. Harrington later sued the state of Iowa for intentionally framing him and the state settled out of court for $12 million (Farwell, 2012).

Criticisms of Brain Fingerprinting

Brain fingerprinting is highly controversial for several reasons. First, although Farwell claims that brain fingerprinting has been rigorously tested and that it has never produced a false positive, Farwell has not made the data from these tests public and the claims have never been subjected to peer review (Meijer, Ben-Shakhar, Verschuere, & Donchin, 2013). Second, P300-MERMERs are produced when stimuli are unexpected, and don't necessarily indicate that a subject has a memory for a stimulus. For example, an innocent murder suspect could be interrogated using brain fingerprinting and could be shown a picture of a knife and be surprised because the suspect believed that the murder weapon was a gun. This would produce a P300-MERMER. Third, brain fingerprinting relies upon suspects paying attention to elements of the crime scene. Meijer, Selle, Elber, and Ben-Shakhar (2014) conducted a laboratory study where participants were taken through an actual crime scenario and found that many of these subjects passed a brain fingerprinting test simply because they did not pay attention to the elements of the scenario. In this same experiment, Meijer et al. (2014) found brain fingerprinting to be less reliable than a standard polygraph. Fifth, brain fingerprinting has a number of practical limitations. Brain fingerprinting cannot be used in cases where facts about the crime are unknown, as when someone disappears and foul play is suspected. It also cannot be used when the suspect claims to have been at the scene of the crime as a witness or when the suspect has already been through a trial related to a crime and has heard every detail in that setting. Finally, brain fingerprinting relies heavily on the assumption that a guilty suspect will have a perfect, undistorted memory of the crime. However, as pointed out by Rosenfeld (2005), it is well established that, even in ideal conditions, not all details of an experience are recorded accurately (e.g., Loftus & Ketcham, 1996); many people commit crimes under extreme stress and/or while intoxicated, which can further weaken the reliability of their memory for the event. Rosenfeld (2005) thus speculates that a guilty individual could appear to "pass" a brain fingerprinting examination simply by not remembering the crime very well. Thus, while brain fingerprinting could sometimes yield evidence of guilty knowledge, most experts agree that the problems with the method far outweigh the benefits it may produce.

Skin Conductivity and Memory Detection

Researchers at the Institute for Frontier Areas of Psychology and Mental Health in Freiburg, Germany, have devised a simple physiological test that can distinguish between false memories and real ones. Ali Baioui and his colleagues used a variation of the Deese-Roediger-McDermott (DRM) paradigm to test their method. The researchers told the participants they were taking part in a study about social perception and emotion and then presented participants with 13 visual images from magazines showing everyday household scenes. Participants were asked to rate the scenes based on their pleasantness. Half of the participants were shown edited versions of the scenes during the study phase while half were shown the original images. Afterward, both groups were hooked up to electrodes that measure skin conductance, breathing, heart rate, and pulse and shown the original images. Participants were asked to indicate whether each image was one that had been presented during the study phase. The autonomic nervous system automatically reacts to new stimuli, so the researchers predicted that participants would have less of a response to scenes they had seen before than to new scenes. The researchers found lower skin conductance for old items than for new ones, even when the participant made an error. This suggests that skin conductance is even more accurate than the participant's recognition at measuring what is in the participant's memory. It is possible that skin conductance, which is somewhat easier to administer than an EEG, may be used as a method of memory detection in the future (Baioui, Ambach, Walter, & Vaitl, 2012).

The Cognitive Interview

The cognitive interview (CI) was developed by Edward Geiselman and Ronald Fisher in the 1980s in an attempt to improve the accuracy of eyewitness testimonies. The techniques used in the CI are based on well-established memory theories, including encoding specificity (see Chapter 6), schemas (see Chapter 7), and recency effects (see Chapter 6). During a CI, the interviewer tries to reinstate the context of the crime for the witness by asking the witness to recount what she or he did that day leading up to the time of the crime. Witnesses are encouraged to recall as much detail as possible, including sights, sounds, feelings, and emotions leading up to the time of the crime. Reinstating context is based on the tenets of encoding specificity, which suggest that retrieval is optimized when it takes place in the same context as encoding. Witnesses are also asked to report the crime from different perspectives, such as the perspective of another witness, or the perspective of the criminal, in order to reduce the witness's dependence on schemas (which can produce inaccurate information). Interviewers also typically ask the witness to report the incident from the end to the beginning in order to take advantage of the fact that recent events tend to be recalled more accurately than less recent events (known as the recency effect).

Finally, at all points during the CI the interviewer listens to the witness while the witness engages in free recall. This helps ensure that the witness provides as much information as possible and does not lose her or his train of thought due to interruptions by the interviewer.

In 1985, Geiselman, Fisher, and their colleagues conducted an experiment to test the efficacy of the cognitive interview. In their experiment, participants viewed a film of a violent crime and were then interviewed two days later by a policeman who used a cognitive interview, or the standard interview method at the time, or an interview by hypnosis. The researchers recorded the number of facts correctly recalled as well as the number of errors. The participants in the cognitive interview condition recalled significantly more facts that participants in the other conditions (Geiselman, Fisher, MacKinnon, & Holland, 1985). It should be noted that, while CIs typically result in more information being recalled, a meta-analysis has revealed that this information is no more accurate than information gleaned using a standard interview (Köhnken, Milne, Memon, & Bull, 1999).

CHAPTER REVIEW

- In the 1970s, Elizabeth Loftus and her colleagues were studying the effect of leading questions on eyewitness memory when they discovered the misinformation effect. This discovery led to questions concerning the accuracy of eyewitness memory.
- Police lineups have been used for centuries to identify perpetrators; however, recent research has revealed that people can easily be misidentified if the lineup procedure is not done correctly. Research suggests that sequential lineups where quick decisions must be made and confidence ratings are collected may produce the most accurate eyewitness identifications. Allowing witnesses to say "I don't know" may also significantly reduce the rates of false identifications.
- Loftus's work also suggested that repressed memories could really be false memories, which ignited a controversy. Many therapists felt repressed memories were real, while psychologists studying the malleability of memory found little evidence for the existence of true repressed memories and felt instead that false memories could easily be implanted in therapeutic settings.
- False memories can also sometimes lead to false confessions.
- The memory of jurors is essential to a fair trial; however, many factors can bias juror memory. Pre-trial publicity can have a significant impact on juror memory even when jurors are instructed to ignore it. This may be because jurors make source memory errors and confuse the publicity with testimony from the trial.

- Research on jurors' memories has revealed that jurors develop a story using information from the trial as well as their personal experience and inferences. This story is used to make decisions about which verdict is most appropriate.
- Research has also shown that note taking during trial improves memory for trial facts, perhaps because it ensures that jurors pay attention during the trial proceedings.
- Jurors better remember trial testimony that evokes negative emotions or is personally relevant than other trial testimony.
- When juries deliberate, it is usually the jurors who are most confident in their memory for the trial who guide the other jurors to a decision, even though those who are more confident are not necessarily more accurate.
- Brain fingerprinting involves looking for patterns in EEG data while questioning suspects with a carefully constructed set of queries. Although the creator of the technique claims it is 100 per cent accurate, data proving its accuracy has never been released and studies conducted by outside parties have found problems with the method.
- Cognitive interviews are a method for questioning witnesses that take advantage of a number of memory theories in order to gain as much information from the witness as possible.

MEMORY ACTIVITY

How Good Is Your Eyewitness Memory?

This chapter began with a case study discussing the life work of Hugo Münsterberg. Without referring back to the case study, can you recall what Hugo Münsterberg looked like? Try sketching a picture of Münsterberg or describing Münsterberg to a friend acting as an amateur sketch artist. Also write down any other details about his appearance that you couldn't include in your drawing and an indication of how confident you are in your recollection. When you have finished, compare your work to the picture of Hugo Münsterberg shown on page 283. Apply what you learned in this chapter to explain possible reasons for your success (or failure) to recall features about Münsterberg.

Questions

1. What is the misinformation effect? Describe an experiment related to this phenomenon.
2. Explain how misinformation comes to be represented in memory according to Loftus (1979).
3. Describe the results from "lost in the mall" paradigm experiments. Explain what implications the results from these experiments have for our understanding of memory.
4. Differentiate between a showup and a lineup.
5. Describe an experiment in which eyewitness confidence was used to compare the diagnostic value of simultaneous lineups to sequential lineups. What were the conclusions of the researchers who conducted this experiment?
6. Describe a new approach to suspect identification that is based on confidence ratings.
7. Explain "the memory war" and describe both positions on the issue.

8. Identify three types of studies that have been used to study repressed memory. Identify possible problems with each of these methods.
9. Describe, in detail, a situation that may cause a person to make a false confession.
10. Describe the experiment that Christine Ruva and Cathy McEvoy conducted to evaluate the effect of pre-trial publicity. What were the results?
11. According to Nancy Pennington and Reid Hastie, what three types of information do jurors use to develop a narrative that they then use during deliberation?
12. Describe an experiment that examined the impact of note taking on juror memory. What do the results suggest about the value of jurors taking notes?
13. Describe an experiment that examined the impact of emotional testimony on juror memory. Discuss how the results may relate to the choice of a trial location and whether accused persons should take the stand in their own defence.
14. Describe an experiment that examined the impact of jury deliberations on juror memory.
15. There have been hundreds of cases of wrongful imprisonment due to incorrect eyewitness identifications. One solution to this problem might be heightened video surveillance. In the United Kingdom, activities in most public places are captured by video cameras and these video recordings have been used to solve thousands of crimes. What do you think about video surveillance in public spaces in Canada? Would it help with the problem of erroneous eyewitness identifications?
16. Explain brain fingerprinting and critique the procedure.
17. How might brain fingerprinting generate a false negative in a criminal investigation?
18. Discuss how skin conductivity might be used for lie detection. List some advantages of this method.
19. Describe a cognitive interview. Explain how memory theory has contributed to the development of this technique.

Key Figures

Stephanie Block p. 304
Neil Brewer p. 298
Ronald Fisher p. 307
Edward Geiselman p. 307
Seth Greenberg p. 304

Gail Goodman p. 304
Reid Hastie p. 302
Elizabeth Loftus p. 283
Cathy McEvoy p. 300
Nancy Pennington p. 302

David Rosenhan p. 302
Christine Ruva p. 300
Nathan Weber p. 298
Gary Wells p. 295

12 Memory and the Marketplace

LEARNING OBJECTIVES

Having read this chapter, you will be able to:

- Describe how brand preferences can develop in very young children.
- Explain how advertisements affect a person's memory of a product's features.
- Explain how advertisements can impact autobiographical memories.
- Compare and contrast explicit and implicit memories for advertisements.
- Predict response to advertisements viewed in full- and divided-attention conditions.
- Describe the effect of repetition on recall for advertisements and explain how this may impact marketing of a product.
- Explain how a political scandal impacts memory for a candidate's political promises.
- Describe the ways in which memory impacts voter decisions.

SCARY MEMORIES SELL PRODUCTS

In 2003, a potentially fatal antibiotic-resistant flu known as severe acute respiratory syndrome, or SARS, became a global epidemic, affecting people in more than 40 countries. People were so afraid of this disease that they went to great lengths to avoid catching it, from wearing surgical masks to avoiding social events. In Canada, visiting hours at hospitals were elimi- nated, and people who

Health workers scan body temperatures on this flight from Auckland in 2009, during the H1N1 outbreak, in an attempt to avoid further international spread of the virus.

were thought to have been exposed to the virus were quarantined, including two dozen newborn babies at Mount Sinai hospital whose neonatal nurse came down with symptoms soon after their births (Priest & Alphonso, 2003). The virus killed 744 people before it was contained in 2006 (Smith, 2006). In 2009, there was another global pan- demic known as the H1N1 influenza virus, or swine flu. The H1N1 outbreak caused even more of a panic than SARS, perhaps because there were nightly news broadcasts about the limited availability of vaccines, and perhaps because H1N1 was a form of in- fluenza, and many people knew influenza killed millions of people worldwide in 1918. Ultimately more than 250,000 people died worldwide from H1N1 in 2009 (Dawood et al., 2012), 438 in Canada (Public Health Agency of Canada, 2010).

Many marketers knew that their consumers would have fearful memories related to these pandemics and seized the opportunity to make sales. Makers of hygiene- related products, like Purell hand sanitizer, Clorox wipes, Kleenex tissues, and Dial soap all created advertisements that reminded people of the flu and then promised that their product could help protect them from the flu (Lindstrom, 2011). The sales of all of the products skyrocketed in 2010 because their advertisements triggered memories of the dangers of SARS and H1N1 even though not one of their products had ever been shown to be effective at preventing airborne illnesses like SARS and H1N1 (Lindstrom, 2011).

In this chapter, we will discuss the many ways that marketers use people's memory to their advantage and how divided attention and repetition affect mem- ories for products. In addition, we will discuss the potential for advertisements to change existing memories for products. For example, we will see that advertise- ments can make people think that they enjoyed a product that they actually disliked. This chapter will also explore memory for political issues, because, after all, political candidates and their stances on issues are marketed to the public in the hopes of manipulating voter choice.

Memory and Advertising

The main goal of most businesses is to convince consumers to spend money on their products. Businesses use advertisements to let consumers know about unique features of their product and also to make their product more familiar to the consumer. In order for any advertisement to influence consumer behaviour, it must interact with a person's memory. In this section, we will explore how advertisers attempt to make this connection with human memory as well as explore research evaluating the efficacy of those methods.

The Development of Brand Preferences

In Chapter 9, we saw that newborns preferred the tastes of garlic or cumin over other tastes if their mother consumed these foods in the weeks before birth, and that newborns could recognize the sound of voices and songs they heard before they were born. The notion that babies can recall experiences from before there are born gains further support from a real-world experiment that took place in an Asian mall. A few years ago, the owners of an Asian mall chain decided to see if they could get pregnant mothers to spend more money at their malls by making the smells and sounds more appealing to them. The mall owners sprayed the scent of Johnson & Johnson baby powder in areas where clothing was sold and an appealing cherry scent in the food-court area. The mall owners also played music from the era when the pregnant mothers were young, hoping that the nostalgia would keep them in the malls longer. The experiment (although not scientific) was a success; the mall saw increased sales after introducing the measures. The experiment had a second effect that the mall owners weren't expecting. About a year after the experiment began, mothers who shopped at the mall when they were pregnant began to report that the mall had a uniquely calming effect on their babies, suggesting that the babies remembered the smells and sounds from before they were born and found them soothing (Lindstrom, 2011). Taken together, results from both intentional and unintentional tests of newborn preferences suggest that marketers can influence preferences of people even before they are born.

Marketing to babies and toddlers may seem strange. After all, babies and toddlers don't shop. However, by marketing to babies and toddlers, companies can help establish preferences that will guide purchasing choices when these babies and toddlers become consumers. Preferences are largely based on familiarity, and thus marketers can create preferences in babies and toddlers just by making sure the babies and toddlers are exposed to the products; knowing what the product is is not important. Martin Lindstrom (who is a marketing expert, not a scientist) tasked SIS International Research to conduct a survey assessing how childhood preferences shape buying habits in adults. In a survey of 2035 individuals, SIS found that more than half of all people choose brands they remember from childhood, particularly when the product is a food or beverage, healthcare product, or household good, proving that

SbytovaMN/iStockphoto

Brand preferences are based largely on familiarity; thus, the sooner marketers can start exposing (future) consumers to their products, the more likely they are to have a loyal customer later.

Zety Akhzar/Shutterstock

Distributors of Kopiko coffee candies gave free samples to women on maternity wards in hopes that the flavour would become familiar to children even before the children were born.

marketers are spending wisely when they market to the very young. Thus, marketers are further motivated to advertise to the youngest possible customers because their goal is to create a lifelong preference for their product *before* the consumer develops a lifelong preference for their competition.

In the early 2000s, distributors of a coffee-flavoured candy called Kopiko began to give samples of the candy to paediatricians and doctors for them to give to women on maternity wards in the Philippines. The distributors were hopeful that exposing babies to the unique taste of Kopiko before they were born would create a sustained taste preference for the candy. The marketing ploy was a huge success. Sales of Kopiko candy increased and when the company released a coffee that tasted that Kopiko, it was an immediate success, especially among children. When marketing researcher Martin Lindstrom later interviewed mothers who had sucked on Kopiko candy while pregnant, mothers reported that they could calm their infants down immediately by giving them a sip of Kopiko coffee! (Lindstrom, 2011)

In 2011, advertisers spent $20 billion on advertising directed at children under four years of age. Advertisers market to children early in an attempt to establish brand preferences, and it works. In 1991 (when it was still legal to advertise cigarettes), a study published in the *Journal of the American Medical Association* reported that almost all six-year-olds living in the United States could identify Joe Camel (a friendly-looking mascot for Camel cigarettes), making him as recognizable to them as Mickey Mouse (Fischer, Schwartz, Richards, Goldstein, & Rojas, 1991). The marketers didn't think that six-year-olds were going to go to the store to buy cigarettes; instead, they hoped that repeated presentations of a cartoon character called Joe Camel would lead to a brand preference and, when the children grew old enough to choose cigarettes themselves, that they would choose Camels. Indeed, in the 1990s, Camels were chosen by one-third of minors purchasing cigarettes (Lindstrom, 2011).

It is estimated that by age 10 a typical child has committed 400 different brands to memory (Lindstrom, 2011), and these memories affect brand preferences. In 2010, Christina Roberto and her colleagues conducted a study to see if packaging affected taste preference in very young children. Roberto, Baik, Harris, and Brownell (2010) found that 40 preschoolers given graham crackers, fruit snacks, and carrots reported that food that came in a package with a licenced character on it tasted better than food that came in plain packaging. In a similar study, Thomas Robinson presented children with hamburgers, chicken nuggets, French fries, milk, and carrots that were identical but either in plain packaging or McDonald's packaging. Robinson, Borzekowski, Matheson, and Kraemer (2007) found that children far preferred the products in McDonald's packaging. At present, there are licenced characters on the packaging of a significant proportion of grocery store items intended for children.

In recent years, young children have begun to use technology more and more, and advertisers have seized this opportunity to expose children to their brands by developing websites and apps featuring free games and a heavy dose of exposure to branded characters. Children can go on virtual adventures with Lucky the Leprechaun from Lucky Charms, they can design and race Hot

Wheels cars, and they can play with Lego. In addition, marketers have found a way to sell items to enhance these games that are essentially advertisements for their products, such as Ganz Webkinz stuffed animals, Lego Mixels, and Disney's Tsum Tsums. In these cases, children actually need to make a purchase in order to play the game, a brilliant ploy by marketers that helps cement the product in the children's memory. Modern parents often choose "commercial-free" television channels for their children; however, most shows are essentially commercials for products associated with licenced characters (e.g., Lego's *Ninjago*, a television show about Lego characters who live in a mythical dojo, markets real-life Lego sets that mimic structures from the show). Most products marketed to children are associated with some brand to which children have mass media exposure. And marketers are hoping that children will stick with that brand as they transition into adult products. For example, most children's toothpastes are branded twice, once with a licenced character (such as *The Avengers* or *Bubble Guppies*) and once with an adult brand name (such as Colgate or Crest). Children who are *Avengers* fans may demand the Colgate *Avengers* toothpaste now and consequently develop a preference for all Colgate products. Companies are careful to keep logos and fonts the same for decades; in this way, preference due to familiarity can be sustained across a lifetime. While children may be able to explicitly recall certain advertisements and experiences, the sense of familiarity that drives preferences is supported by implicit memory. Advertisers who repeatedly expose brand images to young children are creating implicit memories for those brands. These implicit memories for a brand lead to a sense of familiarity and a preference for the brand. Because implicit memories are not prone to forgetting through neurogenesis (see Chapter 8), this sense of familiarity and preference does not change across the course of development and thus brand preferences can be established at a young age and last for a lifetime.

The Effect of Advertisements on Memory for Product Features

Suppose you are a consumer and you need to choose among four brands of orange juice, all of which you have tried in the past. How will you make your decision? If you are like most consumers, you will *believe* your decision must be based on the accurate recall of past experience with each of the different brands and that you will simply choose the brand that had the best taste and texture when you consumed it (Fazio, Zanna, & Cooper, 1978; Hoch & Deighton, 1989; Holbrook & Hirschman, 1982; Smith & Swinyard, 1983). However, there is considerable research suggesting that consumers also develop opinions about products based on advertising (Hoch & Deighton, 1989) and that these advertisements can alter existing memories for a product. So, while you may believe you are choosing brand X orange juice because you previously experienced its superior taste and texture, it is very possible that your memory that brand X had a superior taste and texture came from an advertisement and not from personal experience. This phenomenon is well illustrated in a series of experiments conducted by Kathryn Braun in the late 1990s. Braun (1999) presented participants with an orange-juice sample representing fictitious brands and then tested to see if a consumer's memory for the taste of a sample was affected by subsequent advertisements for the corresponding brand. Key to the experiment was that, unbeknownst to the participants, some of the samples were altered with vinegar and salt in order to make that particular sample taste bad.

First, Braun developed three distinct orange-juice samples by adding varying amounts of water, vinegar, and salt to orange-juice concentrate, creating one "good," one "medium," and one "bad" sample. In her first experiment, Braun (1999) began by telling participants that they would be taste testing a new brand of orange juice called Orange Grove (this was the fictitious brand) and that they would later be asked to evaluate its taste. Depending on their experimental condition, participants were given two ounces of "good," "medium," or "bad" orange juice. Participants were then asked to examine a mock-up of an Orange Grove container. After a delay, participants assigned to the advertising group were told that they were to give feedback on two possible advertisements for Orange Grove juice. The first ad asked viewers to "imagine the taste of fresh-squeezed orange juice . . . it's sweet, pulpy, and pure" (Braun, 1999, p. 322–3). The second ad compared the Orange Grove packaging to the picture of a can of frozen orange juice and stated that Orange Grove "preserves the integrity of Florida orange taste by cutting out the middleman" (Braun, 1999, p. 323). Both advertisements ended with "Orange Grove: Experience the taste Florida's been talking about." After watching both ads, participants rated the commercial on a number of scales and wrote down their thoughts about each ad. There was also a second group who did not see any advertisements. Next, all participants were asked to recall their taste experience with Orange Grove orange juice and to choose three words that they thought best described their memory of Orange Grove's taste. In the final phase of the experiment, participants were presented with five different two-ounce samples of orange juice: the "good," "medium," and "bad" from the first phase of the experiment as well as one that tasted really bad and one that tasted really good. Participants were instructed to attempt to identify the sample they had tasted in the first part of the experiment. All participants rated their confidence in their responses. Finally, all participants rated their overall impression of Orange Grove orange juice.

Braun's (1999) results suggest that postexperience advertising can make consumers believe they had previously sampled a better-tasting juice by altering their memories for the tasting experience. One participant in the advertisement group who had sampled the vinegar- and salt-laden juice later stated, "I thought it tasted real sweet. It quenched my thirst. It would be a nice eye-opener in the morning. It made me want more" (Braun, 1999, p. 325). Another participant, who also tasted the vinegar- and salt-laden juice but saw no advertisement stated, "I thought this juice was pretty terrible. It was bitter and watered down" (Braun, 1999, p. 326). Note that both of these participants tasted the *same* "bad" juice but had very different memories for what it tasted like. Overall, Braun (1999, Experiment 1) found that participants in the no-advertising condition could accurately identify the juice sample they had tasted; however, participants in the advertising condition consistently recalled the juice as tasting better than it had actually tasted.

Braun (1999) found that even with a one-week delay between the advertisement and the taste test, postexperience advertising affected consumer choice. Participants who received the "bad" juice still had more positive memories of the juice if they saw an advertisement for the juice than participants who tasted the "bad" juice and saw no advertisement. Braun (1999) also found that even with a one-week delay, participants who saw the advertisement were less accurate at recalling the juice they had tasted a week before than participants who did not see an advertisement. These findings suggest that postexperience advertisements can change consumer-choice behaviour even when the consumer doesn't like the product, and even when there is a one-week delay between the advertisement and the choice.

The results from Braun's studies imply that memory for advertisements can have a bigger effect on consumer choice than memory for products. This result has several implications for producers. First, this result suggests that advertisements can have a bigger impact on sales than product quality, and that producers may make bigger profits by spending less on producing their products and spending more on advertising them. Second, because of advertising, consumers will always remember name-brand products as being of better quality than no-name products, and thus no-name products will always need to be priced less than name-brand products in order to convince consumers to buy them.

DIY EXPERIMENT

BOX 12.1

Can You Taste the Difference?

The purpose of this experiment is to explore the influence of advertising on the perception of product quality. For this experiment, you will need to purchase a name-brand juice and a no-name juice and two cards, one showing the logo for the name brand and one simply stating "store name." Next, you will need to recruit several participants for a taste test. Have each participant taste each juice in an unmarked glass and rate each on a scale of 1 to 10. Next, have the participant taste and rate each juice again, this time with the appropriate cards in front of each sample. Repeat with multiple participants and compare the scores. Typically, there will be little difference in scores when the samples are not labelled but a preference for the name brand when the samples are labelled, demonstrating the effect of memory for advertising on perceived taste.

The Effect of Advertisements on Autobiographical Memories

A consumer's autobiographical memories are also used to help sell products. Advertisers often show images and play music that they hope will evoke a pleasant personal memory in the consumer so the consumer will in turn associate pleasant feelings with the product being advertised. For example, Walt Disney World advertisements frequently show video of the park from earlier eras, hoping that people who went to the park as children will connect with these ads and have the urge to take their own children to the parks. Marketers tend to use images and music from when their target audience was in their teens and twenties simply because the music we listen to at this age is the music we tend to prefer for life (Lindstrom, 2011). Car advertisements from every era demonstrate this approach well; cars aimed at young consumers are sold using contemporary music and technology, while cars aimed at older consumers are sold using images and music from 20 years ago. A recent ad campaign for a minivan, ostensibly aimed at people with young families, featured images of minivans from the 1990s, when the ad's target audience would have been teens. The advertiser clearly hoped that seeing the old version of the minivan would evoke positive emotions about youth, and that those positive emotions would lead to more sales. When the Chrysler PT Cruiser was introduced, its target market was baby boomers, who grew up riding around in cars with a similar design. There are hundreds of examples of this play on nostalgia. The recent reboot of the Nintendo64 game system is a great illustration; the technology is clearly much better in present day, but autobiographical memories of playing on the old Nintendo64 system will drive many adults to purchase the product anyway. What these campaigns have in common is that they attempt to evoke a memory for an experience and event in the past that actually happened.

It is well established that autobiographical memories can be activated within the context of an advertising message (Baumgartner, Sujan, & Bettman, 1992; Krugman, 1967). Activation of autobiographical memories is more likely to happen when an ad causes the consumer to focus on experiential information (Wells, 1986) or when very dramatic narratives are presented (Boller, 1990). Kathryn Braun, Rhiannon Ellis, and Elizabeth Loftus speculated that because autobiographical memories are malleable (see Chapter 10; see also Schacter, 1995) and because autobiographical memories are activated by some advertisements, certain types of advertisements may alter how people remember their own past.

In 1996, Walt Disney World promoted the twenty-fifth anniversary of the park with an ad campaign called "Remember the Magic." The campaign featured videos of people visiting the park in the 1970s and urging them, as the name of the campaign suggests, to "remember the magic." Braun, Ellis, and Loftus (2002) wondered if the Remember the Magic campaign, which highlights very sentimental personal memories, may actually have had the power to alter some peoples' autobiographical memories, possibly making them think they had been to the park, and been happy there, when they in fact had not. To test this hypothesis, Braun et al. (2002) devised a series of experiments that tested whether advertisements can cause people to become more certain that events actually happened to them as children, including events that were impossible.

In their first experiment, Braun et al. (2002) assessed whether autobiographically focused advertising could directly affect how consumers remember a prior childhood experience. Braun gave participants a list of 20 childhood events and asked to rate whether or not the event happened to them before the age of 10 on a scale of 0 to 100, with a score of 0 indicating the event definitely did not happen to them, and a score of 100 indicating that an event definitely did happen to them. This was known as the Life Experience Inventory (LEI). One item on the list was "Met and shook hands with a favourite TV character at a theme resort." In order to disguise the true purpose of the experiment, Braun et al. (2002) had participants perform a variety of other experiments in addition to the survey. Participants returned one week later and half of them were shown the ad for Walt Disney World depicted in Figure 12.1. The ad encouraged participants to remember the characters of their youth and then includes a description of what it would have been like to meet Mickey Mouse at Walt Disney World. For example, the ad states "You needed no urging, but somehow the closer you got, the bigger he got . . . He doesn't look that big on TV, you thought" and "The excitement rushes through you, you don't know whether you'll faint or explode" (Braun et al., 2002, Figure 1). The experimenters encouraged the participants to imagine themselves experiencing the situation described in the ad and were then asked to write down how the ad made them feel and what the ad made them think about. Participants were then given a five-minute distraction task during which the experimenter from week one came into the lab in a panicked state and said there had been a problem with the autobiographical data and could the participants please fill out the LEI again. Participants completed the life events inventory

Figure 12.1   Autobiographical ad used in Braun et al. (2002) Experiment 1

The advertisement shown to half of the participants in Braun et al. (2002) encourages readers to imagine themselves being at Walt Disney World as a young child.

Source: Braun et al., 2002, Figure 1

and then, after a 15-minute-long distraction task, participants were asked whether they had ever been to Walt Disney World and, if they had visited, to describe their memories from the visit. Finally, participants who had visited Walt Disney World were asked to rate how well they remembered the visit, whether their memory was pleasant or unpleasant, whether they associated emotions with the experience, and whether the memory was central to their childhood.

The researchers were interested in seeing whether a person could be led to believe a previous experience was more probable by imagining that experience through an advertisement. The researchers only analyzed data from participants who reported they were not sure they had met a TV character at a theme park when they completed the survey in week 1. The researchers compared LEI scores at week 1 and week 2 for the target item "Met and shook hands with a favourite TV character at a theme resort." The researchers found that 90 per cent of participants who saw the Walt Disney World ad showed an increase in confidence for the target item from week 1 to week 2, compared to 47 per cent in the control condition. This difference was highly significant. In addition, increases in confidence were significantly larger for the ad group than the control group. The results from Experiment 1 are depicted in Figure 12.2.

In a second experiment, Braun et al. (2002) studied whether false information in advertisements about childhood experiences at Disneyland could make consumers believe that those false events had actually happened to them. This experiment focused on Disneyland, not Walt Disney World, because the participants lived closer to California than Florida. The researchers used the same ad format as in Experiment 1 but included two types of false information. In one ad it was suggested that the participant had shaken hands with Bugs Bunny and that shaking hands with Bugs Bunny was part of every child's experience at Disneyland. This event could not really have taken place because Bugs Bunny is a Warner Brothers character and does not appear at Disneyland, although the participants would have seen Bugs Bunny cartoons frequently when they were 10 years old. In another ad it was suggested that the participant had shaken hands with Ariel, the Little Mermaid, and that shaking hands with Ariel was part of every child's experience at the park. This event could not really have happened because Ariel was not yet introduced when these participants were 10 years old. The researchers also presented a nonautobiographical Disneyland ad that contained information about the park, features of a new ride, and how to order tickets online. The nonautobiographical ad served as the control for the experiment. Participants completed a similar life experience inventory (LEI) as in Experiment 1; however, the target item was changed to "Shaking hands with a cartoon character at a theme park." The participants were asked to rate how confident they were that they had seen specific characters at a theme park; Bugs Bunny and Ariel were embedded in the list. A week later, participants

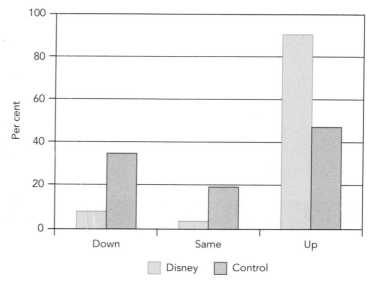

Figure 12.2 The results from Braun et al. (2002) Experiment 1

Participants were asked at week 1 and week 2 how confident they were that they had met and shaken hands with a Disney character. The Disney group saw the ad depicted in Figure 12.1 just before rating their confidence at week 2. The results suggest that autobiographical memories can be influenced by advertisements.

Source: Braun et al., 2002, Figure 2

returned to the lab under the guise of completing a different experiment. During the experiment a panicked researcher again came in and said the LEI data had been lost and the participants were asked to complete the LEI again. After a 15-minute-long distraction task, participants were asked whether they had ever been to Disneyland and, if they had visited, to describe their memories from the visit. Finally, participants who had visited Disneyland were asked to rate how well they remembered the visit, whether their memory was pleasant or unpleasant, whether they associated emotions with the experience, and whether the memory was central to their childhood.

The results from Experiment 2 revealed that 16 per cent of participants who had seen the Bugs Bunny ad falsely recalled shaking hands with Bugs Bunny at Disneyland and 7 per cent of participants who saw the Ariel ad falsely recalled shaking hands with Ariel. The researchers speculated that more people recalled shaking hands with Bugs Bunny because, at the time, Bugs Bunny was a more familiar cartoon character. The results of Experiment 2 thus show that autobiographical advertising can cause people to believe they have experienced events that never really occurred. Further, an examination of peoples' memories for Disney parks following the ads revealed extremely positive sentiments; participants reported wanting to go back to the parks and to talk about their experiences at the parks with their friends. Thus, autobiographical advertising may benefit marketers in two ways: It may change a consumer's purchase intention and it may lead viewers to advertise the brand using word of mouth.

The results from Braun et al. (2002) mirror other experiments that have succeeded in creating false memories, such as those discussed in Chapter 11. Braun et al. (2002) note that the results from their experiments raise the ethical question of whether it is acceptable for advertisers to use campaigns that could potentially alter people's memories for their past. The researchers note that advertisements may change memories even when that is not the intention of an advertisement; even benign advertisements may trigger, and alter, memories. It may therefore not be possible for advertisers to prevent ads from altering memories. In addition, because advertisements tout the benefits of products, it is unlikely that any ad would result in the creation of a negative and harmful memory. However, Braun et al. (2002) note that even though changes in memory due to advertising may be relatively harmless and unavoidable, it may be best, from an ethical standpoint, to inform consumers that advertisements have this power.

Advertisers take advantage of the malleability of autobiographical memory (whether they know it or not) by creating ads that are nostalgic. These ads remind the consumer of the "good old days"; they suggest their product will be "just like Mother used to make"; and use ads from when their target market was young all in an attempt to make the consumer remember (or think they remember) enjoying the product in the past.

DIY EXPERIMENT
BOX 12.2

Memory Manipulation in the Media?

Watch television or another media source with advertising. For at least 10 commercials, note the brand, a brief description of the ad, the types of images shown, and the message.

For each ad, determine whether the advertiser tried to evoke a past memory or nostalgia.

For ads that are clearly nostalgic, consider their target market (i.e., who the marketers hope to influence with their ad) and assess how old the target market was during the time period the nostalgia refers to. Is there a pattern in your data?

Explicit and Implicit Memory and Advertising

Most marketing studies ask consumers to explicitly recall or recognize material from an ad campaign. For example, many companies will recruit consumers and then have them perform what is known as a **day-after recall test**, where consumers are asked to recall or recognize ads they saw the day before. Other times, consumers are shown ads and are asked to indicate if they recall seeing the ads in magazines or online (Shapiro & Krishnan, 2001). Both of these approaches test explicit memory, or the consumer's ability to deliberately recall previously seen campaign information. However, at least two arguments suggest that implicit, not explicit, memory guides many consumer decisions. The first is the speed with which consumers make choices. Researchers have found that most consumers spend just five seconds making decisions about products (Bogart & Tolley, 1988; Park & Hastak, 1994). The second is that implicit memory is strongly correlated with judgments about a product even when explicit memory does not correlate with these judgments (see, e.g., Kardes, 1986; Shedler & Manis, 1986).

In 2001, Stewart Shapiro and Shanker Krishnan set out to study the effects of explicit and implicit memory on consumer choice. Shapiro and Krishnan (2001) focused on two factors: delay between exposure and test, and divided attention during exposure. Both delay and divided attention are related to real-life consumer behaviour; there is often a delay between when an ad is seen and when a product choice must be made, and ads are often presented when consumers are occupied with other tasks (having a conversation, driving, etc.) and are not fully attending to the ad. It is well established that explicit memory is more affected by both the passage of time and divided attention than implicit memory (Debner & Jacoby, 1994; Murdock, 1965; Tulving, Schacter, & Stark, 1982). Shapiro and Krishnan (2001) thus hypothesized that explicit memory retrieval for ads would be hindered both by time delay and divided attention and that implicit memory for these ads would not be as affected by the experimental manipulation.

In the first phase of their experiment, Shapiro and Krishnan (2001) exposed their participants to 12 target ads and 12 distractor ads. All of the ads were for fictitious products and were presented visually. Half of the participants were presented with the ads alone (full-attention condition) while the other half viewed the ad while listening to a radio program that they were instructed to attend to (divided-attention condition). After the ads had all been presented, all participants completed a filler task for 15 minutes. Half of the participants in each of the attention conditions then completed a memory test (no-delay condition) while the other half returned in one week to complete their memory test (delay condition). The memory test was one of three measures. The first was a recognition test designed to require explicit memory. In this test, participants were given a list of 12 product categories and next to each product category were two brand names, one from an ad the participant had seen and one new name. The task was to identify the brand name that the participant had seen. Performance was measured as the proportion of correct responses. The second measure was an implicit memory test. This test was identical to the explicit memory recognition test except that 12 additional product categories, each with two additional brand names, were presented. The inclusion of the new product categories and brand names was an attempt to conceal that the task referred to the prior exposure episode. Participants completing the implicit memory test were told to assume they were purchasing the product and that they should examine the brand names listed and circle the brand name that they would most likely choose. The participants did not need to consciously recall anything from the exposure episode to complete this task and thus the task tapped implicit rather than explicit memory. Performance was measured as the proportion of brand names chosen from

day-after recall test

participants' recall or recognition of ads they saw the day before the target set. The final task was a **process-dissociation procedure (PDP)**, a well-known paradigm designed to get separate estimates of conscious and automatic contributions to retrieval (for a detailed discussion of this procedure, see Jacoby, 1991). In a typical study using the process-dissociation procedure, words (such as SHOWER) are presented on a computer screen for a very brief duration (typically 50 ms) such that they appear as a blip or a flash to the participant. Participants are then given a stem-completion task where they are presented with the first three letters of half of the words that were presented (e.g., SHO___). For one-half of the words, participants are asked to complete the stem but to avoid using words that had just been presented to them. This is known as the exclusion task. In the exclusion task, successful conscious retrieval of the flashed word SHOWER will lead to a decrease in the likelihood of completing the stem SHO___ with SHOWER compared to when no exclusion instructions are given. An increase in the likelihood that a flashed word is used to complete the stem in the exclusion task would only occur if conscious recollection failed and if automatic processes led to the response (Shapiro & Krishnan, 2001). This notion is formalized in the following equation:

$$\text{Exclusion} = (1 - C)A$$

For the other half of the words, participants are again presented with the word stem, but this time they are asked to complete the word stem using words that were flashed to them. This is known as the inclusion task. An increase in the likelihood of using a flashed word in the inclusion task could occur if conscious memory was successful or if conscious memory failed and automatic retrieval occurred. This notion is formalized in the following equation:

$$\text{Inclusion} = C + (1 - C)A$$

Exclusion is the proportion of flashed items used to complete word stems under exclusion instructions and inclusion is the proportion of flashed items used to complete word stems under inclusion instructions. Once exclusion and inclusion are known, it is possible to estimate the amount of conscious influence by solving for C and the amount of automatic influence by solving for A using these equations:

$$C = \text{inclusion} - \text{exclusion}$$
$$A = \text{exclusion}/(1 - C)$$

If the explicit test measures conscious retrieval, then the conscious component of the PDP (C) should show the same effects of delay and divided attention as the explicit memory test. Similarly, if the implicit test measures automatic retrieval then the automatic component of the PDP (A) should show the same effects of delay and divided attention as the implicit memory test.

In the PDP task in Shapiro and Krishnan (2001), participants were shown a list of 12 product categories each with two brand names, one that had been seen before and one that was new. For six of these product categories, participants were told to think back to the exposure episode and choose brands they remembered because those brands received higher ratings in *Consumer Reports* magazine; this is referred to as the inclusion condition. For the other six product categories, participants were told to think back to the exposure episode and not choose brands they remembered because those brands received low ratings in *Consumer Reports* magazine; this is referred to as the exclusion condition. The researchers used PDP equations for C

Table 12.1   The results from Shapiro and Krishnan (2001)

Immediate Test		Explicit Test	Implicit Test	Conscious Component	Automatic Component
		Mean Proportion of Target Brands Chosen			
	Full attention	.78	.40	.39	.31
	Divided attention	.65	.36	.15	.38
Delayed Test					
	Full attention	.43	.35	.15	.31
	Divided attention	.37	.32	.06	.37
Control Group					
		.50 (chance)	.25 (chance)		

Explicit memory was affected by both delay and divided attention while implicit memory was not. The conscious component shows the same pattern as the explicit memory test while the automatic component shows the same pattern as the implicit memory test.

Source: Based on Shapiro & Krishnan, 2001, p. 9

and A to develop estimates of conscious and automatic processing respectively (see Shapiro and Krishnan, 2001).

The results from Shapiro and Krishnan (2001) are shown in Table 12.1. As predicted, Shapiro and Krishnan found performance on the explicit memory test was significantly worse following a delay and when attention was divided. Performance on the implicit memory test, on the other hand, was not affected by delay or divided attention. The distinction between the differing effects of delay and divided attention on explicit and implicit memory tests was validated by the results from the PDP. The conscious influence, which is linked to explicit memory, decreased with delay and divided attention while the automatic influence, which is linked to implicit memory, was not affected by either of these manipulations.

The results from Shapiro and Krishnan (2001) reflect results from the memory literature, showing that explicit memory is affected by time and divided attention and that these factors don't affect implicit memory (see Chapter 5). Shapiro and Krishnan (2001) suggest that these results may have important implications for people designing advertising campaigns. First, Shapiro and Krishnan (2001) argue that measuring ad effectiveness using explicit memory tests is only useful if an advertiser is certain that consumers will engage in an effortful search of their memory for prior information about products before making a purchasing decision; these are referred to as **high-involvement purchases**. This would apply to purchases that are expensive, risky, or of high personal importance to the consumer such as cars, computers, vacations, or investments. In these situations where explicit memory may play a role in purchasing decisions, Shapiro and Krishnan (2001) suggest that advertisers make sure that a consumer sees the ad

high-involvement purchase

when a consumer searches explicit memory for product information before making a purchase decision

many times to ensure that there is the shortest possible delay between seeing the ad and making a purchase decision. In addition, Shapiro and Krishnan (2001) suggest that advertisers focus on advertisements that consumers are likely to pay full attention to, such as magazine or television ads, rather than advertisements that are likely to be encountered in divided-attention scenarios, such as ads played on the radio or presented in ad space on Internet sites. Second, the researchers suggest that implicit memory measures are the best way to gauge the effectiveness of an ad campaign when consumers are not likely to search memory before choosing a product; these are referred to as **low-involvement purchases**. This would apply to purchases that are inexpensive, low risk, and of relatively low personal importance, such as choosing between brands of food items or cleaning products. In these situations where implicit memory likely guides decision making, Shapiro and Krishnan (2001) suggest that advertisers aim for maximum product exposure without being too concerned about grabbing the consumer's attention or having a delay between exposure and the time of the purchase decision. Third, Shapiro and Krishnan (2001) suggest that consumers may use a mix of explicit and implicit memory retrieval to guide their choices and that advertisers may therefore benefit from understanding the relative contribution of conscious and automatic retrieval when designing a campaign. For example, consumers may find themselves in a situation where they are making a high-involvement purchase but fail to consciously retrieve information about a particular brand, perhaps because of a delay since they last saw an ad for the brand. In these cases, implicit memory for the brand may still influence choice. This finding suggests that when designing an ad campaign for an expensive, risky, or highly personal product, advertisers may want to assess memory for the campaign using both explicit and implicit measures.

Thus, explicit and implicit memories affect consumer choice in different ways. Explicit memory is likely to be consulted when making a high-involvement purchase whereas implicit memory will be more likely to guide low-involvement purchases and impulse purchases. Advertisers can capitalize on these differences by designing ad campaigns for high-involvement purchases that are more likely to result in strong explicit memories for the product and counter the possible problems of delay and divided attention. Ad campaigns for low-involvement purchases, on the other hand, should focus on maximum exposure and the advertiser need not be as concerned about delay and divided attention. Finally, advertisers may benefit from assessing their ad campaigns based on the type of memory, be it explicit, implicit, or both, that is likely to influence a consumer who is making a decision about a particular purchase.

low-involvement purchase

when a consumer does not search explicit memory for product information before making a purchase

© Faithiecannoise | Dreamstime.com

Advertisement strategies like the billboards in busy urban areas such as Times Square in New York (pictured above) focus on obtaining maximum exposure rather than undivided attention.

The Effect of Repetition on Memory for Advertisements

One way that advertisers attempt to make their products more memorable is through repetition. The same ad is presented over and over to the same audience in hopes that this repetition will make people remember the product and eventually choose to buy it. Over the past 50 years, researchers have conducted countless studies to assess the effects of repetition

DIY EXPERIMENT

BOX 12.3

Are Advertisers Making the Most of Memory When Designing Ad Campaigns?

Make a list of at least three expensive, risky, or highly personal purchases that you have made in the past year. On a separate list note three inexpensive, low-risk, or impersonal purchases you have made in the past year.

For each item, note how you came to your purchase decision. What features of the product made you choose that product? Determine whether you are likely to have been influenced by explicit memory, implicit memory, or both, when making this purchase.

Next, research the ad campaigns for each product on your list. What types of ads do companies use for these products?

Finally, consider the types of ads used for each product and determine whether the campaign is aimed at maximizing explicit memory or implicit memory.

Compare your assessment of each ad campaign to the reasons you made your product choices. It is most likely that the campaign approach aligns with the reasons you made your choice . . . after all, the advertising worked!

---

on consumer attitudes toward products and memory for advertisements; however, these experiments have yielded conflicting results. Some results suggest that one to three repetitions can be beneficial but more repetitions have no additional benefit (e.g., Gibson, 1996; Krugman, 1972; McDonald, 1971). Other results suggest that many more than three exposures are necessary for consumers to be affected by the advertisement (e.g., Kohli, Harich, & Leuthesser, 2005; Nordhielm, 2002; Zielske, 1959). In 2015, Susanne Schmidt and Martin Eisend conducted a meta-analysis of 312 repetition effects to assess the number of repetitions of an advertisement that lead to maximized attitudes toward a product and maximal recall for the content of the ad. In addition, Schmidt and Eisend (2015) conducted a meta-analysis of a variety of factors that may moderate the effect of repetition on attitudes and recall. These moderating variables included message spacing, advertisement length, brand novelty, measurement delay, and the degree to which the ad makes personal references to the viewer.

First, Schmidt and Eisend's (2015) meta-analysis revealed an inverted U-shaped curve of advertising exposure effect on attitude (see Figure 12.3). Overall they found an initial period of **wear-in**, where repetition had a positive effect on the consumer's attitude toward the product; however, at a certain point this benefit levelled off and eventually gave way to a period of **wear-out**, where additional repetitions had a negative effect on attitudes. Schmidt and Eisend's (2015) finding supports the two-factor theory of repetition effects first proposed by Zajonc (1968). According to this model, both positive and negative factors influence the effect of repetition on attitude. Positive factors include habituation (Berlyne, 1970) and learning (Stang, 1975), and result in positive thoughts about a product. Negative factors include boredom, redundancy (Berlyne, 1970), and fear, which result in negative thoughts about a product. An inverted U-shape results from initial increases in positive thoughts resulting from learning and habituation that are following by a decrease in positive thoughts resulting from boredom when the advertisement is repeated over and over. The results from Schmidt and Eisend (2015) suggest

wear-in

a period of time during which repetition of an ad has a positive effect on the consumer's attitude toward the product

wear-out

a period of time during which additional repetitions have a negative effect on the consumer's attitude toward the product

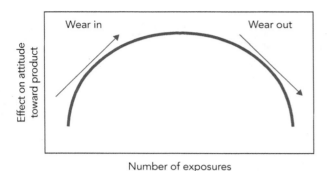

Figure 12.3   Effect on attitude toward product by number of exposures

that repetitions continue to improve attitudes up to about 10 repetitions of an advertisement, after which point negative attitudes begin to develop. Schmidt and Eisend (2015) also found that when an advertisement scores low on involvement (i.e., does not make a direct reference to the consumer), additional repetitions have a larger impact on attitude than when the advertisement scores high on involvement. In addition, the researchers found that attitude was affected more by increased exposures when the exposures were spaced out over time than when they were repeated in close succession. Thus, repetition has its biggest effect on product attitude when the advertisement is low on involvement and is spaced out over time.

Second, Schmidt and Eisend (2015) found that repetition increases the probability of recalling an advertisement, but that this benefit of repetition eventually levels off such that more exposures do not lead to better recall. In addition, the researchers found that recall increased more across repetitions when exposures to the advertisement were close together than when they were spaced further apart.

The results of Schmidt and Eisend (2015) thus suggest that memory for an advertisement, as measured by attitude or by recall, increases to a point and then levels off. This suggests that it is a good strategy to repeat an advertisement until the target audience has seen it about 10 times. The spacing of the exposures is also important. Repetition will have a bigger impact on *attitude* if exposures are spaced out, while repetition will have a bigger impact on *recall* if exposures occur close together. It seems that clustering exposures together across successive days may be the best way to maximize both attitude and recall.

Advertising is not limited to consumer goods. Advertising occurs in all instances where humans are faced with choice. For example, universities advertise to try to attract students, regions advertise to try to attract tourists, and governments advertise to encourage citizens to make safe choices (such as not texting and driving). However, by far the most aggressive advertising for non-consumer goods occurs during political campaigns. In the next section, we will discuss how memory affects how people view political candidates and how people make political decisions.

Memory and Politics

Many voters make their choice on election day based on what they remember from the political campaign. For this reason, many researchers have studied what it is that voters remember about candidates. In this section, we discuss two contentious issues related to political campaigning and memory. The first is the impact that a scandal has on memory for political issues. The second is the impact of memories on voting decisions.

The Impact of Scandal on Memory for Political Policies

Most election campaigns involve scandals. Critics of the media often claim that scandals are problematic because they prevent voters from learning about policies held by political candidates.

It is well established that negative information attracts more attention than positive information. For example, Pratto and John (1991) developed a variation of the Stroop task where participants were asked to identify the colour of a word describing either a positive or negative trait. Participants were slower at identifying negative traits and were more likely to remember negative traits in a subsequent recall test. Pratto and John (1991) concluded that this is because negative stimuli receive more extensive processing (which slows down response times) than positive stimuli. Many other researchers have also found evidence that negative information receives more extensive processing and is better remembered than positive information (e.g., Baumeister, Bratslavsky, Finkenauer, & Vohs, 2001; Bless, Hamilton, & Mackie, 1992; Robinson-Riegler & Winton, 1996).

Thus, negative information is better attended to and better recalled than positive information, but does this have a positive or negative impact on a politician? On the one hand, a voter hearing of a negative scandal may make it more difficult for them to remember previously learned information about the politician through interference (e.g., Gruneberg & Morris, 1992). On the other hand, the fact that negative information garners more attention than positive information could mean that a scandal increases processing of all campaign-related information, leading voters to remember all information about a politician better than they would if no scandal had been reported (Brown & Craik, 2000).

In a 2010 study, Beth Miller chose to investigate the impact of scandal on memory for campaign information. In the first stage of the study, participants registered on a website and provided information about their demographics and political attitudes, and completed a political sophistication quiz. In the second stage of the experiment, participants logged onto the website and read fictitious newspaper articles about a fictitious political candidate running for mayor. In the control condition, participants read five articles that described the politician's views on five different subjects: immigration, abortion, environment, homeland security, and domestic partnership. In the experimental condition, the participants read the same articles except that, instead of reading the article about homeland security, they read an article suggesting that the candidate was about to reveal having had an extramarital affair with a former aide. One to fourteen days after reading the fifth article, participants received an email asking them to complete a questionnaire online. The questionnaire asked participants to recall the candidate's positions on issues and anything else they remembered from the campaign. Finally, participants were also asked to evaluate the candidate because prior research has shown that scandals can have a negative effect on trait assessment and candidate evaluations (see Abramowitz, 2001; Alford & O'Neill, 1994; Dimock & Jacobson, 1995; Fischle, 2000; Funk, 1996; Goren, 2002; Jacobson & Dimock, 1994; Newman, 2002; Rundquist, Strom, & Peters, 1977; Shah, Watts, Domke, & Fan, 2002; Sigal, Hsu, Foodim, & Betman, 1988; Stoker, 1993; Zaller, 1998).

Miller (2010) found that, overall, participants in the scandal conditions recalled a greater proportion of campaign information than participants in the no-scandal condition. Further, participants in the scandal condition were more likely to recall the campaign issues presented before the scandal article than participants in the no-scandal condition, which suggests that hearing of a scandal does not interfere with existing memories about the campaign. Miller (2010) instead suggests that scandals cause participants to pay more attention to a given candidate, which can strengthen memories for all information related to the candidate.

Participants in the scandal condition had more negative evaluations of the candidate than participants in the control group. When compared, Miller (2010) found no difference in the political views of participants in the scandal condition and those in the control condition and thus concluded that the more negative views expressed by participants in the scandal condition must be due to the experimental manipulation. Miller (2010) speculates that exposure to the scandal article enhanced participants' memory for all information related to the candidate, and better enabled these participants to evaluate the political candidate's views against their own opinions about policy. Thus, Miller (2010) suggests that if a participant's views match those of the candidate, scandalous information will have a positive effect on the evaluation of the candidate. However, if the individual's views conflict with the views of the candidate, scandal can lead to more negative evaluations of the candidate. This prediction was borne out in the data; participants who shared political views with the candidate rated the politician more positively in the scandal condition than in the control condition, whereas participants whose political views conflicted with those of the candidate rated the politician more negatively in the scandal condition than in the control condition. Miller (2010) found that scandal can enhance memory for campaign information; however, this enhanced memory for campaign information can have a polarizing effect on candidate evaluations, making positive evaluations more positive in some cases, and negative evaluations more negative in other cases.

The fact that scandal affects peoples' memories is not surprising considering that it is well established that political issues evoke strong emotional responses from people, and people remember emotionally charged information very well. Research suggests that emotions can determine how and when political information is attended to and evaluated, which in turn can impact a person's memory for political issues (Marcus & MacKuen, 1993; Marcus, Neuman, & MacKuen, 2000). In addition, emotions have also been found to influence how people update their evaluations of candidates (Kunda, 1990; Lodge, Taber, & Weber, 2006; Redlawsk, 2002; Redlawsk, Civettini, & Lau, 2007). We explore how emotions can affect memory for political candidates in the next section.

Emotions and Memory for Political Information

In their 2009 paper, Andrew Civettini and David Redlawsk examine the impact of emotional response on later recall of candidate information. In this experiment, participants were required to register as a Democrat or Republican (the participants were all Americans) and were presented with information about four candidates that represented the full range of ideologies from that

party. Participants first completed a computer-based questionnaire measuring their political preferences, their knowledge of politics, and political topics that interested them. The researchers used the responses from this questionnaire to gauge each participant's attitudinal placement on the issues. Participants then had 25 minutes to learn about the candidates by selecting different articles presented to them on a computer. Half of the participants rated their emotional response to each piece of information as anxious, enthusiastic, angry, or evoking no emotion at all; half did not report their emotional response. Participants were assigned to one of five groups, each of which was presented with a different amount of incongruent information associated with their favourite candidate.

Alexandru Nika/Shutterstock

At the end of the review session, participants voted for a candidate, rated each candidate, completed a surprise recall test (where they also recalled emotions) and a surprise cued memory test. On average, participants examined 101 pieces of information in 25 minutes but were only able to recall about 14 per cent of that information and were only able to recognize about 65 per cent of that information. However, emotion seemed to be linked to the information that participants were able to remember. Participants who reported their emotion after reading each article only rated 38 per cent of items as evoking an emotion; however, of those items recalled, 80 per cent were associated with an affective response that the participant could remember. Incongruent items were also more memorable, but only when the congruence was unexpected. When participants encountered large amounts of incongruence, the incongruent items were no better recalled than the congruent items. In sum, Civettini and Redlawsk (2009) found that the likelihood that a campaign item would be remembered was increased if the item evoked an emotional response, but that the actual nature of the emotional response was not important; encountering something that makes a person angry has a similar memory benefit as encountering something that makes a person feel anxious or enthusiastic. In addition, the most significant finding of this experiment was that the more incongruent an item is with the expectations of the participant, the more likely it is to be remembered. Incongruent information seems to be similar to scandals in its impact on memory, and this makes sense, as scandals often involve politicians behaving in ways that are unexpected.

Taken together, the results of Miller (2010) and Civettini and Redlawsk (2009) suggest that campaign events linked to scandal or emotion are more memorable. In the next section, we will explore the extent to which memory plays a role in political decision making.

How Does Memory Influence Voting?

Milton Lodge and his colleagues argue that voters process campaign information online, updating their opinion of candidates as new campaign information becomes available (Lodge, 1995; Lodge, McGraw, & Stroh, 1989; Lodge, Steenbergen, & Brau, 1995; Lodge & Stroh, 1993; McGraw, Lodge, & Stroh, 1990). This online updating results in a real-time tally for each candidate. For example, a person may have a favourable tally for Candidate X and then learn of a policy she or he disagrees with, at which time the tally would be updated to be less favourable. According to Lodge, once the **online tally** regarding a candidate has been updated, the campaign information is no longer relevant. Consequently, Lodge predicts that memory for campaign information will be a weak predictor of voter decision because voters use their tally, not their memory, to make their choices. Lodge's model was based primarily on experiments that monitored participants' opinions of a single candidate over time. In 2001, David Redlawsk tested to see if the claims of Lodge's online model would be supported in an experiment that more accurately depicts a real political campaign, where there were four candidates.

In his experiment, Redlawsk (2001) recruited as participants 99 people ranging in age from 18 to 82 who were registered as Democrats or Republicans in the United States. Participants were then randomly assigned into one of two processing conditions. In the memory-based condition, participants were told that they would be required to list as much as they could remember from the campaign once the election was over, while participants in the online processing condition were not given any specific instructions about what to do with the information and were not forewarned of the memory test. Participants were also randomly assigned into either an easy-choice condition, where they were presented with information about two politicians

online tally

a method a person can use to keep track of her or his view of a public figure; the tally will increase or decrease depending on whether new information is positive or negative

from their political party and four politicians from the other party, or a difficult condition where they were presented with four politicians from their political party and two from the other party. Participants spent 22 minutes reviewing material on all six candidates and then voted for their choice from the party they were affiliated with. Participants were not given complete information about all candidates and some information was only available briefly during the 22-minute period. Participants selected which information to read. Both of these manipulations were intended to make the experiment mirror how information is disseminated in real campaigns. After the vote, all participants were asked to remember as much as they could about all six candidates. Participants in the memory-based condition were expecting this test, while participants in the online processing condition were not expecting the test.

Redlawsk (2001) found that what participants recalled was not representative of what participants actually viewed during the campaign. Individual characteristics and issues were overrepresented in the recall, and other information, such as information about polls and endorsement, was underrepresented. For example, about 36 per cent of the *material reviewed* by participants related to information about the candidate they voted for; however, a full 48 per cent of *memories recalled* related to the candidate they voted for. Conversely, polls comprised about 15 per cent of the information that participants viewed, but comprised only 4 per cent of what they recalled during the memory portion. Participants remembered about 12 per cent of the information they viewed for all six candidates, 14 per cent of the information presented for the party they supported, and 20 per cent of the information viewed about the candidate they ultimately chose in the primary election. Thus, participants not only recalled more information about the candidate they voted for, they were more accurate at recalling information for the candidate they voted for as well.

Redlawsk (2001) also computed an online tally for each candidate depending on the information that the participant viewed. If the participant viewed information about a candidate that was consistent with the political party the participant was affiliated with, the tally was increased. If the participant read information that contradicted her or his view, the tally was decreased. Redlawsk (2001) found that online tally was a better predictor of candidate choice in the online processing condition than in the memory-based condition (which is consistent with the online tally model); however, memory was a better predictor of voter choice in *both* the online tally and the memory-based processing condition.

The online tally voting model presented by Lodge (1995) and others suggests that voters change their opinion of each candidate as new information is received and use that online tally to make election decisions. However, despite the appeal for this model due to its simplicity, the experiment conducted by Redlawsk (2001) demonstrates that, even when voters are not explicitly instructed to remember campaign information, campaign information that is remembered by voters influences voting choice more than online tallies do.

Summary

Most voters would like to believe that their choices are based on a rational assessment of the merits of each available candidate. However, the results from the experiments discussed in this section suggest that memory biases can have a big impact on political opinion and voting. Miller (2010) demonstrated that a scandal can actually help a candidate by making that candidate's views on issues more memorable to people, and this in turn can result in more support for the scandalous candidate if their views match those of a voter. In addition, Civettini and Redlawsk

(2009) showed voters were biased toward remembering political information that evoked an emotional response. Finally, Redlawsk (2001) found that voters cast votes based on what they can remember about different candidates, and don't vote based on a complete assessment of all campaign information.

The results from these experiments suggest that political candidates should only be concerned about political scandal if the scandal conflicts with the politician's stance on an issue. For example, a politician who touts feminist values will be more hurt by a scandal suggesting sexism than a candidate who is not a feminist. In addition, these results indicate that political campaigns are won and lost based on what people remember about the campaign and the candidates, not on a careful comparison of candidates.

CHAPTER REVIEW

- People can begin to develop brand preferences before they are born by experiencing tastes or sounds of the same product over and over again in the womb. Because marketers know that consumers can remain loyal to a brand for a lifetime, they spend billions of dollars each year trying to develop brand loyalty in the very young. This advertising sometimes takes the form of a commercial, but more often is taking the form of full-length television shows, YouTube videos, and apps that appeal to children.
- Memory for product features can be manipulated by advertisements. For example, a consumer who reports a product tastes terrible can later remember that product as tasting very good if the consumer is presented with an effective advertisement.
- Advertisements can alter autobiographical memories if they cause the person to imagine themselves interacting with the product. The processes by which this occurs are similar to those that produce false memories through imagination inflation (see Chapter 11).
- Explicit memories for advertisements are negatively affected by both time and divided attention, while implicit memory for advertisements are not. For some products, consumers make buying decisions by accessing explicit memories about products, as when choosing a car or a cell phone. For these types of products, the most effective ads gain the consumer's attention and make the product seem like it is the best choice when the consumer choice is being made. Other times, consumers make buying decisions without consulting explicit memory, as when picking out gum at the checkout counter. In these cases, where implicit memory guides choice, the most effective ads are those that a consumer sees very often and that make the product feel familiar when the consumer choice is being made.
- Most advertisements need to be repeated to be remembered; however, the effect of advertisements on product memory levels off after about 10 exposures. The spacing between exposures is also important. Repetition will have a bigger impact on attitude if exposures are spaced out, while repetition will have a bigger impact on recall if exposures occur close together. It seems that clustering exposures together across successive days may be the best way to maximize both attitude and recall.
- Political scandals cause individuals to pay more attention to a candidate, and this additional attention may make the candidate's policies more memorable. Overall, scandals appear to have a polarizing effect on memories for candidates, making evaluations much more positive in some cases, and much

more negative in other cases. Emotions also affect memory for political issues. Issues that evoke emotion are much more likely to be recalled than issues that don't evoke emotions. The type of emotion that is evoked doesn't seem to impact memory; anger, enthusiasm, and anxiety all have similar benefits for memory.

- Voters may keep an online tally of candidates, increasing and decreasing their opinion of that candidate as information becomes available through the campaign. Research suggests that while this tally may have some impact, ultimately voter choice is based on explicit recall of campaign information rather than on these online tallies.

MEMORY ACTIVITY

Constructing More Effective Mnemonics

People tend to remember material that is obscene, disgusting, or disturbing better than material that is not, and thus adding one or more of these components to to-be-remembered material can be a very effective mnemonic (Foer, 2011).

In this chapter, you learned about two factors that can impact memory for political campaigns: scandal and emotion. For this activity, you will combine an obscene image with an image of a politician doing something obviously scandalous and obviously emotional. A very tame example would be to imagine your least favourite political candidate in his or her underwear screaming swear words while reading a tabloid newspaper. When you create your image, let your imagination run wild. The more salacious the content, the better you will remember it.

Questions

1. Suppose you are on a marketing team for a new brand of fruit juice. What marketing scheme could you use in an attempt to develop lifelong drinkers of your beverage?
2. Think about a brand that you use every day and would choose over other brands. How could you get a preschooler to develop a preference for that brand?
3. Suppose you make a soft drink that is low in calories but doesn't taste that great. Explain how advertising could help you continue to sell your product. Describe one experiment that supports your plan.
4. No-name products are not advertised. Explain how people's memory for no-name products may differ from their memories for name-brand products.
5. Describe an experiment that tested whether autobiographical memories could be influenced by advertising. Include a description of the results of the experiment.
6. Describe an experiment that tested explicit and implicit memory for an advertisement. Explain how a marketer could use the results from this experiment to develop an effective advertising campaign.
7. Compare and contrast high-involvement purchases and low-involvement purchases. Identify the best advertising approach for each type of item.
8. Describe an experiment that tested the effect of repetition on memory for advertising. Explain what the results of this experiment suggest about the best design for an advertising campaign.

9. Compare and contrast positive and negative outcomes of repeated advertising.

10. Apply your knowledge of the impact of memory on brand selection to explain the pricing of no-name products compared to name-brand products.

11. Describe an experiment that tested the impact of scandal on memory for a political candidate. Describe a situation where a scandal might actually help a political candidate and explain why the scandal may be helpful.

12. Explain how emotions impact memory for political issues. Suggest three ways that a political campaign could use emotion to help voters remember a political issue.

13. Candidate Jones has just made a statement about a political issue. The statement made Maria feel angry, Trevor feel anxious, and Hannah feel enthusiastic. How will the emotions impact the memory of these three voters? Will any of the voters remember the issue better than the others?

14. Describe two hypotheses concerning how voters make decisions on election day. Describe an experiment that compares these two hypotheses and indicate which hypothesis is supported by the result.

Key Figures

13   Memory, the Body, and Health

LEARNING OBJECTIVES

Having read this chapter, you will be able to:

- Differentiate between normal loss of memory that occurs because of aging and dementia.
- Compare and contrast Alzheimer's disease, vascular dementia, dementia with Lewy bodies, and frontotemporal dementia.
- Discuss reversible causes of dementia.
- Identify health conditions that can lead to problems with memory.
- Identify substances that can lead to problems with memory.
- Explain memory problems associated with post-traumatic stress disorder (PTSD).
- Explain how a lack of metamemory skills may contribute to obsessive-compulsive disorder (OCD).
- Identify health behaviours that can improve memory.
- Identify how memory can be used to improve health.
- Discuss the implications of research examining memory for advance directives.
- Explain how memory biases affect individual memory for health-related advice.
- Discuss evolutionary influences on memory.

CLIVE WEARING

Clive Wearing was born in England in 1938. He was an accomplished musicologist who also composed music and conducted orchestras. On March 27, 1985, Wearing contracted herpes viral encephalitis that ravaged his central nervous system. Wearing sustained damage throughout his brain, but his hippocampus was most affected. Although he recovered from the virus, Wearing has had persistent anterograde and retrograde amnesia ever since. His maxi-

Clive Wearing (right, b. 1938) developed extreme anterograde and retrograde amnesia when his hippocampus was damaged by a case of viral encephalitis. He is pictured here with his wife Deborah.

mum span of memory is about 30 seconds. If he stops thinking about something for just a few seconds, it is gone (Wearing, 2005). Throughout each day, Wearing feels as if he has just woken up for the first time. With the help of his caregivers, he keeps a journal. Each time he goes to make an entry he sees his last entry and crosses it out, thinking that someone else must have written in his journal. He then invariably enters something like "I have just woken up for the first time" (Wearing 2005). Wearing has little memory for many of his past life experiences. He knows he has children but does not know their names. He can, however, remember his wife Deborah, whom he married one year before his illness. Wearing has also retained much of his musical ability; he can play piano and sing (Wearing, 2005; France, 2005). Clive Wearing is an example of a case where physiology has directly impacted memory; Clive contracted a virus that destroyed the hippocampus, which in turn affected his memory. Because memories are formed in the brain, they are closely tied to many aspects of human physiology and health. In this chapter, we will explore the physiological aspects of memory, including physiological processes that enhance memory, and physiological processes that can destroy memory. In addition, we will explore the many ways in which memory can impact health outcomes.

Introduction

In this chapter, we explore the many ways that health can influence memory and memory can influence health. In the first section, we will discuss the difference between normal memory loss that occurs with age and dementia, and will then discuss the four most prevalent types of dementia and how each affects memory by affecting the physiological processes of the brain in its own unique way. In the second section, we will discuss a variety of other health conditions that can impact memory, including epilepsy, brain injury, Korsakoff syndrome, sleep patterns, and dissociative amnesia. In the third section, we discuss memory loss due to substance use,

neurocognitive disorder

a general term that describes difficulty with thinking, problem solving, and language that result from disorders affecting the brain and are severe enough to affect everyday activities. Many different disorders can cause dementia.

mini-mental state examination (MMSE)

a test that is used to assess the memory and cognitive functioning of individuals. The MMSE is often used to identify people with dementia.

dementia

a progressive neurocognitive disorder characterized by deficits in cognitive faculties such as memory and/or problem solving

Alzheimer's disease

a form of dementia caused by shrinking of the cerebral cortex and hippocampus. Amyloid plaques may also contribute to cognitive problems.

vascular dementia

a form of dementia caused by the loss of blood flow to the brain

dementia with Lewy bodies

a form of dementia caused by the degeneration of neurons that produce acetylcholine and dopamine

including intentional memory loss due to anaesthesia and accidental memory loss following alcohol consumption. In the fourth section, we turn our attention to how memory can impact health, including post-traumatic stress disorder and obsessive-compulsive disorder. In the fourth section we also consider how memory interacts with health-related behaviours, including how knowledge of memory can help improve the accuracy of advance directives, how exercise can benefit memory, and how false memories may be used to improve people's eating habits. In the final section, we explore how memory biases can affect healthcare using the example of memory for health-related information.

Dementia

Normal Memory Loss vs Dementia

Subtle changes to memory occur frequently as people age. Older people often forget where they put objects and sometimes have difficulty with people's names and finding the correct word when they are speaking. However, as we discussed in Chapter 9, as long as these memory changes do not interfere with everyday life, they are considered normal. So forgetting keys at home, forgetting to put the laundry in the dryer, or forgetting the name of a new neighbour may reflect memory loss due to aging, but is not abnormal. However, forgetting that interferes with day-to-day life, such as forgetting to eat or take medications, getting lost easily, or forgetting where one is or what day it is do not reflect normal memory loss due to aging and instead suggest that the person is experiencing some form of **neurocognitive disorder**, or cognitive disorder that affects not just memory but also the ability to think and reason.

The **mini-mental state examination (MMSE)** is the most frequent test given to determine whether a person is experiencing abnormal impairments in memory and cognition. The test is often administered by family physicians to determine whether a patient has dementia. The 30-item MMSE takes about 10 minutes to complete and assesses memory using tasks that require short-term retention of material, generic recall, and episodic recall. A summary of the items on the MMSE is shown in Table 13.1. Careful scoring of the MMSE can help make a differential diagnosis of cognitive impairment resulting from Alzheimer's disease, vascular disease, dementia with Lewy bodies, or depression (Vertesi et al., 2001).

A person must speak the same language as the interviewer, have no hearing impairments, and have no problems writing or drawing in order for the test to be accurate. An MMSE score of 27 points or more indicates normal cognition. A score between 19 and 24 indicates mild cognitive impairment, a score between 10 and 18 indicates moderate cognitive impairment, and a score of 9 or less indicates severe cognitive impairment. Because each test item requires memory to complete, this test helps demonstrate how important memory is to normal cognitive functioning. If memory is impaired, cognitive functioning breaks down.

There are many different types of neurocognitive disorders. Some neurocognitive disorders are non-progressive, meaning that they do not become worse over time. For example, some people diagnosed with mild cognitive impairment may remain stable, or even improve, over time. Other neurocognitive disorders are degenerative and the symptoms become worse over time; degenerative cognitive decline is referred to as **dementia**. These degenerative disorders vary in severity and include **Alzheimer's disease**, **vascular dementia**, **dementia with Lewy bodies**, and **frontotemporal dementia**.

Table 13.1   Items on the mini-mental state examination (MMSE)

Question Type (total points for question type)	Example
Orientation in time (5 points)	"What time is it?"
Orientation in place (5 points)	"Where is this test being taken?"
Registration (3 points)	"Repeat the words I say right after I say them."
Attention and calculation (5 points)	"Spell the word 'world' backwards."
Recall (3 points)	"Pigeon, oven, doorknob. [pause] Please recall the words I just said."
Language (2 points)	"Name the objects shown in these pictures."
Repetition (1 point)	"The man gave the girl a balloon. Please repeat the phrase back to me."
Complex commands (6 points)	"Make a copy of this drawing."

Source: **Based on Folstein, Folstein, & McHugh, 1975**

Alzheimer's Disease

frontotemporal dementia
a form of dementia caused by the deterioration of spindle neurons in the frontal and temporal lobes

Dr Alois Alzheimer first identified Alzheimer's disease in 1906. Alzheimer's disease accounts for 60 to 70 per cent of neurocognitive disorders and affects between 21 and 35 million people worldwide (which is about 6 per cent of people over the age of 65). Most cases of Alzheimer's disease develop in adults over the age of 65 but 5 per cent of cases occur in younger individuals. Alzheimer's disease is characterized by a buildup of amyloid plaques and tangles in the brain and substantial reduction in the size of the brain. Alzheimer's disease leads to the breakdown of bodily functions and eventually death, usually by pneumonia. The average life expectancy following a diagnosis of Alzheimer's disease is three to nine years. A comparison of a neurotypical brain and a brain of someone with Alzheimer's disease is shown in Figure 13.1.

The first symptom of Alzheimer's disease is usually a problem with short-term memory. The individual may forget the topic of a conversation or forget what task they were about to complete. As the disease progresses, the symptoms become more severe. Shrinking in the cerebral cortex and hippocampus affect the ability to recall old information and to form new memories. As a result, a person with Alzheimer's may lose functions that rely on old memories, like language, as well as abilities that rely on forming new memories, like the ability to stay oriented while walking or driving. In Canada, cholinesterase inhibitors have been approved for the treatment of mild to moderate Alzheimer's disease. These drugs work by improving neural communication. Cholinesterase inhibitors can help people with Alzheimer's for two or three years; however, once major deterioration of neurons has occurred, they are no longer useful. When Alzheimer's disease is moderate or advanced, the neurotransmitter glutamate leaks out of neurons and can cause further damage. Memantine hydrochloride blocks the reabsorption of glutamate into cells.

There is disagreement among researchers as to what causes Alzheimer's disease. There is some evidence to suggest that Alzheimer's disease is genetic. A person with an identical twin who has Alzheimer's is more likely to develop Alzheimer's than a person with a fraternal twin

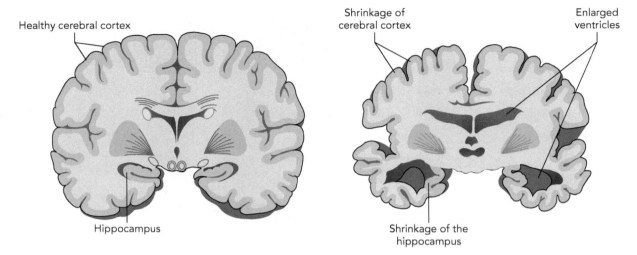

Healthy cerebral cortex

Hippocampus

Shrinkage of cerebral cortex

Enlarged ventricles

Shrinkage of the hippocampus

Figure 13.1   A comparison of a neurotypical brain and a brain of someone with Alzheimer's disease

On the left is a cross-section of a normal brain; on the right is an example of a cross-section of a brain of someone with Alzheimer's disease. A buildup of amyloid plaques and tangles leads to shrinkage in the cerebral cortex, shrinkage in the hippocampus, and an enlargement of the ventricles in the brain. Because the cerebral cortex and hippocampus are central to memory, memory is severely affected by Alzheimer's disease.

Source: Adapted from https://commons.wikimedia.org/wiki/File:ChAlzheimera-obraz-m%C3%B3zguPL.jpg

who has Alzheimer's disease, which indicates that genes play a role. Proponents of this view argue that genetic abnormalities prevent the brain from controlling the amounts of amyloids in the brain (see Figure 13.2), leading to the development of amyloid plaques (Lambert et al., 2013).

Other researchers argue that an amyloid-related mechanism that is involved in the pruning of neurons early in life is triggered in some people later in life and that this pruning leads to the destruction of neurons in people with Alzheimer's disease. This model suggests that the amyloid plaques form because amyloid is a by-product of the destruction of neurons in this way (Nikolaev, McLaughlin, O'Leary, & Tessier-Lavigne, 2009). Alzheimer's disease has also been linked to concussions and to heart disease.

Vascular Dementia

Vascular dementia is a decline in thinking skills caused by reduced blood flow to the brain because of a major stroke or a series of smaller strokes. Vascular dementia is the second most common cause of dementia after Alzheimer's disease. In many cases, vascular dementia co-occurs with

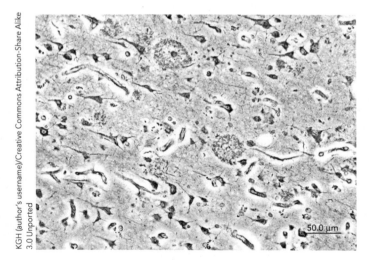

50.0 µm

Figure 13.2   Senile plaques under the microscope

This figure shows senile plaques, which appear as large circular clusters, in the cerebral cortex of a patient with Alzheimer's disease.

RELEVANT RESEARCH

BOX
13.1

The Eye May Hold the Key to Early Detection of Alzheimer's Disease

The symptoms of Alzheimer's are very similar to the symptoms of other forms of dementia that are not related to a buildup of amyloid plaques. It is important to know if someone is developing Alzheimer's early if cholinesterase inhibitors, which can slow the disease, are to be effective. It can also be important to know for sure if someone with dementia does in fact have Alzheimer's disease because other causes of dementia (such as thyroid problems or vitamin deficiencies) can be easily treated. Until recently, only brain biopsies could confirm or rule out Alzheimer's, so researchers set out to find other less invasive, less expensive methods for screening people for Alzheimer's. One option they devised is called retinal amyloid imaging (RAI). The amyloid plaques that cause Alzheimer's disease are also found in the retina of the eye. When an individual undergoes an RAI, they are first administered a substance called cucumin. Cucumin will adhere to any amyloid plaques present in the retina and will cause that area to glow. By imaging the retina, doctors can compute how much amyloid plaque is present based on how much of the retina is glowing. A small amount of amyloid plaque in the eye indicates the early stages of the disease. Amyloid plaques may appear in the retina even before significant cognitive decline has occurred. RAI is inexpensive to administer and could be implemented in large populations for relatively little cost (Hutton, Nagel, & Loewenson, 1984). This test is valuable for identifying early stages of Alzheimer's disease as well as for ruling out Alzheimer's disease as the cause of dementia.

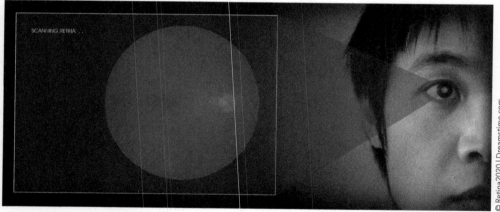

© Retina2020 | Dreamstime.com

Alzheimer's disease because the buildup of amyloid plaques in an Alzheimer's patient causes blood vessels to rupture, leading to vascular dementia. Vascular dementia can cause problems with cognition, movement, behaviour, or emotions depending on what part of the brain is damaged. In cases where Alzheimer's disease is not present, the symptoms typically emerge over a five- to ten-year period with worsening occurring after each stroke. Because the strokes associated with vascular dementia can affect any region of the brain, the symptoms of vascular dementia are more varied than the symptoms of Alzheimer's disease. For example, people with vascular dementia tend to have better recall than people with Alzheimer's disease but are more likely to have problems with speech than people with Alzheimer's disease. This is because vascular dementia can affect any region of the brain, whereas Alzheimer's disease primarily affects the hippocampus and the cerebral cortex. If damage occurs in the frontal lobes, a patient with vascular dementia will have more problems with attention than a patient with Alzheimer's disease and may exhibit apathy and urinary incontinence. The white matter in the brains of individuals with vascular dementia is typically riddled with lesions, broken blood vessels, and a buildup of blood clots, fatty deposits, and calcified arteries.

Vascular dementia can be identified through neuroimaging. Risk factors for vascular dementia include age (most people develop vascular dementia between ages 40 and 80), hypertension, smoking, diabetes, cardiovascular disease, and cerebrovascular disease. Approximately 25 per cent of people who have a stroke develop vascular dementia within one year. Vascular dementia affects about 2.4 per cent of North Americans over the age of 71 (Plassman et al., 2007). There is no treatment for vascular dementia and most people with this disorder need to reside in a nursing home. Vascular dementia can cause death by fatally interrupting the blood supply to the brain.

Dementia with Lewy Bodies

Dementia with Lewy bodies (DLB) is the next most common cause of dementia following Alzheimer's disease and vascular dementia and affects about 15 per cent of people with dementia. DLB is a form of dementia that worsens with time. In addition to difficulty with cognitive tasks, people with DLB often experience fluctuations in alertness, difficulty with movement, mood changes, and visual hallucinations. DLB causes fluctuations in cognitive abilities, alertness, and analytical and abstract thinking. DLB is caused by a buildup of Lewy bodies, which are clumps of alpha-synuclein protein, in neurons. The symptoms of DLB overlap with the symptoms of both Alzheimer's disease and Parkinson's disease. DLB can be distinguished from Alzheimer's disease by examining the disease progression; DLB has a much more rapid onset than Alzheimer's disease. DLB can be distinguished from Parkinson's disease by noting when the symptoms of dementia appeared in relation to difficulties with movement. When the onset of dementia occurs within one year of the onset of motor difficulties, DLB is indicated. When dementia follows the onset of movement difficulties by more than one year, Parkinson's disease is indicated. A differential diagnosis of DLB is very important because medications used to treat Alzheimer's disease and Parkinson's disease can be deadly if taken by someone with DLB. Some symptoms of DLB can be treated (e.g., extreme agitation can be treated with benzodiazepines); however, there is no known cure for the disease. DLB affects about 0.1 per cent of people over the age of 65 (Dickson & Weller, 2011) with a

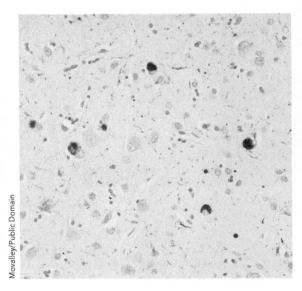

Movalley/Public Domain

Figure 13.3   Lewy bodies up close

This magnified image shows Lewy bodies in the cerebral cortex of a patient with DLB. Lewy bodies appear as brown stains under the microscope.

mean age of onset of 75 years (McKeith, 2002). DLB is slightly more prevalent in men than women (Crystal, 2008). Actor Robin Williams was found to be suffering from DLB when he died by suicide in 2014. It is not clear what role DLB played in his death.

Frontotemporal Dementia

Frontotemporal dementia (FTD) is dementia caused by the deterioration of about 70 per cent of spindle neurons (which are linked to the rapid communication of information throughout the brain) in the frontal and/or temporal lobes. Other neurons are not affected by FTD. The brain degeneration caused by FTD follows a predictable course beginning in the orbitofrontal cortex and ventromedial cortex and later progressing to the dorsolateral cortex and the temporal lobe. FTD is also known as Pick disease after Arnold Pick, who first described the condition in 1892. FTD typically appears between the ages of 55 and 65 although, like Alzheimer's disease, it can sometimes affect younger people. The most common symptom of FTD is a change in social and interpersonal behaviour. People with FTD tend to have blunted emotions, appear apathetic, and have difficulties with both productive and receptive language. However, unlike with other forms of dementia, the cognitive deficits exhibited by people with FTD are not related to memory; memory for material other than language is preserved in people with FTD. Perception, spatial processing, and manual dexterity (praxis) are also preserved in FTD.

It can be difficult to identify FTD in its early stages using neuroimaging; however, researchers have identified several cognitive tests that can indicate whether someone has brain damage consistent with FTD. One example is the faux pas recognition test in which individuals must identify statements or actions that are offensive to others. The orbitofrontal area of the brain, which is damaged in people with FTD, is responsible for feelings of social embarrassment. Other tests of social cognition, including the Iowa gambling task, the hotel task, and the multiple errands task, can also be used to identify people in the early stages of FTD. Some cases of FTD are caused by leaks of cerebrospinal fluid; in these cases, the symptoms of FTD can be reversed. Other forms of FTD are not curable.

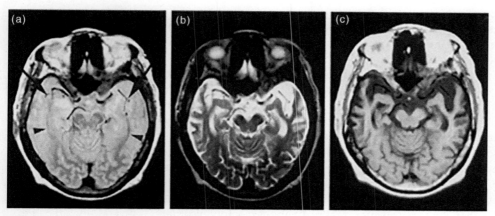

The brain of a 73-year-old woman with temporal dementia is shown above. Images show circumscribed atrophy in both temporal lobes (Kitagaki et al., 1997).

Source: Adapted from Kitagaki, H., Mori, E., Hirono, N., Ikejiri, Y., Ishii, K., Imamura, T., . . . & Nakagawa, Y. (1997). Alteration of white matter MR signal intensity in frontotemporal dementia. *American Journal of Neuroradiology, 18*(2), 367–78.

Reversible Causes of Dementia

Some people develop symptoms of dementia as part of a treatable disorder. In these cases, treating the disorder leads to a significant reduction or elimination of the symptoms of dementia. People with **hypothyroidism** often exhibit poor memory; however, when treated with hormones and other medications to compensate for the under-performing thyroid gland, memory usually returns to normal. In addition, a **vitamin B$_{12}$ deficiency** can cause cognitive impairments and memory problems. When treated with vitamin B$_{12}$, the symptoms disappear. Because these two causes of memory problems are so easy to treat, it is recommended that people exhibiting signs of dementia be screened for hypothyroidism and vitamin B$_{12}$ deficiency.

Some memory loss is expected as people age; however, memory loss that is significant enough to interfere with daily life is not normal and indicates that there is an underlying biological problem. The first step is to determine if hypothyroidism or a vitamin B$_{12}$ deficiency could be the cause of the problem. If thyroid and vitamin problems have been ruled out, then the cause

hypothyroidism
a condition where the thyroid gland does not produce an adequate level of hormones

vitamin B$_{12}$ deficiency
a condition in which the body does not absorb an adequate amount of vitamin B$_{12}$

CASE STUDY

BOX 13.2

Susie McKinnon: A Woman with Severely Deficient Autobiographical Memory

If someone were to ask you about your sixteenth birthday, high school prom, wedding, or other significant life event, chances are you would be able to vividly recall many details from that experience. This is because you have access to autobiographical memory, which is memory of episodes in your life of personal significance. In some rare cases, however, individuals may have severely deficient autobiographical memory (SDAM) and lack specific recollections of life experiences. People with SDAM may know that they turned 16, went to the prom, and got married, but they don't *remember* having done any of these things. Unlike disorders that impair short-term memory (like Alzheimer's disease) or the ability to learn new information (like the cases of Clive Wearing and Henry Molaison), people with SDAM are high functioning and can progress through life completely unaware that there is anything different about their memory. One example is that of Susie McKinnon, who was born in the United States in 1955. The first hint that something was amiss with McKinnon came in 1976 when she was 21 years old and a friend administered the mini-mental state examination (MMSE) to McKinnon as part of a class assignment. McKinnon cannot remember the actual event but she knows that her friend was concerned about some of her responses, particularly when McKinnon was surprised that her friend would be asking her to recall events from her childhood because, as McKinnon put it, "No one remembers that stuff!" (Hayasaki, 2016). McKinnon finished university, was successful at work, and was happily married. Then, in the early 2000s, McKinnon read an article by Endel Tulving that suggested that there may be people with no episodic memory. McKinnon was too nervous to contact Tulving directly (she knew that Tulving was a world-renowned expert on memory), so she contacted Dr Brian Levine, another researcher at the centre where Tulving worked. Levine ran a battery of tests on McKinnon and found that McKinnon lacked not only episodic memory but also mental imagery. Researchers are not sure whether the absence of mental imagery causes SDAM, or whether it is a symptom of SDAM. McKinnon's case illustrates an important point about memory disorders: They are very difficult to identify unless a person has trouble with day-to-day functioning. However, it's important to keep in mind, like Endel Tulving did, that many mild memory disorders may have yet to be discovered.

of the dementia is not likely to be reversible. If a person is exhibiting persistent difficulty with memory tasks, Alzheimer's disease or vascular dementia are the most likely causes for the cognitive problems; however, if memory is not severely affected, it is more likely that the individual is suffering from dementia with Lewy bodies or frontotemporal dementia.

Health Conditions That Can Lead to Memory Loss

Epilepsy

Epilepsy is a group of neurological disorders characterized by epileptic seizures. Epileptic seizures are the result of abnormal excessive or synchronous neuronal activity in the brain. Epileptic seizures, by definition, have no immediate underlying cause; they occur repeatedly and unexpectedly. Epilepsy can sometimes result from brain injury, stroke, brain tumours, or substance abuse; however, the cause of most cases is unknown. Epilepsy affects about 1 per cent of people worldwide. Many people with epilepsy also experience difficulties with memory. Epilepsy and the medications used to treat it can cause problems with attention, which in turn cause problems with learning new things (and remembering things later on). In some cases, the seizures damage the brain and produce **retrograde amnesia**, an inability to remember the past. Sometimes memory is slowly eroded by a series of small seizures such that, years later, events from around the time of the seizures are no longer accessible. In other extreme cases, a single grand mal seizure can produce complete anterograde amnesia.

> **retrograde amnesia**
> the inability to remember facts learned in the past

Brain Injury

Injuries to the brain as a result of accidents or acute disease can also affect memory. When a person is involved in a serious fall or vehicular accident, the brain compresses on impact, often damaging the midbrain, including the hippocampus. Thus, even though the structures most closely associated with memory are in the interior of the brain, they are still vulnerable to damage. This is what happened to Kent Cochrane (1951–2014), a Toronto native who crashed his motorcycle in 1981 when he was 30 years old. Cochrane sustained injuries to the medial temporal lobe and his hippocampus was completely destroyed. Like Molaison before him, Cochrane had complete anterograde amnesia; he could not form new memories. In addition, Cochrane was unable to recall details relating to emotions that occurred before the accident.

Some diseases can also cause memory problems either by causing inflammation that disrupts blood flow to the brain (as with meningitis or encephalitis) or by destroying brain tissue (as with some forms of herpes simplex). Clive Wearing (b. 1938), who is discussed in the chapter-opening case study, had a severe herpes simplex I infection in his brain that led to severe retrograde and anterograde amnesia (Wearing, 2005). Sometimes a person can develop encephalitis from antibodies produced in response to a cancerous tumour in the lung, thymus gland, breast, ovaries, or testes. In February 2015, authorities in California found a disoriented woman with an Australian accent who had no idea where she was from or how she got to California. Doctors soon discovered a volleyball-sized tumour on her ovary and attributed her memory loss to her body's attempt to fight this tumour. The hospital soon launched a worldwide social media campaign and, following three months of waiting, finally identified the woman as Ashley Menatta of San Diego County in July 2015. While Ashley was not Australian, she did have fond memories of visiting Australia in 2013 (Rocha, 2015).

BOX
13.3

CASE STUDY

Moose-Induced Amnesia?

In June 2015, Stephen Bromley from Conche, Newfoundland and Labrador, struck a moose with his car but has no recollection of the event or the days leading up to it. Oddly, this is not the first case of moose-induced amnesia in the province. In 2012, another Newfoundlander drove 40 kilometres after a collision with a moose peeled off the top of her car and has no recollection of the days before the accident, hitting the moose, or driving home after the accident (*CBC News*, 2015). The reason for this pattern of temporary retrograde and anterograde amnesia in these drivers has to do with head trauma. When the brain is impacted it is compressed, and this compression affects the ability of the hippocampus to consolidate new memories. Because it takes several days for a new memory to be fully consolidated, these drivers lost events for several days leading up to the accident. Because it takes some time for the brain to recover, they were unable to consolidate events that occurred after the accident. This pattern of anterograde amnesia and retrograde amnesia is often observed by people who sustain head injuries, and even incidents that may seem highly memorable, like impacting a two-tonne animal, are lost due to suppressed hippocampal functioning following impact.

Blows to the head, including concussions, can also lead to a variety of memory problems. A concussion can disrupt memory consolidation and produce amnesia for the time period surrounding the concussive event. Sustaining multiple concussions can lead to more permanent memory problems. For example, Grant Iverson and his colleagues at the University of British Columbia found that university athletes who had sustained multiple concussions performed much worse on tasks involving working memory and long-term memory than athletes who had sustained only one concussion (Iverson, Gaetz, Lovell, & Collins, 2004).

Korsakoff Syndrome

Korsakoff syndrome

retrograde and anterograde amnesia caused by persistent thiamine (vitamin B_1) deficiency. Korsakoff syndrome is often caused by chronic alcohol misuse.

Korsakoff syndrome is caused by extreme vitamin B_1 (also known as thiamine) deficiency, which causes neurons to develop scar tissue and bleeding that prevents the brain from functioning properly. Korsakoff syndrome is usually caused by years of severe alcohol misuse; however, AIDs, chronic infections, anorexia, and kidney dialysis have also been linked to the disease. Individuals with Korsakoff syndrome display both retrograde amnesia and anterograde amnesia; they cannot remember much of their past and they have significant difficulty learning new information. People with Korsakoff syndrome also have difficulty with short-term memory. In general, people with Korsakoff syndrome have difficulty consciously controlling information; however, these individuals show evidence for the influence of implicit memory on stem-completion tasks. In a stem-completion task, a person is first presented with a list of words but not told that the words will be part of a memory test later. Next, the individual is presented with a series of word stems, which are three-letter strings followed by a blank space, such as LET____. The participant's task is to complete the word stem with any word they choose (see Figure 13.4). Researchers present the stems to hundreds of people to get base rates for each stem completion (e.g., they may discover that 60 per cent of people complete the word stem LET ____ as LETTER, 30 per cent complete the word stem with LETTUCE, and so on). Both neurotypical individuals and people with Korsakoff syndrome use words from the word list more frequently than the base rate for that word. Word-stem completion is thought to be influenced by implicit memory, that is, memory influences that are beyond awareness. While people with Korsakoff syndrome show an influence of implicit memory on word-stem completion tasks, they do not show normal performance on other measures of implicit memory, such as a word-association task where the individual is presented with a word and needs to name the first word that comes to mind. Thus, it is incorrect to say that people with Korsakoff syndrome have preserved implicit memory. It is more accurate to say that the stem-completion task seems to cue people with Korsakoff syndrome to use recently seen words much like it does for neurotypical individuals (Brunfaut & d'Ydewalle, 1996). People with Korsakoff syndrome likely show such widespread memory deficits because all regions of their brain are affected by the thiamine deficiency. About 25 per cent of people with Korsakoff syndrome who receive B_1 vitamin injections recover from the disease.

Word List	Word Stems
GIRLISH	GIR _____
LETTUCE	LET _____
STRANGE	STR _____
BECKON	BEC _____
TRANCE	TRA _____

Figure 13.4   The components of a word-stem completion task experiment

The above is an example of a word list and word stems that may be used in a word-stem completion experiment. The participant is presented with the word list without knowing a memory test is coming. The participant is given the word stems to complete without being told to use the words from the word list. Words from the word list are typically less common than other words that begin with the same three letters. In general, both neurotypical people and people with Korsakoff syndrome complete word stems with words from the word list rather than a more common word, for example completing GIR___ with GIRLISH rather than GIRAFFE.

Dissociative Amnesia

Thus far we have discussed physiological causes of memory failure; however, from time to time psychological processes can result in a type of memory loss called **dissociative amnesia** in which there is a sudden loss of autobiographical memory with no underlying medical cause.

dissociative amnesia

autobiographical memory loss that is not the result of an underlying biological problem

Although often depicted in books and movies (such as *The Bourne Identity* and *Before I Go to Sleep*), dissociative amnesia is an extremely rare condition. It was diagnosed more frequently in the early twentieth century before brain-imaging technology was able to identify underlying biological reasons for memory loss. People with dissociative amnesia are unable to recall past events that relate to themselves and lose their sense of self-identity. They typically do not remember what they look like, do not remember their names, and cannot identify people who are close to them. Each case of dissociative amnesia is unique. Some people lose their autobiographical memory for a few hours or days; others can lose it for years. Dissociative amnesia is often associated with dissatisfying life conditions, such as being in combat, having stressful life conditions, and current or past sexual abuse. Dissociative amnesia often occurs quite suddenly; one day a person has a complete autobiographical memory and the next day does not know who or where she or

People with dissociative amnesia are unable to recall past events that relate to themselves for psychological (as opposed to biological) reasons. Although dissociative amnesia is often portrayed in books, movies, and television, the condition is extremely rare in real life, and doctors are usually able to find a biological cause for amnesic symptoms.

© Imtmphoto | Dreamstime.com

he is. People with dissociative amnesia can remember life events onward from the point when they forgot who they were; forming new autobiographical memories and accessing them is typically not a problem. During the twentieth century, people with dissociative amnesia were often administered drugs that relaxed the nervous system, such as barbiturates or benzodiazepines, before being questioned about their past. However, clinicians soon realized that while under the influence of these medications, the individual was more susceptible to suggestion and no better at accurately recalling events from their past. Hypnosis was also often used; however, because of problems with suggestibility, it is discouraged in contemporary cases of dissociative amnesia. In most (but not all) cases of dissociative amnesia, people eventually recover their memories without any treatment.

dissociative fugue
autobiographical memory loss followed by wandering away from home that is not the result of an underlying biological problem

Dissociative fugue is a type of dissociative amnesia during which the individual with no memory of who she or he is wanders from home. Dissociative fugue with no underlying medical cause is extremely rare. In the present day, most people who present with amnesia or fugue without having any obvious brain trauma are nonetheless found to have abnormalities in their brains in areas associated with autobiographical memory. Area 38 of the right superior temporal sulcus is associated with autobiographical memory and is often found to function abnormally in people with autobiographical amnesia (Calabrese et al., 1996).

In the twentieth century, there were many reported cases of people experiencing a fugue state. In the cases, the individual was found wandering aimlessly with no idea of who she or he was or where she or he came from. Unless it was obvious that the person had sustained some sort of head trauma, it was assumed that fugues were the result of psychological mechanisms. One such case originally assumed to have a psychological origin is that of N.N.

N.N. was a 37-year-old male from Germany about to take his first vacation in more than three years when he went on a bicycle ride to get bread one morning, but instead of returning home he cycled for five days to a city about 600 kilometres south of his home along the Rhine River. Although he doesn't know exactly when the fugue started, by the time he had reached the new city he had no idea who he was or where he came from. He went to the train station seeking help. He was admitted to a hospital where a series of basic medical tests were administered, which all produced normal results. He was then transferred to a psychiatric facility. N.N. seemed happy and got along with other patients but disliked discussing his identity and would try to change the subject whenever it was raised. His family had filed a missing persons report when he didn't return from the trip to the store and they were eventually brought to the hospital to see if N.N. was their lost family member. When they were reunited with N.N., N.N. denied knowing his wife, his brother, and his brother-in-law. Clinicians were able to get a case history by interviewing his wife and brother. The clinicians discovered that for the first two years of his life, N.N.'s mother had treated and dressed him as though he was a girl. Throughout his life he had difficulties with his mother, he had taken his wife's last name when he married, and at the time of the fugue he was not in contact with his mother. The clinicians also discovered that, at the time of his disappearance, N.N. and his wife were having financial difficulties. When they learned of his problems with his mother and his financial problems, clinicians assumed that N.N.'s case was the result of psychological forces that produced the amnesia and the fugue. However, about eight months after the fugue began, Hans Markowitsch of the University of Bielefeld in Germany conducted a series of tests on N.N. to determine whether there were any neurological issues with N.N. that the tests had missed. Markowitsch and his colleagues conducted a battery of tests, including a PET scan. When they reviewed the results from the PET scan, they were surprised to find some significant abnormalities. When N.N. was asked to think about autobiographical events, including events that occurred since his fugue began, Markowitsch found that N.N. used his left superior temporal sulcus when recalling these autobiographical memories instead of the right superior temporal sulcus, which is typically active when people recall life events. The right superior temporal sulcus is believed to be necessary for the successful retrieval of autobiographical information (Markowitsch et al., 1997). The fact that N.N. activated the left, instead of the right, superior temporal sulcus when asked to recall an autobiographical memory suggests an underlying biological cause for N.N.'s fugue state, rather than a psychological one. More and more cases of fugue are being found to be the result of neurological problems that have only recently been identifiable thanks to advances in brain-imaging technology.

Memory Problems Related to Slow-Wave Sleep

In Chapter 4, we discussed the two-stage model of memory, which suggests that memories are consolidated during slow-wave sleep (SWS). According to this theory, an individual needs sufficient slow-wave sleep (SWS) in order to function properly. Consistent with this theory is the observation that many health conditions associated with memory problems are also associated with decreased SWS. Age-related decreases in memory performance may be, in part, the result of reduced SWS with aging. Research suggests that for each additional decade of life after age 20, a person spends 24 fewer minutes per night in slow-wave sleep. This means that by age 80 a person may spend as much as three fewer hours per night in SWS compared to when that person was younger. This decline in SWS means that fewer memories can be reactivated, distributed, and consolidated, which will make it more difficult for older people to form and integrate new memories. In addition, people lose about 10 minutes of REM sleep for every additional year of life after age 20. If REM sleep is important for memory consolidation, this too may contribute to memory problems in older adults (Van Cauter, Leproult, & Plat, 2000). Health conditions that require the use of benzodiazepines, including anxiety disorders and sleep disorders, may indirectly impact memory because benzodiazepines significantly reduce the amount of time a

CASE STUDY

BOX
13.4

What Causes "Baby Brain"?

Many new parents complain that they can't remember things very well. They forget appointments and birthdays. They forget to pay bills. Occasionally they forget to get dressed before leaving the house! The stories of new parents being in a complete fog are endless. It turns out that the problems new parents have with their memories may be linked to that other issue of having a new baby: lack of sleep. Not only does being woken up every three hours (and often more frequently than that) leave you less rested, it seriously disrupts SWS sleep that is needed for new information to be integrated into a person's existing long-term memories. For this reason, new parents not only deal with the short-term memory impairments of sleep deprivation, but also, in the long run, have fewer consolidated memories of the time when their children were very young. I personally have very few memories of the years following the birth of each of my three sons—a flash here, a snippet there, but it is a blur compared to my memories of other years. So, parents who take thousands of pictures of their new babies and document every new achievement on social media are doing themselves a favour, as they may very well have no recollection of these events in a few years.

BOX
13.5

RELEVANT RESEARCH

Do Women Really Forget the Pain of Childbirth?

Expectant mothers are often told by mothers who have had children that they will forget the pain of childbirth as soon as they hold their baby. Is this true? Przemysław Bąbel and colleagues at Jagiellonian University in Krakow, Poland, conducted a study that asked participants who just had a baby by either vaginal delivery or Caesarean section and participants who had just had a gynaecological operation to report their pain intensity levels, anxiety levels, and emotional state. Then, three or six months later, Bąbel asked the participants to recall those levels of pain, anxiety,

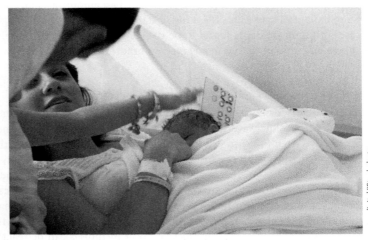

oceandigital/iStockphoto

and emotion. Bąbel found that women who had had a vaginal delivery underestimated the amount of pain they were in after having their baby as well as the amount of anxiety that they were experiencing at the time. The vaginal birth group also had poor accuracy when recalling the emotions they were experiencing at the time of the birth of the child, with a tendency to believe they were experiencing more intense emotions at the time of the birth than they actually were. Women who had Caesarean sections, which involves surgery, were very accurate at recalling the intensity of the pain they were experiencing at the time as well as their levels of anxiety and their emotional state. Women who had had gynaecological surgery tended to overestimate the amount of pain they had experienced and overestimate the amount of negative emotion that they had experienced right after surgery.

Bąbel argues that there may be an evolutionary reason for this pattern of results. In general, people who experience surgical or trauma-related pain remember this pain as being very intense; many go to great lengths to avoid experiencing that type of pain again. From an evolutionary standpoint this makes sense; experiencing accidental pain could incapacitate individuals and limit their ability to pass on their genes. The evolutionary perspective also suggests that there is an evolutionary advantage to forgetting the pain of childbirth, as it needs to be tolerated over and over in order for the maximum number of genes to be passed down. Bąbel suggests that the positive emotions experienced after childbirth help women forget their pain. The evolutionary perspective can also help explain the memories of women in the Caesarean group. Caesarean sections involve surgical pain, which people have a tendency to remember quite well, while childbirth pain is something that women have a tendency to remember poorly. If the mechanisms that cause people to remember surgical pain well compete with the mechanisms that cause women to forget the pain of childbirth, the result should be memory that falls somewhere in between, which is exactly what Bąbel found. Bąbel argues that the memory for pain is therefore influenced by the meaning and affective value of the pain and that this pattern may be directly linked to human evolution (Bąbel, Pieniążek, & Zarotyński, 2015).

person spends in SWS (Roehrs & Roth, 2010). Health conditions that disrupt sleep, including sleep apnea, chronic pain, restless leg syndrome (RLS), or even chronic urinary tract infections (UTIs), can all shorten the amount of SWS individuals get overnight and consequently reduce their ability to form memories.

Substances That Affect Memory

Medications That Affect Memory . . . on Purpose

Many outpatient medical procedures (such as cataract surgery, dental surgery, and colonoscopies) involve **twilight anaesthesia**, in which a mild dose of general anaesthesia is given to reduce a patient's anxiety and to induce anterograde amnesia so that the patient will have no memory of the surgical procedure. Twilight anaesthesia is given in addition to pain medications. Medications that produce the twilight state include nitrous oxide, ketamine, propofol, and midazolam (Bailie et al., 1989). Some medical practitioners (and their patients) want to induce amnesia in case the events of the procedure are either traumatic (such as a dentist needing to climb on a person's chest to extract a stubborn wisdom tooth) or embarrassing (such as the very vulnerable position people are put in during colonoscopies). In the twentieth century, twilight anaesthesia was often used during childbirth as well. Most people recover completely from twilight anaesthesia within a few hours, have little or no memory of events during sedation, and report being happy they chose to be sedated. However, as discussed in Chapter 5, if an individual remains conscious under sedation, she or he may develop implicit memories related to the procedure without explicit recall of those events (Bailie et al., 1989).

twilight anaesthesia
mild anaesthesia intended to reduce anxiety and induce anterograde amnesia in patients undergoing outpatient medical procedures

Alcohol and Memory

Alcohol has diverse effects on memory. In cases of extreme alcohol intoxication, a person can experience a "blackout," or retrograde amnesia. Alcohol can significantly impair executive functions and attention and, because an individual is not attending well to events, they are not encoded and therefore cannot be retrieved. Although alcohol often impairs the acquisition of new memories, it can actually work to enhance memory if consumed in moderation after learning, an effect known as the retrograde enhancement of human memory by alcohol. For example, Robert Mann and his colleagues Jayanti Cho-Young and Muriel Vogel-Sprott at the University of Waterloo had a group of male participants complete a free-recall task before and after consuming alcohol or a placebo. About two hours later, the participants were given a surprise free-recall test. Mann, Cho-Young, and Vogel-Sprott (1984) found that participants in the alcohol group remembered significantly more words from the free-recall lists than did those in the placebo group. The enhancing effect of alcohol on recently learned memories has been replicated dozens of times using a variety of different memory tasks. Researchers speculate that the retrograde enhancement of human memory by alcohol may relate to the stimulating effect of low doses of alcohol. An alternative explanation is that alcohol activates the reward systems within the brain, which enhances the memory for all memories in close temporal proximity such that the rewarding stimuli will be sought out in the future.

Thus far, we have discussed the ways in which health conditions and substance use impact memory, but it is also true that memory can have an impact on health. In the next section, we will discuss the many ways that strong memories or the absence of memories can produce positive and negative health outcomes.

The Effect of Memory on Health and Healthcare
Post-Traumatic Stress Disorder

Post-traumatic stress disorder (PTSD) is a disorder that has a significant impact on memory. PTSD can develop in any person who experiences a traumatic event, although it is most common among people who experience assault-related trauma (such as being in a firefight at war or being attacked in a robbery) than non–assault-related trauma (such as witnessing a traumatic event; Zoladz & Diamond, 2013). Of people who experience assault-related trauma, children under 10 years of age are less likely than adults to develop PTSD, and war veterans are more likely to develop PTSD than other adults who experience trauma. To be diagnosed with PTSD using the DSM-5, an individual must meet five criteria. First, the individual must have been exposed to actual or threatened death, serious injury, or sexual violence. Second, the individual must re-experience the traumatic event, which may mean the individual experiences intrusive thoughts or memories, nightmares related to the event, flashbacks that make it feel like the event is happening again, or psychological difficulty when reminded of the event. Third, the individual must actively try to avoid remembering the event by avoiding thoughts or feelings connected to the event or avoiding people or situations connected to the traumatic event. Fourth, the individual must experience changes in mood and thought patterns that often include memory problems that are exclusive to the event. Fifth, the individual must experience arousal problems such as difficulty concentrating, being easily startled, or being highly irritable.

Individuals with PTSD often complain of having problems with attention and memory. Many empirical studies have found significant memory impairments among people with PTSD (e.g., Gilbertson, Gurvits, Lasko, Orr, & Pitman, 2001). However, many other studies of the effect of PTSD on memory have found no memory problems at all (e.g., Crowell, Kieffer, Siders, & Vanderploeg, 2002). One reason for this discrepancy could be that previous studies have not controlled for the fact that many individuals with PTSD also have depression and abuse alcohol, which both have known negative effects on memory. Kristin Samuelson and her colleagues at the San Francisco Veterans Affairs Medical Center decided to conduct a study testing the memory of veterans with and without PTSD and with and without a history of alcohol abuse while using statistical procedures to control for depression in order to determine if PTSD directly affects memory. Samuelson speculated that if the memory deficits previously observed in people with PTSD were linked to alcohol abuse, then the veterans with and without PTSD who had a history of alcohol abuse should show memory impairments, whereas the veterans with and without PTSD with no history of alcohol abuse should not. If, on the other hand, PTSD directly results in memory deficits, then only veterans with PTSD should show memory deficits and these deficits should be similar regardless of whether the individual with PTSD had a history of substance abuse.

Samuelson et al. (2009) administered a battery of tests, including an intelligence test; a depression inventory; and tests of verbal, visual, and spatial memory to more than 100 American veterans. Samuelson et al. found that individuals with PTSD had significant deficits in verbal memory that could not be explained by a history of alcohol abuse or depression. Individuals also had deficits in working memory. Samuelson et al. did not find that visual memory was worse among participants with PTSD as compared to participants without the disorder; however, visual memory was significantly worse among participants with a history of alcohol abuse

RELEVANT RESEARCH

BOX
13.6

Erasing the Memories of People with PTSD

Each year, thousands of people experience traumatic events that they would like to forget, ranging from assaults, to accidents, to natural disasters. Many people who experiences these types of trauma develop post-traumatic stress disorder (PTSD), which is characterized by nightmares and waking flashbacks related to the traumatic event. PTSD is driven by memory; a person with no memory of a trauma cannot have PTSD. Until recently, memory theorists felt that memories are permanent after they are consolidated; a process that occurs about 24 hours after the memory trace is experienced. Because it takes 24 hours for long-term memories to first consolidate, people who experience head traumas are often unable to recall any events within about a day of their injury. This is because the head trauma halts the consolidation process. Because consolidation was thought to occur only once, memories were believed to be permanent. However recent research suggests that each time a memory is recalled, it is *reconsolidated* through a chemical process that takes place in the amygdala. This led researchers to wonder whether they could interfere with reconsolidation in much the same way that concussions interfere with consolidation. In the late 1990s, researchers discovered (somewhat by accident) that a drug called propranolol, which is normally used to treat hypertension, disrupted the chemical processes required for reconsolidation. Alain Brunet and Roger Pitman led a research team and decided to test the memory-suppressing abilities of propranolol by administering it to emergency room patients (who were chosen because they were at risk for developing PTSD from the events that led them to the emergency room). Brunet and Pitman found that patients who received propranolol were far less likely to develop PTSD than patients who received a placebo in the emergency room. This inspired Brunet to see if they could use propranolol to eliminate PTSD symptoms in people who had already developed the disorder. Volunteers had to come into the lab once a week for six weeks and read a one-page description of their traumatic event. Before reading the one-page story, the volunteers took propranolol. After six weeks, 75 per cent of the PTSD patients who took propranolol and then recalled their trauma had such a reduction in symptoms that they no longer met the clinical criteria for PTSD. Brunet and Pitman's work has inspired researchers to look for more direct methods to completely erase unpleasant memories without affecting the memories that people want to retain (Brunet et al., 2008).

regardless of whether they had PTSD. The results of Samuelson et al.'s experiment suggest that PTSD is associated with decreased memory for verbal material and working memory (Samuelson et al., 2009). The question remains as to why people with PTSD show memory deficits when their condition is not the result of brain injury. Some researchers suggest that hyper-arousal brought on by the disorder results in the over-activity of some neurotransmitters that in turn damage areas of the brain, including those linked to attention and memory. This hypothesis is supported by fMRI studies that show abnormally low levels of activity in their prefrontal cortex (PFC) and ventromedial cortex (vmPFC) (Bremner et al., 2003; Geuze, Vermetten, Ruf, de Kloet, & Westenberg, 2008; Samuelson et al., 2009; Smith & Jonides, 1995; Southwick, Rasmusson, Barron, & Arnsten, 2005). The PFC controls attention; items that are not attended to will not be encoded. This explanation is consistent with the general finding that memory deficits due to PTSD are related to the severity of the disorder.

The Link between Memory and Obsessive-Compulsive Disorder

Obsessive-compulsive disorder (OCD) is a mental disorder characterized by obsessions, which are repetitive thoughts related to a fear of harm (such as "If I don't wash my hands, I will get germs" or "If I leave the stove on, the house will burn down") and compulsions, which are repetitive actions that are conducted in an attempt to reduce the anxiety produced by the obsessions (such as repeatedly hand washing or repeatedly checking to make sure the stove is off). People with OCD and checking problems repeatedly check whether previous attempts to prevent harm, such as turning off the stove or locking the door, were successful. Cognitive theories of OCD explain that the urge to check follows from an inflated sense of responsibility, suggesting that people with OCD feel an overwhelming urge to prevent future harm. While these theories are supported by experiments that show that increasing or decreasing perceived responsibility leads to corresponding increases and decreases in checking behaviour, the theories fail to explain why checking once is not enough. Many people who are responsible for the safety of others, such as airplane pilots or anaesthesiologists, perform regular checks to promote safety, but they do not *repeat* their checks like people with OCD do. **Mnestic deficit theories** attempt to explain this discrepancy by suggesting that OCD checkers have a memory deficit; they do not remember previous checks, so they check again and again. Research that has tested memory performance in OCD checkers has failed to find any significant problems; OCD checkers do not suffer from a general memory deficit (MacDonald, Antony, Macleod, & Richter, 1997). Although OCD checkers do not have a general memory deficit, they do consistently exhibit low memory confidence (Hermans, Martens, De Cort, Pieters, & Eelen, 2003).

Marcel van den Hout and Merel Kindt (2003) from the Netherlands noted that memory confidence depends largely on the vividness and detail of a memory, and that vividness and detail are influenced by familiarity; when an event is more familiar, recollection is less detailed and less vivid. Memories become less vivid with familiarity because repeated exposure makes it more difficult to cue specific instances of the event. Episodic details are thus lost, but general semantic information about the event, which is not affected by repetition, remains. Thus, the more OCD checkers check, the less able they are to retrieve the last checking event, and the less confident they are that they have checked the item that they feel is a threat to them.

Van Den Hout and Kindt (2003) tested the hypothesis that low memory confidence in OCD checkers is the result of repeated checking by developing a computer task in which participants were asked to turn on animated gas stove elements, turn them off, and then check to see if they were off. Participants in the relevant task group completed 20 trials with a gas stove animation, while participants in the irrelevant task group completed 20 trials with a light switch animation. All participants completed a gas stove trial at the very end of the experiment. After the final trial, the experimenters assessed each participant's memory accuracy for which elements had been turned off, recall vividness, memory detail, memory confidence, and outcome confidence. Van den Hout and Kindt (2003) hypothesized that if OCD checkers have low confidence in their memory due to reduced vividness and detail from repeated checking, then participants in the relevant check group should show lower memory vividness, detail, and confidence than members of the irrelevant checking group because they repeated checking gas stoves before the test (while participants in the irrelevant group checked light switches). Indeed, van den Hout and Kindt (2003) found that, while memory accuracy didn't differ between groups, memory vividness, detail, and confidence was significantly lower for the gas stove checking group.

DIY EXPERIMENT

BOX 13.7

Remember to Be Healthy Part I

This experiment is divided into two parts. For the first part, please complete the questionnaire below, recording your answers for future reference. The purpose of this experiment will be explained later.

As you well know, your behaviour can have a significant impact on your health. Take a moment to carefully read the health advice below:

> Eat four servings of vegetables per day.
> Drink eight glasses of water per day.
> Do not engage in dangerous driving.
> Exercise at least one hour per day.
> Eat a diet high in fibre and low in sodium.
> Do not smoke tobacco or marijuana.
> Get eight hours of sleep per day.
> Do not eat a diet that is high in fat.
> Do not drink alcohol in excess.
> Use condoms to reduce the risk of STIs.

Next, review each piece of health advice and record whether you personally follow that advice. Save your answers for later. Make a note to complete Part II of this experiment (Box 13.8 on p. 357) in one week.

Van den Hout and Kindt (2003) argue that this is because repeated checking reduces vividness and detail, resulting in reduced memory confidence. This result suggests that repeated checking in people with OCD may be fuelled by a low tolerance for uncertainty that is perpetuated by memory confidence that reduces with each successive checking of the situation that they feel is a threat to them. As memory confidence erodes, the need to check increases, producing a vicious cycle. This result suggests that people with OCD may lack **metamemory**, or knowledge of how their own memory performs and operates. Thus, exercises designed to build memory confidence in people with OCD may be an effective method for reducing debilitating checking behaviours.

metamemory
personal knowledge of how one's own memory operates

False Memory for End-of-Life Decisions

In the early 2000s, there was intense media attention related to removing life support from a severely brain-damaged Florida woman named Terri Schiavo. Schiavo suffered a massive heart attack in 1990 that resulted in extensive brain damage. In 1998, Schiavo's husband Michael petitioned the Florida court to remove her feeding tube; however, Terri's parents Robert and Mary Schindler opposed him. Michael was Terri's legal guardian and claimed that Terri would not want to be kept alive with no chance for recovery, while Terri's parents claimed that as a Roman Catholic Terri would not want to end her own life. After seven years of appeals, the court finally granted the right for Terri's feeding tube to be removed on March 18, 2005. Terri passed away

13 days later on March 31, 2005. The case of Terri Schiavo brought attention to the importance of **advance directives (AD)**, which are legal documents outlining the medical treatment a person wishes to have should she or he become incapacitated as well as appointing people to make medical decisions on her or his behalf.

Although an AD may have prevented the seven-year-long legal battle in the Terri Schiavo case, several researchers question the effectiveness of ADs during end-of-life decision making (e.g., Ditto, Hawkins, & Pizarro, 2005). One concern, which is supported by research, is that individuals will state preferences in an AD and then change their mind, but not remember the contents of their AD and therefore not change the AD to reflect their current preferences. This could mean people who wish to have life-sustaining treatment don't receive the treatment, or people who wish to avoid life-sustaining treatment could receive that treatment because of what is written in their outdated AD. Stefanie Sharman of the University of South Wales and her colleagues, including Elizabeth Loftus, examined peoples' memories for advance directives over time. In their first study, Sharman, Garry, Jacobson, Loftus, and Ditto (2008) interviewed 332 adults at two points in time. During the first interview, each adult was asked to complete the Life Support Preferences/Predictions Questionnaire developed by Ditto et al. (2001), which is shown in Table 13.2.a. The questionnaire briefly describes nine common end-of-life scenarios and asks participants to rate whether they would want to receive each of the four treatments shown in Table 13.2.b. on a scale of 1 (really would want) to 5 (really would not want). Each participant had a surrogate decision maker. Surrogate decision makers were interviewed separately, made statements predicting what their targets would choose, and reviewed the response the target made to the questionnaire.

Participants and surrogates returned for a follow-up interview 12 months after the initial interview. The second interview followed the same procedure as the initial interview except participants were each also asked to indicate whether the responses had changed since the first interview. Sharman et al. (2008) found that of the 1328 critical decisions made during

Table 13.2   Hypothetical scenarios and treatments presented in Sharman et al. (2008) from Ditto et al. (2001)

a. Scenario	b. Treatment
1. Participant's current health state	1. Antibiotics
2. Alzheimer's disease	2. Cardiopulmonary resuscitation (CPR)
3. Emphysema	3. Gall bladder surgery
4a. Stroke-induced coma with no chance of recovery	4. Artificial nutrition and hydration (tube feeding)
4b. Stroke-induced coma with very slight chance of recovery	
5a. Stroke-induced partial paralysis with no chance of recovery	
5b. Stroke-induced partial paralysis with very slight chance of recovery	
6a. Colon cancer that has spread to the liver requiring no pain relief	
6b. Colon cancer that has spread to the liver requiring pain relief	

Source: Ditto et al., 2001, p. 422

the first interview, 312 (23 per cent) changed by the time of the second interview. Of the participants who changed their decisions, 75 per cent falsely remembered that their decision had not changed; in other words, they stated that their current decision was the same as their original decision when it was not. When the researchers examined the data from the surrogates, the false-memory rate was even higher; 86 per cent of surrogates believed that their target's current decision was the same as the one they had previously reported (about 12 per cent falsely remembered that the decision was different when it was the same). Sharman et al. (2008) replicated their study with a smaller, younger cohort and found a similar result; approximately 86 per cent of participants who changed their decision falsely remembered that they had not changed their decision (only about 8 per cent thought there was a change when there was not). Sharman et al.'s (2008) results suggest that requiring people to update ADs when there is a change may not be an effective way of ensuring an AD is up to date, as many people may falsely remember that their AD is consistent with their current wishes. Sharman et al. (2008) suggest that one solution to this problem may be to have ADs expire after a certain period of time, forcing individuals to frequently update their ADs to ensure that their final wishes are heeded should an advance directive be needed.

Peoples' memories are not flawed only for advance directives. In the next section, we will see cognitive biases shape peoples' memories for their health behaviours as well.

The Impact of Memory Bias on Individual Memory for Health-Related Information and Recommendations

When a person has a health problem, changes in behaviour, including diet, exercise, and medication use, are often recommended. People often ignore medical advice and, while it may seem obvious that they do so because they don't want to change their lifestyle, problems with memory may also contribute to the issue. Research shows that, in general, patients show poor memory for advice from healthcare professionals; recall is often less than 50 per cent accurate. Early arguments as to why this happens included age-related memory problems, information being too complicated, and anxiety about health interfering with recall. However, Marc Kiviniemi and Alexander Rothman noted that these explanations assume **reasoning power** (or the lack of it) is responsible for poor recall of health information and thus predict that *all* medical information is equally likely to be forgotten, when in fact it is well established that whether patients remember a given piece of medical information is closely tied to whether that information is consistent or inconsistent with their beliefs about their health and health issues. In other words, **memory biases**, not processing problems, may be the reason that a lot of medical advice goes unheeded.

To test whether biases may influence memory for medical information, Kiviniemi and Rothman (2006) conducted two studies. In the first study, the researchers tested whether memory for health information is biased based on the individual's pre-existing beliefs about alcohol consumption. The researchers had participants report their attitudes about moderate alcohol consumption in one session and then presented information both for and against moderate alcohol consumption in the second session. Finally, participants were asked to recall the information they had read in the second session. The research found that memory for belief-inconsistent information (information presented in the second session that contradicted the person's attitude about moderate alcohol consumption) was significantly worse than memory for belief-consistent information (information presented in the second session that supported the person's attitude about moderate alcohol consumption), especially when participants held extreme beliefs. This suggests that the participants did in fact have a memory bias favouring their existing attitudes about alcohol

reasoning power

an individual's ability to make decisions based on logic and common sense

memory bias

a tendency to better recall information that is consistent with an individual's beliefs

consumption, suggesting, for example, that people who think that moderate alcohol consumption is not harmful to their health will be less likely to remember the health risks associated with moderate alcohol consumption.

In a second study, Kiviniemi and Rothman (2006) tested whether memory for health-related advice is affected by whether a person is already doing a behaviour. Kiviniemi and Rothman (2006) presented participants with eight common health-behaviour recommendations that were either framed as health promoting (e.g., eating a low-fat diet) or health damaging (e.g., eating a high-fat diet). The behaviours were related to dietary fat consumption, sodium intake, alcohol consumption, aerobic exercise, sugar consumption, caffeine consumption, cholesterol intake, and consumption of fast food. There were two groups in the study. The unhealthy recommendation group was told they were being given a list of behaviours that were thought to be adverse to peoples' health, such as eating high-fat food more than three times a week. The healthy recommendation group was told they were being given a list of behaviours that were thought to have a positive impact on health, such as not eating fast food more than three times a week. The basic information given to both groups was the same (e.g., limit high-fat foods to three times a week) but whether it was framed as healthy or unhealthy varied between groups. After a delay, participants were asked to write down as many of the health recommendations as they could remember and were then asked to report how often they themselves engaged in each of the eight health-related behaviours. When they analyzed the results, Kiviniemi and Rothman (2006) found an interesting pattern. Participants in the healthy recommendation group better remembered health-related behaviours they engaged in, whereas participants in the unhealthy recommendation group remembered more of the unhealthy behaviours they did *not* engage in. Thus, participants in both groups better remembered health recommendations that indicated that they were in good health and not at risk for illness, a clear memory bias. Kiviniemi and Rothman (2006) concluded that memory biases favouring (a) pre-existing beliefs and (b) a view that the individual is healthy may be responsible for patients' noncompliance with health recommendations.

Kiviniemi and Rothman (2006) suggest that good communication between the healthcare provider and the patient may be the best approach to combating these biases. To reduce the bias that favours recall of information that is consistent with pre-existing beliefs, a healthcare professional can have a conversation with the aim of changing the patient's pre-existing beliefs. Patients who do not believe that smoking causes cancer may not heed advice to quit smoking, but if they engage in a conversation that changes their belief about the dangers of smoking, they may be more likely to remember the conversation and heed the advice. To deal with the bias in which people tend to forget information that indicates they are not healthy, the healthcare professional can engage in a conversation in which the patient discusses the threat and its real potential consequence (e.g., explain how smoking affects the lungs and consequently makes them more vulnerable to cancer) and then have patients make concrete statements of how they will change their behaviour (e.g., "I will start on the nicotine patch"; "I will join the smoking cessation program at the local clinic"). The bias against threatening health information only works because the patient is able to ignore the advice, but a patient is unlikely to ignore and forget long conversations about the issue and concrete plans made to help address the problem. One thing is certain from this research: changing health behaviours is difficult and it may be necessary to outsmart cognitive biases to maximize compliance.

In this section, we saw that people have a tendency to recall behaviours that are associated with good health. This finding is linked to a more general phenomenon known as the *survival effect*, which we will discuss next.

DIY EXPERIMENT

BOX
13.8

Remember to Be Healthy Part II

If you have not completed Part I of this activity on page 353, please do so before continuing.

One week ago, you read a list of health advice in this chapter and indicated whether you followed that advice. Without peeking, write down as many pieces of health advice as you can.

Once you have recorded as many pieces of the advice as you can, compare your responses to the list of health advice appearing in Part I of this activity on page 353. Compute your overall per cent recall, your per cent recall for health advice you follow, and your per cent recall for health advice you do not follow. Compare your memory for health advice you follow and don't follow. Was there a difference?

This experiment roughly replicates an experiment conducted by Kiviniemi and Rothman (2006). Kiviniemi and Rothman (2006) found participants were more likely to recall health advice that was consistent with their current health behaviours than health advice that was inconsistent with their current behaviour. Kiviniemi and Rothman (2006) speculate that this pattern emerges because people have a memory bias in favour of information that supports the view that they are healthy. To what extent does your data show evidence of a memory bias? Ways to combat this memory bias for health advice are discussed later in this chapter.

CASE STUDY

BOX
13.9

Full Moon, Saturday Night

People who work in emergency rooms often claim that the weirdest cases occur during a full moon that occurs on a Saturday night. In reality, peoples' behaviour is NOT affected by the phases of the moon, so why is this belief so prevalent? Recall that in Chapter 10 you learned about distinctiveness-based illusory correlations, which are false conclusions about the strength of the relationship between two variables when those variables are very distinctive in memory. Full moons are distinctive events, occurring just once a month, and occurring on Saturday nights only one-seventh of the time (or about 1.5 times a year). Thus, a full

© Sumikophoto | Dreamstime.com

moon on a Saturday night is a very distinct event. Because it is such a distinct event, medical staff are likely to form distinctiveness-based illusory correlations between anything unusual they observe on one of these nights and the fact that it occurred during a full moon on a Saturday night. In reality, the events observed on other Saturday nights are probably very similar, but because they are not distinct, they are not remembered.

The Survival Effect

Adaptation and evolution have resulted in humans who are better able to survive and reproduce than their ancient ancestors. While some adaptations are biological (such as the ability to digest milk), many adaptations are psychological, including the **survival effect**. The survival effect refers to a finding in the memory literature where participants show better performance on memory tasks when the to-be-remembered material bears directly on issues of survival than when it does not. The survival effect has been found for recall and recognition of words as well as memory for the location of objects (Kang, McDermott, & Cohen, 2008).

Early theories explaining the survival effect gave a fairly simple explanation for the phenomenon; individuals who were better able to remember survival-related information were more likely to survive and have offspring (who would better remember survival-related information; Nairne and Pandeirada, 2008). This conclusion was drawn after several experiments revealed that evoking the hunter-gatherer context (under which the survival effect presumably evolved) led to better memory performance. For example, in 2007, James Nairne and his colleagues compared the memory performance of participants who rated words in four contexts, looking specifically to see if thinking about life as a hunter-gatherer (or the **environment of evolutionary adaptiveness [EEA]**) would enhance the survival effect. In the first condition, participants rated words in terms of how important they would be to survival in a foreign grassland (which would evoke the EEA). In the second condition, participants rated items in terms of how important they would be if a person were moving to a new home abroad (where survival is relevant outside of the context of the EEA). In the third condition, participants rated items in terms of pleasantness and in a fourth condition, participants rated items in terms of their self-relevance. Pleasantness and self-relevance are well known to elicit better memory performance; these two conditions were included to see if the survival effect could

The picture of the savannah (left) shows an environment of evolutionary adaptiveness (EEA), while the picture of the city (right) shows how the majority of people in the world live today. Researchers have found that participants are more survival-minded when thinking about life in an EEA than life in a city.

surpass these two oft-observed effects. Nairne, Thompson, & Pandeirada (2007) found that survival-related encoding in the hunter-gatherer (or EEA) context led to both better recall and better recognition. However, some subsequent researchers noted that a problem with such strictly ecologically based explanation for the survival effect (such as Nairne's) is that thinking about survival necessarily evokes thoughts about one's self, and the **self-reference effect** (SRE) can have a powerful positive effect on memory. Sheila Cunningham wondered if the survival effect resulted not from a bias for survival-related information per se, but from the same forces that make all material that is processed in terms of self-reference better remembered (Symons & Johnston, 1997).

Cunningham and her colleagues created a paradigm that was similar to the one used by Nairne et al. (2007) but that manipulated whether participants were thinking about themselves or another person during the task (instead of whether they were thinking about a hunter-gatherer or city environment). Cunningham, Brady-Van den Bos, Gill, and Turk (2013) presented participants with words to evaluate under three sets of instructions. The first was the self-reference condition, in which the person was expected to think most about himself or herself. The instructions were "In this task, try to imagine that you are stranded in the grasslands. You will need to find steady supplies of food and water and protect yourself from predators. You will now be shown a list of words and you are asked rate their relevance to you in this survival situation on a scale of 1–5 (1 being not relevant, 5 being extremely relevant). Some of the words may be relevant and others may not. It is up to you to decide." The second was the other reference condition (where the other person was British Prime Minister David Cameron) and the instructions were "In this task, try to imagine that David Cameron is stranded in the grasslands of a foreign land without basic survival materials. Over the next few months, he will need to find steady supplies of food, water, and protection from predators. You will now be shown a list of words and you are asked to rate their relevance to David Cameron's survival situation using a scale from 1–5 (1 being not relevant, 5 being highly relevant). Some of the words may be relevant, others may not. It is up to you to decide." Finally, there was a semantic coding condition in which the participants had to think about the words in terms of their semantic meaning but not in specific reference to any individual. The instructions for this condition were "In this task, you will be presented with a series of words. Some of these items can be found in the city, others in nature, and some in both. You will be asked to rate these items as follows: 1 = Only found in the city; 2 = Mostly found in the city; 3 = Found in both the city and nature; 4 = Mostly found in nature; and 5 = Only found in nature. It is up to you to decide" (Cunningham et al., 2013, p. 239). Participants were given a surprise recognition test after the encoding phase. In the recognition task, participants were asked to classify 90 items from the encoding phases and 90 new items as either "old" or "new." Correctly identifying an item as old was the measure of recognition.

Cunningham et al. (2013) found that participants recognized the most items from the self-reference conditions (where an average of 86 per cent of items were recognized) and that this was significantly greater than recognition in either of the other reference conditions (where an average of 81 per cent of items were recognized) or the semantic condition (where an average of 79 per cent of items were recognized). Further, participants were no better at recognizing words from the survival condition where they were not thinking about themselves (other reference condition) than in the semantic encoding conditions. Cunningham et al. (2013) conclude that there is a survival effect; however, the survival effect is functionally specific to the self, and not to survival issues in general.

self-reference effect (SRE)

people are better able to recall information when thinking of that information in terms of themselves

Memory and Exercise

Multiple research studies have looked at the effect of aerobic exercise on memory. These studies have two main findings. First, they have consistently shown that aerobic exercise can increase the size of the hippocampus (the brain structure most strongly associated with memory functioning) in people of all ages. Second, people who engage in aerobic exercise consistently show improvement in their visuospatial memory, which is memory for things like maps and other visual material that has a specific spatial organization. They do not show improvement for verbal memory, which is memory for things like word lists. The results from these experiments are particularly relevant to older adults, who often experience a decrease in the volume of their hippocampus and subsequent problems with memory. Aerobic exercise may help reverse or preventing the shrinking of the hippocampus and ameliorate age-related memory issues, including memory for many everyday visuospatial tasks, such as remembering where things are located and how to get from one place to another (Erickson et al., 2011). Health Canada recommends that adults engage in at least two-and-a-half hours of vigorous physical activity each week, and that children exercise at least 60 minutes each day. (For more on Health Canada's guidelines on physical activity, see https://www.canada.ca/en/public-health/services/being-active/physical-activity-your-health.html.) In 2015, Statistics Canada reported that fewer than 2 in 10 adults and 1 in 10 children get the amount of exercise recommended by Health Canada (Statistics Canada, 2015).

Using False Memories to Help People Make Healthier Eating Choices

False memories can be generated for just about any aspect of life, including food. Daniel Bernstein and his colleagues were able to implant false memories of becoming sick as a child as a result of eating either pickles or hard-boiled eggs, and these false memories were found not only to lead participants to avoid these foods, but to avoid related foods as well, such as pickle relish and egg salad (Bernstein, Laney, Morris, & Loftus, 2005). Cara Laney and her colleagues did the reverse; they successfully implanted a false memory of loving asparagus the first time that they tried it in a significant proportion of the participants. The group that had a false memory of loving asparagus was subsequently found to be more likely to choose asparagus from a restaurant menu, rated asparagus higher on a food preference scale, and reported they were willing to pay more for asparagus than participants in a control group that did not have a false memory for asparagus (Laney, Morris, Bernstein, Wakefield, & Loftus, 2008). The results from both Bernstein et al. (2005) and Laney et al. (2008) may have important health implications. First, it may be possible to create food aversions for unhealthy foods, such as fatty foods or foods high in sugar or salt, by implanting a false memory of being made sick by these items as a child. This could have a significant impact on food choices for people struggling to avoid junk food. Second, it may be possible to create food preferences for healthy food by implanting false memories that a person has always loved specific healthy foods, such as food low in fat and salt and high in nutrients. This could also have a significant impact on people's food choices and encourage healthier eating. Indeed, individuals whose diets were hurting their health could have both false memories of illness related to unhealthy food and false memories of enjoying healthy food implanted, which would steer them away from the food that was hurting them and steer them toward foods that could help them become healthier.

CHAPTER REVIEW

- Changes in health can lead to changes in memory. In some cases, memory loss is just a normal sign of aging; however, if an individual's memory loss affects her or his ability to complete day-to-day tasks, it could be a sign of a neurocognitive disorder (commonly referred to as dementia) that affects not just memory but thinking and reasoning as well.

- There are many forms of neurocognitive disorders, including Alzheimer's disease, vascular dementia, dementia with Lewy bodies, and frontotemporal dementia. These disorders differ in cause, symptoms, and prognosis. There are no cures for neurocognitive disorders. A person may also suffer extreme problems with memory due to hypothyroidism or a vitamin B_{12} deficiency. In these cases, medical interventions will restore memory to normal.

- Sometimes diseases have an indirect effect on memory. Epilepsy and the medications used to treat epilepsy can produce both retrograde and anterograde amnesia. In extreme cases, as in the case of Henry Molaison, parts of the brain may need to be removed to prevent seizures, which can also affect memory.

- Injuries to the brain can also lead to memory loss. Brain injuries are sometimes the result of accidents, but other times result from diseases, such as encephalitis, that cause swelling in the brain and damage to brain tissue. Clive Wearing, whose case is discussed in the opening vignette for this chapter, lost his memory following a bout with viral encephalitis.

- Korsakoff syndrome, which occurs following extreme vitamin B_1 deficiencies, is also characterized by permanent retrograde and anterograde amnesia as well as problems with short-term memory. Drugs, including anaesthesia and alcohol, can also cause retrograde amnesia.

- In rare cases, individuals can develop dissociative amnesia, a condition where an individual becomes unable to access autobiographical memories. Sometimes this loss of autobiographical memory leads to wandering, or a fugue state. There is emerging evidence that areas associated with autobiographical memory function abnormally in people with autobiographical amnesia, suggesting a biological cause for autobiographical amnesia.

- Processes related to memory can also affect health and healthcare. Disorders in memory exacerbate the symptoms of post-traumatic stress disorder (PTSD) and obsessive-compulsive disorder (OCD). Treatments based on knowledge of memory processes have been found to be effective for both of these disorders.

- Memory issues can affect choices regarding healthcare. Research clearly shows that people do not accurately recall their end-of-life decisions, suggesting that people should regularly update written records reflecting these preferences to ensure that current wishes are carried out when the time comes.

- Memory biases can impede health. People tend to remember health-related information that sustains their belief that they are healthy and forget information that indicates they may not be healthy. In order to overcome this tendency, healthcare workers need to actively engage individuals in conversations about non-healthy behaviours to increase the likelihood that individuals will remember changes they need to make in their lifestyle.

- Researchers have found that memories that are related to survival are better remembered than other memories. This effect likely results from the self-reference effect rather than preferential processing of survival-related stimuli.

- Memory can be used to promote health. Implanting false memories of healthy food preferences can help people make better choices with their diet.

MEMORY ACTIVITY

Remember the Causes of the Different Dementias

In this chapter, you learned about four types of dementia: Alzheimer's disease, vascular dementia, dementia with Lewy bodies, and frontotemporal dementia. In this activity, you will create a simple mnemonic to help you remember the causes of each of the dementias.

First, review the text and find the cause of each of the dementias and enter the cause in the chart. Next, choose a mnemonic to help you associate the name of the dementia (e.g., Alzheimer's disease) with the cause of the dementia (e.g., a shrinking cortex). Then, find a word that begins with the same letter as the disorder and describes the cause of the disorder, such as *atrophy* in the case of Alzheimer's disease. Finally, review the association between each word and its cue to commit them to memory.

Dementia	Cause	Cue word or phrase
Alzheimer's disease	Shrinking cortex	Atrophy
Vascular dementia		V_____
Dementia with Lewy bodies		D_____
Frontotemporal dementia		F_____

Questions

1. What is normal memory loss associated with aging? How does it differ from dementia?
2. List the eight question types on the MMSE and provide an example of each. Identify which types of questions carry the most weight when calculating a score on the MMSE.
3. Describe Alzheimer's disease. Discuss two aspects of brain functioning that are linked to the disease.
4. Compare and contrast dementia with Lewy bodies and vascular dementia.
5. What are two reversible causes of dementia?
6. Discuss two possible biological causes of memory loss that are not linked to aging.
7. Describe dissociative amnesia and identify a possible cause for this disorder.
8. Briefly describe Korsakoff syndrome. Describe the results of an experiment that explored patterns of memory deficits in patients with this disorder.
9. How does alcohol affect memory?
10. Describe an experiment that has looked for memory deficits in people with post-traumatic stress disorder (PTSD).
11. How might therapists take advantage of natural memory processes to treat PTSD?
12. Describe the mnestic deficit theory of obsessive-compulsive disorder (OCD). Discuss an experiment that supports this theory.
13. What aspects of memory are different in people with OCD?

14. Why is memory for end-of-life decisions important? Discuss an experiment that explored this topic and describe some implications of the results.
15. What advice would you give to someone creating an advance directive and why?
16. How can false memories be used to help people eat more healthily?
17. What are some ways that a person can improve their memory and their health at the same time?
18. What memory-related factors impede people's ability to heed medical advice?
19. Describe an experiment that demonstrated the survival effect.
20. Using an experiment discussed in the text, explain how the self-reference effect can account for the survival effect.

Key Figures

Alois Alzheimer p. 337
Jayanti Cho-Young p. 349
Sheila Cunningham p. 359

Merel Kindt p. 352
Robert Mann p. 349
Kristin Samuelson p. 350

Marcel van den Hout p. 352
Muriel Vogel-Sprott p. 349

14 Exceptional Memory, Mnemonics, and Expertise

LEARNING OBJECTIVES

Having read this chapter, you will be able to:

- Describe the method of loci.
- Identify ways in which memory athletes are similar to sports athletes.
- Identify similarities and differences between memory athletes and the rest of the population.
- Describe the master system and the person-action-object system and explain how these systems can be used to memorize digits.
- Describe skilled memory theory and its three component principles.
- Describe the testing effect and identify the conditions under which a testing effect is most likely to be observed.
- Compare and contrast the efficacy of studying for a test by re-reading material, highlighting key points, and engaging in retrieval practice.
- Explain why delayed feedback is more effective than immediate feedback for multiple-choice tests.
- Describe deliberate practice and explain how it leads to expertise.
- Explain how experts differ from novices in the way they approach their skill.

ALEX MULLEN

In 2017, American medical student Alex Mullen became the first International Association of Memory (IAM) World Memory Champion. Having already won the World Memory Champion title in 2015 and 2016, Alex attended the IAM's first contest, held in Indonesia, and broke several records (a few of them his own) on his way to first place. The IAM championship consists of 10 events and the events vary in both the amount of time given to memorize as much material as possible and the type of material that is to

Courtesy of the University of Mississippi Medical Center

be memorized. During the competition, Alex Mullen memorized 568 digits in five minutes, 133 historic dates in five minutes, 268 words in 15 minutes, 5235 binary numbers in 30 minutes, 3238 numbers in one hour, and an entire deck of shuffled playing cards in just 15.61 seconds (University of Mississippi Medical Centre, 2018)! Mullen also scored high on memorizing names, faces, and abstract images, and recalled digits that had been spoken to him. Although Mullen has done well at school, like all memory athletes he attributes his success to a powerful method of memorizing, not a powerful memory. Alex began to experiment with memory after reading Joshua Foer's 2011 bestseller *Moonwalking with Einstein*, which recounts Foer's own experience going from having an average memory to being the USA Memory Champion in just one year. Mullen used the same method that Foer used, and the same method that all memory athletes use: the **method of loci**. In this chapter, we will discuss why the method of loci is so effective and instruct you on how to use it to accomplish your own feats of memory, which you can use over and over again in your day-to-day life. We will also review the benefits of testing on later recall and identify methods that can help students perform better on tests. Finally, we will discuss the concept of expertise, which represents exceptional memory in a specific domain. The material in this chapter will clearly demonstrate that anyone can become an expert on just about anything, simply by taking advantage of the memory they were born with.

method of loci

a mnemonic that involves visualizing to-be-remembered images at different locations along a well-known path

DIY EXPERIMENT

Memory Capacity

Memorize the following list of items using whatever method you are most comfortable with.

broccoli
noodles
birdseed
order cheques
email Aunt Marg
karate
donate books
water hydrangeas
swim mask
smoke alarm
olives
sparkling water
running shoes
mouse pad
rent a truck

Make a note of what method you used and how long you spent on the material. Ten minutes after you finish trying to encode the items, write down as many items as you can. Then return to this page and check your accuracy.

Memory Athletes

In the early 1990s, Tony Buzan lamented that there were competitions to test skills for just about everything except what he considered the most important skill of all: human memory. Thus, in 1991 Buzan organized the first-ever World Memory Championship, which was held in London, England; there were seven contestants (Foer, 2011). While only seven people competed in 1991, memory competitions grew in popularity very quickly and now dozens of national and international competitions take place every year, including the World Memory Championship that Alex Mullen won in 2015. The competitors in these memory competitions refer to themselves as **memory athletes** because their performance is the result of learning a mnemonic skill and practising it. Memory athletes are the first to admit that, when they don't use mnemonics, their memories are unremarkable; their digit span is in the normal range and they are no more able to remember a list of random items than anyone else. What memory athletes have that the rest of the population lacks is an excellent command of the method of loci, an ancient approach to memorization that takes advantage of human's naturally vivid spatial memory.

memory athlete

an individual who engages in memory training most often for the purpose of entering memory competitions

Memorization throughout History

Until relatively recently, people memorized complex information much more frequently than they do now. Indeed, before the advent of writing around 2500 BCE, information about history, politics, and technology had to be transmitted orally and be memorized or lost to the ages. Most cultures tasked specific groups of people to memorize and teach that culture's most important information. In India, Brahmin priests spent 10 years learning the Vedas; in Arabia, *Rawis* were the official memorizers of the most important poetry; in the east, Buddha's teachings were memorized by priests long before they were written down; and Jewish customs were memorized by people known as *tannaim* (Foer, 2011). In some cases (such as learning the Vedas), memorizers used mnemonics; in other cases, the material itself was designed to be highly memorable. Two good examples of highly memorable material from the west are the poems the *Odyssey* and the *Iliad*, which are often credited to Homer although their true origin is unknown. The *Odyssey* and the *Iliad* are both highly repetitive poems that are riddled with memory cues. For example, the characters are always referred to with an adjective before their name that reminds the reader of a key trait of the individual: there is "*clever* Odysseus," "*swift-footed* Achilles," "*grey-haired* Athena," and "*laughing* Aphrodite." Aphrodite is even referred to as "laughing Aphrodite" when she is in despair (Foer, 2011). In addition to the repetition of names, the stories in the poems follow the same basic formula, first armies are gathered, then heroes take up shields, then rivals challenge each other. Taking up of shields never precedes the gathering of armies, and challenges between rivals never precede taking up of shields, even though the stories may have been a bit more interesting if things were changed around once in a while. The formulaic and liberal use of clichés, rhymes, and alliteration all made the *Odyssey* and the *Iliad* easier to remember, and it is likely that this is why these ancient poems have survived. If there ever was any part of the *Odyssey* or the *Iliad* that was hard to remember, it has been lost to time.

In the fifth century BCE, the Greeks began to write things down on scrolls. Scrolls were made of sheets of papyrus that had been fused together. Scrolls took a long time to create and were rare; they were typically chained to shelves in libraries. However, because an exact copy of a text existed on a scroll (even though that copy may have been very difficult to access), scholars were expected to know the text word for word. While orally presented poems may have been altered a bit by the teller without anyone knowing, the Greeks did not tolerate this sort of transgression. To get around this problem, the Greeks used the method of loci (first introduced in Chapter 1), which was likely already an ancient method of memorization even in ancient Greece.

The earliest known mention of the method of loci is in a book called *Rhetorica Ad Herennium* written by an unknown author in the first century BCE. The author notes that there are two types of memory: **natural memory**, which is embedded in our minds and **artificial memory**, which is a product of art and can be strengthened by training and discipline. Artificial memory, notes the author, is comprised of **backgrounds** and **images**. Backgrounds are defined scenes that can be easily recalled by natural memory, such as a house. An image, says the author, is a portrait of the object we wish to remember. To remember the image, it must be imagined in the background. To remember another image, the rememberer must imagine moving through the background to a different area where the second image can be imagined. This can be repeated for as many images as the rememberer wishes. To recall the images, the rememberer needs only to imagine walking through the background and the images will appear in sequence. According to the author, backgrounds should be deliberately

natural memory

memory that is embedded in our minds and cannot be strengthened

artificial memory

memory that is the product of art and can be strengthened by training

backgrounds

the locations used in the method of loci

images

the visual representations of to-be-remembered material in the method of loci

Scrolls (such as the Torah pictured here) could be bulky, difficult to navigate from page to page, and expensive or time consuming to copy, so memorizing the words was critical to the dissemination of knowledge.

obtained by scholars, and the backgrounds should themselves have few features of interest so that the image can easily be placed on the background and recalled without confusion. Images, unlike backgrounds, should be highly detailed and unique and should contain as much information as possible. Despite being used for thousands of years, the method of loci has never been improved upon; those who use this method today (including World Memory Championship champion Alex Mullen) follow the principles laid out in *Rhetorica Ad Herrenium*. The method of loci is still used for one simple reason: it really works. In the next section, we will put the method of loci to the test and see if you can use it to memorize 15 novel items. Box 14.2 includes a second opportunity to try this method yourself, or perhaps with a friend. Remember, you need a new memory palace for each list (or you need to imagine completely emptying out each item from a previous list before recycling your palace!).

A Demonstration of the Method of Loci

The method of loci involves imagining to-be-remembered items along a well-known route in your imagination. For this first attempt at using the method, I have listed 15 items that could be on anyone's to-do list.

Here are the items that you have to remember:

wash windows
flowers
text Alex
toothpaste
spinach
buttons
go to swim lesson at 4 o'clock
practice pinball
get haircut
clean litter box
cheese
shred documents
pickled eggs
rake leaves
bake a pie

The items on the list are arbitrary. Chances are, if you just practised it over and over you would retain about six or seven items for an immediate recall test—likely items from the start and end of the list. If you were tested tomorrow, you would likely recall even fewer. But with the method of loci, you can commit this list to memory and you should be able to remember all of the items for a long period of time if you put some effort into the encoding process.

First you must choose a background or, as memory athletes call it, a **memory palace**. The best memory palaces are places you know very, very well. If you've used the method of loci before, choose a different location for this exercise (you *always* have to use an "empty" memory palace for the method of loci to work). One good memory palace for present purposes is wherever

memory palace

an imagined location used in the method of loci

you are living right now, if it is sufficiently large, or a childhood home. Choose one and take a moment to imagine this location starting with the area outside the front door and moving clockwise (to the left) through each room, and then clockwise to the next room. It is very important that you end your tour through your home somewhere away from the front door and that you have a smooth, easy to imagine, route. You can go up or down stairs on your route to make more stops; just make sure you take the same path every time. You need 15 memorable locales for this demonstration, so try to imagine travelling through five or six distinct rooms. You can encode using the method of loci by simply reading the paragraphs that follow and imagining items as instructed.

Once you have imagined your memory palace, you can begin putting items from the list in it. The first item is *wash windows* so you can imagine washing the window on your front door, or, if there is no window, imagine that someone has drawn a window on your front door and you are washing the door clean. Next, imagine stepping into your home and seeing *flowers* (the next item on the list) just inside the door. Make your flowers memorable; make them especially beautiful or especially ugly and try to imagine their scent as well as what they look like. Once you have a good image of the flowers, you can move to a new location along the route in your palace where you will place the image for *text Alex*. Your image will be of your own creation but must contain enough information for you to recall "text" and "Alex." You could imagine a person you know named Alex texting, or you could imagine a cell phone with the text "Alex" easily visible on the screen; it's up to you. Continue moving through the palace adding *toothpaste, spinach, buttons, swim lessons at 4 o'clock, pinball, get haircut, clean litter box, cheese, shred documents, pickled eggs, rake leaves,* and *bake a pie* in different locations, making each image unique and adding movement, sound, and scent to your image when possible. When you feel ready, we can begin the test.

To test yourself, you need a sheet of paper (or computer) that can record your thoughts. Don't peek at the list. Imagine moving through your palace from your beginning location in the same order in which you encoded the items. Write each item as you go. The items should come to you spontaneously; you should be able to "see" them in their locations. If, after you test yourself, you don't have 15 items, make a note that you missed one and repeat trying to recall. When you discover your missed item or items, note what they were and ask yourself why they were not very memorable. Was it the location? Was it the image? Try changing the image a bit to add movement, sound, or scent and repeat your test. It is essential to know where you tend to make mistakes if you want to rely on the method of loci in the future.

Most people are able to remember most items from a 15-item list using the method of loci and some coaching, even when they are unable to remember those items using other memory methods.

The method of loci can be used without any other mnemonic devices if the to-be-remembered material is easy to visualize, such as words or actions. However, when the material involves digits, such as *pi*, a memorizer must employ a system that converts the number into an image that can be placed in a memory palace. Digits themselves can't be placed in memory palaces because they are not distinct enough from each other, and also because they repeat. Over the centuries, memorizers have developed many systems for converting digits into images, but the **major system** and the **person-action-object (PAO) system** are most often used by memory athletes (Foer, 2011). The major system involves creating images based on specific phonemes associated with each digit. The person-action-object (PAO) system involves developing complex images associated with pairs of digits ahead of time.

major system

a method that assigns a distinct phoneme to each digit from 0 to 9

person-action-object (PAO) system

a method for creating images from numbers based on memorizing distinct images containing a person, an action, and an object

BOX
14.2

DIY EXPERIMENT

The Method of Loci

This experiment can be modified to serve as a study tool. Simply use your own study list instead of the items provided.

birthday cake
garbage bags
write essay
spaghetti
pay bills online
lemonade
blue cheese dressing
slingshot
make bed
black pepper
eyeglasses
cut toenails
water cactus
pineapple
change light bulb

First, try to learn the items on this list without using the method of loci. Then test your memory and note how many items you were able to remember. Next, try using the method of loci to learn the items. After placing all 15 items in the memory palace, take a break for a couple of minutes and then perform a test, either writing or typing as many items as possible without looking at the list. How did your performance compare to when you didn't use the method of loci?

You can take the experiment one step further and have a friend serve as the participant. Test her or his recall for the list and then teach your friend the method of loci, apply it to these items, and see if recall improves.

To try using the method of loci to learn the key terms from this chapter, see the Memory Activity at the end of this chapter.

The Major System

The major system allows a person to convert digits into words, which can then be used to form images in memory palaces. The first major system was devised by Pierre Herigon sometime in the early 1600s and was refined by Stanislaus Mink von Wennsshein in the early 1700s. The major system is quite simple. Each digit from 0 through 9 is associated with a unique set of phonetic sounds. An example of the major system is shown in Table 14.1.

Vowels are not assigned to digits. Instead, vowels go between the phonemes derived from digits to form words. The major system is referred to as a peg word system because the words are like pegs that hold digits. Table 14.1 shows a single-digit major system where each digit is linked to a distinct word. For example, the digit 2 is converted to the phoneme /n/ and can be linked to the word *honey*. However, memorizers sometimes develop two-digit major systems

Table 14.1   The major system

	Digit									
	0	1	2	3	4	5	6	7	8	9
Phoneme	s or z	t or d	n	m	r	l	ch, sh, or zh	/k/ or /g/	f or v	p or b
Way to remember	zero starts with Z	ONE vertical stroke	TWO vertical strokes	THREE vertical strokes	four ends with /r/ sound	roman numeral for 50 is L	CH, SH, and ZH have six serifs	K and G both appear to have 7s embedded in them	script F looks like an 8	look like 9s
Noun	shoes	tea	honey	womb	ear	eel	witch	psycho	hive	ape
Verb	sew	swat	whine	aim	worry	wail	chew	hack	woof	sob
Adjective	easy	hot	new	yummy	airy	woolly	huge	gooey	heavy	happy

The major system associates digits with distinct phonemes. The phonemes can then be combined with vowels to form words. The phonemes /s/ and /z/ can be used to start words because /s/ and /z/ are associated with the digit zero.

Source: Adapted from Hale-Evans, R. (2006). *Mind performance hacks.* Sebastopol, CA: O'Reilly. p. 14–15

where the two phonemes associated with a letter pair are linked to a single word. For example, the number 67 is converted to the phonemes /ch/ and /k/ and can be linked to the word *chick*. Some memorizers go further and create single words from three-digit combinations. For example, the number 769 is associated with the phonemes /k/, /ch/, and /p/ and can be linked to the word *ketchup*. Memorizers can also use the major system to create a noun, verb, and adjective from a sequence of numbers and combine those into a single image. For example, if memorizers wanted to remember the number 456 they could select a noun with the phoneme /r/ such as *ear*, a verb from the phoneme /l/, such as *wail*, and an adjective from the phoneme /zh/ such as *huge* and combine them into an image of a huge wailing ear. At the time of recall, the memorizer deconstructs the image knowing the first digit stands for the noun, the second for the verb, and the third for the adjective: eaR = 4, waiL = 5, huGE = 6.

A major system can be learned in advance or a person can develop new images as they are needed (as in a memory competition). However, the major system is rarely if ever used by

---

DIY EXPERIMENT

BOX 14.3

Generating Peg Words Using the Internet

There are dozens of websites that generate words for you using the major system. Most will produce a word from digits 1 to 9, numbers 01 to 99 and numbers 001 to 999. First, get to know the major system using Table 14.1. Next, enter chunks of the number into the word generator. For the first chunk, choose a noun; for the second chunk, choose a verb; and for the third chunk, choose an adjective. Then combine these three things into a single image. If you still have more numbers, continue the process. Put the images in a memory palace and test your memory regularly over time to see how effectively you can use the major system. For more, see the Major System Database website: https://major-system.info/en/.

present-day memory athletes; they opt for the person-action-object system (PAO) (Foer, 2011). The PAO system is preferred because it uses highly unusual (and therefore highly memorable) images and there is no awkward image-to-word-to-phoneme translation step, which is both difficult to do and time-consuming in speed competitions.

The Person-Action-Object System

The person-action-object (PAO) system is a method that memory athletes can use to convert digits into images that can then be placed in a memory palace. In this system, every number from 00 to 99 is assigned a unique image consisting of a person, action, and object. The system works best when the person is famous and doing something that is both unique and easy to remember. For example, the number 21 might be Elvis Presley (person) gyrating (action) while holding a microphone (object); number 65 might be Miley Cyrus (person) swinging (action) from a huge ball (object); and the number 07 might be Chris Hadfield (person) floating in space (action) with a guitar (object). The six-digit number 216507 would become the person from number 21 (Elvis Presley), the action from number 65 (swinging on a ball), and the object from 07 (a guitar). The memorizer would envisage Elvis swinging while holding a guitar. The key to this method is non-duplication of items; each person, action, and object can only be used once. Many memory athletes choose very risqué or repulsive images because they are highly memorable (Foer, 2011). Once a person memorizes 100 unique PAO images, the PAO system can be used to remember any number from 0 to 999,999 with a single unique image. When memorizing a deck of 52 playing cards, for example, a memory athlete will typically view three cards at a time, convert the cards into numbers from 01 to 52, and then create an image from those three cards and put it in a location in a memory palace. Thus, an entire deck of cards can be coded as 18 PAO images. If you were able to memorize the 15 items using the method of loci in Box 14.1 (test yourself now if you haven't already), then you can see that memorizing 18 items would probably not be that difficult. If you want to try it yourself, use a spreadsheet to create your 52 images and learn them well. Then assign a number to each playing card (ace of clubs = 01, ace of diamonds = 02, and so on up to king of spades = 52). Get a deck of cards, shuffle them, and deal them three at a time, creating a PAO image for each set of three cards and placing it in a memory palace. You will find you have 17 images combined from three cards and one card left in the deck. Simply make the single PAO image corresponding to this card the eighteenth image. Next, shuffle the cards and then arrange them in the correct sequence based on approaching each image in your memory palace and deconstructing its corresponding numbers.

Some extreme memory athletes have created PAO systems for all numbers from 000 to 1000, allowing them to create a unique image for every number from 0 to 999,999,999. One disadvantage of the PAO system is that memorizers must invest a great deal of time into developing their basic images and memorizing them thoroughly because, unlike with the master system, the association between an image and the digits it represents is completely arbitrary. However, if a person wants to win a memory competition, they are likely highly motivated to invest this time in a method that is likely to be highly effective (Foer, 2011).

Skilled Memory Theory

In the early 1980s, William Chase and Anders Ericsson recruited a graduate student, known only as S.F., to see if practice could affect digit span. Recall that digit span is the number of digits a person can recall in an immediate free-recall test. At the outset of the study, S.F. had a digit

RELEVANT RESEARCH

BOX
14.4

Stage Acting and the Method of Loci

People are notoriously bad at remembering things verbatim, or word for word. A person can demonstrate this easily enough by reading two lines from a page of text and then trying to recite them back. The lines will likely reflect the meaning and the key points of the material but are very unlikely to be recalled word for word (Foer, 2011). Actors must overcome this seemingly natural tendency to recall the gist and not exact sentences when they memorize scripts; actors are a type of memory expert. Helga Noice recruited seven stage actors, provided them with a script, and asked them to record their thought process as they went about learning the script. The actors did not know each other and worked on the task independently. Noice (1992) then transcribed the recordings from all the actors and looked for commonalities. All the actors reported a very similar approach to learning their scripts. First, none of the actors reported trying to learn the script by rote memorization (i.e., repeating lines until they were known well). Second, all of the actors reported that they read the script many times to understand the motivations of the different characters, and to understand what emotional state their character would be in when delivering a given line. Third, all of the actors report only learning the lines verbatim after they learned the blocking, which is the movement and physical actions that take place on stage. All of the actors report that being in a specific location on stage and/or doing a specific action helps cue their memories for the script. Taken together, the results of Noice (1992) suggest that stage actors use a real-world method of loci to retrieve lines from their scripts. Actors first learn the physical movements associated with the script, which creates a memory palace. Next, they place specific verbatim lines of text in each location in this memory palace, which can be retrieved as they enact the play. The emotional and motivational sequence may be paired with the blocking of movements and provide an additional cue to the text at each point in the script (Noice, 1992).

span of about seven digits, which is average. Over the next year, Chase and Ericsson had S.F. spend more than 250 hours storing and retrieving lists of digits. S.F. eventually developed a digit span of 70 digits. Thus, S.F.'s digit span increased tenfold with practice (Chase & Ericsson, 1982; Ericsson, Delaney, Weaver, & Mahadevan, 2004). When interviewed about how he accomplished this improvement, S.F. explained that, as an avid runner, he already had lots of digits stored in long-term memory that were associated with various running times and races, such as Roger Bannister breaking the four-minute mile with a time of 3:59.4, and the distance for a marathon being 26.2 miles. S.F. reported that, after some practice with the digit-span task, he realized that he could use this existing memory to help him recall digits better and began to recode incoming digits as specific running times he already knew. The

According to skilled memory theory, exceptional memory can develop in any individual who follows three basic principles outlined in the model. In the 1980s, research participants S.F. and D.D. used their existing knowledge of running (such as the record-breaking time of runner Roger Bannister, pictured here) to expand their digit span by tenfold or more (Chase & Ericsson, 1982).

Press Association via AP Images

digits 3594, for example, would be stored as "Roger Bannister's record" and so on. S.F. was able to chunk incoming information into groups of three to five digits and then store the digits as well-known running-related facts that he could recall easily later on. To see if this approach could generalize to other people, Chase and Ericsson recruited a second runner, known as D.D., and subjected him to the same amount of practice with the digit-span task. Like S.F., D.D. began with a normal digit span but eventually increased his span to about 80 digits with the help of his existing knowledge of running times and distances.

Chase and Ericsson (1981) developed **skilled memory theory** to account for the digit-span improvement observed in S.F. and D.D. According to skilled memory theory, exceptional memory can develop in any individual when three principles are followed. The first is the **encoding principle**; the individual needs to rely on prior knowledge and patterns to encode the presented items and store them in groups. In the case of S.F. and D.D., this prior knowledge was of running times. The second is the **retrieval-structure principle**; the encoded information needs to be associated with retrieval cues during study that can later trigger LTM retrieval. In the case of S.F. and D.D., the retrieval cue was the associated running feat, which to avid runners is highly memorable. The third is the **speed-up principle**; as individuals gain experience encoding the material, they can learn more information in less time (Ericsson et al., 2004). In the years following the development of skilled memory theory, many researchers tested its assumptions and found increases in memory performance after training that were consistent with the assumptions of the model (see, e.g., Ericsson & Kintsch, 1995; Ericsson & Lehmann, 1996; Higbee, 1997; Kliegl, Smith, & Baltes, 1989; Kliegl, Smith, Heckhausen, & Baltes, 1987; Wenger & Payne, 1997). Skilled memory theory fits well with what is observed among memory athletes; memory athletes devise ways to chunk information (the encoding principle) that is highly memorable (the retrieval-structure principle) and improve their ability to do this over time (the speed-up principle).

A key assumption of skilled memory theory is that exceptional feats of memory are the result of practice; they are not innate. In 1991, Charles Thompson and his colleagues at the University of Kansas began studying Rajan Mahadevan, who was, from 1981 to 1987, the world record holder in memorizing *pi* (π), a mathematical constant used to compute the circumference of a circle that is comprised of an infinite number of digits (see Figure 14.1). Rajan was able to recall 31,811 digits of *pi* correctly on July 5, 1981. What made Rajan appear unusual is that he reportedly had a digit span of 15 digits *before* he began working to memorize *pi*, suggesting that some exceptional memory capacity may be innate. Thompson et al. (1991) noted that Rajan also had a large letter span, suggesting that an inborn ability, and not a mnemonic skill, was behind his exceptional memory. Rajan also claimed not to use mnemonic devices to help him remember. Thompson et al. (1991) thus speculated that, while skilled memory theory may apply in some cases of exceptional memory, it does not apply to all cases of exceptional memory.

In 2005, Anders Ericsson and his colleagues decided to study Rajan to see if his memory was indeed different than the exceptional memories that developed in S.F. and D.D. Ericsson et al. (2004) subjected Rajan to a variety of digit-, letter-, and symbol-span tests involving between 15 and 75 items and analyzed the results very carefully. First, Rajan showed significant serial-position effects within each chunk of digits that he encoded. He recalled items at the beginning and end of each chunk better than those in the middle. This finding is consistent with typical memory and contradicts the notion that Rajan has some sort of "photographic memory" that allows him to encode with perfect precision. Rajan admitted to Ericsson et al. (2004) that he *does* indeed use facts associated with digits to help him remember (e.g., he reported that he coded some groups of

skilled memory theory

a model that asserts that specific memory techniques can lead to greater memory capacity

encoding principle

memory will be better if an individual associates to-be-remembered material with material in long-term memory

retrieval-structure principle

memory will be better when material is associated with easy-to-remember cues

speed-up principle

as people gain experience encoding, they can encode more information in less time

numbers as telephone area codes for specific cities such as "502," others with events that occurred in a given year such as "1861"), contradicting what he had said earlier when being investigated by Thompson et al. (1991). Ericsson et al. (2004) reasoned that if Rajan was in fact associating strings of numbers to facts, and storing those facts in memory, that groups of strings with repeating patterns such as 388383338838 should be much more difficult for him to recall than groups that had distinct digit groups such as 186150291143. Indeed, Rajan recalled 60 per cent fewer digits in the repeating pattern condition than in the random condition, supporting the notion that a mnemonic that produced distinct retrieval cues was assisting his recall.

In a final series of experiments, Ericsson et al. (2004) studied Rajan's ability to recall symbols (such as $, %, #, etc.) and letters. In the first few trials with symbols, Rajan had a span of about six symbols, which was not significantly different from untrained university students. After a few trials, however, Rajan's span began to increase; however, this was because Rajan had learned symbol-digit pairings at this point and could convert symbols into digits and use his highly trained digit-memorization skill to encode them (e.g., ! = 1, (= 2, [= 3, etc.). Rajan also admitted that when presented with letters to remember, he would code them as digits as well (e.g., N = 1, B = 2, C = 3, etc.). When Ericsson et al. (2004) presented Rajan with digit/symbol strings where it would be nearly impossible to recode the string into distinct memory items, such as "444^4^44^^" Rajan never exceeded a span of seven items, which was exactly the same as the control group for the experiment who had no experience memorizing digits. Thus, Ericsson et al. (2004) argue that Rajan, a man who could recite more than 30,000 digits of *pi*, had a basic memory capacity that was no different from that of any other person; his digit span was exceptional because of nurture, not nature.

In 2009, Anders Ericsson had the opportunity to study another **piphilologist**, Chao Lu, who, on November 20, 2005, recited the first 67,890 digits of *pi* with perfect accuracy. Even at a rate

piphilologist

an individual who memorizes the digits of *pi*

3.14159
265358979323
846264338327950288
41971693993751058209 74
944592307816406286208 9986
280348253421170679821 48086513
282306647093844609550 5822317253594
081284811174502841027 019385211055596
446229489549303819644 2881097566593344 6128475
6482337867831652712019 091456485669234603486104 5432664821
33936072602491412737245870066063155881748815209209628292540917
153643678925903600113305305488204665213841469519415116094330572703657595919530 92
18611738193261179310511854807446237996274956735188575272489122793818301194912983367336244065664308602139494639 5224
737190702179860943702770539217176293176752384674818467669405132000568127145263560827785771342757789609173637178721468 44090
1224953430146549585371050792279689258923542019956112129021960864034418159813629774771309960518707211349999998372978049951059731732816096318595024459455346908302642522308 2533446

Figure 14.1 Digits of *pi*

How many digits of *pi* do you think you can memorize? piphilologist Chao Lu translated 67,890 digits of *pi* into a series of more than 30,000 words, which he then memorized. In theory, anyone motivated to memorize *pi* can become a piphilologist.

of about 1.28 digits per second, it still took Chao Lu more than 24 hours to recite all of the digits he had learned (Hu, Ericsson, Yang, & Lu, 2009). In their first experiment, Hu et al. (2009) presented Chao Lu and age-matched controls with a series of digits presented at a fixed rate on a computer screen that they had to encode and then immediately report back. Their digit span was defined as the longest span that they could report correctly on three consecutive trials. Chao Lu's digit span was 8.8 and the control group's was 9.2; there was no statistical difference between the groups. In the next experiment, Hu et al., (2009) presented Chao Lu and the control group with 5×5, 7×7, and 9×9 matrices of random digits printed on paper with a maximum of 10, 15, and 20 minutes, respectively, to memorize each. After the study period was over, participants were given a blank piece of paper and asked to reconstruct the matrix. After completing the test for the 9×9 matrix, Chao Lu was unexpectedly tested on his memory for earlier matrices. Chao Lu recalled all the matrices with 100 per cent accuracy, whereas the control group correctly reported 92 per cent of the 5×5 matrices, 85 per cent of the 7×7 matrices, and 69 per cent of the 9×9 matrices. In addition, Chao Lu spent less time memorizing the matrices. When given a final digit-span test, where Chao Lu determined how much time to spend on each item instead of having them presented at a constant rate, his digit span was vastly superior to controls. Chao Lu reported that he memorized digits in pairs by creating images based on nouns associated with each pair. For example, the series 971376460 corresponded to *goblet, doctor, basketball, tutor, cobra,* and *restroom.* Chao Lu learned this series by creating an image from these words using a system that is highly similar to the PAO system (Hu et al., 2009).

The Brain of the Memory Champion

In the early 2000s, Eleanor Maguire and her colleagues in England studied the brains of highly experienced taxi drivers who knew the location of 25,000 London streets and more than 1000 landmarks. Maguire et al. (2000) found that the posterior hippocampal regions of experienced taxi drivers were significantly larger than normal (for more information, see Chapter 4). Maguire wondered if memory champions would show structural changes in their brains like the changes observed in London taxi drivers. In 2003, Maguire recruited eight participants from the World Memory Championship and examined them on three levels. First, Maguire et al. examined whether people with superior memory (SM) differ from controls in intellectual ability. Second, they examined whether SMs have brain structures that differ from controls (like London taxi drivers). And finally, they examined whether SMs and controls use the same areas of their brain while encoding information.

Maguire, Valentine, Wilding, and Kapur (2003) found no difference in verbal or reasoning skills of the SMs and controls; all had scores in the high average range. The groups also did not differ in their visual memory scores. The only measures where there was a difference related to working memory and long-term verbal memory, where, as expected, the SM group performed significantly better than controls. Maguire et al. (2003) also found no differences in the volume of grey matter or white matter in any brain region between SMs and controls.

Maguire et al. (2003) also compared brain activity during the encoding of visual stimuli of one of three types: digits, faces, or snowflakes. Because SMs and controls will have had more similar experience memorizing faces than digits, they expected a smaller difference for face stimuli than digit stimuli. Also, because neither group is likely to have had any experience memorizing snowflakes, differences were predicted to be the lowest for the snowflakes. As predicted, SMs performed much better than controls when recalling digits, somewhat better than controls when recalling faces, and no differently than controls when recalling snowflakes. When Maguire et al. (2003) analyzed the fMRI data, they found that the SMs had increased activity in the medial parietal cortex, retrosplenial cortex, and right posterior hippocampus, even during the snowflake task where performance of the SMs was the same as performance of controls (see Figure 14.2). These brain areas are linked to spatial memory and navigation (Breathnach, 1980; Burgess, Maguire, & O'Keefe, 2002; Maguire et al., 1998; Maguire et al., 2000) All participants were interviewed after the experiment and it was revealed that, while all SMs used the method of loci, none of the controls used this method, thus explaining why spatial and navigational brain areas were more active in SMs than in controls. Maguire et al. (2003) speculated that even though taxi drivers and SMs were similar in that they relied on spatial information to aid their memory, taxi drivers must learn thousands of distinct routes while SMs can use the same routes over and over, which can explain why the posterior hippocampus is enlarged in taxi drivers but not in SMs.

Why Do Mnemonics Work?

Effective mnemonics take advantage of the strengths of human memory while simultaneously compensating for weaknesses. One reason the method of loci works is that people are extremely good at remembering spatial and visual information. For example, while you probably can't list the names of everyone who was in your second-grade class, you can probably imagine walking through your primary school with ease. When researchers show people in their forties high school yearbook pictures, they are extremely good at recognizing people they went to school with even when they can't remember the person's name. Images and maps stick with us (Bahrick, Bahrick, & Wittlinger, 1975). Chances are you've given directions to someone using "where such and such used to be"; for example, you may have said, "Turn left where that old barn used to be" or "It's in the mall where the Zellers used to be." At first glance, this may seem counterintuitive. How can it be helpful to point someone to a landmark that no longer exists? It is helpful because the landmark *does* still exist in mental representations. Mental maps are so stubborn that memory athletes devote at least a week before each major competition to going through their memory palaces and mentally "emptying" them out so that new material can be added during the competition. (You will have to do this too each

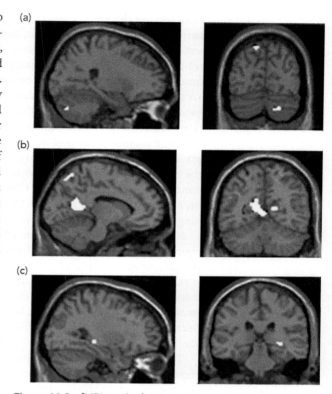

Figure 14.2   fMRI results from Maguire et al. (2003)

Functional MRI results show difference between the SMs and controls. (a) Areas more active for the SMs for all tasks: right cerebellum. (b) Areas active only in the SMs, commonly for all tasks: left medial superior parietal gyrus, bilateral retrosplenial cortex, and (c) right posterior hippocampus. These areas are linked to navigation (Maguire et al., 2003).
Source: Maguire et al., 2003, p. 94, Figure 3

time you use the same memory palace.) The fact that locations stick with people is a major part of what makes the method of loci so effective. Another reason the method of loci works well is that it provides many memory cues when an image includes movement, sounds, and scents. In addition, the private nature of images used in the method of loci allows people to make images highly memorable by making them humorous, salacious, or disgusting. People are much better at remembering funny, lewd, and gross material than mundane material; thus, mnemonics work because they allow mundane things such as the numbers 32908654956 to be remembered as "grandma dancing with a fish in her underwear next to Mike Tyson smearing butter on himself while wearing snow shoes" (for example). The method of loci isn't the only place where highly memorable, funny, lewd, or gross concepts can help memory. For example, the mnemonic "**Dirty Kinky People Can Often Find Great Sex**" is easier for most people to remember than "**Do Kings Play Chess On Fine Green Silk?**" simply because the former is a little funny, and a little salacious. (Both are mnemonics for the taxa of living things: domain, kingdom, phylum, class . . . can you fill in the rest?)

In addition to maximizing the strengths and minimizing the weaknesses of long-term memory, mnemonics also work by reducing working-memory load. Without a mnemonic, a person must use all their working-memory capacity to repeat six to-be-remembered items; however, someone using the method of loci and a 100-item PAO system can instead use her or his working memory to chunk digits into three pairs and then create an image based on these pairs, imagine it in the memory palace, and move on. Indeed, it might be said that it takes *less* effort to create an image from three well-known items from a PAO system than it does to maintain six random digits.

Table 14.2 shows a description of popular memory championship events as well as the world record scores of those events. Note that, in general, memory athletes have a much easier time with events that involve numbers. For example, the world record holder memorized 520 digits in five minutes, but only about 142 historic dates (which are digits linked to words) in five minutes and about 187 names in 15 minutes. These differences clearly demonstrate that it is easier to use a mnemonic to memorize material that is easily converted to digits than other material. This is because digits carry very little meaning of their own and are limited in variety (there are only 10 digits). Digits can thus easily be converted into PAO images and stored in memory palaces. Memory athletes still perform amazing feats for memorizing arbitrary face/name combinations, abstract shapes, and random words but they have to rely on much more arbitrary systems, such as finding a way to get features in a face to relate to the name, or finding a pattern in the order of shapes that can be converted to digits and then words.

For concepts that don't convert neatly into digits, a specific mnemonic can be created. These are difficult to devise on the fly, as evidenced by the fact that some mnemonics have been around for many generations. Examples include BEDMAS (or PEDMAS), the order of operations for arithmetic; FACE and Every Good Boy Deserves Fudge for the spaces and lines of the treble clef; and My Very Educated Mother Just Served Us Nachos for the planets of the solar system. These mnemonics tend to be highly memorable, I recall the word "HHeLiBeBCNOFNeNaMgAlSiPSClArKCa" (which can be pronounced easily with a bit of practice) when I need to spout off the first 20 elements of the periodic table of elements and "is is it he says his son's his aunt" when I need to remember how to conjugate certain French verbs. I learned both of these mnemonics more than 30 years ago and remember them well today.

The best time for a student to invest time in developing a mnemonic is when the material is factual, difficult to learn through rote memorization, highly detailed, and easy to confuse

Table 14.2 Memory competitions that comprise the world memory championship

Event	Memory Time	Recall Time	World Record Score	Description and Scoring
Name and faces	15 min	30 min	187	Recall name when shown face. One point for correct name, 0.5 points for phonetically correct name, −0.5 points for incorrect name, 0 points for blank.
Abstract images	15 min	30 min	599	Recall the order in which abstract images appeared on study sheet. 5 points for a correct row, −1 point for an incorrect row, 0 points for a blank row.
Random words	15 min	40 min	300	Recall words in order. 20 points for correct column, 10 points for one error in column, 0 points for more than one error in column.
Historic dates	5 min	15 min	132	Recall dates associated with historic facts. 1 point for a correct date, −0.5 points for each incorrect date, 0 points for a blank date.
Speed numbers	5 min	15 min	520	Recall digits in order. 40 points for a correct row, 20 points for row with one error, 0 points for row with more than one error.
Spoken number	520 sec	25 min	456	Recall digits in order. 10 digits = 221 points, 20 digits = 313 points, 50 digits = 495 points.
Binary digits	30 min	60 min	5040	Recall binary digits in order. 30 points for a correct row, −15 points for one error in a row, 0 points for more than one error in row.
One-hour numbers	60 min	120 min	3029	Recall digits in order. 40 points for a correct row, 20 points for row with one error, 0 points for row with more than one error.
One-hour cards	60 min	120 min	1612	Recall order of cards. 52 points for a complete pack, 26 points for one error in pack, 0 points for more than one error in pack.
Speed cards	5 min	5 min	20.44 sec	Learn 52 playing cards in order as fast as possible.

Source: Based on material from http://www.world-memory-statistics.co.uk/disciplines.php

with other material. Examples from psychology where a mnemonic may be helpful include the elements of a classical conditioning paradigm, Erikson's stage theory, and the action potential.

Testing Effects

The prevailing assumption among lay people (and even many academics) is that students learn during lectures and studying and that the sole role of tests is to assess what has been learned. However, research contradicts this traditional view and suggests instead that retrieval practice through testing enhances memory. Retrieval practice is typically more effective than studying at establishing long-term retention and at transferring learning to other contexts (Roediger & Butler, 2011). This means that, while attending lectures, taking notes is essential. Most learning will occur when you try to test yourself and try to retrieve the content of those class notes.

The finding that repeated memory retrieval produces better retention than re-reading the same information for an equivalent amount of time is referred to as the **testing effect** (Karpicke & Roediger, 2008). An example of the testing effect was recently demonstrated by Jeffrey Karpicke and Henry Roediger. First, Karpicke and Roediger (2008) had participants learn Swahili–English

testing effect

the finding that repeated memory retrieval produces better retention than re-reading the same information for an equivalent amount of time

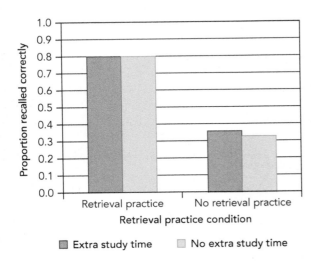

Figure 14.3 The effect of retrieval and extra study time on recall

This figure shows the results from Karpicke and Roediger (2008). Participants first studied Swahili–English word pairs. Half of participants were given retrieval practice, half were not. Half were given the chance for extra study, half were not. While retrieval practice had a significant effect on later recall of the word pairs, extra study time had no effect.

Source: Based on Karpicke & Roediger, 2008, p. 967

word pairs (e.g., mashua–boat). Next, half of the participants practised retrieving the word pairs by entering the English word when the Swahili word was presented. Half of all participants were also given the chance to study the words pairs further if they wished. For the final test, participants were shown the Swahili words and had to enter the corresponding English words. The results from the experiments can be seen in Figure 14.3. The two columns on the left in Figure 14.3 show recall rates for participants who practised retrieving the word pairs; the two columns on the right show participants who did not practise retrieving the word pairs. Participants who practised retrieving word pairs recalled significantly more than participants who did not practise. Further, participants who were given extra time to study the word pairs (shown in purple) did not perform better than participants who did not receive an opportunity to study more.

In 2009, Mary Pyc and Katherine Rawson conducted a series of experiments to determine the best timing for retrieval practice as well as the optimal amount of retrieval practice for long-term retention. Pyc and Rawson (2009) first exposed participants to 70 Swahili–English word pairs. Participants then had a session of retrieval practice, which involved entering the English word that corresponded with the Swahili word presented on the computer screen. Pyc and Rawson (2009) varied the interstimulus interval (ISI) between successive retrieval practice trials of a given word pair by one to six minutes in order to compare performance when retrieval would be easy (short ISI condition) to performance when retrieval would be more difficult because of a time delay (long ISI condition). Pyc and Rawson (2009) also varied how many times a word pair was practised by removing the word pair from the practice roster after it was correctly completed 1, 3, 5, 6, 7, 8, or 10 times. A word pair that was removed after three retrieval practices would have fewer retrieval practices than a word pair removed after seven retrieval practices. The final test occurred following two retention intervals (RIs), 25 minutes or one week. The results from Pyc and Rawson (2009) are shown in Figure 14.4.

The results from Pyc and Rawson show that longer ISIs between retrieval practices result in better performance. Even when retrieval is only practised once and the test occurs one day later, participants in the long ISI condition were four times as likely to recall the item as participants in the short ISI condition. Thus, waiting to practise retrieving material resulted in better performance than practising the material immediately. Pyc and Rawson (2009) also found that additional practice retrieving material benefited retrieval in all conditions except in the short ISI/long RI condition where additional retrieval practice had no effect (and performance was extremely low overall). For the material used in Pyc and Rawson, about seven practice repetitions seemed to produce the maximum benefit such that additional practice did not result in any increase in performance.

Figure 14.4   Results from Pyc and Rawson (2009)

The results from Pyc and Rawson (2009) show that the long ISI (six minutes) always results in better performance than the short ISI (one minute), and that increasing the number of retrieval practices benefits retrieval except in the short ISI/long RI condition. The results suggest that it is best to have a longer delay between exposure and retrieval practice and that maximal benefits result from approximately seven retrieval practices.

Source: Pyc & Rawson, 2009, p. 440

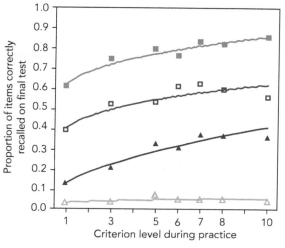

- ■ Long ISI/short RI   ▲ Long ISI/short RI
- ☐ Short ISI/short RI   △ Short ISI/short RI

The results from Pyc and Rawson (2009) suggest that retrieval practice can have a significant impact on recall, but the conditions of retrieval practice are important. The results suggest that individuals are much more likely to see a benefit from retrieval practice if they make the retrieval a little more difficult by delaying practice by a few minutes, and if they repeat retrieval practice about seven times. Typically, additional retrieval practice works better than a single retrieval practice (see Hogan & Kinstch, 1971; Roediger & Karpicke, 2006; and Wheeler & Roediger, 1992). However, both Carpenter (2009) and Carpenter and DeLosh (2006) found that a single retrieval practice benefited recall, and Roediger and Karpicke (2006) and Butler and Roediger (2007) found that single retrieval practices benefited performance even following a long delay. There is also evidence in the literature that suggests that an expanding schedule of retrieval practice, where the interval between practices is increased over time, may be more beneficial than schedules with fixed practice intervals (see Landauer & Bjork, 1978). Short delays early on help ensure that retrieval is accurate, while longer delays later in practice help ensure that retrieval occurs under challenging conditions. Thus, research suggests that students may benefit most from testing themselves on material soon after learning, and then retesting repeatedly with increasing delays between tests.

Feedback

Feedback regarding the accuracy of a given retrieval practice influences the testing effect, both because it allows individuals to correct errors (Pashler, Cepeda, Wixted, & Rohrer, 2005) and because it helps maintain correct responses (Butler, Karpicke, & Roediger, 2008). Not surprisingly, research has shown that when individuals make errors and don't receive feedback, retrieval practice does not benefit later recall (Kang, McDermott, & Roediger, 2007). This means it is important for students to seek feedback for incorrect responses for test material, especially if that material will appear again on a later test. Feedback is argued to be particularly important following multiple-choice tests because the individual has been exposed to incorrect responses as well as the correct response; when an incorrect response is chosen, it is often repeated on subsequent tests (Marsh, Roediger, Bjork, & Bjork, 2007; Butler, Marsh, Goode, & Roediger, 2006; Roediger & Marsh, 2005). Indeed, Butler and Roediger (2008) found that when individuals are given feedback after a multiple-choice test, they do not repeat incorrect responses in the future.

Two types of feedback can be provided for multiple-choice tests; immediate feedback that is provided after each question and delayed feedback that is provided after all the questions have been answered. Wheeler, Ewers, and Buonanno (2003) had students read a passage about a topic and then either take a multiple-choice test or not take a test. One group of students who took the test received immediate feedback, one group received delayed feedback, and one group received no feedback. One week later, all the students took a final test based on the paragraph. The questions on the test were the same as the question stems from the multiple-choice tests but instead of selecting an answer from a list, the students had to retrieve the answer themselves.

The results from Wheeler et al. (2003) clearly show a testing effect; students who practised retrieval performed better than students who did not (see Figure 14.5). Further, there was a significant effect of feedback; participants who received feedback outperformed those who did not, and participants who received delayed feedback performed the best. Butler et al. (2007), Kulhavy and Anderson (1972), Metcalfe, Kornell, and Finn (2009), and Smith and Kimball (2010) also all found superior performance in delayed feedback conditions. Roediger and Butler (2011) speculate that delayed feedback may be a form of **spacing effect**, a phenomenon where material is better recalled if there are intervening items between two presentations of the material than when the material is presented back to back.

Retrieval practice has been shown to result in learning general concepts, not just fixed responses. For example, Andrew Butler had students study six prose passages, each of which contained four concepts that would be tested later. Students then re-studied two of the six passages, re-studied critical sentences containing the concepts from two other passages, and completed multiple-choice tests on the concepts from the final two passages. Students were given feedback after answering each test question; the feedback consisted of the sentences from the passage that related to the concept being tested. One week later, students were given a test comprised of conceptual questions that were related to, but not identical to, the concepts that had been studied. For example, the sentence "Bats are one of the most prevalent species of mammals on earth; more than 1000 species have been identified" is an example of a sentence containing a concept. "There are about 5500 species of mammals on earth. Approximately what per cent of all mammal species are species of bat?" was the corresponding conceptual question. To answer correctly, the student needed to retrieve the fact that there were 1000 bat species and then use this with the other information in the question (that there are about 5500 species of mammals) to get the correct

spacing effect

a phenomenon where material is better recalled if there are intervening items between two presentations of the material than when the material is presented back to back

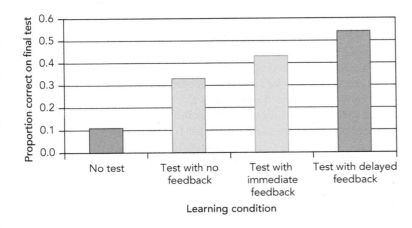

Figure 14.5 The proportion of correct responses on the final test as a function of initial learning condition

Source: Adapted from Wheeler et al., 2003

answer (1000 ÷ 5500 = 18%; Butler, 2010). The results from Butler (2010) are shown in Figure 14.6.

Butler (2010) found that repeated testing significantly improved students' ability to answer the inferential questions about the concepts compared to re-studying passages and re-studying key sentence conditions. Butler (2010) also found that there was no difference in later recall when the student re-read the entire passage and when they re-read only the sentences containing the concepts, even though it is reasonable to assume that students would have had more time to learn the concepts in the latter condition. This result replicated many other studies that have found that re-studying material has a very limited effect on later recall (e.g., Callender & McDaniel, 2009). The results from Butler (2010) demonstrate that testing benefits retrieval even when the testing contexts are very different.

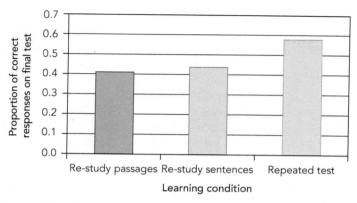

Figure 14.6   The results from Butler (2010) Experiment 1

Students retrieved the most correct information when they repeatedly tested themselves on the study material as compared to re-studying the whole passage or re-studying key sentences from the passages.

Source: Adapted from Butler, 2010

Multiple-Choice Tests Help Learning of Untested (but Related) Material

Many psychology courses include low-stakes multiple-choice quizzes (i.e., tests that aren't worth very many marks) in addition to high-stakes midterms and exams. Not only are low-stakes multiple-choice quizzes easier to administer and mark than other types of tests, there is substantial evidence that answering a multiple-choice question facilitates learning of concepts that are not the correct answer but that appear as incorrect responses on a given question. Jeri Little and Elizabeth Bjork conducted an experiment that compared student performance on a test following either practice multiple-choice questions or practice cued-recall tests. Seventy-two undergraduate students read 800-word passages about Saturn, Yellowstone National Park, and stimulant drugs. The researchers devised 10 pairs of multiple-choice questions for each passage. The pairs tested the same topic (e.g., geysers), and had the same four alternatives (e.g., *Old Faithful, Steamboat Geyser, Castle Geyser,* and *Daisy Geyser*) but had different correct answers. For example, the question "What is the tallest geyser in Yellowstone National Park?" had the correct answer *Steamboat Geyser* whereas the pair to that question, "What is the oldest geyser in Yellowstone National Park?" had the correct answer *Castle Geyser*. The researchers also developed cued-recall questions for each passage that were identical to the multiple-choice questions for that passage, but without alternatives provided. Participants were tested either immediately or 48 hours after learning the material.

Little and Bjork (2012) found that participants better remembered material when given a multiple-choice pretest than when given either a cued-recall pretest or no pretest. Further, superior memory for the material linked to the multiple-choice test was observed in both the five-minute and the 48-hour delay conditions. The results from Little and Bjork (2012) suggest that completing well-structured low-stakes multiple-choice quizzes may benefit students more than short-answer style quizzes, and that these benefits can last for at least two days.

BOX
14.6

CASE STUDY

Michael Phelps

Michael Phelps (b. 1985) is known worldwide as the most decorated Olympian of all time. Between 2008 and 2016, Phelps amassed a total of 28 Olympic medals, including 23 gold medals, in a variety of swimming events. Clearly Michael Phelps is an expert swimmer, but what makes his case interesting from a memory perspective is not that he won so many medals, but that his race times (and the race times of his competitors) have improved dramatically over the course of his career. Take, for example, the 200-metre butterfly. On March 30, 2001, Phelps broke the preceding world record with a time of 1:54.92. Four months later, Phelps broke his own record with a time of 1:54.58 (a difference

© Karaboux | Dreamstime.com

of 34 ms). In July 2003, Phelps beat his old record with a time of 1:53.93 (a difference of 65 ms). In the five years that followed, Phelps beat his own record seven times and shaved three seconds (3000 ms) off his time, completing the event in 1:51:51 on July 1, 2008. While three seconds may not seem like much, consider that the difference between a gold and a silver medal in the 200-metre butterfly is typically less than 20 ms and often less than 10 ms; very little distinguishes first place from second place. Yet time and time again Michael Phelps managed to take that spot. While physical strength likely gives Phelps a lot of his edge, part of his success may also relate to his having a superior memory of how to perform the stroke perfectly. Phelps's continual improvements in his record times are evidence that learning through deliberate practice, not practice alone, makes a person an expert.

Expertise

expertise

special skill or knowledge

deliberate practice

honing a skill by being consciously aware of related actions, even when already highly proficient at a skill

cognitive stage

using conscious effort for all aspects related to completing a task

Anders Ericsson, a professor at Florida State University (FSU), is known for being an expert on **expertise**. He has spent his entire academic career studying how it is that people develop expertise. He has studied Olympic athletes, virtuoso violinists, world-class chess players, and memory athletes and he has concluded that all of these experts have developed their expertise in exactly the same way: through **deliberate practice**. The notion of deliberate practice grew from a model of skill acquisition first proposed by Paul Fitts and Michael Posner in their 1967 book *Human Performance*. According to Fitts and Posner, individuals go through three stages when developing a skill: the **cognitive stage**, the **associative stage**, and the **autonomous stage** (see Figure 14.7).

During the cognitive stage, individuals think carefully about what they are doing and search for strategies on how to complete their goals more efficiently; actions are very deliberate at this stage. People learning to do the butterfly stroke in swimming will think about each movement

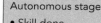

Cognitive stage	Associative stage	Autonomous stage
• Thinking about each aspect of skill • Requires a lot of attention • Skills can be changed	• Some parts of skill done automatically • Attention paid only to difficult aspects of skill • Skills can be changed	• Skill done automatically • No attention needed for skill • Skill cannot be changed

Figure 14.7 Processing stages in skill acquisition according to Fitts and Posner (1967)

Source: Adapted from Fitts & Posner, 1967

required for the stroke and put effort into completing each movement in the correct order. People learning chess may exert a lot of effort to progress the game and defeat their opponent. The cognitive stage often involves an individual comparing her or his current performance to desired performance. Once people acquire an acceptable level of proficiency, they enter the associative stage. During this stage, an individual is able to perform many aspects of the skill easily and uses conscious effort for the more complex aspects of the task. For example, someone learning the butterfly stroke may be able to perform the sequence of movements easily but may need to focus attention on her or his kick or hand position. A person learning chess may know the basics of the game well and may use her or his attention to think about the long-term consequence of each move. Finally, after practice, a person can enter the autonomous stage where no conscious effort is needed for performing a skill. The swimmer can do the butterfly stroke without thinking about individual movements; the chess player can move pieces intuitively and win most of the time. The autonomous stage can be very useful. It means once you learn to walk you don't have to think about walking and you can focus on other things (like not walking into things!).

Anders Ericsson runs The Human Performance Lab at FSU in Tallahassee, Florida, and has been studying experts for decades (Foer, 2011). Ericsson suggests that what separates experts from non-experts in a given field is that experts engage in deliberate practice, which involves consciously avoiding the autonomous stage when performing a skill, and that this practice leads to better memory for details in that field (Ericsson, Krampe, & Tesch-Römer, 1993). According to Ericsson, people wishing to improve their performance must avoid the autonomous stage because skills performed unconsciously are impervious to change, and thus impervious to improvement. Ericsson suggests that people who become experts in a field stay in the cognitive stage of skill acquisition by focusing on their technique, setting goals that exceed their current level of performance, and looking for constant immediate feedback on their performance (Ericsson et al., 1993).

associative stage

using conscious effort for only the most difficult aspects of a task

autonomous stage

using no conscious effort when completing a task

Deliberate Practice

Anders Ericsson and his colleagues argue that experts are unique because of the way they engage in deliberate practice. For example, Ericsson notes that the expertise of musicians is linked to how they practise. Amateur musicians spend their time practising playing music and rarely really improve; they reach the autonomous stage and stay there. Expert musicians, on the other hand, approach music differently, instead of practising pieces they already know how to play, they focus their time on specific, difficult passages of music, which keeps them in the cognitive stage and allows their skill to improve (Ericsson, 2006). A similar pattern is seen among ice skaters. Amateur skaters work on jumps they have mastered while expert skaters, who are constantly improving, spend time challenging themselves with difficult jumps they have not mastered (Deakin & Cobley, 2003). Thus, the difference between people at different levels of expertise in a domain doesn't reflect a difference in innate ability; instead, it reflects a different approach to practice. Those who get to the autonomous stage and don't give learning another thought are competent but don't improve. Those who engage in deliberate practice and stay in the cognitive stage will continue to improve. This capacity to continually improve through deliberate practice can explain why Michael Phelps was able to break his own world record; anyone can get better at anything if they pay attention to the details that matter (see Box 14.6).

There are three components to deliberate practice. One is to study other experts. For example, the best predictor of chess skill is not the number of hours played, but the amount of time that a player has spent working through old games (Charness, Tuffiash, Krampe, Reingold, & Vasyukova, 2005; Foer, 2011). Athletes regularly study the methods of superior athletes. Thinking about what other experts do to perform so well ultimately leads the observer to adopt those habits. A second component of deliberate practice is studying previous mistakes. Elite athletes pore over past performances, identifying exact moments where they could have done better. They think about these mistakes and consciously try to avoid making them in subsequent practice sessions (Deakin & Cobley, 2003). A final method of deliberate practice is to set goals and try to overcome them (Ericsson, 2004). Michael Phelps likely set goals to beat his best time in the 200-metre butterfly and studied other swimmers and his own mistakes until he broke that record.

Feedback plays an essential role in the development of expertise; no one improves without feedback. In 2004, Ericsson found evidence to support this claim by comparing performance change in physicians whose speciality involves immediate feedback (surgeons) to those who don't get feedback for many years (mammographers). Ericsson found that surgeons, whose mistakes are obvious as soon as they are made, tend to improve over time while mammographers, whose mistakes aren't caught for several years (when what was not thought to be a mass grows into a tumour) do not become better at their jobs over time (Ericsson, 2004). Ericsson (2004) suggests that mammographers be trained using mammograms where the outcome is already known so they can receive immediate feedback as to whether they are interpreting features of the mammograms effectively (Ericsson, 2004).

Ericsson's research led him to hypothesize that it takes over 10,000 hours of deliberate practice to become an expert in a given field, and this notion rapidly spread through popular culture (Ericsson et al., 1993). The notion has been the premise for many books, including Malcolm Gladwell's 2008 bestseller *Outliers*. However, Ericsson's argument that deliberate practice is solely responsible for expertise has been questioned by many psychologists who believe that personal factors, such as genetics and willpower, also play a role in superior skill acquisition (see Gardner, 1995; Schneider, 1998; and Sternberg, 1996).

In 2014, David Hambrick and his colleagues set out to determine whether deliberate practice is, as Ericsson suggests, critical for explaining individual differences in expertise. Hambrick et al. (2014) re-analyzed research on the development of expertise in chess and music and assessed the extent to which deliberate practice predicted expertise. Hambrick et al. (2014) found that only 34 per cent of the variance in chess expertise and 29.9 per cent of the variance in music expertise could be explained by deliberate practice, meaning that 66 per cent of chess expertise and 70.1 per cent of music expertise results from factors other than deliberate practice. Hambrick et al. (2014) conclude that, while deliberate practice explains a considerable amount of variance in chess and music performance and appears necessary for expertise, the majority of the variance in these domains remains unexplained by Ericsson's deliberate practice account.

Hambrick et al. (2014) argue that at least four factors in addition to deliberate practice are strong predictors of expertise: age, intelligence, grit, and genes. Hambrick et al. (2014) argue

CASE STUDY

BOX
14.7

Sexing Chicks

Many experts cannot explain how it is they perform their skill. This is because, as we learned in Chapter 5, perceptual memories and movement memories are implicit and outside of conscious awareness. An excellent example of implicit expertise is the chick sexer, trained experts who are very good at what they do without knowing how they do it.

Poultry farmers hatch chicks that are both male (called cockerels) and female (called pullets); however, only pullets are used for meat and egg production. Because it costs money to house and feed chicks, farmers want to know the sex of chicks as soon after hatching as possible; however, newly hatched pullets and cockerels look virtually identical to each other. Only someone who has spent several years practising sexing chicks can tell the cockerels from the pullets; these experts are called chick sexers. Chick sexing was first introduced to North America at a poultry conference held in Ottawa in 1927. At the conference, two Japanese veterinarians explained that, with practice, it is possible to examine a newly hatched chick and determine its sex. These veterinarians created the Zen Nippon Chick Sexing School in Nagoya, Japan, and began training the first chick sexers. The program still exists today and takes a minimum of two years to complete. Only about 5 to 10 per cent of students who begin the program graduate as chick sexers. The chick sexers learn what has come to be known as the *venting method*. Training involves learning about 1000 different configurations of a chick's cloaca, a small vent that holds the chick's genitals. Some examples of vent appearances are shown in Figure 14.8. Note that the differences between the sexes can be very complex and that less common configurations are nearly identical.

To sex the chick, the chick sexer holds the chick gently and squeezes it near its tail, revealing the vent. Checking the vent must be done very quickly as the process of squeezing a chick makes all vents look male after a few seconds. About 20 per cent of the time, chick sexers are lucky and a tiny "bead" is visible in the vent. The chick's sex can be determined based on the size

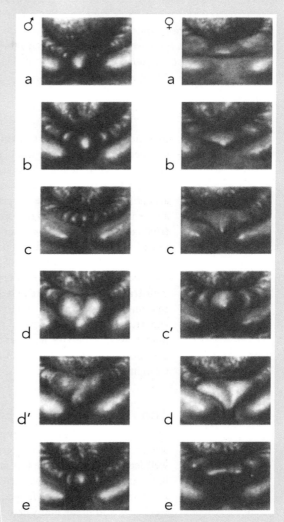

Figure 14.8 Genital eminences of day-old chicks

Common vent configurations for cockerels and pullets. Male genitals are in the left column; female genitals are in the right column. Note that while all vent configurations are very different, there are only subtle differences between the sexes for each configuration.

Source: From Canfield, T.H. (1941). Sex determination of day-old chicks II: Type variations. *Poultry Science, 20,* pp. 327–8. Copyright 1941 by the Poultry Science Association, Inc.

continued

and shape of the bead. However, the other 80 per cent of the time there is no bead and chick sexers must base their decision on experience, somehow matching the configuration they see to one stored in memory. A trained chick sexer can accurately sex a chick in about three seconds and most decisions are made based on intuition; the sexer can't explain how she or he knows the sex of the chick, and yet can sex it accurately. The accuracy of a given chick sexer can be determined for certain about four weeks later, when it is easy to see the cockerels among the pullets based on distinctive feather patterns. Like all forms of expertise, chick sexing relies on memory. Chick sexers go through the cognitive and associative stages while learning their skill; however, because chick sexing must be done very quickly, working chick sexers operate at the autonomous level of skill acquisition.

that individuals who start learning at a younger age are more likely to develop expertise, and that people who are more intelligent are more likely to become experts given the same amount of practice as someone who is less intelligent. In addition, Hambrick et al. (2014) suggest that people who have grit, a personality factor reflected in the accomplishment of long-term goals, are more likely to become experts. Finally, Hambrick et al. (2014) suggest that at least some of a person's ability to excel in a field can be influenced by genes. For example, Coon and Carey (1989) and Vinkhuyzen, van der Sluis, Posthuma, and Boomsma (2009) found exceptional skill to be highly heritable, with 50 per cent to 92 per cent of the variability in talent accounted for by genes.

The results from Hambrick et al. (2014) refute Ericsson's claim that it requires 10,000 hours of deliberate practice (and little else) to become an expert in a given field. Instead, research suggests that many factors in addition to deliberate practice contribute to whether a person becomes an expert, including starting age, intelligence, personality, and genetics. In addition, some people may achieve expertise with far less than 10,000 hours of practice, while other people fail to ever become experts even with copious amounts of practice (Hambrick et al., 2014; Gobet & Compitelli, 2007).

The Neuroscience of Expertise

The model of skill acquisition proposed by Fitts and Posner (1967) suggests that the level of attention given to a task is inversely related to experience. New tasks require a lot of attention; well-learned tasks require less attention. Nicole Hill and Walter Schneider examined both behavioural and fMRI data as participants learned a novel motor skill over the course of one hour. Participants' behaviour changed significantly over the course of the hour. Initially, participants were slow and made many errors, but by the end of the session participants completed the task quickly and made few errors. Hill and Schneider (2006) also found differences in fMRI data over the course of the session, which is shown in Figure 14.9. In the first 20 minutes of the experiment (the novice phase), many parts of the brain were active; however, the researchers found significant decreases in brain activity over the remaining 40 minutes of the experiment. After one hour of practice, brain activity had decreased by 85 per cent. Fitts and Posner's (1967) model, which suggests that less and less attention is needed as a skill is acquired, fits well with the data from Hill and Schneider (2006). The two main regions of the brain associated with attentional control, which is needed to retain conscious control of actions and assess the efficacy of those actions, are the posterior parietal complex (PPC) and the dorsolateral prefrontal cortex (DLPFC) respectively. Hill and Schneider (2006) found that activation in both of these areas decreased as participants became better able to perform the motor-tracking task, while activity in the motor regions stayed about the same, indicating that the motor regions were able to support the task more or less independently after sufficient practice (see Figure 14.9).

The reduced attentional control-network activation with maintained motor activity observed in Hill and Schneider (2006) has been observed in many other experiments using similar paradigms (e.g., Petersen, Van Mier, Fiez, & Riachle, 1998; Poldrack, Desmond, Glover, & Gabrieli, 1998). Researchers suggest that this decrease in activation in the control network is made possible by increased efficiency within the neural network that controls the motor task, such that, with practice, motor neurons fire more strongly, which reduces the need for attentional control processes (see Hill & Schneider, 2006; Petersen et al., 1998; Poldrack et al., 1998). This pattern of reduced control-network activation with maintained motor activity in the brain is the expected result from developing expertise in a perceptual motor task, such as walking, skiing, bicycling, or typing (Hill & Schneider, 2006).

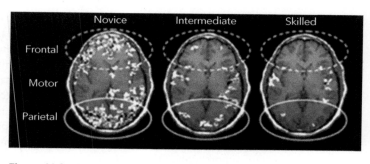

Figure 14.9   Activation of brain as a function of practice

This figure shows activation of the brain as a function of practice in three periods of learning a motor-tracking task in Hill and Schneider (2006). The frontal areas (dashed ellipse) and parietal attention control areas (solid ellipse) show dramatic reductions in activation. The motor areas (middle of images) share fairly preserved activation. Over the course of the one-hour experiment, brain activation decreased by 85 per cent.

Source: Adapted from Hill & Schneider, 2006

In some cases, expertise leads to increased cortical tissue devoted to the task after long periods of training, as with London taxi drivers who have larger-than-average anterior hippocampal regions (Maguire et al., 2000) and expert pianists who have increased cortical density in the primary sensorimotor cortex (Han et al., 2009). In other cases, expertise leads to changes in the brain regions used to complete a given task. As individuals gain expertise, they employ different strategies to complete a task, and these strategies may include tasks that engage different brain regions. For example, when people first try mirror reading (which involves reading text that has been inverted by a mirror), they tend to employ mental rotation as a strategy; however, after practice, the individual comes to recognize the inverted word without having to use mental rotation. In the case of mirror reading, the brain regions associated with mental rotation are active early in practice, but are not involved once the individual has expertise in the skill (Poldrack et al., 1998). Expert chess players also appear to use different regions of their brain to solve chess problems than novice chess players. Merim Bilalić and his colleagues found that expert chess players had much more activation in the fusiform face area (FFA) than novice players when presented with representations of chess positions. The results from Bilalić, Langner, Ulrich, and Grodd (2011) suggest that, with practice, chess players adopt strategies that involve the FFA, which is a brain area that seems specialized for formulating holistic representations of multipart visual stimuli (such as faces), which are comprised of many parts but are perceived as a single unit.

Researchers have also looked at the default mode network (DMN) to gauge the extent of cognitive processing that occurs when experts and novices perform a given skill. The DMN is a set of brain regions including the precuneus/posterior cingulate cortex (P/PCC), the ventral ACC/medial prefrontal cortex (MPFC), angular gyrus (AG), and medial temporal cortex. The DMN shows high levels of activity when an individual is at rest and *decreased* activity when an individual engages in goal-directed cognitive behaviours. Duan et al. (2012) studied activity in the DMN in novice and expert chess players. Duan et al. (2012) found that experts showed a greater decrease in DMN activity (compared to baseline at rest levels) when given chess problems to solve than was observed in novices. Duan et al. (2012) suggest that this difference reflects the fact that expert chess players recruit more cognitive processes to solve chess problems, and that this increased demand for cognitive processing results in greater suppression of the DMN.

CHAPTER REVIEW

- Memory athletes are people who participate in memory competitions. By far the most common mnemonic device used by memory athletes is the method of loci.
- The method of loci involves imagining a well-known location, called a memory palace, and then imagining moving through the memory palace placing to-be-remembered items in different locations along the route. Material can be recalled later by imagining walking through the memory palace.
- Memory athletes often need to memorize long lists of digits. One method is the major system; the other method is the person-action-object (PAO) system. Memory athletes tend to prefer the PAO system to the major system because it is easier to use under time constraint.
- Skilled memory theory is based on the encoding principle, the retrieval-structure principle, and the speed-up principle.
- Memory athletes only differ from other people in how they encode information. Their intelligence and memory spans (when mnemonics cannot be used) are within the normal range.
- Memory athletes engaging in memorization activate regions in their brain associated with visual imagery. This is likely due to the use of the method of loci to memorize material.
- The finding that repeated memory retrieval produces better retention than re-reading the same information for an equivalent amount of time is referred to as the testing effect. Challenging retrieval practice conditions combined with feedback optimize the testing effect.
- Feedback regarding the accuracy of retrieval practice affects the testing effect. Delayed feedback is more helpful than immediate feedback.
- Fitts and Posner (1967) propose that an individual can be in one of three stages when performing a skill: the cognitive stage, the associative stage, or the autonomous stage.
- Anders Ericsson argues that, in order to become an expert, an individual must engage in deliberate practice, which involves remaining in the cognitive stage of skill acquisition. Deliberate practice involves studying other experts, studying one's own mistakes, and setting goals.
- Deliberate practice cannot account for all the variability in expertise. Researchers suggest that starting age, working-memory capacity, grit, and genetics also contribute to a person's ability to achieve expertise in a given field.

- Some expertise involving perceptual processing or physical skill may be difficult to describe because the memories that support the skill are implicit. An example of this is chick sexers, who can sex chicks accurately but cannot explain how they do so.
- Experts use their brains differently than novices. Experts performing a well-practiced skill are less dependent on attentional control than novices. In addition, experts often perform different cognitive tasks than novices, which in turn recruit different brain areas. For example, novice mirror readers utilize areas associated with mental rotation while expert mirror readers do not.
- The default mode network (DMN) is active when a person is at rest and inactive when a person is engaged in goal-directed behaviour. Experts tend to show greater decreases in DMN activity than novices performing the same task. This result suggests that experts recruit more cognitive processes when performing a skill than novices do.

MEMORY ACTIVITY

The Method of Loci

The method of loci has been used as a memory aid for thousands of years. In this activity, you will create a memory palace to help you remember the key terms from this chapter and their definitions. For example, for "cognitive stage" you may imagine a spot in your memory palace where there is a brain on a stage doing a difficult juggling task alone. When your palace is complete, test yourself on your knowledge of each key term and modify your palace until your recall is perfect! Next, try applying this method to other material from this text.

Chapter 14 Key Term	Definition
method of loci	a mnemonic that involves visualizing to-be-remembered images at different locations along a well-known path
memory athlete	an individual who engages in memory training most often for the purpose of entering memory competitions
expertise	special skill or knowledge
deliberate practice	honing a skill by being consciously aware of related actions, even when already highly proficient at a skill
cognitive stage	using conscious effort for all aspects related to completing a task
associative stage	using conscious effort for only the most difficult aspects of a task
autonomous stage	using no conscious effort when completing a task
skilled memory theory	a model that asserts that specific memory techniques can lead to greater memory capacity
encoding principle	memory will be better if an individual associates to-be-remembered material with material in long-term memory
retrieval-structure principle	memory will be better when material is associated with easy-to-remember cues
speed-up principle	as people gain experience encoding, they can encode more information in less time
piphilologist	an individual who memorizes the digits of *pi*

continued

testing effect	the finding that repeated memory retrieval produces better retention than re-reading the same information for an equivalent amount of time
spacing effect	a phenomenon where material is better recalled if there are intervening items between two presentations of the material than when the material is presented back to back
major system	a method that assigns a distinct phoneme to each digit from 0 to 9
person-action-object (PAO) system	a method for creating images from numbers based on memorizing distinct images containing a person, an action, and an object
memory palace	an imagined location used in the method of loci
natural memory	memory that is embedded in our minds and cannot be strengthened
artificial memory	memory that is the product of art and can be strengthened by training
backgrounds	the locations used in the method of loci
images	the visual representations of to-be-remembered material in the method of loci

Questions

1. Memory competitors call themselves "memory athletes." Is this comparison to sport reasonable? Support your answer.
2. What aspects of a memory champion's memory are similar to those of other people and what aspects appear to be different?
3. Describe some memory competitions for which the PAO system may work well and some memory competitions for which the PAO system will not likely work well.
4. Suppose you were presented with six people and were told that three were memory champions and three were not. If you could use an fMRI, how could you determine who was a memory champion and who was not without asking participants directly?
5. Develop a detailed method for approaching studying for a midterm based on research on testing effects.
6. Describe the potential benefits of completing low-stakes multiple-choice quizzes. What components need to be present in the quiz for it to have maximal benefit?
7. Provide three reasons why the PAO system combined with the method of loci is an effective mnemonic device.
8. Suppose you are tutoring a friend who is preparing for an upcoming psychology test. What sort of materials would you develop to help your friend prepare and what sort of feedback would you provide?
9. Explain why delayed feedback is more effective than immediate feedback.
10. Describe the three stages of skill acquisition according to Fitts and Posner (1967).
11. What is deliberate practice? How could a person who wishes to become an expert juggler use the principles of deliberate practice to hone her or his skill?
12. Critique the deliberate practice account of expertise.
13. Use the notion of deliberate practice to explain how Michael Phelps broke his own world record in the 200-metre butterfly over and over again.
14. Use Fitts and Posner's (1967) model of skill development to explain how people come to be expert chick sexers.
15. Describe an experiment that demonstrated that experts utilize different brain processes than novices.

16. If you looked at fMRIs taken every 10 minutes of a person learning a motor skill that takes about one hour to master, what change(s) would you expect to see in the fMRIs as time progressed?

17. Explain how activity in the default mode network can be used to gauge the level of cognitive processing a person is engaging in.

Key Figures

Elizabeth Bjork p. 383
Andrew Butler p. 382
Anders Ericsson p. 384
David Hambrick p. 386

Jeffrey Karpicke p. 379
Jeri Little p. 383
Eleanor Maguire p. 376
Helga Noice p. 373

Mary Pyc p. 380
Katherine Rawson p. 380
Henry Roediger p. 379
Charles Thompson p. 374

Glossary

absent-mindedness when inattention leads to the inability to recall information

action potential the brief reversal of polarity in a neuron that occurs when a neuron is stimulated

advance directive (AD) a legal document that details the medical treatment that a person wishes to have and/or who is to make medical decisions on her or his behalf should she or he become incapacitated

agnosia the loss of memory for words

agrammatism the loss of the ability to create grammatically correct sentences

altered stimulus conditions when the context at the time of test is different than the context at the time of learning

altricial a term describing an animal born in an undeveloped state that requires care and feeding by the parents

Alzheimer's disease a form of dementia caused by shrinking of the cerebral cortex and hippocampus. Amyloid plaques may also contribute to cognitive problems.

amodal to be independent of perceptual and motor representations

anoetic consciousness a state of mind associated with pure perception and emotion without cognitive content

anterograde amnesia the loss of the ability to form new memories

artificial grammar a set of rules governing how a string of letters can be combined

artificial memory memory that is the product of art and can be strengthened by training

associationist a philosopher who believed that ideas are brought to consciousness through associations with other ideas

associations links between ideas that give rise to memories

associative priming faster recognition of a word when the word is preceded by a related word than when a word is preceded by an unrelated word

associative stage using conscious effort for only the most difficult aspects of a task

attention a capacity-limited cognitive mechanism that is used for both stimuli selection and the control of cognitive tasks

audience tuning when speakers recall events based on the nature of the audience they are speaking to

autobiographical knowledge base knowledge of the self that can be used by the individual to determine what the self is, what the self was, and what the self can be

autobiographical memory one's recall of experiencing events from one's own life

autonoetic consciousness the ability for one to imagine oneself in past, future, or counterfactual situations

autonomous stage using no conscious effort when completing a task

baby boom a large cohort of North Americans born between 1945 and 1963

backgrounds the locations used in the method of loci

behaviourist era a time in the history of psychology when the majority of research focused on the observable effects of experience on behaviour

beneffectance the tendency to take credit for events that have favourable outcomes and to blame other for events that have unfavourable outcomes

benefit of forgetting in a directed-forgetting paradigm, better memory performance in the forget condition than the remember condition

bias when a person's state of mind causes the recollection of some items but not others

blocking when a person is unable to retrieve an item because of the unwanted recall of another item

brain fingerprinting a process that attempts to detect a match between criminal evidence and the memory of a suspect

Brown-Peterson paradigm a paradigm designed to test the rate of primary memory decay by preventing the rehearsal of to-be-remembered items through the use of a concurrent counting task

case studies a research report style in which an individual researcher reports the details of an individual case

central executive a supervisory system that controls the flow of information in and out of working memory

classical conditioning a learning process in which an innate response to a potent stimulus comes to be elicited in response to a previously neutral stimulus

cocktail party effect the phenomenon whereby a person attending to one auditory channel is able to detect important information conveyed in an unattended auditory channel

cognitive dissonance a mental state in which a person holds two contradictory beliefs or values at the same time

cognitive maps an animal's internal representation of the spatial relationship among objects in the environment

cognitive revolution the period in the early 1960s during which psychologists began to use the experimental methods developed by the behaviourists to develop theories about cognitive functioning

cognitive skill how to perform a task that requires thinking, such as playing chess or completing a Sudoku

cognitive stage using conscious effort for all aspects related to completing a task

collaborative inhibition when nominal recall is greater than group recall, indicating that the act of collaboration inhibited recall in one or more group members

collective memory memories shared by members of the same social group that relate to their group identity

competition-induced interference when having to inhibit retrieval of an item results in later forgetting of that same item

compound-cue model a model that assumes recognition of an item is based on a measure of familiarity determined by the compounded effects of a number of cues including context, cues that result from sharing associations with items that have recently been presented, and cues from associations in memory

concept a general idea derived or inferred from specific instances or occurrences

concreteness effect words that easily evoke visual images, such as *cat*, are better remembered than words that are less easy to imagine, such as *justice*

conditioned response (CR) a response that is made as a result of classical conditioning

conditioned stimulus (CS) a previously neutral stimulus that, after becoming associated with the unconditioned stimulus, eventually comes to trigger a conditioned response

confederate a person who is working on behalf of the experimenter to say and do specific things during an experiment. Other participants are not aware that the confederate is playing a role.

confession contamination when police provide a suspect of a crime information that only the culprit would know and that information is later included in a confession

consciousness the mind's level of responsiveness to incoming sensory information

conservatism the tendency to seek information that confirms existing beliefs

consolidation a general term for neurological processes that make it possible for a memory trace to be sustained over time

context cue in compound-cue theory, this is the extent to which the learning context serves as a cue for an item in generic memory

cost of forgetting in a directed-forgetting paradigm, worse memory performance for to-be-forgotten items than to-be-remembered items

cross-race effect (CRE) eyewitnesses are less accurate at making identifications when the suspects are of a different race

cue-driven principle a principle of memory that states that all memories are retrieved through cues

day-after recall test participants' recall or recognition of ads they saw the day before

decay theory of forgetting forgetting occurs because of a decline in the memory trace due to some biological mechanism

decision criterion a threshold of activation that must be met in order for an item to be retrieved from generic memory

déjà vécu the experience of perceiving a new situation as though it has occurred before

deliberate practice honing a skill by being consciously aware of related actions, even when already highly proficient at a skill

dementia a progressive neurocognitive disorder characterized by deficits in cognitive faculties such as memory and/or problem solving

dementia with Lewy bodies a form of dementia caused by the degeneration of neurons that produce acetylcholine and dopamine

dissociative amnesia autobiographical memory loss that is not the result of an underlying biological problem

dissociative fugue autobiographical memory loss followed by wandering away from home that is not the result of an underlying biological problem

distinctiveness-based illusory correlation incorrect judgments about the relationship between two variables based on the co-occurrence of distinctive stimulus events

distributed practice practice that takes place over several learning sessions

double-blind procedure when neither the police officer administering the lineup nor the witness knows who is the suspect in the lineup

echoic memory a large-capacity, short-duration memory store for auditory information

ecological model of memory development explains changes in memory performance across infancy as resulting from changes in the ecological niche occupied by infants of different ages

ecologically valid when the parameters of an experiment mirror the real-world situations to which the results of the experiments are to be applied

effect of articulatory suppression a decrement in recall for verbally presented words when the participant is given a concurrent task involving speech

egocentricity the tendency to remember one's own behaviours better than the behaviours of others

electroencephalogram (EEG)   a method for measuring the electrical activity occurring in the brain in real time using conductors applied to the scalp

embedded-processes model   a model of short-term memory in which short-term memory is envisaged as the component of long-term memory that is currently active

emotional working memory (eWM) training   an *n*-back working memory task that includes stimuli designed to evoke emotions, such as angry faces or emotional words

empiricist   a person who believes that knowledge is gained through observation

encoding principle   memory will be better if an individual associates to-be-remembered material with material in long-term memory

encoding suppression   any process that makes encoding less likely to be successful

encoding/retrieval specificity   a common experimental finding that participants more easily recall episodic memories when asked to retrieve them in the same context in which they originally learned the material

encoding/retrieval specificity effects   an experimental finding in which similarity between conditions at encoding and retrieval predicts greater probability of memory retrieval

engram   a specific location in the brain holding the trace of a specific memory

Enlightenment   an era from the 1650s to the 1780s in which cultural and intellectual forces in western Europe emphasized reason, analysis, and individualism rather than traditional lines of authority

environment of evolutionary adaptiveness   a term used to describe living conditions present when humans were last under the most ecological pressure to adapt

environmental cues   cues in the external world such as people, places, or things

episodic buffer   a component of working memory that can hold about four chunks of multidimensional code

episodic memory   a type of long-term memory comprised of memories of specific situations, experiences, or events

error correction   when incorrect memories are identified and corrected through the process of gathering new information

event-specific knowledge   highly detailed information about specific life events

exceptional memory   memory that exceeds what is typical in the population; for example, being able to remember events from every day for the past 20 years or being able to recite *pi* to 200 decimal places

expertise   special skill or knowledge

explicit memory system   a memory system that evolved so that animals could be consciously aware of previous experiences and could use consciousness to deliberately recall information. This system operates within consciousness.

explicit memory   a memory that an individual can bring into conscious awareness

exposure learning   a method for studying memory in which the individual is exposed to stimuli, such as a specific song, and then response to this song is compared to response to an unfamiliar song. A difference in behaviour in the two conditions is inferred to indicate memory for the familiar song.

extinction   when the CS no longer elicits the CR

false confession   when a person takes responsibility for a crime that she or he did not commit

false memory   a psychological phenomenon in which a person recalls information that did not actually occur

false memory of abuse   a memory of being abused that is not based on events that actually happened

false-fame effect   participants being more likely to rate a non-famous name as famous when they have seen the name before compared to when the name is unfamiliar

familiarity   a feeling that an item has been encountered before

fast mapping   when learning can occur with a single brief exposure to the stimulus

filler   an individual presented in a lineup who is not associated with the crime

flashbulb memory   a highly detailed memory of a surprising event of personal significance

forgetting curve   a negatively accelerated function over time predicting that most forgetting occurs soon after learning, and that as time goes on less and less additional forgetting occurs

free recall   an experimental paradigm where participants are asked to report items from a list without regard to serial order

frontoparietal cognitive control network   a collection of brain areas linked to attention and cognitive control that includes the dorsolateral prefrontal cortex (PFC), the inferior parietal cortex, and the anterior cingulate

frontotemporal dementia   a form of dementia caused by the deterioration of spindle neurons in the frontal and temporal lobes

general event   an aspect of the autobiographical knowledge base that is comprised of either multiple representations of repeated events or a sequence of related events that are related to achieving or failing at personal goals

generation effect   material that is generated by the participant is better remembered than material that is provided to the participant by an outside source

generic memory   memory for facts, concepts, and meanings that is context free and not associated with a particular point in time

Gestalt approach   to always see the whole as greater than the sum of the individual parts

granule cells   cells that eventually develop into neurons

group recall score   the number of items that a group jointly recalls during collaborative recall

habituation   a decrement in response to a stimulus following repeated presentation of the same stimulus

Hebb's postulate   the notion that when cell A persistently causes the firing of cell B, there is a metabolic change such that cell A will more easily cause cell B to fire in the future

Hebbian plasticity   the notion that synapses are created by metabolic changes resulting from the simultaneous firing of neurons

heuristic   a loosely defined approach to solving a problem

hierarchical-network model   a model of generic memory in which concepts are organized from the most general at the top to the most specific at the bottom, with facts about a concept attached to the highest level of the hierarchy to which they apply

high-involvement purchase   when a consumer searches explicit memory for product information before making a purchase decision

high-amplitude sucking paradigm   an experimental method in which an infants' rate of sucking on a pressure-sensitive pacifier is used to assess an infant's interest or disinterest in a stimulus

hub-and-spoke model of generic memory   a model by Pobric et al. (2010), which proposes that six types of modality-specific representations all meet at a central hub in the anterior temporal lobe

hyperthymesia   a rare condition in which a person has exceptionally accurate episodic memory for events of personal relevance

hypothyroidism   a condition in which the thyroid gland does not produce an adequate level of hormones

ibotenic acid   a substance that destroys the neuron attached to dendrites it comes in contact with without affecting axons that pass through the injection site

iconic memory   a large-capacity, short-duration memory store for visual information

illusory correlation   the incorrect belief that two variables are related, such as the full moon and violent crime

illusory-truth effect   when participants are more likely to rate a statement as being true when they have seen the statement before compared to when the statement is unfamiliar

images   the visual representations of to-be-remembered material in the method of loci

imagination inflation   when a person comes to believe that her or his memory of an imagined event represents a memory for an event that occurred

implicit memory   a general term for memories that an individual cannot be consciously aware of, such as how to perform an action

implicit memory system   a memory system that evolved to help animals adapt to their environments and learn new behaviours. This system operates outside of awareness.

incidental forgetting   forgetting that occurs without cognitive activity related to suppressing encoding or retrieval

infantile amnesia   the inability for adults to remember events from early in life

information persistence   the availability of stimulus information after the stimulus has been removed

information-sampling bias   a phenomenon where members of a group will not discuss an item if no one else in the group mentions it

in-group   a social group that a person feels she or he belongs to

intentional forgetting: forgetting that results from deliberate attempts to suppress certain memories

interference theory of forgetting   forgetting occurs because of a conflict between new and old information

inter-item cue   in compound-cue theory, this is the extent to which an item learned with another item serves as a cue for an item in generic memory

inter-item presentation interval (IPI)   the amount of time that separates the presentation of two items

internal cues   cues that come from within a person, such as thoughts or other memories

irrelevant-speech effect   a decrement in recall performance when participants hear unrelated speech sounds when trying to learn a list of words

isomorphic   being of identical or similar form, shape, or structure

item-method DF paradigm   a paradigm in which participants are instructed to forget specific items from a single list immediately after the item is presented

Jost's Law   when two memories are of similar strength, the older memory will decay at a slower rate than the newer memory

jury deliberation process   when the jurors from a trial convene to decide on a verdict

Korsakoff syndrome   retrograde and anterograde amnesia caused by persistent thiamine (vitamin B,) deficiency. Korsakoff syndrome is often caused by chronic alcohol misuse.

leading question   a question that by its form or content suggests the desired answer to the witness, or leads the witness to the desired answer

learning curve   a negatively accelerating function in which additional practice is very helpful in the early stages of learning but has less benefit over time

learning   a behaviour that facilitates the acquisition of new information

lifetime period   an aspect of the autobiographical knowledge base that contains information about activities, relationships, locations, and timeframes associated with various themes in one's life

lineup procedure   an identification procedure wherein the suspect's picture is mixed in with pictures of similar-looking individuals who are not associated with the crime. The witness is asked if anyone in the picture array committed the crime.

list-method DF paradigm   a paradigm in which participants are instructed to forget an entire list of items after it has been presented

long-term depotentiation (LTD)   when a cell loses its ability to create an action potential

long-term memory   all the memories a person has stored in memory

long-term potentiation (LTP)   a persistent strengthening of a synapse based on recent patterns of activity

long-term store   in the two-stage model of memory, the long-term store learns slowly and holds memories for long periods of time

low-involvement purchase   when a consumer does not search explicit memory for product information before making a purchase

major system   a method that assigns a distinct phoneme to each digit from 0 to 9

massed practice   learning that occurs during one long practice session

mediated priming effect   the finding that words that are associated by way of several other words can often prime each other. For example, *mane* can prime *stripe* even though they are not directly related concepts.

memory   a record of learning

memory athlete   an individual who engages in memory training most often for the purpose of entering memory competitions

memory bias   a tendency to better recall information that is consistent with an individual's beliefs

memory palace   an imagined location used in the method of loci

memory pooling   the sharing of memories of many individual experiences of a single event, such as the proceedings of a trial

memory-trace consolidation   a strengthening of the connection between neurons comprising a given memory

memory war, the   a scholarly debate over whether or not traumatic memories could be repressed and later recovered

mental time travel   a sense of one's self in the past that is typically accompanied by imagery featuring perceptual details related to the recollections

mere exposure effect   when a person comes to prefer stimuli merely because she or he has been exposed to the stimulus repeatedly

metamemory   personal knowledge of how one's own memory operates

metaphor   a figure of speech in which a term or phrase is applied to something to which it is not literally applicable in order to suggest a resemblance

method of loci   a mnemonic that involves visualizing to-be-remembered images at different locations along a well-known path

mini-mental state examination (MMSE)   a test that is used to assess the memory and cognitive functioning of individuals. The MMSE is often used to identify people with dementia.

misattribution   when a person recalls a piece of information but incorrectly recalls the source of that information

misinformation effect   the observation that people often recall post-event misinformation when recalling a witnessed event

mnemonic silences   memories related to conversational topics that are not retrieved as part of the conversation

mnemonic   a device that aids in improving memory

mnestic deficit theories   theories that explain actions as a result of poor memory

modal model of memory   a heuristic, first introduced by Atkinson and Shiffrin (1968), for thinking about how memory processes work. The modal model includes three main components: sensory memory, short-term memory and long-term memory.

modality effect   the improved recall of the final items of a list when that list is presented verbally in comparison with a visual presentation

motivated forgetting   forgetting that occurs because of conscious strategies to forget, or because of cognitive processes whose by-product is forgetting

multicomponent model   a model of memory first proposed by Alan Baddeley in which working memory is comprised of a phonological loop, a visuospatial sketchpad, and an episodic buffer, which are all controlled by a central executive

multiple-trace theory   a theory that suggests that generic memories are formed from multiple episodic traces

multi-voxel pattern analysis (MVPA)   a popular analytical technique in neuroscience that involves identifying patterns in fMRI BOLD signal data that are predictive of task conditions

natural memory   memory that is embedded in our minds and cannot be strengthened

n-back procedure (n-back task)   an experimental paradigm in which the participant must indicate whether the stimulus on the current trial matches the stimulus presented *n* trials before

n-back task (n-back procedure)   an experimental paradigm in which the participant must indicate whether the stimulus on the current trial matches the stimulus presented *n* trials before

negative memory bias   the tendency to better recall events that are associated with negative emotions than those associated with positive emotions

negative priming   when response times are slowed for stimuli that have been ignored on previous trials

negative PTP   pre-trial publicity that depicts the defendant in a way that suggests the defendant committed the crime or was capable of committing the crime she or he is accused of committing

negative transfer   the extent to which learning of one ability interferes with the learning of another ability

neuroanatomical model of memory development   explains changes in memory performance across infancy as resulting from maturation of the hippocampus

neurocognitive disorder   a general term that describes difficulty with thinking, problem solving, and language that result from disorders affecting the brain and are severe enough to affect everyday activities. Many different disorders can cause dementia.

neurogenesis   the growth of new neurons

neurogenesis-dependent decay   forgetting that is the result of impaired pattern completion following the integration of new neurons in the hippocampus

neurotypical   a nervous system that is functioning normally

noetic consciousness   a state of mind associated with knowledge and intellect

nominal recall score   the number of items that an individual recalls on her or his own during the control phase of a collaborative learning experiment

nonsense syllables   pronounceable strings of letters that are not actual words, examples in English would include dak, ver, and maz.

normative influence   when a person conforms with another person in order to avoid social costs

nostalgia inventory   a measure for assessing the extent to which an individual misses different parts of her or his past

nostalgia   a sentimental longing or wistful affection for the past

obsessive-compulsive disorder (OCD)   a mental disorder characterized by obsessions, which are repetitive thoughts of potential harm that cause anxiety, and compulsions, which are actions intended to reduce anxiety produced by obsessions

online tally   a method a person can use to keep track of her or his view of a public figure; the tally will increase or decrease depending on whether new information is positive or negative

oratory   the art of public speaking.

orthogonal   when two representations do not overlap

orthogonal coding   when a unique set of neurons is used to form a memory

out-group   a social group that a person feels she or he does not belong to

output interference   when the act of retrieval itself interferes with retrieval

overshadowing   when a stimulus is less well learned when presented along with a stronger, more salient stimulus than when it is presented alone

paired-comparison task   an experimental paradigm in which an individual is familiarized with a stimulus and then, following a delay, presented with that stimulus and a novel stimulus during a test phase. Researchers measure the amount of time spent looking at each stimulus during the test phase.

paired-associate paradigm   a research paradigm where participants study word pairs (such as DOG–horse) and then later learn new word pairs that partially overlap with the old pairs (such as DOG–chair)

parsimony   the notion that when given the choice, the hypothesis that makes the fewest assumptions should be chosen

partial-list cueing effect   when participants study a list and are given some items as cues at recall, participants recall fewer items than when not given part of the list as a cue

partial-report advantage   when the partial-report score is greater than the number of letters that are reported on whole-report trials

partial-report paradigm   an experimental paradigm where participants are shown an array of several rows of items and are then presented with a cue indicating which row of items they should report

partial-report score   a measure used to estimate how much material is available to participants reporting only one row from an array. The partial report score is computed by multiplying the number of letters reported by the number of rows in the array.

pattern completion   matching an existing memory to a cue

pattern-learning paradigm   a paradigm in which participants must indicate the location of asterisks presented on a computer screen. Asterisks are presented very quickly to limit conscious processing of the stimuli.

pattern separation   the production of distinct neural codes for distinct episodic events

perforant path   the connection between the entorhinal complex and the dentate gyrus in the hippocampus

perseveration   the process by which memories are consolidated

persistence   the unwanted recall of distressing memories

person-action-object (PAO) system   a method for creating images from numbers based on memorizing distinct images containing a person, an action, and an object

PGO waves   high-amplitude bursts of activity that originate in the brainstem and move toward the hippocampus

phonological loop   a portion of working memory in Baddeley and Hitch's multicomponent model that consists of the short-term phonological store and an articulatory rehearsal mechanism

phonological-similarity effect   a decrement in recall performance that occurs when to-be-remembered words all sound similar (e.g., *pen, when, hen*)

phrenology   a popular nineteenth century pseudoscience in which measurements of the skull are used to predict elements of an individual's personality and intellect

physical skill   how to perform a task using the body, such as riding a bicycle or playing a violin

piphilologist   an individual who memorizes the digits of *pi*

population coding   when a unique set of neurons is used to form a memory

population spike   a shift in electrical potential in a neuron that occurs after the neuron fires

positive memory bias   the tendency to better recall events that are associated with positive emotions than those associated with negative emotions

positive PTP   pre-trial publicity that depicts the defendant in a way that suggests the defendant would not or could not commit the crime she or he is accused of committing

post-categorical   information that has been processed to the point of having meaning

post-event misinformation   inaccurate facts about an event that was witnessed by a person that are sometimes deliberately created for experimental purposes, but can also occur naturally

postsynaptic neuron   a neuron that receives a signal across a synapse

potentiation   when a stimulus is better learned when presented along with a stronger, more salient, stimulus than when it is presented alone

pre-categorical   a stimulus that has not been processed to the point of having meaning. Because the stimulus has no meaning, whether it is a letter, number, word, or nonword is not known.

precocial   a term describing an animal born in an advanced state that is able to feed itself almost immediately

pressure-sensitive pacifier   a tool used by infant researchers to record sucking rates of infants in high-amplitude sucking paradigm experiments

presynaptic neuron   a neuron that sends a signal across a synapse

pre-trial publicity (PTP)   media coverage of a crime that occurs before the case is brought to trial

primacy effect   higher probability of free recall for items presented at the beginning of a to-be-remembered list as compared to items from the middle of the list

primary memory   a synonym for short-term memory

priming effect   when the recognition of an item is facilitated by previous exposure to a related item

principles approach   an approach to memory that looks to commonalities in memory research across different experimental settings

proactive interference   a reduction in the ability to create new memories because of existing memories

procedural memory   a type of long-term memory comprised of knowledge of how to perform actions

process-dissociation procedure   a well-known procedure designed to get separate estimates of conscious and automatic contributions to retrieval

processing approach   an approach to memory that presumes that memory traces vary based on how the to-be-remembered information has been processed

promiscuous encoding   the encoding of all events that are experienced by an organism

propinquity effect   a finding that people who spend time together tend to like each other

prospective studies   a method of gathering data where researchers identify a group and then look for evidence related to their hypothesis as time passes

psychogenic amnesia   significant memory loss resulting from psychological factors

p-system   the part of primary memory that consists of conscious thought

pursuit-rotor task   a task used to assess procedural learning where the goal is to keep a stylus on a specific spot within a rotating circle that is embedded on a disk also rotating, but in the opposite direction

rationalist   a person who believes that using reason, rather than experience, authority, or spiritual revelation, provides the primary basis for knowledge

reasoning power   an individual's ability to make decisions based on logic and common sense

recall   the act of retrieving a target based on a cue that does not include the target

recency effect   recently acquired memories are more likely to be recalled than memories from further in the past

recognition   the act of retrieving a target based on a cue that includes the target

recollection   the reinstatement of an event from memory that includes contextual details and an accompanying sense of self

reconsolidation   when a static memory is activated, becomes labile, and is returned to a static state again

relational binding   the process by which different memories of the same object are linked together

reminiscence bump   the tendency for older adults to recall autobiographical events from adolescence and early adulthood

repetition priming   when previous exposure to a stimulus facilitates processing in some way

response competition   when a query results in more than one item being retrieved in such a way that the correct response is not indicated

retention interval   the period of time between a learning event and a test of memory for that event

retrieval-disruption hypothesis   the claim that collaborative inhibition occurs because one group member's retrieval strategy disrupts retrieval strategies that would lead to better recall in other group members

retrieval-induced forgetting   forgetting that occurs because in order to retrieve one item accurately, similar items must be inhibited

retrieval-structure principle   memory will be better when material is associated with easy-to-remember cues

retrieval suppression   a process by which a person stops an encoded memory from entering conscious awareness

retroactive interference   a reduction in the ability to retrieve old memories because of newly learned information

retrograde amnesia   the inability to remember facts learned in the past

retrospective studies   a method of gathering data where researchers look for evidence related to their hypothesis by looking at events that have already happened

rhetoric   the art of speaking in a way that informs, persuades, or motivates particular audiences in specific situations

savings   refers to the fact that it takes less time to learn material on subsequent attempts, compared to the first time

schema   a cognitive framework that helps to organize and interpret information

scripts   knowledge about the components of events and the order in which the components are to occur

secondary memory   a synonym for long-term memory

self-reference effect   people are better able to recall information when thinking of that information in terms of themselves

self-self cue   in compound-cue theory, this is the cue that represents a sense of familiarity and is the extent to which an item serves as a cue for itself in generic memory

semantic dementia   a condition associated with damage to the anterior temporal lobe where generic memory is lost while episodic memory remains intact

semantic memory   a type of long-term memory comprised of meanings and concepts.

sensory memory   a general term referring to a very brief, very large-capacity memory store that retains information for a given sense (sight, hearing, taste, touch, or smell)

sensory preconditioning (SPC)   an association that is developed in the absence of reinforcement

sensory recruitment model   assumes that the brain areas that support STM for a stimulus are the same areas responsible for perceptual processing of that stimulus

sensory register   a point where information from modality-specific sensory memories comes together into one store

sentence-verification task   a paradigm in which participants are presented with statements such as "A bird can fly" or "A fish eats rocks" and must indicate as quickly and accurately as possible whether the sentence is true or false

serial position curve   a way of presenting data from free-recall experiments where proportion correct is presented on the vertical axis and the relative position of an item on the to-be-remembered list is shown on the horizontal axis

set   the portion of generic memory that is currently active

shared memory   memories that many people possess but that are not necessarily linked to a social identity

sharp-wave ripples   high-amplitude bursts of EEG activity in the hippocampal region of the brain

short-term memory   a memory store that holds about four pieces of information for about 15 to 30 seconds without rehearsal

showup procedure   an identification procedure wherein the witness is shown a single picture of a suspect and asked if the person in the picture was the person who committed the crime

sins of commission   when an error results in the failure to retrieve an item

sins of omission   memory failure that occurs because a process is not performed

skilled memory theory   a model that asserts that specific memory techniques can lead to greater memory capacity

sleep spindles   bursts of high-frequency high-amplitude EEG activity in the thalamo-cortical region of the brain

slow oscillations   slow-wave EEG activity in the neocortex

social conformity   changing one's beliefs or behaviours in order to fit in with the group

social contagion   the spread of ideas through interpersonal contact, interaction, or communication

source attribution error   a memory error wherein an individual believes that a piece of information came from one source when really it came from a different source

source confusion   a phenomenon in which a person cannot recall the original source of a memory

spacing effect   a phenomenon where material is better recalled if there are intervening items between two presentations of the material than when the material is presented back-to-back

speed-up principle   as people gain experience encoding, they can encode more information in less time

spindle cells   large neurons found only in the anterior cingulate cortex and frontal lobes of a few large-brained mammals. These neurons likely evolved to transmit information quickly across long distances.

spontaneous recovery   a weak conditioned response that occurs when an organism remembers a CS-CR association but forgets that the association is no longer useful

spreading activation model   a model of the relationship among concepts in memory based on the ideas that related concepts are connected in a network, and that concepts that share more properties will have more links between them

spreading depression   inhibition in brain activity caused by recent brain trauma

s-system   the part of primary memory that holds information in pre-categorical form

stability–plasticity dilemma   a problem in neuroscience concerning how it is possible for the brain to keep existing memories stable while integrating new memories

state-dependent memory   a phenomenon in which memory is enhanced when the individual is in the same state of consciousness at the time of learning and the time of retrieval

state-dependent memory effects   an experimental finding in which congruence between mood at the time of encoding and mood at the time of retrieval predicts a greater probability of memory retrieval

stereotype   a widely held but fixed and oversimplified image or idea of a particular type of person or thing

stimulus persistence   residual neurological activity resulting from a stimulus presentation that fades rapidly over time

suffix effect   recall is better when to-be-remembered items are followed by a suffix that is a non-speech sound than when followed by a suffix that is a speech-like sound

suggestibility   when a recollection is changed because an outside source indicates that the recollection is incorrect

survival effect   memories that are related to survival are better remembered than other memories

synapse   the location where a nervous impulse passes from one neuron to another neuron

systems approach   an approach to memory that presumes that memory is comprised of multiple independent systems, such as a short-term memory system, a long-term memory system, a procedural memory system, etc.

temporary store   in the two-stage model of memory, the temporary store holds new memories for short periods of time

testing effect   the finding that repeated memory retrieval produces better retention than re-reading the same information for an equivalent amount of time

tetani   high-frequency electrical stimulations of a single neuron

theta waves   a pattern of EEG activity that is similar to activity observed when a person is awake

three-factor theory of forgetting   a theory that proposes that forgetting results from response competition, altered stimulus conditions, or set

transactive memory   when people share a memory task and fill in the gaps of each other's recall

transfer   the extent to which learning of one ability accelerates learning of another ability

transience   the loss of information over time

transitivity   when stimuli become associated because they are each independently associated with the same stimulus

triarchic model of memory   a model of memory proposed by Endel Tulving in which different types of memory are distinguished by different types of consciousness.

twilight anaesthesia   mild anaesthesia intended to reduce anxiety and induce anterograde amnesia in patients undergoing outpatient medical procedures

two-stage model   a model of memory proposing that memories are consolidated through two processes: reactivation and redistribution

typicality effect   the finding that response times in a sentence-verification task are faster for more typical instances of a category than less typical instances. For example, "A robin is a bird" is recognized more quickly than "An ostrich is a bird."

unconditioned response (UR)   an automatic response to a stimulus

unconditioned stimulus (US)   a stimulus that produces an automatic response

unconscious transference   when previous exposure to a suspect leads to a feeling of familiarity that provides the sole basis for the identification of the suspect

vascular dementia   a form of dementia caused by the loss of blood flow to the brain

visuospatial sketchpad   a part of short-term memory that retains both visual and spatial information in a realistic representation

vitamin B_{12} deficiency   a condition in which the body does not absorb an adequate amount of vitamin B_{12}

wear-in   a period of time during which repetition of an ad has a positive effect on the consumer's attitude toward the product

wear-out   a period of time during which additional repetitions have a negative effect on the consumer's attitude toward the product

whole-report paradigm   an experimental paradigm where participants are shown an array of several rows of items and are required to report as many letters as they can from anywhere in the array

word-fragment completion (WFC) paradigm   participants are presented with letters and blank spaces and are asked to fill in the blank spaces with letters to form a proper word. The WFC task is used to assess implicit memory.

word-length effect   a decrement in recall performance when words take longer to verbalize

word-stem completion (WSC) paradigm   participants are presented with three letters and are asked to use the letters to complete a real word. The WSC can be used to assess implicit memory.

working memory   the part of short-term memory that is responsible for immediate conscious perceptual, cognitive, and linguistic processing.

working self   a set of personal goals and self-images that are organized in a hierarchy

References

Chapter 1

Atkinson, R.C. & Shiffrin, R.M. (1968). Human memory: A proposed system and its control processes. *The Psychology of Learning and Motivation, 2*, 89–195.

Baddeley, A., Eysenck, M., & Anderson, M. (2015). *Memory*. New York, NY: Psychology Press.

Banaji, M.R. & Crowder, R.G. (1989). The bankruptcy of everyday memory. *American Psychologist, 44*(9), 1185.

Bartlett, F.C. (1932). *Remembering: A study in experimental and social psychology*. Cambridge, England: Cambridge University Press.

Bower, G.H. (2000). A brief history of memory research. In E. Tulving & F.I. Craik (Eds.), *The Oxford handbook of memory* (pp. 3–32). New York, NY: Oxford University Press.

Broadbent, D.E. (1958). *Perception and communication*. Elmsford, NY: Pergamon Press.

Bruce, I. (1998). *Plato's theory of forms*. No pages. Online: http://www.ccs.neu.edu/course/com3118/Plato.html.

Chomsky, N. (1959). A review of B.F. Skinner's verbal behavior. *Language, 35*(1), 26–58.

Craik, F.I. & Lockhart, R.S. (1972). Levels of processing: A framework for memory research. *Journal of Verbal Learning and Verbal Behavior, 11*(6), 671–84.

Gall, F.J. (1835). *On the functions of the brain and of each of its parts: With observations on the possibility of determining the instincts, propensities, and talents, or the moral and intellectual dispositions of men and animals, by the configuration of the brain and head*, Volume 1. Marsh, Capen & Lyon.

Hebb, D.O. (1949). *The organization of behavior: A neuropsychological approach*. John Wiley & Sons.

Kolb, B. & Whishaw, I.Q. (2012). *Fundamentals of human neuropsychology*. New York, NY: Macmillan.

Lashley, K.S. (1929). *Brain mechanisms and intelligence: A quantitative study of injuries to the brain*. Chicago, IL: University of Chicago Press.

Marks, D.F. (1973). Visual imagery differences in the recall of pictures. *British Journal of Psychology, 64*(1), 1–24.

Miller, G.A. (1956). The magical number seven, plus or minus two: Some limits on our capacity for processing information. *Psychological Review, 63*(2), 81.

Newell, A. & Simon, H.A. (1961). Computer simulation of human thinking. *Science, 134*, 2011–7.

Nicoll, R.A. & Roche, K.W. (2013). Long-term potentiation: Peeling the onion. *Neuropharmacology, 74*, 18–22.

Penfield, W. (1952). Memory mechanisms. *Archives of Neurology and Psychiatry, 67*(2), 178.

Porter, L.W. & Duncan, C.P. (1953). Negative transfer in verbal learning. *Journal of Experimental Psychology, 46*(1), 61.

Ray, W.J. (2013). *Evolutionary psychology: Neuroscience perspectives concerning human behavior and experience*. Los Angeles, CA: Sage Publishing.

Ross, W.D. (Ed.). (1930). *The works of Aristotle: Vol. II* (R.P. Hardie & R.K. Gaye, Trans.) Oxford: Clarendon Press.

Schacter, D.L. (1987). Implicit expressions of memory in organic amnesia: Learning of new facts and associations. *Human Neurobiology, 6*(2), 107–18.

Schacter, D.L., Eich, J.E., & Tulving, E. (1978). Richard Semon's theory of memory. *Journal of Verbal Learning and Verbal Behavior, 17*(6), 721–43.

Scoville, W.B. & Milner, B. (1957). Loss of recent memory after bilateral hippocampal lesions. *Journal of Neurology, Neurosurgery, and Psychiatry, 20*(1), 11.

Semon, R. (1921). *The mneme*. London: George Allen & Unwin.

Squire, L.R. & Wixted, J.T. (2011). The cognitive neuroscience of human memory since HM. *Annual Review of Neuroscience, 34*, 259.

Surprenant, A.M. & Neath, I. (2013). *Principles of memory*. Psychology Press.

Walsh, R.T., Teo, T., & Baydala, A. (2014). *A critical history and philosophy of psychology: Diversity of context, thought, and practice*. Cambridge University Press.

Yates, F.A. (1966). *The art of memory*. Chicago: University of Chicago Press.

Chapter 2

Beste, C., Schneider, D., Epplen, J.T., & Arning, L. (2011). The functional BDNF Val66Met polymorphism affects functions of pre-attentive visual sensory memory processes. *Neuropharmacology*, 60(2–3), 467–71.

Cherry, E.C. (1953). Some experiments on the recognition of speech, with one and with two ears. *The Journal of the Acoustical Society of America*, 25(5), 975–9.

Conrad, R. & Hull, A.J. (1968). Input modality and the serial position curve in short-term memory. *Psychonomic Science*, 10(4), 135–6.

Darwin, C.J., Turvey, M.T., & Crowder, R.G. (1972). An auditory analogue of the Sperling partial report procedure: Evidence for brief auditory storage. *Cognitive Psychology*, 3(2), 255–67.

Di Lollo, V. (1980). Temporal integration in visual memory. *Journal of Experimental Psychology: General*. 109(1) 75–97.

Di Lollo, V. & Dixon, P. (1988). Two forms of persistence in visual information processing. *Journal of Experimental Psychology: Human Perception and Performance*, 14(4), 671.

Driver, J. (2001). A selective review of selective attention research from the past century. *British Journal of Psychology*, 92(1), 53–78.

Efron, R. (1970). The minimum duration of a perception. *Neuropsychologia*, 8(1), 57–63.

Haber, R.N. (1983). The impending demise of the icon: A critique of the concept of iconic storage in visual information processing. *Behavioral and Brain Sciences*, 6(1), 1–11.

Irwin, D. & Thomas, L. (2008). Neural basis of sensory memory. In S. Luck and A. Hollingworth (Eds.). *Visual memory* (pp. 32–5). New York, NY: Oxford University Press.

Irwin, D.E. & Yeomans, J.M. (1986). Sensory registration and informational persistence. *Journal of Experimental Psychology: Human Perception and Performance*, 12, 343–60.

Keysers, C., Xiao, D.K., Földiák, P., & Perrett, D.I. (2005). Out of sight but not out of mind: The neurophysiology of iconic memory in the superior temporal sulcus. *Cognitive Neuropsychology*, 22(3–4), 316–32.

Kojima, T., Karino, S., Yumoto, M., & Funayama, M. (2014). A stroke patient with impairment of auditory sensory (echoic) memory. *Neurocase*, 20(2), 133–43.

Loftus, G.R. & Irwin, D.E. (1998). On the relations among different measures of visible and informational persistence. *Cognitive Psychology*, 35(2), 135–99.

Marks, D.F. (1973). Visual imagery differences in the recall of pictures. *British Journal of Psychology*, 64(1), 17–24.

Merikle, P.M. (1980). Selection from visual persistence by perceptual groups and category membership. *Journal of Experimental Psychology: General*, 109(3), 279.

Mewhort, D.J.K., Campbell, A.J., Marchetti, F.M., & Campbell, J.I. (1981). Identification, localization, and "iconic memory": An evaluation of the bar-probe task. *Memory & Cognition*, 9(1), 50–67.

Morton, J., Crowder, R.G., & Prussin, H.A. (1971). Experiments with the stimulus suffix effect. *Journal of Experimental Psychology*, 91(1), 169–90.

Nairne, J.S. (2003). Sensory and working memory. *Handbook of Psychology*, 423–44.

Neath, I., Bireta, T.J., & Surprenant, A.M. (2003). The time-based word length effect and stimulus set specificity. *Psychonomic Bulletin & Review*, 10(2), 430–4.

Neath, I., Surprenant, A.M., & Crowder, R.G. (1993). The context-dependent stimulus suffix effect. *Journal of Experimental Psychology: Learning, Memory, and Cognition*, 19(3), 698.

Neisser, U. (1967). *Cognitive psychology*. East Norwalk, CT, US: Appleton-Century-Crofts.

Sperling, G. (1960). The information available in brief visual presentations. *Psychological Monographs: General and Applied*, 74(11), 1.

Sperling, G. (1967). Successive approximations to a model for short term memory. Acta psychologica, 27, 285–92.

Spoehr, K.T. & Corin, W.J. (1978). The stimulus suffix effect as a memory coding phenomenon. *Memory & Cognition*, 6(6), 583–9.

Straube, E.R. & Germer, C. K. (1979). Dichotic shadowing and selective attention to word meanings in schizophrenia. *Journal of Abnormal Psychology*, 88(4), 346.

Surprenant, A.M. & Neath, I. (2013). *Principles of memory*. New York: NY: Psychology Press.

Urakawa, T., Inui, K., Yamashiro, K., Tanaka, E., & Kakigi, R. (2010). Cortical dynamics of visual change detection based on sensory memory. *Neuroimage*, 52(1), 302–8.

Vlassova, A. & Pearson, J. (2013). Look before you leap: Sensory memory improves decision making. *Psychological Science*, 24(9), 1635–43.

Wood, N. & Cowan, N. (1995). The cocktail party phenomenon revisited: How frequent are attention shifts to one's name in an irrelevant auditory channel? *Journal of Experimental Psychology: Learning, Memory, and Cognition*, 21(1), 255.

Chapter 3

Allen, R.J., Baddeley, A.D., & Hitch, G.J. (2006). Is the binding of visual features in working memory resource-demanding? *Journal of Experimental Psychology: General*, 135(2), 298.

Atkinson, R.C. & Shiffrin, R.M. (1968). Human memory: A proposed system and its control processes. *The Psychology of Learning and Motivation*, 2, 89–195.

Baddeley, A.D. (1966). The influence of acoustic and semantic similarity on long-term memory for word sequences. *The Quarterly Journal of Experimental Psychology*, 18(4), 302–9.

Baddeley, A.D. (1968). How does acoustic similarity influence short-term memory? *The Quarterly Journal of Experimental Psychology*, 20(3), 249–64.

Baddeley, A. (1986). *Oxford psychology series, No. 11. Working memory.* New York, NY: Clarendon Press/Oxford University Press.

Baddeley, A. (2000). The episodic buffer: A new component of working memory? *Trends in Cognitive Sciences, 4*(11), 417–23.

Baddeley, A. (2007). *Working memory, thought, and action.* Oxford: Oxford University Press.

Baddeley, A. (2012). Working memory: Theories, models, and controversies. *Annual Review of Psychology, 63,* 1–29.

Baddeley, A.D. (2015). Working memory in second language learning. In *Working memory in second language acquisition and processing,* 17–28.

Baddeley, A., Banse, R., Huang, Y.M., & Page, M. (2012). Working memory and emotion: Detecting the hedonic detector. *Journal of Cognitive Psychology, 24*(1), 6–16.

Baddeley, A.D. & Hitch, G. (1974). Working memory. In *Psychology of Learning and Motivation* (Vol. 8, pp. 47–89). Academic Press.

Baddeley, A.D., Hitch, G.J., & Allen, R.J. (2009). Working memory and binding in sentence recall. *Journal of Memory and Language, 61*(3), 438–56.

Baddeley, A.D., Thomson, N., & Buchanan, M. (1975). Word length and the structure of short-term memory. *Journal of Verbal Learning and Verbal Behavior, 14*(6), 575–89.

Baddeley, A.D. & Wilson, B. (1985). Phonological coding and short-term memory in patients without speech. *Journal of Memory and Language, 24*(4), 490–502.

Banich, M.T., Mackiewicz, K.L., Depue, B.E., Whitmer, A.J., Miller, G.A., & Heller, W. (2009). Cognitive control mechanisms, emotion and memory: A neural perspective with implications for psychopathology. *Neuroscience & Biobehavioral Reviews, 33*(5), 613–30.

Bjork, R.A. & Whitten, W.B. (1974). Recency-sensitive retrieval processes in long-term free recall. *Cognitive Psychology, 6*(2), 173–89.

Brener, R. (1940). An experimental investigation of memory span. *Journal of Experimental Psychology, 26*(5), 467.

Broadbent, D.E. (1958). *Perception and communication.* Elmsford, NY: Pergamon Press.

Bush, G., Luu, P., & Posner, M.I. (2000). Cognitive and emotional influences in anterior cingulate cortex. *Trends in Cognitive Sciences, 4*(6), 215–22.

Colle, H.A. & Welsh, A. (1976). Acoustic masking in primary memory. *Journal of Verbal Learning and Verbal Behavior, 15*(1), 17–31.

Conrad, R. (1964). Acoustic confusions in immediate memory. *British Journal of Psychology, 55*(1), 75–84.

Conrad, R. & Hull, A. J. (1964). Information, acoustic confusion and memory span. *British Journal of Psychology, 55*(4), 429–32.

Cowan, N. (1988). Evolving conceptions of memory storage, selective attention and their mutual constraints within the human information processing system. *Psychological Bulletin, 104,* 163–91.

Cowan, N. (1999). An embedded-processes model of working memory. In A. Miyake & P. Shah (Eds.), *Models of working memory: Mechanisms of active maintenance and executive control* (pp. 62–101). New York, NY: Cambridge University Press.

Denis, M., Logie, R., & Cornoldo, C. (2012). The processing of visuo-spatial information: Neuropsychological and neuroimaging investigations. In M. Denis, R. H. Logie, C. Cornoldi, M. de Vega, & J. Engelkamp (Eds.), *Imagery, language and visuo-spatial thinking* (pp. 81–102). Hove, UK: Psychology Press.

Duncan, J. (2010). The multiple-demand (MD) system of the primate brain: Mental programs for intelligent behaviour. *Trends in Cognitive Sciences, 14*(4), 172–9.

Duncan, J. & Owen, A.M. (2000). Common regions of the human frontal lobe recruited by diverse cognitive demands. *Trends in Neurosciences, 23*(10), 475–83.

Gathercole, S. & Alloway, T.P. (2008). *Working memory and learning: A practical guide for teachers.* Sage.

Gathercole, S.E. & Baddeley, A.D. (1989). Evaluation of the role of phonological STM in the development of vocabulary in children: A longitudinal study. *Journal of Memory and Language, 28*(2), 200–13.

Gathercole, S.E. & Baddeley, A.D. (1990). Phonological memory deficits in language disordered children: Is there a causal connection? *Journal of Memory and Language, 29*(3), 336–60.

Gathercole, S.E., Pickering, S.J., Knight, C., & Stegmann, Z. (2004). Working memory skills and educational attainment: Evidence from national curriculum assessments at 7 and 14 years of age. *Applied Cognitive Psychology, 18*(1), 1–16.

Ghent, L., Mishkin, M., & Teuber, H.L. (1962). Short-term memory after frontal-lobe injury in man. *Journal of Comparative and Physiological Psychology, 55*(5), 705.

Glanzer, M. & Cunitz, A.R. (1966). Two storage mechanisms in free recall. *Journal of Verbal Learning and Verbal Behavior, 5*(4), 351–60.

Holmes, J. & Gathercole, S.E. (2014). Taking working memory training from the laboratory into schools. *Educational Psychology, 34*(4), 440–50.

Isen, A.M. (2008). Some ways in which positive affect influences decision making and problem solving. *Handbook of Emotions, 3,* 548–73.

Jacobsen, C.F. (1936). The functions of the frontal association areas in monkeys. *Comparative Psychology Monographs, 13,* 1–60.

Jolicoeur, P. & Kosslyn, S.M. (1985). Is time to scan visual images due to demand characteristics? *Memory & Cognition, 13*(4), 320–32.

Koppenaal, L. & Glanzer, M. (1990). An examination of the continuous distractor task and the "long-term recency effect." *Memory & Cognition, 18*(2), 183–95.

Kosslyn, S.M. (1975). Information representation in visual images. *Cognitive Psychology, 7*(3), 341–70.

Kosslyn, S.M. (1976). Can imagery be distinguished from other forms of internal representation? Evidence from studies of information retrieval times. *Memory & Cognition, 4*(3), 291–7.

Kosslyn, S.M. (1980). *Image and mind.* Harvard University Press.

Kosslyn, S.M., Alpert, N.M., Thompson, W.K., Maljkovic, V., Weise, S.B., Chabris, C.F., . . . & Buonanno, F. (1993). Visual mental imagery activates topographically organized visual cortex: PET investigations. *Journal of Cognitive Neuroscience, 5*(3), 263–87.

Kosslyn, S.M. & Pomerantz, J.R. (1977). Imagery, propositions, and the form of internal representations. *Cognitive Psychology, 9*(1), 52–76.

Lakin, J.L., Giesler, R.B., Morris, K.A., & Vosmik, J.R. (2007). HOMER as an acronym for the scientific method. *Teaching of Psychology, 34*(2), 94–6.

Langerock, N., Vergauwe, E., & Barrouillet, P. (2014). The maintenance of cross-domain associations in the episodic buffer. *Journal of Experimental Psychology: Learning, Memory, and Cognition, 40*(4), 1096.

Malmo, R.B. (1942). Interference factors in delayed response in monkeys after removal of frontal lobes. *Journal of Neurophysiology, 5*, 296–308.

Miller, G.A. (1956). The magical number seven, plus or minus two: Some limits on our capacity for processing information. *Psychological Review, 63*(2), 81.

Milner, B.A. (1982). Some cognitive effects of frontal-lobe lesions in man. *Philosophical transactions of the Royal Society of London. B, Biological Sciences, 298*(1089), 211–26.

Murdoch, W.W. (1972). The functional response of predators. *Biological Control, 15*, 237–40.

Murray, D.J. (1968). Articulation and acoustic confusability in short-term memory. *Journal of Experimental Psychology, 78*(4p1), 679.

Nairne, J.S. (1996). Short-term/working memory. *Memory, 10*, 101–26.

Nairne, J.S. (2003). The myth of the encoding/retrieval match. *Memory, 10*(5–6), 389–395.

Nairne, J.S., Neath, I., Serra, M., & Byun, E. (1997). Positional distinctiveness and the ratio rule in free recall. *Journal of Memory and Language, 37*(2), 155–66.

Neath, I. (1993). Contextual and distinctive processes and the serial position function. *Journal of Memory and Language, 32*(6), 820–40.

Paivio, A., Yuille, J.C., & Madigan, S.A. (1968). Concreteness, imagery, and meaningfulness values for 925 nouns. *Journal of Experimental Psychology, 76*(1p2), 1.

Paulesu, E., Frith, C.D., & Frackowiak, R.S. (1993). The neural correlates of the verbal component of working memory. *Nature, 362*(6418), 342–5.

Pearson, D.G., Logie, R.H., & Gilhooly, K.J. (1999). Verbal representations and spatial manipulation during mental synthesis. *European Journal of Cognitive Psychology, 11*(3), 295–314.

Peterson, L.R. & Johnson, S.T. (1971). Some effects of minimizing articulation on short-term retention. *Journal of Verbal Learning and Verbal Behavior, 10*(4), 346–54.

Peterson, L. & Peterson, M.J. (1959). Short-term retention of individual verbal items. *Journal of Experimental Psychology, 58*(3), 193.

Pope, H.G. & Yurgelun-Todd, D. (1996). The residual cognitive effects of heavy marijuana use in college students. *JAMA, 275*(7), 521–7.

Postle, B.R. (2016). The hippocampus, memory, and consciousness. In *The neurology of consciousness* (2nd ed., pp. 349–63).

Ranganathan, M. & D'Souza, D.C. (2006). The acute effects of cannabinoids on memory in humans: A review. *Pharmacology, 188*, 425–44.

Roodenrys, S. & Quinlan, P.T. (2000). The effects of stimulus set size and word frequency on verbal serial recall. *Memory, 8*(2), 71–8.

Rothbart, M.K. & Rueda, M.R. (2005). The development of effortful control. In *Developing individuality in the human brain: A tribute to Michael I. Posner*, 167–88.

Rundus, D. (1971). Analysis of rehearsal processes in free recall. *Journal of Experimental Psychology, 89*(1), 63.

Rundus, D. & Atkinson, R.C. (1970). Rehearsal processes in free recall: A procedure for direct observation. *Journal of Verbal Learning and Verbal Behavior, 9*(1), 99–105.

Scharinger, C., Soutschek, A., Schubert, T., & Gerjets, P. (2015). When flanker meets the n-back: What EEG and pupil dilation data reveal about the interplay between the two central-executive working memory functions inhibition and updating. *Psychophysiology, 52*(10), 1293–304.

Schweizer, S., Grahn, J., Hampshire, A., Mobbs, D., & Dalgleish, T. (2013). Training the emotional brain: Improving affective control through emotional working memory training. *The Journal of Neuroscience, 33*(12), 5301–11.

Scoville, W.B. & Milner, B. (1957). Loss of recent memory after bilateral hippocampal lesions. *Journal of Neurology, Neurosurgery, and Psychiatry, 20*(1), 11.

Serences, J.T., Ester, E.F., Vogel, E.K., & Awh, E. (2009). Stimulus-specific delay activity in human primary visual cortex. *Psychological Science, 20*(2), 207–14.

Shepard, R.N. & Metzler, J. (1971). Mental rotation of three-dimensional objects. *Science, 171*(3972), 701–3.

Simon, H.A. (1974). How big is a chunk? By combining data from several experiments, a basic human memory unit can be identified and measured. *Science, 183*(4124), 482–8.

Smith, E.E., Jonides, J., & Koeppe, R.A. (1996). Dissociating verbal and spatial working memory using PET. *Cerebral Cortex, 6*(1), 11–20.

Sperling, G. (1960). The information available in brief visual presentations. *Psychological monographs: General and applied, 74*(11), 1.

Stanton, A., Unkrich, L., Walters, G., Lasseter, J. Peterson, B., Reynolds, D., & Brooks, A. (2003). *Finding Nemo.*

Tan, L. & Ward, G. (2000). A recency-based account of the primacy effect in free recall. *Journal of Experimental Psychology: Learning, Memory, and Cognition, 26*(6), 1589.

Walker, I. & Hulme, C. (1999). Concrete words are easier to recall than abstract words: Evidence for a semantic contribution to short-term serial recall. *Journal of Experimental Psychology: Learning, Memory, and Cognition, 25*(5), 1256.

Warrington, E.K., & Weiskrantz, L. (1970). Amnesic syndrome: Consolidation or retrieval? *Nature, 228*(5272), 628.

Watkins, M.J., Neath, I., & Sechler, E.S. (1989). Recency effect in recall of a word list when an immediate memory task is performed after each word presentation. *The American Journal of Psychology, 35, 102*(2), 265–70.

Waugh, N.C. & Norman, D.A. (1965). Primary memory. *Psychological Review, 72*(2), 89.

Welch, G.B. & Burnett, C.T. (1924). Is primacy a factor in association formation? *The American Journal of Psychology, 35,* 396–401.

Yang, H., Yang, S., & Isen, A.M. (2013). Positive affect improves working memory: Implications for controlled cognitive processing. *Cognition & Emotion, 27*(3), 474–82.

Chapter 4

Alpern, H.P. & Crabbe, J.C. (1972). Facilitation of the long-term store of memory with strychnine. *Science, 177*(4050), 722–4.

Berger, R.J. & Phillips, N.H. (1995). Energy conservation and sleep. *Behavioural Brain Research, 69*(1), 65–73.

Bliss, T.V. & Lømo, T. (1973). Long-lasting potentiation of synaptic transmission in the dentate area of the anaesthetized rabbit following stimulation of the perforant path. *The Journal of Physiology, 232*(2), 331–56.

Born, J. & Wilhelm, I. (2012). System consolidation of memory during sleep. *Psychological Research, 76*(2), 192–203.

Carpenter, G.A. & Grossberg, S. (1988). The ART of adaptive pattern recognition by a self-organizing neural network. *Computer, 21*(3), 77–88.

Carr, M.F., Jadhav, S.P., & Frank, L.M. (2011). Hippocampal replay in the awake state: A potential substrate for memory consolidation and retrieval. *Nature Neuroscience, 14*(2), 147–53.

Diekelmann, S. & Born, J. (2007). One memory, two ways to consolidate? *Nature Neuroscience, 10*(9), 1085-6.

Diekelmann, S. & Born, J. (2010). The memory function of sleep. *Nature Reviews Neuroscience, 11*(2), 114–26.

Diekelmann, S., Wilhelm, I., Wagner, U., & Born, J. (2013). Sleep to implement an intention. *Sleep, 36*(1), 149.

Eichenbaum, H. & Cohen, N.J. (2004). *From conditioning to conscious recollection: Memory systems of the brain.* Oxford University Press.

Fischer, S. & Born, J. (2009). Anticipated reward enhances offline learning during sleep. *Journal of Experimental Psychology: Learning, Memory, and Cognition, 35*(6), 1586.

Gordon, W.C. (1977). Susceptibility of a reactivated memory to the effects of strychnine: A time-dependent phenomenon. *Physiology & Behavior, 18*(1), 95–9.

Hebb, D.O. (1949). *The organization of behavior: A neuropsychological approach.* John Wiley & Sons.

Howard, M.W. & Kahana, M.J. (2002). A distributed representation of temporal context. *Journal of Mathematical Psychology, 46*(3), 269–99.

Hupbach, A., Hardt, O., Gomez, R., & Nadel, L. (2008). The dynamics of memory: Context-dependent updating. *Learning & Memory, 15*(8), 574–9.

Knutson, K.L. & Van Cauter, E. (2008). Associations between sleep loss and increased risk of obesity and diabetes. *Annals of the New York Academy of Sciences, 1129*(1), 287–304.

Lømo, T. (2003). The discovery of long-term potentiation. *Philosophical Transactions of the Royal Society of London B: Biological Sciences, 358*(1432), 617–20.

Maguire, E.A., Woollett, K., & Spiers, H.J. (2006). London taxi drivers and bus drivers: A structural MRI and neuropsychological analysis. *Hippocampus, 16*(12), 1091–101.

Marr, D., Willshaw, D., & McNaughton, B. (1991). *Simple memory: A theory for archicortex* (pp. 59-128). Birkhäuser Boston.

McClelland, J.L., McNaughton, B.L., & O'Reilly, R.C. (1995). Why there are complementary learning systems in the hippocampus and neocortex: Insights from the successes and failures of connectionist models of learning and memory. *Psychological Review, 102*(3), 419.

McDaniel, M.A., Anderson, J.L., Derbish, M.H., & Morrisette, N. (2007). Testing the testing effect in the classroom. *European Journal of Cognitive Psychology, 19*(4–5), 494–513.

Morris, R.G.M., Anderson, E., Lynch, G.A., & Baudry, M. (1986). Selective impairment of learning and blockade of long-term potentiation by an N-methyl-D-aspartate receptor antagonist, AP5, *Nature. 319*(6056), 774–6.

Murray, E.A., Bussey, T.J., & Saksida, L.M. (2007). Visual perception and memory: A new view of medial temporal lobe function in primates and rodents. *Annual Review of Neuroscience, 30,* 99–122.

Nadel, L. & Moscovitch, M. (1998). Hippocampal contributions to cortical plasticity. *Neuropharmacology, 37*(4), 431–9.

Nader, K. & Hardt, O. (2009). A single standard for memory: The case for reconsolidation. *Nature Reviews Neuroscience, 10*(3), 224–34.

Nader, K., Schafe, G.E., & LeDoux, J.E. (2000). Fear memories require protein synthesis in the amygdala for reconsolidation after retrieval. *Nature, 406*(6797), 722–6.

Norman, K.A., Schacter, D.L., & Reder, L.M. (1996). Implicit memory, explicit memory, and false recollection: A cognitive neuroscience perspective. In L.M. Reder (Ed.), *Implicit memory and metacognition* (pp. 229–58). Hillsdale, NJ: Erlbaum Associates.

Olsen, R.K., Lee, Y., Kube, J., Rosenbaum, R.S., Grady, C.L., Moscovitch, M., & Ryan, J.D. (2015). The role of relational binding in item memory: Evidence from face recognition in a case of developmental amnesia. *Journal of Neuroscience, 35*(13), 5342–50.

Oswald, I. (1980). Sleep as a restorative process: Human clues. *Progress in Brain Research, 53,* 279–88.

Page, S., & Robertson, E., (2000). "Pinch Me". PINCH ME. Words and Music by STEVEN PAGE and ED ROBERTSON. Copyright © 2000 WB MUSIC CORP. and TREAT BAKER MUSIC. All Rights Administered by WB MUSIC CORP. All Rights Reserved. Used By Permission of ALFRED MUSIC.

Polyn, S.M., Natu, V.S., Cohen, J.D., & Norman, K.A. (2005). Category-specific cortical activity precedes retrieval during memory search. *Science, 310*(5756), 1963–6.

Rao, V.R. & Finkbeiner, S. (2007). NMDA and AMPA receptors: Old channels, new tricks. *Trends in Neurosciences, 30*(6), 284–91.

Rasch, B., Büchel, C., Gais, S., & Born, J. (2007). Odor cues during slow-wave sleep prompt declarative memory consolidation. *Science, 315*(5817), 1426–9.

Rechtschaffen, A. & Bergmann, B.M. (1995). Sleep deprivation in the rat by the disk-over-water method. *Behavioural Brain Research, 69*(1), 55–63.

Schafe, G.E. & LeDoux, J.E. (2000). Memory consolidation of auditory Pavlovian fear conditioning requires protein synthesis and protein kinase A in the amygdala. *Journal of Neuroscience, 20*(18), RC96.

Squire, L.R. (1992). Declarative and nondeclarative memory: Multiple brain systems supporting learning and memory. *Journal of Cognitive Neuroscience, 4*(3), 232–43.

Terry, L. & Holliday, J.H. (1972). Retrograde amnesia produced by electroconvulsive shock after reactivation of a consolidated memory trace: A replication. *Psychonomic Science, 29*(3), 137–8.

Wierzynski, C.M., Lubenov, E.V., Gu, M., & Siapas, A.G. (2009). State-dependent spike-timing relationships between hippocampal and prefrontal circuits during sleep. *Neuron, 61*(4), 587–96.

Wilhelm, I., Diekelmann, S., Molzow, I., Ayoub, A., Mölle, M., & Born, J. (2011). Sleep selectively enhances memory expected to be of future relevance. *The Journal of Neuroscience, 31*(5), 1563–9.

Chapter 5

Bacon, F.T. (1979). Credibility of repeated statements: Memory for trivia. *Journal of Experimental Psychology: Human Learning and Memory, 5*(3), 241.

Begg, I.M., Anas, A., & Farinacci, S. (1992). Dissociation of processes in belief: Source recollection, statement familiarity, and the illusion of truth. *Journal of Experimental Psychology: General, 121*(4), 446.

Blaxton, T.A. (1989). Investigating dissociations among memory measures: Support for a transfer-appropriate processing framework. *Journal of Experimental Psychology: Learning, Memory, and Cognition, 15*(4), 657.

Crick, F. & Koch, C. (1998). Consciousness and neuroscience. *Cerebral Cortex, 8*(2), 97–107.

Cutting, J.E. (2003). Gustave Caillebotte, French impressionism, and mere exposure. *Psychonomic Bulletin & Review, 10*(2), 319–43.

Damasio, A.R. (2000). *The feeling of what happens: Body, emotion and the making of consciousness.* Random House.

DeSchepper, B. & Treisman, A. (1996). Visual memory for novel shapes: Implicit coding without attention. *Journal of Experimental Psychology: Learning, Memory, and Cognition, 22*(1), 27.

Diekelmann, S. & Born, J. (2010). The memory function of sleep. *Nature Reviews Neuroscience, 11*(2), 114–26.

Geiger, F. & Wolfgram, L. (2013). Overshadowing as prevention of anticipatory nausea and vomiting in pediatric cancer patients: Study protocol for a randomized controlled trial. *Trials, 14*(1), 103.

Gollin, E.S. (1960). Developmental studies of visual recognition of incomplete objects. *Perceptual and Motor Skills, 11*(3), 289–98.

Graf, P. & Mandler, G. (1984). Activation makes words more accessible, but not necessarily more retrievable. *Journal of Verbal Learning and Verbal Behavior, 23*(5), 553–68.

Greenwald, A.G., McGhee, D.E., & Schwartz, J.L. (1998). Measuring individual differences in implicit cognition: The implicit association test. *Journal of Personality and Social Psychology, 74*(6), 1464.

Hasher, L., Goldstein, D., & Toppino, T. (1977). Frequency and the conference of referential validity. *Journal of Verbal Learning and Verbal Behavior, 16*(1), 107–12.

Heindel, W., Salmon D., Shults, C., Walicke, P., & Butters, N. (1989). Neuropsychological evidence for multiple implicit memory systems: A comparison of Alzheimer's, Huntington's, and Parkinson's disease patients. *The Journal of Neuroscience 9*(2), 582–7.

Jacoby, L.L. (1983). Remembering the data: Analyzing interactive processes in reading. *Journal of Verbal Learning and Verbal Behavior, 22*(5), 485–508.

Jacoby, L.L., Woloshyn, V., & Kelley, C. (1989). Becoming famous without being recognized: Unconscious influences of memory produced by dividing attention. *Journal of Experimental Psychology: General, 118*(2), 115.

Kolb, B., & Whishaw, I. (Eds.). (2016). Brain and Behaviour: Revisiting the Classic Studies. Sage.

Levinson, B.W. (1965). States of awareness under general anaesthesia. A case history. *Medical Proceedings (S-Afr)*, 243–5.

Liu, T. & Cooper, L.A. (2001). The influence of task requirements on priming in object decision and matching. *Memory & Cognition, 29*(6), 874–82.

Masters, R.S. (1992). Knowledge, knerves and know-how: The role of explicit versus implicit knowledge in the breakdown of a complex motor skill under pressure. *British Journal of Psychology, 83*(3), 343–58.

Merikle, P.M. & Daneman, M. (1996). Memory for unconsciously perceived events: Evidence from anesthetized patients. *Consciousness and Cognition, 5*(4), 525–41.

Mishkin, M. (1982). A memory system in the monkey. *Philosophical Transactions of the Royal Society of London. Series B: Biological Sciences, 298*(1089), 85–95.

Mishkin, M., Suzuki, W.A., Gadian, D.G., & Vargha–Khadem, F. (1997). Hierarchical organization of cognitive memory. *Philosophical Transactions of the Royal Society of London. Series of London. Series B: Biological Sciences, 352*(1360), 1461–7.

Nissen, M.J. & Bullemer, P. (1987). Attentional requirements of learning: Evidence from performance measures. *Cognitive Psychology, 19*(1), 1–32.

Rajaram, S. & Roediger, H.L. (1993). Direct comparison of four implicit memory tests. *Journal of Experimental Psychology: Learning, Memory, and Cognition, 19*(4), 765.

Reber, A.S. (1967). Implicit learning of artificial grammars. *Journal of Verbal Learning and Verbal Behavior, 6*(6), 855–63.

Russell, I.F. & Wang, M. (1997). Absence of memory for intraoperative information during surgery under adequate general anaesthesia. *British Journal of Anaesthesia*, 78(1), 3–9.

Shimamura, A.P. (1986). Priming effects in amnesia: Evidence for a dissociable memory function. *The Quarterly Journal of Experimental Psychology Section A*, 38(4), 619–44.

Squire, L.R. (1992). Declarative and nondeclarative memory: Multiple brain systems supporting learning and memory. *Journal of Cognitive Neuroscience*, 4(3), 232–43.

Squire, L.R., Shimamura, A.P., & Graf, P. (1987). Strength and duration of priming effects in normal subjects and amnesic patients. *Neuropsychologia*, 25(1), 195–210.

Stadler, M.A. (1995). Role of attention in implicit learning. *Journal of Experimental Psychology: Learning, Memory, and Cognition*, 21(3), 674.

Tulving, E., Schacter, D.L., & Stark, H.A. (1982). Priming effects in word-fragment completion are independent of recognition memory. *Journal of Experimental Psychology: Learning, Memory, and Cognition*, 8(4), 336.

Wang, M. (2010). Implicit memory, anesthesia and sedation. In G.W. Davies, D. (Ed.), *Current issues in applied memory research* (pp.165–184). London: Psychology Press.

Wang, M., Russell, I.F., & Logan, C.D. (2004). Light anaesthesia without explicit recall during hysterectomy is associated with increased postoperative anxiety over a 3-month follow-up period. *British Journal of Anaesthesia*, 93(3), 492P–3P.

Wang, M., Russell, I.F., & Nicholson, J. (2004). A 10-yr retrospective follow-up of alfentanil-midazolam patients who indicated intraoperative pain without explicit recall. *British Journal of Anaesthesia*, 93(3), 493P–3P.

Warrington, E.K. & Weiskrantz, L. (1970). Amnesic syndrome: Consolidation or retrieval? *Nature*, 228(5272), 628–30.

Zajonc, R.B. (2001). Mere exposure: A gateway to the subliminal. *Current Directions in Psychological Science*, 10(6), 224–8.

Chapter 6

Batcho, K.I. (1995). Nostalgia: A psychological perspective. *Perceptual and motor skills*, 80(1), 131–43.

Berntsen, D. & Rubin, D.C. (2002). Emotionally charged autobiographical memories across the life span: The recall of happy, sad, traumatic, and involuntary memories. *Psychology & Aging*, 17, 636–52.

Bohannon III, J.N. (1988). Flashbulb memories for the space shuttle disaster: A tale of two theories. *Cognition*, 29(2), 179–96.

Brenner, M. (1973). The next-in-line effect. *Journal of Verbal Learning and Verbal Behaviour*, 12, 320-3.

Brown, R. & Kulik, (1977). Flashbulb memories. *Cognition*, 5(1), 73–99.

Buzsáki, G. (2006). *Rhythms of the brain*. Oxford: Oxford University Press.

Chinnakkaruppan, A., Wintzer, M.E., McHugh, T.J., & Rosenblum, K. (2014). Differential contribution of hippocampal subfields to components of associative taste learning. *The Journal of Neuroscience*, 34(33), 11007–15.

Conway, M.A. (2005). Memory and the self. *Journal of memory and language*, 53(4), 594–628.

Conway M.A. (2009). Episodic memory. *Neuropsychologia*, 47, 2305–6.

Conway, M.A., Anderson, S.J., Larsen, S.F., Donnelly, C.M., McDaniel, M.A., McClelland, A.G., Rawles, R.E., & Logie, R.H. (1994). The formation of flashbulb memories. *Memory & Cognition*, 22(3), 326–43.

Conway, M.A. & Fthenaki, A. (2000). Disruption and loss of autobiographical memory. In L.S. Cermak (Ed.), *Handbook of neuropsychology: Memory and its disorders* (pp. 281-312). Amsterdam, Netherlands: Elsevier Science Publishers B.V.

Conway, M.A. & Pleydell-Pearce, C.W. (2000). The construction of autobiographical memories in the self-memory system. *Psychological Review*, 107(2), 261.

Conway, M.A., Pleydell-Pearce, C.W., & Whitecross, S.E. (2001). The neuroanatomy of autobiographical memory: A slow cortical potential study of autobiographical memory retrieval. *Journal of Memory and Language*, 45(3), 493–524.

Conway, M.A., Wang, Q., Hanyu, K., & Haque, S. (2005). A cross-cultural investigation of autobiographical memory. *Journal of Cross-Cultural Psychology* 36, 739–49.

Elliotson, J. (1835). *Human physiology* (p. 646). London: Longman, Orme, Browne, Green, and Longman.

Erdelyi, M., Buschke, H., & Finkelstein, S. (1977). Hypermnesia for Socratic stimuli: The growth of recall for an internally generated memory list abstracted from a series of riddles. *Memory & Cognition*, 5(3), 283–6.

Ferguson, T.J., Rule, B.G., & Carlson, D. (1983). Memory for personally relevant information. *Journal of Personality and Social Psychology*, 44(2), 251.

Girden, E. & Culler, E. (1937). Conditioned responses in curarized striate muscle in dogs. *Journal of Comparative Psychology*, 23(2), 261.

Godden, D.R. & Baddeley, A.D. (1975). Context-dependent memory in two natural environments: On land and underwater. *British Journal of Psychology*, 66(3), 325–31.

Greenwald, A.G. (1980). The totalitarian ego: Fabrication and revision of personal history. *American Psychologist*, 35(7), 603.

Hassabis, D. & Maguire, E.A. (2007). Deconstructing episodic memory with construction. *Trends in Cognitive Sciences*, 11(7), 299–306.

Janowsky, J.S., Shimamura, A.P., & Squire L.R. (1989). Source memory impairment in patients with frontal lobe lesions. *Neuropsychologia*, 27(8), 1043–56.

Janssen, S., Chessa, A., & Murre, J. (2005). The reminiscence bump in autobiographical memory: Effects of age, gender, education, and culture. *Memory* 13(6), 658–668.

Janssen, S.M., Chessa, A.G., & Murre, J.M. (2007). Temporal distribution of favourite books, movies, and records: Differential encoding and re-sampling. *Memory*, 15(7), 755–67.

Leist, A.K., Ferring, D., & Filipp, S.-H. (2010). Remembering positive and negative life events: Associations with future time perspective and functions of autobiographical memory. *GeroPsych: The Journal of Gerontopsychology and Geriatric Psychiatry, 23*(3), 137–147.

Levine, B., Turner, G.R., Tisserand, D., Hevenor, S.J., Graham, S.J., & McIntosh, A.R. (2004). The functional neuroanatomy of episodic and semantic autobiographical remembering: A prospective functional MRI study. *Journal of Cognitive Neuroscience, 16,* 1633–46.

Libby, L.K. & Eibach, R.P. (2002). Looking back in time: Self-concept change affects visual perspective in autobiographical memory. *Journal of Personality and Social Psychology, 82*(2), 167.

Lisman, J.E. (1999). Relating hippocampal circuitry to function: Recall of memory sequences by reciprocal dentate–CA3 interactions. *Neuron, 22,* 233–42.

Mishkin, M. (1982). A memory system in the monkey. *Philosophical transactions of the Royal Society of London. Series B: Biological Sciences, 298*(1089), 85–95.

Lotterman, J.H. & Bonanno, G.A. (2014). Those were the days: Memory bias for the frequency of positive events, depression, and self-enhancement. *Memory, 22*(8), 925–36.

"My Favorite Things" music by Richard Rodgers, lyrics by Oscar Hammerstein II © 1959 (Renewed) by Williamson Music (ASCAP), a division of The Rodgers & Hammerstein Organization: a Concord Music Company International Copyright Secured. All Rights Reserved. Used by Permission.

Mystkowski, J.L., Mineka, S., Vernon, L.L., & Zinbarg, R.E. (2003). Changes in caffeine states enhance return of fear in spider phobia. *Journal of Consulting and Clinical Psychology, 71*(2), 243–50.

Nairne, J.S. (2002). The myth of the encoding/retrieval match. *Memory, 10*(5–6), 389–95.

Neisser, U. (1982). Memory: What are the important questions? In *Memory observed: Remembering in natural contexts* (pp. 3–19). Macmillan.

Nutt, R.M., & Lam, D. (2011). Comparison of mood-dependent memory in bipolar disorder and normal controls. *Clinical Psychology and Psychotherapy, 18,* 379–86.

O'Connor, A.R., Lever, C., & Moulin, C.J. (2010). Novel insights into false recollection: A model of déjà vécu. *Cognitive Neuropsychiatry, 15*(1–3), 118–44.

Overton, D.A. (1964). State dependent or "dissociated" learning produced with pentobarbital. *Journal of Comparative and Physiological Psychology, 57*(1), 3.

Pearce, S.A., Isherwood, S., Hrouda, D., Richardson, P.H., Erskine, A., & Skinner, J. (1990). Memory and pain: Tests of mood congruity and state dependence learning in experimentally induced and clinical pain. *Pain, 43,* 187–93.

Pillemer, D.B. (2001). Momentous events and the life story. *Review of General Psychology, 5*(2), 123.

Rathbone, C.J., Moulin, C.J., & Conway, M.A. (2008). Self-centered memories: The reminiscence bump and the self. *Memory and Cognition 36*(8), 1403–14.

Rogers, T.B., Kuiper, N.A., & Kirker, W.S. (1977). Self-reference and the encoding of personal information. *Journal of Personality and Social Psychology, 35*(9), 677.

Routledge, C., Arndt, J., Sedikides, C., & Wildschut, T. (2008). A blast from the past: The terror management function of nostalgia. *Journal of Experimental Social Psychology, 44,* 132–40.

Routledge C., Arndt, J., Wildschut, T., Sedikides, C., Hart, C., Juhl, J., & Schlotz, W. (2011). The past makes the present meaningful: Nostalgia as an existential resource. *Journal of Personality and Social Psychology, 101,* 638–52.

Rubin, D.C., Rahhal, T.A., & Poon, L.W. (1998). Things learned in early adulthood are remembered best. *Memory & Cognition, 26,* 3–19.

Schmolck, H.H., Buffalo, E.A., & Squire, L.R. (2000). Memory distortions develop over time: Recollections of the O.J. Simpson trial verdict after 15 and 32 months. *Psychological Science 11*(1), 39–45.

Sheen, M., Kemp, S., & Rubin, D. (2001). Twins dispute memory ownership: A new false memory phenomenon. *Memory & Cognition, 29*(6), 779–88.

Surprenant, A.M. & Neath, I. (2013). *Principles of memory.* Psychology Press.

Swanson, J.M. & Kinsbourne, M. (1976). Stimulant-related state-dependent learning in hyperactive children. *Science, 192*(4246), 1354–7.

Talarico, J.M. & Rubin, D.C. (2003). Confidence, not consistency, characterizes flashbulb memories. *Psychological Science, 14*(5), 455–61.

Tulving, E. (1972). Episodic and semantic memory. In E. Tulving & W. Donaldson (Eds.), *Organization of memory* (p. 402). Oxford, England: Academic Press.

Tulving, E. & Thomson, D.M. (1973). Encoding specificity and retrieval processes in episodic memory. *Psychological Review, 80*(5), 352.

Turner, R.N., Wildschut, T., & Sedikides, C. (2012). Dropping the weight stigma: Nostalgia improves attitudes toward persons who are overweight. *Journal of Experimental Social Psychology, 48,* 130–7.

Vess, M., Arndt, J., Routledge, C., Sedikides, C., & Wildschut, T. (2012). Nostalgia as a resource for the self. *Self and Identity, 11*(3), 273–84.

Von Restorff, H. (1933). Über die wirkung von bereichsbildungen im spurenfeld. *Psychologische Forschung, 18*(1), 299–342.

Wang, Q. & Conway, M.A. (2004). The stories we keep: Autobiographical memory in American and Chinese middle-aged adults. *Journal of Personality, 72,* 911–38.

Weingartner, H., Adefris, W., Eich, J.E., & Murphy, D.L., (1976). Encoding-imagery specificity in alcohol state-dependent learning. *Journal of Experimental Psychology—Human Learning and Memory, 2*(1), 83–7.

Weingartner, H., Miller, H., & Murphy, D.L. (1977). Mood-dependent retrieval of verbal associations, *Journal of Abnormal Psychology, 86*(3), 276–84.

Wildschut, T., Sedikides, C., Arndt, J., & Routledge, C. (2006). Nostalgia: Content, triggers, functions. *Journal of Personality and Social Psychology, 91*(5), 975.

Wildschut, T., Sedikides, C., Routledge, C., Arndt, J., & Cordaro, P. (2010). Nostalgia as a repository of social connectedness: The role of attachment-related avoidance. *Journal of Personality and Social Psychology, 98*, 573–86.

Widner, R.L., Otani, H., & Winkelman, S.E. (2005). Tip-of-the-tongue experiences are not merely. *The Journal of General Psychology, 132*(4), 392–407.

Chapter 7

Bak, T.H., O'Donovan, D.G., Xuereb, J.H., Boniface, S., & Hodges, J.R. (2001). Selective impairment of verb processing associated with pathological changes in Brodmann areas 44 and 45 in the motor neurone disease–dementia–aphasia syndrome. *Brain, 124*(1), 103–20.

Baron-Cohen, S., Burt, L., Smith-Laittan, F., Harrison, J., & Bolton, P. (1996). Synaesthesia: Prevalence and familiality. *Perception, 25*(9), 1073–9.

Barsalou, L.W. (1982). Context-independent and context-dependent information in concepts. *Memory & Cognition, 10*(1), 82–93.

Bower, G.H. (1970). Analysis of a mnemonic device: Modern psychology uncovers the powerful components of an ancient system for improving memory. *American Scientist, 58*(5), 496–510.

Bowers, J.S. (2009). On the biological plausibility of grandmother cells: Implications for neural network theories in psychology and neuroscience. *Psychological Review, 116*(1), 220.

Bransford, J.D. & Johnson, M.K. (1972). Contextual prerequisites for understanding: Some investigations of comprehension and recall. *Journal of Verbal Learning and Verbal Behavior, 11*(6), 717–26.

Butters, N. & Cermak, L.S. (1980). *Alcoholic Korsakoff's syndrome: An information-processing approach to amnesia.* Academic Press.

Caramazza, A. & Shelton, J.R. (1998). Domain-specific knowledge systems in the brain: The animate-inanimate distinction. *Journal of Cognitive Neuroscience, 10*(1), 1–34.

Carey, S. (1988). Conceptual differences between children and adults. *Mind & Language, 3*(3), 167–81.

Chiou, R. & Rich, A.N. (2014). The role of conceptual knowledge in understanding synesthesia: Evaluating contemporary findings from a "hub-and-spokes" perspective. *Frontiers in Psychology, 5*, 8. doi: 10.3389/fpsyg.2014.00105

Collins, A.M. & Loftus, E.F. (1975). A spreading-activation theory of semantic processing. *Psychological Review, 82*(6), 407.

Collins, A.M. & Quillian, M.R. (1969). Retrieval time from semantic memory. *Journal of Verbal Learning and Verbal Behavior, 8*(2), 240–7.

Conrad, C. (1972). Cognitive economy in semantic memory. *Journal of Experimental Psychology, 92*(2), 149–54.

Cosentino, S., Chute, D., Libon, D., Moore, P., & Grossman, M. (2006). How does the brain support script comprehension? A study of executive processes and semantic knowledge in dementia. *Neuropsychology, 20*(3), 307.

Cotelli, M., Manenti, R., Cappa, S.F., Geroldi, C., Zanetti, O., Rossini, P.M., & Miniussi, C. (2006). Effect of transcranial magnetic stimulation on action naming in patients with Alzheimer disease. *Archives of Neurology, 63*(11), 1602–4.

Dagenbach, D., Horst, S., & Carr, T.H. (1990). Adding new information to semantic memory: How much learning is enough to produce automatic priming? *Journal of Experimental Psychology: Learning, Memory, and Cognition, 16*(4), 581.

Daniele, A., Giustolisi, L., Silveri, M.C., Colosimo, C., & Gainotti, G. (1994). Evidence for a possible neuroanatomical basis for lexical processing of nouns and verbs. *Neuropsychologia, 32*(11), 1325–41.

Farah, M.J. & McClelland, J.L. (1991). A computational model of semantic memory impairment: Modality specificity and emergent category specificity. *Journal of Experimental Psychology: General, 120*(4), 339.

Funnell, E. (1996). Response biases in oral reading: An account of the co-occurrence of surface dyslexia and semantic dementia. *The Quarterly Journal of Experimental Psychology: Section A, 49*(2), 417–46.

Gainotti, G. (2004). A metanalysis of impaired and spared naming for different categories of knowledge in patients with a visuo-verbal disconnection. *Neuropsychologia, 42*(3), 299–319.

Gainotti, G., Silveri, M.C., Daniele, A., & Giustolisi, L. (1995). Neuroanatomical correlates of category-specific semantic disorders: A critical survey. *Memory, 3*(3–4), 247–63.

Gelman, S.A. & Markman, E.M. (1986). Categories and induction in young children. *Cognition, 23*(3), 183–209.

González, J., Barros-Loscertales, A., Pulvermüller, F., Meseguer, V., Sanjuán, A., Belloch, V., & Ávila, C. (2006). Reading cinnamon activates olfactory brain regions. *Neuroimage, 32*(2), 906–12.

Hart, J. & Gordon, B. (1992). Neural subsystems for object knowledge. *Nature, 359*(6390), 60–4.

Hauk, O., Johnsrude, I., & Pulvermüller, F. (2004). Somatotopic representation of action words in human motor and premotor cortex. *Neuron, 41*(2), 301–7.

Hoenig, K., Sim, E.J., Bochev, V., Herrnberger, B., & Kiefer, M. (2008). Conceptual flexibility in the human brain: dynamic recruitment of semantic maps from visual, motor, and motion-related areas. *Journal of Cognitive Neuroscience, 20*(10), 1799–814.

Joordens, S. & Becker, S. (1997). The long and short of semantic priming effects in lexical decision. *Journal of Experimental Psychology: Learning, Memory, and Cognition, 23*(5), 1083.

Keil, F.C. & Kelly, M.H. (1987). Developmental changes in category structure. In S. Harnad (Ed.), *Categorical perception: The groundwork of cognition* (pp. 491–510). Cambridge University Press.

Kiefer, M. (2005). Repetition-priming modulates category-related effects on event-related potentials: further evidence for multiple cortical semantic systems. *Journal of Cognitive Neuroscience, 17*(2), 199–211.

Kiefer, M. & Barsalou, L.W. (2013). Grounding the human conceptual system in perception, action, and internal states. *Action science: Foundations of an emerging discipline*, 381–401.

Kiefer, M. & Pulvermüller, F. (2012). Conceptual representations in mind and brain: Theoretical developments, current evidence and future directions. *Cortex*, 48(7), 805–25.

Kiefer, M., Sim, E. J., Liebich, S., Hauk, O., & Tanaka, J. (2007). Experience-dependent plasticity of conceptual representations in human sensory-motor areas. *Journal of Cognitive Neuroscience*, 19(3), 525–42.

Lakoff, G. (1987). *Women, Fire, and Dangerous Things What categories reveal about the mind*. Chicago, IL: University of Chicago Press.

Lashley, K.S. (1929). *Brain mechanisms and intelligence: A quantitative study of injuries to the brain*. Chicago, IL: University of Chicago Press.

Lashley, K.S. (1958). Cerebral organization and behavior. *Research Publications of the Association for Research in Nervous & Mental Disease*, 36, 1–4 and 14–18.

Manns, J.R., Hopkins, R.O., & Squire, L.R. (2003). Semantic memory and the human hippocampus. *Neuron*, 38(1), 127–33.

Markman, E.M. (1987). How children constrain the possible meanings of words. In U. Neisser (Ed.), *Emory symposia in cognition, 1. Concepts and conceptual development: Ecological and intellectual factors in categorization* (pp. 255–87). New York, NY: Cambridge University Press.

Massey, C.M. & Gelman, R. (1988). Preschooler's ability to decide whether a photographed unfamiliar object can move itself. *Developmental Psychology*, 24(3), 307.

McClelland, J.L. & Rogers, T.T. (2003). The parallel distributed processing approach to semantic cognition. *Nature Reviews Neuroscience*, 4(4), 310–22.

McClelland, J.L., McNaughton, B.L., & O'Reilly, R.C. (1995). Why there are complementary learning systems in the hippocampus and neocortex: Insights from the successes and failures of connectionist models of learning and memory. *Psychological Review*, 102(3), 419.

McNamara, T.P. (1992). Theories of priming: I. Associative distance and lag. *Journal of Experimental Psychology: Learning, Memory, and Cognition*, 18(6), 1173.

Medin, D.L. (1989). Concepts and conceptual structure. *American Psychologist*, 44(12), 1469.

Medin, D.L. & Shoben, E.J. (1988). Context and structure in conceptual combination. *Cognitive Psychology*, 20(2), 158–90.

Murphy, G.L. & Medin, D.L. (1985). The role of theories in conceptual coherence. *Psychological Review*, 92(3), 289.

Neely, J.H. (1977). Semantic priming and retrieval from lexical memory: Roles of inhibitionless spreading activation and limited-capacity attention. *Journal of Experimental Psychology: General*, 106(3), 226.

Oden, G.C. (1987). Concept, knowledge, and thought. *Annual Review of Psychology*, 38(1), 203–27.

Patterson, K., Nestor, P.J., & Rogers, T.T. (2007). Where do you know what you know? The representation of semantic knowledge in the human brain. *Nature Reviews Neuroscience*, 8(12), 976–87.

Pexman, P.M., Hargreaves, I.S., Edwards, J.D., Henry, L.C., & Goodyear, B.G. (2007). Neural correlates of concreteness in semantic categorization. *Journal of Cognitive Neuroscience*, 19(8), 1407–19.

Pobric, G., Jefferies, E., & Ralph, M.A.L. (2010). Category-specific versus category-general semantic impairment induced by transcranial magnetic stimulation. *Current Biology*, 20(10), 964–8.

Posner, M.I. & Keele, S.W. (1968). On the genesis of abstract ideas. *Journal of Experimental Psychology*, 77(3p1), 353.

Quiroga, R.Q., Reddy, L., Kreiman, G., Koch, C., & Fried, I. (2005). Invariant visual representation by single neurons in the human brain. *Nature*, 435(7045), 1102–7.

Rascovsky, K., Growdon, M.E., Pardo, I.R., Grossman, S., & Miller, B.L. (2009). "The quicksand of forgetfulness": Semantic dementia in *One Hundred Years of Solitude*. *Brain*, 132(9), 2609–16.

Ratcliff, R. & McKoon, G. (1988). A retrieval theory of priming in memory. *Psychological Review*, 95(3), 385.

Rips, L.J., Shoben, E.J., & Smith, E.E. (1973). Semantic distance and the verification of semantic relations. *Journal of Verbal Learning and Verbal Behavior*, 12(1), 1–20.

Rogers, T.T., Lambon Ralph, M.A., Garrard, P., Bozeat, S., McClelland, J.L., Hodges, J.R., & Patterson, K. (2004). Structure and deterioration of semantic memory: A neuropsychological and computational investigation. *Psychological Review*, 111(1), 205.

Rosch, E.H. (1973). On the internal structure of perceptual and semantic categories. In T.E. Moore (Ed.), *Cognitive development and the acquisition of language*. Oxford, England: Academic Press.

Rosch, E. (1975). Cognitive reference points. *Cognitive Psychology*, 7(4), 532–47.

Rosch, E., Mervis, C.B., Gray, W.D., Johnson, D.M., & Boyes-Braem, P. (1976). Basic objects in natural categories. *Cognitive Psychology*, 8(3), 382–439.

Sánchez-Casas, R., Ferré, P., García-Albea, J., & Guasch, M. (2006). The nature of semantic priming: Effects of the degree of semantic similarity between primes and targets in Spanish. *European Journal of Cognitive Psychology*, 18(2), 161–84.

Schank, R.C., Collins, G.C., & Hunter, L.E. (1986). Transcending inductive category formation in learning. *Behavioral and Brain Sciences*, 9(04), 639–51.

Sirigu, A., Zalla, T., Pillon, B., Grafman, J., Agid, Y., & Dubois, B. (1995). Selective impairments in managerial knowledge following pre-frontal cortex damage. *Cortex*, 31(2), 301–16.

Staniloiu, A. & Markowitsch, H. (2012). Towards solving the riddle of forgetting in functional amnesia: Recent advances and current opinions. *Frontiers in Psychology*, 3, 1664–78.

Surprenant, A.M. & Neath, I. (2013). *Principles of memory*. Psychology Press.

Tanaka, J.W. & Taylor, M. (1991). Object categories and expertise: Is the basic level in the eye of the beholder? *Cognitive Psychology, 23*(3), 457–82.

Tranel, D., Damasio, H., & Damasio, A.R. (1997). A neural basis for the retrieval of conceptual knowledge. *Neuropsychologia, 35*(10), 1319–27.

Tranel, D., Kemmerer, D., Adolphs, R., Damasio, H., & Damasio, A.R. (2003). Neural correlates of conceptual knowledge for actions. *Cognitive Neuropsychology, 20*(3–6), 409–32.

Wagner, A.D., Paré-Blagoev, E.J., Clark, J., & Poldrack, R.A. (2001). Recovering meaning: Left prefrontal cortex guides controlled semantic retrieval. *Neuron, 31*(2), 329–38.

Warrington, E.K. & McCarthy, R. (1983). Category specific access dysphasia. *Brain, 106*(4), 859–78.

Warrington, E.K. & McCarthy, R.A. (1987). Categories of knowledge: Further fractionations and an attempted integration. *Brain, 110*(5), 1273–96.

Warrington, E.K. & Shallice, T. (1984). Category specific semantic impairments. *Brain, 107*(3), 829–53.

Wilson-Mendenhall, C.D., Barrett, L.F., Simmons, W.K., & Barsalou, L.W. (2011). Grounding emotion in situated conceptualization. *Neuropsychologia, 49*(5), 1105–27.

Wittgenstein, L. (1953). *Philosophical investigations. Philosophische Untersuchungen.* Oxford, England: Macmillan.

Chapter 8

Abernethy, E.M. (1940). The effect of changed environmental conditions upon the results of college examinations. *The Journal of Psychology, 10*(2), 293–301.

Acsády, L., Kamondi, A., Sík, A., Freund, T., & Buzsáki, G. (1998). GABAergic cells are the major postsynaptic targets of mossy fibers in the rat hippocampus. *The Journal of Neuroscience, 18*(9), 3386–403.

Altman, J. & Das, G.D. (1965). Autoradiographic and histological evidence of postnatal hippocampal neurogenesis in rats. *Journal of Comparative Neurology, 124*(3), 319–35.

Anderson, M.C. & Green, C. (2001). Suppressing unwanted memories by executive control. *Nature, 410*(6826), 366.

Anderson, M.C. & Hanslmayr, S. (2014). Neural mechanisms of motivated forgetting. *Trends in Cognitive Sciences, 18*(6), 279–92.

Anderson, M.C. & Spellman, B.A. (1995). On the status of inhibitory mechanisms in cognition: Memory retrieval as a model case. *Psychological Review, 102*(1), 68.

Anderson, M.C., Bjork, R.A., & Bjork, E.L. (1994). Remembering can cause forgetting: Retrieval dynamics in long-term memory. *Journal of Experimental Psychology: Learning, Memory, and Cognition, 20*(5), 1063.

Anderson, M.C., Ochsner, K.N., Kuhl, B., Cooper, J., Robertson, E., Gabrieli, S.W., ... & Gabrieli, J.D. (2004). Neural systems underlying the suppression of unwanted memories. *Science, 303*(5655), 232–5.

Badre, D. & Wagner, A.D. (2007). Left ventrolateral prefrontal cortex and the cognitive control of memory. *Neuropsychologia, 45*(13), 2883–901.

Basden, B.H. & Basden, D.R. (1996). Directed forgetting: Further comparisons of the item and list methods. *Memory, 4*(6), 633–54.

Basden, B.H., Basden, D.R., & Gargano, G.J. (1993). Directed forgetting in implicit and explicit memory tests: A comparison of methods. *Journal of Experimental Psychology: Learning, Memory, and Cognition, 19*(3), 603.

Bäuml, K.H., Hanslmayr, S., Pastötter, B., & Klimesch, W. (2008). Oscillatory correlates of intentional updating in episodic memory. *NeuroImage, 41*(2), 596–604.

Benoit, R.G. & Anderson, M.C. (2012). Opposing mechanisms support the voluntary forgetting of unwanted memories. *Neuron, 76*(2), 450–60.

Bjork, E.L., Bjork, R.A., & Anderson, M.C. (1998). Varieties of goal-directed forgetting. In J.M. Golding & C.M. MacLeod (Eds.) *Intentional forgetting: Interdisciplinary approaches* (pp. 103–37). Mahwah, NJ: Lawrence Erlbaum Associates Publishers..

Brun, V.H., Ytterbø, K., Morris, R.G., Moser, M.B., & Moser, E.I. (2001). Retrograde amnesia for spatial memory induced by NMDA receptor-mediated long-term potentiation. *The Journal of Neuroscience, 21*(1), 356–62.

Cameron, H.A. & McKay, R.D. (2001). Adult neurogenesis produces a large pool of new granule cells in the dentate gyrus. *Journal of Comparative Neurology, 435*(4), 406–17.

Campbell, B.A. & Campbell, E.H. (1962). Retention and extinction of learned fear in infant and adult rats. *Journal of Comparative and Physiological Psychology, 55*(1), 1.

Campbell, B.A., Misanin, J.R., White, B.C., & Lytle, L.D. (1974). Species differences in ontogeny of memory: Indirect support for neural maturation as a determinant of forgetting. *Journal of Comparative and Physiological Psychology, 87*(2), 193.

Cowan, N., Beschin, N., & Della Sala, S. (2004). Verbal recall in amnesiacs under conditions of diminished retroactive interference. *Brain, 127*(4), 825–34.

Deng, W., Aimone, J.B., & Gage, F.H. (2010). New neurons and new memories: How does adult hippocampal neurogenesis affect learning and memory? *Nature Reviews Neuroscience, 11*(5), 339–50.

Dewar, M., Garcia, Y.F., Cowan, N., & Della Sala, S. (2009). Delaying interference enhances memory consolidation in amnesic patients. *Neuropsychology, 23*(5), 627.

Ebbinghaus, H. (1885). *Über das gedächtnis: Untersuchungen zur experimentellen psychologie.* Books on Demand.

Foster, N.L. & Sahakyan, L. (2011). The role of forget-cue salience in list-method directed forgetting. *Memory, 19*(1), 110–17.

Frankland, P.W., Köhler, S., & Josselyn, S.A. (2013). Hippocampal neurogenesis and forgetting. *Trends in Neurosciences, 36*(9), 497–503.

Geiselman, R.E. (1974). Positive forgetting of sentence material. *Memory & Cognition, 2*(4), 677–82.

Hardt, O., Nader, K., & Nadel, L. (2013). Decay happens: The role of active forgetting in memory. *Trends in Cognitive Sciences, 17*(3), 111–20.

Harley, K. & Reese, E. (1999). Origins of autobiographical memory. *Developmental Psychology, 35*(5), 1338.

Hebb, D.O. (1949). *The organization of behavior: A neuropsychological approach.* John Wiley & Sons.

Hockley, W.E. (1992). Item versus associative information: Further comparisons of forgetting rates. *Journal of Experimental Psychology: Learning, Memory, and Cognition, 18*(6), 1321.

Hupbach, A., Gomez, R., Hardt, O., & Nadel, L. (2007). Reconsolidation of episodic memories: A subtle reminder triggers integration of new information. *Learning & Memory, 14*(1–2), 47–53.

Huttenlocher, P.R. & Dabholkar, A.S. (1997). Regional differences in synaptogenesis in human cerebral cortex. *Journal of Comparative Neurology, 387*(2), 167–78.

Inokuchi, K. (2011). Adult neurogenesis and modulation of neural circuit function. *Current Opinion in Neurobiology, 21*(2), 360–4.

Jabès, A. & Nelson, C.A. (2015). 20 years after "The ontogeny of human memory: A cognitive neuroscience perspective," where are we? *International Journal of Behavioral Development,* doi: 0165025415575766.

Jenkins, J.G. & Dallenbach, K.M. (1924). Obliviscence during sleep and waking. *The American Journal of Psychology, 35*(4), 605–12.

Johnson, S.K. & Anderson, M.C. (2004). The role of inhibitory control in forgetting semantic knowledge. *Psychological Science, 15*(7), 448–53.

Jonker, T.R., Seli, P., & MacLeod, C.M. (2013). Putting retrieval-induced forgetting in context: An inhibition-free, context-based account. *Psychological Review, 120*(4), 852.

Joslyn, S.L. & Oakes, M.A. (2005). Directed forgetting of autobiographical events. *Memory & Cognition, 33*(4), 577–87.

Josselyn, S.A. & Frankland, P.W. (2012). Infantile amnesia: A neurogenic hypothesis. *Learning & Memory, 19*(9), 423–33.

Jost, A. (1897). *Die assoziationsfestigkeit in ihrer abhängigkeit von der verteilung der wiederholungen.* Leopold Voss.

Kikuchi, H., Fujii, T., Abe, N., Suzuki, M., Takagi, M., Mugikura, S., . . . & Mori, E. (2010). Memory repression: Brain mechanisms underlying dissociative amnesia. *Journal of Cognitive Neuroscience, 22*(3), 602–13.

Kitamura, T., Saitoh, Y., Takashima, N., Murayama, A., Niibori, Y., Ageta, H., . . . & Inokuchi, K. (2009). Adult neurogenesis modulates the hippocampus-dependent period of associative fear memory. *Cell, 139*(4), 814–27.

Knoth, R., Singec, I., Ditter, M., Pantazis, G., Capetian, P., Meyer, R.P., . . . & Kempermann, G. (2010). Murine features of neurogenesis in the human hippocampus across the lifespan from 0 to 100 years. *PloS One, 5*(1), e8809.

Ko, H.G., Jang, D.J., Son, J., Kwak, C., Choi, J.H., Ji, Y.H., Lee, Y.S., Son, H., & Kaang, B.K. (2009). Effect of ablated hippocampal neurogenesis on the formation and extinction of contextual fear memory. *Molecular Brain, 2*(1), 1.

Kolb, B. & Whishaw, I.Q. (2009). *Fundamentals of human neuropsychology.* Macmillan.

Kuhl, P. & Rivera-Gaxiola, M. (2008). Neural substrates of language acquisition. *Annual Review of Neuroscience, 31*, 511–34.

Lambert, A.J., Good, K.S., & Kirk, I.J. (2010). Testing the repression hypothesis: Effects of emotional valence on memory suppression in the think-no think task. *Consciousness and Cognition, 19*(1), 281–93.

Levy, B.J. & Anderson, M.C. (2002). Inhibitory processes and the control of memory retrieval. *Trends in Cognitive Sciences, 6*(7), 299–305.

Luria, A.R. & Solotaroff, L.T. (1987). *The mind of a mnemonist: A little book about a vast memory.* Harvard University Press.

McGeoch, J.A. (1932). The influence of degree of interpolated learning upon retroactive inhibition. *The American Journal of Psychology, 44*(4), 695–708.

Mecacci, L. (2103). Solomon V. Shereshevsky: The great Russian mnemonist. *Cortex 49*(8), 2260–3.

Meeter, M., Murre, J.M.J., & Janssen, S.M.J. (2005). Remembering the news: Modeling retention data from a study with 14,000 participants. *Memory & Cognition, 33*(5), 793–810.

Meltzer, L.A., Yabaluri, R., & Deisseroth, K. (2005). A role for circuit homeostasis in adult neurogenesis. *Trends in Neurosciences, 28*(12), 653–60.

Migues, P.V., Hardt, O., Wu, D.C., Gamache, K., Sacktor, T.C., Wang, Y.T., & Nader, K. (2010). PKM [zeta] maintains memories by regulating GluR2-dependent AMPA receptor trafficking. *Nature Neuroscience, 13*(5), 630-4.

Minami, H. & Dallenbach, K.M. (1946). The effect of activity upon learning and retention in the cockroach, Periplaneta americana. *The American Journal of Psychology, 59*(1), 1–58.

Müller, G.E. & Pilzecker, A. (1900). *Experimentelle beiträge zur lehre vom gedächtniss* (Vol. 1). JA Barth.

Nelson, K. (1993). The psychological and social origins of autobiographical memory. *Psychological science, 4*(1), 7–14.

Niibori, Y., Yu, T.S., Epp, J.R., Akers, K.G., Josselyn, S.A., & Frankland, P.W. (2012). Suppression of adult neurogenesis impairs population coding of similar contexts in hippocampal CA3 region. *Nature Communications, 3*, 1253.

Osten, P., Valsamis, L., Harris, A., & Sacktor, T.C. (1996). Protein synthesis-dependent formation of protein kinase Mzeta in long-term potentiation. *The Journal of Neuroscience, 16*(8), 2444–51.

Parker, E.S., Cahill, L., & McGaugh, J.L. (2006). A case of unusual autobiographical remembering. *Neurocase, 12*(1), 35–49.

Peterson, C. (2002). Children's long-term memory for autobiographical events. *Developmental Review, 22*(3), 370–402.

Rizio, A.A. & Dennis, N.A. (2013). The neural correlates of cognitive control: Successful remembering and intentional forgetting. *Journal of Cognitive Neuroscience, 25*(2), 297–312.

Rogers, T.B., Kuiper, N.A., & Kirker, W.S. (1977). Self-reference and the encoding of personal information. *Journal of Personality and Social Psychology, 35*(9), 677.

Rovee-Collier, C. & Cuevas, K. (2009). Multiple memory systems are unnecessary to account for infant memory development: An ecological model. *Developmental Psychology, 45*(1), 160.

Rubin, D.C. (1982). On the retention function for autobiographical memory. *Journal of Verbal Learning and Verbal Behavior, 21*(1), 21–38.

Rubin, D.C. (2002). Autobiographical memory across the lifespan. In P. Graf & N. Ohta (Eds.), *Lifespan development of human memory* (pp. 159–84). Cambridge, MA: The MIT Press.

Rubin, D.C. & Schulkind, M.D. (1997). Distribution of important and word-cued autobiographical memories in 20-, 35-, and 70-year-old adults. *Psychology and Aging, 12*(3), 524.

Sadeh, T., Ozubko, J.D., Winocur, G., & Moscovitch, M. (2014). How we forget may depend on how we remember. *Trends in Cognitive Sciences, 18*(1), 26–36.

Sahakyan, L., Delaney, P.F., Foster, N.L., & Abushanab, B. (2013). List-method directed forgetting in cognitive and clinical research: A theoretical and methodological review. *The Psychology of Learning and Motivation, 59*, 131.

Sahay, A., Scobie, K.N., Hill, A.S., O'Carroll, C.M., Kheirbek, M.A., Burghardt, N.S., . . . & Hen, R. (2011). Increasing adult hippocampal neurogenesis is sufficient to improve pattern separation. *Nature, 472*(7344), 466–70.

Saunders, J.O. & MacLeod, M.D. (2006). Can inhibition resolve retrieval competition through the control of spreading activation? *Memory & Cognition, 34*(2), 307–22.

Schacter, D.L. (2002). *The seven sins of memory: How the mind forgets and remembers.* Houghton Mifflin Harcourt.

Seki, T. & Arai, Y. (1993). Highly polysialylated neural cell adhesion molecule (NCAM-H) is expressed by newly generated granule cells in the dentate gyrus of the adult rat. *The Journal of Neuroscience, 13*(6), 2351–8.

Serrano, P., Friedman, E.L., Kenney, J., Taubenfeld, S.M., Zimmerman, J.M., Hanna, J., Alberini, C, Kelley, A., Maren, S., Rudy, J., Yin, J. C., Sacktor, T., & Fenton, A. (2008). PKMζ maintains spatial, instrumental, and classically conditioned long-term memories. *PLoS Biology, 6*(12), e318.

Shors, T.J., Miesegaes, G., Beylin, A., Zhao, M., Rydel, T., & Gould, E. (2001). Neurogenesis in the adult is involved in the formation of trace memories. *Nature, 410*, 372–6.

Sierra, A., Encinas, J.M., & Maletic-Savatic, M. (2011). Adult human neurogenesis: From microscopy to magnetic resonance imaging. *Frontiers in Neuroscience, 5*, 47.

Simcock, G. & Hayne, H. (2002). Breaking the barrier? Children fail to translate their preverbal memories into language. *Psychological Science, 13*(3), 225–31.

Simon, E. (1979). Depth and elaboration of processing in relation to age. *Journal of Experimental Psychology: Human Learning & Memory, 5*(2), 115–24.

Storm, B.C. & Nestojko, J.F. (2010). Successful inhibition, unsuccessful retrieval: Manipulating time and success during retrieval practice. *Memory, 18*(2), 99–114.

Thorndike, E.L. (1913). *The psychology of learning* (Vol. 2). Teachers College, Columbia University.

Tulving, E. (1974). Cue-dependent forgetting: When we forget something we once knew, it does not necessarily mean that the memory trace has been lost; it may only be inaccessible. *American Scientist, 62*(1), 74–82.

Villarreal, D.M., Do, V., Haddad, E., & Derrick, B.E. (2002). NMDA receptor antagonists sustain LTP and spatial memory: Active processes mediate LTP decay. *Nature Neuroscience, 5*(1), 48–52.

Wetzler, S. E. & Sweeney, J. A. (1986). Childhood amnesia: An empirical demonstration. In D. C. Rubin (Ed.), *Autobiographical memory* (pp. 191–201). New York, NY: Cambridge University Press.

Winocur, G. & Moscovitch, M. (2011). Memory transformation and systems consolidation. *Journal of the International Neuropsychological Society, 17*(05), 766–80.

Wixted, J.T. (2005). A theory about why we forget what we once knew. *Current Directions in Psychological Science, 14*(1), 6-9.

Chapter 9

Anderson, N.D. & Craik, F.I. (2000). Memory in the aging brain. In E. Tulving & F. Craik (Eds.), *The Oxford handbook of memory* (pp. 411–25). New York, NY: Oxford University Press.

Antonini, A., Leenders, K.L., Meier, D., Oertel, W.H., Boesiger, P., & Anliker, M. (1993). T2 relaxation time in patients with Parkinson's disease. *Neurology, 43*(4), 697.

Bäckman, L., Almkvist, O., Andersson, J., Nordberg, A., Winblad, B., Reineck, R., & Långström, B. (1997). Brain activation in young and older adults during implicit and explicit retrieval. *Journal of Cognitive Neuroscience, 9*(3), 378–91.

Bäckman, L., Ginovart, N., Dixon, R.A., Wahlin, T.B.R., Wahlin, Å., Halldin, C., & Farde, L. (2000). Age-related cognitive deficits mediated by changes in the striatal dopamine system. *American Journal of Psychiatry, 157*(4), 635–7.

Baddeley, A. (2012). Working memory: Theories, models, and controversies. *Annual Review of Psychology, 63*, 1–29.

Bahrick, L.E. & Pickens, J.N. (1995). Infant memory for object motion across a period of three months: Implications for a four-phase attention function. *Journal of Experimental Child Psychology, 59*(3), 343–71.

Barr, R., Marrott, H., & Rovee-Collier, C. (2003). The role of sensory preconditioning in memory retrieval by preverbal infants. *Animal Learning & Behavior, 31*(2), 111–23.

Barr, R., Vieira, A., & Rovee-Collier, C. (2001). Mediated imitation in 6-month-olds: Remembering by association. *Journal of Experimental Child Psychology, 79*(3), 229–52.

Barr, R., Vieira, A., & Rovee-Collier, C. (2002). Bidirectional priming in infants. *Memory & Cognition, 30*(2), 246–55.

Bauer, P.J. (2008). Toward a neuro-developmental account of the development of declarative memory. *Developmental Psychobiology, 50*(1), 19–31.

Bauer, P.J. (2009). Learning and memory: Like a horse and carriage. In A. Woodward & A. Needham (Eds.), *Learning and the infant mind* (pp. 3–28). New York, NY: Oxford University Press.

Bhatt, R.S. & Rovee-Collier, C. (1994). Perception and 24-hour retention of feature relations in infancy. *Developmental Psychology*, *30*(2), 142.

Bhatt, R.S. & Rovee-Collier, C. (1996). Infants' forgetting of correlated attributes and object recognition. *Child Development*, *67*(1), 172–87.

Boller, K. (1997). Preexposure effects on infant learning and memory. *Developmental psychobiology*, *31*(2), 93–105.

Brown, R.G. & Marsden, C.D. (1990). Cognitive function in Parkinson's disease: From description to theory. *Trends in Neurosciences*, *13*(1), 21–9.

Brown, T.T., Kuperman, J.M., Chung, Y., Erhart, M., McCabe, C., Hagler, D.J., Jr., et al. (2012). Neuroanatomical assessment of biological maturity. *Current Biology*, 22, 1693–8.

Burzynska, A.Z., Nagel, I.E., Preuschhof, C., Li, S.C., Lindenberger, U., Bäckman, L., & Heekeren, H.R. (2011). Microstructure of frontoparietal connections predicts cortical responsivity and working memory performance. *Cerebral Cortex*, *21*(10), 2261–71.

Butler, J. & Rovee-Collier, C. (1989). Contextual gating of memory retrieval. *Developmental Psychobiology*, *22*(6), 533–52.

Cabeza, R. (2002). Hemispheric asymmetry reduction in older adults: The HAROLD model. *Psychology and Aging*, *17*(1), 85.

Cabeza, R. & Nyberg, L. (2000). Imaging cognition II: An empirical review of 275 PET and fMRI studies. *Journal of Cognitive Neuroscience*, *12*(1), 1–47.

Cabeza, R., Daselaar, S.M., Dolcos, F., Prince, S.E., Budde, M., & Nyberg, L. (2004). Task-independent and task-specific age effects on brain activity during working memory, visual attention and episodic retrieval. *Cerebral Cortex*, *14*(4), 364–75.

Campanella, J. & Rovee-Collier, C. (2005). Latent learning and deferred imitation at 3 months. *Infancy*, *7*(3), 243–62.

Campbell, B.A. & Campbell, E.H. (1962). Retention and extinction of learned fear in infant and adult rats. *Journal of Comparative and Physiological Psychology*, *55*(1), 1.

Carey, S. & Bartlett, E. (1978). Acquiring a single new word. *Proceedings of the Stanford Child Language Conference*, *15*, 17–29.

Carver, L.J. & Bauer, P.J. (2001). The dawning of a past: The emergence of long-term explicit memory in infancy. *Journal of Experimental Psychology: General*, *130*(4), 726.

Charles, S.T., Mather, M., & Carstensen, L.L. (2003). Aging and emotional memory: The forgettable nature of negative images for older adults. *Journal of Experimental Psychology: General*, *132*(2), 310.

Chen, W.J., Lariviere, N.A., Heyser, C.J., Spear, L.P., & Spear, N.E. (1991). Age-related differences in sensory conditioning in rats. *Developmental Psychobiology*, *24*(5), 307–26.

Cheslock, S.J., Varlinskaya, E.I., High, J.M., & Spear, N.E. (2003). Higher-order conditioning in the newborn rat: Effects of temporal disparity imply infantile encoding of simultaneous events. *Infancy*, *4*(2), 157–76.

Cockburn, J. & Smith, P.T. (1988). Effects of age and intelligence on everyday memory tasks. *Practical aspects of memory: Current research and issues*, *2*, 132–6.

Cockburn, J. & Smith, P.T. (1991). The relative influence of intelligence and age on everyday memory. *Journal of Gerontology*, *46*(1), P31–6.

Conklin, H.M., Luciana, M., Hooper, C.J., & Yarger, R.S. (2007). Working memory performance in typically developing children and adolescents: Behavioral evidence of protracted frontal lobe development. *Developmental Neuropsychology*, *31*(1), 103–28.

Cowan, N., Day, L., Saults, J.S., Keller, T.A., Johnson, T., & Flores, L. (1992). The role of verbal output time in the effects of word length on immediate memory. *Journal of memory and language*, *31*(1), 1–17.

Craik, F.I. (1985). Paradigms in human memory research. In L.-G. Nilsson & T. Archer (Eds.), *Series in comparative cognition and neuroscience. Perspectives on learning and memory* (pp. 197–221). Hillsdale, NJ: Lawrence Erlbaum Associates, Inc.

Craik, F.I. (1986). A functional account of age differences in memory. In F. Klix & H. Hagendorf (Eds.), *Human memory and cognitive capabilities: Mechanisms and performances* (pp. 409–22). North Holland: Elsevier Science Publishers.

Craik, F.I., Byrd, M., & Swanson, J.M. (1987). Patterns of memory loss in three elderly samples. *Psychology and Aging*, *2*(1), 79–86.

Craik, F.I. & McDowd, J.M. (1987). Age differences in recall and recognition. *Journal of Experimental Psychology: Learning, Memory, and Cognition*, *13*(3), 474.

Crone, E.A., Wendelken, C., Donohue, S., van Leijenhorst, L., & Bunge, S.A. (2006). Neurocognitive development of the ability to manipulate information in working memory. *Proceedings of the National Academy of Sciences*, *103*(24), 9315–20.

Cuevas, K. (2009). Transitions in the temporal parameters of sensory preconditioning during the first year of life. Dissertation. Rutgers University, New Brunswick, NJ.

Cuevas, K., Giles, A. B., & Rovee-Collier, C. (2009). Developmental shifts in sensory preconditioning: Deferred imitation, looking time, verbal and motor skills, and number of trials. Poster presented at the Biennial Meeting of the Society for Research in Child Development, Denver, CO.

Cuevas, K., Rovee-Collier, C., & Learmonth, A.E. (2006). Infants form associations between memory representations of stimuli that are absent. *Psychological Science*, *17*(6), 543–9.

Daneman, M. & Carpenter, P.A. (1980). Individual differences in working memory and reading. *Journal of Verbal Learning and Verbal Behavior*, *19*(4), 450–66.

DeCasper, A.J. & Fifer, W.P. (1980). Of human bonding: Newborns prefer their mothers' voices. *Science*, *208*(4448), 1174–6.

DeCasper, A.J. & Spence, M.J. (1986). Prenatal maternal speech influences newborns' perception of speech sounds. *Infant Behavior and Development*, *9*(2), 133–50.

DeLoache, J.S., Cassidy, D.J., & Brown, A.L. (1985). Precursors of mnemonic strategies in very young children's memory. *Child Development*, *56*(1), 125–37.

De Wall, C.D., Wilson, B.A., & Baddeley, A.D. (1994). The Extended Rivermead Behavioural Memory Test: A measure of everyday memory performance in normal adults. *Memory*, *2*(2), 149–66.

Einstein, G.O., Holland, L.J., McDaniel, M.A., & Guynn, M.J. (1992). Age-related deficits in prospective memory: The influence of task complexity. *Psychology and Aging, 7*(3), 471.

Finn, A.S., Kalra, P.B., Goetz, C., Leonard, J.A., Sheridan, M.A., & Gabrieli, J.D. (2016). Developmental dissociation between the maturation of procedural memory and declarative memory. *Journal of Experimental Child Psychology, 142*, 212–20.

Flavell, J.H., Beach, D.R., & Chinsky, J.M. (1966). Spontaneous verbal rehearsal in a memory task as a function of age. *Child Development, 37*(2), 283–99.

Fox, M.W. (1971). Overview and critique of stages and periods in canine development. *Developmental Psychobiology, 4*(1), 37–54.

Gathercole, S.E., Pickering, S.J., Ambridge, B., & Wearing, H. (2004). The structure of working memory from 4 to 15 years of age. *Developmental Psychology, 40*(2), 177.

Gerton, B.K., Brown, T.T., Meyer-Lindenberg, A., Kohn, P., Holt, J.L., Olsen, R.K., & Berman, K.F. (2004). Shared and distinct neurophysiological components of the digits forward and backward tasks as revealed by functional neuroimaging. *Neuropsychologia, 42*(13), 1781–7.

Goldkrand, J.W. & Litvack, B.L. (1991). Demonstration of fetal habituation and patterns of fetal heart rate response to vibroacoustic stimulation in normal and high-risk pregnancies. *Journal of Perinatology: Official Journal of the California Perinatal Association, 11*(1), 25–9.

Greco, C., Rovee-Collier, C., Hayne, H., Griesler, P., & Earley, L. (1986). Ontogeny of early event memory: I. Forgetting and retrieval by 2- and 3-month-olds. *Infant Behavior and Development, 9*(4), 441–60.

Green, P.C. (1962). Learning, extinction, and generalization of conditioned responses by young monkeys. *Psychological Reports, 10*, 731–8.

Hartshorn, K.L., Collamer, M., Auerbach, M., Myers, J.B., Pavlotsky, N., & Tauber, A.I. (1988). Effects of influenza A virus on human neutrophil calcium metabolism. *The Journal of Immunology, 141*(4), 1295–301.

Hartshorn, K., & Rovee-Collier, C. (1997). Infant learning and long-term memory at 6 months: A confirming analysis. *Developmental Psychobiology, 30*(1), 71–85.

Hartshorn, K., Rovee-Collier, C., Gerhardstein, P., Bhatt, R.S., Wondoloski, T.L., Klein, P., . . . & Campos-de-Carvalho, M. (1998). The ontogeny of long-term memory over the first year-and-a-half of life. *Developmental Psychobiology, 32*(2), 69–89.

Hepper, P.G. (1991). An examination of fetal learning before and after birth. *The Irish Journal of Psychology, 12*(2), 95–107.

Hepper, P.G. (1997). Memory in utero? *Developmental Medicine & Child Neurology, 39*(5), 343–6.

Herbert, J. & Hayne, H. (2000). Memory retrieval by 18–30-month-olds: Age-related changes in representational flexibility. *Developmental Psychology, 36*(4), 473.

Hill, W.L., Borovsky, D., & Rovee-Collier, C. (1988). Continuities in infant memory development. *Developmental Psychobiology: The Journal of the International Society for Developmental Psychobiology, 21*(1), 43–62.

Howard, D.V., & Howard, J.H., Jr. (1992). Adult age differences in the rate of learning serial patterns: Evidence from direct and indirect tests. *Psychology and Aging, 7*, 232–41.

Howard, D.V., Shaw, R.J., & Heisey, J.G. (1986). Aging and the time course of semantic activation. *Journal of Gerontology, 41*(2), 195–203.

Hsu, V.C., & Rovee-Collier, C. (2009). The time window construct in early memory development. *New Directions in Developmental Psychobiology,* 1–22.

Hulme, C., Thompson, N., Muir, C., & Lawrence, A. (1984). Speech rate and the development of spoken words: The role of rehearsal and item identification processes. *Journal of Experimental Child Psychology, 38*, 241–53.

Hultsch, D.F., Hertzog, C., Small, B.J., & Dixon, R.A. (1999). Use it or lose it: Engaged lifestyle as a buffer of cognitive decline in aging? *Psychology and Aging, 14*(2), 245.

Jack, F. & Hayne, H. (2007). Eliciting adults' earliest memories: Does it matter how we ask the question? *Memory, 15*(6), 647–63.

Jack, F., Simcock, G., & Hayne, H. (2012). Magic memories: Young children's verbal recall after a 6-year delay. *Child Development, 83*(1), 159–72.

Jackson, J.H. (1884). The Croonian lectures on evolution and dissolution of the nervous system. *British Medical Journal, 1*(1215), 703.

Java, R.I. & Gardiner, J.M. (1991). Priming and aging: Further evidence of preserved memory function. *The American Journal of Psychology, 104*(1) 89–100.

Johnson, M.K., De Leonardis, D.M., Hashtroudi, S., & Ferguson, S.A. (1995). Aging and single versus multiple cues in source monitoring. *Psychology and Aging, 10*(4), 507.

Kail, R. & Salthouse, T.A. (1994). Processing speed as a mental capacity. *Acta Psychologica, 86*(2–3), 199–225.

Kausler, D.H. & Puckett, J.M. (1980). Adult age differences in recognition memory for a nonsemantic attribute. *Experimental Aging Research, 6*(4), 349–55.

Kausler, D.H. & Puckett, J.M. (1981). Adult age differences in memory for sex of voice. *Journal of Gerontology, 36*(1), 44–50.

Kennedy, Q., Mather, M., & Carstensen, L.L. (2004). The role of motivation in the age-related positivity effect in autobiographical memory. *Psychological Science, 15*(3), 208–14.

Kihlstrom, J.F. & Harackiewicz, J.M. (1982). The earliest recollection: A new survey. *Journal of Personality, 50*(2), 134–48.

Klingberg, T. (2006). Development of a superior frontal–intraparietal network for visuo-spatial working memory. *Neuropsychologia, 44*(11), 2171–7.

Klingberg, T., Forssberg, H., & Westerberg, H. (2002). Increased brain activity in frontal and parietal cortex underlies the development of visuospatial working memory capacity during childhood. *Journal of Cognitive Neuroscience, 14*(1), 1–10.

Knight, B.G., Maines, M.L., & Robinson, G.S. (2002). The effects of sad mood on memory in older adults: A test of the mood congruence effect. *Psychology and Aging, 17*(4), 653.

Kwon, H., Reiss, A.L., & Menon, V. (2002). Neural basis of protracted developmental changes in visuo-spatial working memory. *Proceedings of the National Academy of Sciences, 99*(20), 13336–41.

Leader, L.R. & Baillie, P. (1991). The assessment and significance of habituation in normal and high-risk pregnancies. *Journal of Perinatology, 11*, 25–9.

Leader, L.R., Baillie, P., Martin, B., Molteno, C., & Wynchank, S. (1984). Fetal responses to vibrotactile stimulation, a possible predictor of fetal and neonatal outcome. *Australian and New Zealand Journal of Obstetrics and Gynaecology, 24*(4), 251–6.

Lenroot, R.K., Gogtay, N., Greenstein, D.K., Wells, E.M., Wallace, G.L., Clasen, L.S., . . . & Thompson, P.M. (2007). Sexual dimorphism of brain developmental trajectories during childhood and adolescence. *Neuroimage, 36*(4), 1065–73.

Light, L.L. & Singh, A. (1987). Implicit and explicit memory in young and older adults. *Journal of Experimental Psychology: Learning, Memory, and Cognition, 13*(4), 531.

Luna, B., Garver, K.E., Urban, T.A., Lazar, N.A., & Sweeney, J.A. (2004). Maturation of cognitive processes from late childhood to adulthood. *Child Development, 75*(5), 1357–72.

MacDonald, S., Uesiliana, K., & Hayne, H. (2000). Cross-cultural and gender differences in childhood amnesia. *Memory, 8*(6), 365–76.

Mather, M. & Carstensen, L.L. (2005). Aging and motivated cognition: The positivity effect in attention and memory. *Trends in Cognitive Sciences, 9*(10), 496–502.

Mather, M. & Johnson, M.K. (2000). Choice-supportive source monitoring: Do our decisions seem better to us as we age? *Psychology and Aging, 15*(4), 596.

Mather, M., Knight, M., & McCaffrey, M. (2005). The allure of the alignable: Younger and older adults' false memories of choice features. *Journal of Experimental Psychology: General, 134*(1), 38.

May, C.P., Hasher, L., & Kane, M.J. (1999). The role of interference in memory span. *Memory & Cognition, 27*(5), 759–67.

Maylor, E.A. (1993). Aging and forgetting in prospective and retrospective memory tasks. *Psychology and Aging, 8*(3), 420.

Maylor, E.A. (1996). Age-related impairment in an event-based prospective-memory task. *Psychology and Aging, 11*(1), 74.

Micco, A. & Masson, M.E. (1992). Age-related differences in the specificity of verbal encoding. *Memory & Cognition, 20*(3), 244–53.

Michalczyk, K., Malstädt, N., Worgt, M., Könen, T., & Hasselhorn, M. (2013). Age differences and measurement invariance of working memory in 5- to 12-year-old children. *European Journal of Psychological Assessment, 29*(3), 220–9.

Miller, R.R. & Berk, A.M. (1977). Retention over metamorphosis in the African claw-toed frog. *Journal of Experimental Psychology: Animal Behavior Processes, 3*(4), 343.

Moscovitch, M. (1982). A neuropsychological approach to perception and memory in normal and pathological aging. In F. Craik & S. Trehub (Eds.), *Aging and Cognitive Processes* (pp. 55–78). Boston, MA: Springer.

Nagy, Z.M. (1979). Development of learning and memory processes in infant mice. In N. E. Spear & B. A. Campbell (Eds.), *Ontogeny of Learning and Memory* (pp. 101–33). Hillsdale, NJ: Lawrence Erlbaum.

Nelson, C.A. (1995). The ontogeny of human memory: A cognitive neuroscience perspective. *Developmental Psychology, 31*(5), 723.

Olesen, P.J., Nagy, Z., Westerberg, H., & Klingberg, T. (2003). Combined analysis of DTI and fMRI data reveals a joint maturation of white and grey matter in a fronto-parietal network. *Cognitive Brain Research, 18*(1), 48–57.

Ornstein, P.A., Naus, M.J., & Liberty, C. (1975). Rehearsal and organizational processes in children's memory. *Child Development, 46*(4), 818–30.

Owen, A.M., McMillan, K.M., Laird, A.R., & Bullmore, E. (2005). N-back working memory paradigm: A meta-analysis of normative functional neuroimaging studies. *Human Brain Mapping, 25*(1), 46–59.

Park, D.C., Hertzog, C., Kidder, D.P., Morrell, R.W., & Mayhorn, C.B. (1997). Effect of age on event-based and time-based prospective memory. *Psychology and Aging, 12*(2), 314.

Parkin, A.J. & Streete, S. (1988). Implicit and explicit memory in young children and adults. *British Journal of Psychology, 79*(3), 361–9.

Parkin, A.J. & Walter, B.M. (1992). Recollective experience, normal aging, and frontal dysfunction. *Psychology and Aging, 7*(2), 290.

Parkinson, S.R., Inman, V.W., & Dannenbaum, S.E. (1985). Adult age differences in short-term forgetting. *Acta Psychologica, 60*(1), 83–101.

Perez, L.A., Peynircioğlu, Z.F., & Blaxton, T.A. (1998). Developmental differences in implicit and explicit memory performance. *Journal of Experimental Child Psychology, 70*(3), 167–85.

Peters, J.J. & Isaacson, R.L. (1963). Acquisition of active and passive responses in two breeds of chickens. *Journal of Comparative and Physiological Psychology, 56*(4), 793.

Poon, L.W. & Schaffer, G. (1982, August). *Prospective memory in young and elderly adults.* Paper presented at the annual meeting of the American Psychological Association, Washington, DC.

Raz, N. (2000). Aging of the brain and its impact on cognitive performance: Integration of structural and functional findings. In F.I.M. Craik & T.A. Salthouse (Eds.), *The handbook of aging and cognition* (pp. 1–90). Mahwah, NJ: Lawrence Erlbaum Associates Publishers.

Rendell, P.G., & Thomson, D.M. (1993). The effect of ageing on remembering to remember: An investigation of simulated medication regimens. Australian Journal on Ageing, 12(1), 11–18.

Rendell, P.G. & Thomson, D.M. (1999). Aging and prospective memory: Differences between naturalistic and laboratory tasks. *The Journals of Gerontology Series B: Psychological Sciences and Social Sciences, 54*(4), P256–69.

Reynolds, B. & Rovee-Collier, C. (2005). *Forgetting of latent associations in the second half-year of life.* Presented at Aresti Undergraduate Research Conference. Rutgers University, New Brunswick, NJ.

Richmond, J. & Nelson, C.A. (2007). Accounting for change in declarative memory: A cognitive neuroscience perspective. *Developmental Review, 27*(3), 349–73.

Rovee-Collier, C. & Giles, A. (2010). Why a neuromaturational model of memory fails: Exuberant learning in early infancy. *Behavioural Processes*, 83(2), 197–206.

Rovee-Collier, C. & Cuevas, K. (2009). Multiple memory systems are unnecessary to account for infant memory development: An ecological model. *Developmental Psychology*, 45(1), 160.

Rovee-Collier, C., Schechter, A., Shyi, G.C., & Shields, P.J. (1992). Perceptual identification of contextual attributes and infant memory retrieval. *Developmental Psychology*, 28(2), 307.

Salthouse, T.A. (1994). The aging of working memory. *Neuropsychology*, 8(4), 535.

Salthouse, T.A. & Babcock, R.L. (1991). Decomposing adult age differences in working memory. *Developmental Psychology*, 27(5), 763.

Salthouse, T.A., Kausler, D.H., & Saults, J.S. (1988). Utilization of path-analytic procedures to investigate the role of processing resources in cognitive aging. *Psychology and Aging*, 3(2), 158.

Samuel, A.G. (1978). Organizational vs retrieval factors in the development of digit span. *Journal of Experimental Child Psychology*, 26(2), 308–19.

Schacter, D.L. & Moscovitch, M. (1984). Infants, amnesics, and dissociable memory systems. In M. Moscovitch (Ed.), *Infant memory* (pp. 173–216). Boston, MA: Springer.

Scherf, K.S., Sweeney, J.A., & Luna, B. (2006). Brain basis of developmental change in visuospatial working memory. *Journal of Cognitive Neuroscience*, 18(7), 1045–58.

Schleepen, T.M. & Jonkman, L.M. (2012). Children's use of semantic organizational strategies is mediated by working memory capacity. *Cognitive Development*, 27(3), 255–69.

Schneider, W., Knopf, M., & Stefanek, J. (2002). The development of verbal memory in childhood and adolescence: Findings from the Munich Longitudinal Study. *Journal of Educational Psychology*, 94(4), 751.

Simcock, G. & Hayne, H. (2002). Breaking the barrier? Children fail to translate their preverbal memories into language. *Psychological Science*, 13(3), 225–31.

Simcock, G. & Hayne, H. (2003). Age-related changes in verbal and nonverbal memory during early childhood. *Developmental Psychology*, 39(5), 805.

Simon, E. (1979). Depth and elaboration of processing in relation to age. *Journal of Experimental Psychology: Human Learning & Memory*, 5(2), 115–24.

Snitz, B.E., O'Meara, E.S., Carlson, M.C., Arnold, A.M., Ives, D.G., Rapp, S.R., . . . & DeKosky, S.T. (2009). Ginkgo biloba for preventing cognitive decline in older adults: A randomized trial. *JAMA*, 302(24), 2663–70.

Spinnler, H., Della Sala, S., Bandera, R., & Baddeley, A. (1988). Dementia, ageing, and the structure of human memory. *Cognitive Neuropsychology*, 5(2), 193–211.

Swain, I.U., Zelazo, P.R., & Clifton, R.K. (1993). Newborn infants' memory for speech sounds retained over 24 hours. *Developmental Psychology*, 29(2), 312.

Tamnes, C.K., Walhovd, K.B., Grydeland, H., Holland, D., Østby, Y., Dale, A.M., & Fjell, A.M. (2013). Longitudinal working memory development is related to structural maturation of frontal and parietal cortices. *Journal of Cognitive Neuroscience*, 25(10), 1611–23.

Tiemeier, H., Lenroot, R.K., Greenstein, D.K., Tran, L., Pierson, R., & Giedd, J.N. (2010). Cerebellum development during childhood and adolescence: A longitudinal morphometric MRI study. *Neuroimage*, 49(1), 63–70.

Tustin, K. & Hayne, H. (2010). Defining the boundary: Age-related changes in childhood amnesia. *Developmental Psychology*, 46(5), 1049.

Van Soelen, I.L.C., Brouwer, R.M., van Baal, G.C.M., Schnack, H.G., Peper, J.S., Collins, D.L., . . . & Pol, H.H. (2012). Genetic influences on thinning of the cerebral cortex during development. *Neuroimage*, 59(4), 3871–80.

Vellas, B., Coley, N., Ousset, P.J., Berrut, G., Dartigues, J.F., Dubois, B., . . . & Touchon, J. (2012). Long-term use of standardised Ginkgo biloba extract for the prevention of Alzheimer's disease (GuidAge): A randomised placebo-controlled trial. *The Lancet Neurology*, 11(10), 851–9.

Verhaeghen, P., Marcoen, A., & Goossens, L. (1993). Facts and fiction about memory aging: A quantitative integration of research findings. *Journal of Gerontology*, 48(4), P157–71.

Wager, T.D. & Smith, E.E. (2003). Neuroimaging studies of working memory. *Cognitive, Affective, & Behavioral Neuroscience*, 3(4), 255–74.

Willingham, D.B. & Winter, E. (1995). Comparison of motor skill learning in elderly and young human subjects. In *Society for Neuroscience Abstracts* (Vol. 21, p. 1440). Washington, DC: Society for Neuroscience.

Vander Linde, E., Morrongiello, B.A., & Rovee-Collier, C. (1985). Determinants of retention in 8-week-old infants. *Developmental Psychology*, 21(4), 601.

Chapter 10

Asch, S.E. (1956). Studies of independence and conformity: I. A minority of one against a unanimous majority. *Psychological Monographs: General and Applied*, 70(9), 1.

Baron, R.S., Vandello, J.A., & Brunsman, B. (1996). The forgotten variable in conformity research: Impact of task importance on social influence. *Journal of Personality and Social Psychology*, 71(5), 915.

Bartlett, F.C. (1932). *Remembering: A study in experimental and social psychology*. Cambridge, England; Cambridge University Press.

Basden, B.H., Basden, D.R., Bryner, S., & Thomas III, R.L. (1997). A comparison of group and individual remembering: Does collaboration disrupt retrieval strategies? *Journal of Experimental Psychology: Learning, Memory, and Cognition*, 23(5), 1176.

Blair, I.V., Ma, J.E., & Lenton, A.P. (2001). Imagining stereotypes away: The moderation of implicit stereotypes through mental imagery. *Journal of Personality and Social Psychology*, 81(5), 828.

Boon, J.C. & Baxter, J.S. (2000). Minimizing interrogative suggestibility. *Legal and Criminological Psychology*, 5(2), 273–84.

Bornstein, R.F. (1989). Exposure and affect: Overview and meta-analysis of research, 1968–1987. *Psychological Bulletin, 106*(2), 265.

Chapman, L.J. (1967). Illusory correlation in observational report. *Journal of Verbal Learning and Verbal Behavior, 6*(1), 151–5.

Coman, A. & Hirst, W. (2012). Cognition through a social network: The propagation of induced forgetting and practice effects. *Journal of Experimental Psychology: General, 141*(2), 321.

Congleton, A.R. & Rajaram, S. (2011). The influence of learning methods on collaboration: Prior repeated retrieval enhances retrieval organization, abolishes collaborative inhibition, and promotes post-collaborative memory. *Journal of Experimental Psychology: General, 140*(4), 535.

Cuc, A., Koppel, J., & Hirst, W. (2007). Silence is not golden: A case for socially shared retrieval-induced forgetting. *Psychological Science, 18*(8), 727–33.

Dasgupta, N. & Asgari, S. (2004). Seeing is believing: Exposure to counterstereotypic women leaders and its effect on the malleability of automatic gender stereotyping. *Journal of Experimental Social Psychology, 40*(5), 642–58.

Dudukovic, N.M., Marsh, E.J., & Tversky, B. (2004). Telling a story or telling it straight: The effects of entertaining versus accurate retellings on memory. *Applied Cognitive Psychology, 18*(2), 125–43.

Echterhoff, G., Higgins, E.T., & Levine, J.M. (2009). Shared reality experiencing commonality with others' inner states about the world. *Perspectives on Psychological Science, 4*(5), 496–521.

Echterhoff, G., Hirst, W., & Hussy, W. (2005). How eyewitnesses resist misinformation: Social postwarnings and the monitoring of memory characteristics. *Memory & Cognition, 33*(5), 770–82.

Festinger, L. (1962). *A theory of cognitive dissonance* (Vol. 2). Stanford University Press.

Finlay, F., Hitch, G.J., & Meudell, P.R. (2000). Mutual inhibition in collaborative recall: Evidence for a retrieval-based account. *Journal of Experimental Psychology: Learning, Memory, and Cognition, 26*(6), 1556.

Greenwald, A.G. & Banaji, M.R. (1995). Implicit social cognition: Attitudes, self-esteem, and stereotypes. *Psychological Review, 102*(1), 4.

Greenwald, A.G., McGhee, D.E., & Schwartz, J.L. (1998). Measuring individual differences in implicit cognition: The implicit association test. *Journal of Personality and Social Psychology, 74*(6), 1464.

Grice, H.P. (1975). *Logic and conversation*. In P. Cole, & J. L. Morgan. (Eds.), *Syntax and Semantics*, Vol. 3, *Speech Acts* (pp. 41–58). New York, NY: Academic Press.

Hamilton, D.L., & Gifford, R.K. (1976). Illusory correlation in interpersonal perception: A cognitive basis of stereotypic judgments. *Journal of Experimental Social Psychology, 12*(4), 392–407.

Hasher, L., Goldstein, D., & Toppino, T. (1977). Frequency and the conference of referential validity. *Journal of Verbal Learning and Verbal Behavior, 16*(1), 107–12.

Hirst, W. & Echterhoff, G. (2012). Remembering in conversations: The social sharing and reshaping of memories. *Psychology, 63*(1), 55.

Hollingshead, A.B. & Brandon, D.P. (2003). Potential benefits of communication in transactive memory systems. *Human Communication Research, 29*(4), 607–15.

Kerr, N.L. & Tindale, R.S. (2004). Group performance and decision making. *Annual Review of Psychology, 55*, 623–55.

Lyons, A. & Kashima, Y. (2003). How are stereotypes maintained through communication? The influence of stereotype sharedness. *Journal of Personality and Social Psychology, 85*(6), 989.

Marsh, E.J. (2007). Retelling is not the same as recalling: Implications for memory. *Current Directions in Psychological Science, 16*(1), 16–20.

Meade, M.L. & Roediger, H.L. (2002). Explorations in the social contagion of memory. *Memory & Cognition, 30*(7), 995–1009.

Mitchell, K.J. & Johnson, M.K. (2009). Source monitoring 15 years later: What have we learned from fMRI about the neural mechanisms of source memory? *Psychological Bulletin, 135*(4), 638.

Mullen, B. & Johnson, C. (1990). Distinctiveness-based illusory correlations and stereotyping: A meta-analytic integration. *British Journal of Social Psychology, 29*(1), 11–28.

Pereira-Pasarin, L.P. & Rajaram, S. (2011). Study repetition and divided attention: Effects of encoding manipulations on collaborative inhibition in group recall. *Memory & Cognition, 39*(6), 968–76.

Rajaram, S. & Pereira-Pasarin, L.P. (2010). Collaborative memory: Cognitive research and theory. *Perspectives on Psychological Science, 5*(6), 649–63.

Rodriguez, D.N. & Strange, D. (2014a). Dissonance-induced false memories: Evidence from a free-choice paradigm. *Journal of Cognitive Psychology, 26*(5), 571–9.

Rodriguez, D.N. & Strange, D. (2014b). False memories for dissonance inducing events. *Memory*, (ahead-of-print), 1–10.

Schacter, D.L. (1987). Implicit expressions of memory in organic amnesia: Learning of new facts and associations. *Human Neurobiology, 6*(2), 107–18.

Sinclair, L. & Kunda, Z. (1999). Reactions to a black professional: Motivated inhibition and activation of conflicting stereotypes. *Journal of Personality and Social Psychology, 77*(5), 885.

Slamecka, N.J. & Graf, P. (1978). The generation effect: Delineation of a phenomenon. *Journal of Experimental Psychology: Human Learning and Memory, 4*(6), 592.

Stone, C.B., Coman, A., Brown, A.D., Koppel, J., & Hirst, W. (2012). Toward a science of silence: The consequences of leaving a memory unsaid. *Perspectives on Psychological Science, 7*(1), 39–53.

Truth and Reconciliation Commission of Canada (TRC). (2015). *Canada's Residential Schools: The Final Report of the Truth and Reconciliation Commission of Canada* (Vol. 1). McGill-Queen's Press-MQUP.

Vandierendonck, A. & Van Damme, R. (1988). Schema anticipation in recall: Memory process or report strategy? *Psychological Research, 50*(2), 116–22.

Van Veen, V., Krug, M.K., Schooler, J.W., & Carter, C.S. (2009). Neural activity predicts attitude change in cognitive dissonance. *Nature Neuroscience, 12*(11), 1469–74.

Weldon, M.S. (2000). Remembering as a social process. *Psychology of Learning and Motivation, 40,* 67–120.

Wittenbaum, G.M. & Park, E.S. (2001). The collective preference for shared information. *Current Directions in Psychological Science, 10*(2), 70–3.

Wittenbaum, G.M., Hollingshead, A.B., & Botero, I.C. (2004). From cooperative to motivated information sharing in groups: Moving beyond the hidden profile paradigm. *Communication Monographs, 71*(3), 286–310.

Wixted, J.T. (2004). The psychology and neuroscience of forgetting. *Annual Review of Psychology, 55,* 235–69.

Zajonc, R.B. (1980). Feeling and thinking: Preferences need no inferences. *American Psychologist, 35*(2), 151.

Chapter 11

Baioui, A., Ambach, W., Walter, B., & Vaitl, D. (2012). Psychophysiology of false memories in a Deese-Roediger-McDermott paradigm with visual scenes. *PloS One, 7*(1), e30416.

Bernbach, H.A. (1971). Strength theory and confidence ratings in recall. *Psychological Review, 78*(4), 338–40.

Bernbach, H.A. (1973). Processing strategies for recognition and recall. *Journal of Experimental Psychology, 99*(3), 409.

Bernstein, M.J., Young, S.G., & Hugenberg, K. (2007). The cross-category effect: Mere social categorization is sufficient to elicit an own-group bias in face recognition. *Psychological Science, 18*(8), 706–12.

Block, S.D., Greenberg, S.N., & Goodman, G.S. (2009). Remembrance of eyewitness testimony: Effects of emotional content, self-relevance, and emotional tone 1. *Journal of Applied Social Psychology, 39*(12), 2859–78.

Brewer, N. & Wells, G.L. (2011). Eyewitness identification. *Current Directions in Psychological Science, 20*(1), 24–7.

Briere, J. & Conte, J. (1993). Self-reported amnesia for abuse in adults molested as children. *Journal of Traumatic Stress, 6*(1), 21–31.

Burke, A., Heuer, F., & Reisberg, D. (1992). Remembering emotional events. *Memory & Cognition, 20*(3), 277–90.

Busey, T.A. & Loftus, G.R. (2007). Cognitive science and the law. *Trends in Cognitive Sciences, 11*(3), 111–17.

Cleary, A.M. & Greene, R.L. (2000). Recognition without identification. *Journal of Experimental Psychology: Learning, Memory, and Cognition, 26*(4), 1063.

Farwell, L.A. (2012). Brain fingerprinting: A comprehensive tutorial review of detection of concealed information with event-related brain potentials. *Cognitive Neurodynamics, 6*(2), 115–54.

Fivush, R. & Edwards, V.J. (2004). Remembering and forgetting childhood sexual abuse. *Journal of Child Sexual Abuse, 13*(2), 1–19.

Geiselman, R.E., Fisher, R.P., MacKinnon, D.P., & Holland, H.L. (1985). Eyewitness memory enhancement in the police interview: Cognitive retrieval mnemonics versus hypnosis. *Journal of Applied Psychology, 70*(2), 401.

Goodman-Brown, T.B., Edelstein, R.S., Goodman, G.S., Jones, D.P., & Gordon, D.S. (2003). Why children tell: A model of children's disclosure of sexual abuse. *Child Abuse & Neglect, 27*(5), 525–40.

Harland-Logan, S. (2019). Thomas Sophonow. *Innocence Canada.* Retrieved from http://www.innocencecanada.com/exonerations /thomas-sophonow/

Harris, C.R. & Pashler, H. (2005). Enhanced memory for negatively emotionally charged pictures without selective rumination. *Emotion, 5*(2), 191.

Holmes, D.S. (1990). The evidence for repression: An examination of sixty years of research. In J.L. Singer (Ed.), *Repression and dissociation* (pp. 85–102). University of Chicago Press.

Innocence Project (n.d.). Frank Sterling. *Innocence Project.* Accessed 27 Feb 2019. Retrieved from https://www.innocenceproject.org /cases/frank-sterling/

Jackiw, L.B., Arbuthnott, K.D., Pfeifer, J.E., Marcon, J.L., & Meissner, C.A. (2008). Examining the cross-race effect in lineup identification using Caucasian and First Nations samples. *Canadian Journal of Behavioural Science/Revue canadienne des sciences du comportement, 40*(1), 52.

Kensinger, E.A. & Corkin, S. (2003). Memory enhancement for emotional words: Are emotional words more vividly remembered than neutral words? *Memory & Cognition, 31*(8), 1169–80.

Köhnken, G., Milne, R., Memon, A., & Bull, R. (1999). The cognitive interview: A meta-analysis. *Psychology, Crime & Law, 5*(1–2), 3–27.

Loftus, E.F. (1979). Reactions to blatantly contradictory information. *Memory & Cognition, 7*(5), 368–74.

Loftus, E.F. (1993). The reality of repressed memories. *American Psychologist, 48*(5), 518.

Loftus, E.F. (1999). Lost in the mall: Misrepresentations and misunderstandings. *Ethics & Behavior, 9*(1), 51–60.

Loftus, E.F. (2003). Memory in Canadian courts of law. *Canadian Psychology/Psychologie canadienne, 44*(3), 207–12.

Loftus, E.F. (2013). Memory distortions: Problems solved and unsolved. In M. Garry & H. Hayne (Eds.), *Do justice and let the sky fall* (pp. 14–27). Psychology Press.

Loftus, E.F. & Davis, D. (2006). Recovered memories. *Annual Review of Clinical Psychology, 2,* 469–98.

Loftus, E.F. & Guyer, M.J. (2002). Who abused Jane Doe? The hazards of the single case history part 2. *Skeptical Inquirer, 26*(4), 37–40.

Loftus, E.F. & Ketcham, K. (1996). The myth of repressed memory: False memories and allegations of sexual abuse. Macmillan.

Loftus, E.F. & Palmer, J.C. (1974). Reconstruction of automobile destruction: An example of the interaction between language and memory. *Journal of Verbal Learning and Verbal Behavior, 13*(5), 585–9.

Loftus, E.F. & Pickrell, J.E. (1995). The formation of false memories. *Psychiatric Annals, 25*(12), 720–5.

Loftus, E.F., Miller, D.G., & Burns, H.J. (1978). Semantic integration of verbal information into a visual memory. *Journal of Experimental Psychology: Human Learning and Memory*, *4*(1), 19.

Meijer, E.H., Ben-Shakhar, G., Verschuere, B., & Donchin, E. (2013). A comment on Farwell (2012): Brain fingerprinting: A comprehensive tutorial review of detection of concealed information with event-related brain potentials. *Cognitive Neurodynamics*, *7*(2), 155–8.

Meijer, E.H., Selle, N.K., Elber, L., & Ben-Shakhar, G. (2014). Memory detection with the Concealed Information Test: A meta analysis of skin conductance, respiration, heart rate, and P300 data. *Psychophysiology*, *51*(9), 879–904.

Meissner, C.A. & Brigham, J.C. (2001). Thirty years of investigating the own-race bias in memory for faces: A meta-analytic review. *Psychology, Public Policy, and Law*, *7*(1), 3.

Münsterberg, H. (1908). *On the witness stand*. Doubleday.

Pennington, N. & Hastie, R. (1992). Explaining the evidence: Tests of the story model for juror decision making. *Journal of Personality and Social Psychology*, *62*(2), 189.

Phelps, E.A. (2004). Human emotion and memory: Interactions of the amygdala and hippocampal complex. *Current Opinion in Neurobiology*, *14*(2), 198–202.

Pritchard, M.E. & Keenan, J.M. (2002). Does jury deliberation really improve jurors' memories?. *Applied Cognitive Psychology*, *16*(5), 589–601.

Rosenfeld, J.P. (2005). Brain fingerprinting: A critical analysis. *The Scientific Review of Mental Health Practice*, *4*(1), 20–37.

Rosenhan, D.L., Eisner, S.L., & Robinson, R.J. (1994). Notetaking can aid juror recall. *Law and Human Behavior*, *18*(1), 53.

Ruva, C.L. & Guenther, C.C. (2015). From the shadows into the light: How pretrial publicity and deliberation affect mock jurors' decisions, impressions, and memory. *Law and Human Behavior*, *39*(3), 294.

Ruva, C.L. & McEvoy, C. (2008). Negative and positive pretrial publicity affect juror memory and decision making. *Journal of Experimental Psychology: Applied*, *14*(3), 226.

Ruva, C.L., McEvoy, C., & Bryant, J.B. (2007). Effects of pre-trial publicity and jury deliberation on juror bias and source memory errors. *Applied Cognitive Psychology*, *21*(1), 45–67.

Schooler, J.W., Bendiksen, M., & Ambadar, Z. (1997). Taking the middle line: Can we accommodate both fabricated and recovered memories of sexual abuse? In M. Conway (Ed.), *Recovered memories and false memories* (p. 251). Oxford University Press.

Van Bavel, J.J., Packer, D.J., & Cunningham, W.A. (2011). Modulation of the fusiform face area following minimal exposure to motivationally relevant faces: Evidence of in-group enhancement (not out-group disregard). *Journal of Cognitive Neuroscience*, *23*(11), 3343–54.

Weber, N. & Perfect, T.J. (2012). Improving eyewitness identification accuracy by screening out those who say they don't know. *Law and Human Behavior*, *36*(1), 28.

Williams, L.M. (1994). Recall of childhood trauma: A prospective study of women's memories of child sexual abuse. *Journal of Consulting and Clinical Psychology*, *62*(6), 1167.

Wilson, J.P., Hugenberg, K., & Bernstein, M.J. (2013). The cross-race effect and eyewitness identification: How to improve recognition and reduce decision errors in eyewitness situations. *Social Issues and Policy Review*, *7*(1), 83–113.

Chapter 12

Abramowitz, A. (2001). The time for change model and the 2000 election. *American Politics Research*, *29*(3), 279–82.

Alford, J. & O'Neill, D. (Eds.). (1994). *The contract state: Public management and the Kennett government*. Centre for Applied Social Research, Deakin University.

Baumeister, R.F., Bratslavsky, E., Finkenauer, C., & Vohs, K.D. (2001). Bad is stronger than good. *Review of General Psychology*, *5*(4), 323.

Baumgartner, H., Sujan, M., & Bettman, J.R. (1992). Autobiographical memories, affect, and consumer information processing. *Journal of Consumer Psychology*, *1*(1), 53–82.

Berlyne, D.E. (1970). Novelty, complexity, and hedonic value. *Perception & Psychophysics*, *8*(5), 279–86.

Bless, H., Hamilton, D.L., & Mackie, D.M. (1992). Mood effects on the organization of person information. *European Journal of Social Psychology*, *22*(5), 497–509.

Bogart, L. & Tolley, B.S. (1988). The search for information in newspaper advertising. *Journal of Advertising Research*, *28*(2), 9–19.

Boller, G.W. (1990). The vicissitudes of product experience: "Songs of our consuming selves" in drama ads. In M.E. Goldberg, G.J. Gorn, & R.W. Pollay (Eds.), *Advances in consumer research* (Vol. 17, pp. 621-625). Association for Consumer Research.

Braun, K.A. (1999). Postexperience advertising effects on consumer memory. *Journal of Consumer Research*, *25*, 319–34.

Braun, K.A., Ellis, R., & Loftus, E.F. (2002). Make my memory: How advertising can change our memories of the past. *Psychology & Marketing*, *19*(1), 1–23.

Brown, S.C. & Craik, F.I. (2000). Encoding and retrieval of information. In E. Tulving and F.I. Craik (Eds.), *The Oxford handbook of memory* (pp 93–107). New York, NY: Oxford University Press.

Civettini, A.J. & Redlawsk, D.P. (2009). Voters, emotions, and memory. *Political Psychology*, *30*(1), 125–51.

Dawood, F.S., Juliano, A.D., Reed, C., Meltzer, M.I., Shay, D.K., Cheng, P.Y. . . . & Widdowson, M.A. (September 2012). Estimated global mortality associated with the first 12 months of 2009 pandemic influenza A H1N1 virus circulation: A modelling study. *Lancet Infectious Diseases*, *12*(9), 687–95.

Debner, J.A. & Jacoby, L.L. (1994). Unconscious perception: Attention, awareness, and control. *Journal of Experimental Psychology: Learning, Memory, and Cognition*, *20*(2), 304.

Dimock, M.A. & Jacobson, G.C. (1995). Checks and choices: The House bank scandal's impact on voters in 1992. *Journal of Politics*, *57*, 1143–59.

Fazio, R.H., Zanna, M.P., & Cooper, J. (1978). Direct experience and attitude-behavior consistency: An information processing analysis. *Personality and Social Psychology Bulletin, 4*(1), 48–51.

Fischer, P.M., Schwartz, M.P., Richards, J.W., Goldstein, A.O., & Rojas, T.H. (1991). Brand logo recognition by children aged 3 to 6 years: Mickey Mouse and Old Joe the Camel. *JAMA, 266*(22), 3145–8.

Fischle, M. (2000). Mass response to the Lewinsky scandal: Motivated reasoning or Bayesian updating? *Political Psychology, 21*(1), 135–59.

Foer, J. (2011). *Moonwalking with Einstein: The art and science of remembering everything.* Penguin.

Funk, C.L. (1996). The impact of scandal on candidate evaluations: An experimental test of the role of candidate traits. *Political Behavior, 18*(1), 1–24.

Gibson, L.D. (1996). What can one TV exposure do? *Journal of Advertising Research, 36*(2), 9–18.

Goren, P. (2002). Character weakness, partisan bias, and presidential evaluation. *American Journal of Political Science, 46*(3), 627–41.

Gruneberg, M.M, & Morris, P.E. (1992). Applying memory research. In M.M. Gruneberg & P.E. Morris (Eds.), *Aspects of memory: The practical aspects* (pp. 1–17). Florence: Taylor & Francis/ Routledge.

Hoch, S.J. & Deighton, J. (1989). Managing what consumers learn from experience. *The Journal of Marketing, 53*(2), 1–20.

Holbrook, M.B. & Hirschman, E.C. (1982). The experiential aspects of consumption: Consumer fantasies, feelings, and fun. *Journal of Consumer Research, 9*(2), 132–40.

Jacobson, G.C. & Dimock, M.A. (1994). Checking out: The effects of bank overdrafts on the 1992 House elections. *American Journal of Political Science,* 601–24.

Jacoby, L.L. (1991). A process dissociation framework: Separating automatic from intentional uses of memory. *Journal of Memory and Language, 30*(5), 513–41.

Kardes, F.R. (1986). Effects of initial product judgments on subsequent memory-based judgments. *Journal of Consumer Research, 13*(1), 1–11.

Kohli, C. S., Harich, K.R., & Leuthesser, L. (2005). Creating brand identity: A study of evaluation of new brand names. *Journal of Business Research, 58*(11), 1506–15.

Krugman, H.E. (1967). The measurement of advertising involvement. *Public Opinion Quarterly, 30,* 349–56.

Krugman, H.E. (1972). Why three exposures may be enough. *Journal of Advertising Research, 12*(6), 11–14.

Kunda, Z. (1990). The case for motivated reasoning. *Psychological Bulletin, 108*(3), 480.

Lindstrom, M. (2011). *Brandwashed: Tricks companies use to manipulate our minds and persuade us to buy.* Crown Business.

Lodge, M. (1995). Toward a procedural model of candidate evaluation. In M. Lodge & K. McGraw (Eds.), *Political judgment: Structure and process* (pp. 111–40). University of Michigan Press.

Lodge, M., McGraw, K.M., & Stroh, P. (1989). An impression-driven model of candidate evaluation. *American Political Science Review, 83*(2), 399–419.

Lodge, M., Steenbergen, M.R., & Brau, S. (1995). The responsive voter: Campaign information and the dynamics of candidate evaluation. *American Political Science Review, 89*(2), 309–26.

Lodge, M. & Stroh, P. (1993). Inside the mental voting booth: An impression-driven process model of candidate evaluation. In S. Iyengar W. McGuire (Eds.), *Explorations in political psychology* (pp. 225–263). Durham, NC: Duke University Press.

Lodge, M., Taber, C., & Weber, C. (2006). First steps toward a dual-process accessibility model of political beliefs, attitudes, and behavior. In D. Redlawsk (Ed.), *Feeling politics: Emotion in political information processing* (pp. 11–30). Palgrave Macmillan US.

Marcus, G.E. & MacKuen, M.B. (1993). Anxiety, enthusiasm, and the vote: The emotional underpinnings of learning and involvement during presidential campaigns. *American Political Science Review, 87*(03), 672–85.

Marcus, G.E., Neuman, W.R., & MacKuen, M. (2000). *Affective intelligence and political judgment.* University of Chicago Press.

McDonald, C. (1971). What is the short-term effect of advertising? Working Paper 71-142, Marketing Science Institute.

McGraw, K.M., Lodge, M., & Stroh, P. (1990). On-line processing in candidate evaluation: The effects of issue order, issue importance, and sophistication. *Political Behavior, 12*(1), 41–58.

Miller, B. (2010). The effects of scandalous information on recall of policy-related information. *Political Psychology, 31*(6), 887–914.

Murdock, B.B. (1965). Effects of a subsidiary task on short-term memory. *British Journal of Psychology, 56*(4), 413–19.

Newman, B. (2002). Bill Clinton's approval ratings: The more things change, the more they stay the same. *Political Research Quarterly, 55*(4), 781–804.

Nordhielm, C.L. (2002). The influence of level of processing on advertising repetition effects. *Journal of Consumer Research, 29*(3), 371–82.

Park, J.W. & Hastak, M. (1994). Memory-based product judgments: Effects of involvement at encoding and retrieval. *Journal of Consumer Research, 21*(3), 534–47.

Pratto, F. & John, O.P. (1991). Automatic vigilance: The attention-grabbing power of negative social information. *Journal of Personality and Social Psychology, 61,* 380–91.

Priest, L. & Alphonso, C. (2003). Two dozen new mothers panicked by SARS. *The Globe and Mail,* June 7, 2003.

Public Health Agency of Canada. (2010). Bi-weekly and cumulative number of deaths due to Pandemic (H1N1) 2009, by province /territory, Canada. Archived from the original on 5 August 2009. Retrieved 4 February 2010.

Redlawsk, D.P. (2001). You must remember this: A test of the on-line model of voting. *The Journal of Politics, 63*(1), 29–58.

Redlawsk, D.P. (2002). Hot cognition or cool consideration? Testing the effects of motivated reasoning on political decision making. *The Journal of Politics, 64*(4), 1021–44.

Redlawsk, D.P., Civettini, A.J., & Lau, R.R. (2007). Affective intelligence and voting: Information processing and learning in a campaign. In W.R. Neuman, G.E. Marcus, & M. MacKuen (Eds.),

The affect effect: Dynamics of emotion in political thinking and behavior (pp. 152–79). University of Chicago Press.

Roberto, C.A., Baik, J., Harris, J.L., & Brownell, K.D. (2010). Influence of licensed characters on children's taste and snack preferences. *Pediatrics, 126*(1), 88–93.

Robinson, T.N., Borzekowski, D.L., Matheson, D.M., & Kraemer, H.C. (2007). Effects of fast food branding on young children's taste preferences. *Archives of Pediatrics & Adolescent Medicine, 161*(8), 792–7.

Robinson-Riegler, G.L. & Winton, W.M. (1996). The role of conscious recollection in recognition of affective material: Evidence for positive-negative asymmetry. *The Journal of General Psychology, 123*(2), 93–104.

Rundquist, B.S., Strom, G.S., & Peters, J.G. (1977). Corrupt politicians and their electoral support: Some experimental observations. *American Political Science Review, 71*(3), 954–63.

Schacter, D.L. (1995). *Memory distortion.* Cambridge, MA: Harvard University Press.

Schmidt, S. & Eisend, M. (2015). Advertising repetition: A meta-analysis on effective frequency in advertising. *Journal of Advertising, 44*(4), 415–28.

Shah, D.V., Watts, M.D., Domke, D., & Fan, D.P. (2002). News framing and cueing of issue regimes: Explaining Clinton's public approval in spite of scandal. *Public Opinion Quarterly, 66*(3), 339–70.

Shapiro, S. & Krishnan, H.S. (2001). Memory-based measures for assessing advertising effects: A comparison of explicit and implicit memory effects. *Journal of Advertising, 30*(3), 1–13.

Shedler, J. & Manis, M. (1986). Can the availability heuristic explain vividness effects? *Journal of Personality and Social Psychology, 51*(1), 26.

Sigal, J., Hsu, L., Foodim, S., & Betman, J. (1988). Factors affecting perceptions of political candidates accused of sexual and financial misconduct. *Political Psychology, 9,* 273–80.

Smith, R.D. (2006). Responding to global infectious disease outbreaks: Lessons from SARS on the role of risk perception, communication and management. *Social Science & Medicine, 63*(12), 3113–23.

Smith, R.E. & Swinyard, W.R. (1983). Attitude-behavior consistency: The impact of product trial versus advertising. *Journal of Marketing Research, 20*(3), 257–67.

Stang, D.J. (1975). Effects of "mere exposure" on learning and affect. *Journal of Personality and Social Psychology, 31*(1), 7.

Stoker, L. (1993). Judging presidential character: The demise of Gary Hart. *Political Behavior, 15,* 193–223.

Tulving, E., Schacter, D.L., & Stark, H.A. (1982). Priming effects in word-fragment completion are independent of recognition memory. *Journal of Experimental Psychology: Learning, Memory, and Cognition, 8*(4), 336.

Wells, W.D. (1986). Three useful ideas. In R.J. Lutz (Ed.), *Advances in consumer research* (Vol. 13, pp. 9–12). Provo, UT: Association for Consumer Research.

Zajonc, R.B. (1968). Attitudinal effects of mere exposure. *Journal of Personality and Social Psychology, 9*(2p2), 1.

Zaller, J.R. (1998). Monica Lewinsky's contribution to political science. *Political Science and Politics, 31,* 182–9.

Zielske, H.A. (1959). The remembering and forgetting of advertising. *The Journal of Marketing, 23,* 239–43.

Chapter 13

Bąbel, P., Pieniążek, L., & Zarotyński, D. (2015). The effect of the type of pain on the accuracy of memory of pain and affect. *European Journal of Pain, 19*(3), 358–68.

Bailie, R., Christmas, L., Price, N., Restall, J., Simpson, P., & Wesnes, K. (1989). Effects of temazepam premedication on cognitive recovery following alfentanil—propofol anaesthesia. *British Journal of Anaesthesia, 63*(1), 68–75.

Bernstein, D.M., Laney, C., Morris, E.K., & Loftus, E.F. (2005). False memories about food can lead to food avoidance. *Social Cognition, 23*(1), 11–34.

Bremner, J.D., Vythilingam, M., Vermetten, E., Southwick, S.M., McGlashan, T., Staib, L.H., . . . & Charney, D.S. (2003). Neural correlates of declarative memory for emotionally valenced words in women with posttraumatic stress disorder related to early childhood sexual abuse. *Biological Psychiatry, 53*(10), 879–89.

Brunet, A., Orr, S.P., Tremblay, J., Robertson, K., Nader, K., & Pitman, R.K. (2008). Effect of post-retrieval propranolol on psychophysiologic responding during subsequent script-driven traumatic imagery in post-traumatic stress disorder. *Journal of Psychiatric Research, 42*(6), 503–6.

Brunfaut, E. & d'Ydewalle, G. (1996). A comparison of implicit memory tasks in Korsakoff and alcoholic patients. *Neuropsychologia, 34*(12), 1143–50.

Calabrese, P., Markowitsch, H.J., Durwen, H.F., Widlitzek, H., Haupts, M., Holinka, B., & Gehlen, W. (1996). Right temporofrontal cortex as critical locus for the ecphory of old episodic memories. *Journal of Neurology, Neurosurgery & Psychiatry, 61*(3), 304–10.

CBC News. (2015, June 24). Man from Conce, N.L., hits moose, but can't remember it. Retrieved from https://www.cbc.ca/news/canada/newfoundland-labrador/man-from-conche-n-l-hits-moose-but-can-t-remember-it-1.3126446

Crowell, T.A., Kieffer, K.M., Siders, C.A., & Vanderploeg, R.D. (2002). Neuropsychological findings in combat-related post-traumatic stress disorder. *The Clinical Neuropsychologist, 16*(3), 310–21.

Crystal, H.A. (2008). *Dementia with Lewy bodies.* Emedicine.

Cunningham, S.J., Brady-Van den Bos, M., Gill, L., & Turk, D.J. (2013). Survival of the selfish: Contrasting self-referential and survival-based encoding. *Consciousness and Cognition, 22*(1), 237–44.

Dickson, D. & Weller, R.O. (Eds.). (2011). *Neurodegeneration: The molecular pathology of dementia and movement disorders.* John Wiley & Sons.

Ditto, P.H., Danks, J.H., Smucker, W.D., Bookwala, J., Coppola, K.M., Dresser, R., . . . & Zyzanski, S. (2001). Advance directives as acts of communication: A randomized controlled trial. *Archives of Internal Medicine, 161*(3), 421–30.

Ditto, P.H., Hawkins, N.A., & Pizarro, D.A. (2005). Imagining the end of life: On the psychology of advance medical decision making. *Motivation and Emotion, 29*(4), 475–96.

Erickson, K.I., Voss, M.W., Prakash, R.S., Basak, C., Szabo, A., Chaddock, L., . . . & Wojcicki, T.R. (2011). Exercise training increases size of hippocampus and improves memory. *Proceedings of the National Academy of Sciences, 108*(7), 3017–22.

Folstein, M.F., Folstein, S.E., & McHugh, P.R. (1975). "Mini-mental state": A practical method for grading the cognitive state of patients for the clinician. *Journal of Psychiatric Research, 12*(3), 189–98.

France, L. (2005, January 23). The death of yesterday. *The Observer.*

Geuze, E., Vermetten, E., Ruf, M., de Kloet, C.S., & Westenberg, H.G. (2008). Neural correlates of associative learning and memory in veterans with posttraumatic stress disorder. *Journal of Psychiatric Research, 42*(8), 659–69.

Gilbertson, M.W., Gurvits, T.V., Lasko, N.B., Orr, S.P., & Pitman, R.K. (2001). Multivariate assessment of explicit memory function in combat veterans with posttraumatic stress disorder. *Journal of Traumatic Stress, 14*(2), 413–32.

Hayasaki, E. (2016, April). In a perpetual present. *Wired.* Accessed June 15, 2019.

Hermans, D., Martens, K., De Cort, K., Pieters, G., & Eelen, P. (2003). Reality monitoring and metacognitive beliefs related to cognitive confidence in obsessive–compulsive disorder. *Behaviour Research and Therapy, 41*(4), 383–401.

Hutton, J.T., Nagel, J.A., & Loewenson, R.B. (1984). Eye tracking dysfunction in Alzheimer-type dementia. *Neurology, 34*(1), 99.

Iverson, G.L., Gaetz, M., Lovell, M.R., & Collins, M.W. (2004). Cumulative effects of concussion in amateur athletes. *Brain Injury, 18*(5), 433–43.

Kang, S.H., McDermott, K.B., & Roediger III, H.L. (2007). Test format and corrective feedback modify the effect of testing on long-term retention. *European Journal of Cognitive Psychology, 19*(4-5), 528–58.

Kang, S.H., McDermott, K.B. & Cohen, S.M. (2008). The mnemonic advantage of processing fitness-relevant information. *Memory & Cognition, 36*(6), 1151. https://doi.org/10.3758/MC.36.6.1151

Kiviniemi, M.T. & Rothman, A.J. (2006). Selective memory biases in individuals' memory for health-related information and behavior recommendations. *Psychology & Health, 21*(2), 247–72.

Lambert, J.C., Ibrahim-Verbaas, C.A., Harold, D., Naj, A.C., Sims, R., Bellenguez, C., . . . & Evans, D. (2013). Meta-analysis of 74,046 individuals identifies 11 new susceptibility loci for Alzheimer's disease. *Nature Genetics, 45*(12), 1452–8.

Laney, C., Morris, E.K., Bernstein, D.M., Wakefield, B.M., & Loftus, E.F. (2008). Asparagus, a love story: Healthier eating could be just a false memory away. *Experimental Psychology, 55*(5), 291–300.

MacDonald, P.A., Antony, M.M., Macleod, C.M., & Richter, M.A. (1997). Memory and confidence in memory judgments among individuals with obsessive compulsive disorder and non-clinical controls. *Behaviour Research and Therapy, 35*(6), 497–505.

Mann, R.E., Cho-Young, J., & Vogel-Sprott, M. (1984). Retrograde enhancement by alcohol of delayed free recall performance. *Pharmacology Biochemistry and Behavior, 20*(4), 639–42.

Markowitsch, H.J., Fink, G.R., Thone, A., Kessler, J., & Heiss, W.D. (1997). A PET study of persistent psychogenic amnesia covering the whole life span. *Cognitive Neuropsychiatry, 2*(2), 135–58.

McKeith, I.G. (2002). Dementia with Lewy bodies. *The British Journal of Psychiatry, 180*(2), 144–7.

Nairne, J.S. & Pandeirada, J.N. (2008). Adaptive memory: Is survival processing special? *Journal of Memory and Language, 59*(3), 377–85.

Nairne, J.S., Thompson, S.R., & Pandeirada, J.N. (2007). Adaptive memory: Survival processing enhances retention. *Journal of Experimental Psychology: Learning, Memory, and Cognition, 33*(2), 263.

Nikolaev, A., McLaughlin, T., O'Leary, D.D., & Tessier-Lavigne, M. (2009). APP binds DR6 to trigger axon pruning and neuron death via distinct caspases. *Nature, 457*(7232), 981–9.

Plassman, B.L., Langa, K.M., Fisher, G.G., Heeringa, S.G., Weir, D.R., Ofstedal, M.B., . . . & Steffens, D.C. (2007). Prevalence of dementia in the United States: The aging, demographics, and memory study. *Neuroepidemiology, 29*(1–2), 125–32.

Rocha, V. (2015, July 2). Woman with amnesia and cancer identified; family found. *Los Angeles Times.* https://www.latimes.com/local/lanow/la-me-ln-woman-with-amnesia-identified-20150701-story.html. Accessed June 15, 2016.

Roehrs, T. & Roth, T. (2010). Drug-related sleep stage changes: Functional significance and clinical relevance. *Sleep Medicine Clinics, 5*(4), 559–70.

Samuelson, K.W., Neylan, T.C., Lenoci, M., Metzler, T.J., Cardenas, V., Weiner, M.W., & Marmar, C.R. (2009). Longitudinal effects of PTSD on memory functioning. *Journal of the International Neuropsychological Society, 15*(06), 853–61.

Sharman, S.J., Garry, M., Jacobson, J.A., Loftus, E.F., & Ditto, P.H. (2008). False memories for end-of-life decisions. *Health Psychology, 27*(2), 291.

Smith, E.E. & Jonides, J. (1995). *Working memory in humans: Neuropsychological evidence.* The MIT Press.

Southwick, S.M., Rasmusson, A.M., Barron, J., & Arnsten, A. (2005). Neurobiological and neurocognitive alterations in PTSD: A focus on norepinephrine, serotonin, and the HPA axis. In J.J. Vasterling & C.R. Brewin (Eds.), *Neuropsychology of PTSD: Biological, cognitive, and clinical perspectives* (pp. 27–58). New York, NY: The Guilford Press.

Statistics Canada. (2015). Table 117-0019—Distribution of the household population meeting/not meeting the Canadian physical activity guidelines, by sex and age group, occasional (percentage) [Data File]. Retrieved on May 26, 2015.

Symons, C.S. & Johnson, B.T. (1997). The self-reference effect in memory: A meta-analysis. *Psychological Bulletin, 121*(3), 371.

Van Cauter, E., Leproult, R., & Plat, L. (2000). Age-related changes in slow wave sleep and REM sleep and relationship with growth hormone and cortisol levels in healthy men. *JAMA, 284*(7), 861–8.

van den Hout, M. & Kindt, M. (2003). Repeated checking causes memory distrust. *Behaviour Research and Therapy, 41*(3), 301–16.

Vertesi, A., Lever, J.A., Molloy, D.W., Sanderson, B., Tuttle, I., Pokoradi, L., & Principi, E. (2001). Standardized Mini-Mental State Examination. Use and interpretation. *Canadian Family Physician, 47*(10), 2018–23.

Wearing, D. (2005, January 12). The man who keeps falling in love with his wife. *The Telegraph.*

Zoladz, P.R. & Diamond, D.M. (2013). Current status on behavioral and biological markers of PTSD: A search for clarity in a conflicting literature. *Neuroscience & Biobehavioral Reviews, 37*(5), 860–95.

Chapter 14

Bahrick, H.P., Bahrick, P.O., & Wittlinger, R.P. (1975). Fifty years of memory for names and faces: A cross-sectional approach. *Journal of Experimental Psychology: General, 104*(1), 54.

Bilalić, M., Langner, R., Ulrich, R., & Grodd, W. (2011). Many faces of expertise: Fusiform face area in chess experts and novices. *The Journal of Neuroscience, 31*(28), 10206–14.

Breathnach, C.S. (1980). The hippocampus as a cognitive map. *Philosophical Studies, 27*, 263–7.

Burgess, N., Maguire, E.A., & O'Keefe, J. (2002). The human hippocampus and spatial and episodic memory. *Neuron, 35*(4), 625–41.

Butler, A.C. (2010). Repeated testing produces superior transfer of learning relative to repeated studying. *Journal of Experimental Psychology: Learning, Memory, and Cognition, 36*(5), 1118.

Butler, A.C. & Roediger, H.L. (2008). Feedback enhances the positive effects and reduces the negative effects of multiple-choice testing. *Memory & Cognition, 36*(3), 604–16.

Butler, A.C. & Roediger, III, H.L. (2007). Testing improves long-term retention in a simulated classroom setting. *European Journal of Cognitive Psychology, 19*(4–5), 514–27.

Butler, A.C., Karpicke, J.D., & Roediger III, H.L. (2007). The effect of type and timing of feedback on learning from multiple-choice tests. *Journal of Experimental Psychology: Applied, 13*(4), 273.

Butler, A.C., Karpicke, J.D., & Roediger III, H.L. (2008). Correcting a metacognitive error: Feedback increases retention of low-confidence correct responses. *Journal of Experimental Psychology: Learning, Memory, and Cognition, 34*(4), 918.

Butler, A.C., Marsh, E.J., Goode, M.K., & Roediger, H.L. (2006). When additional multiple-choice lures aid versus hinder later memory. *Applied Cognitive Psychology, 20*(7), 941–56.

Callender, A.A. & McDaniel, M.A. (2009). The limited benefits of rereading educational texts. *Contemporary Educational Psychology, 34*(1), 30–41.

Carpenter, S.K. (2009). Cue strength as a moderator of the testing effect: The benefits of elaborative retrieval. *Journal of Experimental Psychology: Learning, Memory and Cognition, 35*(6) 1563–69.

Carpenter, S.K. & DeLosh, E.L. (2006). Impoverished cue support enhances subsequent retention: Support for the elaborative retrieval explanation of the testing effect. *Memory and Cognition, 34*(2), 268–76.

Charness, N., Tuffiash, M., Krampe, R., Reingold, E., & Vasyukova, E. (2005). The role of deliberate practice in chess expertise. *Applied Cognitive Psychology, 19*(2), 151–65.

Chase, W.G. & Ericsson, K.A. (1981). Skilled memory. In J.R. Anderson (Ed.), *Cognitive skills and their acquisition* (pp. 141–89). Hillsdale, NJ: Lawrence Erlbaum.

Chase, W.G. & Ericsson, K.A. (1982). Skill and working memory. *Psychology of Learning and Motivation, 16*, 1–58.

Coon, H. & Carey, G. (1989). Genetic and environmental determinants of musical ability in twins. *Behavior Genetics, 19*, 183–93.

Deakin, J.M. & Cobley, S. (2003). An examination of the practice environments in figure skating and volleyball: A search for deliberate practice. In J.L. Starkes & K.A. Ericsson (Eds.), *Expert performance in sports: Advances in research on sport expertise* (pp. 90–113). Champaign, IL: Human Kinetics.

Duan, X., Liao, W., Liang, D., Qiu, L., Gao, Q., Liu, C., . . . & Chen, H. (2012). Large-scale brain networks in board game experts: Insights from a domain-related task and task-free resting state. *PloS One, 7*(3), e32532.

Ericsson, K. (2004). Deliberate practice and the acquisition and maintenance of expert performance in medicine and related domains. *Academic Medicine, 79*(10), 870–81.

Ericsson, K.A. (2006). The influence of experience and deliberate practice on the development of superior expert performance. In K.A. Ericsson, N. Charness, P.J. Feltovich, & R.R. Hoffman (Eds.), *The Cambridge handbook of expertise and expert performance* (pp. 685–705). Cambridge University Press.

Ericsson, K.A. & Lehmann, A.C. (1996). Expert and exceptional performance: Evidence of maximal adaptation to task constraints. *Annual Review of Psychology, 47*(1), 273–305.

Ericsson, K.A., Delaney, P.F., Weaver, G., & Mahadevan, R. (2004). Uncovering the structure of a memorist's superior "basic" memory capacity. *Cognitive Psychology, 49*(3), 191–237.

Ericsson, K.A. & Kintsch, W. (1995). Long-term working memory. *Psychological Review, 102*(2), 211.

Ericsson, K.A., Krampe, R.T., & Tesch-Römer, C. (1993). The role of deliberate practice in the acquisition of expert performance. *Psychological Review, 100*(3), 363.

Fitts, P.M. & Posner, M.I. (1967). *Human performance.* Oxford, England: Brooks/Cole.

Foer, J. (2011). *Moonwalking with Einstein: The art and science of remembering everything.* Penguin.

Gardner, H. (1995). Expert performance: Its structure and acquisition: Comment. *American Psychologist, 50*, 802–3.

Gladwell, M. (2008). *Outliers: The story of success.* New York, NY: Little, Brown, and Co.

Gobet, F. & Campitelli, G. (2007). The role of domain-specific practice, handedness, and starting age in chess. *Developmental Psychology, 43*, 159–72.

Hambrick, D.Z., Oswald, F.L., Altmann, E.M., Meinz, E.J., Gobet, F., & Campitelli, G. (2014). Deliberate practice: Is that all it takes to become an expert? *Intelligence, 45*, 34–45.

Han, Y., Yang, H., Lv, Y.T., Zhu, C.Z., He, Y., Tang, H.H., . . . & Dong, Q. (2009). Gray matter density and white matter integrity in pianists' brain: A combined structural and diffusion tensor MRI study. *Neuroscience Letters, 459*(1), 3–6.

Higbee, K.L. (1997). Novices, apprentices, and mnemonists: Acquiring expertise with the phonetic mnemonic. *Applied Cognitive Psychology, 11*(2), 147–61.

Hill, N.M. & Schneider, W. (2006). Brain changes in the development of expertise: Neuroanatomical and neurophysiological evidence about skill-based adaptations. In K.A. Ericsson, N. Charness, P.J. Feltovich, & R.R. Hoffman (Eds.), *The Cambridge handbook of expertise and expert performance* (pp. 653–82). Cambridge University Press.

Hogan, R.M. & Kintsch, W. (1971). Differential effects of study and test trials on long-term recognition and recall. *Journal of Verbal Learning and Verbal Behaviour, 10*, 562–7.

Hu, Y., Ericsson, K.A., Yang, D., & Lu, C. (2009). Superior self-paced memorization of digits in spite of a normal digit span: The structure of a memorist's skill. *Journal of Experimental Psychology: Learning, Memory, and Cognition, 35*(6), 1426.

Kang, S.H., McDermott, K.B., & Roediger III, H.L. (2007). Test format and corrective feedback modify the effect of testing on long-term retention. *European Journal of Cognitive Psychology, 19*(4–5), 528–58.

Karpicke, J.D. & Roediger, H.L. (2008). The critical importance of retrieval for learning. *Science, 319*(5865), 966–8.

Kliegl, R., Smith, J., & Baltes, P.B. (1989). Testing-the-limits and the study of adult age differences in cognitive plasticity of a mnemonic skill. *Developmental Psychology, 25*(2), 247.

Kliegl, R., Smith, J., Heckhausen, J., & Baltes, P.B. (1987). Mnemonic training for the acquisition of skilled digit memory. *Cognition and Instruction, 4*(4), 203–23.

Kulhavy, R.W. & Anderson, R.C. (1972). Delay-retention effect with multiple-choice tests. *Journal of Educational Psychology, 63*(5), 505.

Landauer, T.K. & Bjork, R.A. (1978). Optimum rehearsal patterns and name learning. In M.M. Gruneberg et al., (Eds.), *Practical aspects of memory* (pp. 625–32). Academic Press.

Little, J.L. & Bjork, E.L. (2012, August). The persisting benefits of using multiple-choice tests as learning events. In *Proceedings of the 34th annual conference of The Cognitive Science Society* (pp. 683-688).

Maguire, E.A., Burgess, N., Donnett, J.G., Frackowiak, R.S., Frith, C.D., & O'Keefe, J. (1998). Knowing where and getting there: A human navigation network. *Science, 280*(5365), 921–4.

Maguire, E.A., Gadian, D.G., Johnsrude, I.S., Good, C.D., Ashburner, J., Frackowiak, R.S., & Frith, C.D. (2000). Navigation-related structural change in the hippocampi of taxi drivers. *Proceedings of the National Academy of Sciences, 97*(8), 4398–403.

Maguire, E.A., Valentine, E.R., Wilding, J.M., & Kapur, N. (2003). Routes to remembering: The brains behind superior memory. *Nature Neuroscience, 6*(1), 90–5.

Marsh, E.J., Roediger, H.L., Bjork, R.A., & Bjork, E.L. (2007). The memorial consequences of multiple-choice testing. *Psychonomic Bulletin & Review, 14*(2), 194–9.

Metcalfe, J., Kornell, N., & Finn, B. (2009). Delayed versus immediate feedback in children's and adults' vocabulary learning. *Memory & Cognition, 37*(8), 1077–87.

Noice, H. (1992). Elaborative memory strategies of professional actors. *Applied Cognitive Psychology, 6*(5), 417–27.

Pashler, H., Cepeda, N.J., Wixted, J.T., & Rohrer, D. (2005). When does feedback facilitate learning of words? *Journal of Experimental Psychology: Learning, Memory, and Cognition, 31*(1), 3.

Petersen, S.E., Van Mier, H., Fiez, J.A., & Raichle, M.E. (1998). The effects of practice on the functional anatomy of task performance. *Proceedings of the National Academy of Sciences, 95*(3), 853–60.

Poldrack, R.A., Desmond, J.E., Glover, G.H., & Gabrieli, J.D. (1998). The neural basis of visual skill learning: An fMRI study of mirror reading. *Cerebral Cortex, 8*(1), 1–10.

Pyc, M.A. & Rawson, K.A. (2009). Testing the retrieval effort hypothesis: Does greater difficulty correctly recalling information lead to higher levels of memory? *Journal of Memory and Language, 60*(4), 437–47.

Roediger, H.L. & Butler, A.C. (2011). The critical role of retrieval practice in long-term retention. *Trends in Cognitive Sciences, 15*(1), 20–7.

Roediger, III, H.L. & Karpicke, J.D. (2006). Test-enhanced learning: Taking memory tests improves long-term retention. *Psychological Science, 17*(3), 249–55.

Roediger III, H.L. & Marsh, E.J. (2005). The positive and negative consequences of multiple-choice testing. *Journal of Experimental Psychology: Learning, Memory, and Cognition, 31*(5), 1155.

Schneider, W. (1998). Innate talent or deliberate practice as determinants of exceptional performance: Are we asking the right question? *The Behavioral and Brain Sciences, 21*(3), 423–4.

Smith, T.A. & Kimball, D.R. (2010). Learning from feedback: Spacing and the delay–retention effect. *Journal of Experimental Psychology: Learning, Memory, and Cognition, 36*(1), 80.

Sternberg, R.J. (1996). Costs of expertise. In K.A. Ericsson (Ed.), *The road to excellence: The acquisition of expert performance in the arts and sciences, sports, and games* (pp. 347–354). Mahwah, NJ: Lawrence Erlbaum.

Thompson, C.P., Cowan, T., Frieman, J., Mahadevan, R.S., Vogl, R.J., & Frieman, J. (1991). Rajan: A study of a memorist. *Journal of Memory and Language, 30*(6), 702–24.

University of Mississippi Medical Centre (2018, January 25). Alex Mullen's memory, again, holds all the cards. *UMMC News.* Retrieved from https://www.umc.edu/news/News_Articles/2018 /01/alex-mullens-memory-again-holds-all-the-cards-.html

Vinkhuyzen, A.E., van der Sluis, S., Posthuma, D., & Boomsma, D.I. (2009). The heritability of aptitude and exceptional talent across different domains in adolescents and young adults. *Behavior Genetics, 39*(4), 380–392.

Wenger, M.J. & Payne, D.G. (1997). Cue integration across study tasks and direct and indirect retrieval instructions: Implications for the study of retrieval processes. *Journal of Experimental Psychology: Learning, Memory, and Cognition, 23*(1), 102.

Wheeler, M., Ewers, M., & Buonanno, J. (2003). Different rates of forgetting following study versus test trials. *Memory, 11*(6), 571–80.

Wheeler, M.A. & Roediger III, H.L. (1992). Disparate effects of repeated testing: Reconciling Ballard's (1913) and Bartlett's (1932) results. *Psychological Science, 3*(4), 240–5.

Index